COGNITIVE PROCESSING IN BILINGUALS

ADVANCES
IN
PSYCHOLOGY

83

Editors:

G. E. STELMACH
P. A. VROON

NORTH-HOLLAND
AMSTERDAM • LONDON • NEW YORK • TOKYO

COGNITIVE PROCESSING IN BILINGUALS

Edited by

Richard Jackson HARRIS

Department of Psychology
Bluemont Hall
Kansas State University
Manhattan, KS, U.S.A.

1992

NORTH-HOLLAND
AMSTERDAM • LONDON • NEW YORK • TOKYO

NORTH-HOLLAND
ELSEVIER SCIENCE PUBLISHERS B.V.
Sara Burgerhartstraat 25
P.O. Box 211, 1000 AE Amsterdam, The Netherlands

Distributors for the United States and Canada:
ELSEVIER SCIENCE PUBLISHING COMPANY, INC.
655 Avenue of the Americas
New York, N.Y. 10010, U.S.A.

Library of Congress Cataloging-in-Publication Data

Cognitive processing in bilinguals / edited by Richard Jackson Harris.
     p.   cm. -- (Advances in psychology ; 83)
   Includes bibliographical references and indexes.
   ISBN 0-444-88922-1
   1. Cognition. 2. Bilingualism. 3. Bilingualism--Psychological
aspects.   I. Harris, Richard Jackson. II. Series: Advances in
psychology (Amsterdam, Netherlands) ; 83.
BF311.C55182   1992
153--dc20   91-40682
                                                                CIP

ISBN: 0 444 88922 1

© 1992 ELSEVIER SCIENCE PUBLISHERS B.V. All rights reserved.

Printed in The Netherlands

Preface

This volume arose essentially through my frustration of not easily finding published research on cognitive processing in bilinguals. As a cognitive psychologist interested in this population, I found only very occasional treatment of the problem in standard cognitive journals. Slowly but surely I discovered more and more such research published, but it was very widely scattered in many journals and books, some with much less readership than the work deserved. While certain aspects of bilingualism, such as second-language acquisition and bilingual education, were widely covered, there seemed to be a need for a gathering in one source of research on cognitive processing by adult bilinguals.

In mid-1990 I began by soliciting chapters from several prominent researchers widely known in the area. There was, however, a commitment to also include high quality research by young scholars and by those outside the international academic mainstream of North America and Western Europe. Recommendations of such people were solicited from early contributors. Thus the original list of contributors grew steadily to the roster actually appearing in this volume. It is my commitment that the study of cognition in bilinguals is best advanced by examination of both established international scholars and new researchers and those in societies from around the world.

Thanks to Kees Michielsen of Elsevier for catching the vision of this volume, and to Alison Carter for her technical editing. This book would never have been possible without the hours of typing, *de facto* editing, and computer disk shuffling by Sharon Sterling. Thanks also to Patrick Knight, Julia Pounds, and Beth Nelson for help at various stages. Thanks to the Council for International Exchange of Scholars for a Fulbright Lecturing award for Brazil where I had the opportunity to observe myself becoming bilingual and thus became forever intrigued with multilingualism and multiculturalism. Finally, thanks to my wife Caprice Becker, who realized I was doing something important with this book, and to my children Clinton, Natalie, and Grady.

Manhattan, Kansas USA   August 1991

Table of Contents

Part I:

WHO ARE THE BILINGUALS?

Cognitive Processing in Bilinguals – R.J. Harris (Editor)
© *1992 Elsevier Science Publishers B.V. All rights reserved.*

Bilingualism: Not the Exception Any More

Richard Jackson Harris and Elizabeth Marie McGhee Nelson
Kansas State University

Abstract

This chapter introduces the topic of bilingualism in its broad social context
and briefly lays out several of the areas of study of the cognition in bilinguals.
We conclude with an overview of the book and recommended further reading
on cognition in bilinguals.

This chapter introduces the volume by presenting a very broad context for
bilingualism.[1] While the emphasis in this volume is not social, cultural, or political, it
is helpful to have the "big picture." This chapter provides some social and cultural
background for bilingualism and a brief introduction to some basic measurement and
cognitive issues.

Bilingualism in the World

On a worldwide basis, bilingualism is very common and much more the rule than
the exception in most places. Even many largely monolingual countries, such as many
in western and central Europe, are relatively small in area and surrounded by other
nations speaking different languages. Larger monolingual immigrant societies like the
United States, Brazil, Argentina, or Australia have culturally and linguistically
overwhelmed (if not almost exterminated) their indigenous languages. Residents of
such nations are the most likely to be truly monolingual. Such nations, however, are
relatively few in number, and even in these societies, many individual residents are
bilingual.   Today's unprecedented "permanent" migration across international
boundaries seems likely to accelerate this trend.

There is also some tendency for recent immigrant groups to show signs of greater
resistance to linguistic assimilation than occurred in earlier generations. For example,
the USA is already the sixth largest Spanish-speaking country in the world, with its
Spanish-speaking population being one of the fastest-growing social groups. Cities like
Miami and Los Angeles may become largely Spanish-speaking in the next decade.
Even historically monolingual and monocultural countries of western Europe are facing
cultural and linguistic pluralism on an unprecedented scale. North African emigration
to southern France is making Marseille the largest Arabic-speaking Muslim city outside
the Arab world. Large-scale African, Caribbean, and South Asian emigration to Great
Britain has forced that nation to face issues of racism and multiculturalism that it
formerly could ignore. Internal strife and hard times in the Soviet Union threaten to
send massive emigrations westward with unknown effects.

The issue of language, and bilingualism specifically, may be an important social and political issue in either a unifying or divisive sense. For example, while the English-French bilingualism of Canada is a major part of its national cultural identity, it has at times also threatened to split the country into separate nations, most seriously in the early 1970s. Unlike Canada, where Anglophones vastly outnumber Francophones, Belgium has much closer to an even division of its French and Dutch speakers. Switzerland has for centuries existed peacefully in its quadrilingual state with German, French, Italian, and Romansch in far from equal importance. India has at least 20 languages spoken by over 1 million and several others spoken by fewer. In that context, English has survived well past the colonial period as a useful tongue that is "neutral" in terms of regional identity.

Although most bilingual or multilingual nations actually are composed of distinct regions, each using primarily its own language, there are a few cases where bilingualism is actually characteristic of most residents. Sometimes there is a second language which is almost universally spoken. For example, most residents of the Germanic-speaking countries of northern Europe of middle age or younger have extensively studied and used English. Alone in the Americas, Paraguay shows widespread bilingualism with the European language (Spanish) and an indigenous language (Guaraní), with most Paraguayans bilingual in the two. The Guaraní language has become a part of general Paraguayan nationalism in a way that no other native American language has in a modern nation.

Language may also be a source of regional consciousness. For example, the old Celtic tongues survive in varying degrees of Britain, Ireland, and Brittany. Welsh is the most widely used Celtic vernacular, with 15-20% of Wales residents speaking Welsh as a first language, though virtually all of these are bilingual in English. Irish is studied in all schools in the Republic of Ireland, although it is the first language of almost no one. Catalan and Basque are central aspects of regional cultural consciousness in Catalonia and the Basque country of Spain. Both have experienced a resurgence since the end of the repressive Franco era in 1975. Regional languages in the Soviet republics (e.g., Estonian, Lithuanian, Georgian, Azerbaijani) are in most cases a strong part of the national and independence movements in those republics beginning in 1989-90.

Sometimes a bilingual society or subculture will show status differences between the languages. This condition, called **diglossia**, usually sees a high-status formal language and a low-status everyday language. For example, diglossia was once common in much of the colonized Third World, as in Africa, where English, French, or Portuguese was the language of government, commerce, and education. Often the colonial language has survived as the unifying language in a nation composed of distinct cultures. For example, English continues to be very important in Nigeria, since, unlike Yoruba, Ibo, Hausa, or any other local language, it is subculturally neutral throughout the country. Large segments of the population of Peru and Bolivia speak Quechua or Aymará as a first or only language, though education and services of the nation are in Spanish. The status difference may sometimes be taught or reinforced with children, for example by schools punishing children for using their native language in the classroom or even at play.

Sometimes the social inequity inherent in diglossia perseveres because one of the languages is widely perceived as being more instrumental outside the region or nation than is the other language. For example, part of what makes Canadian francophones feel so threatened is that English is so much more useful than French outside Canada, most notably in the neighboring U.S., that immigrants to Quebec speaking a third language have more motivation to learn English than French. English has survived as a vernacular for many in the Tagalog-speaking Philippines long after the U.S. colonial rule ended because of its perceived instrumental value in the world at large. One of the major precipitating events of the Soweto riots in South Africa in 1976 was the Afrikaner government's decree that education in the black townships had to be in Afrikaans rather than English. Though both were perceived as "foreign" and "white" languages, English was seen by blacks as widely useful outside South Africa, while Afrikaans was spoken nowhere and was also identified as the language of "the oppressors" locally.

Appendix 1 presents the "family trees" of many of the world's languages, including all of those mentioned in this volume.

What is Bilingualism?

Simply defining bilingualism operationally turns out to be far from simple. Language use may be grossly divided into the four basic skills of reading, writing, speaking, and listening, and any given person's ability may differ vastly in these four skills. For example, many advanced students throughout the world have learned to read English for academic purposes but have little oral facility in the language. On the other hand, some persons living temporarily in another culture many acquire some degree of oral comprehension skills (and perhaps speaking as well) without much reading or writing ability. In fact, there are probably few truly balanced bilinguals. People develop skills as needed for particular circumstances. A complete description of the "bilingual" sample is critical to an adequate interpretation of any research on bilingualism (see Palij & Aaronson, this volume). Most often one's best language is the one learned first, but that is not necessarily the case. There are many people who live the first few years of their lives in a foreign culture and acquire its language first and that of their own culture shortly thereafter (or both simultaneously). In such cases fluency in the first language may be largely lost (or at least felt to be lost) after a family move removes the need and opportunity for using that tongue.

Measuring Bilingualism

Measuring bilingualism has proven as complex as defining it. The purpose of the measurement often dictates what tests of bilingualism are used. Rating scales have been used to assess the bilingual's language background and language use. Often, the bilingual is asked to make self-ratings on the skills of reading, writing, listening and speaking in both languages. Self-ratings have sometimes proven to be adequate measures of fluency when a homogeneous group of bilinguals is desired.

Fluency tests are given as an interview or written test. In the interview, the bilingual may be asked to read aloud, answer questions and follow oral instructions. This is a common method for testing bilinguals who wish to work in government or who wish to be foreign language teachers in the public schools. On the written test, bilinguals may be asked to name pictures or complete sentences with appropriate expressions. This method of measurement is often used in college placement tests to evaluate the fluency level of the beginning language student.

Flexibility tests and dominance tests have been used by researchers interested in determining whether a bilingual is balanced in both languages. In the flexibility tests, the bilingual is asked to name in both languages as many synonyms and associations as possible to a list of words in both languages. The assumption is that a balanced bilingual will produce an equal number of words in both languages. Similarly, in dominance tests the bilingual looks at a word or phrase which could belong to either language (e.g., Les) and then pronounces and defines it (in French, the plural definite article; in English, a nickname). Again, it is assumed that the balanced bilingual will use one language as frequently as the other.

For specific purposes such as determining student proficiency, these measurements are satisfactory. But if the goal of the measurement is to research bilingual processes, other factors, such as socio-cultural determinants of language use, must be taken into consideration. See Baetens Beardsmore (1982), Macnamara (1969), and chapters by Keatley, Palij and Aaronson, and Votaw in this volume for further discussion of this issue.

The Bilingual Personality

We have emphasized that the situation is an important factor to take into account when investigating a bilingual's language use. Anecdotal evidence would lead to the conclusion that it is something about the bilingual person which leads him or her to switch from one language to another. For example, a French-German bilingual might use French for flirting and German for swearing. It seems more probable, however, that the choice of language is determined, not by a personality trait characteristic of bilinguals, but by the cultural and social context of the language use. The situation produces attitudes and behaviors, including choice of language.

Although there may not be a bilingual personality, i.e., one which changes with the language used, bilinguals do hold attitudes toward their bilingualism which may make their personality different from that of a monolingual. Very few bilinguals feel marginal in their cultural affiliation, nor do they see their two languages as interfering with each other. Such attitudes are more typical of inferences made by monolinguals about bilinguals.

Bilinguals, for the most part, feel there are no disadvantages to being bilingual. They have positive attitudes toward their bilingualism. They feel a strong cultural and social identification. By knowing two languages, they understand more than one way of thinking. They perceive the world in different ways. More practical advantages include being able to read literature in its original language and to communicate with people from other countries in their native language. Unfortunately, these positive attitudes can be overpowered by the negative attitudes of some monolinguals. Whereas the wealthy and educated bilingual will be admired for his or her language proficency, the poor and uneducated bilingual will be pitied. These attitudes indicate that the bilingual personality is the product of the interaction of socio-cultural factors and language ability (Grosjean, 1982).

Positive and Negative Effects

Translations of the Binet test were used in the early twentieth century to measure the intelligence of the vast numbers of immigrants to the United States. These bilinguals were found to be lower in intelligence than monolinguals (Goddard, 1917). Some argued that the lower intelligence was due to genetic differences between bilinguals and monolinguals (Brigham, 1923; Goodenough, 1926). Others believed that it was the experience of learning a second language which produced the lower intelligence (Smith, 1939). It was later found that this difference in intelligence between bilinguals and monolinguals disappeared when certain factors were controlled for: age, gender, education, socio-economic background and fluency in both languages (Hakuta, 1986).

Later research indicated that, in fact, balanced bilinguals had certain advantages in cognitive processes (Bain & Yu, 1980; Diaz, 1983; Peal & Lambert, 1962). They were better at concept formation and in tasks that required symbol manipulation and mental flexibility. The problem with this research was that the bilingual selection process picked out the more intelligent subjects (Hakuta, 1986). The cognitive capabilities which allowed them to successfully learn two languages also led to their higher performance on the tasks. Additional research found that when subjects were randomly assigned to conditions and were tested for cognitive abilities before learning a second language, no differences were found between the bilinguals and monolinguals. Being bilingual appears to have neither an overall positive nor a negative effect on cognition (Hakuta, 1986). There are, however, some differences between monolinguals and bilinguals in several aspects of cognitive processing, as pointed out in numerous chapters in this book.

Overview of this Volume

The focus in this volume is on <u>cognitive</u> aspects of bilingualism. We have defined "cognitive" fairly broadly, but in every chapter the focus of the discussion is on thought processes in bilinguals. In most cases the emphasis is on adults rather than children, though a few chapters focus on children. The emphasis is not on the acquisition of a second language, nor is it on issues in education. These problems have been covered extensively elsewhere. Following this chapter, Catharine Keatley offers a review of the history of bilingualism research in cognitive psychology, François Grosjean suggests a new way to conceptualize the bilingual, and Michael Palij and Doris Aaronson argue that language background should be taken into account in any study of bilingualism or even cognition in general.

Part II contains several papers dealing with memory in bilinguals. Following a general paper on bilingual memory by Roberto Heredia and Barry McLaughlin, Gordon Brown and Charles Hulme examine the role of short-term memory on L2 processing. Michael Harrington looks at the limited capacity of working memory as a constraint in L2 development, and Nick Ellis examines a more specific working memory effect, that of bilingual word length. The two papers by Jeanette Altarriba and J. Y. Opoku examine the role of translation equivalents in bilingual memory. In the final paper, Judith Kroll and Alexandra Sholl examine lexical versus conceptual memory in bilinguals, a topic that serves as transition to the next section.

The next set of papers (Part III) is narrower in focus and examines the issue of word recognition and lexical access in bilinguals, primarily drawing on reserach using the lexical decision paradigm. Jonathan Grainger and Ton Dijkstra present a theoretical model of word recognition in bilinguals. Cecile Beauvillain examines orthographic properties, Estelle Doctor and Denise Klein focus on phonological processing, and Hsuan-chih Chen looks at L2 proficiency in lexical access. Cheryl Frenck-Mestre and Jyotsna Vaid examine lexical access in number words versus "ordinary" words and its implications for theories of word recognition. Helena-Fivi Chitiri, Yilin Sun, Dale Willows, and Insup Taylor focus specifically on word recognition in reading. Finally, Marianne Votaw offers an integrative review of the bilingual lexical access literature, arguing the necessity of a functional view of the problem.

The three papers in Part IV expand the scope of bilingual cognition to consider the role of syntax in bilingual processing. Janet McDonald and Kathy Heilenman look at the bilingual's development of word-order strategies. Kerry Kilborn examines on-line integrative processing in bilinguals. Finally, Kenneth Hyltenstam focuses on the issue of the bilingual's ultimate attainment in L2 and argues that even highly fluent and balanced bilinguals do show some processing differences from L1 speakers.

The papers in Part V look at issues of language transfer and code switching. Brian MacWhinney uses the framework of the Competition Model to examine the issue of transfer from L1 to L2, while Aydin Durgunoglu and Barbara Hancin examine research on components of the reading process to understand the role of L1 transfer at each level. Beatrice de Gelder and Jean Vroomen examine the role of L1 orthography and mastery of alphabetic skills in speech perception. Wei Ling Lee, Ghim Choo Wee, Ovid Tzeng, and Daisy Hung compare the effect of type of orthography on Stroop task performance. Abdelali Bentahila and Eirlys Davies present a qualitative analysis of social and psychological factors in code-switching, and Monica Lasisi and Anthony Onyehalu look at the role of cultural knowledge in the bilingual's language comprehension.

Although each of the papers in Part VI examines metalinguistic skills in bilinguals in some way, they approach the problem from vastly different angles. In three papers studying child bilinguals, Lenore Arnberg and Peter Arnberg look at bilingual awareness and language separation, Marguerite Malakoff examines the process of translation, and Ellen Bialystok argues that bilingual children excel in selective attention compared to monolinguals. Finally, Jacqueline Thomas discusses metalinguistic awareness in adult bilinguals and trilinguals.

Taking a very different approach than the other papers in this volume, the last section (Part VII) offers two papers (by Edith Mägiste and Rumjahn Hoosain) on the role of cerebral lateralization in bilingual cognitive processing.

Recommended Reading

The most readable introduction to bilingualism is François Grosjean's (1982) *Life with Two Languages*. While fully referenced to the empirical research, Grosjean also presents numerous first-person testimonies called "Bilinguals Speak" which give a wonderful phenomenological sense of being bilingual. This book simply cannot be recommended too highly, and it contains chapters on the social aspects of bilingualism as well as the cognitive and interpersonal aspects and a chapter on the bilingual child. A somewhat briefer book in the same vein is Hakuta (1986), which, unlike Grosjean, contains overview chapters on bilingual education and bilingualism and intelligence. For a look at bilingualism from a sociolinguistic and developmental perspective, see Romaine (1989).

For earlier empirical papers, including many by contributors to the present volume, see Vaid (1986). Readers interested in bilingualism and second-language acquisition in children should read McLaughlin (1984, 1985). For a good set of papers on childhood bilingualism, see Homel, Palij, and Aaronson (1987). For readings on bilingualism across the entire life span, see Hyltenstam and Obler (1989). Those interested in second-language acquisition in adults should read Krashen (1981) and Klein (1986). For the specific topic of cross-linguistic influence, see Odlin (1989), and for communication strategies in L2, see Bialystok (1990). Genesee (1987) examines results of immersion and bilingual education programs. Reynolds (1991) contains several integrative papers on different aspects of bilingualism.

Curiously, bilingualism is barely mentioned in most cognitive psychology texts, even those that treat language fairly extensively. The most thorough chapter on bilingualism in psycholinguistics texts is Taylor and Taylor (1990), and Paivio and Begg (1981) also have one. Other texts in psycholinguistics treat bilingualism only very lightly, if at all.

Finally, for a tremendously moving testimony of the personal costs of diglossia and being educated out of one's native language and culture, see Richard Rodriguez' (1982) *Hunger of Memory*.

Footnote

[1]We struggle over whether to use the term "bilingualism" or "multilingualism." On the one hand, there is a denotative difference of whether two or more than two languages are involved. Nonetheless, we and most of the authors in this book have opted for "bilingual," on the grounds that (1) that term is the more familiar one in the literature, and (2) most, though not all, of the research in the area studies bilingual rather than multilingual people. Still, however, it is worth bearing in mind that many people and cultures we label "bilingual" may in fact be multilingual, and no slighting of this fact is intended.

References

Baetens Beardsmore, H. (1982). *Bilingualism: Basic principles*. Clevedon, UK: Tieto Ltd.

Bain, B., and Yu, A. (1980). Cognitive consequences of raising children bilingually: "One parent, one language." *Canadian Journal of Psychology*, 34, 304-313.

Bialystok, E. (1990). *Communication strategies: A psychological analysis of second-language use*. Oxford UK: Basil Blackwell.

Brigham, C. C. (1923). *A study of American intelligence*. Princeton, NJ: Princeton University Press.

Diaz, R. (1983). Thought and two languages: The impact of bilingualism on cognitive development. *Review of Research in Education*, 10, 23-54.

Genesee, F. (1987). *Learning through two languages: Studies of immersion and bilingual education*. New York: Newbury/Harper & Row.

Goddard, H. H. (1917). Mental tests and the immigrant. *Journal of Delinquency*, 2, 243-277.

Goodenough, F. (1926). Racial differences in the intelligence of school children. *Journal of Experimental Psychology*, 9, 388-397.

Grosjean, F. (1982). *Life with two languages*. Cambridge, MA: Harvard University Press.

Hakuta, K. (1986). *Mirror of language*. New York: Basic Books.

Homel, P., Palij, M., & Aaronson, D. (Eds.) (1987). *Childhood bilingualism: Aspects of linguistic, cognitive, and social development*. Hillsdale, NJ: Lawrence Erlbaum Associates.

Hyltenstam, K., & Obler, L. K. (Eds.) (1989). *Bilingualism across the lifespan.* Cambridge, UK: Cambridge University Press.

Klein, W. (1986). *Second language acquisition.* Cambridge, UK: Cambridge University Press.

Krashen, S. (1981). *Second language acquisition and second language learning.* Oxford, UK: Pergamon Press.

Macnamara, J. (1969). How can one measure the extent of one's verbal proficiency? In L. G. Kelly (Ed.) *Description and measurement of bilingualism.* Toronto: University of Toronto Press. Pp. 80-119.

McLaughlin, B. (1984). *Second-language acquisition in childhood: Vol. 1. Preschool children.* (2nd ed.). Hillsdale, NJ: Lawrence Erlbaum Associates.

McLaughlin, B. (1985). *Second-language acquisition in childhood: Vol. 2. School-age children.* (2nd ed.). Hillsdale, NJ: Lawrence Erlbaum Associates.

Odlin, T. (1989). *Language transfer.* Cambridge, UK: Cambridge University Press.

Paivio, A., & Begg, I. (1981). *Psychology of language.* Englewood Cliffs, NJ: Prentice-Hall.

Peal, E., & Lambert, W. E. (1962). The relation of bilingualism to intelligence. *Psychological Monographs, 76* (27, Whole No. 546).

Reynolds, A. G. (Ed.). (1991). *Bilingualism, multiculturalism, and second language learning.* Hillsdale, NJ: Lawrence Erlbaum Associates.

Rodriguez, R. (1982). *Hunger of memory: The education of Richard Rodriguez.* Boston: D. R. Godine.

Romaine, S. (1989). *Bilingualism.* Oxford UK: Basil Blackwell.

Smith, M. E. (1939). Some light on the problem of bilingualism as found from a study of the progress in mastery of English among pre-school children of non-American ancestry in Hawaii. *Genetic Psychology Monographs, 21,* 119-284.

Taylor, I., & Taylor, M. M. (1990). *Psycholinguistics.* Englewood Cliffs, NJ: Prentice-Hall.

Vaid, J. (Ed.) (1986). *Language processing in bilinguals.* Hillsdale, NJ: Lawrence Erlbaum Associates.

Appendix 1: Languages of the World Family Trees

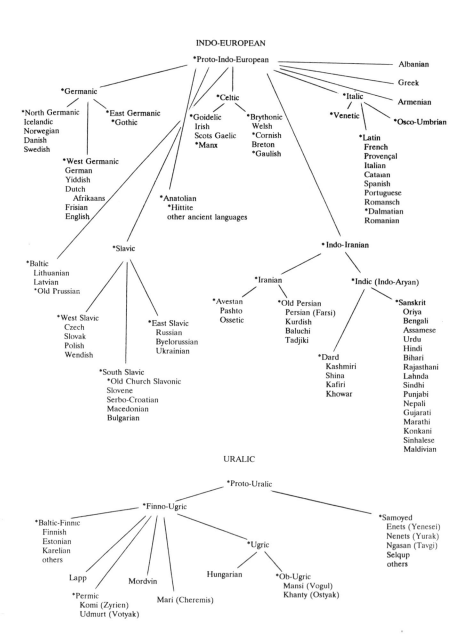

INDO-EUROPEAN

*Proto-Indo-European — Albanian

Greek

*Germanic

Armenian

*Celtic

*Italic

*North Germanic   *East Germanic
Icelandic   *Gothic
Norwegian
Danish
Swedish

*Goidelic   *Brythonic
Irish   Welsh
Scots Gaelic *Cornish
*Manx   Breton
             *Gaulish

*Venetic

*Osco-Umbrian

*West Germanic
German
Yiddish
Dutch
Afrikaans
Frisian
English

*Latin
French
Provençal
Italian
Cataıan
Spanish
Portuguese
Romansch
*Dalmatian
Romanian

*Anatolian
*Hittite
other ancient languages

*Slavic

• Indo-Iranian

*Baltic
Lithuanian
Latvian
*Old Prussian

*Iranian

*Indic (Indo-Aryan)

*Avestan
Pashto
Ossetic

*Old Persian
Persian (Farsi)
Kurdish
Baluchi
Tadjiki

*Sanskrit
Oriya
Bengali
Assamese
Urdu
Hindi
Bihari
Rajasthani
Lahnda
Sindhi
Punjabi
Nepali
Gujarati
Marathi
Konkani
Sinhalese
Maldivian

*West Slavic
Czech
Slovak
Polish
Wendish

*East Slavic
Russian
Byelorussian
Ukrainian

*Dard
Kashmiri
Shina
Kafiri
Khowar

*South Slavic
*Old Church Slavonic
Slovene
Serbo-Croatian
Macedonian
Bulgarian

URALIC

*Proto-Uralic

*Finno-Ugric

*Baltic-Finnic
Finnish
Estonian
Karelian
others

*Samoyed
Enets (Yenesei)
Nenets (Yurak)
Ngasan (Tavgi)
Selqup
others

*Ugric

Lapp

Mordvin

Hungarian

*Ob-Ugric
Mansi (Vogul)
Khanty (Ostyak)

*Permic
Komi (Zyrien)
Udmurt (Votyak)

Mari (Cheremis)

Appendix 1: Languages of the World Family Trees (cont.)

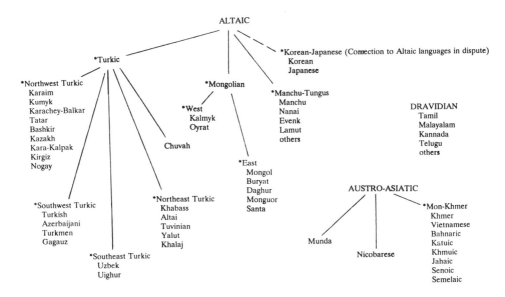

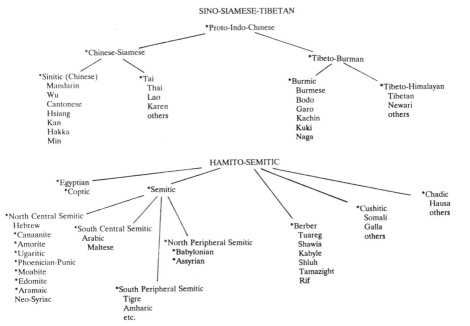

Appendix 1: Languages of the World Family Trees (cont.)

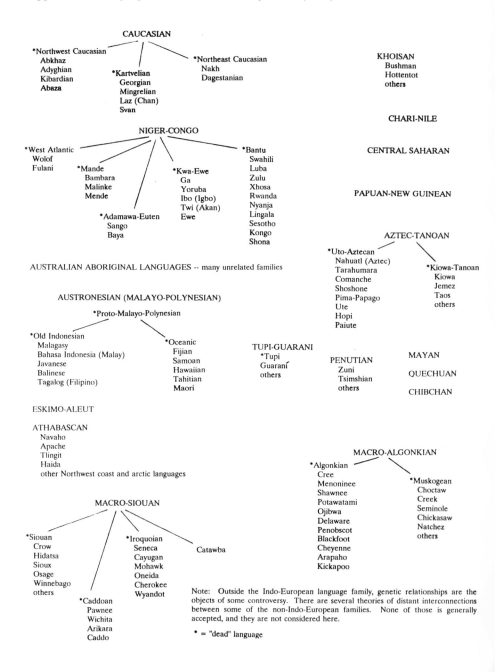

CAUCASIAN

*Northwest Caucasian
Abkhaz
Adyghian
Kibardian
Abaza

*Kartvelian
Georgian
Mingrelian
Laz (Chan)
Svan

*Northeast Caucasian
Nakh
Dagestanian

KHOISAN
Bushman
Hottentot
others

CHARI-NILE

NIGER-CONGO

*West Atlantic
Wolof
Fulani

*Mande
Bambara
Malinke
Mende

*Adamawa-Euten
Sango
Baya

*Kwa-Ewe
Ga
Yoruba
Ibo (Igbo)
Twi (Akan)
Ewe

*Bantu
Swahili
Luba
Zulu
Xhosa
Rwanda
Nyanja
Lingala
Sesotho
Kongo
Shona

CENTRAL SAHARAN

PAPUAN-NEW GUINEAN

AZTEC-TANOAN

*Uto-Aztecan
Nahuatl (Aztec)
Tarahumara
Comanche
Shoshone
Pima-Papago
Ute
Hopi
Paiute

*Kiowa-Tanoan
Kiowa
Jemez
Taos
others

AUSTRALIAN ABORIGINAL LANGUAGES -- many unrelated families

AUSTRONESIAN (MALAYO-POLYNESIAN)

*Proto-Malayo-Polynesian

*Old Indonesian
Malagasy
Bahasa Indonesia (Malay)
Javanese
Balinese
Tagalog (Filipino)

*Oceanic
Fijian
Samoan
Hawaiian
Tahitian
Maori

TUPI-GUARANI
*Tupi
Guaraní
others

PENUTIAN
Zuni
Tsimshian
others

MAYAN

QUECHUAN

CHIBCHAN

ESKIMO-ALEUT

ATHABASCAN
Navaho
Apache
Tlingit
Haida
other Northwest coast and arctic languages

MACRO-ALGONKIAN

*Algonkian
Cree
Menoninee
Shawnee
Potawatami
Ojibwa
Delaware
Penobscot
Blackfoot
Cheyenne
Arapaho
Kickapoo

*Muskogean
Choctaw
Creek
Seminole
Chickasaw
Natchez
others

MACRO-SIOUAN

*Siouan
Crow
Hidatsa
Sioux
Osage
Winnebago
others

*Iroquoian
Seneca
Cayugan
Mohawk
Oneida
Cherokee
Wyandot

Catawba

*Caddoan
Pawnee
Wichita
Arikara
Caddo

Note: Outside the Indo-European language family, genetic relationships are the
objects of some controversy. There are several theories of distant interconnections
between some of the non-Indo-European families. None of those is generally
accepted, and they are not considered here.

* = "dead" language

Cognitive Processing in Bilinguals – R.J. Harris (Editor)

History of Bilingualism Research in Cognitive Psychology

Catharine W. Keatley
Tilburg University

Abstract

A review of the history of the research in cognitive psychology on bilingualism reveals that it is emerging as a discrete field of study. The historical perspective allows three separate trends to be identified in the literature. These trends have different histories, assumptions and foci. The story of the bilingual research is the story of how these trends have developed, sometimes together and sometimes independently, over the past forty years.

Introduction

The research on the cognitive psychology of bilingualism is just emerging as a coherent body. The experiments are often closely linked to theories, models, and research from other areas. This results in differences between experiments which can obscure the common threads that hold them together. A pattern is identifiable, however, in the differences between experiments. Much of the research can be roughly divided into three subgroups. Each of these subgroups has a slightly different history, theoretical foundation and focus. The story of how these subgroups have developed demonstrates that there is a cumulative body of knowledge on the cognitive psychology of bilingualism which now exists as a discrete field of research.

The largest group of studies has been carried out using bilingualism as a means of determining whether the meanings of words expressed in different languages are represented in memory in a single shared store, or whether they are represented in separate, different memory systems. This group is strongly related to general psychological models of memory. Another group focuses on whether there are influences from an inactive language on behavior in an active language. They focus on creating models of language functioning, not necessarily of memory organization. These experiments are often more closely related to linguistic models of language functioning than the experiments in the other two groups. The third group does not ask if memory is separate or shared but, assuming that memory is shared, focuses on how words in the two different languages access the shared conceptual representations.

The experiments reviewed in this paper have been grouped according to paradigms or focus. Within each group, the experiments are organized chronologically, although occasionally chronology is broken in order to present highly related experiments together. The order of the sections has been determined partially by when the paradigm became important and partially by the development of the theories. Generally, the earlier research included experiments employing recall and recognition measures, while the later research has emphasized reaction time measures; especially reaction time on the lexical decision task. Within the limits of a single chapter it is not possible to include all the published experiments on bilingualism. Thus, the criterion for inclusion is whether the research has had an important impact on the body of experimental research. Experiments that focus on educational issues and psychophysiology are not included. These constitute a rich and complex literature which interact with, but do not form a constituent part of, the experimental literature.

Earlier Research Paradigms: Emphasis on Recall and Recognition Measures

The Compound-Coordinate Distinction

Throughout the late nineteenth and early twentieth centuries, psychologists generally left issues of bilingual processing to educators and linguists. The main exceptions were Cattell's experiments in 1887 (see the section on Comparisons of Reaction Times). The first detailed description of bilingual memory organization did not appear until 1953, and was written by a linguist, Weinreich. He proposed that three kinds of bilingual memory systems exist: coexistent bilingualism, merged bilingualism and subordinative bilingualism.

In 1954, Ervin and Osgood published a psychological model of bilingual memory which incorporated ideas similar to those of Weinrich. Ervin and Osgood's compound-coordinate model reflected the behavioristic climate in psychology prevalant at that time by emphasizing mechanisms of memory, and not the nature of the representations. They suggested that bilinguals who learn their languages in different environments develop a coordinate memory system in which representations of words in different languages are separate (Weinreich's coexistent model). Bilinguals who learn their languages by using them interchangeably develop a memory system where the representations are compounded, which means they are the same for translation equivalent words (Weinreich's merged model). Weinreich suggested that if a bilingual learned a second language on the basis of a first language, the referents of the new words would be their translation equivalents in the first language. He called this subordinative bilingualism. This idea was dropped for years, but has reappeared as the word association hypothesis (see section on Comparisons of Reaction Times). Ervin and Osgood included subordinative bilingualism in their compounded model. They did not see the compound and coordinate models as mutually exclusive, but rather as often coexisting in the same individual.

In the 1950's and early 1960's there was a flurry of research on the compound-coordinate model, much of which supported the model. Experiments were conducted on bilinguals with compound and coordinate histories to determine if their performance on memory experiments with bilingual stimuli reflected coordinate and compound memory systems. For example, Lambert, Havelka and Crosby (1958) found on the semantic differential (a system of rating words according to their connotations) that compound bilinguals showed more uniformity of responses across languages and coordinates more diversity. Another example is a study by Jacobovits and Lambert (1961), which reported that subjects with a compound language history showed effects of semantic satiation across languages, while subjects with a coordinate history did not.

Other research, however, did not support the model. One example is the study by Kolers (1963) reported below, in which he found no difference in the associations produced by compound and coordinate bilinguals. Diller (1974) wrote an adamant attack on experiments which did support the compound-coordinate model. He found the means of classifying subjects as coordinate and compound to be unclear and changing from experiment to experiment. Further he claimed that the results of the experiments were inconclusive because alternative explanations could be provided for most of the data.

The compound-coordinate model of bilingualism was the first statement of the shared and separate store hypotheses of bilingual memory which would provide the basis for most research in bilingual memory over the next 30 years. However, consideration of the compound-coordinate model was generally dropped by the end of the 1960s. Perhaps this was due to problems within both model and research, but it was probably also caused by the general excitement within psychology about models based on information processing frameworks. These models linked questions about memory organization to those about the nature of representations.

Experiments on the Generation of Cross-Language Associations

In 1963 Paul Kolers wrote an important paper which linked the models of the organization of bilingual memory to models of the nature of representation. He described what was essentially Ervin and Osgood's (1954) compound model and called it the "shared" model. e linked the shared model to a "supralinguistic" characterization of representations. This argues that concepts are stored in some sort of non-linguistic, abstract form such as the proposition. He described what was essentially Ervin and Osgood's coordinate model and called this the "separate store model." This he linked to a view of representation in which the representations are formed specifically by the means of the encoding experience. In a bilingual, the representation of a word encoded in a specific language would be stored in a form that in some way is specific to that language.

By linking the separate and shared models to questions about the actual nature of representations, Kolers' schema could not propose that both forms of bilingualism exist in one individual. Rather they became conflicting models of the same phenomena.

Studies on the generation of cross-language associations are embedded in associationist models of memory and focus on determining the organization of representations in memory. Kolers assumed in his 1963 paper that primary associates generated by subjects reveal the organization of the representations of concepts in memory. He tested the separate and shared models by asking bilingual subjects to generate associates to words within and across languages. While there was no difference between the responses of subjects with compound and cooordinate language histories, Kolers found that for all the subjects, about two-thirds of the associations to translation equivalents were different. He concluded that experiences and memories are stored separately by representations specific to the original language.

Macnamara (1967) asked subjects to produce associates either in one language or to switch between languages in their responses, and found that they produced more associates in the unilingual condition. Taylor (1971) repeated this result, and also found that subjects produce more within-language primary associates than across-language associates. Macnamara and Taylor both concluded, along with Kolers, that there are more associations within than across languages. Therefore this data supports the position that representations of words expressed in different languages are separate. However, they also found some cross-language associations.

The Language Switch

The above-reviewed studies on the associates produced by bilinguals became entangled with research on the question of how bilinguals switch between one language system and the other. While switching reduced the associations generated, it was demonstrated that subjects could produce some associations across languages, suggesting that the two language systems were not entirely cut off from each other in memory. Psychologists addressed the question of defining the mechanism which controls the bilingual's ability to change from one language system to another. While the generation of associations literature was firmly based on models of memory, the language switch literature had a different genesis. The idea that a mechanism exists came from neurophysiological theory. Hebb (1958) suggested that a neurophysiological "switch" exists which mediates between independent "neural sets." This idea was applied to bilingual memory specifically by Penfield and Roberts (1959) who proposed that the functional separation of languages is carried out by an automatic switch at the neurophysiological level. No evidence for such a neurophysiological switch mechanism has been found, but the idea of such a mechanism prompted a group of studies in the 1960s and early 1970s which will be briefly reviewed below. (For a complete review of this research see Albert and Obler, 1978). The literature now is a hybrid based on linguistic models of language functioning and cognitive models of memory. Conclusions drawn from the research are related to grammar systems rather than to representations. However, the question and models parallel those in the studies designed to examine memory organization. These experiments look at language switching under natural conditions and try to determine what controls this code-switching behavior: a supralinguiustic grammar or the meshing of the grammars of the two languages.

Kolers (1966b) conducted the first experiments on language switching. He asked subjects to read passages under various conditions in which he mixed bilingual text. Comprehension seemed unaffected by mixing the languages, but speed of reading was slower in the mixed-language conditions. Kolers concluded that the meanings of words are represented in a language-free form in long term memory, but at the encoding level there is a language switch that mediates between encodings of language specific stimuli. In addition, the functioning of the language switch takes time.

This experiment was repeated in various forms by a number of other researchers. Dalrymple-Alford and Aamiry (1967) tested comprehension time of unilingual and bilingual two-word stimuli and found no evidence of a switch in encoding the stimuli. Macnamara, Krauthammer and Bolgar (1968) found evidence for a switch between languages when subjects made verbal responses and concluded a switch does mediate between language-specific verbal production systems. Macnamara and Kushnir (1971) reported that as the number of language switches increased in the sentences, the time necessary for subjects to make true-false judgements about the sentences also increased. They concluded that the separation between the languages included a separation in the representations of the meanings of the words.

Albert and Obler (1978) proposed an alternative mechanism which they called a "continuous operating monitor system." They saw it as a more general system for controlling the processing of incoming stimuli from different modalities and in different languages both in monolinguals and bilinguals. Chan, Chau and Hoosain (1983) tested subjects by using materials that were "naturally" switched. The naturally-mixed text was read at the same rate as text written entirely in the subjects' first language. The authors concluded that the time attributed to the operation of the switch in various experimental tasks is the result of the experimental situation, and decided the continuously operating monitor system provided a better explanation for their data. Dalrymple-Alford (1985) varied relatedness as well as language in word lists, and also concluded that the increased time attributed to the switch was a result of the unnatural experimental materials rather than evidence for a cognitive mechanism.

Whether or not a specific cognitive switch exists disappeared as an issue during most of the 1980s. It was generally agreed that evidence for the switch came from the unnatural experimental stimuli and not from the act of changing languages. It was observed that many bilinguals switch between languages in normal discourse, and their natural code-switching does not take time. Examinations of natural code-switching behavior indicated that the switches are not arbitrary but rule-based (Clyne, 1980; Pfaff, 1979; Poplack, 1980). A new question emerged: what governs this switching behavior? Pfaff (1979) argued that it is governed by structural and semantic constraints which are the natural result of the two grammars meshing. Sridhar and Sridhar (1980) concluded that the two grammar systems are separate but interact to form code-switched sentences. Clyne (1980) proposed that language switching affects only the surface structure of communication, while the meanings of words and sentences are stored in a deeper metalinguistic level of representation. Poplack (1980) held that code-switching is a discrete mode of speaking with a grammar discrete from those of its constituent languages.

The code-switching literature and the general switch literature share a basic question: how is linguistic switching behavior governed? Is there a single supralinguistic grammar or switch, or is language changing the inevitable result of meshing two language systems without recourse to a supralinguistic or metalinguistic system?

Although the idea of a specific language switch has been dropped, the question of how bilinguals functionally separate their languages remains a theme throughout much of the literature. An important question is whether bilinguals actually do keep their languages apart, or whether there are subtle differences between bilinguals and monolinguals which demonstrate influences across languages. These question are taken up in later sections of this survey. (For a good description of code-switching as well as an excellent general discussion of bilingualism, see Grosjean, 1982.)

Transfer of Learning and Interference Across Languages

In the 1970s a number of studies inspired by Learning Theory models were conducted to examine whether learning in one language transferred to another language system. These studies grew out of learning theory research which assumed a basic associationist model of memory. Transfer across language systems was taken as indicating shared representation; lack of transfer, separate representation. These experiments used classic learning theory experimental designs such as serial list learning and paired associate learning. Generally they tested whether learning words in a list in one language affected how translation equivalent words were learned in a later list.

Young and Saegert (1966) studied cross-language transfer in serial list learning by English-Spanish bilinguals. They found both positive and negative transfer of learning across translation equivalents. Lopez and Young (1974), using a similar design, also found position transfer across languages. Young and Webber (1967) extended the experiment to learning lists of paired associates. Again, this provided evidence of transfer of learning across languages. These results were essentially duplicated by Young and Navar (1968) and by Lopez, Hicks and Young (1974). In 1973, Saegert, Obermeyer and Kazarian found within- and cross-language language negative transfer in a part-whole list learning experiment. McLeod (1976) used a list-learning procedure to see if a savings effect would occur across languages when the second list occurred after five weeks or a full year of the initial exposure. He found that the words in the first list facilitated the learning of translation equivalents as well as exact repetitions in later presented lists, even when subjects could not recall the words from the first list. Since all these experiments found transfer of learning across language systems, they were taken as support for the single store model of bilingual memory organization.

Kintsch and Kintsch (1969) carried out a slightly different experiment. They tested learning rates of short bilingual word lists in which all words on each list were paired with the same digit. In the learning sessions, the authors found evidence of cross-language interference across translation equivalents. A second experiment, employing a probe technique, produced no apparent interference. The authors concluded that interlingual interference occurs in secondary memory rather than in primary memory. This important interpretation marks the beginnings of the idea that word meanings are shared in a "deeper" memory, but not in a more shallow or transient memory. Kintsch (1970) carried out a related experiment which found that subjects confused translation equivalents and repetitions on a continuous learning task. He concluded that subjects can code words either in terms of language specific cues or in terms of semantic content; the task itself determines which encoding system will predominate. This was taken up later by Durgunoglu and Roediger (1987) (see section on Effects of Repetition on Recall).

The Learning Theory based experimental designs described above generally produced results which demonstrated that learning a word in one language affected how its translation equivalent was learned later. This was taken as support for a shared model of bilingual memory. However, the paradigm was abandoned for the most part after the middle 1970s. Information processing models replaced the learning theory models which inspired this literature. These newer models allowed stages, or levels, of processing which were applied to the bilingual literature to account for findings such as those of Kintsch and Kintsch (1969), that on some tasks bilingual memory appears to be shared, while on others, separate.

Release from Proactive Interference

The research on release from Proactive Interference (P.I.) in bilinguals was based on monolingual research on memory, and its results are considered in the light of models of memory organization. In the unilingual list learning experiments it had been demonstrated that if the category of words in a to-be-recalled list is changed after a number of items, then recall is increased. This is explained as release from Proactive Interference (P.I.); interference caused by previously learned items which tap the same structures in memory. In the bilingual version, the language of presentation of the stimuli is changed.

Goggin and Wickens (1971) conducted an important experiment where they found that bilinguals produced as much release from P.I. in recall when the language of the words changed as when the category in a unilingual list changed. Proficient bilinguals had a greater release from P.I. with a language switch than less proficient bilinguals. Goggin and Wickens interpreted these results as support for a separate store model of memory. Dillon, McCormack, Petrusic, Cook and Lafleur (1973) essentially repeated the experiment with the same results but were neutral on how to interpret them. Later McCormack (1977) argued that these results support the language-tagging model of bilingual memory, to be discussed below.

A more recent study by O'Neill and Huot (1984) used consonant-vowel-consonant nonwords which could be pronounced with either a French or English accent, instead of words in different languages. Presentation was auditory. The results indicated that a pronunciation shift with meaningless syllables was sufficent to produce significant release from P.I. O'Neill and Huot concluded that the data supports a model of separate phonological decoding systems for the two languages, but does not test a model of how the meanings of words are stored.

Although the results of these experiments are uncontested, the question is how to interpret them. Goggin and Wickens' interpretation that the results support a separate as opposed to shared store model of representation reflects the shared-separate dichotomy as it was posed by Kolers in 1963. O'Neill and Huot's interpretation is based on the the more current assumption that there are different levels or structures involved in the processing of words and that while phonological coding processes may be separate, the representations of meaning may still be shared. The first appeal to this idea in the context of bilingual memory was the application of attribute-tagging models of memory to bilingual representation. This will be introduced in the next section.

Organization of Recall of Categories in Bilingual Lists

While the literature reviewed above examined the effect of changing the category membership of words in lists, a small group of experiments focused on the relative strength of bonds between words in the same language, and bonds between words across languages that represent members of the same category. This research is based on an associationist model of memory; its focus is to test models of memory organization. It is in the context of this literature that the attribute-tagging model of memory was first applied to bilingual memory. This model has been used to explain how a shared memory system with amodal, abstract representations can also incorporate information about specific perceptual/sensory modes or specific symbolic codes (such as the language a word is expressed in). It holds that this sort of information is stored as a tag attached to the abstract representation which neither influences nor contributes to the meaning. Subjects in an experiment may attend to the conceptual representations or to the linguistic tags, depending on the demands of the task. If subjects are required to focus on the concepts, the tags may be disconnected in decoding and lost, leading to wrong-language errors. (For a full description see Anderson and Bower, 1972; for a description of how the model is applied to bilingual memory, see McCormack,1976, 1977.)

Lambert, Ignatow, and Krauthammer (1968) reported that mixing language of presentation of words in a list did not affect recall; however, mixing category membership of words interfered with recall from unilingual lists and interfered even more with recall from bilingual lists. They found, however, that on bilingual lists, subjects still tended to group together words that named objects belonging to the same category. Also, in this cross-language condition, they observed a number of wrong-language errors. Neither the shared nor the separate models as stated by Kolers (1963) could account for this finding and the authors concluded that a simple associationist model was inadequate to explain the results.

The same year, Nott and Lambert (1968) published a similar study where they found that if words on bilingual lists belonged to a small number of categories, recall was better than when the lists had words that could not be categorized. On the bilingual category lists, subjects made a significant number of wrong-language errors. The authors interpreted these results as supporting the language-tagging hypothesis. They took the wrong-language errors, which occurred only when subjects could categorize words across languages, as evidence that subjects were decoding words semantically, and the language tags were getting lost in the process. These experiments by Lambert were followed by an experiment of Dalrymple-Alford and Aamiry (1969) who, using three languages and three categories, found the same results.

Champagnol (1975) in a similar experiment also obtained the same general results. In addition, he found that, as proficiency in the second language increased, the clustering of recalled items on bilingual lists became more dependent on semantic category and less dependent on language.

The research on the organization of categories across languages demonstrated that bilingual memory did not appear to be either fully shared or fully separate. Rather, models that could account for strong bonds within languages, but also bonds between languages were needed. Kolers' 1963 statement of the simple separate and shared positions could not provide such a framework. The language-tagging model, however, could because it assumed that the meanings of translation equivalent words are stored as shared representations, while the language specific tags are separate.

Recall of the Language of Presentation of a Stimulus

While the experiments in the previous section examined the strength of bonds between words expressed in the same language as compared to bonds between semantically related words across languages, the experiments reviewed in this section looked at how well subjects remember what language words are expressed in on a first presentation. This research focuses on using bilingual memory as a test for the attribute-tagging model of memory. If the language of presentation is easily forgotten, this would suggest that it is a tagged attribute. However, if language of presentation is retained this suggests that it is an integral part of the representation of a word.

Kolers (1965) asked subjects to learn lists of words. In one condition they were to remember the language of the words in a bilingual list; in the other condition they were to remember which of two colours the words were written in. Remembering the language of words did not affect recall at all, remembering the colour the words were written in reduced recall by one-half. Kolers interpreted these results as indicating that while color takes up an item in memory, language does not. He concluded that language is not just an arbitrary coding scheme, a tagged attribute in memory, but rather forms an integral part of the representation of the word.

Rose and Carroll (1974) and Rose, Rose, King and Perez (1975) found that recall of the language of presentation was very good for both words in lists and words in sentences. Saegert, Hamayan and Ahmar (1975) reported that recognition of "old" words and recall of the language of presentation was very high in trilinguals, but lower when the words were embedded in sentences than when they were in lists. They concluded that these results supported the language-tagging model, which they interpreted as predicting that subjects can selectively attend either to the linguistic attributes of words or to the semantic aspects of words.

From the mid-1970s until the mid-1980s the question of recall of the language of presentation of stimuli was largely ignored. In 1986 Cristoffanini, Kirsner and Milech, as part of an experimental series asked subjects to read words in a bilingual list and then gave them a recognition test. Some of the words were translation equivalents and some were cognates, translation equivalents which differed orthographically only slightly across languages. Memory for language of presentation was very good for noncognates and very poor for cognates. Cristoffanini et al. interpreted these results as support for an attribute-tagging model of memory where morphology rather than language per se determines how shared representations in memory are tagged. Language is not an attribute according to this model, only the relations of letter patterns and meaning, i.e., morphology, determines the boundaries between what are usually taken as language categories in memory. They propose that this process is continuous with monolingual word processing where, according to the same model, words are organized according to principles based on their morphology. The representations of the meanings of words are always assumed to be shared.

This point of view was expanded in a paper by Kirsner (1986) where he argued that it is not necessary to propose a special model of bilingual memory. Rather, he argued that overall, some attributes are more important than others in determining recall. In memory for language of presentation, similarity of morphology is more important than similarity of meaning. The more similar the morphology, the more a first encoding facilitates a morphologically similar second encoding. Hence, the better recall and recognition will be for morphologically similar repeated words, whether they belong to the same language or not and whether they share the same meaning or not.

Effects of Repetition Across Languages on Recall

The experiments to be reviewed in this section examine the effects of within- and cross-language repetition on recall and recognition. Repetition across languages means that the second presentation is the translation equivalent of the word in the first presentation. Results from these experiments are taken as support for a diversity of models of bilingual memory; the dual-coding model, the language-tagging model, and the means specific or transfer appropriate approach to bilingual memory. These positions all provide more complex explanations of bilingual memory than the first description of Kolers (1963). They focus on why bilinguals produce different kinds of responses on different tasks. It is particularly evident in these studies that the models are taken from more general models of memory organization, and their results have implications not only for bilingual memory, but for general models of memory.

It was Kolers (1966a) again who conducted the seminal experiment. On unilingual lists recall of words increases with the frequency of presentation by n/2. Kolers' bilingual subjects saw lists where the number of repetitions varied within and across languages. The results showed that the probability of recall was the same whether the repetitions were within or across languages. Kolers' conclusions were that translation equivalent words share the same representation of semantic meaning.

Tulving and Colotla (1970) used a slightly different design. They asked subjects to freely recall words from lists which were monolingual, bilingual and trilingual. A large proportion of the items across the lists were translation equivalents. Recall from unilingual lists was best, recall from bilingual lists next best, and recall was worst from trilingual lists. Recall of words on multilingual lists was the most impaired in the subjects' dominant language. The authors concluded that these results supported the separate store hypothesis. Liepmann and Saegert (1974) basically repeated Tulving and Colotla's experiment and reported the same results for overall recall. However, they also found that performance deteriorated and wrong-language errors increased as a function of the number of lists learned. They argued this demonstrated subjects had to make discriminations on the basis of language as well as on the basis of list membership. The number of wrong-language errors was taken as support for the position that the meaning of the words are stored in a single memory system where the language attribute is tagged to the propositional representation.

Glanzer and Duarte (1971) carried out an experiment to see if the distribution effect, an increase of recall with an increase of lag between items, occurred on bilingual lists as it was known to occur on unilingual lists. The distribution effect was generally attributed to additive encodings of the repeated stimulus in long-term memory. The results of this experiment were that the distribution effect held for repetitions within and across languages. Whereas in Kolers' experiment repetitions across languages produced as much increase in recall as repetition within languages, in this experiment cross-language repetitions produced more recall. This was due particularly to the repetitions with short lags. The data suggested that the representations of translation equivalent words in different languages did not overlap completely in short-term or long-term memory; however, the authors did not specifically link their conclusions to a particular model of memory.

Kolers and Gonzalez (1980) carried out two cross-language repetition experiments in order to study why Kolers (1966a) had found equal within- and cross-language increase in recall with repetitions. By 1980, Kolers had become more an advocate of a means-specific approach to representation. They found that while repetition with synonyms produced some increase of recall over single presentations, identical repetition and repetition with translation equivalents produced much more increase in recall. The authors argued that these results demonstrate that, contrary to the tenets of the attribute-tagging model or any other shared store model, words with the same meaning do not share the same representations within or across languages. They assumed that the increase in recall when words are repeated as translation equivalents was due to subject strategy based on different criteria for word similarity within and across languages.

Kolers and his colleagues (Kolers & Brison, 1984; Kolers & Roediger, 1984; Kolers & Smythe, 1984) have argued, in the context of the means specific theory, that words can be encoded according to a number of different attributes, depending on the context and the purposes of the individual, not just in terms of the language of presentation. They hold that the single-separate dichotomy is an empty dichotomy; the question of whether memory is separate or shared an empty question, since it is neither. Rather, Kolers emphasized the importance of the similarity of encodings, and of the means of the encodings, in determining when recall will be increased by repetition. This idea was developed by Durgunoglu and Roediger (1987), as discussed below.

Paivio does not agree that the shared-separate dichotomy is empty. He believes in the separate model of memory and has developed the dual-coding model of bilingual memory (Paivio, 1986; Paivio, Clark & Lambert, 1988; Paivio & Desrochers, 1980; Paivio & Lambert, 1981) based on his dual-coding model of memory for images and words (Paivio, 1971, 1986; Paivio & Begg, 1981). His model contends that word representations in different languages are in different and separate memory stores which can function independently. In normal processing, these word meanings are derived from interconnections between representations within and across separate memory systems. In bilingual memory there are connections between representations across language systems, especially between translation equivalents. Representations of translation equivalent words may have connections to the same image representations, which means they can provide indirect links between the separate language systems.

Paivio and Lambert (1981) tested the model by asking subjects to recall words after performing various tasks, and found that tasks which activate the hypothesized image representations or associative pathways increased recall, especially of concrete words. Paivio, Clark and Lambert (1988) showed lists of words to subjects, in which they varied lag, kinds of repetition (identical repetitions and semantic repetitions, which were either synonyms or translation equivalents) and concreteness of the words. The results generally confirmed the findings of previous experiments. The most important new finding was that with short lags, recall of semantic repetitions, (both translations and synonyms) was greater than recall of identical repetitions. In the discussion, the authors demonstrated how the effects of lag and type of repetition observed in this and other experiments are predicted by the constructs of the dual-coding model.

Durgunoglu and Roediger (1987), in a paper which reflects many of the ideas developed by Kolers and Roediger (1984), suggested that the results of these recall experiments reflect the processing demands of retrieval tasks rather than different forms of memory organization. Performance, such as recall, depends upon how closely the test situation resembles the encoding condition, and not upon memory organization by languages. They suggested an essential difference between different tasks is whether they are conceptually-driven or data-driven: Whether they require the subjects to focus on the concepts the stimuli represent, or on the physical aspects of stimuli. Free recall is assumed to be conceptually-driven while word-fragment completion, (subjects see a few letters of a word and must add the other letters) is assumed to be data-driven. Lexical decision would be another example of a data-driven task. Recognition, they argued, is a task which can be either conceptually-driven or data-driven. Therefore, they tested whether, under identical encoding conditions and with the identical materials, the task demands of free recall, recognition and fragment completion can determine the results obtained. Their results confirmed the prediction.

The authors concluded, as had Kolers and his colleagues, including Roediger (see above), that the separate versus shared dichotomy is an unresolvable issue and perhaps a meaningless question. Rather, they suggested that studying bilingual phenomena within the framework of transfer appropriate processing, would provide more interesting keys to understanding bilingual memory organization.

Cristoffanini et al.'s (1986) and Kirsner's (1986) modified tagged-attribute model, plus the means-specific approach of and Kolers and Gonzalez (1980) and the transfer appropriate hypothesis of Durgunoglu and Roediger (1987), all represent a move away from the separate and shared dichotomy in bilingual memory models. These approaches reject the idea that representations necessarily are encoded by language. Instead, they emphasize that words can be encoded according to a number of attributes. These positions can be contrasted with the assumptions of the dual-coding model, which states that the code (such as language) determines the organization of representations in separate memory systems.

Most newer models of bilingual memory follow one of two paths. They either reject the separate and shared dichotomy and suggest that representations are encoded according to a different set of principles, or they propose a number of different levels and structures in word processing, some shared and some separate. These models will be described below in the survey of experiments employing reaction time measures.

Later Research: Emphasis on Reaction Time Measures

The Trend Toward Reaction Time Measures in Bilingual Research

Durgunoglu and Roediger's argument that results from memory experiments reflect the retrieval demands of specific tasks was not new (although they extended this argument to suggest that results from any experiment will reflect subject strategy which depends on the nature of the task). In the 1970s, experiments using recall and recognition often were criticized for reflecting subject strategy or controlled processing rather than a more basic organization of representations (see for example Kolers & Gonzalez, 1980; Posner, 1978). This criticism reflects a belief which was gaining acceptance in the larger field of cognitive psychology: the belief that a basic organization of conceptual representations exists in memory which is reflected in automatic processing, but which can be distorted when processing is guided by consciousness or controlled processing (see for example Neely, 1977; Posner & Snyder, 1975).

In the 1980s there was a change in methodology in bilingual research, away from recall and recognition studies, towards studies using reaction time as the measure. Although the recall and reaction time experiments are separated in this paper, the actual chronology of the change is not so neat. The Stroop task was a part of bilingualism research from the 1950s. Reaction time experiments were, as will be seen below, always the backbone of experiments which focus on comparisons of processing times across languages. These experiments, however, were not influential until the 1980s, when most bilingual research became based on designs employing reaction time measures rather than recall or recognition. Research in the 1980s and early 1990s includes a number of different experimental designs which employ reaction time as the measure, but the lexical decision task had been used the most frequently, as illustrated in the experiments reviewed below.

Comparisons of Processing Times in Different Languages

These experiments usually are not grouped together to form a subset of the literature. However, when the experimental bilingual research is examined in its totality, they cohere due to their shared assumptions, shared methodology, and similar foci. The earliest experiments were based on a classic associationist model of memory which assumed that translation equivalent words were associated with the same concept in mind. They posed the question of whether knowledge of words in a second language interfered with associations between concepts and words in the first language. This assumption about how concepts are stored in memory has continued throughout the literature, whether in the classic associationist form (Mägiste), or in the more elaborated information processing models, such as the three-code model. The shared methodology is to compare processing times of bilinguals in their two languages, often across tasks. This allows researchers to make deductions about how the conceptual representations are accessed by words in the bilinguals' different languages.

The first studies of bilinguals by an experimental psychologist were conducted by Cattell in 1887. He thought that learning a second language might interfere with speed of associating concepts to words in the first language. He compared processing times in the first language (L1) and the second language (L2) in naming objects, reading object names and translating concepts. He found more time was needed to name objects in L2 than in L1, and more to translate in either direction than to name objects. Cattell concluded that bilinguals may pay a cognitive price for being able to communicate in two languages, "These numbers show that foreign languages take up much time even after they have been learned, and may lead us once more to weigh the gain and loss of a polyglot mental life" (Cattell, 1887, p. 70).

From that time until the 1950s there were no psychological experiments on bilingualism. Any discussions of bilingual memory or performance during these sixty years were treated as educational or linguistic issues. (For a good review of this literature see Weinreich, 1953). Psychological research on bilingual behavior began in the 1950s, but most studies used recall and recognition measures. In 1973 Oller and Tullius compared processing times of native and non-native, but fluent, readers of English in reading English text. They found that non-native readers produced the same number of fixations and regressions as did native readers, but their fixations were much longer. Like Cattell's results, these indicated that bilinguals process symbols more slowly in their second language. Marsh and Maki (1976) found a similar result when measuring the time bilinguals needed to compute answers to simple mathematical problems: they computed much faster in their preferred language.

These experiments all demonstrated that bilingual subjects process information more quickly in their first language. However, this did not address the question of whether bilinguals are also slower or less efficient in their first language than monolinguals. Edith Mägiste (1979, 1980) conducted experiments in which she tested monolinguals, bilinguals and trilinguals on a series of simple naming, encoding, and reading tasks in L1 and L2. The monolinguals were the fastest, the bilinguals were slower, and the trilinguals were the slowest. Mägiste concluded, like Cattell (1887), that the bilingual experiences interference from competing language systems. She also suggested bilinguals are slower than monolinguals because they have less automaticity in either language. This occurs because the bilinguals have less time to practice language processing in either language.

Ransdell and Fischler (1987) tested monolingual and bilingual subjects in their first language only and found much less dramatic differences than did Mägiste. However, bilinguals were slower at recognizing words and making lexical decisions. The authors concluded these differences occurred because the tasks were data-driven (see discussion of Durgunoglu and Roediger in previous section). They suggested, as did Mägiste, that bilinguals are at a disadvantage on data-driven tasks because they spend less time processing words in their first language.

The above experiments examined whether knowledge of a second language interferes with the access of L1 words of the shared conceptual store. Meanwhile, Potter, So, Von Eckhardt and Feldman (1984) compared processing times to test more precise hypotheses about how the L2 words access the conceptual representations. One hypothesis, the word association hypothesis, holds that when words in L2 access conceptual representations they must first access the lexical representations of translation equivalent words in the L1 language-specific lexicon. This is essentially the subordinative bilingualism model proposed by Weinreich (1953; see section above on the Compound-Coordinate Distinction). The other hypothesis, the conceptual mediation hypothesis, holds that an L2 representation can directly access conceptual representations in memory. This hypothesis is embedded in the three-code model of bilingual memory.

The three-code model of bilingual memory contends there are different levels of word processing, with words having different representations in the different levels. At the more superficial level, a word has a lexical representation which is language specific, representing the word name but not its meaning. At a deeper level, the word meaning is stored in a shared conceptual memory system within which representations of concepts are amodal and unrelated to any language or perceptual/sensory system. These shared conceptual representations mediate between separate language-specific representations of translation equivalent words at the lexical level (Potter et al., 1984; Snodgrass, 1984).

Potter et al. tested the two hypotheses by comparing processing times on various tasks. They found that subjects could name a picture in L2 as fast as they could translate the name from L1 to L2. This demonstrated that they did not need to access the translation equivalent of an L2 word in L1 in order to access the conceptual representation of the picture. In addition, categorization of items was carried out with equal speed whether the category and item were named in the same or in different languages. This result was also reported earlier by Caramazza and Brones (1980). Both findings supported the conceptual mediation hypothesis. In a second experiment, Potter et al. used less fluent bilingual subjects and obtained the same results in the picture naming and translating tasks. They took this as evidence that L2 words directly access the conceptual store even for beginner language learners.

This last conclusion has been explored further in other experiments. Kroll and Curley (1988), using the translation and picture naming tasks, found evidence that early beginner language students do seem to access translation equivalents in order to access the conceptual representation. They suggested Potter et al.'s non-fluent subjects were more fluent than the beginners they used in this experiment. Chen and Leung (1989) found evidence that early language learners use a familiar mediating stimulus to access the conceptual representation, but later language learners seem to change to a direct access of the conceptual store.

The research reviewed in this section forms a distinct subset of the bilingual literature because the experiments used the same methods and the designs all incorporated a shared store assumption for the representations of the meanings of words in bilingual memory. Although forming a coherent subset, the experiments and theories also interacted with and influenced other research. This can be seen in the reviews given below, where the three-code model is used to explain complex patterns of bilingual behavior.

Cross-Language Stroop Task

The Stroop task has been used in bilingual studies since the 1950s. In early experiments, Stroop task results were closely tied to the language switch literature. While the switch literature demonstrated that bilinguals can change languages, the Stroop test tried to determine if such switches were complete. For the most part, Stroop experiments focused on the question of whether the functional language systems of a bilingual are entirely separate, or if processing in one language is influenced by knowledge of an inactive language. The experiments in the previous section assumed that conceptual representations are shared, but much of the Stroop literature remains neutral on memory organization per se.

In the original monolingual Stroop (1935) experiment subjects read colour names printed in different colours of ink which may be congruent (colour of ink and colour name are the same) or incongruent (colour of ink and colour name are different). The subjects name the colour of the ink. Usually they respond more slowly in the incongruent condition. This is attributed to an automatic processing of the word meaning which interferes with production of the name of the colour of the ink. In the bilingual version, the word name can be printed in the subjects' first language, with the response in the second language, or vice versa.

Preston and Lambert (1969) conducted the first cross-language Stroop task experiment and found within-language interference to be generally greater than cross-language interference, but they did also find significant cross-language interference. The degree of cross-language interference appeared to depend on two factors: If subjects were more proficient in one language, it tended to cause more interference in naming ink colours in the other, weaker, language. Also, if stimuli were similar across the two languages (that is, if the colour names looked or sounded similar), there was greater interference across languages. Preston and Lambert concluded that when one language is active, the other remains at least partially operative.

Similar experiments using other languages produced the same general results and conclusions. These include Dalrymple-Alford (1968), Dyer (1971), Albert and Obler (1978), and Fang, Tzeng and Alva (1981). Hamers and Lambert (1972) reported an auditory Stroop test which found interference across languages. Ehri and Ryan (1980) used a picture-word version of the Stroop task, with results again that the greatest amount of interference occurred in the within-language condition. They concluded that this supported the shared model of bilingual memory.

Preston and Lambert's finding that the similarity between stimuli across languages increases cross-language Stroop interference was further explored by Fang, Tzeng, and Alva (1981) when they compared interference between languages across a number of experiments. They included languages written in different orthographies. The authors found that cross-language interference increased, relative to within-language interference, with similarity of orthographies. They concluded the different orthographies require different cognitive strategies and processing mechanisms, but they did not extend this conclusion to the processing of word meanings in different languages.

Mägiste (1984, 1985, 1986), like Preston and Lambert (1969), found patterns of Stroop interference depended upon the subjects' relative proficiency. With very balanced subjects, the between-language interference was as great as within-language interference. She concluded that the relative amount of experience in processing each of the specific languages is the determiner of Stroop interference. However, Mägiste did not believe the Stroop task could be used to test questions of memory organization. Since the written words are the controlling stimuli for the supposedly inactive language, she argued that the "inactive" language cannot be completely turned off.

Chen and Ho (1986) conducted a number of Stroop tests on Chinese-English bilinguals of different levels of proficiency in English. They always found greater within- than cross-language interference when Chinese was the language the subjects used to name the ink colour. However, they found different results when English, L2, was the response language for proficient English speakers and beginners: The more proficient produced more within-language interference (English words-English response) than between-language interference (Chinese words-English response), while the beginner English speakers produced more cross-language interference in this condition and less within-language interference. Chen and Ho took these results as more support for a two-stage model of second language acquisition, which is based on a three-code, concept mediation, model of memory (see previous section. Although this experiment used the Stroop task design, it is closer in theoretical assumptions and in focus to experiments surveyed in the previous section, which assume a concept mediation model of memory, and focus on how words in L1 and L2 access conceptual representations.

The chief finding of the Stroop experiments is that Stroop interference occurs within and across languages, but the within-language interference is stronger. This suggests the switch across languages is not complete, and that both processing systems remain active during language processing. The next section reviews a few experiments which examine the same question, but use different experimental designs.

Influence of an Inactive Language on an Active Language

The experiments in this section also focus on the question of whether knowledge of an inactive language influences functioning in an active language. Ervin (1961) studied this by observing how monolingual Navaho and bilingual Navaho-English subjects label colours, for the colour label categories are different in the two languages. She found the bilinguals labeled colours differently from the monolinguals in their native language, with differences consistent with the organization of colour labels in the inactive language, English. This indicated that the knowledge of English had influenced the bilinguals' processing in their native language.

Anisfeld, Anisfeld and Semogas (1969) asked English-Lithuanian bilinguals and English monolinguals to judge nonwords for acceptability as the name of a new product in a native English community and a native Lithuanian community. The nonwords were constructed to follow the sound sequences of English, Lithuanian or neither. Bilinguals, in contrast to monolinguals, judged nonwords based on Lithuanian sound sequences to be acceptable for an English community. Altenberg and Cairns (1983) reported a similar experiment with the same results. Guttentag, Haith, Goodman and Hauch (1984) asked subjects to match tachistoscopically presented words to categories, while ignoring flanker words which were either in the same language as the target words or in the other language. Results indicated the flanker words influenced the subjects' response times in both the same-language and different-language conditions.

Soares and Grosjean (1984) conducted an auditory version of the lexical decision task where bilingual and monolingual subjects heard sentences and made lexical decisions (decision of whether the stimulus is an existing word or a made-up nonword) to words containing pre-determined phonemes (the phoneme-triggered LDT). They included two speech modes; one monolingual and one bilingual, where the sentences were naturally code-switched (see above). Monolingual and bilingual subjects produced exactly the same responses to real words in the monolingual mode; however, bilinguals were slower in responding to nonwords. In the bilingual mode, bilinguals were slower to respond to code-switched words than words in the monolingual mode, and again they were slower at rejecting nonwords. These results provided more evidence that both language systems of a bilingual are active while processing linguistic stimuli. The results also suggested that bilinguals, even when in a monolingual mode, search both lexicons when confronted with nonwords. This issue of whether bilinguals search one or both lexicons was explored further by a group of studies which examined whether bilinguals can reject real words in an inactive language as nonwords as fast as real nonwords on the lexical decision task.

The above experiments, like the Stroop task experiments, all indicate that an inactive language influences behavior in an active language, at least when stimuli are present which can activate the supposedly inactive linguistic system. Experiments in the next section also test the influence of an inactive language.

The Lexical Decision Task

Rejecting words in a non-target language. Experiments reviewed in this section were designed to determine if bilingual subjects can ignore the lexical meaning of words in an inactive language while making lexical decisions about words in an active language. Typically, in the visual lexical decision task, subjects are shown a list of "words" tachistoscopically. Some are real words and some are nonwords, created by changing one or two letters of a real word. The subject is asked to respond by pressing a button to indicate whether the stimulus is a real word or a nonword. If the subjects reject real words in a second language at the same rate as nonwords, this suggests they can function in one language while completely turning off processing in the other. However, if subjects are slower rejecting pseudo-nonwords (which are actually real words in an inactive language), than rejecting ordinary nonwords, this suggests they process these words as linguistic symbols and are unable to turn off the supposedly inactive language system.

Gerard Nas (1983) asked bilingual subjects to make lexical decisions to words in their second language. Some of the "nonwords" were actually real words in their first language, or nonwords which were homophonous with real words when read according to the first language phonology. He found that the subjects were slower in responding to both kinds of pseudo-nonwords than in responding to conventional nonwords. Nas concluded that representation in the bilingual lexicon is shared. Altenberg and Cairns (1983) carried out a similar experiment and found similar results. Their conclusion, however, was that when processing language stimuli, all language-specific processing systems are simultaneously activated. They did not feel these results could be extended to issues of memory representation.

Scarborough, Gerard and Cortese (1984, Experiment 2) when comparing the performance of monolingual English and bilingual English-Spanish subjects on the rejection of nonwords, found a different result. Both groups rejected nonwords, which were actually real words in Spanish, at the same rate. The authors concluded that bilinguals can process stimuli employing their knowledge of one language system or the other selectively. Gerard and Scarborough (1989) repeated the basic experiment with similar results.

It is not clear why in the earlier experiments subjects seemed unable to treat real words in an inactive language as nonwords, and why in the Scarborough et al. (1984) and the Gerard and Scarborough (1989) experiments they rejected real words in the second language as fast as nonwords. The answer may lie in how much the experimental designs encouraged them to focus on representations in the "inactive" language. While these experiments, and those in the last two sections, examined influence and interference in functioning across languages, the next sections review lexical decision experiments which test questions of bilingual memory organization.

Cross-language repetition effects.   Earlier, this survey reviewed several studies which looked at the effects of repeating concepts across languages on recall and on learning rate. In general they found cross-language repetition (repetitions of concepts with translation equivalents) increases recall, and also increases learning rate on the second presentation. Research has also examined effects of cross-language repetitions on response time on the LDT. An increase in response speed to the second presentation of a concept (a translation equivalent), is assumed to indicate that a shared store model exists. It is assumed the effect results from additive activations of the same representation in memory. Meanwhile, a lack of repetition effect across translation equivalents indicates the existence of separate memory stores. The results of these experiments are surprising when compared to the recall and transfer of learning research.

Kirsner, Brown, Abrol, Chandra and Sharma (1980) found that subjects responded significantly faster on the second presentation of words which were within-language repetitions, but found no difference in response speed when the repetition was a translation equivalent. Similar results were reported by Scarborough, Gerard and Cortese (1984 Experiment 1) and Kirsner, Smith, Lockhart, King and Jain (1984, Experiment 1).

Kirsner, et al. (1984, Experiments 2 & 3) found a cross-language repetition effect occurred only when subjects' attention was directed specifically to the physical aspect of translation equivalent words. They concluded that repetition effects across languages can occur if the subject activates representations in the inactive memory system of the appearances of the words, but that repetition effects do not occur automatically for translation equivalents across languages.

Brown, Sharma and Kirsner (1984) found a cross-language repetition effect with bialphabetic subjects. At that time, the authors concluded the results provided evidence for the attribute-tagging model of bilingual memory. Later, Kirsner (1986) renalyzed the data and found the subjects were highly Urdu dominant and that the results were probably based on covert translation in the Hindi-Urdu conditions.

All these experiments provide evidence of some separation between representations of translation equivalent words. This is inconsistent with results of other studies which examined the effects of cross-language repetition on recall and transfer of learning. It is also surprising in view of evidence for influences across languages from the Stroop test and from LDT experiments on rejecting non-words in an inactive language. Researchers have tried to reconcile these inconsistencies in several ways: One solution is the appeal to the idea that language processing occurs at a number of different levels, such as the lexical and the conceptual levels, some of which are shared and some of which are separate. This approach is taken by proponents of the three-code and attribute-tagging models. Another solution claims that evidence for a shared store model reflects subject strategy and task demands rather than the actual organization of representations in separate memory stores. This position is taken by proponents of the dual-coding or the more general separate store position. These different approaches which have already been seen in the context of the recall experiments, run throughout research on the priming effect on the lexical decision task discussed in the next section.

The cross-language priming effects. Research on the repetition effect demonstrated that within-language repetitions led to faster responses on the second presentation of the word, while cross-language repetition effects only occurred under special circumstances. Research using the primed LDT, however, produced cross-language priming effects. As models were developed incorporating the idea that there are different levels and structures in processing words, experimenters became concerned whether their tests reflected the level of processing they sought to describe. The primed LDT was at first taken as a good vehicle for revealing the organization of the representations of concepts. Soon, however, researchers began to argue that it may reflect other processes in memory. The arguments that surround how to interpret the results of the primed LDT, and the arguments about the organization of bilingual memory, share a theoretical basis. Both issues are based on a multi-layer model of memory and a belief in a "basic" organization of representations that is either shared or separate. One result of these assumptions is that the more current models of memory which are tested are very specific and concrete about the nature of the levels of processing and the forms of representation in the different levels.

In the monolingual primed LDT, subjects see two words, a prime and a target, normally with one shown before the other. When the prime and target are related, responses are usually faster than when they are unrelated. (Meyer & Schvaneveldt, 1971). This is often attributed to a hypothetical construct called spreading activation.

This is activation which is assumed to automatically flow from an activated representation of the prime to the representation of the target and to all other related concepts in memory (Collins & Loftus, 1975). In the bilingual test, the primes and targets are presented in different languages in cross-language conditions.

For the bilingual literature, the most important assumption of the primed LDT is that the priming effect reflects the basic organization of semantic representations of word stimuli in memory. This assumption has been questioned, however, on a number of grounds: subjects may use strategies (Becker, 1979; Eisenberg & Becker,1982), and strategy is influenced by the proportion of related pairs and the stimulus onset asynchrony (SOA) (the time between the onset of the prime and the onset of the target) (Den Heyer, Briand & Dannenberg, 1983; de Groot, 1984; Neely, 1977; Tweedy, Lapinski, & Schvaneveldt, 1977). (For a review of the LDT literature, see Neely, 1990). In addition, priming is sometimes caused by a decision process that occurs after lexical access of the target word (Balota & Chumbley, 1984; de Groot, Thomassen & Hudson, 1982), which may be based on an attempt to integrate meanings of the two words (de Groot et al., 1982). The consensus, however, is that useful information can be obtained from the primed LDT but that interpretations must be constrained by the limitations of the paradigm and the individual experiments.

Meyer and Ruddy (1974) conducted the first cross-language primed LDT experiment. They used simultaneous presentation of primary associate prime-target pairs, and found within and cross-language priming effects. However, the responses to cross-language pairs were longer than those to within-language pairs. The authors attributed this to a switching mechanism, an accepted concept at that time (see section on the Cross-Language Switch). Meyer and Ruddy felt the results supported a model of memory which was either a shared model or a separate model where cross-language representations were highly connected. However, Scarborough, Gerard, and Cortese (1984) suggested Meyer and Ruddy's cross-language priming effect may have resulted from subjects using a covert translation strategy encouraged by simultaneous presentation of word pairs. In other words, they suggested the results reflected something other than the "basic" organization of representations.

Kirsner, et al. (1984, Experiment 5) conducted a cross-language primed LDT experiment with associated words presented at four-second intervals. Facilitation occurred both within and across languages with related words, but only when they appeared one after the other. More facilitation occurred within languages than between languages. Kirsner et al. compared this finding to within-language repetition effects, in which faster responses to the second presentation of a word can occur after quite long lags. They argued that the differing priming effects are caused by different processes. Priming from semantic repetition, they suggested, is due to a short lived activation between semantic representations within and across languages, while identical repetition priming is due to reactivation of identical representations. Like Meyer and Ruddy, Kirsner et al. decided their results supported either of two models: the concept mediation model and the highly interconnected separate model.

Schwanenflugel and Rey (1986, Experiment 2) reported an experiment which, using category names and exemplars as stimuli, found equal amounts of within- and cross-language priming. Also, overall reaction times to same-language pairs were the same as those to different-language pairs. They argued their data supported the conceptual mediation shared store model of bilingual memory rather than the highly interconnected model.

Jin and Fischler (1987) included prime-target pairs with primes which were the translation equivalents of the targets, and found priming greater for translation equivalents than for related targets. They attributed this to a semantic priming effect which they suggested occurred across languages in this experiment, but not in other repetition experiments, because of the experimental design: In this experiment there was a 0-lag between primes and targets, while other studies used longer lags. This argument, they pointed out, was consistent with the findings of Kirsner et al. (1984), that the semantic priming effect is short-lived and does not occur when there are items between the prime and the target. Jin and Fischler also controlled the concreteness of their stimuli, and found priming to be greater with concrete word pairs. This they attributed to task demands and not to the activation of image representations as predicted by the dual-coding model.

Grainger and Beauvillain (1988) suggested that evidence for shared conceptual representations across languages results from predictive strategies of subjects. They conducted an experiment employing two SOA's, 750 ms and 150 ms, and found within-language priming in both SOA conditions, but cross-language priming only with the longer SOA. They argued that since subject strategy requires controlled processing, and controlled processing requires time between the prime and target, that the cross-language priming effect found in other studies was due to subject strategy. In addition, overall response time to cross-language pairs was longer than was overall response time to within-language pairs.   The authors concluded the data supports an interconnected but separate model of bilingual memory, and not a concept mediation model. In contrast to Grainger and Beauvillain's results, Chen and Ng (1989) found equal within- and between-language facilitation and equal overall response times to targets in the two conditions when employing a 300 ms SOA. They concluded their results, together with those of Schwanenflugel and Rey (1986), supported a concept mediation model of bilingual memory. As in the Jin and Fischler (1987) experiment, a translation prime condition was included which produced more priming than that from related pairs. The authors argued that this finding also supported the concept mediation model which holds that translation equivalent words share conceptual nodes.

De Groot and Nas (1991, Experiments 3 & 4) included a masked condition in their cross-language primed LDT experiment. Like Chen and Ng, they also included pairs which were translation equivalents. When the primes were masked, within-language associative priming effects were found, while between-language associate priming disappeared. There was also significant repetition priming, both with exact repetition and repetitions with translation equivalents, in the masked prime condition. These results led the authors to conclude, like Grainger and Beauvillain (1988), that evidence for cross-language associative links is due to predictive strategies or post-lexical access integration strategies, and not to spreading activation. Further, they concluded the representations of related words across languages, are, at a conceptual level, separate and language-specific; while translation equivalent words are connected across languages at the lexical level.

The finding of de Groot and Nas, namely that between-language priming disappears when opportunities for strategies or post-lexical processing are eliminated, was also found by Keatley and de Gelder (1991). When subjects were encouraged to respond quickly, within 600 ms, priming from primary associate words across languages disappeared though it persisted within languages. Priming across translation equivalent prime-target pairs also persisted when subjects responded quickly.

The experiments which employ the cross-language primed LDT differ from each other in so many ways that it is difficult to compare them directly. No one factor can account for differences between experiments which find cross-language priming and those that do not. However, it is possible that combinations of factors may explain these differences. In general, these experiments were designed to test specific information processing models of memory with different levels for different processes. The arguments about what the data really mean are based on a belief in a "basic" organization of the representations of meaning in memory, whether separate or shared. This approach differs from some of those developed in the context of the recall literature reviewed above, which move away from the separate and shared models and toward a view that language does not necessarily determine how words or their concepts are represented in memory (Cristoffanini et al., 1986; Kirsner, 1986; Durgunoglu & Roediger, 1987). In the next section the two approaches will be seen again in the research on cognates.

Priming effects with cognates. The experiments reviewed above introduced a cross-language translation equivalent priming condition similar to cross-language repetition experiments surveyed earlier. However, in priming experiments the prime and target were presented consecutively, while in repetition experiments they were usually separated by a number of items. This suggests repetition priming effects may be due to two different processes; one related to the physical identity of stimuli and one related to semantic identity. Research on cognates addresses this question.

Experiments reviewed here are based on theories of memory organization, but these models are less specific and concrete than those underpinning the experiments in the previous section. Several of these experiments produced conclusions which reject the separate-shared dichotomy. The first three experiments in this section examine a slightly different question from those addressed so far. These three tried to determine if the route of a representation of a word to its meaning is guided by the word's identification as a member of a specific language system, or if this conceptual access is non-language specific. With cognates, the graphemic pattern of the word is non-language specific because it is the same, or almost the same, for the words in both languages. Pronunciation, however, is language-specific. Meaning is the same for cognate translations and different for homographic noncognates. Comparisons of repetition effects across these different kinds of words allow researchers to study which aspects determine how they are encoded. The final experiment, de Groot and Nas (1991), is more similar to the experiments in the last section in that it seeks to determine directly the organization of representations through effects of spreading activation.

Caramazza and Brones (1980) carried out an experiment using cognates to determine how a lexical unit accesses a conceptual representation in memory. Unbalanced bilingual subjects responded at the same rate whether cognates were embedded in L1 lists, L2 lists or bilingual lists. This indicated that access to representations for these words was due entirely to their orthographic pattern and not to language specific aspects.

Cristoffanini, Kirsner and Milech, (1986 Experiment 1) carried out a cross-language repetition LDT experiment which included stimuli that were either exact repetitions, identical and orthographically similar cognates, or translation equivalents. The cognates produced a repetition effect while the morphologically different translation equivalents did not. Like Caramazza and Brones, the authors concluded that the letter pattern of a word, rather than language, determines lexical access. Cristoffanini et al. however, held that the analysis of the letter pattern, or the graphemic representation, is morphological, related to how units of letters relate to meanings. As already described, they proposed a modified attribute-tagging model of bilingual memory in which morphology is a salient attribute of words which determines how linguistic experiences are encoded in and retrieved from memory. This model represents a move away from more traditional models of bilingual memory which assume that language is the central attribute determining the organization of representations. (Also see Kirsner 1986.)

Beauvillain and Grainger (1987), used homographic noncognates (words that look alike but represent different meanings across languages) in a primed lexical decision task experiment, and they found, with a short SOA, that priming occurred from homographic noncognate words whose meaning, in the given language reading of the primes, was unrelated to the cross-language target. However, priming disappeared with a longer SOA. Further, they found the frequencies of occurrence of different meanings of the homographic noncognates seemed to determine the patterns of priming. The authors concluded that when language processing is automatic, the process by which words access conceptual representations is guided by the frequency of the given reading of the orthographic form and not by language.

Gerard and Scarborough (1989 Experiment 2) conducted an experiment similar to that of Cristoffanini et al. However, they included homographic noncognates such as those used in the Beauvillain and Grainger (1987) experiment. They found no repetition effect for noncognate translation equivalents, though there was an equal repetition effect for cognates and for homographic noncognates. Gerard and Scarborough argued that this indicates there exists a language-independent encoding process that occurs before lexical access. This is the level at which repetition effects from repetitions of orthographic patterns occur. However, they argued that lexical access is language specific because noncognate translation equivalents do not produce repetition effects, and there is no difference in the repetition effects occurring for words that look alike and mean the same, and for words that look alike and have different meanings.

De Groot and Nas (1991) gave a slightly different focus to their primed LDT experiment with cognates. Theirs was designed to determine if the representations of words in different languages are separate or shared at the lexical and the conceptual levels. They conducted a series of experiments: two with cognate pairs (Experiments 1 & 2) and two with non-cognates (Experiments 3 & 4, see section on the Cross-Language Primed LDT). With cognates, the subjects saw cross-language primary associate pairs and cognate pairs, as well as within-language pairs. In one condition the primes were masked, as in the primed LDT experiment described above using noncognates, leaving them unaware of the nature of the prime. In the masked condition, a priming effect occurred in both the repetition and the associative priming conditions. By contrast, with noncognates it was found that that associative priming disappeared between languages in the masked condition. The authors concluded cognates have linked representations at the lexical level and shared representations at the conceptual level, while noncognate translations are connected at the lexical level but have separate representations at the conceptual level. A general principle proposed by de Groot and Nas was that whether representations of translations are shared or separate depends upon characteristics of the words, such as graphemic similarity or concreteness (referring to the study by Jin and Fischler, 1987) rather than on a more general format of memory organization. This position again reflects the trend away from the shared-separate dichotomy toward a search for principles other than language which may govern how words in different languages are encoded.

Conclusion

The research on cognates reflects trends seen in reviews of other research paradigms. Models of bilingualism are developing simultaneously in several directions. One group relies on multi-layer information processing models of memory, but retains at its center separate or shared assumptions about representations of the meanings of words in different languages. Another trend is to move away from the separate-shared dichotomy in search of other principles which determine how words are encoded, especially principles that can be applied to monolingual as well as bilingual linguistic processing. A third trend assumes concepts have shared representations in memory and, based on that assumption, examines how words in different languages access the shared conceptual store.

Research on bilingualism has functioned to a large degree as a testing ground for developed, more general, models of memory or language processing. This partly explains the strong influences of different theoretical and research traditions on the different trends in the bilingual research. However, as can be seen in this survey, a change is occurring. Instead of only testing existing theories, the bilingual research is now generating models of cognitive functioning which can be extended to more general models of cognition. As a source of models and theory, the bilingual research promises to play an important role in cognitive psychology research in the years to come.

However, there is no grand consensus in current research on the nature of bilingual memory. Nor is there consensus on what may be assumed nor on what questions can, or should, be asked. What is evident, however, is a growing belief that any description of bilingual memory must be able to explain extremely complex and varied behavior.

Acknowledgment Note

Some of this paper appeared in an earlier form in Keatley (1988).

References

Albert, M., & Obler, L. (1978). *The bilingual brain.* New York: Academic Press.

Altenberg, E. P., & Cairns, H. S. (1983). The effects of phonosyntactic constraints on lexical processing in bilingual and monolingual subjects. *Journal of Verbal Learning and Verbal Behavior, 22*, 174-188.

Anderson, J. R., & Bower, G. H. (1972). Recognition and retrieval processes in free recall. *Psychological Review, 79*, 97-123.

Anisfeld, M., Anisfeld, E., & Semogas, R. (1969). Cross-influences between the phonological systems of Lithuanian-English bilinguals. *Journal of Verbal Learning and Verbal Behavior, 8*, 257-261.

Balota, D. A., & Chumbley, J. I. (1984). Are lexical decisions a good measure of lexical access? The role of word frequency in the neglected decision stage. *Journal of Experimental Psychology: Human Perception and Performance, 10*, 340-357.

Beauvillain, C., & Grainger, J. (1987). Accessing interlexical homographs: Some limitations of a language-selective access. *Journal of Memory and Language, 26*, 658-672.

Becker, C. A. (1979). Semantic context and word frequency effects in visual word recognition. *Journal of Experimental Psychology: Human Perception and Performance, 3*, 252-259.

Brown, H., Sharma, N. K., & Kirsner, K. (1984). The role of script and phonology in lexical representation. *Quarterly Journal of Experimental Psychology*, 36A, 491-505.

Caramazza, A., & Brones, I. (1980). Semantic classification by bilinguals. *Canadian Journal of Psychology*, 34, 77-81.

Cattell, J. M. (1887). Experiments on the association of ideas. *Mind*, 12, 68-74.

Champagnol, R. (1975). Organization sémantique et linguistique dans le rappel libre bilingue [Semantic and linguistic organization in bilingual free recall]. *Année Psychologique*, 73, 115-134.

Chan, M.-C., Chau, H. L. H., & Hoosain, R. (1983). Input/output switch in bilingual code switching. *Journal of Psycholinguistic Research*, 12, 407-416.

Chen, H.-C., & Ho, C., (1986). Development of Stroop interference in Chinese-English bilinguals. *Journal of Experimental Psychology: Learning, Memory and Cognition*, 12, 397-401.

Chen, H.-C., & Leung, Y.-S. (1989). Patterns of lexical processing in a nonnative language. *Journal of Experimental Psychology: Learning, Memory and Cognition*, 15, 316-325.

Chen, H.-C., & Ng, M.-L. (1989). Semantic facilitation and translation priming effects in Chinese-English bilinguals. *Memory and Cognition*, 17, 454-462.

Clyne, M. G. (1980) Triggering and language processing. *Canadian Journal of Psychology*, 34, 400-406.

Collins, A. M., & Loftus, E. (1975). A spreading-activation theory of semantic processing. *Psychological Review*, 82, 407-428.

Cristoffanini, P. K., Kirsner, K., & Milech, D. (1986). Bilingual lexical representation: The status of Spanish-English cognates. *Quarterly Journal of Experimental Psychology*, 38A, 367-393.

Dalrymple-Alford, E. C. (1968). Interlingual interference in a colour-naming task. *Psychonomic Science*, 10, 215-216.

Dalrymple-Alford, E. C. (1985). Language switching during bilingual reading. *British Journal of Psychology*, 76, 111-122.

Dalrymple-Alford, E. C., & Aamiry, A. (1967). Speed of responding to mixed language signals. *Psychonomic Science*, 9, 535-536.

Dalrymple-Alford, E. C., & Aamiry, A. (1969). Language and category clustering in bilingual free recall. *Journal of Verbal Learning and Verbal Behavior*, 8, 762-768.

Den Heyer, K., Briand, K., & Dannenberg, G. (1983). Strategic factors in a lexical-decision task: Evidence for automatic and attention-driven processes. *Memory and Cognition*, 11, 374-381.

Diller, K. (1974). "Compound" and "coordinate" bilingualism: A conceptual artifact. *Word*, 26, 254-261.

Dillon, R. F., McCormack, P. D., Petrusic, W. M., Cook, G. M., & Lafleur, L. (1973). Release from proactive interference in compound and coordinate bilinguals. *Bulletin of the Psychonomic Society*, 2, 293-294.

Durgunoglu, A. Y., & Roediger, H. L. (1987). Test differences in accessing bilingual memory. *Journal of Memory and Language*, 26, 377-391.

Dyer, F. N. (1971). Colour naming interference in monolinguals and bilinguals. *Journal of Verbal Learning and Verbal Behavior*, 10, 297-302.

Ehri, L. C., & Ryan, E. B. (1980). Performance of bilinguals in a picture-word interference task. *Journal of Psycholinguistic Research*, 9, 285-302.

Eisenberg, P., & Becker, C. A. (1982). Semantic context effects in visual word recognition, sentence processing, and reading: Evidence for semantic strategies. *Journal of Experimental Psychology: Human Perception and Performance*, 8, 739-756.

Ervin, S. (1961). Semantic shift in bilingualism. *American Journal of Psychology*, 4, 233-241.

Ervin, S., & Osgood, C. (1954). Psycholinguistics: A survey of theory and research problems. In C. Osgood & T. Seboek (Eds.), *Psycholinguistics* (pp. 139-146). Baltimore: Waverly Press.

Fang, S.-P., Tzeng, O. J., & Alva, L. (1981). Intralanguage and interlanguage Stroop effects in two types of writing systems. *Memory and Cognition*, 9, 609-617.

Gerard, L., & Scarborough, D. (1989). Language-specific lexical access of homographs by bilinguals. *Journal of Experimental Psychology: Learning, Memory and Cognition*, 15, 305-315.

Glanzer, M., & Duarte, A. (1971). Repetition between and within languages in free recall. *Journal of Verbal Learning and Verbal Behavior*, 10, 625-630.

Goggin, J., & Wickens, D. D. (1971). Proactive interference and language change in short-term memory. *Journal of Verbal Learning and Verbal Behavior*, 10, 453-458.

Grainger, J., & Beauvillain, C. (1988). Associative priming in bilinguals: Some limits of interlingual facilitation effects. *Canadian Journal of Psychology*, 42, 261-273.

Groot, A. M. B. de (1984). Primed lexical decision: Combined effects of the proportion of related prime-target pairs and the stimulus onset asynchrony of prime and target. *Quarterly Journal of Experimental Psychology*, 36A, 253-280.

Groot, A. M. B. de, & Nas, G. L. (1991). Lexical representation of cognates and noncognates in compound bilinguals. *Journal of Memory and Language*, 30, 90-123.

Groot, A. M. B. de, Thomassen, A. J., & Hudson, P. T. (1982). Associative facilitation of word recognition as measured from a neutral prime. *Memory and Cognition*, 10, 358-370.

Grosjean, F. (1982). *Life with two languages: An introduction to bilingualism.* Cambridge, MA: Harvard University Press.

Guttentag, R. E., Haith, M., Goodman, G., & Hauch, J. (1984). Semantic processing of unattended words by bilinguals: A test of the input switch mechanism. *Journal of Verbal Learning and Verbal Behavior*, 23, 178-188.

Hamers, J., & Lambert, W. E. (1972). Bilingual interdependencies in auditory perception. *Journal of Verbal Learning and Verbal Behavior*, 11, 303-310.

Hebb, D. O. (1958). *A textbook of psychology.* Philadelphia: W. B. Saunders Co.

Jacobovits, L. A., & Lambert, W. E. (1961). Semantic satiation among bilinguals. *Journal of Experimental Psychology*, 2, 576-582.

Jin, Y.-S., & Fischler, I. (1987). Effects of concreteness on cross-language priming of lexical decision. Paper presented at the Southeastern Psychological Association Meeting, Atlanta, Georgia.

Keatley, C. W. (1988). *Cross-language facilitation on the primed lexical decision task.* Doctoral dissertation, University of Hong Kong.

Keatley, C. W., & de Gelder, B. (1991). *Semantic facilitation between languages: Evidence for language-specific representation.* Tilburg University, The Netherlands.

Kintsch, W. (1970). Recognition memory in bilingual subjects. *Journal of Verbal Learning and Verbal Behavior*, 9, 405-409.

Kintsch, W., & Kintsch, E. (1969). Interlingual interference and memory processes. *Journal of Verbal Learning and Verbal Behavio*r, 8, 16-19.

Kirsner, K. (1986) Lexical function: Is a bilingual account necessary? In J. Vaid (Ed.), *Language processing in bilinguals: Psycholinguistic and neuropsychological perspectives.* London: Lawrence Erlbaum Associates.

Kirsner, K., Brown, H., Abrol, S., Chandra, N., & Sharma, K. (1980). Bilingualism and lexical representation. *Quarterly Journal of Experimental Psychology,* 32, 585-594.

Kirsner, K., Smith, M., Lockhart, R., King, M. & Jain, M. (1984). The bilingual lexicon: Language specific limits in an integrated network. *Journal of Verbal Learning and Verbal Behavior,* 23, 519-539.

Kolers, P. A. (1963). Interlingual word associations. *Journal of Verbal Learning and Verbal Behavior,* 2, 291-300.

Kolers, P. A. (1965). Bilingualism and bicodalism. *Language and Speech,* 8, 122-126.

Kolers, P. A. (1966a). Interlingual facilitation of short-term memory. *Journal of Verbal Learning and Verbal Behavior,* 5, 314-319.

Kolers, P. A. (1966b). Reading and talking bilingually. *The American Journal of Psychology,* 79, 357-377.

Kolers, P. A., & Brison, S. J. (1984). Commentary: On pictures, words, and their mental representation. *Journal of Verbal Learning and Verbal Behavior,* 23, 105-113.

Kolers, P. A., & Gonzalez, E. (1980). Memory for words, synonyms and translations. *Journal of Experimental Psychology: Human Learning and Memory,* 6, 53-65.

Kolers, P. A., & Roediger, H. L. (1984). Procedures of mind. *Journal of Verbal Learning and Verbal Behavior,* 23, 425-449.

Kolers, P. A., & Smythe, W. E. (1984). Symbol manipulation: Alternatives to the computational view of mind. *Journal of Verbal Learning and Verbal Behavior,* 23, 289-314.

Kroll, J. F., & Curley, J. (1988). Lexical memory in novice bilinguals: The role of concepts in retrieving second language words. In M. Gruneberg, P. Morris, & R. Sykes (Eds.), *Practical aspects of memory,* (Vol. 2). Chichester: John Wiley & Sons.

Lambert, W. E., Havelka, J., & Crosby, C. (1958). The influence of language acquisition contexts on bilingualism. *Journal of Abnormal and Social Psychology*, 56, 239-244.

Lambert, W. E., Ignatow, M., & Krauthamer, M. (1968). Bilingual organization in free recall. *Journal of Verbal Learning and Verbal Behavior*, 7, 207-214.

Liepmann, D., & Saegert, J. (1974). Language tagging in bilingual free recall. *Journal of Experimental Psychology*, 103, 1137-1141.

Lopez, M., Hicks, R. E., & Young, R. K. (1974). Retroactive inhibition in a bilingual a - b, a - b' paradigm. *Journal of Experimental Psychology*, 103, 85-90.

Lopez, M., & Young, R. K. (1974). The linguistic interdependence of bilinguals. *Journal of Experimental Psychology*, 102, 981-983.

Macnamara, J. (1967). The linguistic independence of bilinguals. *Journal of Verbal Learning and Verbal Behavior*, 6, 729-736.

Macnamara, J., Krauthammer, M., & Bolgar, M. (1968). Language switching in bilinguals as a function of stimulus and response uncertainty. *Journal of Experimental Psychology*, 78, 208-215.

Macnamara, J., & Kushnir, S. L. (1971). Linguistic independence of bilinguals: The input switch. *Journal of Verbal Learning and Verbal Behavior*, 10, 480-487.

Mägiste, E. (1979). The competing language systems of the multilingual: A developmental study of decoding and encoding processes. *Journal of Verbal Learning and Verbal Behavior*, 18, 79-89.

Mägiste, E. (1980). Memory for numbers in monolinguals and bilinguals. *Acta Psychologica*, 46, 63-68.

Mägiste, E. (1984). Stroop tasks and dichotic translations: The development of interference patterns in bilinguals. *Journal of Experimental Psychology: Learning, Memory and Cognition*, 10, 304-315.

Mägiste, E. (1985). Development of intra- and interlingual interference in bilinguals. *Journal of Psycholinguistic Research*, 14, 137-154.

Mägiste, E. (1986). Selected issues in second and third language learning. In J. Vaid (Ed.), *Language processing in bilinguals: Psycholinguistic and neuropsychological perspectives* (pp. 97-122). London: Lawrence Erlbaum Associates.

Marsh, L. G., & Maki, R. H. (1976). Efficiency of arithmetic operations in bilinguals as a function of language. *Memory and Cognition*, 4, 459-464.

McCormack, P. D. (1976). Language as an attribute of memory. *Canadian Journal of Psychology*, 30, 238-248.

McCormack, P. D. (1977). Bilingual linguistic memory: The independence-interdependence issue revisited. In P. A. Hornby (Ed.), *Bilingualism: Psychological, social, educational implications.* New York: Academic Press.

McLeod, C. M. (1976). Bilingual episodic memory: Acquisition and forgetting. *Journal of Verbal Learning and Verbal Behavior*, 15, 347-364.

Meyer, D. E., & Ruddy, M. G. (1974). *Bilingual word-recognition: Organization and retrieval of alternative lexical codes.* Paper presented to the Eastern Psychological Association, Philadelphia.

Meyer, D. E., & Schvaneveldt, R. W. (1971). Facilitation in recognizing pairs of words: Evidence of a dependence between retrieval operations. *Journal of Experimental Psychology*, 90, 227-234.

Nas, G. (1983). Visual word recognition in bilinguals: Evidence for a cooperation between visual and sound based codes during access to common lexical store. *Journal of Verbal Learning and Verbal Behavior*, 22, 526-534.

Neely, J. H. (1977). Semantic priming and retrieval from lexical memory: Roles of inhibitionless spreading activation and limited-capacity attention. *Journal of Experimental Psychology: General*, 106, 1-66.

Neely, J. H. (1990). Semantic priming effects in visual word recognition: A selective review of current findings and theories. In D. Besner & G. Humphreys (Eds.), *Basic Processes in reading: Visual word recognition.* Hillsdale, N.J.: Lawrence Erlbaum Associates.

Nott, R. C., & Lambert, W. E. (1968). Free recall in bilinguals. *Journal of Verbal Learning and Verbal Behavior*, 7, 1065-1071.

Oller, J. W., & Tullius, J. R. (1973). Reading skills of non-native speakers of English. *International Review of Applied Linguistics*, 11, 69-80.

O'Neill, W., & Huot, R. (1984). Release from proactive inhibition as a function of a language of pronunciation shift in bilinguals. *Canadian Journal of Psychology*, 38, 54-62.

Paivio, A. (1971). *Imagery and verbal processes.* Toronto: Holt, Rinehart and Winston.

Paivio, A. (1986). *Mental representations: A dual coding approach.* Oxford: Oxford University Press.

Paivio, A., & Begg, I. (1981). *Psychology of language.* Englewood Cliffs, N.J.: Prentice Hall.

Paivio, A., Clark, J. M., & Lambert, W. E. (1988). Bilingual dual-coding theory and semantic repetition effects on recall. *Journal of Experimental Psychology: Learning, Memory and Cognition*, 14, 163-172.

Paivio, A., & Desrochers, A. (1980). A dual-coding approach to bilingual memory. *Canadian Journal of Psychology*, 34, 388-399.

Paivio, A., & Lambert, W. E. (1981). Dual-coding and bilingual memory. *Journal of Verbal Learning and Verbal Behavior*, 20, 532-539.

Penfield, W., & Roberts, L. (1959). *Speech and brain mechanisms.* Princeton, N.J.: Princeton University Press.

Pfaff, C. W. (1979). Constraints on language mixing: Intrasentential code-switching and borrowing in Spanish/English. *Language*, 55, 291-318.

Poplack, S. (1980). Sometimes I'll start a sentence in English and y termino en español: Toward a typology of code-switching. *Linguistics*, 18, 581-618.

Posner, M. (1978). *Chronometric explorations of mind.* Hillsdale, NJ: Lawrence Erlbaum Associates.

Posner, M., & Snyder, C. (1975). Facilitation and inhibition in the processing of signals. In P. Rabbitt and S. Dornic (Eds.), *Attention and performance V*, (pp. 669-683). New York: Academic Press.

Potter, M. C., So, K.-F., Von Eckardt, B., & Feldman, L.B. (1984). Lexical and conceptual representation in beginning and proficient bilinguals. *Journal of Verbal Learning and Verbal Behavior*, 23, 23-38.

Preston, M. S., & Lambert, W. E. (1969). Interlingual interference in a bilingual version of the Stroop colour-word task. *Journal of Verbal Learning and Verbal Behavior*, 8, 295-301.

Ransdell, S. E., & Fischler, I. (1987). Memory in a monolingual mode: When are bilinguals at a disadvantage? *Journal of Memory and Language*, 26, 392-405.

Rose, R. G., & Carroll, J. F. (1974). Free recall of a mixed language list. *Bulletin of the Psychonomic Society*, 3, 267-268.

Rose, R. G., Rose, P. R., King, N., & Perez, A. (1975). Bilingual memory for related and unrelated sentences. *Journal of Experimental Psychology: Human Learning and Memory*, 1, 599-606.

Saegert, J., Hamayan, E., & Ahmar, H. (1975). Memory for language of input in polyglots. *Journal of Experimental Psychology: Human Learning and Memory,* 1, 607-613.

Saegert, J., Obermeyer, J., & Kazarian, S. (1973). Organizational factors in free recall of bilingually mixed lists. *Journal of Experimental Psychology,* 97, 397-399.

Scarborough, D., Gerard, L., & Cortese, C. (1984). Independence of lexical access in bilingual word recognition. *Journal of Verbal Learning & Verbal Behavior,* 23, 84-99.

Schwanenflugel, P., & Rey, M. (1986). Interlingual semantic facilitation: Evidence for a common representational system in the bilingual lexicon. *Journal of Memory and Language,* 25, 605-618.

Snodgrass, J. G. (1984). Concepts and their surface representations. *Journal of Verbal Learning and Verbal Behavior,* 23, 3-22.

Soares, C., & Grosjean, F. (1984). Bilinguals in a monolingual and a bilingual speech mode: The effect on lexical access. *Memory and Cognition,* 12, 380-386.

Sridhar, S., & Sridhar, K. (1980). The syntax and psycholinguistics of bilingual code mixing. *Canadian Journal of Psychology,* 34, 407-416.

Stroop, J. R. (1935). Studies of interference in serial verbal reactions. *Journal of Experimental Psychology,* 18, 643-661.

Taylor, I. (1971). How are words from two languages organized in bilingual memory. *Canadian Journal of Psychology,* 25, 228-240.

Tulving, E., & Colotla, U. (1970). Free recall of trilingual lists. *Cognitive Psychology,* 1, 86-98.

Tweedy, J. R., Lapinski, R. H., & Schvaneveldt, R. W. (1977). Semantic-context effects on word recognition: Influence of varying the proportion of items presented in an appropriate context. *Memory and Cognition,* 5, 84-89.

Weinreich,U. (1953). *Languages in Contact.* New York: The Linguistic Circle of New York.

Young, R. K., & Navar, I. M. (1968). Retroactive inhibition with bilinguals. *Journal of Experimental Psychlogy,* 77, 109-115.

Young, R. K., & Saegert, J. (1966). Transfer with bilinguals. *Psychonomic Science,* 6, 161-162.

Young, R. K., & Webber, A. (1967). Positive and negative transfer with bilinguals. *Journal of Verbal Learning and Verbal Behavior,* 6, 874-877.

Cognitive Processing in Bilinguals – R.J. Harris (Editor)
© *1992 Elsevier Science Publishers B.V. All rights reserved.*   51

Another View of Bilingualism

François Grosjean
Université de Neuchâtel

Abstract

A particular view of bilingualism--the monolingual (or fractional) view--is first spelled out, and the negative consequences it has had on various areas of bilingual research are discussed. A bilingual (or wholistic) view is then proposed. According to it, the bilingual is not the sum of two complete or incomplete monolinguals but a unique and specific speaker-hearer. Four areas of research are discussed in this light: comparing monolinguals and bilinguals, language learning and language forgetting, the bilingual child and 'semilingualism', and the bilingual's speech modes. A description of research in mixed language processing concludes the chapter.

Only rarely do researchers working on the many facets of bilingualism take the opportunity to sit back from their on-going work and reflect on some fundamental issues regarding bilingualism and the bilingual person. Among the many issues that should be kept at the forefront of research, we find the following:

1. What do we mean when we use the terms 'bilingual' and 'bilingualism'?

2. Is the bilingual person the 'sum' of two monolinguals or a specific speaker-hearer in his or her own right?

3. Can one adequately compare monolinguals and bilinguals, and if so, can one continue to do so with traditional procedures?

4. Can the linguistic tools and methods developed to study monolinguals be used without reservation to study bilinguals?

These are some of the questions that will be raised in this chapter. A particular view of bilingualism that has been prevalent in the field for decades and that we refer to as the monolingual (or fractional) view of bilingualism will first be discussed. A different view of bilingualism, called the bilingual (or wholistic) view, will then be evoked and a number of areas of bilingual research that are affected by this different perspective will be discussed. Finally, a series of studies aimed at obtaining a better understanding of the processing of mixed speech will be summarized. Before proceeding, however, it is important that we state what we understand by the terms 'bilingualism' and 'bilingual'. Bilingualism is the regular use of two (or more) languages, and bilinguals are those people who need and use two (or more) languages in their everyday lives.

The Monolingual (or Fractional) View of Bilingualism

We wish to argue that a monolingual (or fractional) view of bilingualism has played too great a role in our study of people who use two languages in their everyday lives. According to a strong version of this view, the bilingual has (or should have) two separate and isolable language competencies; these competencies are (or should be) similar to those of the two corresponding monolinguals; therefore, the bilingual is (or should be) two monolinguals in one person.

It is interesting to ask why this view of bilingualism has been so prevalent among researchers and educators, as well as among lay persons, be they monolingual or bilingual. Perhaps the main reason is that language sciences have developed primarily through the study of monolinguals who have been the models of the 'normal' speaker-hearer. The methods of investigation developed to study monolingual speech and language have been used with little, if any, modification to study bilinguals; strong monolingual biases have influenced bilingual research, and the yardstick against which any bilingual has been measured has inevitably been the ideal--monolingual--speaker-hearer. (One should add to this the strong impact of writing systems which are always monolingual.) It is worth asking how the research on bilingualism would have evolved and what state it would be in today, had the scholars in the field all been bi- or multilingual (in fact and in spirit) and had the research been conducted in societies where bi- or multi-lingualism was the norm and not the exception.

The monolingual (or fractional) view of bilingualism has had a number of consequences, among which we find:

a) Bilinguals have been described and evaluated in terms of the fluency and balance they have in their two languages

The 'real' bilingual has long been seen as the one who is equally and fully fluent in two languages. He or she is the 'ideal', the 'true', the 'balanced', the 'perfect' bilingual. All the others (in fact, the vast majority of people who use two languages in their everyday life) are 'not really' bilingual or are 'special types' of bilinguals; hence the numerous qualifiers found in the literature: 'dominant', 'unbalanced', 'semilingual', 'alingual', etc. This search for the 'true' bilingual has used traditional language tests as well as psycholinguistic tests which are constructed around the notion of 'balance'; among these we find tests in which visual stimuli have to be named as fast as possible in one language or the other, or tests in which associations have to be given to stimuli in each of the two languages. Invariably, the ideal bilingual subject is the one who does as well in one language as in the other. All other subjects are somehow 'less bilingual' and are put into an indeterminate category--they are neither monolingual nor 'really bilingual'!

b) Language skills in bilinguals have almost always been appraised in terms of monolingual standards

The tests used with bilinguals are often quite simply the tests employed with the monolinguals of the two corresponding language groups. These tests rarely take into account the bilingual's differential needs for the two languages or the different social functions of these languages (what a language is used for, with whom and where). The results obtained from these tests invariably show that bilinguals are less proficient than the corresponding monolinguals. This, in turn, is seen as a problem by the monolingual environment. It would appear that much of the current controversy surrounding so-called 'semilingualism' or 'alingualism' in children is affected by the prevalence of the monolingual viewpoint and by the monolingual tests which have been used. These may be appropriate for monolingual children but not for the other kinds of children: those who are monolingual in the other language, those who are in the process of becoming bilingual, or those who have attained a stable level of bilingualism. Monolingual tests are, for the most part, quite inappropriate to evaluate the language skills of bilinguals.

c) The effects of bilingualism have been closely scrutinized

Because the monolingual viewpoint considers bilingualism as the exception (when, in fact, half of the world's population is bilingual) and because bilinguals should be two monolinguals in one person, the cognitive and developmental consequences of bilingualism have received close scrutiny. (One can wonder why the cognitive consequences of monolingualism have not been investigated with the same care!). Numerous studies have 'pushed' the apparent negative effects or the apparent positive effects of bilingualism, and have done so with such force that it is rare to find an educator or a lay person who does not have an opinion on the subject. What we fail to remember is that numerous problems still surround the 'effects' literature: children have rarely been tested in the appropriate language or languages (how many tests use mixed language with children whose normal input and output is mixed language? how many tests use the language variety the child is used to? etc.); matching and sampling procedures remain questionable despite all the criticisms that have been made; and few studies manage to show a direct, unambiguous, causal relationship between using two languages in one's everyday life and various cognitive effects.

d) The contact of the bilingual's two languages is seen as accidental and anomalous

Because bilinguals are (or should be) two separate monolinguals in one person, covert or overt contact between their two languages should be rare. The two language systems should be autonomous and should remain so at all times. If there is contact, it is accidental and is simply the result of language interference; 'borrowings' and 'code-switches', which are often conscious and intentional in conversations with other bilinguals, are either included in the interference category or are explained away as the product of 'sloppy' language.

e) Research on bilingualism is in large part conducted in terms of the bilingual's individual and separate languages

The monolingual view of bilingualism has influenced the many domains of bilingualism research. For example, researchers studying language acquisition have too often concentrated solely on the development of the new language system and, with few exceptions, have paid no real attention to what happens concurrently to the first language as it restructures itself in contact with L2. In addition, researchers have invariably used the monolingual child as the yardstick against which to judge the bilingual. Sociolinguists have long been interested in what the bilingual's languages are used for, when they are used, with whom, etc. and yet many surveys are still done solely in terms of the two separate languages; they then have problems categorizing the 'Both languages at the same time' answers. Psycholinguists have been interested in how the bilingual's two languages are activated one at a time, how one language gets switched on while the other gets switched off, and hence have paid little attention to the simultaneous activation of the two languages as in the case of borrowing and code-switching. Linguists have shown little interest in the bilingual's language competence in the Chomskyan sense, maybe because the bilingual can never be an 'ideal speaker-hearer' in the same way that the monolingual supposedly can; there is no real acceptance among linguists that the bilingual's two grammars can be quite different from the corresponding monolingual grammars or that language competence (and especially first language competence) can actually change when it comes into contact with another language. Finally, many speech therapists and neurolinguists are still using standard monolingual tests with their bilingual subjects; these tests very rarely take into account the situations and domains the languages are used in, nor do they take into account the type and amount of code-mixing the person is involved in on a daily basis. Thus, much of what we know about bilingualism today is tainted--in part at least--by a monolingual, fractional, view of bilingualism.

(f) Bilinguals rarely evaluate their language competencies as adequate

The monolingual view of bilingualism is assumed and amplified by most bilinguals, and they exteriorize this in different ways: some criticize their own language competence: 'Yes, I use English every day at work, but I speak it so badly that I'm not really bilingual'; 'I mix my languages all the time, so I'm not a real bilingual', etc.; others strive their hardest to reach monolingual norms (how many bilinguals have been put down by other bilinguals who strive to be 'pure' monolinguals?); and still other hide their knowledge of their 'weaker' language.

To conclude this section, it is important to stress how negative--often destructive--the monolingual view of bilingualism has been, and in many areas, still is. It is time that we accept the fact that bilinguals are not two monolinguals in one person, but different, perfectly competent speaker-hearers in their own right. It is this view that that will now be developed.

The Bilingual (or Wholistic) View of Bilingualism

The bilingual or wholistic view of bilingualism (Grosjean, 1982, 1985) proposes that the bilingual is an integrated whole which cannot easily be decomposed into two separate parts. The bilingual is NOT the sum of two complete or incomplete monolinguals; rather, he or she has a unique and specific linguistic configuration. The co-existence and constant interaction of the two languages in the bilingual has produced a different but complete language system. An analogy comes from the domain of track and field. The high hurdler blends two types of competencies, that of high jumping and that of sprinting. When compared individually with the sprinter or the high jumper, the hurdler meets neither level of competence, and yet when taken as a whole the hurdler is an athlete in his or her own right. No expert in track and field would ever compare a high hurdler to a sprinter or to a high jumper, even though the former blends certain characteristics of the latter two. A high hurdler is an integrated whole, a unique and specific athlete, who can attain the highest levels of world competition in the same way that the sprinter and the high jumper can. In many ways, the bilingual is like the high hurdler: an integrated whole, a unique and specific speaker-hearer, and not the sum of two complete or incomplete monolinguals. Another analogy comes from the neighbouring domain of biculturalism. The bicultural person (the Mexican-American, for example) is not two monoculturals; instead, he or she combines and blends aspects of the two cultures to produce a unique cultural configuration.

According to the wholistic view, then, the bilingual is a fully competent speaker-hearer; he or she has developed competencies (in the two languages and possibly in a third system that is a combination of the first two) to the extent required by his or her needs and those of the environment. The bilingual uses the two languages-- separately or together--for different purposes, in different domains of life, with different people. Because the needs and uses of the two languages are usually quite different, the bilingual is rarely equally or completely fluent in the two languages. Levels of fluency in a language will depend on the need for the language and will be extremely domain specific (hence the 'fossilized' competencies of many bilinguals in each of their two languages).

Because the bilingual is a human communicator (as is the monolingual), he or she has developed a communicative competence that is sufficient for everyday life. This competence will make use of one language, of the other language or of the two together (in the form of mixed speech) depending on the situation, the topic, the interlocutor, etc. The bilingual's communicative competence cannot be evaluated correctly through only one language; it must be studied instead through the bilingual's total language repertoire as it is used in his or her everyday life.

A number of areas of research are affected by this wholistic view of bilingualism; a few will be discussed below.

Comparing Monolinguals and Bilinguals

A wholistic view of bilingualism and the bilingual should lead, hopefully, to a more complete and fairer comparison of bilinguals and monolinguals in terms of language competence, language performance, language learning, etc. The comparison will need to stress the many specificities of the bilingual:

- the structure and organization of the bilingual's language competencies; it may well be that these competencies are in some ways different from those of the two corresponding monolinguals;

- the structure and organization of the bilingual's mixed language competence; that is, the language system(s) that is (are) activated when the bilingual is in a bilingual (mixed) speech mode and is borrowing and code-switching with other bilinguals.

- the bilingual's language processing systems when the language input and output are monolingual (as when the bilingual is speaking to monolinguals; we know that in such cases the other language is never totally deactivated);

- the linguistic and psycholinguistic operations involved in producing and perceiving mixed speech.

But the comparison of bilinguals and monolinguals will also need to stress the many similarities that exist between the two at the level of communicative competence. A first question that needs to be answered is the following: Does the stable bilingual (and not the person in the process of learning or restructuring a language) meet his or her everyday communicative needs with two languages--used separately or together-- and this to the same extent as the monolingual with one language? Because the bilingual, like the monolingual, is a human communicator with similar needs to communicate with others, we hypothesize that the answer to this question can only be affirmative. The bilingual will develop a communicative competence that is equivalent to that of other speaker-hearers, be they monolingual, bilingual, or multilingual, even though the outward manifestations of this competence may at first appear quite abnormal to the monolingual researcher (as in the case of mixed speech, which so often is seen as a reflection of semilingualism or alingualism). To answer the communicative needs question, we will need to develop new testing procedures. Traditional language tests that put more stress on the form of the language than on the speaker's ability to communicate in context are not appropriate. Having shown that bilinguals do indeed have the same communicative competence as monolinguals, one will then need to study in more detail how the two types of speaker-hearers implement this competence; that is, how the bilingual and the monolingual meet their everyday communicative needs so differently on the surface; the former with his or her two languages, used separately or together, and the monolingual with just the one language.

Language Learning and Language Forgetting

If the bilingual is indeed an integrated whole, then it is interesting to study the wax and wane of languages in that person; in other words, how changes in the language environment, and therefore in language needs, affect his or her linguistic competence in the one language and in the other, but not in his or her communicative competence in general. The following hypothesis can be made: a person can go in and out of bilingualism, can shift totally from one language to the other (in the sense of acquiring one language and forgetting the other totally), but will never depart (except in transitional periods of language learning or restructuring) from a necessary level of communicative competence needed by the environment. Because bilinguals, like monolinguals, have an innate capacity for language and are by essence communicators, they will develop competence in each of their languages to the extent needed by the environment (their linguistic competence in one language may therefore be quite rudimentary, as the interlanguage literature has shown) but they will always maintain a necessary level of communicative competence. New situations, new environments, and new interlocutors will involve new linguistic needs in one language, in the other, or in both simultaneously, and will therefore change the language configuration of the persons involved; but this will in no way modify their communicative competence. After a period of adjustment (of language restructuring) they will meet their new communicative needs to the fullest.

It is critical to differentiate between the process of restructuring a language and the outcome of restructuring, in other words, between becoming bilingual or re-adjusting one's bilingualism and attaining stability in one's bilingualism. It is also important to study what is happening to the two languages (and to the interaction of the two) during this period of readjustment. In the long run, the really interesting question of language learning and language forgetting is how the human communicator adjusts to and uses one, two or more languages--separately or together--to maintain a necessary level of communicative competence, and not what level of grammatical competence is reached in each language taken individually and out of context. Unfortunately, too much stress has been put on the latter in bilingual research, especially when children are being studied.

The Bilingual Child and 'Semilingualism'

Much has been written about the 'semilingualism' or 'alingualism' of certain bilingual children and adolescents. And yet before coming to rapid conclusions about language deficit in these children, it is important that we consider the points made so far on comparing bilinguals to monolinguals and on language learning and language forgetting. We will then be ready to answer the following questions:

- Is the child in the process of becoming bilingual (structuring or restructuring his or her language competencies), either because he or she is learning two languages simultaneously and is in the fusion stage (a stage often found in infant bilinguals), or because he or she is simply in the process of learning a second language (or a different variety of the first language)? Could so-called 'language deficit' simply be a reflection of language learning or language restructuring in process?

- Is the child mostly in a 'bilingual speech mode' at home? In other words, is the language input usually mixed and the output therefore also mixed? Is the child only just discovering the monolingual versions of the two languages (as when a bilingual is speaking to a monolingual)? Can one expect the child to know how to behave in the monolingual mode when he or she has had no experience with this mode? Learning to use only one language at a time, when the two have always been used in a mixed language mode, takes time to get used to and needs the appropriate environment and feedback.

- Finally, is the child meeting his or her communicative needs in the home environment? Could 'language deficit' simply be a reflection of the absence of particular formal skills that the child has never needed until he or she arrived in school?

These questions, among others, must be asked before concluding that a child is 'semilingual'. It is important that we not talk of 'language deficit' until we are sure the child has had the chance, and has been given every opportunity, to learn and use the new language or new language variety that is employed in school. Learning or restructuring a language (or variety) takes time, and yet the child is often tagged as 'semilingual' or 'alingual' before he or she has had the time to adjust to the new language environment. Time is a critical factor, as are need and motivation: the child must feel the necessity to learn the new language and must be motivated to do so. If neither need nor motivation is present, then the child will not become bilingual, but through no fault of his or hers. It is clearly up to the school system and the adult environment to motivate language acquisition and to create the opportunity for the child to learn the new language or language variety. Does the child meet his or her everyday communicative needs by remaining monolingual in the minority language? In a sense, the answer is 'yes', as communicating in school, with the majority language, has never become a need for many children. For various reasons, they have not been given the opportunity to become bilingual and remain therefore monolingual in the minority language.

The Bilingual's Speech Modes

An aspect of bilingual behavior that takes on added dimensions when seen from the wholistic perspective concerns the bilingual's speech modes. In everyday life, bilinguals find themselves at various points along a situational continuum which induces a particular speech mode. At one end of the continuum, bilinguals are in a totally monolingual speech mode in that they are speaking to monolinguals of either language A or language B. At the other end of the continuum, bilinguals find themselves in a bilingual speech mode in that they are speaking to bilinguals who share languages A and B and with whom they normally mix languages (code-switch and borrow). For convenience, we will refer to the two ends of the continuum when speaking of the monolingual or bilingual speech modes, but we should keep in mind that these are end points and that intermediary modes do exist between the two.

It is important to note two things before describing these end points. First, bilinguals differ among themselves as to the extent they travel along the continuum; some rarely find themselves at the bilingual end (purists, language teachers, etc.) whereas others rarely leave this end (bilinguals who live in tight knit bilingual communities where the language norm is mixed language). Second, it is critical to know which speech mode a bilingual is in before making any claims about the individual's language processing or language competence. For example, what might be seen as the accidental (or permanent) interference of one language on the other during language production, may in fact be a perfectly conscious borrowing or code-switch in the bilingual speech mode. Rare are the bilingual corpora that clearly indicate the speech mode the bilinguals were in when their speech was recorded; as a consequence, many unfounded claims are made about the bilingual's knowledge of his or her languages.

In the monolingual speech mode, bilinguals adopt the language of the monolingual interlocutor. They also deactivate, as best they can, the other language This de-activation has led to much theorizing and much controversy around the notion of a language switch or a monitor system. What is certain, however, is that bilinguals rarely deactivate the other language totally, and this leads to the following question: In what way is the language processing of bilinguals in the monolingual speech mode different from that of monolinguals, given that there is always some residual activation of the other language in bilinguals? The specific processing operations that will be uncovered in the future will only strengthen the view that the bilingual is a unique speaker-hearer.

In the bilingual speech mode, both languages are activated. Bilinguals usually choose a base language to use with their bilingual interlocutor (i.e., the main language of interaction) but can, within the same conversation, decide to switch base languages if the situation, topic, interlocutor, etc. require it. Once a particular base language has been chosen, bilinguals can bring in the other language in various ways. One of these ways is to code-switch, that is to shift completely to the other language for a word, a phrase, a sentence. (For example, 'Va chercher Marc and bribe him avec un chocolat chaud with cream on top'). Code-switching has received considerable attention from linguists who have asked questions such as: What rules or constraints govern the switching? Is there a code-switching grammar? Sociolinguists have also studied code-switching extensively and have concentrated on when and why it takes place in the social context. The actual production and perception of code-switches have received much less attention however. The other way bilinguals can mix languages is to borrow a word from the other, less activated, language and to adapt it phonologically and morphologically into the base language ('bruncher' or 'switcher' in French, for example). Again, the linguistic aspects of borrowings have been investigated carefully, but much less is known about their processing.

Research on the production and perception of language in bilinguals will have to take into account the speech mode the bilingual is in when speaking or listening. As things stand, many published studies have not controlled for this variable and much of the data obtained is thus quite ambiguous. It is time that the complexity of the bilingual's speech modes is taken into account by researchers.

Processing Mixed Speech

For the last few years, we have been conducting research aimed at obtaining a better understanding of the underlying operations that are involved in the production and perception of mixed speech, that is utterances and discourse that include both code-switches and borrowings. Our ultimate goal is to explain how two languages interact during processing in the bilingual mode, be it production or in perception. In a first study (Soares & Grosjean, 1984), we investigated the lexical access of base language and code-switched words (and nonwords) in English-Portuguese bilinguals. We found that although subjects accessed real words in English as rapidly as monolinguals, they were substantially slower at responding to nonwords. We hypothesized that a nonword triggers a complete search of the base language lexicon which is then followed by at least a partial search of the other, less active, lexicon, and this before the stimulus is classified as a nonword. We also found that bilinguals took longer to access code-switched words in the bilingual speech mode than they did base language words in the monolingual speech mode. We later accounted for these results (Grosjean & Soares, 1986) by isolating such factors as cross-language coarticulation, delay or absence of certain segmental and suprasegmental language switches in the speaker's production, the listener's base language expectation, and his or her tendency to assimilate ambiguous items during the perception of code-switches.

Subsequently, the importance of the base language context was investigated in depth by means of a categorical perception paradigm (Bürki-Cohen, Grosjean, & Miller, 1989). French-English bilinguals identified stimuli from computer-edited series that ranged from an English to a French word. It was found that the base language had a contrastive effect on the perception of a code-switched word when the endpoints of the between-language series were phonetically marked as English and French respectively. However, when the endpoints of the series were phonetically unmarked and thus compatible with either language, no effect of the base language was found. Thus, the results provided evidence that the perception of a code-switched word is influenced by the base language context in which it occurs and, moreover, that the nature of the effect depends on the acoustic-phonetic characteristics of the code-switched words.

In another study (Grosjean, 1988), we investigated further the factors that account for the recognition of code-switched and borrowed words during the perception and comprehension of mixed speech. Different types of English words, varying in phototactic configuration and lexicon membership, were embedded in French sentences and were produced either as code-switches or borrowings. The gating paradigm (Grosjean, 1980) was used to present these words to French-English bilingual listeners in order to determine the role played by word type and language phonetics in the lexical access of guest words, as well as to uncover the underlying operations involved in the recognition process. Results showed that the phonotactics of a guest word (whether it is marked clearly as belonging to one or the other lexicon), the presence or absence of a base language homophone, the language phonetics of the word (that is, the pronunciation of the guest word in one language or in the other), and the language that precedes the word (the base language context), all play a role in the recognition process. An interactive activation model was proposed to accommodate these results. Its main characteristics are as follows: When the bilingual is in a bilingual speech mode, both language networks are activated but the base language network is more strongly activated; the activation of a unit (e.g., phoneme, syllable, word, etc.) in one network and of its "counterpart" in the other (if it exists) depends on their degree of similarity; the activation of units specific to one language increases the overall activation of that language network and thus speeds up the recognition of words in that language; finally, the activation of words that are similar in the two lexicons will normally slow down the recognition of guest language words.

Research at the University of Neuchâtel (Switzerland) is continuing along these lines and is aimed at understanding how processing in mixed language takes place so rapidly and so efficiently despite, as we have just seen, many intricate underlying operations.

Conclusion

To conclude, it is our hope that the bilingual or wholistic view of bilingualism will increasingly affect our thinking and our research on bilingualism, and that an increasing number of researchers will consider the bilingual as a unique and specific speaker-hearer, a communicator of a different sort.

This will have a number of positive consequences:

(a) It will encourage us to study the bilingual as a whole. We will no longer examine one of the bilingual's languages without examining the other; rather we will study how the bilingual structures and uses the two languages, separately or together, to meet his or her everyday communicative needs.

(b) It will force us to use tests that are appropriate to the domains of language use: domains that involve mixed language will be tested in mixed language; domains requiring a monolingual speech mode will be tested monolingually, etc. Great care will be taken not to give bilinguals (and especially bi- or monolingual children) batteries of tests that have little to do with their knowledge and use of the two languages.

(c) It will stimulate us to identify (or control) the speech mode the bilingual is in before recording or testing him or her. Too many studies have failed to pay attention to the speech mode issue and the results or data they have obtained are therefore difficult to appraise.

(d) It will force us to differentiate between the person or child who is in the process of becoming bilingual, and the one who has reached a (more or less) stable level of bilingualism (whatever the ultimate level of proficiency attained in the two languages).

(e)   Finally, it will encourage us to study the bilingual as such and not always in
       relation to the monolingual, unless it is at a level of analysis that makes the
       comparison possible (for example, the level of communicative competence
       as opposed to formal competence). We should keep in mind that half the
       world's population is bilingual and that using the monolingual as a yardstick
       is questionable.

Each type of human communicator, whether he or she uses a spoken or a sign
language, one or two languages, has a particular language competence, a unique and
specific linguistic configuration. Our role as researchers is to recognize this and to
develop our methods of analysis to reflect this. It is only when we start studying
bilingualism in itself and for itself that we will make additional headway in this field.

References

Bürki-Cohen, J., Grosjean, F., & Miller, J. (1989). Base language effects on word
    identification in bilingual speech: Evidence from categorical perception
    experiments. *Language and Speech*, <u>32</u>(4), 355-371.

Grosjean, F. (1980). Spoken word recognition processes and the gating paradigm.
    Perception and Psychophysics, <u>28</u>, 267-283.

Grosjean, F. (1982). *Life with two languages: An introduction to bilingualism*.
    Cambridge, Mass: Harvard University Press.

Grosjean, F. (1985). The bilingual as a competent but specific speaker-hearer.
    Journal of Multilingual and Multicultural Development, <u>6</u>, 467-477.

Grosjean, F. (1988). Exploring the recognition of guest words in bilingual speech.
    Language and Cognitive Processes, <u>3</u>(3), 233-274.

Grosjean, F., & Soares, C. (1986). Processing mixed language: Some preliminary
    findings. In Vaid, J. (Ed.). *Language processing in bilinguals: Psycholinguistic and
    neuropsychological perspectives*. Hillsdale, New Jersey: Lawrence Erlbaum.

Soares, C., & Grosjean, F. (1984). Bilinguals in a monolingual and a bilingual speech
    mode: The effect on lexical access. *Memory and Cognition*, <u>12</u>(4), 380-386.

Footnote

The greater part of this chapter first appeared in "The bilingual as a competent but
specific speaker-hearer", *Journal of Multilingual and Multicultural Development*, 1985,
<u>6</u>, 467-477. The author wishes to thank Multilingual Matters Ltd, Bank House, 8A Hill
Road, Clevedon, Avon BS21 7HH, England, for permission to reprint it.

Cognitive Processing in Bilinguals – R.J. Harris (Editor)
63

The Role of Language Background in Cognitive Processing

Michael Palij & Doris Aaronson
New York University

Abstract

The language background of experimental subjects is important and should be systematically evaluated because (a) the number of bilinguals in college subject pools and in the general population is increasing, and (b) the subjects' background affects their cognitive processing and interacts with other experimental variables. We provide a taxonomy for grouping people on the basis of language background, discuss how language background can affect cognitive processing, and evaluate experimental design concerns. We illustrate these points with examples from our own research (a) on age of English acquisition effects in memory tasks, and (b) on language-specific effects on sentence processing in Chinese-English and Spanish-English bilinguals.

Overview: The Study of the Psychological Processing of Language, the Native Speaker of English Criterion, and the Nature of Psychology Department Subject Pools

Traditional psychological study of language processing and usage, as conducted in the United States, has usually had a strong monolingual bias, with an emphasis on the study of English usage by Native Speakers of English. The reasons for this are many but some of them might include the following: (a) lack of interest on the part of U. S. cognitive psychologists in non-English language processing and bilingualism, (b) lack of access to a convenient pool of subjects with heterogeneous language ability and experience, and (c) the theoretical assumption that Native Speakers, especially those with limited or no experience in another language, serve as the ideal subjects for psycholinguistic research because these subjects should manifest relatively pure processing within a language.

However, research during the past decade shows that the psychological study of non-English language processing and bilingualism has been increasing (Homel, Palij, & Aaronson, 1987). Moreover, college enrollments have undergone dramatic demographic changes and now provide an excellent source of subjects with heterogeneous language backgrounds, as we discuss below. Finally, although the intuitions of Native Speakers were considered to be decisive for testing linguistic theories (e.g., Chomsky, 1957/1978; but see also the alternative comments of Paikeday, 1985), recent research suggests that the Native Speaker criterion is an ambiguous and potentially discriminatory criterion, as we discuss below.

For ease of communication, we take an approach that focuses on English as a target or reference language. This should not be interpreted as assigning special status to English, and researchers who adopt some of the conceptions presented here should feel free to apply them to any language.

Who and What are Native Speakers of English?

It is tempting to think of a Native Speaker of English, or of any language, as coming from a homogenous class of language speakers who have a common language history and experience and who process their native language in more or less the same way. Cognitive psychologists and psycholinguists often implicitly (and sometimes explicitly) make this assumption, especially when advertising for experimental subjects (Palij, 1988). It is assumed that non-native speakers will differ in some systematic fashion from native speakers, though how or why these differences occur is left to others to investigate. Non-native speakers are either prevented from participating in many experiments or, if allowed to participate, their data are often thrown out without statistical evaluation.

The notion of a homogeneous class of Native Speakers can be seriously misleading. There are several factors that should be considered when talking about Native Speakers. These are illustrated in the Figure 1 classification tree, using English as an example.

(1) Is the Native Speaker a monolingual or a bilingual? It may come as a surprise to some but there is no reason why a person cannot be a Native Speaker in two or more languages or a Native Speaker in one language and a proficient language user in a second or third language that was acquired later in life. It is also possible for a person not to be a Native Speaker in any language. For example, a person may acquire Spanish as a child, then come to the United States, undergo a process of subtractive bilingualism and end up as a monolingual English speaker as an adult. Spanish was the person's native language but now it is (apparently) gone. To take into account people with this type of language background we would need to expand the classification tree to include these types of bilinguals, which we do later.

(2) If the person is a bilingual Native Speaker of English, when was the second language acquired? Although age of language acquisition is a continuous variable (i.e., a language can be acquired at any age), we restrict our attention to the first 20 or so years of life, to approximate the age range of departmental subject pools, and trichotomize it into three age periods: (a) from birth to age 6, (b) from age 6 to age 12, (c) after age 12. The rationale for this grouping is that the experience of language acquisition may differ substantially among these three age groups. Language acquisition from birth to age 6 may be based (a) on a small number of contexts or environments, (b) on communication with a small number of people (e.g., immediate family), and (c) on a limited scope of topics. In contrast, language acquisition in the age range from 6 to 12 will occur in contexts outside of the home, with individuals outside of one's family, and with a broad range of topics. Finally, if a language is

acquired after age 12, then, from a neurologically based critical period perspective, one might claim that language ability may never match that of a Native Speaker.

(3) Are the Contexts of Language Acquisition Equivalent? A bilingual may or may not have used both languages in the same situations. For example, a Hispanic child who is exposed to English in school but uses Spanish at home may have a very different language experience in the two languages relative to a child who uses both languages in both contexts or uses only one language in both contexts (e.g., Spanish at home and in school). The language context may also provide cultural definition for behavior and have more general effects on understanding and interpretation. For example, sociolinguistic information about appropriate expression, through vocabulary and style of communication, is likely to vary and to be relatively language and culture specific. It would most likely be conditioned on cultural context (e.g., one doesn't talk to one's teacher or elders in the same way that one talks to one's friends or age peers).

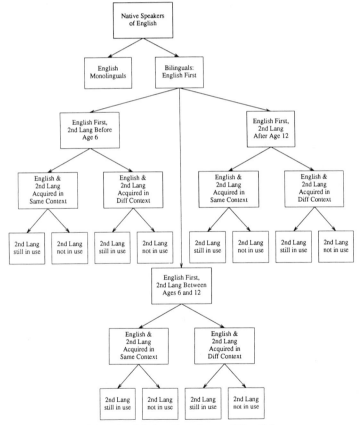

Figure 1. Classification Tree for Native Speakers of English.

(4) Is the Second, Non-English Language Still in Use? A person who is currently bilingual is most likely to be cognitively different from a person who is historically bilingual, that is, a person who was previously bilingual but who is presently proficient in only one language. A currently proficient bilingual should experience far more language interaction in cognitive processing than a historical bilingual, and there should be significant across-language facilitation or interference.

The combination of the above-mentioned factors give rise to the 13 different groups of Native English Speakers shown in Figure 1. Doubtless, other factors can be identified which would further subdivide these groups. What and who, then, is a Native Speaker of English? The answer, of course, is that all of these different groups are Native Speakers of English. But to leave the matter at that gross a level confuses issues. Is it more than likely that the factors above might interact with other factors in experiments. If we ignore these additional background factors we risk eliminating any external or ecological validity of the conclusions. Indeed, since most researchers just ask whether English is a subject's first language, it is not clear to which group of Native Speakers one should generalize. One solution might be to limit participation of subjects to, say, only English monolinguals. But this is generally not feasible as an examination of the language backgrounds of the people in a departmental subject pool will reveal.

Who is in Psychology Department Subject Pools and Can We Afford to Focus Exclusively on Native Speakers of English?

For the past few years we have surveyed the language background of subject pool students in the NYU Psychology Department. The initial survey results are reported elsewhere (Palij, 1987, 1990) and a summary of several semesters' results is currently being prepared. An excerpt of some these results is presented below.

Our main interest in acquiring language background information was specifically for stratification of subjects who would participate in experiments in memory and language processing. The stratification was based on the following factors, which are graphically displayed in Figure 2 and described below: a) Monolingual vs. Bilingual, b) Age of Second Language Acquisition, and c) Age of English Acquisition. These factors are similar to ones identified for grouping Native Speakers of a language but the tree is now expanded to include Non-Native Speakers of English, that is, those people who acquire English as a second or later language. Within the Native Speaker of English branch in Figure 2, we limit the growth of groups to the English monolingual vs Bilingual Native Speaker branch, the latter has age of second language acquisition as the final factor. To limit the complexity of subject grouping (and avoid obtaining very small sample sizes) we have eliminated the context of acquisition and second language current usage factors from the grouping scheme.

   The second major branch, that of acquiring English as a second language, is further trichotomized into age of English Acquisition. This scheme gives rise to only 7 groups with the most important language factors represented. One may ask why these factors are important. We have the following answers. The monolingual- bilingual distinction is important because monolinguals do not experience the language interactions that bilinguals have. The age of second language acquisition was identified as a factor in the Native Speaker classification and we provide some additional details here.

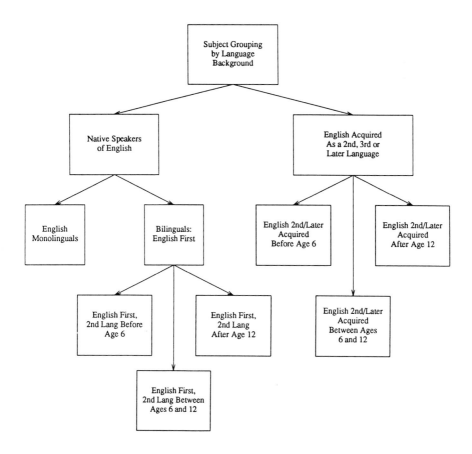

Figure 2. Classification Tree for General Language Background (based on Figure 1 from Palij, 1990)

The age of second language acquisition has played a major role in other classifications of bilinguals, the most significant for cognitive psychology being the compound-coordinate distinction, which was initially proposed by the linguist Weinreich (1953) and translated into psychological terms (via mediation theory) by Ervin and Osgood (1954). Compound bilinguals are individuals who acquired both languages from birth and within the same context. Coordinate bilinguals are individuals who acquired their second language later in life, usually in a context different from that of the first language. The compound-coordinate distinction actually confounds age of acquisition with context of acquisition (it represents only two cells in the four cell factorial representation for the two factors) and is implicitly included in Figure 1 where all combinations of the two factors are represented.

The compound-coordinate distinction served as the basis for the interdependent-independent bilingual memory distinction that several investigators promoted as a model of bilingual memory. That is, compound bilinguals supposedly had interdependent memory systems for their two languages, because the common context of acquisition and usage served as the basis for the common memory representations. Coordinate bilinguals had independent memory systems for their two languages, which developed in two different contexts. This theoretical distinction led to the infamous "tanks" view of bilingual memory, as instantiated by Kolers (1968) and still presented in some textbooks (e.g., Reynolds & Flagg, 1983). The problem with the distinction was that it gave rise to inconsistent patterns of results on the independent-interdependent attributes for coordinate and compound bilinguals. A model suggesting how these findings can be reconciled into a single processing system is provided by Palij and Homel (1987). At present, the best usage of the compound-coordinate distinction is as a description of one's language background experience without implications for cognitive or memory processing.

The final factor, that of age of **English** acquisition, has significance even beyond the more general category of age of second language acquisition, and is thus explicitly identified in Figure 2. English is rapidly becoming the new common language of international communication and millions of children, adolescents, and adults are learning it every year. And, as we shall see, it also has some important cognitive consequences.

How do language background factors affect indicators of language ability and processing?

Language background surveys of the participants of the New York University Psychology Subject Pool have been conducted for the past four years. Table 1 provides the number and percentage of participants in the subject pool who fall into the seven categories defined by Figure 2, plus some minor additions (VIII-X). Results from the first year and the latest year are provided to help identify changes that have occurred over the four year interval. The first thing to notice about Table 1 is that most of the participants can be assigned to the 8 language background categories; approximately 98% provided sufficient information for classification. Second, notice that self-described English monolinguals make up a small proportion of the subject pool, ranging from 1% to 10%. At first glance this may seem curious until one remembers that (a) like most universities, NYU requires most of its incoming students to have had foreign language instruction in high school, and (b) we ask the participants to list any language to which they have had systematic exposure, not just languages in which they are proficient. Third, notice in Table 1 that Native Speakers of English constitute only a relatively small majority of the subject pool. In Spring 1987 the percentage of Native Speakers of English was about 62%, in Fall 1987 it was just under 62%, in Fall 1990 it was about 56%, and in Spring 1991 it was about 55%. The number of Native Speakers of English appears to be declining over time, which is consistent with the national trend for increasing numbers of recent immigrants and foreign students to enter U.S. colleges.

Effect of Age of English Acquisition on Ratings of One's Ability in English

Given that we can assign subjects to the groups in Figure 2, what can we say about the validity of the classification scheme? Does it in fact reflect language experience factors that may affect cognitive processing in English? As reported in Palij (1987, 1990), ratings of ability to read, write, listen, and speak in English and in a bilingual's Native Language appear to be strongly related to a person's Age of English Acquisition (AEA). In Figure 3 we have ratings of English ability plotted against age of English Acquisition (in grouped form). There is a clear decline in rated ability across the groups, i.e., rated **current** ability in English becomes progressively lower, as English is acquired later in life.

Effect of Age of English Acquisition on Ratings of Ability in One's Native, Non-English Language

In Figure 4 we have ratings by bilinguals of their ability in their non-English native language. Note that the x-axis is again the Age of English Acquisition Grouping. We see that current rated ability in one's native language is higher the later that one acquires English. That is, the earlier one acquires English as a second language, the lower one's current ability in the native language. This result suggests that these bilinguals do not develop or maintain equal levels of proficiency in both languages, i.e., that English displaces the native language.

Effect of Age of English Acquisition on Scholastic Aptitude Test (SAT) Verbal Performance

In Figure 5 we provide a scattergram plotting SAT Verbal score as a function of Age of English Acquisition. There is a strong negative relationship present, Pearson $r(58) = -.596$, $p < .001$, and the regression equation indicates that for every year of delay in acquiring English, there is an almost 13 point drop in SAT verbal score. The SAT verbal score is a composite score representing performance on four verbal subtests: (1) antonym selection, (2) sentence completion, (3) text comprehension, and (4) analogies. The current results do not provide information on the extent to which

Table 1. Frequency and percentage distribution for subjects divided into bilingualism groupings.

Bilingualism Groupings	Spring 1987 N	%	Fall 1987 N	%	Fall 1990 N	%	Spring 1991 N	%
I. English monolinguals	24	10.13	32	8.29	20	5.56	4	1.30
II. English acquired first, Other language before 6	38	16.03	53	13.73	87	23.32	83	26.60
III. English first, Other language between 6 & 12	28	11.81	59	15.28	59	15.82	43	13.60
IV. English first, Other language after 12	57	24.05	95	24.61	43	11.53	42	13.50
V. Other language acquired first, English before 6	40	16.88	86	22.28	97	26.00	73	23.40
VI. Other language first, English between 6 & 12	22	9.28	36	9.33	21	5.63	24	7.70
VII. Other language first, English after 12	6	2.53	5	1.29	9	2.41	7	2.20
VIII. Other two languages first, English third	15	6.33	17	4.40	32	8.58	34	10.90
IX. Bilinguals, indeterminate background	5	2.11	3	0.78	1	0.27	2	0.60
X. Indeterminate language background	2	0.84	3	0.78	4	1.07	4	1.30
Total	237	100.00	386	100.00	373	100.00	316	100.00

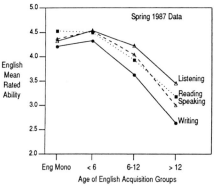

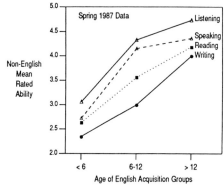

Figure 3. Rated ability to listen, read, speak, and write in English as a function of age of English acquisition grouping.

Figure 4. Rated ability in the other, non-English language to listen, read, speak, and write as a function of age of English acquisition grouping.

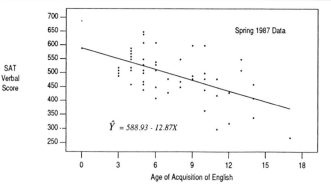

$$\hat{Y} = 588.93 - 12.87X$$

Figure 5. Scatterplot of SAT verbal score as a function of age of English acquisition.

(Part of Table 1 and Figures 3-5 are based on material in Palij, 1990)

the various subtests are affected by age of English acquisition, but results from an experiment utilizing an abbreviated version of the SAT suggests that all four subtests are affected (Palij & Aaronson, 1990).

Effect of Age of English Acquisition on Recall and Recognition Memory Performance

The negative relationship between SAT verbal score and age of English acquisition raises an important question: For people who acquire English later in life, is all cognitive processing in English negatively affected or are only selective processes affected? If all cognitive processing is affected, then we would expect even simple memory for English words to be poor for people who acquire English late. But if only certain higher order processes, such as those involved in reasoning, are affected, then basic memory for English should not be affected regardless of the age of English acquisition.

To examine whether basic memory processes are influenced by age of English acquisition, we have conducted delayed free recall and recognition memory studies to determine if a relationship exists (Palij & Aaronson, 1989, 1990). These studies are currently being prepared for publication but both give unambiguous conclusions: the ability to recall or recognize English words does not appear to be dependent upon the age at which one acquires English. That is, a person who acquires English in their teens will recall and recognize English words as accurately as a Native Speaker of English (for the types of tasks that we used). From these results it appears that the effect manifested with the SAT verbal score may be based on a higher level processing of English, which may require processing of syntactic and/or complex semantic relationships.

The conclusion that one can draw from the preceding results is that language background factors, especially those like age of English acquisition, may have a strong impact on current language processing in English, both from a subjective perspective, as revealed by rated ability, and from a more objective perspective, as shown by SAT verbal scores. However, other cognitive processes, such as basic verbal memory, do not appear to be affected. This suggests that we should expect to find selective effects of language background on cognitive processing, that is, language background interacts with cognitive processing.

Implications Of Language Background Effects For Psychological Research

Optimal Use of University Subject Pools

Over the past 20 years there have been several surveys concerning the sources of subjects for human behavioral research in American universities (e.g., Jung, 1969; Kulich, Seldon, Richardson & Servies, 1978; Sieber & Saks, 1989). All of these reports indicated that from 70% to over 90% of the research subjects are obtained from undergraduate "subject pools" generally by placing "academic" requirements on students in lower-level courses to serve as subjects. Although there is extensive discussion of research ethics in the use of such subject pools (e.g., confidentiality, considerate treatment, educational value), those reports have not focused on discrimination against "non-native English speakers" in the subject selection procedures used, nor its impact on the subjects or the research (Palij, 1988).

Disadvantages of Omitting Bilinguals from Cognitive Research

In many universities the proportion of bilingual subjects is rather large: French-English bilinguals in some Canadian provinces, Asian-English bilinguals in large cities along the east and west coasts, Spanish-English bilinguals in the southern states, and recently, Russian (and other Slavic languages)-English bilinguals in the northeast. As indicated earlier 30% to 50% of the available research subjects may be non-native English speakers (See Table 1 for NYU). Nevertheless, a large percentage of the available experimenters may not want the bilinguals' data, as the experimenters expect biased data, or at least high variance. As a result, many experimenters either explicitly exclude bilingual subjects or throw out the data. Either alternative is a waste of human resources, both the subjects' and the experimenters', although there are often alternative approaches.

By not including the bilinguals' data, perhaps as separate subject groups or in separate data analyses, for starters researchers are compromising their ability to **generalize** their results to the population at large, as much of the population is bilingual (Padilla, Lindholm, Chen, Duran, Hakuta, Lambert & Tucker, 1991).

Secondly, the exclusion of bilinguals may lead to **distorted results**. For example, in the '60s and '70s many American researchers were excited about new developments in psycholinguistics, including some strong theories of syntax and its cognitive processing, as well as ideas about linguistic universals (Chomsky, 1965). During those years, some critics of the new "movement" joked that "psycholinguistics" should be renamed "psycho-English." In part because of the narrow focus, erroneous conclusions were made about supposed linguistic universals at lexical (processing units), syntactic (transformations) and semantic (conceptual relations) levels, which might have been avoided if bilinguals' data for English and other languages had been studied.

Third, careful use of bilingual data can reveal **new phenomena** not easily observed in monolinguals. Previous studies have revealed increased amounts and types of cognitive flexibility, metalinguistic awareness, concept formation strategies and creativity often observed in "balanced" bilinguals but not in monolinguals (Cummins, 1987; Hakuta & Garcia, 1989; Lambert, 1987).

Fourth, bilinguals of carefully selected languages can be used as **research tools** to test theoretical ideas that would otherwise be difficult to study. For example, Chinese- and Japanese-English bilinguals have been used to test notions regarding hemispheric laterality in information processing, with studies using both ideograms and alphabetic stimuli (Hung & Tzeng, 1981; Tzeng, 1985). Hebrew-English bilinguals have been used to study differences and similarities in left-to-right (English) and right-to-left (Hebrew) processing strategies in reading as well as differential coding of functors (English words vs. Hebrew prefixes) (Koriat, Greenberg & Goldshmid, 1991). German-English and Italian-English bilinguals have been used to study word-order based coding strategies, as German and Italian have less rigid syntactic constraints on word order than English does (Bates & MacWhinney, 1981; MacWhinney, Bates & Kliegl, 1984).

Fifth, the use of bilinguals as subjects is necessary for research on many **applied problems** that directly concern those populations, such as second language learning (Hakuta, 1987; Lambert, 1972) or the optimal language for psychotherapy (Bracero, 1990; Javier, 1982; Rivera, 1987; Schneider, 1981).

Sixth, as is obvious from the table of contents of this book, **bilingualism** is an important topic in its own right within cognitive psychology. This includes an understanding of the extent to which two languages are processed independently or interactively during language perception, comprehension, production and memory.

Ways to Include Bilinguals in Cognitive Research

Other chapters in this book focus on experiments that were explicitly designed to shed light on cognitive and linguistic processing in bilinguals. In contrast, this section deals with ways to enrich cognitive research designed primarily for other purposes, by incorporating bilinguals. In that context one must consider two research issues: selecting the subjects based on various demographic and/or performance attributes, and analyzing the data in ways that can provide new information.

Subject Selection. As involvement of bilinguals as subjects is potentially relevant to everyone using a departmental subject pool, selection procedures should begin at that level. Rapid preliminary classification or screening of subjects within a pool can be done in any (or all) of four ways: subjective questionnaires, objective standardized test scores, language-specific behavioral data, or experiment-relevant behavioral data. Because a fair amount of useful information can be obtained within a short amount of class time, some schools administer a selection "battery" to hundreds of students in the introductory psychology course.

The data described in the first part of this chapter were obtained from a <u>subjective questionnaire</u>, and contain both demographic and performance information. Although some researchers have reservations about subjective rating procedures, this might be the most valid and efficient means of assessing the potential subjects' cognitive abilities for their relevant languages, as the subjects themselves are the most knowledgeable about their own backgrounds. However, a check on one supposedly objective piece of data on the NYU questionnaire did suggest concerns about subject-reports. The native English speakers' self-reported SAT scores were overestimates of their actual scores.

As <u>objective classification measures</u>, universities often have on file the students' SAT verbal (and quantitative) scores, as well as TOEFL (Test of English as a Foreign Language) scores. Computer accessible transcript information may exist on the number of foreign language courses students have taken, their grades, or for scores on foreign language proficiency tests.

<u>Language-specific assessment procedures</u> could be designed to handle the few dominant foreign languages at universities that have heavy concentrations of recent immigrants. For example, at NYU only two languages (Chinese and Spanish) comprise about 46% of the subject pool's non-English native languages. A simple screening test might include a few printed pages in each dominant language plus a dozen multiple-choice comprehension questions. A request to mark the last word read in one or two minutes, plus the accuracy score for each language, could assess the **relative** proficiency in English and the subjects' native language. More specific tests using only English could highlight those language errors frequently made by people with particular non-English backgrounds. For example, Russians (and other Slavic language speakers) have problems with English articles whereas Chinese (and other Asian language speakers) have problems with English tense and number. A half-dozen or so well chosen English mini-tests could be useful in assessing English proficiency.

Finally, <u>experiment-related behavioral data</u> could be obtained to assess English language proficiency. To be included in a departmental screening battery, however, the procedures must be quick and potentially relevant to research in several different labs. Such data would be useful in evaluating language (and cognitive) proficiency of native as well as non-native speakers. For example, at a lexical processing level, within a few minutes in a classroom context, subjects could check off 50 to 100 YES/NO word pairs as consisting of (a) synonyms, (b) antonyms, or (c) category exemplars of a superordinate category. If 100 stimulus pairs of each type were given with a 1 minute time period per type, both speed and accuracy could be assessed. Such a 3-minute screening test could provide a valuable covariate for various experiments on verbal memory, psycholinguistics, concept formation, or even research that uses RT responses to verbal stimuli having relevance to social psychology (e.g., racial prejudice), personality psychology (e.g., honesty; extroversion), or clinical psychology (e.g., self-esteem; learned helplessness).

As suggested earlier, the "native speaker" criterion, used so often to exclude bilingual subjects from research projects, may not be appropriate. Instead, general language proficiency tests, based on both time and accuracy data, may be more valid screening tests for English proficiency regardless of the underlying causes (bilingualism, foreign speaking parents, learning disabilities, or earlier education in a poor-quality school system).

Data Analyses. Data from many of the above four types of background language assessment procedures could be used in a variety of ways that could provide empirically and theoretically useful information. If there were sufficient numbers of bilingual speakers to form relatively homogeneous subgroups for use in **analysis of variance** designs (e.g., consistent with Figure 2), that would often be optimal. Such groups could be based on the specific native (or primary) language or language-family, on age of English acquisition or number of years speaking English, or on any subjective or objective measures of English proficiency.

However, in many situations there will be high variance along the above dimensions rather than homogeneity. In that case it would be better to use subjective or objective language background or proficiency data as extra variables in **regression analyses**, or possibly as **covariates** to reduce the error variance and improve the statistical sensitivity along other dimensions being studied.

For many research areas within psychology, particularly within cognitive psychology and psycholinguistics, it would be useful to know **whether or not** language background is a significant factor in the experimental results. Such a study, designed to evaluate metalinguistic ratings for English sentences will be considered below, as the bilinguals included in the normal subject pool sample differed from others in theoretically important ways. Many standard research procedures can obtain interesting data on cognitive differences between bilinguals and monolinguals with little research investment beyond that needed for studying only the monolinguals.

Effects of Language Background on Linguistic Processing

Procedure. A study of metalinguistic ratings on the contributions of **English words** to sentential **meaning** and **structure** used only native English speakers from the NYU subject pool. Based on language background questionnaires, subjects were classified into monolingual English speakers, fully bilingual (from birth) Chinese-English and Spanish-English, and miscellaneous bilinguals not considered here. We found theoretically interesting and statistically reliable differences for the Chinese-English bilinguals in comparison to the English monolinguals (to be called "Chinese" and "Americans" respectively). The data for the Spanish speakers are considered later in this chapter. All subjects had been asked to rate on a 5-point scale the contributions of 3 underlined words per sentence (for 90 sentences) to (a) the meaning and (b) the structure of the sentence. The instructions were general, indicating that these attributes depended upon (a) the particular **word** itself, (b) its local and total sentence

context and (c) the knowledge and orientation of the reader. Some sample stimuli are in Table 2 and the sample sizes of the various lexical categories used are in Table 3.

Theoretical Framework. Before we consider the empirical results, we consider some theoretical concepts and hypotheses. We'll take a cognitive, rather than strictly linguistic, approach. For example, the coding of **structural** information from words may be based on both linguistic attributes, such as their syntactic or functional role in the surface structure, and also verbal attributes such as word length, rhythmic, stress and intonation patterns. Likewise, the coding of **meaning** information from words may depend primarily on semantic attributes, but also on word frequency or familiarity, emotional associations, referential relations to other text components and to worldly entities.

To account for differences between "Chinese" and "American" ratings of **English words**, we suggest a **Comparison Hypothesis: Bilinguals process English words in relation to their past combined linguistic experience in both languages, whereas monolinguals process English words in relation to their past experience with English.** As diagrammed in Figure 6, suppose that English words, on the average, convey more meaning or structure than broadly analogous Chinese "words" (including the large number of monomorphemic ideograms, as discussed below) comprising part of a bilingual's **adaptation level** (i.e., the average ongoing perception of linguistic contributions of words that the bilingual experiences on a daily basis). Then, when both groups perceive the same **English** words, the bilinguals should assign correspondingly higher ratings. These are indicated in Figure 6 by the **distances** between words and the relevant adaptation level for each group.

Chinese-English Differences. To provide a background for applying the Comparison Hypothesis in this specific case, let us consider some linguistic differences between Chinese and English that are listed in Table 4. When useful, we provide examples that characterize many or all written Chinese dialects, but are drawn primarily from the Beijing dialect of Mandarin, now the "national" language of China.

As indicated in the top of Table 4 the minimal free form in Chinese is the single character monosyllabic ideogram (Henne, Rungen & Hansen 1977; Karlgren, 1962). According to Bloomfield and other linguists the minimal free form (as opposed to bound forms such as affixes) defines a word (Lyons, 1979). Chinese sentences consist of alternating characters and spaces, where each character or ideogram represents a single morpheme of meaning. In contrast, English words are generally multicharacter, multisyllabic and often multimorphemic. Although not used very often, Chinese has 3 ways to form multimorphemic, generally 2 syllable, words (Chao, 1968, Henne, et al., 1977; Li & Thompson, 1981): compounds (e.g., feng-chi=wind-vehicle=windmill), reduplication (e.g., xie=rest; xie-xie=nap), and a few affixes for semantic or grammatical attributes. Chen (1982), based on analyses of the Liu, Chaung & Wang (1975) word frequency corpus, reports 1,177,984 characters for 982,110 words, yielding a ratio of about 1.2 for Chinese, as an "isolation" ratio (i.e., the extent to which an isolated morpheme forms a complete word). In contrast Lyons (1979) reports English

Table 2: SAMPLE STIMULUS SENTENCES

1. Only the lower economic section of Washington was burned by the militants.
2. In a meeting with the cabinet the President made known his feelings about foreign policy.
3. Because of the doctor's new cure the patient was able to continue his work.
4. After many long hours of debate the housing bill was approved by the legislature.
5. Within all of the government only the office of the President issued a statement about the arms treaty.

Table 3: SAMPLING OF LEXICAL CATEGORIES

Lexical category	N for S,M ratings	Lexical category	N for S,M ratings
Content words	93	Function words	161
Verb set	45	Organizational set	61
Lexical verbs	15	Conjunctions	17
Auxiliary verbs	15	Prepositions	44
Adverbs for verbs	15		
		Definiteness set	100
Noun set	48	A, an	17
Nouns	15	The	36
Adjectives	18	Absolute pronouns	33
Adverbs for adjectives	15	Relative pronouns	14

Table 4: LINGUISTIC PROPERTIES OF CHINESE AND ENGLISH LEXICAL UNITS

Property	Chinese	English
Basic units		
1. Minimal free form	1. Ideogram	1. Word
2. Syllabification	2. Monosyllabic	2. Multisyllabic
3. Sentence units	3. Morpheme strings	3. Word strings
4. Spaces	4. Between ideograms	4. Between words
Linguistic attributes		
1. Inherent categories	1. Questionable	1. Generally yes
2. Word types	2. Full/empty	2. Content/function
3. Inflections	3. Generally no	3. Generally yes
4. Function words	4. Generally optional	4. Generally obligatory

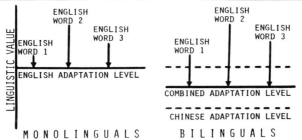

Figure 6. The Comparison Hypothesis as a metalinguistic model for Chinese-English bilinguals. [Adapted from Aaronson & Ferres (1986)].

and Eskimo to have ratios of 1.7 and 3.7 respectively. Ratios for English newspapers and high school texts generally exceed 2.0. Thus, Sinologists generally consider the Chinese word to be a single character, or very close to that (Chao, 1968). As we will see, these linguistic differences between Chinese and English **words** are important for the amount of meaning and structure they may convey to subjects, as suggested by the Figure 6 representation of the Comparison Hypothesis.

The bottom of Table 4 indicates yet other **lexical** attributes that are relevant to the Comparison Hypothesis. The existence and nature of Chinese lexical categories is questioned by linguists (Halliday, 1956; Simon, 1937), and many linguists maintain that Chinese words have no **inherent** lexical categories (e.g., noun, adjective) because a given morpheme can generally serve as many different "parts of speech," depending on the context. Sinologists often divide ideograms into two categories: "full" words having semantic content, and "empty" words which are grammatical markers devoid of substance (Forrest, 1973; Kratochvil, 1968). For example, an empty word might indicate that prior characters modify a subsequent character. English has no pure grammatical markers. Thus, Chinese full and empty words do **not** completely correspond to English content and function words. Further, English words often have grammatical inflections (e.g., **-ed** or **-ing** for tense), but Chinese does not (Karlgren, 1962; Kratochvil, 1968; Li & Thompson, 1981). Finally, it is syntactically permissible to omit most Chinese function words, if the result would not be hopelessly ambiguous (Karlgren, 1962; Li & Thompson, 1981) whereas that would generally render English sentences ungrammatical.

Results and Discussion.   The 5-point (1=low) rating data from "American" monolinguals and "Chinese" bilinguals are presented together with a discussion of linguistic differences that could lead to the rating differences. Most of the data are in Figure 7, and Table 5 provides an outline of the relevant linguistic information. First, we discuss meaning ratings and then structure ratings. For each of these rating types we consider the classes of content and function words listed in Table 3.

Meaning Ratings: Content Words.   Figure 7 compares ratings for pairs of content and function categories that have related functional roles in English sentences but that differ in semantic value (e.g., noun/pronoun). Figure 7A-7D illustrate three trends for the meaning ratings. (1) Both subject groups give higher meaning ratings to content than function words (F test, $p < .05$). Because this trend would be expected based on the semantic attributes of these English word classes, and holds for both subject groups we won't discuss it further. (2) The interaction for meaning ratings between subject group and lexical category (content, function) will be discussed later along with the complementary interaction for structure ratings in Figure 7E-7H (both F-tests, $p < .05$). (3) The meaning ratings are consistently higher for the bilinguals than the monolinguals for every lexical category, (F test, $p < .05$). Thus, the "Chinese" may perceive English words to be semantically richer than the "Americans" do, in accord with the Comparison Hypothesis. The top of Table 5 lists three linguistic reasons for this rating trend that are consistent with the Comparison hypothesis. First, linguistic data indicate that the amount of meaning associated with a single English content word is often spread over several Chinese "words," usually 1-character morphemes, as indicated earlier and in Table 4 (Forrest, 1973). For example, the single English word "greater" would correspond to a string of Chinese "words" equivalent to "great compared (with) me." The present stimulus content words, averaging 2.1 syllables and 1.8 morphemes, are typical of English in general and close to double the morphemic content of Chinese words.

Second, English content words generally have one or only a few well defined and relatively context-free meanings, whereas Chinese words are highly polysemous and heavily **context-dependent**. Karlgren (1962) reports an average of 10 meanings per Chinese ideogram for a dictionary, of 4200 words, with some words having 60 to 70 different meanings. Thus, the meaning of a Chinese word is generally not inherent in the word itself. Rather, the word is often highly ambiguous, and context (both linguistic and real-world) is necessary for its realization.

Third, bilinguals may perceive English words to be more meaningful because they are often more abstract than Chinese ideograms. For example, Chinese has a relative lack of particular affixes, such as **poly-, super-, -tion, -ment, -ist**, that serve to increase a word's abstractness in English (Chao, 1968; Forrest, 1973). Further, Chinese often uses a string of concrete words instead of a single abstract word, e.g., in Chinese "turn over one's body" means "emancipate" (Karlgren, 1962; Venezky, 1985). Finally, Chinese often lacks an abstract superordinate term for concrete exemplars (e.g., there are words for many specific types of oranges, but no general word "orange;" words for many modes and means of carrying, but no general word "carry.") (Forrest, 1973).

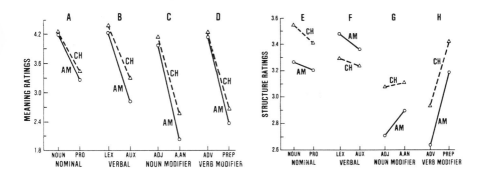

Figure 7. Meaning (A-D) and structure (E-H) ratings for related pairs of content and function words for monolinguals (AM) and bilinguals (CH). PRO = pronouns; LEX = Lexical verbs; AUX = auxiliary verbs; ADJ = adjectives; ADV = adverbs; PREP = adverbial preposition.

Table 5: LINGUISTIC DIFFERENCES BETWEEN ENGLISH AND CHINESE WHICH COULD LEAD TO THE RATING DIFFERENCES BETWEEN BILINGUALS AND MONOLINGUALS

Meaning ratings: Bilinguals > Monolinguals
For content and function words, on the average:
1. English words have more meaning per unit than Chinese.
2. English words are less contextually dependent than Chinese.
3. English words are more abstract than Chinese.

Structure ratings: Bilinguals > Monolinguals
For content words, on the average:
1. English words have less overlap among grammatical categories than Chinese.
2. English words have grammatical inflections more often than Chinese.
For function words on the average:
1. English words serve multiple syntactic functions less often than Chinese.
2. English words are optional (vs. obligatory) less often than Chinese.

In sum, the linguistics literature provides three reasons why English content **words** might be perceived as containing more meaning than Chinese **words**. These should yield higher meaning ratings by Chinese-English bilinguals than by English monolinguals, supporting the Comparison Hypothesis. Linguistic information inherent in **individual** English words appears to be carried at higher contextual levels in Chinese.

Meaning Ratings: Function Words. Analogous linguistic explanations account for the fact that function words are also rated higher in meaning by bilinguals than monolinguals. First, the equivalent of some English function words do not exist in Chinese, and "empty" syntactic markers partially serve the purposes of other English function words. For example, Chinese has no real articles and very few pronouns: **he**, **him, she, her** and **it** are all translated as "ta," perhaps making Chinese a nonsexist language (Henne et al., 1977). Chinese does have a few real prepositions and conjunctions but they are not often used, as they are grammatically optional and generally omitted if that would not lead to ambiguity. For example "Ji bu chi le" could mean "The chickens are not eating any more" (on a farm) or "As for chicken, I am not going to eat any more" (at a restaurant) (Li, 1971).

Second, function words also have multiple meanings as well as multiple syntactic functions, so that their precise meaning is heavily context dependent (Brandt, 1943; Henne et al., 1977; Tewksbury, 1948). For example, the character "gen" can mean "with," "together," "and," "using," "following," "as," or "from."

In sum, a number of important language-specific differences between Chinese and English could lead bilinguals to view English **words** as contributing more meaning to their sentences than the average Chinese word, whereas monolinguals would not make such comparisons when processing English words. These are consistent with both the Figure 7 data and the Comparison Hypothesis.

Structure Ratings: Content Words. The Figures 7E-7H structure ratings show (a) a category by language interaction (F-test, $p < .05$) (complementing the interaction in 7A-7D), which we will discuss later and (b) additional support for the Comparison Hypothesis, with structure ratings higher for Chinese than Americans (for all categories but verbs) (F-test, $p < .05$). Again, differences between the two languages should lead to these rating differences, as indicated in the bottom of Table 5. First, there is heavy overlap among grammatical categories for Chinese words. Although English has some overlap (e.g, **to plant, the plant**), those lexical categories are so reliable that (a) school children are taught "parts of speech," (b) linguists agree on the category system, and (c) on how particular words are to be classified, and (d) dictionaries specify those categories. The lexical category system has such commonality across languages that it has been hypothesized as a "universal" property (Halliday, 1956). But Chinese may be an exception (Kratochvil, 1968). The relative lack of **inherent** grammatical categories for Chinese has led to Scrabble-type sentence games and poetry styles that have sentences in two dimensions with words playing different syntactic roles each way (Herdan, 1964). That would be almost impossible in English. However, Chinese does have a dozen linguistic devices to indicate the **functional** (as opposed to lexical) role of a word within its sentence. But most of these are (a) semantic, (b) at higher contextual levels than the word, (c) only partially reliable, and (d) generally optional (Chao, 1968; Li & Thompson, 1981; Simon, 1937). Thus, we see syntactic as well as semantic evidence that English is relatively context-free while Chinese is heavily context-sensitive as a communication vehicle.

A second linguistic cause for the structure rating trends in Figure 7 is the relative paucity of grammatical inflections for Chinese content words. In English such inflections signal a word's lexical category (noun), functional role (subject), and grammatical relations to other words. Generally, Chinese doesn't use inflections for number, gender or case for nouns, tense for verbs, comparative forms for adjectives, or tags for adverbs. Occasionally there are grammatical affixes, but the absence of those affixes for the appropriate words does **not** imply the absence of the corresponding grammatical features!

Note again, that Chinese does have some partially reliable linguistic devices to indicate such lexical information, but they are **not inherent** in the words. For example, plural can be expressed semantically by words for "some" or "many", and tense can be expressed by adding words for "tomorrow" or "yesterday." The different linguistic levels for communicating such information may encourage different cognitive and metalinguistic processing strategies that can persist across languages for bilinguals.

Structure Ratings: Function Words. Bilinguals also rate English function words as contributing more to sentential structure than do monolinguals (Figure 7). The bottom of Table 5 indicates two reasons. First, the frequency and extent to which Chinese functors and markers have multiple roles far exceeds that in English. Some words may have 9-12 different functions, as determined by their contexts. Thus, their reliability as **psychological cues** in processing other sentential information is low. In contrast, English function words provide very reliable cues for upcoming text. For example, articles are followed by nouns (or perhaps by adjectives that are followed by nouns), and relative pronouns (e.g., **who, which**) are followed by clauses, etc. When we read an English function word, we quickly build an expectancy of what will follow and set in place a cognitive strategy to do the appropriate processing. It would be difficult to build up such expectancies in Chinese if a dozen different syntactic patterns could follow. Second, as mentioned earlier, even the few ambiguous Chinese function words and markers are optional, and they are indeed omitted most of the time. As a description of the use of five Chinese functors, the key sentence in a standard Chinese grammar text is instructive: "No rules are given for their use, and their proper usage can only be acquired by close attention to the manner in which the Chinese use them" (Brandt, 1943, p. 133).

The fact that structure ratings in Figure 7 for verbs show a reversed pattern is consistent with Chinese-English differences in at least two ways. In contrast to other Chinese content words, verbs, or more accurately "verbals," have an extensive set of affixes (i.e., bound particles) to convey aspectual and modal information (and possibly tense, although that is questioned). Further, verbals are the "central" aspect of a Chinese sentence, and are a required part of sentences. In fact, in Chinese one can often find sentences composed entirely of a single verb or verbal. This is rare in English (e.g., the command, "Run!").

Structure Ratings: Spanish-English Bilinguals. In accord with the Comparison Hypothesis, if structure ratings were obtained from bilinguals who spoke a language that was more strongly inflected than English, their ratings of English should be **lower** than those of monolingual English speakers. Our two Spanish subjects, while certainly not a large sample size, can provide a suggestive test of this idea. Indeed, their averaged structure ratings were **lower** than those of English monolinguals for seven of the eight lexical categories in Figure 2. The exception category was pronouns. However, even this exception would be predicted based on Spanish-English differences. Spanish pronouns as syntactic subjects are optional and are often omitted. Thus, Spanish sentences would have an inflected verb but no subject. This would not be grammatically acceptable in English. It would be interesting to follow up this suggestive trend with more Spanish-English bilinguals and those speaking other highly inflected languages.

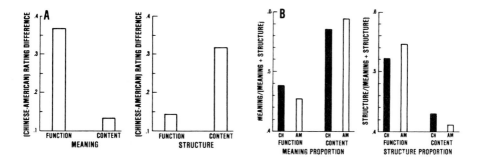

Figure 8. Interactions between language populations and lexical categories.
A. Chinese-American rating differences for meaning (left) and structure (right).
B. Proportion of "linguistic value" devoted to meaning (left) and structure (right).

Interactions Between Language Background and Lexical Category. Figure 7 shows interactions that are presented more simply in Figure 8. Figure 8A shows that the meaning difference between language groups is greater for function than content words, but the structure difference is greater for content than function words. These rating differences correspond to differences in "adaptation level" in the Figure 6 model. Figure 8B shows the same information as ratios: the relative proportion of the "linguistic value" (i.e., structure+meaning) devoted to meaning (8B left) or to structure (8B right). These graphs, normalized for total linguistic value, provide evidence that the data cannot be attributed simply to a response bias toward higher overall ratings for Chinese.

The Figure 8 rating differences are consistent with the relative magnitude of Chinese-English language differences. Although function words in both languages provide syntactic cues, Chinese-English semantic differences for function words are large. As mentioned earlier, many Chinese "function" words are (a) syntactic markers devoid of meaning (i.e., "empty") (b) that are often omitted entirely. Although content words in both languages are semantically rich, Chinese-English syntactic differences for content words are large. Chinese content words (a) generally don't have inherently marked lexical categories or inflections, and (b) those words often serve equally well as nouns, verbs, adjectives or adverbs. Thus, supporting the Comparison Hypothesis, bilinguals' meaning perceptions should differ from their adaptation level more for function than content words, and their structure perceptions should differ more for content than function words, in accord with Figure 8 data.

In sum, we have evidence for interesting language-specific interactions between a bilingual's two languages. As Chinese is more context dependent and less word dependent than English, its speakers have different perceptions than monolingual English speakers of the various English lexical categories. This may, in turn, influence bilingual performance in other cognitive tasks, such as reading, where their allocation of time (a) to word vs. contextual processing and (b) among the various lexical categories may differ from that of monolinguals.

In ending, let us note that all of our subjects met the "Native English Speaker" criterion so often invoked by cognitive researchers to "purify" their data. As many of our subjects were also native speakers of another language, their cognitions and data reflected their language background. Thus, future researchers should be cautioned to consider their subjects' backgrounds in more detail, and to take advantage of the rich diversity when analyzing the data.

Acknowledgements

This research was supported in part by PHS Grant MH-16,496 to New York University and by an NYU Research Challenge Grant. We thank Steve Ferres for help in data collection, and Deborah Weinstock for comments on an earlier draft of this chapter. Communication regarding this research can be addressed to the Authors at the Psychology Department, New York University, 6 Washington Place, 8th Floor, New York, NY 10003 USA.

References

Aaronson, D., & Ferres, S. (1986). Sentence processing in Chinese-American bilinguals. *Journal of Memory and Language*, 25, 136-162.

Bates, E., & MacWhinney, B. (1981). Second-language acquisition from a functionalist perspective: Pragmatic, semantic and perceptual strategies. In H. Winitz (Ed.), *Native language and foreign language acquisition*. New York: New York Academy of Science.

Bracero, W. (1990). *Bilingualism in the TAT response of normal Puerto Rican women.* Ph.D. dissertation, New York University.

Brandt, J. J. (1943). *Introduction to spoken Chinese* (Amer. ed.). North Manchester, IN: Heckman Bindery.

Chao, Y. R. (1968). *A grammar of spoken Chinese*. Berkeley, CA: University of California Press.

Chomsky, N. (1957/1978). *Syntactic structures*. The Hague: Mouton.

Chomsky, N. (1965). *Aspects of the theory of syntax*. Cambridge, MA: MIT Press.

Chen, C. -M. (1982). Analysis of present day Mandarin. *Journal of Chinese Linguistics*, 10, 282-358.

Cummins, J. (1987). Bilingualism, language proficiency, and metalinguistic development. In P. Homel, M. Palij, & D. Aaronson (Eds.) *Childhood bilingualism: Aspects of linguistic, cognitive, and social development.* Hillsdale, NJ: Erlbaum.

Ervin, S. M. & Osgood, C. E. (1954). Second language learning and bilingualism. *Journal of Abnormal and Social Psychology*, 49, 139-146.

Forrest, R. A. D. (1973). *The Chinese language.* London: Faber & Faber.

Hakuta, K. (1987). The second-language learner in the context of the study of language acquisition. In P. Homel, M. Palij, & D. Aaronson (Eds.) *Childhood bilingualism: Aspects of linguistic, cognitive, and social development.* Hillsdale, NJ: Erlbaum.

Hakuta, K. & Garcia, E. E. (1989). Bilingualism and education. *American Psychologist*, 44, 374-379.

Halliday, M. A. K., (1956). Grammatical categories in modern Chinese. *Transactions of the Philological* Society, 178-224.

Henne, H., Rongen, O. B., & Hansen, L. J. (1977). *A handbook on Chinese language structure.* Oslo: Universitetsforlaget.

Herdan, G. (1964). *The structuralistic approach to Chinese grammar and vocabulary.* The Hague: Mouton.

Homel, P., Palij, M., & Aaronson, D. (1987). (Eds.) *Childhood bilingualism: Aspects of linguistic, cognitive, and social development.* Hillsdale, NJ: Erlbaum.

Hung, D. G. & Tzeng, O. J. L. (1981). Orthographic variations and visual information processing. *Psychological Bulletin*, 90, 377-414.

Javier, R. A. (1982). *The effects of stress on the language independence phenomenon in coordinate bilinguals.* Ph.D. dissertation, New York University.

Jung, J. (1969). Current practices and problems in the use of college students for psychological research. *The Canadian Psychologist*, 9, 59-66.

Karlgren, B. (1962). *Sound and symbol in China.* Hong Kong: Cathay.

Kolers, P. A. (1968). Bilingualism and information processing. *Scientific American*, 218, 78-86.

Koriat, A., Greenberg, S. N., & Goldshmid, Y. (1991). The missing-letter effect in Hebrew: Word-frequency or word function. *Journal of Experimental Psychology: Learning, Memory, and Cognition*, 17, 66-80.

Kratochvil, P. (1968). *The Chinese language today*. London: Hutchinson Univ. Press.

Kulich, R. J., Seldon, J. W., Richardson, K., & Servies, S. (1978, May) *Frequency of employing undergraduate samples in psychological research and subject reaction to forced participation*. Paper presented at the meeting of the Midwest Psychological Association, Chicago.

Lambert, W. E. (1972). *Language, psychology, and culture*. Stanford: Stanford University Press.

Lambert, W. E. (1987). The effects of bilingual and bicultural experiences on children's attitudes and social perspectives. In P. Homel, M. Palij & D. Aaronson (Eds.), *Childhood bilingualism: Aspects of linguistic, cognitive, and social development*. Hillsdale, NJ: Erlbaum.

Li, C. N., & Thompson, S. A. (1981). *Mandarin Chinese: A functional reference grammar*. Berkeley, CA: Univ. of California Press.

Li, Y. C. (1971). *An investigation of case in Chinese grammar*. South Orange, NJ: Seton Hall Univ. Press.

Liu, I. M., Chaung, C. J., & Wang, S. C. (1975). *Frequency county of 40,000 Chinese words*. Taipei Taiwan: Lucky Books.

Lyons, J. (1979). *Introduction to theoretical linguistics*. London: Cambridge Univ. Press.

MacWhinney, B., Bates, E., & Kliegl, R. (1984). Cues validity and sentence interpretation in English, German and Italian. *Journal of Verbal Learning and Verbal Behavior*, 23, 127-150.

Padilla, A. M., Lindholm, K. J., Chen, A., Duran, R., Hakuta, K., Lambert, W., Tucker, G. R. (1991). The English-Only Movement. *American Psychologist*, 46, 120-130.

Paikeday, T. M. (1985). *The native speaker is dead!* Toronto: Paikeday Pub.

Palij, M. (1987). *Assessing language background differences* (Report WPP 87-1). Working Papers in Psycholinguistics (ERIC Document Reproduction Service No. ED 299 814). New York: Department of Psychology, New York University.

Palij, M. (1988). What happens to the unwanted subject? Comment on the value of undergraduate participation in research. *American Psychologist*, 43, 404-405.

Palij, M. (1990). Acquiring English at different ages: The English displacement effect and other findings. *Journal of Psycholinguistic Research*, 19, 57-70.

Palij, M. & Aaronson, D. (1989). *Age of English acquisition and the recall of English words*. Paper presented at the 30th annual meeting of the Psychonomic Society, Atlanta, Georgia.

Palij, M. & Aaronson, D. (1990). *Age of English acquisition and the recognition of English words*. Paper presented at the 31th annual meeting of the Psychonomic Society, New Orleans, Louisiana.

Palij, M. & Homel, P. (1987). The relationship of bilingualism to cognitive development: Historical, methodological, and theoretical considerations. In P. Homel, M. Palij, & D. Aaronson (Eds.) *Childhood bilingualism: Aspects of linguistic, cognitive, and social development*. Hillsdale, NJ: Erlbaum.

Reynolds, A. G. & Flagg, P. W. (1983). *Cognitive Psychology* (2nd Ed). Boston: Little, Brown.

Rivera, H. (1987). *The relation between bilingualism and primary process thinking*. Ph.D. dissertation, New York University.

Schneider, H. (1981). *Emotional expression and bilingual: The effect of the language independence phenomenon*. Ph.D. dissertation, New York University.

Sieber, J. E. & Saks, M. J. (1989). A census of subject pool characteristics and policies. *American Psychologist*, 44, 1053-1061.

Simon, W. (1937). Has the Chinese language parts of speech? *Transactions of the Philological Society*, 99-119.

Tewksbury, M. G. (1948). *Speak Chinese*. New Haven, CT: Far Eastern Publications, Yale University.

Tzeng, O. J. L. (1985). Some psycholinguistic issues in reading Chinese. In J. Y. Mei (Ed.) *Reading in China*. New York: National Committee on US-China Relations.

Venezky, R. (1985). Language, script and reading in China. In J. Y. Mei (Ed.). *Reading in China*. New York: National Committee on US-China Relations.

Weinreich, U. (1953). *Languages in contact*. New York: Linguistic Circle of New York.

Part II:

BILINGUAL MEMORY

Cognitive Processing in Bilinguals – R.J. Harris (Editor)
© *1992 Elsevier Science Publishers B.V. All rights reserved.*

Bilingual Memory Revisited

Roberto Heredia and Barry McLaughlin
University of California at Santa Cruz

Abstract

In this paper we address the question of how the bilingual stores information.
We begin with a brief review of the research on bilingual memory. Our aim
here is not to be exhaustive but representative. Next we turn to some recent
work to bear on the question of bilingual memory. We conclude with a
discussion of the implications for our understanding of how the bilingual mind
is organized.

From ancient times the question of the capacity of the bilingual mind fascinated
people. The Romans were concerned that their children would not learn Latin well
if they were taught Greek at a young age by Greek tutors. This was an early instance
of the "limited brain" argument that is still used by some opponents of bilingual
education.

The concern over how the bilingual brain is organized has a long history in
modern experimental psychology. There has been a vast amount of research on the
question of bilingual memory. One particular issue has proven especially intractable--
the question of whether there is a single memory store for both languages or a
separate store for each? However, some recent work, we feel, resolves some of the
apparent contradictions in past research.

Research on Bilingual Memory

The position that there is a single memory store for both languages has become
known as the *interdependence* model. This model assumes that items or concepts are
stored in the bilingual's memory in the form of language-free concepts with a single
conceptual or semantic representation subserving the two lexical entries (Caramazza
& Brones, 1980; Marshall & Caraveo-Ramos, 1984). Moreover, the model assumes
that bilinguals store words in terms of their semantic features only, with some means
of "tagging" the items with the proper language at the time of the output (Lopez &
Young, 1974). The evidence for this hypothesis comes from free recall experiments,
including those using repetition and distance paradigms (e.g., Glanzer & Duarte, 1971;
Kolers & Gonzalez, 1980; however, see Paivio, Clark & Lambert, 1988; Tulving &
Colotla, 1970).

In contrast, proponents of an *independence* model contend that bilinguals
organize their storage system in two distinct memories--one memory for each language,
with information in one language not readily available to the other system (Kolers,
1966; Lopez & Young, 1974). This model assumes two distinct memory

codes for each language (Kirsner, Brown, Abrol, Chadha, & Sharma, 1980; Kirsner, Smith, Lockhart, King, & Jain, 1984; Sharma, 1984; Watkins & Peynircioglu, 1983). Furthermore, the model assumes that an "input switch" turns off one language while the other is active (Macnamara & Kushnir, 1971). In general, word-fragment identification and lexical decision tasks are consistent with this model (e.g., Chen, 1990; Chen & Ng, 1989; Durgunoglu & Roediger, 1987; Kirsner et al.,1980; Kirsner et al., 1984; Sharma, 1984; Watkins & Peynircioglu, 1983).

Although the experimental evidence is equivocal, some have argued that an interdependence model explains some aspects of language, while the independence model was more appropriate for other aspects. Thus Kolers (1966) suggested that bilinguals had neither separate nor shared memories; some information was restricted to the language of encoding, while some was accessible to both linguistic systems.

Most of the research on bilingual memory representation has utilized free recall, recognition, and lexical decision tasks (for a review, see Heredia, 1988; Heredia, Weldon, & McLaughlin, 1991). This research has been criticized because it constrains language to isolated individual items. This point was made by Hummel (1986) and Ransdell and Fischler (1989) who argued that the nature of bilingual memory representations cannot be conclusively demonstrated when the principal experimental stimulus is the lexical item divorced from a grammatical context. A similar argument was made over twenty years ago by Macnamara (1967). However, recent experimental work with prose material has not resolved the debate about the nature of bilingual memory representation. Evidence has been found supporting both the independence (Hummel, 1986) and the interdependence hypotheses (Ransdell & Fischler, 1989).

Romaine (1989) and Grosjean (1982) have argued that the procedures used in bilingual memory research fail to distinguish between general concept memory, which is language independent, and a more linguistic specific, and constrained semantic store. It was this line of reasoning that led Paradis (1981) to propose a three-store model, according to which a bilingual possesses two language memory stores, one for each language, and a more general conceptual memory representation. In both language stores, units of meaning in each language are grouped together with conceptual features in different ways. The conceptual store corresponds to the bilingual's experiential and conceptual information, and contains mental representations of things and events (Grosjean, 1982; Romaine, 1989). Such model would represent words in different languages at the surface level by independent lexical representations but at the conceptual level by a common representation (Kroll & Stewart, 1990). The empirical evidence for this hypothetical model is presently lacking, however.

Recent Research on Memory

In the past few years, there is important experimental research on human memory that may clarify the traditional work on bilingual memory. This work makes a central theoretical distinction between *explicit* and *implicit* memory retrieval tasks (Graf & Schacter, 1985). Explicit memory tasks are those tasks that require conscious recollection of studied material directly tested on episodes from recent experience (Richardson-Klavehn & Bjork, 1988). In performing these tests subjects are instructed to remember events and presumably are aware that they are recollecting recent experiences. Traditional free recall, recognition, and paired-associate learning are included in this category. Implicit tasks, on the other hand, refer to tests that involve no reference to an event in the subject's personal history, but are nonetheless influenced by such events (Richardson-Klavehn & Bjork, 1988). That is, the task does not require conscious recollection, but retention is measured by transfer from a prior experience relative to an appropriate baseline. Any improvement over baseline is referred to as a priming effect. Word-fragment completion tasks, lexical decision tasks, and word identification tasks are considered implicit tasks.

Differences in performance on explicit and implicit memory tasks relates to comparisons between priming effects and recall or recognition. This task incongruency is known as memory dissociation. For instance, comparison of explicit and implicit tasks has shown that amnesic patients whose performance in recall or recognition is gravely impaired, exhibit normal or near-normal priming effects on implicit tasks (Roediger, 1990). Other research has shown that it is possible to produce significant effects on free recall and recognition, with little or no influence on priming (Graf & Mandler, 1984; but see Hamman, 1990). Furthermore, research on the generation effect--the advantage of later recall produced by generating an item (e.g., a synonym or translation) rather than reading a given item during the study phase--shows explicit and implicit memory dissociations as well (Blaxton, 1985). Research on picture-word stimuli shows similar effects (e.g., Weldon & Roediger, 1987; Weldon, Roediger, & Challis, 1989).

As pointed out by Richardson-Klavehn and Bjork (1988), the underlying assumption of task-comparison methods is that different tasks make different informational demands on the subjects. Based on patterns of dissociations and parallel effects across tasks as a function of critical independent variables, inferences can be made about the similarities and differences between the mental states and processes necessary to comply with the information demands of the respective tasks (Roediger, et al., 1989).

Differences in performance on implicit and explicit tasks have led to two possible explanations for memory dissociations. These are the *multi-memory* approach and the *unitary-system processing* approach. The leading proponents of multi-memory systems are Tulving (1986), who makes the distinction between episodic and semantic systems, and Squire (1987) and numerous other investigators who distinguish procedural and declarative systems. Tulving argues that dissociation between implicit and explicit support his distinction between episodic and semantic memory, because research shows that it is possible to tap one particular type of memory (episodic) without being able to tap the other (semantic). Squire makes a similar argument with regard to procedural and declarative systems.

However, other researchers take a somewhat different approach (Blaxton 1985; Jacoby 1983; Roediger & Blaxton 1987; Roediger et al., 1989; Weldon et al., 1989). They argue that differences on implicit and explicit tests should be understood in terms of a distinction between data-driven or surface processing, and conceptually-driven or semantic processing, with the additional assumption that tasks may vary considerably with respect to the nature of the appropriateness of the processes involved. The underlying memory representation is a unitary system (Jacoby, 1983; Roediger & Blaxton, 1987; Weldon & Roediger, 1987). That is, it is not necessary to postulate more than one memory system to account for these dissociations.

The principle of *transfer-appropriate processing* (Morris, Bransford, & Franks, 1977) is central to this characterization of the relation between implicit and explicit memory. The argument is that performance on an implicit memory task is often more dependent on the match between perceptual conditions at study and test phases than is performance on explicit tasks. However, it is important to note that the there is no necessary equivalence between data-driven and implicit and conceptually-driven and explicit memory. Implicit tasks can be conceptually-driven (e.g., cued recall, word-fragment identification translations), and recognition memory tests usually involve a blend of data-driven and conceptually-driven processing (Jacoby, 1983; Durgunoglu & Roediger, 1987; Hamman, 1990; Graf & Ryan, 1990).

Some Recent Research on Bilingual Memory

What are the implications of this research on implicit/explicit memory for research on bilingual memory? We will argue that this framework helps us understand some of the contradictory findings in bilingual memory research. To this end, we review some recent experimental work that uses conceptually-driven versus data-driven tasks to explore the question of whether bilinguals represent their two languages in one (interdependent) or two memory (independent) systems.

Durgunoglu and Associates

The pioneering work in this area was carried out by Durgunoglu and Roediger (1987), who argued that discrepancies and inconsistencies in past research were due to failure to distinguish the processes involved in the memory tasks. The distinction between conceptually-driven processes and data-driven processes suggests that bilingual memory tasks measure two different processes. The conceptual task measures the bilingual's semantic and conceptual word representation, and supports a one-memory system. Data-driven tasks, on the other hand, involve identifying language-specific patterns, or the languages' orthographical features (Watkins & Peynircioglu, 1983), and hence retrieval improves when the language of study matches the language of test.

Thus Durgunoglu and Roediger maintained that recall tasks that involved semantic and conceptual processes (e.g., Caramazza & Brones, 1980; Glanzer & Duarte, 1971; Lopez & Young, 1974; Marshall & Caraveo-Ramos, 1984) yield results consistent with the interdependence model. On the other hand, tasks that involved data-driven processes generally produce results that show language-specific features, thus supporting the independence model. For example, experiments employing priming paradigms and lexical decision tasks (Chen & Ng, 1989; Kirsner et al., 1980; Kirsner et al., 1984) or fragment completion tasks (Watkins & Peynircioglu, 1983) suggest that items from the same language facilitate memory retrieval; more priming results from encoding conditions that involve processing of similar perceptual surface features (Watkins & Peynircioglu, 1983; Weldon & Roediger, 1987).

To test the hypothesis that evidence for one or two memory systems depends on the type of processing, Durgunoglu and Roediger (1987) utilized free recall and word-fragment completion tasks. For the conceptually-driven processing of free recall, they predicted support for the interdependence hypothesis. The data-driven fragment completion task was expected to support the independence model. Their study employed five encoding conditions: subjects saw words twice in (a) Spanish and (b) English or in (c) both languages. For other words, subjects saw words in (d) Spanish and English and also generated the English equivalent in writing, or (e) saw the word twice in Spanish and generated an image of its referent. The conditions requiring more elaboration (e.g., generation and translation) were expected to evoke conceptually-driven processing and enhance recall, but have little effect on priming in fragment completion. Variation in language of study was expected to have minimum effect on the conceptually-driven free recall task, but to affect the word fragment completion task. The fragment completion task was in English, therefore greater priming was anticipated from studying the stimuli words in English than Spanish.

Durgunoglu and Roediger's (1987) results demonstrated that in free recall the language studied was unimportant. Generating word translations and forming an image of the referent word facilitated retrieval. However, elaboration during study did not improve word-fragment completion rates. If the studied language matched the test language, fragment completion rates were significantly higher than the rate for non-studied items. However, if the study language did not match the test language, the fragment completion rates did not differ from the non-studied items.

To further investigate the importance of task dependency, Durgunoglu and Garcia (1989) extended Durgunoglu and Roediger's (1987) experiment to include an implicit task with explicit memory instructions. Durgunoglu and Garcia kept the retrieval cues constant (i.e, word-fragments), but the retrieval strategies (explicit instructions) differed between the two groups of subjects. Following the study phase, one group of subjects completed a word-fragment test, and the other group performed a recall test using the same fragments as cues. All materials were in English. They predicted that if the data-driven processing elicited by the retrieval cues had a greater effect than the task strategy required by the explicit instructions (fragment-cued recall), then both groups would show comparable retrieval rates.

In general, Durgunoglu and Garcia (1989) replicated Durgunoglu and Roediger's (1987) study. The results showed that explicit memory instructions were unable to overcome the effects of the surface features in the fragment-cued recall task. Like Durgunoglu and Roediger, Durgunoglu and Garcia (1989) concluded that in studying bilingual memory, retrieval task requirements are critical to the outcome. Both studies support Durgunoglu and Roediger's contention that the manner in which bilinguals organize their two languages--in one memory or in two memories depends on the processing demands required by the type of memory task.

Heredia, Weldon, and McLaughlin

This section describes two recent experiments we have carried out using a different memory paradigm to extend the generality of the findings of Durgunoglu and her associates. In this study bilingual subjects were given lists with words repeated in the same language (within-language repetitions) and lists with words that were translation equivalents in the other language (between-language repetitions). This paradigm had been employed by Glanzer and Duarte (1971), who investigated what they termed "the bilingual equivalence effect"--that within-language and between-language repetitions would increase the amount recalled by the same amount. This effect is a variant of the interdependence hypothesis, namely that for a bilingual the two languages are equivalent, and hence both types of repetitions should produce equivalent results. Glanzer and Duarte (1971) found support for the bilingual equivalence effect in that the probability of recall was an orderly function of distance between repetitions for both within- and between-language repetitions. As distance increased, so did the probability of recall. Between-language repetitions gave higher recall overall than within-language repetitions, especially for massed repetitions.

We used the repetition paradigm to test the effects of conceptually-driven versus data-driven processes in bilingual memory. The aim of the study was to verify Durgunoglu and Roediger's (1987) contention that bilingual's organize their two languages in one or two memory storages depending on the processing demands required by the type of memory task. Subjects were exposed to either a free recall task or a fragment identification task. Because of the conceptually-driven processes of free recall, the results of this task were expected to support the bilingual equivalence effect (Glanzer & Duarte, 1971; Kolers & Gonzalez, 1980; Paivio et al., 1988). As distance increased, the probability of recall was expected to increase for both the bilingual (between-language) and monolingual (within-language) repetitions. However, the word-fragment identification task was expected to exhibit English specific patterns (Watkins & Peynircioglu, 1983; Durgunoglu & Garcia, 1989; Durgunoglu & Roediger, 1987). Because the fragment identification task involved data-driven processes, the results were expected to contradict the bilingual equivalence effect and to show superior performance resulting from monolingual repetitions.

A second experiment was motivated by Durgunoglu and Garcia (1989) who used explicit instructions in an implicit task in an attempt to overcome the effects surface features in an implicit task. By having subjects employ English fragments as stimuli for generating Spanish translations, the experimenters hoped to minimize the perceptual advantage of the English surface cues.

Both experiments used the same procedures. Bilingual Spanish-English subjects saw lists of words in which some words were repeated either in the same language or in their translation equivalent. Lists were counterbalanced to minimize position effects. Twelve sets were constructed. Each set contained 24 lists, and each list contained 24 items. Half of the words in each list were in English and half in Spanish. Each list contained two Spanish-Spanish (S-S) repetitions, two English-English (E-E) repetitions, two English-Spanish (E-S) repetitions and two Spanish-English (S-E) repetitions. In addition to the 16 target repetitions, each list contained four unrepeated Spanish items and four unrepeated English items. The repetitions in each list were evenly divided with 0, 1, 2, or 5 intervening items. Across the 24 lists, the pairs for each of the 16 targets appeared once at each possible serial position.

For the word-fragment identification task, words were normed so that 25 to 30 percent of the fragmented items could be completed without previous exposure or practice. The word fragmentation was done by a computer program that placed white squares at random locations over the rectangular area occupied by the words. A randomized answer-sheet was constructed. Each answer-sheet contained eight of the original 16 repetitions, four Spanish non-repeated items, four English non-repeated items and four non-studied items. All items in the answer sheet were in English.

The experiment consisted of a study and a test phase. During the study phase, subjects sat individually in front of a computer monitor and viewed two practice lists. Then 24 experimental lists were presented, each followed by either a free recall or a word fragment identification task. In the free recall condition, subjects were told to recall as many words as they could in any order. For the fragment identification task, subjects were instructed to complete as many word-fragments as possible. They were not informed that the answer sheets contained non-studied items. Subjects in both conditions viewed the same words. The experimenter read the instruction in Spanish and English, and advised subjects to pronounce the words aloud.

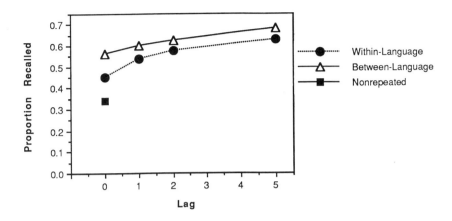

Figure 1. Free Recall at Varying Repetition Distances

Retrieval results for the first experiment showed that for the conceptually-driven free recall task, the bilingual equivalence effect was obtained. The probability of recall for the between- and within-languages conditions increased as the distance increased (Figure 1). Bilingual repetitions gave higher recall rates than monolingual repetitions. This advantage was most noticeable for massed repetitions, especially at distance 0. The advantage of the bilingual over the monolingual condition in massed conditions could be due to encoding variability (Madigan, 1969), or to processing the second occurrence of the item more fully when the format is altered (Jacoby, 1978; Dellarosa & Bourne 1985; however see Slamecka & Katsaiti, 1987). As expected, these results supported the interdependence model and replicated Glanzer and Duarte's (1977) experiment.

However, on the data-driven task (i.e., word-fragment identification task) language made a difference: there was no bilingual equivalence effect. The E-E condition produced greater word-fragment identifications than did S-S repetitions (Figure 2). Only when the tested language matched the language of study was there an improvement in retrieval. Distance between repeated items had an effect on E-E retrieval only. In short, the word-fragment identification task showed English specific patterns, thus supporting the independence model (Durgunoglu & Garcia, 1989; Durgunoglu & Roediger, 1987; Watkins & Peynircioglu, 1983).

Like Durgunoglu and Roediger (1987), we concluded that the free recall task measures the semantic and conceptual meaning of the two languages, while the word-fragment identification measures the perceptual features of the language. The results from the free recall task and the word-fragment identification task in the first experiment suggest that the question of whether bilinguals' memory is independent or interdependent cannot be answered without addressing the conceptually-driven and the data-driven issue. That is, these results suggest that processing demands, i.e., test appropriate processing (Morris, Bransford, Franks, 1977), need to be considered when interpreting results of bilingual memory (Durgunoglu & Garcia, 1989; Durgunoglu & Roediger, 1987).

R. Heredia and B. McLaughlin

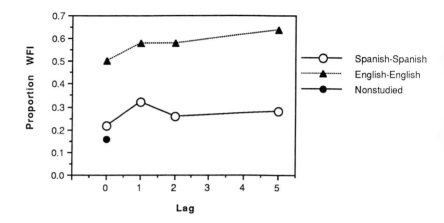

Figure 2. Word-Fragment Identification at Varying Repetition Distances.

   Inspection of Figure 2 indicates that despite the fact that the word-identification task was expected to evoke only data-driven processes, it seemed to involve both data-driven and conceptually-driven processing. Contrary to the results of Durgunoglu and Roediger (1987) and Durgunoglu and Garcia (1989), the S-S condition benefited from priming, which suggests that conceptually-driven processes were involved to some degree. It is likely that subjects in the S-S condition translated from Spanish to English to solve the English fragment task, an activity that may involve conceptually-driven processes.

   If this is the case, it may be possible to overcome the perceptual features of the E-E condition by requiring subjects in this condition to translate from English to Spanish. This was what we attempted to do in Experiment 2. We wanted to determine whether we could provide subjects on an implicit memory task with explicit instructions that would increase conceptually-driven processing. This had been attempted by Durgunoglu and Garcia (1989) but without success. Their task involved using the fragment as a retrieval cue for recall. Subjects in this condition did not differ from subjects in the word fragment completion condition.

   In our second experiment we gave subjects explicit memory instructions on an implicit task. Our reasoning was similar to that of Richardson-Klavehn and Bjork (1988), who argued that it is not enough to show dissociations among tasks unless the nature of the processing that is assumed to produce these dissociations is also analyzed. They argued that it is important to examine the role of explicit (strategically based) and implicit contributions to performance on implicit memory tests. Hence in Experiment 2 subjects were told to employ English fragments as cues to generate Spanish translations after viewing monolingual and bilingual Spanish and English lists.

   If the language differences on the word identification test in Experiment 1 were due to the surface features of the E-E cues, the explicit instructions should not override the perceptual features of the implicit task, because the perceptual retrieval cues will remain in English. That is, the E-E condition should produce significantly better performance than the S-S condition, which would be congruent with Durgunoglu and Garcia's (1989) findings. However, if translations are able to tap conceptually-driven processing, the test should yield results more like a conceptually-driven (e.g., free recall) task.

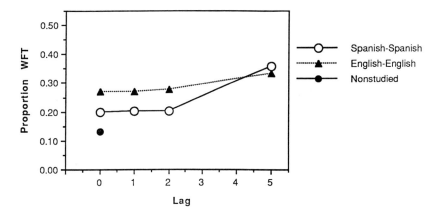

Figure 3. Correct Responses at Varying Distances on Experiment 2.

As predicted, the results showed that when subjects were required to generate Spanish translations from the English fragments, performance for the E-E and S-S conditions did not differ significantly (Figure 3). As the repetition distance increased, the probability for both S-S and E-E language conditions increased equally. These results suggest that the S-S priming found in Experiment 1 may have been due to extra effort (e.g., translation) during the decoding phase. These results also suggest that the procedure used in the second experiment was successful in equating S-S and E-E retrieving strategies.

In short, the Heredia et al. (1991) study supports Durgunoglu and Roediger's (1987) contention that in measuring bilingual memory both encoding and retrieval assumption, as well as task processing requirements should be considered. The results of the second experiment indicate that interpretations concerning the nature of bilingual memory do not simply depend on the type of task used (whether it involves implicit or explicit memory tests), but also on the operations and strategies used in performance. It is not simply a question of words versus fragments; the nature and use of retrieval strategies (explicit search of memory versus no explicit search) is critical to interpreting the results.

Conclusions

We are in agreement with Durgunoglu and Roediger (1987) who contended that the question of whether bilinguals have a common, language-independent conceptual representation for the words in their two languages, or separate, language-specific representations is indeterminate. We agree that the question of task requirements is a primary variable in determining language independence or language specificity in bilingual memory. But the task requirements need to be carefully analyzed. Our data show that a fragment-identification task can require explicit search of memory that overrides the data-driven processing elicited by word fragments.

The argument of this paper is that recent work on the implicit/explicit memory distinction has important implications for understanding bilingual memory. As Glucksberg (1984) pointed out, the form of an ultimate model of human conceptual functioning demands specification of the conditions under which performance is modality specific. Task requirements are a primary consideration in determining the form that bilingual memory takes.

As was noted earlier, Durgunoglu and Roediger argued that it is not necessary to invent hypothetical memory systems, such as distinguish procedural and declarative knowledge or episodic and semantic memory. A more parsimonious approach is to consider dissociations among measures of retention as the result of varying procedural requirements across retention tests and encoding activities. Thus the question of transfer appropriate processing across memory tasks becomes crucial to understanding performance measures. How is bilingual memory organized? It depends.

References

Blaxton, T. A. (1985). *Investigating dissociations among memory measures: Support for a transfer appropriate processing framework.* Doctoral dissertation, Purdue University.

Caramazza, A. & Brones, I. (1980). Semantic classification by bilinguals. *Canadian Journal of Psychology, 34,* 77-81.

Chen, H. (1990). Lexical processing in a non-native language: Effects of language proficiency and learning strategy. *Memory & Cognition, 18,* 279-288.

Chen, H., & Ng, M. (1989). Semantic facilitation and translation priming effects in Chinese-English bilinguals. *Memory & Cognition, 17,* 454-462.

Dellarosa, D., & Bourne, L. E. (1985). Surface form and the spacing effect. *Memory & Cognition, 13,* 529-537.

Durgunoglu, A. Y., & Garcia, E. G. (1989, November). *Effects of implicit or explicit memory instructions on bilingual memory.* Paper presented at the Psychonomic Society, Atlanta, GA. Atlanta.

Durgunoglu, A. Y., & Roediger, H. L. (1987). Test differences in accessing bilingual memory. *Journal of Memory and Language, 26,* 377-391.

Glanzer, M., & Duarte, A. (1971). Repetition between and within languages in free recall. *Journal of Verbal Learning and Verbal Behavior, 10,* 625-630.

Glucksberg, S. (1984). Commentary: The functional equivalence of common and multiple codes. *Journal of Verbal Learning and Verbal Behavior, 10,* 625-630.

Graf, P., & Mandler, G. (1984). Activation makes words more accessible, but not necessarily more retrievable. *Journal of Verbal Learning and Verbal Behavior, 23,* 553-568.

Graf, P. & Ryan, L. (1990). Transfer-appropriate processing for implicit and explicit memory. *Journal of Experimental Psychology: Learning, Memory, & Cognition, 16,* 978-992.

Graf, P., & Schacter, D. L. (1985). Implicit and explicit memory for new dissociations in normal and amnesic subjects. *Journal of Experimental Psychology: Learning, Memory, & Cognition, 11,* 501-518.

Grosjean, F. (1982). *Life with two languages: An introduction to bilingualism.* Cambridge, MA: Harvard University Press.

Hamman, S. B. (1990). Level-of-processing effects in conceptually driven implicit tasks. *Journal of Experimental Psychology: Learning, Memory, & Cognition, 16,* 970-977.

Heredia, R. R. (1988). *Do bilinguals have one memory store for each language?* Unpublished manuscript, University of California, Davis.

Heredia, R. R., Weldon, M.S. & McLaughlin, B. (1991). *Conceptually driven versus data-driven processes in bilingual memory: One or two memory systems?* University of California, Santa Cruz.

Hummel, K. M. (1986). Memory for bilingual prose. In J. Vaid (Ed.), *Language processing in bilinguals: Psycholinguistic and neuropsychological perspectives* (pp.47-64). Hillsdale, NJ: Erlbaum.

Jacoby, L. (1978). On interpreting the effects of repetition: Solving a problem versus remembering a solution. *Journal of Verbal Learning and Verbal Behavior, 17,* 649-667.

Jacoby, L. L. (1983). Remembering the data: Analyzing interactive processes in reading. *Journal of Verbal Learning and Verbal Behavior, 22,* 485-508.

Kirsner, K., Brown, H. L., Abrol, S., Chadha, N. K., & Sharma, N. K. (1980). Bilingualism and lexical representation. *Quarterly Journal of Experimental Psychology, 32,* 585-594.

Kirsner, K., Smith, M. C., Lockhart, R. S., King, M. L. & Jain, M. (1984). The bilingual lexicon: Language-specific units in an integrated network. *Journal of Verbal Learning and Verbal Behavior, 23,* 519-539.

Kolers, P. A. (1966). Interlingual facilitation of short-term memory. *Journal of Verbal Learning and Verbal Behavior, 5,* 314-319.

Kolers, P. A., & Gonzalez, E. (1980). Memory for words, synonyms, and translations. *Journal of Experimental Psychology: Human Learning and Memory, 6,* 53-65.

Kroll, J. F., Stewart, E. (1990, November). *Concept mediation in bilingual translation.* Paper presented at the annual meeting of the Psychonomic Society, New Orleans, LA.

Lopez, M. & Young, R. K. (1974). The linguistic interdependence of bilinguals. *Journal of Experimental Psychology, 6,* 981-983.

Macnamara, J. (1967). The bilingual's linguistic performance: a psychological overview. *Journal of Social Sciences, 23,* 59-77.

Macnamara, J. & Kushnir, S. (1971). Linguistic independence of bilinguals: The input switch. *Journal of Verbal Learning and Verbal Behavior, 10,* 480-487.

Madigan, S. A. (1969). Intraserial repetition and coding processes in free recall. *Journal of Verbal Learning and Verbal Behavior, 8,* 828-835.

Marshall, P. H. & Caraveo-Ramos, L. E. (1983). Bilingual frequency encoding. *Journal of Psycholinguistic Research, 13,* 295-306.

Morris, C. D., Bransford, J. D., Franks, J. J. (1977). Levels of processing versus transfer appropriate processing. *Journal of Verbal Learning and Verbal Behavior, 16,* 519-533.

Paivio, A., Clark, J. M. & Lambert, W. E. (1988). Bilingual dual-coding theory and semantic repetition effect on recall. *Journal of Experimental Psychology: Learning, Memory, and Cognition, 14, 163-172.*

Paradis, M. (1981). Neurolinguistic organization of a bilingual's two languages. In J. E. Copeland & P. W. Davis (Eds.), *The seventh LACUS forum* (486-494). Columbia, SC: Horn Beam Press.

Ransdell, S. E., & Fischler, I. (1989). Effects of concreteness and task context on recall of prose among bilingual and monolingual speakers. *Journal of Memory and Language, 28,* 278-291.

Richardson-Klavehn, A., & Bjork, R. A. (1988). Measures of memory. *Annual Review of Psychology, 39,* 475-543.

Roediger, H. L. (1990). Implicit memory: Retention without remembering. *American Psychologist, 45,* 1043-1056.

Roediger, H. L. & Blaxton, T. A. (1987). Retrieval modes produce dissociations in memory for surface information. In D. S. Gorfein & R. R. Hoffman (Eds.), *The Ebbinghaus centennial conference* (pp. 349-379). Hillsdale, NJ: Erlbaum.

Roediger, H. L., Weldon, M. S., & Challis, B. H. (1989). Explaining dissociations between implicit and explicit measures of retention: A processing account. In H. L. Roediger & F. I. M. Craik (Eds.) *Varieties of memory and consciousness.* (pp. 3-41). Hillsdale, NJ: Erlbaum.

Romaine, S. (1989). *Bilingualism.* New York: Basil Blackwell.

Sharma, N. K. (1984). Bilingualism and the representation of linguistic information in memory. *Psycho-Lingua, 1,* 19-34.

Slamecka, N. J. & Katsaiti, L. T. (1987). The generation effect is an artifact of selective displaced rehearsal. *Journal of Memory and Language, 26,* 589-607.

Squire, L. R. (1987). *Memory and Brain.* New York: Oxford University Press.

Tulving, E. (1986). What kind of hypothesis is the distinction between episodic and semantic memory? *Journal of Experimental Psychology: Learning, Memory, & Cognition, 12,* 307-311.

Tulving, E. & Colotla, V. A. (1970). Free recall of trilingual lists. *Cognitive Psychology, 1,* 86-98.

Watkins, M. J., & Peynircioglu, Z. F. (1983). On the nature of word recall: Evidence for linguistic specificity. *Journal of Verbal Learning and Verbal Behavior, 22,* 336-394.

Weldon, M. S., & Roediger, H. L. (1987). Altering retrieval demands reverses the picture superiority effect. *Memory & Cognition, 15,* 269-280.

Weldon, M. S., Roediger, H. L., & Challis, B. H. (1989). The properties of retrieval cues constrain the picture superiority effect. *Memory & Cognition, 17,* 95-105.

Cognitive Processing in Bilinguals – R.J. Harris (Editor)
© *1992 Elsevier Science Publishers B.V. All rights reserved.*   105

Cognitive Psychology and Second Language Processing:
The Role of Short-Term Memory

Gordon D. A. Brown
University of Wales at Bangor
and
Charles Hulme
University of York

Abstract

In this chapter recent research on the psychology of short-term memory is discussed. The chapter begins with evidence which suggests that phonological short-term memory is indeed required both for syntactic processing and for first and second language acquisition. Current psychological models of short-term memory, and their explanation for the reduced memory span size that is observed in a less familiar language, are then summarised. These accounts are criticised, and the results of several studies that test an alternative explanation for the reduced memory span observed in a second language are described. It is concluded that reduced short-term memory capacity can arise because of the lack of strong phonological lexical representations for second language items in long term memory.

Introduction

The aim of this chapter is to show how recent advances in our understanding of the cognitive psychology of short-term memory can shed new light on the nature of language processing in second language learners. Furthermore, we summarise the results of several experiments we have conducted to investigate subjects' short-term memory capacity for materials in a second language.

The evidence that we discuss is relevant to three critical theoretical questions. The first question is simply this: why do people show a reduced short-term memory capacity for material in a less familiar language? Secondly, what are the consequences of a reduced short-term memory capacity for the nature of processing in the second language? The third theoretical question that we focus on concerns the nature of the relationship between short-term memory capacity in a second language, and competence in that language. Does short-term memory causally affect the second language acquisition process?

The chapter is organized in the following way. In the first section, we review evidence concerning the role of short-term memory in language processing generally, and show that short-term memory does indeed play a major role both in language acquisition and in the normal skilled processing of language by fluent adults. In the next section, we discuss current models of short-term memory within cognitive psychology, and describe how they attempt to account for the reduced short-term memory span in a second language. These models, and the explanation they give for reduced second language short-term memory capacity, are then criticised. We then describe a series of experiments we have conducted which investigate short-term memory in different languages, and develop an account which suggests that short-term memory capacity in a second language is reduced for two quite separate reasons: because speech rate is reduced in a second language, and also because long-term memory for the phonological forms of words is reduced in a second language. We conclude by discussing the implications of our results both for models of short-term memory and for models of second language processing and acquisition.

The Role of Short-Term Memory in Language Processing

Short-term memory is widely assumed to be implicated in language processing and language learning. Here we simply summarise some of the main evidence in this area, in order to motivate our subsequent discussion of short-term memory and bilingualism. If short-term memory is indeed important in a wide range of language processing skills, and if short-term memory capacity is reduced in a second language (Dornic, 1980), then our understanding of short-term or immediate memory is important if we are to understand the psychology of second language processing.

Short-Term Memory and Reading

One source of evidence comes from comparing readers of different ability levels. Some studies have claimed that poorer readers have smaller immediate memory capacities than age-matched good readers (e.g. Brady, Shankweiler & Mann, 1983), and exhibit reduced phonemic confusability effects (e.g. Shankweiler, Liberman, Mark, Fowler & Fischer, 1979). This has been taken as evidence of an association between short-term memory and reading capacity, although this line of evidence has recently been called into question (e.g. Johnston, Rugg & Scott, 1987). Studies which have attempted to correlate short-term memory capacity (as assessed by span) with reading ability have generally found rather low correlations. Higher correlations are generally found when more complex measures of "working memory" capacity are used (e.g. Baddeley, Logie, Nimmo-Smith & Brereton, 1985; Daneman & Carpenter, 1983). However, several different studies have suggested that temporary storage of the phonological forms of items occurs during sentence comprehension. For example, Black, Coltheart and Byng (1987) present evidence which suggests that filling the gaps in verb-gapped sentences makes use of phonological representations from earlier parts of the sentence.

More specific hypotheses concerning the role of a phonological buffer in syntactic comprehension have been evaluated by examining the performance of brain-damaged patients who have reduced memory spans. For example, Baddeley, Vallar and Wilson (1987) found that span-impaired patients had difficulty in comprehending long and complex sentences. It appears not to be the mere length of a sentence that is problematic; it is necessary also that the sentence be syntactically complex and/or contain semantically reversible terms (Vallar & Baddeley, 1984; see also the papers in Vallar & Shallice, 1990). The cognitive neuropsychological evidence suggests that the phonological store does appear to have some backup function in speech comprehension (although see Butterworth, Campbell & Howard, 1986, who report the case of a patient who had problems with sentence repetition but not with syntactic analysis and comprehension).

Thus there is mixed evidence concerning the role of phonological short-term memory in reading, but there is enough to suggest a causal role of some kind. Clearer evidence comes from the study of language learning, particularly vocabulary acquisition.

Short-Term Memory and Learning

For some years it was believed that information had to pass through a short-term memory system in order to enter long-term memory. This view came to be abandoned in the light of cognitive neuropsychological work on head-injured patients, for patients were found who have severely impaired short-term memory spans but intact long-term memory learning (e.g. Shallice & Warrington, 1970; see Vallar & Shallice, 1990, for review). In recent years there has, however, been more attention paid to the role of short-term phonological memory in the learning of new verbal material (as, for example, in foreign language vocabulary acquisition). Baddeley, Papagno and Vallar (1988) found that a patient with a short-term memory deficit had great difficulty in associating familiar words with foreign language items, although she was able to learn associations between previously familiar items. Baddeley et al. concluded that short-term memory may play an important role in vocabulary acquisition.

This assumption receives some support from work by Gathercole and Baddeley (1990), who found that children who had trouble in repeating back non-words (a task assumed to tap phonological short-term memory) were less able than other children to learn phonologically unfamiliar names. One possible problem with this approach is that the task of non-word repetition requires phonological segmentation and other non-lexical skills, as well as pure short-term memory (see Snowling, Chiat & Hulme, in press, for further discussion of these problems). Papagno, Valentine and Baddeley (1991) directly examined the question of whether phonological short-term memory plays a causal role in foreign language vocabulary learning. In a series of experiments they found that articulatory suppression (a manipulation designed to prevent the use of the subvocal articulatory rehearsal procedure in short-term memory) impaired the learning of both nonsense syllables and phonologically unfamiliar words in a foreign language (both Finnish and Russian words were used, with English and Italian subjects).

Further evidence for the causal role of phonological short-term memory in the learning of both native and foreign language vocabulary comes from longitudinal studies. Such studies look for causal relationships between subskills by seeing whether some ability (e.g. repetition ability) predicts some aspect of performance (e.g. vocabulary size) in the same individual at some later date. Gathercole and Baddeley (1989) reported longitudinal data that were consistent with a causal role for short-term memory in vocabulary acquisition, for they found that non-word repetition skill in four-year-old children was a good predictor of vocabulary size a year later (although cf. the point made above, that non-word repetition may involve skills other than pure short-term memory). Furthermore, Ellis (1990) has shown in a longitudinal study that short-term memory is causally implicated at certain stages of reading development in the native language.

Finally, Service (1989) has shown that non-word repetition skill predicts subsequent success in learning English as a foreign language. These data are also interpreted as evidence for the causal role of phonological immediate memory in language acquisition.

Current Models of Short-term Memory

In this section we review current cognitive models of short-term memory. Early work (e.g. Miller, 1956) viewed short-term memory as limited in terms of the number of items that could be held in the store at one time. Miller suggested a capacity of "seven plus or minus two" items as the capacity of the store. However, subsequent work has shown that memory span varies with the type of material that must be remembered. Over two decades ago it was observed that memory span for phonemically confusable items (whether words or letters) was smaller than span for non-confusable items (e.g. Conrad, 1964). This was taken as evidence that the short-term memory store is best characterised as a speech-based system of some kind. A considerable amount of further evidence for this view accumulated in the 1970s and 1980s. Baddeley, Thomson and Buchanan (1975) found that subjects could remember fewer words when the words took a long time to articulate - memory span is larger for short words than for long words, when span is measured in terms of number of items. However, when capacity is assessed in terms of the amount of time it takes to articulate the items to be remembered, a roughly constant time interval is obtained. Estimates of this constant time interval vary, but average around two seconds. In subsequent research, the suggestion that immediate memory span for familiar materials such as words and digits will be equal to the amount of material that can be rehearsed subvocally in a fixed time interval has been widely accepted. This has lead to a model of short-term memory known as the verbal trace decay model. Perhaps the most well-known variant on this theme is the "articulatory loop" model of Baddeley (see Baddeley, 1986, for an overview; see also Brown & Hulme, in press, for a detailed model of some of the relevant processes). This model assumes that items are registered in an immediate memory store when they are presented, but the memory traces in the store decay over time. The trace can however be refreshed by using a subvocal rehearsal procedure. If the trace takes a constant amount of time to decay, then the capacity of the store will be limited to the amount of material that can be rehearsed in a fixed time interval, i.e., the time it takes for the trace to decay. The number of items that can be rehearsed will therefore depend in a straightforward manner on the length of time it takes to rehearse the items subvocally. Subvocal rehearsal rate is generally assumed to be highly correlated with the rate at which items can be overtly pronounced.

Thus, this general class of model predicts that immediate memory span and the rate of articulation of the material to be remembered will be highly correlated. Much evidence supports this conclusion. One source of evidence comes from developmental psychology. The observed increases in memory span in children as they grow older are accompanied by a corresponding increase in speech rate (Hulme, Thomson, Muir & Lawrence, 1984; Hulme & Muir, 1985; Nicolson, 1981). Furthermore, the rate at which adults can articulate materials is correlated with memory span for those materials (e.g. Baddeley et al., 1975). These results, and many others, have all been taken as supportive of the general type of model outlined above, according to which memory span is equal to the amount of material that can be rehearsed in a fixed time period.

Explaining Memory Span in a Second Language

The above account of phonological short-term memory gave rise to an explanation of why memory span for digits is not always the same in different languages. Languages differ in the speed of articulation with which digit names can be articulated by skilled speakers of the language, and it is also likely that speakers in the early stages of learning a second language will be less skilled, and slower, in articulating the words of that language. Both of these factors could lead to altered short-term memory capacity for various types of material and, as we have seen above, this can have important implications for language processing strategies.

Some studies have examined digit span in bilingual subjects, and the results have generally been in accord with the predictions of the trace decay model of short-term memory outlined above (see Ellis, this volume, for a review of this work). Ellis and Hennelly (1980) found that Welsh-English bilinguals articulated digit names more slowly in Welsh than in English, despite being equally fluent in both languages. There was a corresponding reduction in digit span in Welsh. As Ellis and Hennelly pointed out, not only is this result in accordance with the predictions of trace decay models but it also has implications for the assessment of intelligence, as many standard intelligence tests have digit span as an important subcomponent.

Other researchers who have compared the performance of subjects who speak different languages have come to a similar conclusion. Naveh-Benjamin and Ayres (1986) found that reading rate and memory span varied in the expected ways in English, Spanish, Hebrew and Arabic. We discuss these findings in more detail below. Stigler, Lee and Stevenson (1986) compared digit span for native speakers of English and of Chinese, and again found that memory span measured in number of digits was greater for the language in which the digit names are articulated more rapidly (Chinese).

There are, then, two separate claims that can be made on the basis of the simple account presented so far. First, bilingual subjects may have different digit spans in their different languages, even though they are equally fluent in those languages. This is a reflection of the differing articulatory characteristics of digit names in the two languages. Secondly, memory span for any type of material in a second and less familiar language will be reduced just to the extent that articulatory speed is reduced in the second language. This would have important implications for the processing of the language because, as we have shown above, there is considerable evidence that short-term memory is heavily implicated in a wide range of language processing and learning tasks.

On the basis of the model of short-term memory outlined above, it is tempting to suggest that there could be benefits associated with focussing effort, during the second language learning process, on increasing subjects' fluency of articulation. This could then lead to improved short-term memory capacity, with consequences for general language processing ability. However, as we see below, this conclusion must be modified in the light of recent advances in our theoretical understanding of the processes underlying short-term memory.

A Long-Term Memory Contribution to Memory Span

We have argued above that there is considerable evidence that phonological short-term memory plays an important role in both the acquisition and the processing of language. Secondly, we have described the widespread claim that the reduced short-term memory span in a second language is a direct result of the lower rate at which the less familiar second language material can be subvocally rehearsed. Below, we report studies which call into question the claim that rehearsal rate is the sole determinant of short-term memory capacity. First, however, we review earlier work which is also difficult to reconcile with the idea that the whole of memory span is causally determined by rehearsal rate.

Several researchers have recently argued against the simple but widespread view that the articulatory loop is the sole determinant of span (Gregg, Freedman & Smith, 1989; Tehan & Humphreys, 1988; Watkins, 1977; Wright, 1979). An important source of evidence comes from experiments which attempt to prevent subjects making use of the articulatory rehearsal procedure. This is done by requiring subjects to suppress articulation by constantly reciting irrelevant material. This experimental manipulation reduces immediate memory span considerably, but by no means abolishes it altogether (e.g. Baddeley et al., 1975; Baddeley, Lewis & Vallar, 1984; Ellis & Hennelly, 1980). Typically a "residual span" of between three and four digits or words is obtained even when subjects are required to suppress articulation, compared with a span of around seven when no suppression is required. This residual span, equal to around half the normal immediate memory span, cannot plausibly be attributed to operation of the subvocal rehearsal process. Craik (1971) has attributed this component of span to the operation of long-term memory, e.g. "My conclusion is that the traditional span measure of STM includes a SM [Secondary Memory] component" (1971; p. 233).

This research leads to the hypothesis that the reduced memory span that is observed in a second language is partly due to the lack of a strong long-term memory contribution to short-term memory capacity, rather than simply differences in articulation rate for material in the two different languages.

Our Experiments

The experimental results we now describe will be used to assess the hypotheses, outlined above, that the reduced short-term memory capacity in a second language is due to the lack of strong long-term memory representations for lexical items in those languages as well as, or instead of, the reduced rate at which items in the second language can be rehearsed. The studies we summarise here are reported in more detail in Hulme, Maughan and Brown (in press) and Brown, Hulme, McMahon, Scholey and Cook (1991).

One function of the experiments is to constrain theoretical accounts of the short-term memory limitation in a second language. However, they also illustrate the way in which second-language research can feed back in to our understanding of monolingual processing. As Cook (1981) has pointed out, there is evidence that general cognitive strategies will to a large extent be carried over to the second language learning process. The study of second language learning therefore provides a method of unconfounding specific language skills from general cognitive strategies. These two factors are of course correlated in first language learning, because general cognitive development proceeds hand in hand with language acquisition.

Study 1: Memory for Words and Non-words

In the early stages of learning a second language, many words in the new language will not be known to the subjects. They are thus effectively non-words for the language learners. In the first study we describe here, we measured short-term memory span for English words and non-words in order to assess the separate contributions of long-term memory representations and articulatory rehearsal to memory span. The logic of the experiment is as follows. The non-words, like unlearned words in a second language, will lack representations in long-term memory. We should therefore expect inferior memory span for these items. However, the articulatory rehearsal procedure will contribute to memory for span for both the words and the non-words. An index of the extent of the rehearsal loop contribution can be obtained by measuring span for words and non-words of different spoken durations. The difference between span for items of different lengths can be represented as the slope of a function relating rehearsal rate to memory span.

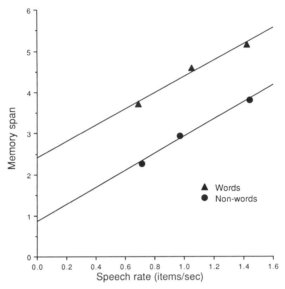

Figure 1. Memory span and speech rate for words and non-words of different lengths

We therefore measured memory span and speech rate for short, medium and long words, and short, medium and long non-words. The results can be seen in Figure 1, which plots memory span against speech rate for both the words and the non-words. It can be seen that there is a straight-line relationship between memory span and speech rate for both the words and the non-words, such that faster-articulated items are associated with greater memory spans. This is expected, and replicates previous findings described earlier. However it is also clear that memory span is reduced for non-words compared with words, and that this reduction applies at all item lengths. Thus this lexicality effect is reflected in the intercept of the speech-rate recall function. We suggest that this reduced intercept of the function for non-words as compared with words reflects the lack of long-term memory representations for the non-word items. An obvious question, then, is whether the intercept of this function will increase when subjects learn the meanings of initially unfamiliar items, as will occur in second language acquisition. This is the question we set out to address in our second study.

Study 2: Learning Italian Words

The first phase of this experiment was identical to that of the one just described, except that subjects were given memory span and speech rate assessments for English words and Italian words of different lengths. None of the subjects were Italian speakers, and so all the Italian words were equivalent to non-words for them at the beginning of the experiment. In the second phase of the experiment, subjects were

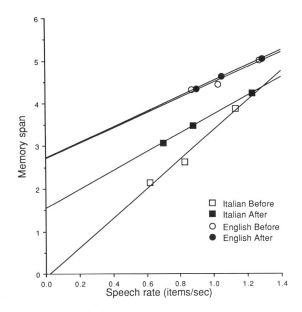

Figure 2. Memory span and speech rate for English and Italian words before and after learning

taught the Italian words, and then their speech rate and memory span for the English and Italian words was again assessed. If our suggestion that the reduced memory for non-words in the first study, and the lower intercept for the speech-rate / recall function, is due to the lack of long-term memory representations for the non-words, then teaching subjects the Italian words should increase the intercept of the speech-rate / recall function for those items.

Inspection of Figure 2, which shows the results of this study, reveals that the expected pattern of results was obtained. When subjects have learned the meanings of the Italian words, their memory span for those items improves, and this is reflected primarily in an increase in the intercept of the recall function for those items. There is also a reduction in the slope of the speech-rate/recall function; this is attributed to the phonotactic unfamiliarity of the Italian items initially (see Hulme et al., in press).

Given the importance of short-term memory in second language processing, this result has obvious implications for second language learning. The construction of good long-term memory representations for the second language vocabulary will have advantages over and above the obvious benefits of a larger vocabulary per se, because syntactic and other processing will also be facilitated by the availability of the improved short-term memory capacity which will result from the long-term memory representations.

Study 3: Learning Phonological Representations

The studies reported above provide good evidence that the availability of a long-term memory representation for items leads to improvements in short-term memory capacity for those items. However, they leave open the question of what the precise nature of the relevant long term memory representation is. When subjects were taught the Italian words in Study 2 above, they learned both phonological and semantic representations of the initially unfamiliar items. Which of these was responsible for the observed increase in memory span? The purpose of the present experiment was to test the suggestion that it is the availability of a long-term phonological representation for an item that gives rise to increased span for familiar items. We tested this by deriving speech-rate/recall functions for non-words before and after teaching subjects the phonological forms of the non-words, without any semantic information being provided. These functions could then be compared with an equivalent function for words.

The prediction, then, is straightforward. If the long-term memory contribution to short-term memory span is phonological in nature, then teaching subjects the phonological forms of the non-words should increase the intercept of the speech-rate/recall function, on the assumption that the intercept of this function can be taken as a reflection of the long-term memory contribution to span. Thus the design of this study was similar to that of the second study, except that subjects were asked to learn the phonological forms of the non-words used. Subjects were tested on their knowledge of the phonological forms of the non-words by presenting them with pairs consisting of each actual non-word and another non-word which differed by only one phonetic feature. The subjects were required to identify which of the pair of items was in the list of non-words.

The results can be seen in Figure 3, which shows the speech-rate recall function for non-words before and after subjects learned the phonological forms of the non-words. The subjects' speech rate and memory span for words was also measured, and this is also presented in Figure 3.

The results were as expected on the hypothesis that it is long-term memory representations of the phonological forms of items that is responsible for the increased memory span for those items. The intercept of the speech-rate/recall function for the words increased substantially after subjects learned the phonological forms of the items, even though they they had not learned any semantic information. This result strongly suggests that the benefits to short-term memory seen in the study described above, where subjects learned the translations of the Italian words, was due not to the provision of semantic information about the Italian words, but due instead to the increased quality of phonological representations for those items.

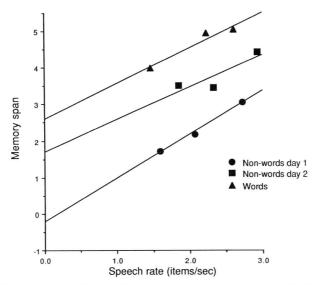

Figure 3. Memory span and speech rate for words and non-words before and after training

The results of these first three studies seriously compromise the widespread belief that changed memory span in a less familiar second language, especially the reduced span in an unfamiliar language, is entirely due to the different rate of articulatory rehearsal for items in that language. Rather, they suggest that the availability of phonological representations in long-term memory is crucial. The next study attempts to obtain further evidence on this question, using a different methodology.

Study 4: Memory Span for Digits in a Second Language

This study can be seen as a more direct test of the idea that memory span differences between languages cannot be entirely attributed to rehearsal rate differences between the languages.

We also attempted to generalise our conclusions in this experiment by using only words (digit names) rather than non-words. Thus our conclusion will be strengthened if it could be shown that the quality of long-term memory representations for words influences memory span independently of articulation rate. In this study, then, we assessed memory span for digits in both French and English, using subjects (school children) who were in the relatively early stages of learning French as a second language. It would be expected that both speech rate and memory span would be reduced in French compared to English. We attempted to prevent subjects from subvocal rehearsal during memory span assessment, on the grounds that any difference in memory span between the two languages when subvocal rehearsal was prevented must reflect factors other than rate of subvocal rehearsal. Material was presented visually in this experiment.

We therefore needed an experimental manipulation that would selectively affect the rehearsal process. The manipulation designed to prevent use of the subvocal rehearsal procedure was articulatory suppression (in our case, concurrent recitation of the irrelevant word "double"). It is safe to assume that articulatory suppression does prevent subvocal rehearsal, for it largely or completely abolishes the word length effect (Baddeley et al. 1975; 1984). Two further methodological points need to be made regarding the use of articulatory suppression as a secondary task. First, Besner, Davies and Daniels (1981) have shown that rate of articulatory suppression can determine whether or not an effect of suppression is obtained. We therefore ensured that our subjects suppressed at least at a rate rather faster than rates which have previously been shown to abolish the word length effect, and we monitored suppression rate throughout the experiment. Second, Baddeley et al. (1984) have shown that it is sometimes necessary to continue suppression through the recall stages of the task to prevent subjects translating items into an articulatory code immediately prior to recall; we therefore ensured that our subjects did this.

In this experiment, then, memory span and speech rate were assessed for digit names in both English and French. Memory span was measured both with and without articulatory suppression. The results can be seen in Table 1.

The results of this experiment were straightforward. Both memory span and speech rate were reduced in the subjects' less familiar language (French). The articulatory suppression, which was designed to prevent subjects using the subvocal rehearsal procedure, significantly reduced memory span in both French and English. The most crucial effect, however, was a significant effect of language on memory span even under conditions where subvocalisation was prevented. In other words, preventing subvocal rehearsal does not abolish differences in memory span between familiar and less familiar languages.

Table 1

English and French digit spans and speech rates with and without articulatory suppression (AS).

	Digit Span		Speech rate (items/sec)
	No A.S.	A.S.	
English	6.1	3.6	4.5
French	4.8	2.9	3.4

We take this as strong evidence that, contrary to the suggestions made by previous investigators, rehearsal rate differences cannot completely account for memory span differences between a first and a second, less familiar language. However we should note that in this experiment, as in others reported in the literature, articulatory suppression largely abolished individual differences in memory span. This result strongly suggests that rate of rehearsal is indeed a causal determinant of memory span.

Conclusions

On the basis of our literature review, and the studies we have reported, we believe that some definite conclusions can be drawn. First, it appears that phonological short-term memory is important both in the processing of fluent language, and in the acquisition of both a first and second language. Second, we have argued that rate of subvocal rehearsal may well be an important determinant of span, but it cannot completely explain the differences in memory span between familiar and less familiar languages. Some of the differences in memory span are due to the availability of better phonological long-term memory for words in the more familiar language. Third, the use of second-language methodology has added to our knowledge of phonological short-term memory, and provided further evidence for a long-term memory contribution to short-term memory span.

Other evidence that goes against the idea that short-term memory capacity is determined entirely by subvocal rehearsal rate is reviewed in Hulme et al. (in press) and Brown et al. (1991). In the latter paper, we claim that the estimates of trace duration that have been observed within and across languages are not in fact constant, as has been widely assumed, but vary in systematic ways. Variation between experiments, which has been high, can be assumed to be due to methodological differences, mainly in the method of assessing rehearsal rate. Even within experiments, however, systematic variations in the estimates of trace duration can be observed. In the cross-linguistic study of Naveh-Benjamin and Ayres (1986), for example, estimates of trace decay time for four different languages are reported, and the trace decay estimates are shorter for those languages in which digits are articulated more quickly and digit span is higher. If it is assumed that the long-term memory contribution to digit span will be the same for all languages, then a constant of two or three items can be subtracted from the estimates of digit span in various languages to give an estimate of the amount of capacity that is due to rehearsal alone. When this is done for the data reported by Naveh-Benjamin and Ayres, the estimate of trace decay time becomes much closer to an exact constant. For example, subtracting a constant three items from the memory spans found by Naveh-Benjamin and Ayres reduces the variation on trace decay estimates for their four languages from 0.3 seconds to 0.1 seconds. The pattern is the same across a variety of cross-linguistic studies (Ellis & Hennelly, 1980; Stigler et al., 1986), although the differences between within-study estimates of trace duration are generally either not analysed or are too small to be significant. Thus the estimates of trace decay that have been obtained even within different studies are not in fact constant, and they vary in systematic ways that are predictable on the assumption that there is a secondary memory contribution to span. This point is discussed in more detail in Brown et al. (1991).

The research has some implications for the second language teaching process. Given the importance of short-term memory in fluent language processing, any teaching strategy that leads to improvements in short-term memory capacity will be beneficial. The results of the experiments we have described suggest that any part of the learning process that increases either rate of articulation of materials in the second language, or that increases the quality of long-term phonological representations of items in the language, will prove useful.

Author Note

This work was supported by grants to the first author from the Medical Research Council (U.K.), reference number G8809938N, and to the first and second authors from the Economic and Social Research Council (U.K.), reference number R000232576. We are grateful to the staff and pupils of Colchester Royal Grammar School for their assistance, and to V. J. Cook who collaborated in Study 4. Address all correspondence to: Gordon Brown, Cognitive Neurocomputation Unit, Department of Psychology, University of Wales, Bangor, LL57 2DG, United Kingdom.

References

Baddeley, A. D. (1986). *Working Memory*. Oxford: Oxford University Press.

Baddeley, A. D., Lewis, V. & Vallar, G. (1984). Exploring the articulatory loop. *Quarterly Journal of Experimental Psychology*, 36A, 281-289.

Baddeley, A. D., Logie, R., Nimmo-Smith, I., & Brereton, N. (1985). Components of fluent reading. *Journal of Memory and Language*, 24, 119-131.

Baddeley, A. D., Papagno, C., Vallar, G. (1988). When long-term learning depends on short-term storage. *Journal of Memory and Language*, 27, 586-595.

Baddeley, A. D., Thomson, N. & Buchanan, M. (1975). Word length and the structure of short-term memory. *Journal of Verbal Learning and Verbal Behavior*, 14, 575-589.

Baddeley, A. D., Vallar, G., & Wilson, B. (1987). Comprehension and the articulatory loop: Some neuropsychological evidence. In M. Coltheart (Ed.), *Attention and Performance XII*. London: Erlbaum.

Besner, J., Davies, J., & Daniels, S. (1981). Reading for meaning: The effects of concurrent articulation. *Quarterly Journal of Experimental Psychology*, 33A, 415-437.

Black, M., Coltheart, M., & Byng, S. (1987). Forms of coding in sentence comprehension during reading. In M. Coltheart (Ed.), *Attention and Performance XII*. London: Erlbaum.

Brady, S., Shankweiler, D., & Mann, V. (1983). Speech perception and memory coding in relation to reading ability. *Journal of Experimental Child Psychology*, 35, 345-367.

Brown, G.D.A., & Hulme, C. (in press). Connectionist models of human short-term memory. In O. Omidvar (Ed.), *Progress in Neural Networks*. Norwood, NJ: Ablex.

Brown, G.D.A., Hulme, C., McMahon, J., Scholey, K., & Cook, V. J. (1991). The causal determinants of memory span: Against simple trace decay. Manuscript submitted for publication.

Butterworth, B., Campbell, R., & Howard, D. (1986). The uses of short-term memory: A case study. *Quarterly Journal of Experimental Psychology*, 38A, 705-738.

Conrad, R. (1964). Acoustic confusion in immediate memory. *British Journal of Psychology*, 55, 75-84.

Cook, V. J. (1981). Some uses for second-language learning research. *Annals of the New York Academy of Sciences*, 371, 251-258.

Craik, F. I. M. (1971). Primary memory. *British Medical Bulletin*, 27, 232-236.

Daneman, M., & Carpenter, P. A. (1983). Individual differences in integrating information between and within sentences. *Journal of Experimental Psychology: Learning, Memory and Cognition*, 9, 561-584.

Dornic, S. (1980). Language dominance, spare capacity and perceived effort in bilinguals. *Ergonomics*, 23, 369-377.

Ellis, N. C. (1990). Reading, phonological processing and STM: Interactive tributaries of development. *Journal of Research in Reading*, 13, 107-122.

Ellis, N. C., & Hennelly, R. A. (1980). A bilingual word-length effect: Implications for intelligence testing and the relative ease of mental calculation in Welsh and English. *British Journal of Psychology*, 71, 43-51.

Gathercole, S., & Baddeley, A. D. (1989). Evaluation of the role of phonological STM in the development of vocabulary in children: A longitudinal study. *Journal of Memory and Language*, 28, 200-213.

Gathercole, S., & Baddeley, A. D. (1990). The role of phonological memory in vocabulary acquisition: A study of young children learning new names. *British Journal of Psychology*, 81, 439-454.

Gregg, V. H., Freedman, C. M., & Smith, D. K. (1989). Word frequency, articulatory suppression and memory span. *British Journal of Psychology*, 80, 363-374.

Hulme, C., & Muir, C. (1985) Developmental changes in speech rate and memory span: A causal relationship? *British Journal of Developmental Psychology*, 3, 175-181.

Hulme, C., Thomson, N., Muir, C., & Lawrence, A. (1984) Speech rate and the development of short-term memory span. *Journal of Experimental Child Psychology*, 38, 241-253.

Hulme, C., Maughan, S., & Brown, G.D.A. (in press). Memory for words and non-words: Evidence for a long-term memory contribution to short-term memory tasks. *Journal of Memory and Language*.

Johnston, R. S., Rugg, M. D., & Scott, T. (1987). Phonological similarity effects, memory span and developmental reading disorders: The nature of the relationship. *British Journal of Psychology*, 78, 205-211.

Miller, G. A. (1956). The magical number seven, plus or minus two: Some limits on our capacity for processing information. *Psychological Review*, 63, 81-97.

Naveh-Benjamin, M., & Ayres, T. J. (1986). Digit span, reading rate, and linguistic relativity. *Quarterly Journal of Experimental Psychology*, 38A, 739-751.

Nicolson, R. (1981). The relationship between memory span and processing speed. In M. Friedman, J. P Das, & N. O'Connor (Eds.), *Intelligence and Learning*. New York: Plenum Press.

Papagno, C., Valentine, T., & Baddeley, A. D. (1991). Phonological short-term memory and foreign-language vocabulary learning. *Journal of Memory and Language,* 30, 331-347.

Shankweiler, D., Liberman, I. Y., Mark, L. S., Fowler, C. A. & Fischer, F. W. (1979). The speech code and learning to read. *Journal of Experimental Psychology: Human Learning and Memory*, 5, 531-545.

Service, E. (1989). Phonological coding in working memory and foreign language learning. *General Psychology Monographs B 9*, University of Helsinki.

Shallice, T., & Warrington, E. K. (1970). Independent functioning of the verbal memory stores: A neuropsychological study. *Quarterly Journal of Experimental Psychology*, 22, 261-273.

Snowling, M., Chiat, S., & Hulme, C. (in press). Words, non-words and phonological processes: Some comments on Gathercole, Willis, Emslie and Baddeley. *Applied Psycholinguistics*.

Stigler, J. W., Lee, S-Y., & Stevenson, H. W. (1986). Digit memory in Chinese and English: Evidence for temporally limited store. *Cognition*, 23, 1-20.

Tehan, G., & Humphreys, M. S. (1988). Articulatory loop explanations of memory span and pronunciation rate correspondences: A cautionary note. *Bulletin of the Psychonomic Society*, 26, 293-296.

Vallar, G., & Baddeley, A. D. (1984). Phonological short-term store, phonological processing and sentence comprehension: A neuropsychological case study. *Cognitive Neuropsychology*, 1, 121-141.

Vallar, G. & Shallice, T. (Eds.). (1990). *Neuropsychological impairments of short-term memory*. Cambridge: Cambridge University Press.

Watkins, M. J. (1977). The intricacy of memory span. *Memory & Cognition*, 5, 529-534.

Wright, C. C. (1979). Duration differences between rare and common words and their implications for the interpretation of word frequency effects. *Memory & Cognition*, 7, 411-419.

Cognitive Processing in Bilinguals – R.J. Harris (Editor)

Working Memory Capacity as a Constraint on L2 Development

Michael Harrington
University of California at Santa Cruz

Abstract

This chapter examines the role of working memory capacity in L2 development. The first part of the chapter traces the development of working memory as an explanatory construct in individual differences models of language processing and use. The research paradigm developed to measure working memory capacity is described and research relating capacity to individual differences in L1 reading skill is presented. In the second part the working memory construct is applied to L2 development and evidence for the role of working memory capacity in L2 reading is presented. Although preliminary evidence suggests a role for working memory capacity in explaining differences in L2 development, key methodological and theoretical issues in the approach remain unresolved. In the concluding part these issues are discussed and directions for future research on capacity limitations on L2 development are considered.

A fundamental difference between first and second language acquisition is the tremendous range of individual differences evident in L2 learner outcomes. Although individual differences in size of lexis, reading skill, etc., exist in the L1, such differences pale in comparison to those evident in L2 acquisition, where ultimate attainment ranges from virtual ignorance to near native-like fluency in the target language. Attempts to account for these differences have focused on linguistic, social and cognitive factors, and there is a consensus that L2 success--however defined--will be the result of multiple variables. Variables investigated include *social-psychological*, such as attitude and motivation (Gardner, 1985); *cognitive*, as in learner strategies (O'Malley, Chamot & Walker, 1987) and metalinguistic awareness (Bialystok & Bouchard Ryan, 1985); *personality-based*, including introversion-extroversion and risk-taking (Strong, 1984; Ely, 1986); and *aptitude*, comprised of such traits as the ability to make sound-symbol associations, the sensitivity to grammatical form, the ability to induce form-meaning correspondences, and rote-learning ability (Carroll, 1981). This chapter examines working memory capacity, that is, the relative capacity to intake and integrate information in immediate, on-line processing. The notion of working

A portion of the data reported here is from research funded by a grant from the University of California, Pacific Rim Research Program, Barry McLauglin, principal investigator. Acknowledgements to Bill Murdoch, Jane Stanely and Mark Sawyer for comments on the preparation of this chapter.

memory capacity as a constraint on language development is in the tradition of aptitude trait models (see Skehan, 1989 for a review of aptitude research), but differs from the traditional foreign language learning traits in its applicability across a range of cognitive processing domains (e.g., reading, spatial reasoning, quantitative reasoning).

Recent research on individual differences in L2 learning has paid minimal attention to aptitude issues. This is due in part to the putative 'fixed' nature of such traits: longitudinal research suggests that aptitude traits are innate, or at least highly stable across the developmental sequence (Skehan, 1989). Resistant to modification through teaching or experience, aptitude traits elicit little interest from researchers interested mainly in interventions that facilitate learning. Also, the notion of fixed cognitive predispositions for L2 learning, or any other cognitive skill, strike some as elitist in tone (McLaughlin, In press.). Alternatively there is the belief that aptitude traits, even if present, play only a minor role in accounting for differences observed in learning outcomes, particularly outside of the formal classroom setting (Gardner, 1985). The basic research methodology used in aptitude research is also an issue. Findings that link L2 learning outcomes with aptitude traits, as measured by instruments like the Modern Language Aptitude Test (Carroll & Sapon, 1959), are based on statistical correlations. Although legitimate for establishing the predictive validity of the traits, correlational findings in and of themselves have very limited explanatory value.

Aptitude traits reflect differences in the speed and manner in which individuals process information. Such traits are of interest to models of L2 learning to the extent that they can provide an independently motivated explanation for observed individual differences in L2 development. Although individual differences research, by definition, addresses what is unique in the language learning process, a better understanding of the factors that are responsible for variation across learners may also provide insights into the systematic aspects of L2 development and use. The focus in this chapter is on the status of the working memory capacity construct as an independent constraint on L2 development.

The interest in working memory capacity as a constraint on L2 development fits squarely into the framework of information processing models of L2 learning (McLaughlin, Rossman & McLeod, 1983; Hulstijn & Hulstijn, 1984; Bialystok & Bouchard Ryan, 1985; Pienemann & Johnston, 1987). L2 learning is viewed as the development of a cognitive skill, and the researcher is interested in accounting for the development of the mental representations comprising L2 knowledge and the processes that act upon them. The mental representations include phonological, lexical, syntactic and pragmatic knowledge structures, and the processes range from the perceptual encoding of orthographic or phonological information, activating and accessing word meaning, and the encoding of basic propositions, up to such higher order processes as integrating schema and contextual knowledge with linguistic cues, drawing inferences, and sustaining discourse coherence. Skill development in the L2 is characterized as a process of moving from the controlled, effortful command of the component subskills, to routinized integration of the skills in relatively effort-free automatic processing

Working memory capacity is proposed as a possible independent constraint on this process.

Working memory capacity and individual differences in L1 reading

Memory research has long made a basic distinction between immediate, short-term memory processes and the long-term storage of knowledge structures. As early as the end of the 19th century, William James proposed a bipartite memory system consisting of a short-term or "primary" memory of immediate consciousness, and a long term (or "secondary") memory that serves as the repository of our cumulative experiences (James, 1890-1983). The short- versus long-term distinction was at the heart of the information processing models of memory that dominated memory research in the 1960s and 1970s. One of the most widely-cited models was the three-stage model of Atkinson and Shiffrin (1968). The model consisted of a bank of sensory buffer stores that accepted and temporarily stored information from the different sense modalities, (visual, auditory, tactile, etc). The second stage consisted of a limited-capacity short-term store, which received information from the sensory buffers and both fed information to, and extracted information from, the long-term store. The third stage was the long-term store that held past experiences and knowledge structures constructed from that experience.

The Atkinson and Shiffrin model and models like it were extremely influential at the time, but were ultimately abandoned. (see Baddeley, 1986, for a review). One problem was the conception of the short term memory store. Short-term memory was seen as a passive storage buffer in which information was held until processed. Capacity was essentially static and reflected the ability to passively store bits of unstructured information, e.g. strings of random digits or words. Miller's classic study set the capacity of the short-term store at seven, plus or minus two, bits of information (Miller, 1956). The problem was that the size of the bit was never defined and it appeared to vary according to the type of information processed; subsequent research showed that subjects were able to recall seven familiar sentences as easily as seven random words. This variability suggested that active processing was also taking place in the short-term store, with relative capacity to handle information a function of both processing and storage. Additionally, and of relevance to individual differences research, static short-term memory capacity (i.e. memory for lists of random words or digits) has proven to be a very poor predictor of skill in reading and other higher-order cognitive processes (Perfetti, 1985).

The notion of a *working* memory dates back to Newell (1973), and emphasizes both processing and storage functions. In this view, working memory serves as a "computational arena" in which processes are executed and partial products of these processes stored in the course of ongoing processing (Carpenter & Just, 1989, p.35). A central assumption is that the processes and knowledge structures compete for shared limited capacity. Information may be lost through decay of activation strength or by displacement, if the additional structures that are encoded, activated, or constructed exceed capacity. A task that makes heavy processing demands should therefore decrease the amount of additional information that can be maintained, because more attention is required for more demanding processes, and hence more capacity is used for processing that otherwise would be available for storage. In contrast to the earlier short-term store that was defined in terms of units of static storage space, working memory capacity is defined in terms of an operational capacity relative to a specific cognitive processing domain, and serves as an index of relative processing efficiency (Carpenter & Just, 1989). The elasticity of working memory capacity distinguishes it from the more traditional aptitude traits which appear to remain relatively fixed over a long period of time (Carroll, 1981).

Working memory capacity is measured by means of a concurrent processing task designed to tap both processing and storage functions in immediate processing. The subject typically performs a primary memory task while simultaneously carrying out a simple processing task that also makes demands on processing resources. In Daneman and Carpenter's (1980) reading span test, the subject is required to read aloud a set of sentences while simultaneously remembering the final word of each sentence. At the end of each set the subject is signalled to recall all the final words of the sentences in the set. The number of sentences in a set - and thus the number of sentence-final words to be remembered - is steadily increased, placing an increasingly greater processing load on the subject. An individual's working memory capacity is indexed as the number of final words correctly recalled, either in criterial terms, that is the maximum set size in which all or a portion of the sentence-final words were correctly recalled (Daneman & Carpenter, 1980; Carpenter & Just, 1989), or in the absolute number of final words recalled (Turner & Engle, 1989).

The relationship between reading span capacity and L1 reading skill has been studied extensively. Individual reading span sizes have strong, positive correlation with measures of overall reading comprehension, as well as with specific reading skills (Daneman & Carpenter, 1980; Daneman & Carpenter, 1983; Daneman & Green, 1986; Daneman & Tardif, 1987; Turner & Engle, 1989). In the original Daneman and Carpenter study reading span measures correlated with scores on standardized measures of general reading proficiency such as the SAT and the Nelson-Denny Reading Test (r = .4 to .6). For specific reading skills, such as the ability to recover the pronoun referent, the correlations were as high as r = .9. Other reading skills have been investigated as well. Differences in working memory capacity have been related to discourse processing, specifically the ability to make comprehension-facilitating elaborative inferences (Whitney, Ritchie & Clark, 1990). Capacity differences have also been implicated in syntactic processing during reading. In research on reading ambiguous 'garden-path' sentences, eye movement data reveals that readers with larger reading spans appear to keep alternative syntactic interpretations activated longer than readers with smaller reading span, who commit early to a single, often erroneous, interpretation early in the sentence (Just & Carpenter, 1989).

The correlational nature of the evidence linking working memory capacity and reading skill requires cautious interpretation. Performance by subjects on the various reading tasks may be a function of working memory capacity, as reflected in the reading span score, or it may be that performance on the reading span task merely reflects a higher level of reading skill - or it is possible that a third factor is responsible for performance on both tasks. Although the relationship between working memory and L1 reading appears robust correlations alone prevent inferences as to the direction of any causal relationship. Converging evidence will be required before the status of working memory capacity as in independent constraint on language development can be established. What form such evidence might take will be considered below.

Working memory capacity and L2 development

It has been proposed that working memory capacity may serve as a source of individual differences L1 language development and use. But what of L2? There are qualitative and quantitative reasons why working memory capacity may play a relatively greater role in the development of L2 skill by the adult learner than it does in the case of the L1. Attainment of native fluency in the L1 is the result of the interaction of linguistic, cognitive and biological factors. Some factors, such as those related to maturation, are irrelevant to the adult L2 learner, while the availability of others, like the principles of universal grammar, is questionable. Although UG-based principles are generally assumed to play an important role in L1 acquisition, there is substantial evidence that these principles are not available - or available only in a highly restricted way - to adult L2 learners (Bley-Vroman, 1989). As a result, L2 learning may rely to a greater degree on general cognitive learning principles that are involved in the acquisition of higher order cognitive skills across different knowledge domains. A class of "production" models have been proposed that attribute a key role to working memory capacity in the development of complex cognitive skills such as computer programming or L2 learning (Anderson, 1983).

There is also a quantitative difference between L1 and adult L2 development. It is a commonplace that the L2 learner rarely reaches a level of fluency approaching that of the native speaker. Less facility in processing means the L2 learner often spends more time on the lower-level, "bottom-up" processes, thus placing greater demands on attentional resources and a greater load on working memory. This is evident in L2 reading, where less skilled L2 readers tend to focus on graphic cues at the expense of higher level semantic or inferential processes (Cziko, 1980; McLeod & McLaughlin, 1986), and even skilled bilinguals will tend to activate word meanings more slowly, and at a shallower level in their L2 than in their L1 (Favreau & Segalowitz, 1983; Magiste, 1986; Segalowitz, 1986). The greater capacity demands made by the slow, effortful processing of the less fluent L2 learner may result in working memory capacity playing a relatively greater role in constraining development of the L2.

Both of these factors suggest that differences in working memory capacity may provide some insight into the development of L2 skill. Harrington & Sawyer (In press), examined the relationship between L2 working memory capacity and L2 reading skill in advanced Japanese ESL learners. Subjects in the study were given a battery of memory tests consisting of random digit strings, random word strings, and a modified version of the reading span test (Daneman & Carpenter, 1980) in the L2 English[2]. As in the earlier studies, subjects read sets of test

----
[2] The test were also administered in the Japanese L1 in order to provide crosslinguistic comparisons. The results generally reflected the L2 English findings, although there were problems with several of tests and the

sentences aloud and then recalled the final word in each sentence. The number of
sentences per set, and thus the number of sentence-final words, increased over
the course of the task, with the individual's reading span indexed by the absolute
number of words correctly recalled (Turner & Engle, 1989). The random word
and digit tests, assumed to tap static storage capacity alone, provided a form of
discriminant validity for the reading span test as a measure of processing and
storage capacity. Scores on the three memory tests were then correlated with
measures of L2 reading skill, as reflected in performance on the Grammar (Part
2) and on the Reading (Part 3) sections of TOEFL, as well as on a cloze passage.

The results are presented in Table 1. Readers with higher L2 reading span
scores did better on the L2 reading tasks, as reflected in the relatively strong
correlations between the L2 reading span measure and the TOEFL Grammar
and TOEFL Reading scores. In contrast, the random word and digit spans only
weakly correlated with the L2 reading

Table 1.

Correlations among L2 Memory and Reading Scores

Memory span scores	TOEFL2 Grammar	TOEFL3 Reading	Cloze
English Digit span	.25	.23	.15
English Word span	.21	.24	.28
English Reading span	.57**	.54**	.33

p < .001 **
n = 32

(From Harrington & Sawyer, In press)

comprehension measures and with the L2 reading span measure, indicating that
the reading span measure was tapping more than passive, short-term memory
capacity. The reading span thus appears to serve as an index of L2 working
memory capacity that is defined functionally in terms of a trade-off between
active processing and storage, and that relates to global reading skill in the L2.
Although replicating results from the L1 literature, the status of the reading
span as an independent measure of L2 working memory capacity remains
unclear. As noted above, the correlational nature of the evidence linking L2
reading span and L2 reading skill prevents inferences as to the direction of the
relationship. Performance by the subjects on the L2 reading tasks may be a
function of L2 working memory capacity, or it may be that the reading span task
merely reflects a higher level of L2 reading skill - or some other third factor
common to both.

---

measure of overall Japanese reading proficiency was found to be unsuitable. For details see Harrington &
Sawyer (In press).

One possible factor mediating performance on the reading span and reading skill measures is the degree of L2 lexical development. This would manifest itself in a larger lexicon, and on-line in faster lexical access and a stronger level of activation for the words accessed. Another factor contributing to performance on both measures is the degree of command over syntactic processing in the L2, reflected in L2 grammatical knowledge, and on-line in terms of less effortful, more automatic processing (McLaughlin, Rossman & McLeod, 1983). These lexical and syntactic skills are assumed to draw on working memory capacity, but are not synonymous with it; they are posited to share capacity with other processes (e.g. integrating lexical, syntactic and pragmatic information into the ongoing discourse interpretation) that comprise the more general working memory construct. Should the lexical and syntactic processes alone account for the variance shared in the L2 reading span-reading skill relationship, then the working memory construct becomes superfluous.

Harrington (1991) examined the role of vocabulary and grammatical knowledge on performance of L2 reading and the L2 reading span tasks. In the study measures of vocabulary knowledge (two 75-item multiple-choice vocabulary tests), grammatical knowledge (scores on a comprehensive grammar test and grammar course grades), L2 reading skill (TOEFL Reading) and reading span size were obtained from advanced Japanese ESL subjects. See Table 2. Replicating results from Harrington & Sawyer (In press), performance on the L2 English

Table 2.

Correlations among L2 Memory and Reading Scores

	Read span	Read test	Voc1	Voc2	Grm1	Grm2
Reading span	1					
Reading test	.51*	1				
Vocabulary score 1	.46*	.61*	1			
Vocabulary score 2	.42*	.76*	.82*	1		
Grammar score 1	.35*	.62*	.67*	.59*	1	
Grammar score 2_a	.32	.53*	.49*	.48*	.29	1

$p < .001$ $n = 55$ $n_a = 36$

(From Harrington, 1991)

reading span measure correlated reliably with L2 reading ability. The reading span measure correlated with the vocabulary and grammar measures as well, although to a lesser degree.

The substantial intercorrelations among the measures illustrate the problems inherent in this line of research, where the different measures tap processes that are closely related. In an attempt to account for the unique contributions of grammar and vocabulary knowledge to the correlation of reading span and reading skill, a hierarchical regression model was used. The goal was to see if, after partialling out the contribution of vocabulary and grammatical knowledge to L2 reading skill, there was was still significant variance left to be accounted for by the reading span measure (Cohen & Cohen, 1982). Using L2 reading scores as the dependent measure, a hierarchical model was specified in which sets representing vocabulary and grammar knowledge and reading span were entered sequentially. The analysis indicated that the reading span measure accounted for a small amount of unique variance in the L2 reading scores, after partialling for the effects of L2 vocabulary and grammatical knowledge. (See Table 3.) The results suggest that the reading span taps more than just vocabulary and grammatical knowledge, but the findings and any conclusions based on them are tentative. The measures of lexical and grammatical knowledge used were quite general and were administered off-line, thus only indirectly reflecting any processing advantages. More sensitive on-line measures of lexical and grammatical knowledge are needed, as for example, the measure of lexical activation strength used in Woltz (1988). The use of TOEFL Reading (Part 3) as the sole measure of L2 reading skill is problematic, as is the treatment of reading skill itself as a monolithic entity. These issues will be taken up in the final part of the chapter.

Table 3.

Components of L2 Reading Skill: Partial Correlation Coefficients for Vocabulary, Grammar and Reading span measures.

	cum R2	pR2	F	df	p
Vocabulary	.579	*	35.13	2,54	.001
Grammar	.637	.159	7.98	1,50	.01
Readspan	.707	.143	6.41	1,49	.05

(From Harrington, 1991)

Thus far it has been shown that the reading span as a putative index of working memory capacity correlates with reading skill in both L1 and L2. Furthermore, in the case of the L2, the reading span size appears to be more than just the reflection of the individual's lexical and grammatical knowledge. The problems inherent in correlational nature of the research paradigm were also noted. In the next part the relevance of the working memory construct to L2 theory is considered. Examined will be methodological and theoretical issues that need to be resolved before working memory capacity can be established as an independent constraint on L2 development.

Working memory capacity and models of L2 development.

Capacity limitations are of theoretical interest to models of L2 learning to the extent that they are motivated independently of the L2 skills they are posited to constrain. The lack of direct access to the processes in question means that indirect measures like the reading span are necessary, with a resulting reliance on correlational evidence. Thus it will be necessary to obtain evidence for the construct from converging operations. Three research directions can be identified that will allow researchers to assess the status of working memory capacity as an independent constraint. The three lines of research are: aptitude by treatment designs assessing the link between capacity and performance on specific skills, crosslinguistic comparisons within L2 learners, and longitudinal studies examining how capacity and skill level covary over time.

Experimental research on working memory has used an aptitude by treatment design, in which subjects are grouped according to working memory capacity and then tested on a particular skill, as in the investigation of elaborative inferencing in Whitney et al., (1990). This approach allows the researcher to isolate a specific component of a global skill, like reading, and assess how performance in that skill varies as a function of working memory capacity (Skehan, 1989). By piecing together evidence from a range of component skills, a picture will emerge of which aspects of L2 development are affected and how they are affected by individual differences in capacity. It is likely that the effect of working memory capacity will vary according to skill and degree of skill development. One area deserving attention is how working memory capacity differences relate to models of L2 syntactic development that incorporate such constraints as explanatory variables (McLaughlin, Rossman & McLeod, 1983; Hulstijn & Hulstijn, 1984; Bialystok & Bouchard Ryan, 1985; Pienemann & Johnston, 1987). Pienemann and Johnston (1987) propose a two-dimensional model of L2 development consisting of a hierarchical sequence of key morpho-syntactic structures that are acquired in a fixed order by all learners of a given L2, and a set of variational features whose acquisition is more idiosyncratic. Both dimensions contribute to overall L2 skill but differ in psycholinguistic status. Progression through the hierarchical sequence depends on overcoming processing constraints of increasing complexity, similar in form to Slobin's operating principles (Slobin, 1973). Acquisition of the variational features reflects a range of other linguistic and social psychological factors. It would be of interest to see how the reading span measure relates to the two proposed dimensions of development. A strong relationship between reading span size and relative morphosyntactic development along the uniform sequence would provide a degree of independent support for the model's processing constraints, which are presently defined, in a circular manner, in terms of the perceived complexity of the given syntactic structure. Divergence between the correlation of reading span with morphosyntactic development and the correlation of reading span size with overall proficiency - which reflects development along both the universal and variation dimensions - would indicate that the reading span and the processing constraints are tapping different kinds of capacity limitations.

A comparison of the relationship between reading span size and skill across the learner's L1 and L2 will also be relevant to the issue of independence. If relative processing efficiency is independent of specific language development, it is expected that relative working memory capacity in the L1 will also be evident in the L2. Further, it would be expected that individuals with larger L1 working memory capacity will be better, possibly faster learners of the L2. This advantage, of course, is only a necessary condition for establishing working memory as an independent constraint, and any effects would be relative, as working memory capacity is assumed to vary within the individual learner as a function of skill development. As noted above there is always the possibility that other factors are involved. What such evidence would allow is the comparison of the relative effects of working memory across L1 and L2, and thus insight into the relative contribution of such constraints on the development in the two languages. It would also provide a test of the reading span measure itself as a valid measure in languages other than English. Harrington and Sawyer (In press) found a moderate correlation between L1 and L2 reading spans (r = .40), but there were a number of methodological problems with the crosslinguistic data.

Evidence may also come from the study of development of L2 reading span size across time. Such longitudinal evidence could be obtained by collecting measures of memory capacity and skill at several points in time and then testing causal models representing alternative causal directions. Such evidence would provide a profile of how L2 working memory capacity and L2 comprehension skill covary in the course of development and move beyond simple bivariate correlations and the attendant problems with inferring causal direction. A combination of longitudinal and crosslinguistic approaches is also possible, allowing the relative effect of the development of the development of one on the other to be examined.

In conclusion, it remains unclear whether working memory capacity, as operationalized in the reading span measure, is independently motivated. The predictive power of the reading span measure for both L1 and L2 is supported, but the evidence to date precludes any claims as to the causal role such capacity might have in the development of language skill - L1 or L2. To the degree that researchers are able to obtain such evidence, the construct will be of interest to researchers interested in aptitude-based individual differences among L2 learners, and the role these differences play in L2 development.

References

Anderson, J. (1983). *The architecture of cognition*. Cambridge, MA: Harvard University Press.

Atkinson, R. C., & Shiffrin, R.M. (1968). Human memory: A proposed system and its control processes. In K. W. Spence (Ed.), *The psychology of learning and motivation: Advances in research and theory* (Vol. 2). New York: Academic Press.

Baddeley, A. (1986). *Working memory*. Oxford: Clarendon Press.

Bialystok, E., & Bouchard Ryan, E. (1985). A metacognitive framework for the development of first and second language skills. In D. L. Forrest-Pressley, G. E. MacKinnon, & T. G. Waller (Eds.), *Metacognition, cognition and human performance* (Vol.1). New York: Academic Press.

Bley-Vroman, R. (1989). What is the logical problem of foreign language learning? In S. Gass, & J. Schacter (Eds.), *Linguistic perspectives on second language acquisition*. Cambridge, UK: Cambridge University Press.

Carpenter, P. A., & Just, M. A. (1989). The role of working memory in language comprehension. In D. Klahr, & K. Kotovsky (Eds.), *Complex information processing: The impact of Herbert A. Simon*. Hillsdale, N.J.: Lawrence Erlbaum Associates.

Carroll, J. (1981). Twenty-five years of research on foreign language aptitude. In K. Diller, (Ed.) *Individual differences and universals in language learning aptitude*. Rowley, MA. : Newbury House.

Carroll. J., & Sapon, S. (1959). *Modern Languages Aptitude Test*. New York: The Psychological Corporation.

Cohen, J. & Cohen, J. (1982). *Applied multivariate statistics for the behavioral sciences*. Hillsdale, N.J.: Lawrence Erlbaum.

Cziko, G. (1980). Language competence and reading strategies: A comparison of first- and second-language oral reading errors. *Language Learning, 30,* 2, 101-116.

Daneman, M., & Carpenter, P. A. (1980). Individual differences in working memory and reading. *Journal of Verbal Learning and Verbal Behavior, 19,* 450-466.

Daneman, M., & Carpenter, P. A. (1983). Individual differences in integrating information between and within sentences. *Journal of Experimental Psychology: Learning, Memory, and Cognition, 9,* 561-583.

Daneman, M., & Green, I. (1986). Individual differences in comprehending and producing words in context. *Journal of Memory and Language, 25,* 1-18.

Daneman, M., & Tardif, T. (1987). Working memory and reading skill re-examined. In M. Coltheart (Ed.), *Attention and performance XII*. London: Lawrence Erlbaum Associates.

Ely, C. M. (1986). An analysis of discomfort, risktaking, sociability, and motivation in the L2 classroom. *Language Learning, 36,* 1, 1-25.

Favreau, M., & Segalowitz, N. (1983). Automatic and controlled processes in reading a second language. *Memory and Cognition, 11,* 565-574.

Gardner, R. C. (1985). *Social psychology and second language learning: The role of attitudes and motivation*. London: Edward Arnold.

Harrington, M. (1991). Individual differences in L2 reading: Processing capacity versus linguistic knowledge. A paper presented at the Annual Meeting of the American Association of Applied Linguists, March 12, 1991. New York.

Harrington, M., & Sawyer, M. (In press). L2 working memory capacity and L2 reading skill. To appear in *Studies in Second Language Acquisition*.

Hulstijn, J. H., & Hulstijn, W. (1984). Grammatical errors as a function of processing constraints and explicit knowledge. *Language Learning, 34,* 1, 23-43.

James, W. (1890-1983). *The principles of psychology.* Cambridge, MA.: Harvard University Press.

Just, M.A., & Carpenter, P.A. (1989). Individual differences in comprehension due to working memory. A paper presented at the annual meeting of the Psychonomic Society, November 19, 1989. Atlanta, GA.

Magiste, E. (1986). Selected issues in second and third language learning. In J. Vaid (Ed.), *Language processing in bilinguals: Psycholinguistic and neuro-psychological perspectives.* Hillsdale, NJ: Lawrence Erlbaum Associates.

McLaughlin, B. (In press). Another look at aptitude. To appear in *Modern Language Journal.*

McLaughlin, B., Rossman, T., & McLeod, B. (1983). Second language learning: an information-processing perspective. *Language Learning,* 33, 135-158.

McLeod, B.,& McLaughlin, B. (1986). Restructuring of automaticity? Reading in a second language. *Language Learning, 36,* 2, 109-124.

Miller, G. A. (1956). The magical number seven, plus or minus two: some limits of our capacity for processing information. *Psychological Review, 63,* 81-87.

Newell, A. (1973). Production systems: Models of control structures. In W. G. Chase (Ed.), *Visual information processing.* New York: Academic Press.

O'Malley, J. M., Chamot, A.U., & Walker, C. (1987). Some applications of cognitive theory to second language learning. *Studies in Second Language Acquisition, 9,* 287-306.

Perfetti, C. A. (1985). *Reading ability.* New York: Oxford University Press.

Pienemann, M., & Johnston, M. (1987). Factors influencing the development of language proficiency. In D. Nunan (Ed.), *Applying second language acquisition research.* Adelaide: National Curriculum Resource   Centre.

Segalowitz, N. (1986). Skilled reading in a second language. In J. Vaid (Ed.), *Language processing in bilinguals: psycholinguistic and neuropsychological perspectives.* Hillsdale, NJ: Lawrence Erlbaum Associates.

Skehan, P. (1989). *Individual differences in second language learning.* London: Edward Arnold.

Slobin, D. I. (1973). Cognitive prerequisites for the development of grammar. In C. A. Ferguson & D. I. Slobin (Eds.), *Studies of child language development.* New York: Holt, Rinehart & Winston.

Strong, M. H. (1984). Integrative motivation: Cause or result of successful language acquisition? *Language Learning, 34,* 3, 1-14.

Turner, M. L., & Engle, R. W. (1989). Is working memory capacity task dependent? *Journal of Memory and Language, 28,* 127-145.

Whitney, P., Ritchie, B. G., & Clark, M. B. (1990). Working memory capacity and the use of elaborative inferencing in text comprehension. Unpublished manuscript. Washington State University.

Woltz, D. G. (1988). An investigation of the role of working memory in procedural skill acquisition. *Journal of Experimental Psychology: General, 117,* 319-331.

Cognitive Processing in Bilinguals – R.J. Harris (Editor)
© *1992 Elsevier Science Publishers B.V. All rights reserved.*

Linguistic Relativity Revisited: The Bilingual Word-length Effect In Working Memory
During Counting, Remembering Numbers, and Mental Calculation.

Nick Ellis
University College of North Wales

ABSTRACT

In different languages the names of numbers take different times to articulate. This chapter considers the role of language and representation in arithmetic. It reviews studies which demonstrate that digit word-length limits the short-term memory for digit sequences (such as telephone numbers or digit span as used in many intelligence tests). Three experiments are reported which show that a language's number name word-lengths have a determinative influence upon the ease of mental calculation and counting in that language - some languages are more conducive to mental arithmetic than others. More general aspects of the effects of language word-length are also considered.

INTRODUCTION

The facility of human cognitive processes depends on the internalisation of effective representational systems and the greatest of all such systems is language. "Human beings do not live in the objective world alone, nor alone in the world of social activity as ordinarily understood, but are very much at the mercy of the particular language that has become the medium of expression for their society" (Sapir, in Spier, 1941). "A change in language can transform our appreciation of the Cosmos." (Whorf, 1956). "'This way,' says the word, 'is an interesting thought: come and find it.' And so we are led on to rediscover old knowledge." (Cooley, 1962). "Speech is the best show man puts on. It is his own 'act' on the stage of evolution, in which he comes before the cosmic backdrop and really 'does his stuff'." (Whorf, 1942).

"The mathematical formula that enables a physicist to adjust some coils of wire, tinfoil plates, diaphragms, and other quite inert and innocent gadgets into a configuration in which they can project music to a far country puts the physicist's consciousness on to a level strange to the untrained man. ... We do not think of the designing of a radio station or a power plant as a linguistic process, but it is one nonetheless. The necessary mathematics is a linguistic apparatus, and, without its correct specification of essential patterning, the assembled gadgets would be out of proportion and adjustment, and would remain inert. ... the mathematics used in such a case is a *specialised* formula-language, contrived for making available a specialised type of force manifestation through metallic bodies only, namely, *electricity*, as we today define what we call by that name." (Whorf, 1942).

The history of mathematics, of logic, of computation, even of thought, is marked with the milestones of the developments of representational systems.

In the case of mathematics the invention of positional notation was of enormous significance for civilisation. Early systems of numeration used by the Egyptians, Hebrews, Greeks and Romans were based on a purely additive system. Thus in the Roman symbolism, for example, one wrote:　　　　　CXVIII = one hundred + ten + five + one + one + one.

A disadvantage of such additive notations was that more and more new symbols were needed as numbers got larger. But the chief problem was that computation with numbers was so difficult that only the specialist could handle any but the simplest problems. To realise the efficiency of our present positional notation, we have only to try to perform an addition by means of Roman numerals, for example:

CCLXVI	266
MDCCCVII	1807
DCL	650
MLXXX	1080
MMMDCCCIII	3803

Without converting the Roman numerals into our modern system the problem is difficult, if not impossible to solve. And this is only an addition - multiplication or division would be even worse. Such systems do not lend themselves to calculation because of the static nature of their basic numerals, which are essentially only abbreviations for recording the results of calculations already done by means of a counting board or abacus. "That is why, from the beginning of history until the advent of our modern positional numeration, so little progress was made in the art of reckoning." (Dantzig, 1930).

Additive systems are quite different from place-value (positional) systems which were independently conceived only four times in history. Three of these conceptions were by the Babylonians (in the early second millennium B.C.), the Mayas (probably in the Classic Period, third to ninth centuries A.D.), and the Chinese (shortly before the beginning of the Christian era). But these place-value systems were defective in comparison with the numeration developed by the Hindus that is still in use. This positional system has the agreeable property that all numbers, however large or small, can be represented by the use of a small set of different digit symbols (in the decimal system these are the Arabic numerals 0, 1, 2, ..., 9) and the place-value principle is used consistently with powers of the base 10. In conjunction with the place-value principle, discovery of the zero made the decisive stage in a process of development without which we cannot imagine the progress of modern mathematics, science, and technology. The zero freed human intelligence from the counting board that had held it prisoner for thousands of years, eliminated all ambiguity in the written expression of numbers, revolutionized the art of reckoning, and made it accessible to everyone (Ifrah, 1987). The most important advantage is that of ease of computation. The rules of reckoning with numbers represented in positional notation can be stated in the form of addition and multiplication tables for the digits, and these can be memorised once and for all. As Courant & Robbins (1941) extol: "The ancient art of computation, once confined to a few adepts, is now taught in elementary school. There are not many instances where scientific progress has so deeply affected and facilitated everyday life."

Another key example of the crucial importance of representation is to be found later in the development of mathematics where we have retained the notation of Leibniz, dx/dy for the derivative, $f'(x)$ and $\int f(x)\, dx$ for the integral because it is extremely useful, allowing the limits of quotients and sums to be handled 'as if' they were actual quotients or sums, notwithstanding the fact that Leibniz' explanations and theory was clearly surpassed by Newton's - "Leibniz' notation is at least an excellent notation for the limit process; as a matter of fact, it is almost indispensable in the more advanced parts of the theory." (Courant & Robbins, 1941, p. 435).

As written representations vary in their efficiency, so do mental representations. Our entry into mathematics, the very beginnings which may one day allow us to consider the sublime calculus and beyond, lies in our being taught about number, counting and simple arithmetic. And each language has its own names for the digits and the operations thereon. These surface features of language are, at first sight, an unlikely locus for cognitive constraint. Yet this chapter will demonstrate that such a simple feature as the time it takes to pronounce the names of the digits affects the ability of a native speaker of a language to remember numbers, to count, and to perform mental calculations.

DIGIT LENGTH AND SHORT-TERM MEMORY

BILINGUAL DIGIT NAMING RATE

In Gwynedd in North Wales over 60% of the population speak Welsh (Baker, 1985). In 1978 I was attempting to learn the language. Casual observation suggested that it mostly takes longer to articulate the names for digits in the Welsh language (*dim, un, dau, tri, pedwar, pump, chwech, saith, wyth, naw, deg*) than their English equivalents (*nought, one, two, three, four, five, six, seven, eight, nine, ten*). Ellis & Hennelly (1980) therefore tested this in 12 bilingual subjects who were required to read aloud as fast as possible 200 instances of randomly ordered digits in English, and in Welsh. There was a highly significant difference in reading time for the two languages: even though only one-third of the subjects rated themselves more competent in English than in Welsh, every subject read the digits faster in English. It took on average 385 ms to read a Welsh digit compared with 321 ms to read an English digit. That is, on average, a subject would read six digits in English in the time taken to read five in Welsh.

These cross-language digit name length differences may affect performance in tasks where vocal or subvocal articulation of digit names is involved, i.e. in short-term memory (STM) for digits, in counting, and in mental arithmetic.

BILINGUAL STM SPAN

Baddeley, Thomson & Buchanan (1975) demonstrated that immediate memory span for short words is greater than that for long words. This effect cannot be solely attributed to the number of syllables or phonemes in the stimulus. Rather the effect is truly one of word-length: even when the number of syllables and phonemes is held constant, the memory span for words which take a short time to articulate (e.g. wicket, phallic) is greater than that for words which take a long time to articulate (e.g. zygote, coerce). In general the span could be predicted on the basis of the number of words which the subject could read in approximately 2 s. Baddeley (1986) interprets such word-length effects in terms of the Working Memory model. In the original formulation (Baddeley & Hitch, 1974) items are encoded in STM in an articulatory code. Loss of information occurs by passive decay, but this can be countered by rehearsing the traces of decaying items. As long as all the items in a sequence can be refreshed within the decay time of the store, they can be maintained more or less indefinitely. If, however, the length of a sequence of spoken items exceeds the decay time, errors in recall will occur. Thus the rehearsal process is limited by temporal duration, and the articulatory loop is seen to be analogous to a tape loop of specific length which can hold a message which fits onto that length of tape. Thus subjects' STM capacity is limited to roughly the amount of material that can be rehearsed sub-vocally in about 2 seconds (Baddeley, 1986; but see Gordon Brown [this volume] for some qualifications of this).

In combination with the bilingual digit-name length differences, these findings led to the prediction that the immediate memory span for English digits will be greater than for Welsh digits, even in subjects who consider themselves more competent in the Welsh language. Ellis & Hennelly (1980) therefore tested the same 12 subjects for their STM for Welsh and English digits.

For each condition the stimuli consisted of three trials at each length of string from two to ten digits and these were presented in ascending order of length. The subject listened to the string and, upon a cue to respond, tried to repeat the digits in the correct order and the same language of presentation, continuing in this fashion until there had been incorrect responses on three consecutive trials. STM span was calculated as 1 + (number of trials correct/3).

The mean STM span for English was 6.55 which was significantly greater than that of 5.77 for Welsh digits ($p< 0.01$). This was the case even though the majority of subjects were more proficient in the Welsh language and the difference is consistent with an explanation that it results from the word-length effect whereby Welsh digits take longer to articulate than English digits.

Baddeley *et al.* (1975) demonstrated that a subject's span could be predicted to be the number of words that could be read in approximately 2 s, and concomitantly demonstrated a significant correlation between subjects' reading speed and memory span. Both of these findings were confirmed in Ellis & Hennelly (1980): (i) A Spearman rank-order correlation between the 12 subjects' digit reading speeds and their STM spans was significant at rho = 0.47 ($p< 0.05$); (ii) The mean time taken to read a Welsh digit was 385 ms, the mean Welsh span was 5.77; this number of digits could thus be read in 2.2 s. Comparable figures for the English language are a digit span of 6.55 items which at a reading rate of 321 ms/digit could be read in 2.1 s.

BILINGUAL STM SPAN UNDER ARTICULATORY SUPPRESSION

Digit span measured in the Welsh language is thus smaller than that measured in English. It is not possible to conclude, however, that this is necessarily an effect of word-length: both the span and reading rate differences might be attributable either to word-length differentials or to differences in degree of familiarity. This latter possibility must be considered as it seems that Welsh speakers do on occasion preferentially use English number names. For example, the year of the Ellis & Hennelly experiments was often referred to as 'nineteen seventy-eight' in preference to 'mil naw saith wyth' or the more clumsy 'un mil naw cant saith deg wyth'. It is thus possible that numbers are a special case of language usage, and therefore the language competence self-ratings obtained for our bilingual subjects may not represent their language of preference when dealing with numbers.

Effects of word-length and familiarity can be distinguished if articulatory suppression is used as an interference task. The word-length effect, which Baddeley *et al.* (1975) attribute to the functioning of the articulatory loop, is much reduced with visual stimulus presentation if the subject's articulation is simultaneously suppressed by their repeatedly whispering an irrelevant phrase such as 'the the the ...'. Therefore if the difference between English and Welsh digit spans is the result of the differential articulation time of the digit names, i.e. if it is a word-length effect, this difference should be either absent under articulatory suppression, or, if present, present in a much reduced form.

Eight bilingual subjects were therefore tested for their digit spans in Welsh and English with visual presentation and articulatory suppression. The digit strings were presented sequentially on a memory drum at a rate of one item per second. To ensure that the stimuli were processed in the required language, digit words were presented, e.g. 'pedwar' or 'four', as opposed to the digit figures. The subjects were again required to report the component digits of the strings in the correct order at the end of string presentation. The major difference between this and the prior procedure was that throughout the period of digit string presentation the subject was to whisper the sequence 'a-b-c-d' in a continuous cycle at the fastest rate compatible with clarity of pronunciation. The subjects were tested on both conditions with order of presentation counterbalanced.

The mean digit spans under articulatory suppression in Welsh and English were 3.75 and 4.00 respectively, a non- significant difference. These figures are to be compared with those of 5.77 and 6.55 where no suppression was used and stimulus presentation was auditory.

It must therefore be concluded that the bilingual digit span differential is a word-length effect. Even for subjects who consider themselves more proficient in Welsh, the structure of the Welsh digit names necessitates that it is easier to remember lists of numbers in English. This effect, albeit relatively small (the English span being 114 per cent that of the Welsh span) must be assumed to be operative in everyday situations such as the short-term remembering of telephone numbers.

INTELLIGENCE TESTING

Individual differences in the span of immediate memory, as measured using strings of random digits as stimuli, have commonly been utilized as sub-components of intelligence tests. In the Terman-Merrill (1974), for example, a 10 year old child is tested on their ability to repeat six-digit strings in the correct order. Similarly, in the Wechsler Intelligence Scale for Children (WISC, 1949) the same age child is tested for their ability to repeat digit strings both in their original and reversed order. The sum of forwards and reversed spans measured on this test are compared with the norm score of 9 for a child of this age.

The development or modification of intelligence tests for use with different languages or dialects must be accompanied by re-normalisation. As Burt (1939) stated in reference to the use of the WISC in England: testers in England 'should be supplied with a standardised procedure and with standardised norms - a procedure which has been experimentally adjusted to English idioms and to English customs, norms which have been statistically deduced from extensive trials with English children, trained in English homes and taught in English schools.' Norms for different adaptations of an intelligence test should not be directly compared with an aim to deducing intellectual differences between the populations from which these norms were derived. Our demonstrations reinforce this claim - cross-lingual differences in word-length result in different magnitudes of digit span as measured in those languages and this entails that digit span norms cannot be compared across languages as an indicator of cultural intellectual differences.

Table 1
Digit span scores (sum of digit spans forwards and reversed) for the American population tested in English on the WISC procedure, and the Welsh population tested in Welsh on the WCIS translation of WISC digit span procedure.

Subject age (years)	6.10	7.10	8.10	9.10	10.10	11.10	12.10	13.10	14.10	15.10
WISC digit span score	7	8	8	9	9	10	10	10	11	11
WCIS digit span score	7	7	8	8	8	9	9	9	9	10

William & Roberts (1972) developed a Welsh language Children's Intelligence Scale (WCIS) by modifying and translating the Wechsler Intelligence Scale for Children (WISC).

The WISC was experimentally adjusted to Welsh idioms and to Welsh customs and norms were statistically deduced from extensive trials with Welsh-speaking children taught in Welsh schools. The digit span sub-test of the WCIS, was in effect, a direct translation of that of the WISC, the same digit strings are used. The norms on this test are compared to those of the original WISC in Table 1 where the digit span figures represent the sum of digit span forwards and digit span reversed. It can be seen that the norms for the Welsh sample are reliably less than those of the American sample. However this cannot be taken to imply intellectual differences between the two populations, rather they are the result of the differing languages - English digits are easier to remember than Welsh digits as a consequence of their word-length.

RECENT CONFIRMATIONS IN OTHER LANGUAGES

Ellis & Hennelly (1980) suggested that this digit name length effect would also operate in other languages, i.e. languages would be more or less conducive to number memorability and manipulation/calculation as a function of the word-length of the languages' number names. They called for a survey of the word-lengths of the digit names in a wide variety of languages and there have since been a number of replications in other languages.

Stigler, Lee & Stevenson (1986) demonstrated that Mandarin Chinese number words (*i, er, san, si, wu, liu, chi, ba, jiou, shi*) were of a significantly shorter pronunciation (0.40 s per digit for university students) than English number words (0.53 s per digit; see also Liu & Shen, 1977). {Note that here and hereafter, mean digit naming times are not comparable *across* studies because of differences in procedures and subjects in the different experiments}. Associated with these differences the mean digit span for the Chinese subjects was 9.2 whilst that of the Americans was 7.2. {We might speculate that, had George Miller (1956) been of Chinese extraction, the magical number would have been 9!}. As in the Working Memory model, Stigler *et al.* (1986) interpret the finding that the total pronunciation duration for a subject's maximum span did not differ between Chinese and Americans as evidence for a temporally limited store.

Naveh-Benjamin & Ayres (1988) investigated digit word-length and memory span in English, Spanish, Hebrew and Arabic. The mean number of syllables per word for the digits used (0-6, 8-9) were 1.0, 1.6, 1.9, and 2.3 respectively and this led to reliable differences in digit naming time with English fastest at 0.26 s per digit and Arabic slowest at 0.37 s per digit. As a result the digit STM spans in these languages were 7.2, 6.4, 6.5 and 5.8 respectively. Again digit span was approximately predicted by the number of digits that could be read in 2 s.

As Baddeley (1990) observes, the record so far for speed of articulation goes to Cantonese speakers of Chinese residing in Hong Kong. Hoosain (1979) had demonstrated that the digit span for such undergraduates was 9.9 and Hoosain (1986, 1987) and Hoosain and Salili (1987) showed this to be a result of the pronunciation speed and sound duration (0.31 s per digit) of Cantonese number names compared to English (0.38 s per digit). Hoosain and Salili used the identical procedure as Ellis & Hennelly to measure digit reading speed in Chinese and this resulted in an estimate of 0.26 s per digit compared with 0.32 s for English and 0.39 s for Welsh in Ellis & Hennelly.

In summary, it is clear that there are differences between languages in the lengths of their digit names and these affect the time it takes a native speaker to articulate them. Material in STM decays rapidly unless it is refreshed by the use of the articulatory loop for rehearsal. Thus bilingual digit-name length differences affect performance in tasks such as short-term memory for digits which involve vocal or subvocal articulation of digit names. Other potential tasks where these surface features of language might play a determining role include counting and mental arithmetic.

DIGIT LENGTH AND MENTAL CALCULATION

Mental arithmetic falls into two distinct classes: associative and procedural. Some answers (e.g. 5 x 9 = ?) we just 'know' - the answer is stored in long-term memory and the association is recalled directly. Other problems (e.g. 254 x 187 = ?) have not been learned, but most people do know *how* to compute them and, by following the rules of multiplication, the appropriate answers can be produced. In this type of problem the procedural routines applicable to its solution are stored, the numerical product per se is not. These types of sum have been considered (Hunter, 1957) to involve short-term storage of (a) the original problem (if e.g. presented auditorily), (b) the results of interim calculation stages or routines, (c) the particular stage the subject is at in the calculation as a whole. The similarity between the short-term storage involved in digit span tasks and that in mental calculation is illuminated in the following stream of consciousness from Joyce:

"- Bill, sir? she said, halting. Well, it's seven mornings a pint at twopence is seven twos is a shilling and twopence over and these three mornings a quart at fourpence is three quarts is a shilling and one and two is two and two, sir."

In working out a complex problem the fundamental difficulty is not a lack of number facts, but rather it is trying to remember where we are in the problem and what has been achieved at each stage. As the complexity of the problem increases, the amount of temporary information to be kept track of also increases and this can defeat our short-term memory capacity leading to resort to pencil and paper for external scratch-pad memory.

It is clear from introspection that we use internal speech in keeping track during reconstructive arithmetic problems. If you are not convinced, try doing the following sum under Articulatory Suppression (i.e. whilst repeatedly saying 'the the the ...'): 4798 x 7. It is likely that you find it very difficult, if not impossible, when you are denied the short-term storage facility afforded by internal speech. But you can probably do this sum quite easily under normal conditions. There is also experimental confirmation. Groen & Parkman (1972) demonstrated that 6-7 year old children counted to themselves when doing simple additions - they would start with the larger of the two digits presented (whatever the order of presentation) and increment the counter a number of times equivalent to the smaller of the two digits with a time of about 0.4 seconds per increment, a rate consistent with that of their counting aloud. In adults simple addition has become a highly over-learned skill and the slope of the regression line is now a mere 20 milliseconds, much faster than the rate of internal speech counting which is at best one number every 150 msec (Landauer, 1962; Restle, 1970; Groen & Parkman, 1972; Ashcraft & Fierman, 1982). However, adults still resort to short-term memory and articulatory rehearsal to keep track during more complicated sums as is shown by Sokolov (1972) who recorded the electromyogram activity of the speech musculature of adults performing mental arithmetic and thus revealed their considerable sub-vocal articulatory activity. Sokolov (1972) also demonstrates that suppressing covert articulation by having subjects pronounce irrelevant speech sounds during mental calculation impairs performance.

Lindsay and Norman (1972) and Kahneman (1973) similarly argue that such mental calculations are limited by the need to hold information temporarily in a transient working store and Hitch (1978a,b) demonstrates that forgetting increases during the course of calculation as a function of the number of calculational stages intervening between initial presentation and subsequent utilisation of information.

On the basis of the findings of Ellis & Hennelly (1980) it may be predicted that bilingual differences will also be found in mental calculation tasks which involve short-term storage. If this storage in any way involves articulatory encoding (the level at which word-length effects are thought to operate, see Baddeley *et al.*, 1975) then bilingual differences in efficiency should be found. We should note, however, that the analysis given here is the normative one. People can choose or learn different ways of doing mental arithmetic. For example learning to use a mental abacus as a calculational tool affects the mathematical competence and digit spans of those who acquire this skill (Hatano, Miyake, & Binks, 1977; Stigler, 1984), and expert calculators have a wide range of idiosyncratic number knowledge and routines (Hunter, 1977).

As bilingual number-name word-length differences show their effects at a short-term storage level, bilingual differences are not expected in associative mental arithmetic problems (e.g. 5 x 9) where little or no short-term storage or manipulation is involved and the answer is directly retrieved from long-term memory. Similarly, bilingual differences are less to be expected in written calculation where the child can (but may not) use the visible page as a permanent working store which provides an efficient substitute for human working storage (Hitch, 1978; Lindsay and Norman, 1972).

The prediction is therefore that Welsh/English number-name word-length differences will result in slower and less accurate calculation in Welsh for problems which involve an appreciable short-term working storage load.

EXPERIMENT 1

Subjects

25 bilingual 'Welsh' and 25 'English' children between the ages 9-12 years were tested individually. The 'Welsh' children were drawn from 3 schools, the 'English' children from 4. The criteria for 'Welsh' and 'English' were (a) attendance at a predominantly Welsh/English speaking school, and (b) the same main language had to be used both at home and at school. The 'Welsh' children performed the mental calculations in their preferred Welsh, the 'English' children in English.

The two groups were matched for age, intelligence as determined using the Deeside intelligence test, and, as far as possible, socio-economic background. All the children were of average or above average intelligence as determined using the intelligence tests. The 'Welsh' children attended schools in Gwynedd, as did some of the 'English' children, the remainder being from Wolverhampton.

Apparatus and procedure

Practice sums and 24 test sums were presented on a Commodore Pet 2001 Personal Computer. The children were individually instructed, in their own language, that they could start a trial by pressing a key, and that, using the numeric keys, they were to type in the answer to the sum which appeared on the screen as soon as they had worked it out. This was to be followed by pressing the 'return' button. The completion times accurate to 1/60s were recorded for each sum, as were the responses.

There were 6 examples of four sum types in the test trials:

Type 1	Simple multiplication	e.g. $5 \times 3 =$
Type 2	Simple multiple-figure (3, 2) addition	e.g. $305 + 42 =$
Type 3	Complex multiple-figure (3, 2) addition with carrying	e.g. $134 + 88 =$
Type 4	Multiple figure (9) addition	e.g. $5 + 3 + 7 + 4 + 9 + 8 + 6 + 5 + 3 =$

These were presented in standard format with addens aligned vertically. The sum remained displayed throughout the trial. No interim workings (either written or keyed) were allowed, and the answer was to be input in left to right order (i.e. 305 + 42 requires a '347' response rather than that in the typical order of calculation '743').

It can be seen that sum type 1 is associative (should the child have learnt his tables), sum type 2 requires use of reconstructive strategies with little associated short-term memory involvement, and sum types 3 and 4 require reconstructive strategies with carrying and a considerably greater short-term memory load is incurred.

Results

The response time data were analysed as a 3 factor ANOVA (2 Groups x 4 Sum types x 6 Sums) with subjects nested within groups. The Groups factor (F(1,48) = 6.75, p < 0.05) demonstrates that on average the 'English' children solved the sums faster than the 'Welsh' children (mean response times 18.9s and 24.1s respectively). The Sum type factor (F(3,144) = 153.5, p < 0.01) is significant, a Duncan's Multiple Range Test demonstrates that Type 1 sums produced the fastest responses, Type 2 the next fastest, and Types 3 and 4, which did not differ from each other significantly, produced the slowest responses. The most interesting finding is the significance of the Group x Sum type interaction (F(3,144) = 3.84, p < 0.05). The relevant interaction means can be seen in Table 2. A Duncan's Multiple Range Test shows that whilst the 'Welsh' children do not differ significantly from the 'English' children in the average speed at which they answer Type 1 or Type 2 sums, the 'Welsh' children are significantly (p < 0.01) slower at answering Type 3 and 4 sums which involve carrying and many interim stages.

Table 2

Mean Response Latencies (s) for the 'Welsh' and 'English' Children on the Four types of Sum.

	Sum Type	'Welsh'	'English'	difference	p
1	Simple multiplication	8.77	7.25	1.52	n.s.
2	Simple multiple-figure addition	14.45	12.43	2.02	n.s.
3	Complex multiple-figure addition	35.86	27.73	8.13	p < .01
4	Multiple figure addition	37.15	28.02	9.13	p < .01

Table 3

Mean Errors out of 6 for the 'Welsh' and 'English' Children on the Four types of Sum.

	Sum Type	'Welsh'	'English'	d	p
1	Simple multiplication	0.24	0.16	0.08	n.s.
2	Simple multiple-figure addition	0.64	0.20	0.44	n.s.
3	Complex multiple-figure addition	1.96	1.56	0.40	n.s.
4	Multiple figure addition	1.60	0.96	0.64	p=.06
	Total	4.44	2.88		p< .01

The 'Welsh' children also differed from the 'English' children in that they made significantly more errors (Group means 4.44 and 2.88 respectively). A 3 factor ANOVA demonstrates a significant Group difference (F(1,48)=7.2, p<.01), a significant effect of Sum type (F(3,144)=27.28, p<.01) but the Group by Sum type interaction failed to reach significance (F(3,144)=0.69, n.s.). In Table 3 there is a numerical trend whereby there is a greater difference between the Groups on the non-associative sums, and independent samples t tests assessing group differences on each of the Sum types fail to reach significance except in the case of the multiple figure addition sums which was marginally significant at p=.06. These data are illustrated in the left-hand graphs of Figure 1.

EXPERIMENT 2

Experiment 1 demonstrates an interaction whereby Welsh children are slower and more error-prone on sums which involve considerable working storage. However, these are also the sums which involve more calculational steps and so, notwithstanding the matching of the children for intelligence and SES, it might be argued that it is calculational complexity rather than the temporary storage demands that underlie these effects.

In order to clarify this issue we therefore ran a second study where any need for calculation was removed and the dependent variable was simply the time to pass through typical interim numerical solutions. We asked a subject to do aloud the mental calculations for the sums in Experiment 1 and we transcribed the interim numbers that he generated. Thus a Type 1 sum '7 x 3' transcribes as '7 3 21' corresponding to '7 times 3 is 21'; a Type 2 sum '204 + 41' as '1 4 5 4 0 4 2 245' corresponding to '1 and 4 is 5, 4 and 0 is 4, 2 answer 245'; a Type 3 sum '688 + 75' as '8 5 13 3 1 7 8 8 16 6 1 6 7 763' corresponding to '8 and 5 is 13, 3 down carry 1 and 7 is 8 and 8 is 16, 6 down carry 1 and 6 is 7, answer 763'; a Type 4 sum '9 + 4 + 3 + 6 + 7 + 4 + 3 + 7 + 6' as '9 4 13 3 16 6 22 7 29 4 33 3 36 7 43 6 49'. The transcriptions for the six sums of each type were written on cards, with one card for each sum type.

Subjects

Three groups of 25 subjects each were used. These were all shop-keepers or assistants in the Bangor-Caernarfon area of North Wales. Their ages ranged from 17 to 67. Two of the groups were bilingual in that they claimed their proficiency in Welsh was better than that in English but both languages had been acquired in childhood. The third group comprised monoglot English speakers.

Procedure

The subjects were approached in their shops early in the morning whilst trading was quiet. They were asked to read the numbers on the cards at a comfortable fast rate making as few mistakes as possible. Twenty five of the bilingual subjects were randomly chosen and asked to read the numbers in Welsh and 25 in English. The English group read in English. The subjects were timed for each card and also for the time it took them to count from 1 to 100 as quickly as possible.

Results

The reading times for the 6 sums of each type and the counting times are shown in the right-hand graph of Figure 1 where it can be seen that there is no difference between the bilingual subjects performing in English and the English subjects, but bilingual subjects are slower reading out the interim numbers in Welsh, and this is more pronounced with sum types 3 and 4. This is confirmed by ANOVA with a significant group effect (F(2,72)=40.3, p<.001), a significant sum type effect (F(2,288)=567.2, p<.001) and a significant group by sum type interaction (F(8,288)=25.1, p<.001). Figure 1 also shows the solution times and the error rates for the subjects actually doing these sums in Experiment 1. The scale differences on the two graphs involving time reflect (i) the differing subjects in the two experiments, and (ii) reading times for Experiment 2 are for 6 sums but involve no calculations.

FIGURE 1

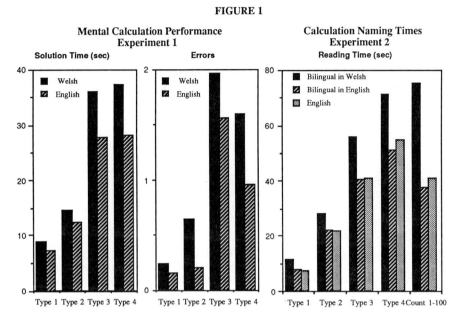

Mental Calculation Performance
Experiment 1

Solution Time (sec)   Errors

Calculation Naming Times
Experiment 2

Reading Time (sec)

There is a clear correspondence between the time it takes here to name the numbers involved in the interim calculations and the actual times taken and the errors made when people to do the sums in the two languages.

Discussion

It is clear that the relative time differences between the languages on the different types of sum are preserved even when we take out the calculation components and simply record the articulation times for the interim 'workings'. The close relationship between these interim 'workings' naming latencies and the actual times taken to do the sums suggest that people do go through these stages of interim calculation and that the latency effects found in Experiment 1 really are a result of the differing articulation rates for numbers in Welsh and English. The fact that the differential error rates on the sums closely parallel these latencies is consistent with the notion of the involvement of a temporally limited STM store. Loss from this store affects computational accuracy and is greater with longer names for the digits involved.

EXPERIMENT 3

The procedure of the first experiment was strictly controlled, and the sum types, with prevention of interim written working, perhaps artificial. To determine whether these results are of any significance in the classroom a field study was undertaken.

Method

74 Primary Schools in Gwynedd and Clwyd were randomly selected from the telephone directory and the head-teachers of these schools were asked whether they would arrange for their 9, 10 and 11 year old children to attempt the sums on a test sheet. This sheet of 60 sums contained 6 examples of the following types of sum: $3 + 4$; 7×6; $9 + 2 + 8 + 4 + 6 + 3$; $754 - 231$; $384 - 197$; 563×2; $84990 + 52529$; $36 + 59 + 42 + 19 + 36 + 54$; $224 \div 4$; 29×24. Those head-teachers who responded were sent the necessary number of forms, and were asked to administer the test ensuring that the children noted both the language(s) of math teaching and the language they used in mental calculation. No other instructions were given. Children were assigned to the Welsh or the English group on the basis of the language used in mental calculation.

As a result, error data for 88 nine year olds, 118 ten year olds and 43 eleven year olds were obtained for each group, i.e. 249 Welsh and 249 English children.

The 'English' children used in this study represented a random sample by age from a considerably larger pool of respondents since it was much more difficult to find children performing the test in Welsh even though the mathematics instruction in the vast majority of the schools was bilingual.

Results

The average number of errors was 9.7 for the 'Welsh' children and 7.0 for the 'English' children (Mann-Whitney U Test, $z = 2.34$, $p < 0.01$, 1 tailed). This difference, although statistically significant, is small, being of the order of 3 sums out of a possible 60.

Discussion

The results of Experiment 1 confirm the speculation that the longer word-length of Welsh digit-names which result in smaller Welsh digit span (Ellis and Hennelly, 1980) also result in relative slowness and increased errors in reconstructive mental calculation in Welsh.

It might be claimed that the procedure of Experiment 1 was artificial in that no written workings were allowed. However, bilingual differences were found at their largest in long addition, sum type 4, where typically no interim workings are used. These sums were designed to represent analogues of the calculations performed traditionally by shop-keepers albeit the case that the mental solution of this type of problem has now been made unnecessary by the advent of the electronic till.

In a less rigourously controlled environment, with subjects under no time stress and where memory loads are reduced by the use of written scratchpad memory (Experiment 3), bilingual differences can be seen to a lesser extent in the significant difference between the number of sums which the 'Welsh' and 'English' children could attempt successfully. Such differences were also perhaps reflected by the fact that in these bilingual schools surveyed it was considerably easier to find children who perform mental calculation in English. One headmaster, totally unprompted, enclosed a note with the return of the test sheets. This reads "...I would like to add that they are Welsh speaking and taught in their mother tongue, but one and all prefer to calculate in English. The answer apparently is 'It's easier in English'!"

Although the differences obtained in this study are statistically significant, they are fairly small in Experiment 3 where written calculation is used. These bilingual differences, although interesting, are therefore considered of less significance in the real-world educational setting where few situations demand calculation without the use of external memory of paper, calculator or fingers.

Relative Welsh/English number name word-length has been shown to affect both the memorability of digit strings (e.g. telephone numbers) (Ellis and Hennelly, 1980), and the ease of mental calculation in these languages. There is no reason to doubt that this effect also operates in other languages. Languages will be more or less conducive to number memorability and calculation, and this will be dependent upon the word-length of the languages' number names.

COUNTING

Figure 1 illustrates the difference in time taken for bilingual individuals to count from 1 to 100 in Welsh and English. It is apparent that this difference is greater than that found for the reading of interim (one or two digit) calculations for sum types 1 through 4. It is likely that this effect is a result of the even greater redundancies in Welsh counting above ten. Thus there is no equivalent to the '-ty' suffix in English, but rather each decade must be expressed as two words (10 *deg*, 20 *dau ddeg*, 30 *tri deg*, 40 *pedwar deg*, etc.), a contrast clearly illustrated by the economy of, e.g. *forty four* in comparison with *pedwar deg pedwar*. Welsh, like other Celtic languages, Breton and Irish, also allows a more traditional, and even longer, form of counting in a system centring on twenties (and, to a lesser extent fifteens). Thus 15 is *pymtheg*, 19 *pedwar ar bymtheg*, 20 *ugain*, 31 *un ar ddeg ar hugain*, 40 *deugain*, etc. Welsh is by no means the only language which uses bases other than ten. Thus in French *vingt* and *quatre-vingts* for 20 and 80 suggest that for some purposes a system with base 20 might have been used. In Danish the word for 70, *halvfirsindstyve* means half way (from three times) to four times twenty. The Eskimos of Greenland, the Tamanas of Venezuela, and the Ainus of Japan are three of the many other people who count by the scores, showing a universal tendency for people to take off their socks as well as their gloves in order to count. Thus for 53, for example, the Greenland Eskimos use the expression *inup pinga-jugsane arkanek-pingasut*, "of the third man, three on the first foot" (Ifrah, 1987). The Babylonian astronomers took a system of notation that was partly sexagesimal (base 60) from their predecessors, the Sumerians, and this is believed to account for the customary division of the hour and the angular degree into 60 minutes (Courant & Robbins, 1941).

There are various processes underlying the counting of the number of objects in an array. Kaufman, Lord, Reese & Volkmann (1949) demonstrate that adults can provide a rapid, confident, and accurate report of the numerosity of small arrays of elements (up to six or seven items) presented for short durations - they name this phenomenon *subitizing*. With larger arrays subjects become increasingly inaccurate unless display times are lengthened to allow actual counting. Logie & Baddeley (1987) show that there is a linear increase in time taken for subjects to count the number of items (between 8 and 25) in arrays, with a slope of approximately 0.32 s per additional item. This latency increase is close to that which one would expect for subvocal counting. Furthermore, the fact that articulatory suppression affects both counting time and accuracy suggests that internal articulation (i.e. subvocalisation of a running total) is required for the accurate counting of arrays of elements. Although we have not directly investigated effects of language digit word-length on subjects' latency of counting the number of elements in an array, we have demonstrated clear differences in the time taken to count from 1->100 in different languages, and this taken together with the Logie & Baddeley findings, provides clear reason to suggest that language digit word-length effects will also operate here.

Hurford (1975) has produced a linguistic theory of numbering systems, distinguishing between a set of primitive numbers (e.g. in English and typically 0 to 9 and units such as the '-ty' in twenty) combined according to base rules to form compound numbers such as 29.

Compound numbers cannot be directly combined - thus 20 + 9 is *twenty-nine*, but 20 + 11 is not *twenty-eleven*. Combining compound numbers such as 20 + 11 involves first their unpacking into primitives (e.g. 20 + 10 + 1) and then repacking them so that the larger leftmost units take on the largest possible value. Thus *twenty-eleven* is ill-formed but *thirty-one* is not. One problem of the English counting system is the idiosyncratic way in which names are formed for numbers in the teens. Number names from 20 to 99 are formed by suffixing a decade name with a unit value. But number names such as *eleven* and *twelve* do not preserve the decade name, and the later teens must be addressed by a 'Switch' rule (Hurford, 1975) whereby the unit value precedes the decade name, with the decade name being the special term *teen*. The reported examples of non-standard numbers being produced by American children consist of the improper concatenation of legitimate number names, and Miller & Stigler (1987) demonstrate that American children have a particular problem with the non-standard teens (e.g. treating them as primitives and generating non-standard numbers like *forty-twelve* for 52) whereas Chinese children never make such errors, Mandarin having no equivalent to the teens, but rather forming these by the regular compounding of a decade value with a unit value. Chinese also lacks the special (and slightly confusing) decade names such as twenty, decades are the compound of the value and *ten* (*twenty seven* is, in effect, *two-ten-seven : er shi qi*).

Here again we see clear effects of linguistic legacy on mental arithmetic. The transparent Chinese counting system makes it easier for Chinese children to induce the difference between primitive and compound numbers. This induction is more difficult in English, and children frequently show confusion over what is or is not a primitive number that can be combined in forming compound numbers. Thus there are large country differences generally favouring Chinese over American children in counting (Miller & Stigler, 1987).

More important is the realisation that counting is the entrée to mathematics. The child's ability to reason arithmetically rests on their representations of numerosity. Developmental investigations make it clear that the young child obtains such representations of by counting - "the judgement of equivalence or order, the application of the operations of addition, subtraction, and identity, and the process of solving all depend on counting" (Gelman & Gallistel, 1978; p. 244; Miller & Gelman, 1983). Furthermore, counting provides an important source of feedback for the learning of arithmetical relationships (Siegler & Robinson, 1982). This view is confirmed by studies of children with specific arithmetical learning disability (ALD). ALD children have a specific working memory deficit in relation to processing numerical information - they are particularly poor at working memory tasks involving counting but not those involving more general language processing (Siegel & Ryan, 1989). Performance on working memory tasks which involve counting increases as a function of speed of counting, and asking adults to count in an unfamiliar language causes a drop in their performance on counting-working-memory tasks to levels of 6 years old children (Case, Kurland & Goldberg, 1982). In line with this, Hitch & McAuley (in press) demonstrate that it is impaired counting that affects the acquisition of arithmetical skills as well as their execution in ALD children.

The counting systems of a language, and the names that it has for its numbers, affect the ease of counting in that language. This, in turn, affects the development of arithmetical competence in its speakers.

MORE GENERAL ASPECTS OF LANGUAGES' WORD-LENGTHS

Languages differ on many dimensions relevant to efficient communication. Cherry (1966) states "The relationship between the whole structure of a language (the morphemic, syntactic grammatical formalism) and the outside world associations (its semantic functioning) is extremely complicated; it is essentially empirical and, above all, varies between different languages. Again, redundancy is built into the structural forms of different languages in diverse ways. No general laws exist."

In considering word-length we are addressing just one of the factors contributing to the redundancy of a language. Within this limited area, however, there do appear general laws. Cherry (1966) observes "... under the natural stress of human economising; the most frequently used words are the shortest; when a word comes into frequent and popular use we tend to abbreviate it (UNESCO, NATO, gas)." Zipf (1935) formulated the law of abbreviation: whenever a long word or phrase suddenly becomes common, we tend to shorten it. Similarly Miller and Newman (1958) suggest that an evolutionary process of selection has been working in favour of short words and demonstrated empirically that the average frequency of words of *i* letters in length is a reciprocal function of their average rank with respect to increasing length.

If the value of some redundancy in allowing detection of errors in transmission or reception under non-optimal conditions is for the present ignored (cf. e.g. van Amerongen, 1975), then it can be seen that having a minimum-redundancy code is desirable. Miller and Chomsky (1963) demonstrate this from an economic viewpoint: there is a cost to communication and the average length of the message is an appropriate measure of this cost since it takes either more time or more equipment to transmit more symbols. In a given period of time, more information can be transmitted using a low redundancy short code. High frequency words, by definition, are those commonly used for communication. It is these which have apparently evolved to be of short word-length and low redundancy.

If languages are compared for average word-length, moreover, gross differences can be seen. Fuchs (1968) devised the following mathematical relationship for the mean frequency distribution h_i of i-syllabic words when the mean number of syllables is $\bar{i}$:

$$h_i = \frac{(\bar{i} - 1)^{i-1}}{(i - 1)!} \, e^{-(\bar{i}-1)}$$

This relationship appears valid for all languages. The only criterion that varies from one language to another is the value $\bar{i}$ for the average number of syllables. For example, in nine languages investigated by Fuchs, this value was as small as 1.41 for English, ranging through 2.10 for Arabic and Greek, and as large as 2.46 for Turkish. The English language appeared to contain the highest proportion of monosyllabic words i.e. it requires the least number of syllables to convey a given amount of information, and proponents of English as a *lingua franca* have suggested (van Amerongen, 1975) that this may be one reason why English has to so great an extent become adopted as an international language.

These considerations of language efficiency as a function of word-length have arisen from the viewpoint of interpersonal communication. In addition, however, word-length has been shown to affect a number of functions involved in intrapersonal information processing and manipulation, e.g.. reading and short term memory span (Baddeley *et al.* 1975) and mental calculation (Ellis and Hennelly, 1980 and the experiments reported here).

Word-length effects operate at an articulatory encoding level. It must therefore be concluded that efficiency at any task which involves articulation will to some extent be a function of the length of the words to be so encoded. The generation of speech is the most obvious example of such a task. In addition, Kleiman (1975) speculates that any condition in which information enters the system more rapidly than it can be semantically processed may cause the subject to use articulatory encoding as a back-up store. Given the large cross-lingual differences in average word-length it can be concluded that, as a function of word-length, languages differ in the efficiency at which they can be used to communicate and manipulate information.

CONCLUSIONS AND BROADER CONSIDERATIONS

We have demonstrated a range of effects of languages' numbering systems, their word length and their transparencies in forming number names from primitives, that affect the facility of speakers of that language in remembering numbers, in counting, and in mental calculation.

There are very large national and cultural differences in mathematics ability (Husén, 1967; Stevenson, Lee & Stigler, 1986; Stigler, Lee & Stevenson, 1987). Thus American children lag behind Japanese and Chinese children in mathematics ability (Stevenson et al., 1986) and Israeli children clearly surpass English who in turn are better than Swedish children at 13 years old (Husén, 1967). The linguistic relativity effects reviewed here play but one role in determining these. We must remember that counting and mental arithmetic are merely the portals of mathematics and play little role in the abstractions of algebra, geometry, sets, calculus, proofs, logic, ..., and mathematical creativity. Also important in determining this skill-base in the populace are the children's schooling, the attitudes of their parents and their culture towards mathematics, the involvement of parents and children in school-work, teacher training and competence, and the child's expectations and aspirations (Husén, 1967; Stevenson et al., 1986; Stigler et al., 1987).

ACKNOWLEDGEMENTS

I gratefully acknowledge the help of the teachers and pupils of the co-operating schools and of the Director of Education for Gwynedd. I thank my students, Rick Hennelly, Sue Kettle and Janet Morris for helping me run these experiments, and Colin Baker, Graham Hitch, Paul Coackley, and Alan Beaton for comments on an earlier draft of this chapter.

REFERENCES

Ashcraft, M.H. & Fierman, B.A. (1982) Mental addition in third, fourth, and sixth graders. *Journal of Experimental Child Psychology*, **33**, 216-234.

Baddeley, A.D. (1986) *Working Memory*. Oxford: Clarendon Press.

Baddeley, A.D. (1990) *Human Memory: Theory and Practice*. Hove and London: Lawrence Erlbaum Associates.

Baddeley, A. D. & Hitch, G. J. (1974). Working memory. In G. A. Bower (ed.), *The Psychology of Learning and Motivation: Advances in Research and Theory,* **8**, pp. 47-89. New York: Academic Press.

Baddeley, A.D., Thomson, N. & Buchanan, M. (1975) Word-length and the structure of short-term memory. *Journal of Verbal Learning and Verbal Behaviour*, 14, 575-589.

Baker, C. (1985) *Aspects of Bilingualism in Wales*. Clevedon: Multilingual Matters.

Burt, C. (1939). *Mental and Scholastic Tests*. London: King.

Case, R., Kurland, D.M., & Goldberg, J. (1982) Operational efficiency and the growth of short-term memory span. *Journal of Experimental Child Psychology*, **33**, 386-404.

Cherry, C. (1966) *On Human Communication*. Cambridge, Mass.: M.I.T. Press. 2nd Edition.

Cooley, C.H. (1962) *Social Organisation*. New York: Schoken Books.

Courant, R. & Robbins, H. (1941) *What is Mathematics?* Oxford: Oxford University Press.

Dantzig, T. (1930) *Number: The Language of Science*. New York: Macmillan Company.

Ellis, N.C. & Hennelly, R.A. (1980) A bilingual word-length effect: implications for intelligence testing and the relative ease of mental calculation in Welsh and English. *British Journal of Psychology*, **71**, 43-51.

Fuchs, W. (1968) *Nach allen Regeln der Kunst*. Stuttgart: Deutsche Verlags-Anstalt.

Gelman, R. & Gallistel, C.R. (1978) *The Child's Understanding of Number*. Cambridge, Mass.: Harvard University Press.

Groen, G.J. & Parkman, J.M. (1972) A chronometric analysis of simple addition. *Psychological Review*, **79**, 329-343.

Hatano, G., Miyake, Y. & Binks, M.G. (1977) Performance of expert abacus operators. *Cognition*, **5**, 47-55.

Hitch, G.J. (1978a) Mental arithmetic: short-term storage and information processing in a cognitive skill. In A.M. Lesgold, J.W. Pellegrino, S.D. Fokkema & R. Glaser (Eds.) *Cognitive Psychology and Instruction*. New York: Plenum Publishing Corporation.

Hitch, G.J. (1978b) The role of short-term working memory in mental arithmetic. *Cognitive Psychology*, **10**, 302-323.

Hitch, G.J. & McAuley, E. (In press). Working memory in children with specific arithmetical difficulties. *British Journal of Psychology*. In press.

Hoosain, R. (1979) Forward and backward digit span in the languages of the bilingual. *The Journal of Genetic Psychology*, **135**, 263-268.

Hoosain, R. (1986) Language, orthography and cognitive processes: Chinese perspectives for the Sapir-Whorf hypothesis. *International Journal of Behavioural Development*, **9**, 507-525.

Hoosain, R. (1987) Correlation between pronunciation speed and digit span size. *Perceptual and Motor Skills*, **55**, 1128.

Hoosain, R. & Salili, F. (1987) Language differences in pronunciation speed for numbers, digit span, and mathematical ability. *Psychologia*, **30**, 34-38.

Hunter, I.M.L. (1964) *Memory*. Harmondsworth: Penguin.

Hunter, I.M.L. (1977) Mental calculation. In P.N. Johnson-Laird & P.C. Wason (Eds.) *Thinking: Readings in Cognitive Science*. Cambridge: Cambridge University Press.

Hurford, J.R. (1975) *The Linguistic Theory of Numerals*. Cambridge: Cambridge University Press.

Husén, T. (1967) *International Study of Achievement in Mathematics.* Volumes I and II. New York: John Wiley & Sons.

Ifrah, G. (1987) *From One to Zero: A Universal History of Numbers.* New York: Viking Penguin.

Joyce, J. (1969) *Ulysses.* Harmondsworth: Penguin.

Kahneman, D. (1973) *Attention and Effort.* Englewood Cliffs, N.J.: Prentice-Hall.

Kaufman, E.L., Lord, M.W., Reese, T.W. & Volkman, J. (1949) The discrimination of visual number. *American Journal of Psychology,* **62,** 498-525.

Kleiman, G.M. (1975) Speech Recoding in Reading. *Journal of Verbal Learning and Verbal Behaviour,* **14,** 323-339.

Landauer, T.K. (1962) Rate of implicit speech. *Perceptual and Motor Skills,* **15,** 646.

Lindsay, P.H. & Norman, D.A. (1972) *Human information processing: An introduction to psychology.* New York: Academic Press.

Liu, K.S. & Shen, H.M. (1977) Effects of language structure and intertrial interval on the speed of silent reading. *Acta Psychologica Taiwanica,* **19,** 57-59.

Logie, R.H. & Baddeley. A.D. (1987) Cognitive processes in counting. *Journal of Experimental Psychology: Learning, Memory, and Cognition,* **13,** 310-326.

Miller, G.A. (1956) The magical number seven, plus or minus two: Some limits on our capacity for processing information. *Psychological Review,* **63,** 81-97.

Miller, G.A. (1965) Introduction to Zipf, G.K. *The Psycho-Biology of Language.* Cambridge, Mass: M.I.T. Press.

Miller, G.A. & Chomsky, N. (1963) Finitary Models of Language Users. In Luce, R.D., Bush, R.R. and Galanter, E. (eds) *Handbook of Mathematical Psychology,* Volume II. New York: John Wiley.

Miller, G.A. & Newman, E.B. (1958) Tests of a statistical explanation of the rank- frequency relation for words in written English. *American Journal of Psychology,* **71,** 209-258.

Miller, K. & Gelman, R. (1983) The child's representation of number: a multidimensional scaling analysis. *Child Development,* **54,** 1470-1479.

Miller, K.F. & Stigler, J.W. (1987) Counting in Chinese: Cultural variation in a basic cognitive skill. *Cognitive Development,* **2,** 279-305.

Naveh-Benjamin, M. & Ayres, T.J. (1986) Digit span, reading rate, and linguistic relativity. *Quarterly Journal of Experimental Psychology,* **38,** 739-751.

Restle, F. (1970) Speed of adding and comparing numbers. *Journal of Experimental Psychology,* **83,** 274-278.

Spier, L. (Ed.) (1941) *Language, Culture and Personality: Essays in Memory of Edward Sapir.* Menasha, Wis.: Sapir Memorial Publication Fund.

Siegel, L.S. & Ryan, E.B. (1989) The development of working memory in normally achieving and subtypes of learning disabled children. *Child Development,* **60**, 973-980.

Siegler, R.S. & Robinson, M. (1982) The development of numerical understandings. In H. Reese & L.P. Lipsitt (Eds.) *Advances in Child Development and Behaviour, Vol. 16.* New York: Academic Press.

Sokolov, A.N. (1972) *Inner Speech and Thought.* Translated by G. T. Onischenko. New York: Plenum Publishing Co.

Stevenson, H.W., Lee, S.-Y., & Stigler, J.W. (1986) Mathematics achievement of Chinese, Japanese, and American children. *Science,* **231**, 693-699.

Stigler, J.W. (1984) "Mental abacus": The effects of abacus training on Chinese children's mental calculation. *Cognitive Psychology,* **16**, 145-176.

Stigler, J.W., Lee, S.-Y. & Stevenson, H.W. (1986) Digit memory in Chinese and English: Evidence for a temporally limited store. *Cognition,* **23**, 1-20.

Stigler, J.W., Lee, S.-Y. & Stevenson, H.W. (1987) Mathematics classrooms in Japan, Taiwan, and the United States. *Child Development,* **58**, 1272-1285.

Terman, L. M. & Merrill, M. A. (1960). *Stanford-Binet Intelligence Scale: Manual for the Third Revision.* Boston: Houghton Mifflin.

Van Amerongen, C. (1975) *The Way Things Work Book of the Computer.* London: George Allen and Unwin Ltd.

Wechsler, D. (1949). *Manual for the Wechsler Intelligence Scale for Children.* New York: The Psychological Corporation.

Whorf, B.J. (1942) Language, Mind and Reality. January and April Issues, *The Theosophist.*

Whorf, B.J. (1956) *Language, Thought and Reality. Selected Writings of Benjamin Lee Whorf.* New York: John Wiley.

William, U. & Roberts, G. (1972). *The Welsh Children's Intelligence Scale.* Windsor: NFER.

Zipf, G.K. (1949) *Human Behaviour and the Principle of Least Effort.* Cambridge, Mass: Addison-Wesley.

Cognitive Processing in Bilinguals – *R.J. Harris (Editor)*

The Representation of Translation Equivalents in Bilingual Memory

Jeanette Altarriba
University of Massachusetts at Amherst

Abstract

A fluent bilingual generally has two lexical representations for a single concept in memory, one in each of two languages. Researchers in bilingual memory have investigated the structure of the representation of a word and its translation in memory. Early research focused on translation equivalents in episodic memory while more recent research has focused on their representation in semantic memory. Current studies on facilitation effects in priming for translation equivalents suggest that in fluent bilinguals both words are linked at a conceptual level in memory. It appears that translation equivalents share a common semantic representation. Implications for learning a second language are discussed.

Introduction

The acquisition of a second language generally begins by learning the translation equivalents for words already known in one's first language. In translating from one language to another, the lexical code is varied while a particular concept remains invariant (Leont'ev, 1973). As learning translation equivalents is fundamental to the acquisition of a second language, it appears useful to investigate the structure of their representation in memory and the process by which the two lexical codes are connected.

A primary debate in the bilingual literature centers on the issue of whether a bilingual has two unique memory stores, one for each language, or a single semantic store in which words are "tagged" as to language at the time of output. The first view has been referred to as the independent or dual- store view while the second has been referred to as the interdependent or single-store view (Kolers, 1966; McCormack, 1974, 1977). Another way to characterize this distinction is in terms of semantic or conceptual representation. That is, do translation equivalents have separate semantic representations or do they share a common semantic representation? The aim of this chapter is to review the experimental evidence regarding the representation of translation equivalents in both episodic and semantic memory and to present new data which suggests that for fluent bilinguals, translation equivalents are connected at a conceptual level.

Translation Equivalents in Episodic Memory

Experimental Evidence

Free recall.   Lopez and Young (1974) investigated language representation in bilinguals by examining transfer effects for translation equivalents. In their experiment, subjects were familiarized with a list of either Spanish words or English words, i.e., they were asked to read the list several times. Subjects were then placed in one of three conditions. They learned either the same list they had studied, a list containing translation equivalents of the words they had originally studied, or a new list of words. In the learning phase, the word list was presented auditorily, and the subjects then participated in free recall. The subjects were bilingual in English and Spanish and rated themselves higher in English fluency than Spanish fluency. Subjects in the experimental conditions recalled significantly more words than subjects in the control condition, and there was no difference in the amount of transfer observed for the two experimental conditions. Facilitation was equal in the Spanish to English and the English to Spanish conditions. These results appear to support an interdependent view of bilingual memory. If the familiarization of a word or its translation equivalent results in the activation of the same semantic representation, then this familiarization should result in equal amounts of transfer in learning regardless of whether or not the learning is in the same language as the familiarization. These results should also occur regardless of which language is dominant.

Although Lopez and Young (1974) discussed their results in terms of the semantic representation of words in memory, their task involved the episodic processing of words and their translation equivalents. In most free recall tasks, memory is episodic and involves memory for a particular event rather than one's long-term, semantic memory. However, a possible flaw in this study is that subjects might have translated the words during familiarization producing a transfer effect in learning. This might have been true especially if subjects had been asked to rate their fluency prior to participating in the experiment and were aware of the nature of the study.

Liepmann and Saegert (1974) also used list learning to investigate the representation of translation equivalents. Arabic-English bilinguals were shown fifteen lists of words in English or mixed in English and Arabic. Items overlapped across lists. In the English lists, a subset of items was repeated across lists. In the mixed lists, the language of a subset of items alternated across lists. The words were presented on slides, and subjects participated in free recall immediately following each list. Recall for successive lists was found to decrease for the mixed lists as compared to the unilingual lists. For mixed lists, subjects had to retain information as to which list and which language an item appeared in whereas for the unilingual lists, subjects only had to remember which list an item appeared in. The results appear to support an interdependent view of language representation in episodic memory. If items had been stored separately or had separate representations in memory, then subjects' performance would have been better with the mixed lists than with the unilingual lists because subjects would have been able to use language to mark items more effectively and would have had less overlap in items from successive lists.

In contrast, the results of another recall study seem to suggest that a word and its translation are represented independently. Watkins and Peynircioglu (1983) investigated the extent to which a word in a study list would facilitate the completion of a word fragment of its translation in a subsequent cued-recall test. Turkish-English bilinguals were presented lists of words in either Turkish or English. The authors hoped that this would minimize translation during study as might have occurred in Lopez and Young's (1974) study. Each list contained 60 words, 10 of which were buffer words. The words were presented auditorily along with line drawings of each word at a rate of 1 word every 4 seconds. Immediately following the study period, subjects participated in free recall. Subjects were then shown fragment cues for 25 of the 50 words presented in the study list (the consistent condition) and for the translations of the other 25 (the inconsistent condition). Subjects were also shown 50 fragment cues for words that had not been presented in the study list, 25 in Turkish and 25 in English (the no-presentation condition).

Subjects performed best in the consistent condition, and their performance was equal for the inconsistent and the no- presentation conditions. There were no facilitation effects in cued recall for the translations of studied words. These results seem to suggest that a word and its translation equivalent do not share the same conceptual representation in episodic memory. The authors concluded that word recall can be direct rather than concept-mediated.

Savings. MacLeod (1976) also investigated the representation of information in episodic memory. He used a savings method to examine the information that remained in episodic memory for items that were not recalled (i.e., forgotten) after a five-week retention period. French-English bilinguals learned a list of number-word paired associates in which the words were either in English or in French (e.g., **81-apple**; **81-pomme**). Five weeks later, subjects were tested for their retention of the words. They were presented with the numbers and were asked to recall the corresponding words. For those words that were forgotten, new words were substituted that matched the original words in meaning or in language. Savings is found when the residual information in the forgotten word facilitates relearning of the new word as compared to an unrelated new word. Subjects showed a savings effect for the meaning of the original words but not for the language in which they appeared. It appears that the savings residual for nonrecallable words contained semantic information in a relatively language-free form. These results appear to support the notion of a single underlying concept for translation equivalents in episodic memory.

The translation effect. Clifton, Sorce, Schaye, and Fiszman (1978) used a memory search task to investigate language representation. Spanish-English bilinguals saw sets of 1 to 4 Spanish or 1 to 4 English words. After each set, they were presented with a probe word that was either a word from the set or a translation of a word that had been in the set. Before beginning each session, subjects were told what type of probe to expect. Subjects' mean reaction times were longer when the probe word was a translation of an item in the set than when the probe was an actual item from the set. It appears that in the translation condition, subjects held both the presented and translated forms of the words in memory. Subjects then searched through both the presented forms and the translated forms before making a decision. Thus, response times were longer in this condition than in the "no translation" condition. The authors concluded that when a task encourages encoding in a language-specific manner, subjects are able to do so. Although one might be tempted to conclude that the representation of translation equivalents is language- specific, these results reflect task demands of the experiment and do not address issues of conceptual representation.

Limitations of Episodic Memory Tasks

The tasks described above reflect the means by which translation equivalents are encoded rather than the structure of their semantic representations. The results suggest that bilingual subjects have the ability to encode information in a language-specific manner when necessary. However, subjects can also attend to the meanings of words to the apparent exclusion of language information. Thus, these tasks are informative about language processing in episodic memory and demonstrate how bilinguals can use their language skills to organize information and enhance performance. These studies do not provide sufficient evidence to distinguish the independent from the interdependent view of semantic representation described above.

The following section is a review of bilingual studies involving semantic memory tasks. These studies investigated the representation of translation equivalents at a conceptual level in semantic memory.

Translation Equivalents in Semantic Memory

Experimental Evidence

Visual masking. Another paradigm that has been used to examine the representation of translation equivalents is visual masking. O'Neill (1977) used a masking procedure to test the hypothesis that translation equivalents functioned like superordinate-subordinate associates (e.g., **animal-horse**). Ten French-English balanced bilinguals participated in this study. Target-mask pairs were either translation equivalents, unrelated French and English words, bilingual homophones (e.g., **phone-faune**), unilingual superordinates and subordinates, or unrelated unilingual words. On each trial, subjects were presented with a target word for 20 milliseconds (ms) followed by a 10-ms delay interval. The mask was then presented for 120 ms. The delay interval was increased in steps of 5 ms until the subject correctly identified the target. The results are shown in Table 1.

Table 1

Mean Masking Thresholds as a Function of Target-Mask Relation
(adapted from O'Neill, 1977)

Target-Mask Relation	Mean Masking Threshold (ms)
unilingual superordinate-subordinate	77
translation equivalents	93
unilingual unrelated words	125
bilingual unrelated words	149
homophones	165

There was no significant difference in mean masking threshold for the first two conditions above. Masking thresholds for translation equivalents differed significantly from masking thresholds for bilingual unrelated words. The mean threshold for homophones was significantly greater than the mean threshold for unilingual unrelated words.

The results from O'Neill's (1977) study suggested that the relationship between translation equivalents in memory is similar to that between same-language superordinate and subordinate words. Translation equivalents were less effective masks than different-language unrelated masks demonstrating the facilitative effect of semantic relatedness in the masking procedure. These results support the idea that translation equivalents share a common conceptual representation in bilingual memory.

Priming. A large part of the evidence regarding the organization of words or concepts in bilingual memory comes from studies examining priming effects in lexical decisions for words and their translation equivalents. In a typical lexical decision trial, a subject is presented with one or two strings of letters on a computer screen and is asked to decide whether or not the letters form a real word. Lists include both words and nonwords (e.g., **blit**). Response time is measured to a target item following presentation of a related prime. The time interval or stimulus onset asynchrony (SOA) between the presentation of the prime and the target may vary. It is assumed that a long SOA leads to more elaborate processing of the prime.

One effect that regularly occurs in the lexical decision task is semantic priming (e.g., Meyer & Schvaneveldt, 1971). That is, a subject's decision as to whether a letter string is a word or a nonword is facilitated when the target word (e.g., **tiger**) is preceded by a semantically-related word (e.g., **lion**).

Results of this kind are predicted by the theory of spreading activation (Quillian, 1962). In this theory, concepts are viewed as nodes in a semantic network. The nodes are connected through associative pathways. Activation spreads through the pathways to related areas when the network becomes activated. This spread of activation makes the related areas more available for future processing. Spreading activation theory assumes that when an event is processed, other events are activated to the extent that they are closely related to that event. In the bilingual case, if the recognition of a word (e.g., **dog**) is facilitated by the previous presentation of its translation equivalent (e.g., **perro**) it may be assumed that a word and its translation are linked through an underlying concept in semantic memory.

Although several studies have examined cross-language priming for semantically-related prime-target pairs (see, e.g., Altarriba, 1990; Frenck & Pynte, 1987; Grainger & Beauvillain, 1988; Keatley, Spinks, & de Gelder, 1990; Kirsner, Smith, Lockhart, King, & Jain, 1984; Meyer & Ruddy, 1974; Schwanenflugel & Rey, 1986), few studies have examined priming for translation equivalents. Kirsner, Brown, Abrol, Chadha, and Sharma (1980), Kirsner et al. (1984), Experiments 1 and 3, and Scarborough, Gerard, and Cortese (1984) failed to find facilitation effects in priming for translation equivalents. However, these studies included relatively long intervals of 10 minutes or more between the presentation of the primes and the targets. These studies were designed to examine the repetition effect, i.e., faster recognition of a word following its repetition as compared to its first presentation. Scarborough et al. argued that the repetition effect at long lags depends on the physical similarity of the stimuli rather than processing at a conceptual level. Therefore, failure to find a repetition effect for translation equivalents does not imply the absence of a common conceptual representation for translation equivalents.

Three experiments examined translation priming effects with very short lags between the presentation of the prime and the target. One of these was a study conducted by Chen and Ng (1989). In this study, semantic facilitation and translation priming effects in Chinese-English bilingual speakers were demonstrated with a lexical decision task. Subjects were presented with two blocks of prime-target pairs, one with 30 Chinese-English pairs and another with 30 English-Chinese pairs. Each trial of the experiment began with the presentation of a star signal for one second in the center of the visual field, followed immediately by the display of a prime item for 300 ms. The prime was then replaced by the target item. The subjects' task was to decide whether the presented target was a word or not.

Subjects' lexical decision responses were facilitated to a greater extent when primed with a translation equivalent than with an unrelated, between-language word. However, this study had several methodological problems that raise questions as to the validity of the results. The SOA (300 ms) might have been long enough to permit the translation of the prime or the use of other strategies on the part of the subjects. Also, the response times averaged over 800 ms in the translation condition. This is quite a departure from the 600-700 ms average reported in previous studies with similar procedures (see Neely & Keefe, 1989, and Neely, 1990, for complete reviews).

If subjects were not responding quickly to the targets, the results might have been influenced by strategic processes.

A second study that examined translation priming effects with short prime-target intervals was a study conducted by Jin (1990). Korean-English bilinguals were shown 50 Korean-English pairs and 50 English-Korean pairs in a lexical decision task. Word-word pairs included translation equivalents, associates, and unrelated prime-target pairs. In each trial, a fixation point was shown in the center of a computer screen for 750 ms followed by the presentation of the prime word for 150 ms. The target replaced the prime word, and the subject's task was to decide whether or not the target was a legitimate word. These results support the view that translation equivalents are closely integrated through a common, conceptual representation.

Significant facilitation effects in priming were found for translation equivalents as compared to unrelated target words. These effects were significantly greater for Korean-English word pairs (150 ms) than for English-Korean word pairs (36 ms). One problem with this study, however, was the high proportion of related prime-target word pairs in the stimulus lists (.67). The relatedness proportion effect is the finding that semantic priming increases in magnitude with increases in the proportion of related prime-target word trials (de Groot, 1984; Neely, Keefe, & Ross, 1989; Tweedy & Lapinski, 1981). Tweedy and Lapinski (1981) found that a gradual increase in the number of related prime-target pairs per block of trials enhanced the priming effect in successive blocks presented to the same subjects. A decrease in the number of related prime-target pairs in successive blocks presented to a second group of subjects reduced the effect. One explanation for this effect is that as subjects become aware of the presence of related prime-target pairs, they begin to expect a target to be related to a preceding prime. Subjects may use this information to facilitate their response as they go through a stimulus list. As a result, they will be quick to respond "yes" to the target.

Another aspect of the stimulus list that may influence the size of the priming effect is the nonword ratio. This ratio is the probability that a target is a nonword, given that it is unrelated to its prime. Researchers have noted that subjects in the lexical decision task check whether the target is related or unrelated to its preceding word prime (e.g., Balota & Lorch, 1986; de Groot, 1984; McNamara & Altarriba, 1988; Neely, 1976, 1977; Neely & Keefe, 1989). Subjects use information about prime-target relatedness to facilitate their word/nonword response. The stimulus lists used by Jin (1990) had a high nonword ratio (.54), and subjects might have used this information to bias a "nonword" response. Again, their results might have been influenced by strategic processes. In order to reduce the use of semantic checking strategies, Neely et al. (1989) suggested using a low nonword ratio.

A third study conducted by de Groot and Nas (1991, Experiment 3) examined priming for cognates and translation equivalents in masked and unmasked conditions. The authors argued that when primes are clearly visible, subjects may try to use strategies such as the ones mentioned above to facilitate their responses to target words. Thus, masking the prime should minimize the use of strategies and lead to automatic processing. Dutch-English bilinguals performed lexical decisions on English-English or Dutch-English word pairs. In the masked condition, the prime was preceded by a row of 11 hash marks for 480 ms followed by a 20 ms blank interval. The prime was then presented for 40 ms, and 20 ms later the target appeared. In the unmasked condition the SOA was 240 ms. Cross-language priming for translation equivalents was found in both the masked and unmasked conditions (35 ms and 113 ms, respectively). Although it appears that the masking procedure may have minimized the use of controlled strategies by the subjects, it is unclear whether the subjects actually perceived the prime in a sufficient number of trials (this information was reported for Experiment 2 but not for Experiment 3). Also, as noted by the authors, it is difficult to disentangle the effects of masking vs. SOA as the SOA was always larger in the unmasked condition (240 ms) than in the masked condition (60 ms).

The important point in reference to the present discussion is that de Groot and Nas (1991) did not control relatedness proportion and nonword ratio within their stimulus lists. There has been only one bilingual priming study in which the proportion of related prime-target pairs within stimulus lists was controlled. Keatley et al., (1990) used a relatedness proportion of .25 in their study of cross-language priming in Chinese-English and Belgian-Dutch bilinguals and found evidence of facilitation effects in priming for semantically-related word pairs as compared to unrelated word pairs. However, they investigated priming for primary associates and did not include prime-target word pairs that were translation equivalents. The study described below investigated priming for translation equivalents under conditions that were designed to minimize subjects' use of the strategies mentioned above.

Priming for Translation Equivalents in Contextually Constrained Conditions: A Study

Previous cross-language priming experiments have reported facilitation in reaction time for paired translation equivalents. However, a critical examination of this literature suggests that the observed facilitation effects may be attributed to the operation of predictive strategies and, therefore, do not necessarily imply the existence of structural links between the two languages. In some cases, subjects might have had time to translate the prime before processing the target word, and any priming effects observed could have been purely intralingual rather than interlingual.

The current study provides a more appropriate test of whether or not translation equivalents are connected at a conceptual level by constraining the lexical decision task to insure that primes will be read without enabling the use of active translations or other conscious, effortful strategies. The approach taken by Neely et al. (1989) in minimizing the role of prime-generated expectancies was adopted here. Spanish-English bilinguals performed lexical decisions on within- and cross-language word pairs. The proportion of related word-prime/word-target trials (RP) and the nonword ratio (NR) within the stimulus lists were held low and constant (.33), while the stimulus onset asynchrony (SOA) between prime and target was manipulated (200 ms and 1000 ms).

Method

Subjects.   Sixty-four Spanish-English bilinguals were recruited from Florida International University, Miami, Florida to participate in this study. Subjects received credit or payment in the amount of $7.00 for their participation. Table 2 contains a summary of their language backgrounds.

Table 2

Summary of Subjects' Language Histories

		SOA Group	
		200 SOA N=32	1000 SOA N=32
Mean age in years		24	25
Mean number of years in the U.S.		16	17
Mean number of years in U.S. schools		11	12
Mean number of years each language spoken:	English	16	18
	Spanish	24	24
Ratings on a 7-point scale (1=strongly disagree, 7=strongly agree)			
I read Spanish very well		5.9	5.7
I read English very well		6.7	6.4
Percentage of the day each language spoken:	English	59%	54%
	Spanish	41%	46%

Design.   The design included one between-subjects factor, SOA (200 ms vs. 1000 ms), and three within-subjects factors, prime-target relation (semantically related, semantically unrelated, direct translation, and neutral), prime language (English and Spanish), and target language (English and Spanish).

Materials. English word primes were chosen from the association word norms of Postman and Keppel (1970). These primes were then translated into Spanish (Smith, Davies, & Hall, 1989). Thirty Spanish-English bilinguals at Florida International University were asked to provide word associations to the Spanish primes. The most frequently given response in both languages was chosen as the target in each pair for the semantically-related condition. Examples of the words used in this study can be seen in Table 3. Word-nonword pairs were also included. Nonwords were formed by changing one or two letters in unrelated words chosen from the same source as the critical stimuli.

Table 3

Examples of Stimulus Pairs Used in This Study

Relation	Language	
	Same	Different
semantically-related	SUGAR-sweet	SUGAR-dulce
	AZUCAR-dulce	AZUCAR-sweet
unrelated	DIRT-sweet	DIRT-dulce
	TIERRA-dulce	TIERRA-sweet
repetition/translation	SWEET-sweet	SWEET-dulce
	DULCE-dulce	DULCE-sweet
neutral	READY-sweet	READY-dulce
	LISTO-dulce	LISTO-sweet

Note. As the present discussion focuses on the representation of translation equivalents, only the response times for those pairs will be discussed in the results. A complete description of the results can be found in Altarriba (1990).

Table 4 shows the number of items per stimulus list used as a function of RP and NR. Critical items were counterbalanced across lists and varied from list to list. A total of sixteen stimulus lists were formed. Each subject saw one list of 256 pairs which was presented with one of the following block orders: EE SE SS ES; SE SS ES EE; SS ES EE SE; or ES EE SE SS. Each of the four blocks was preceded by a practice block of 16 trials. Four observations were collected for each subject in each experimental condition.

Table 4

Number of Items per Stimulus List as a Function of RP (.33) and NR (.33)

	TP*	CP*
Word prime		
related word targets	32	32
semantically related	(16)	(16)
translations	(16)	(16)
unrelated word targets	64	16
nonword targets	32	16
Neutral prime		
word targets	96	16
nonword targets	32	16
TOTAL	256	96

*TP=Total pairs; CP=Critical pairs

Note. To clarify, the 256 trials were divided equally into the four language blocks within each list with the constraint that the RP and NR were maintained within each block as well as within each list overall.

Procedure. Subjects were given written instructions which informed them that they would be shown pairs of letter strings on a computer screen and that their task was to decide whether or not the second letter string of each pair was a word in a particular language. A message appeared on the screen at the beginning of each block of trials informing subjects of the language of the primes and targets in that particular block. Subjects were instructed to press the "m" key on the computer keyboard if the second letter string was a real word or the "z" key if it was not. Subjects were encouraged to respond as quickly and as accurately as possible.

On each trial, the first letter string appeared in uppercase, left-justified in the center of the screen. After a 200- or 1000-ms delay, the second letter string replaced the first. The second letter string was presented in lower-case letters. Successive letter string pairs appeared as subjects responded. If subjects responded with the wrong key, the word "ERROR" appeared centered on the computer screen.

Following the lexical decision task, subjects completed a Language History Questionnaire. An experimental session lasted approximately 45 minutes.

Results and Discussion

Mean reaction times were computed for each subject and each condition and are shown in Table 5. Response times outside the "upper outer fence" (Tukey, 1977) for each condition were classified as outliers and not included in the analyses of response times. In order to obtain a MSe for the evaluation of the planned contrasts, the data were submitted to separate 3 (priming condition: related, repetition/translation, or neutral) X 2 (prime language: English or Spanish) X 2 (target language: English or Spanish) ANOVAs for each SOA group.

Table 5

Mean Response Times (ms) to Word Targets in the Unrelated and Translation Priming Conditions and Mean Priming Effects

SOA Group/Prime-Target Language

Condition	200		1000	
	SE	ES	SE	ES
Unrelated	609	749	613	697
Translation	592	679	561	621
Priming Effects:	+17	+70*	+52*	+76*

Note. Priming effects in the translation condition were computed by subtracting the reaction times in that condition from the reaction times in the unrelated condition. The least significant difference for each facilitation effect was based on the MSe for the Priming Condition X Prime Language X Target Language interaction for each of the two SOA groups: 200-ms SOA = 3,779 and 1000-ms SOA = 3,542. SOA = stimulus onset asynchrony. SE = Spanish-English. ES = English-Spanish.
*p < .005, two-tailed.

Translation priming effects were highly significant for English-Spanish word pairs at both levels of SOA. Priming effects were also significant for Spanish-English word pairs at the long SOA but not at the short SOA. As explained above, increases in SOA lead to increases in the magnitude of the priming effect as subjects have more time to elaborate and perhaps translate the prime word before responding to the target word.

It appears that priming effects were greater for English- Spanish word pairs than for Spanish-English word pairs, although this difference was not significant at the long SOA ($p > .05$). These results were similar to those reported by Jin (1990). In his study, translation priming effects were greater when the primes were in the subjects' first language than when the primes were in the subjects' second language. In the present study, the subjects appeared to be more proficient in reading English than reading Spanish. When asked to rate how well they read in each language, the subjects rated English higher than Spanish in the 200-SOA group ($\underline{F}(1,31) = 7.54$, $\underline{MSe} = 1.194$, $\underline{p} = .01$) and in the 1000-SOA group ($\underline{F}(1,31) = 6.10$, $\underline{MSe} = 1.24$, $\underline{p} = .02$) (see Table 2). Based on this result and the fact that the subjects have been in United States schools for an average of 12 years, it appears that subjects might best be described as English-Spanish bilinguals for the purposes of this study. Thus, the trend in the data suggests that translation priming effects may be stronger from L1 to L2 than from L2 to L1. This result will be addressed in the final section of this chapter.

Conclusions

An important issue that has been studied in the area of bilingual memory is whether the two languages of a bilingual are stored independently or are mediated through a common conceptual representation. Early investigations involved episodic or short-term memory tasks in which subjects were given an initial orienting task during a study period and were then unexpectedly tested on their retention for the studied material. The language of both the study and test materials was varied. These studies addressed issues of language processing and the representation of meaning in episodic memory rather than the representation of meaning in long-term, semantic memory.

Semantic memory tasks have also been used to investigate bilingual memory. Most of the experimental evidence regarding semantic representation in bilinguals has been gathered using visual masking and semantic priming techniques. Response times to target words are measured following the presentation of a translation equivalent or a semantically-related prime word. The new evidence presented here strongly suggests that translation equivalents share an underlying conceptual representation, and that this representation mediates facilitation in priming between the two words.

Although not included in this review, two other tasks that have been used to investigate bilingual memory are bilingual naming and translation (see, e.g., Chen, 1990; Chen & Leung, 1989; Kroll & Curley, 1987; Potter, So, Von Eckardt, & Feldman, 1984). In these tasks, subjects either name words or pictures in a particular language or translate words presented in one language into another language. These tasks are most informative about the nature of lexical processing in bilinguals. Their results suggest that both methods of language acquisition and proficiency in a non-native language are important determinants for the patterns of lexical processing in bilinguals.

The following section discusses the implications of the current results for issues concerning second language acquisition and language development.

Acquiring a Second Language

Research on first- and second- language acquisition is of interest for both theoretical and practical reasons, as research findings may be utilized to teach a second language (see, e.g., Winitz, 1981). A model of language representation recently developed by Kroll and Stewart (1990) and discussed by Kroll, Altarriba, Sholl, Mazibuko, and Stewart (1991) is supported by the current results and illustrates a developmental process in second language acquisition. The model assumes that a bilingual has a large lexical store for his/her first language and a smaller store for the second language. A third store, a conceptual store, is closely linked to the bilingual's first language. As the bilingual acquires words in the second language, those words are connected via lexical links to words in the first language store. Subsequently, as a bilingual becomes more proficient in the second language, direct conceptual links from the second language store to conceptual memory are also acquired.

The model assumes that conceptual links between languages are stronger from L1 to L2 than from L2 to L1, as the former links are the first to be acquired. Therefore, priming is facilitated to the degree that the prime is a member of the larger language store. As a bilingual becomes more proficient in the second language to the point of becoming equally proficient in both languages, it is predicted that facilitation should be about equal in both directions.

The above developmental model suggests that as one becomes more proficient in a second language, one is able to directly access conceptual memory from a word in the second language. This conclusion suggests that new methodologies in teaching should be aimed at enhancing conceptual mediation to facilitate second language acquisition. Methods emphasizing concepts and conceptual representation in addition to lexical, word-to-word representation are to be preferred.

Acknowledgments

This work was supported by NIH Grant HD07327 for training in psycholinguistics and NIMH Grant MH44246 awarded to Judith F. Kroll. The research reported here was based on a doctoral dissertation submitted by the author to Vanderbilt University.

References

Altarriba, J. (1990). *Constraints on interlingual facilitation effects in priming in m Spanish-English bilinguals.* Unpublished doctoral dissertation, Vanderbilt University.

Balota, D. A., & Lorch, R. F. (1986). Depth of semantic spreading activation: Mediated priming effects in pronunciation but not in lexical decision. *Journal of Experimental Psychology: Learning, Memory, and Cognition,* 12, 336-345.

Chen, H.-C. (1990). Lexical processing in a non-native language: Effects of language proficiency and learning strategy. *Memory and Cognition*, 18, 279-288.

Chen, H.-C., & Leung, Y. S. (1989). Patterns of lexical processing in a non-native language. *Journal of Experimental Psychology: Learning, Memory, & Cognition*, 15, 316-325.

Chen, H.-C., & Ng, M.-L. (1989). Semantic facilitation and translation priming effects in Chinese-English bilinguals. *Memory & Cognition*, 17, 454-462.

Clifton, C., Sorce, P., Schaye, P., & Fiszman, A. (1978). Translation between language in memory. *American Journal of Psychology*, 91, 237-249.

de Groot, A. M. B. (1984). Primed lexical decision: Combined effects of the proportion of related prime-target pairs and the stimulus-onset asynchrony of prime and target. *Quarterly Journal of Experimental Psychology*, 36A, 253-280.

de Groot, A. M. B., & Nas, G. L. J. (1991). Lexical representation of cognates and noncognates in compound bilinguals. *Journal of Memory and Language*, 30, 90-123.

Frenck, C., & Pynte, J. (1987). Semantic representation and surface forms: A look at across-language priming in bilinguals. *Journal of Psycholinguistic Research*, 16, 383-396.

Grainger, J., & Beauvillain, C. (1988). Associative priming in bilinguals: Some limits of interlingual facilitation effects. *Canadian Journal of Psychology*, 42, 261-273.

Jin, Y.-S. (1990). Effects of concreteness on cross-language priming in lexical decisions. *Perceptual and Motor Skills*, 70, 1139-1154.

Keatley, C., Spinks, J., & de Gelder, B. (1990). *Asymmetrical semantic facilitation between languages: Evidence for separate representational systems in bilingual memory.* Unpublished manuscript, University of Tilberg, The Netherlands.

Kirsner, K., Brown, H. L., Abrol, S., Chadha, N. K., & Sharma, N. K. (1980). Bilingualism and lexical representation. *Quarterly Journal of Experimental Psychology*, 32, 585-594.

Kirsner, K., Smith, M. C., Lockhart, R. L. S., King, M. L., & Jain, M. (1984). The bilingual lexicon: Language-specific units in an integrated network. *Journal of Verbal Learning and Verbal Behavior*, 23, 519-539.

Kolers, P. A. (1966). Interlingual facilitation of short-term memory. *Journal of Verbal Learning and Verbal Behavior*, 5, 314-319.

Kroll, J. F., Altarriba, J., Sholl, A., Mazibuko, T., & Stewart, E. (1991, June). *Asymmetric connections in bilingual memory.* Poster presented at the annual meeting of the American Psychological Society, Washington, D.C.

Kroll, J. F., & Curley, J. (1987). Lexical memory in novice bilinguals: The role of concepts in retrieving second language words. In M. M. Gruneberg, P. E. Morris, & R. N. Sykes (Eds.), *Practical aspects of memory: Current research and issues* Vol. 2 (pp. 389-395). London: Wiley.

Kroll, J. F., & Stewart, E. (1990, November). *Concept mediation in bilingual translation.* Paper presented at the annual meeting of the Psychonomic Society, New Orleans.

Leont'ev, A. (1973). Some psychological aspects of language acquisition: Verbal memory, translation, and the significance of errors. *Soviet Psychology*, 11, 84-92.

Liepmann, D., & Saegert, J. (1974). Language tagging in bilingual free recall. *Journal of Experimental Psychology*, 103, 1137-1141.

Lopez, M., & Young, R. K. (1974). The linguistic interdependence of bilinguals. *Journal of Experimental Psychology*, 102, 981-983.

MacLeod, C. M. (1976). Bilingual episodic memory: Acquisition and forgetting. *Journal of Verbal Learning and Verbal Behavior*, 15, 347-364.

McCormack, P. D. (1974). Bilingual linguistic memory: Independence or interdependence: Two stores or one? In S. T. Carey (ed.), *Bilingualism, biculturalism and education.* Edmonton, Canada: University of Alberta.

McCormack, P. D. (1977). Bilingual linguistic memory: The independence-interdependence issue revisited. In P. A. Hornby (Ed.), *Bilingualism.* New York: Academic Press.

McNamara, T. P., & Altarriba, J. (1988). Depth of spreading activation revisited: Semantic mediated priming occurs in lexical decisions. *Journal of Memory and Language*, 27, 545-559.

Meyer, D. E., & Ruddy, M. G. (1974, April). *Bilingual word recognition: Organization and retrieval of alternative lexical codes.* Paper presented at the annual meeting of the Eastern Psychological Association, Philadelphia, PA.

Meyer, D. E., & Schvaneveldt, R. W. (1971). Facilitation in recognizing pairs of words: Evidence of dependence between retrieval operations. *Journal of Experimental Psychology*, 90, 227-234.

Neely, J. H. (1976). Semantic priming and retrieval from lexical memory: Evidence for facilatory and inhibitory processes. *Memory & Cognition*, 4, 648-654.

Neely, J. H. (1977). Semantic priming and retrieval from lexical memory: Roles of inhibitionless spreading activation and limited capacity attention. *Journal of Experimental Psychology: General*, 106, 226-254.

Neely, J. H. (1990). Semantic priming effects in visual word recognition: A selective review of current findings and theories. In D. Besner & G. Humphreys (Eds.), *Basic processes in reading: Visual word recognition* (pp. 264-336). Hillsdale, N. J.: Erlbaum.

Neely, J. H., & Keefe, D. E. (1989). Semantic context effects on visual word processing: A hybrid prospective/retrospective processing theory. In G. H. Bower (Ed.), *The psychology of learning and motivation: Advances in research and theory* Vol. 24, (pp. 207-248). New York: Academic Press.

Neely, J. H., Keefe, D. E., & Ross, K. L. (1989). Semantic priming in the lexical decision task: Roles of prospective prime-generated expectancies and retrospective semantic matching. *Journal of Experimental Psychology: Learning, Memory, and Cognition*, 15, 1003-1019.

O'Neill, W. (1977). Visual masking by translation equivalents in bilinguals. *Perceptual and Motor Skills*, 45, 1311-1314.

Postman, L., & Keppel, G. (Eds.) (1970). *Norms of word association*. New York: Academic Press.

Potter, M. C., So, K.-F., Von Eckardt, B., & Feldman, L. B. (1984). Lexical and conceptual representation in beginning and proficient bilinguals. *Journal of Verbal Learning and Verbal Behavior*, 23, 23-38.

Quillian, M. R. (1962). A revised design for an understanding machine. *Mechanical Translation*, 7, 17-29.

Scarborough, D. L., Gerard, L., & Cortese, C. (1984). Independence of lexical access in bilingual word recognition. *Journal of Verbal Learning and Verbal Behavior*, 23, 84-99.

Schwanenflugel, P. J., & Rey, M. (1986). Interlingual semantic facilitation: Evidence for a common representational system in the bilingual lexicon. *Journal of Memory and Language*, 25, 605-618.

Smith, C. C., Davies, G. A., & Hall, H. B. (1989). *Langenscheidt's compact Spanish dictionary*. New York: Langenscheidt.

Tukey, J. W. (1977). *Exploratory data analysis.* Reading, MA: Addison-Wesley.

Tweedy, J. R., & Lapinski, R. H. (1981). Facilitating word recognition: Evidence for strategic and automatic factors. *Quarterly Journal of Experimental Psychology,* 33A, 51-59.

Watkins, M. J., & Peynircioglu, Z. F. (1983). On the nature of word recall: Evidence for linguistic specificity. *Journal of Verbal Learning and Verbal Behavior,* 22, 385-394.

Winitz, H. (Ed.) (1981). *Native language and foreign language acquisition.* New York: New York Academy of Sciences.

Cognitive Processing in Bilinguals – R.J. Harris (Editor)
© *1992 Elsevier Science Publishers B.V. All rights reserved.*

The Influence of Semantic Cues in Learning Among Bilinguals at Different Levels of Proficiency in English[1]

J. Y. Opoku
University of Ghana

Abstract

Four groups of bilinguals at different levels of proficiency in English, their second language, participated in a study aimed at determining the influence of semantic cues in learning at the different levels of proficiency in English. Subjects at each level of proficiency learned two lists of sentences, first in one language, then in the other. The sentences of the two lists were either semantically unrelated or translations. Performance was measured by the degree and direction of "transfer" from one language to the other. Findings showed that only bilinguals at higher levels of proficiency in English derived some benefit on the tasks.

The influence that a second language of a bilingual could exercise on the first language and vice versa is of linguistic, educational, and psychological interest. The linguistic interest is mainly concerned with the question of interference from one language to the other, while the educational interest is mainly on the effect of the language of instruction in learning the school curriculum (see for example: Spencer, 1971; Bamgbose, 1976).

The psychological interest has centered mainly on questions of the type of storage or representational systems that bilinguals possess for their two languages. Two main theories have been formulated. One theory holds that there is a common store of information that the two languages merely tap (e.g., Anderson, 1976; Kintsch, 1974; Norman & Rumelhart, 1975). The other theory holds that there are separate stores for bilinguals and the acquisition of information is language- or means-dependent (e.g., Kolers, 1978; Kolers & Gonzalez, 1980; Paivio, 1971, 1978).

In developing countries where a second language is the Lingua Franca owing to colonial heritage, the questions posed above may still be relevant, but new theories which can take account of the peculiar bilingual situations in such countries need to be formulated. In addition, the important question of what cognitive processes go on when a bilingual is functioning in one language has not been properly addressed by language scholars and psychologists.

In previous research reports, the author has argued that while competent adult bilinguals in developing countries may possess separate representational systems for their two languages, young bilinguals who are still in the process of achieving adequate proficiency in their second language (which is a foreign language) may possess a common representational system. It was argued and partially supported by findings that there is a development from a common (fused) representational system to separate representational systems with increasing proficiency in the second language (Opoku, 1983). Further research however, revealed that proficiency in a second language may not be the sole determinant of the degree of separation of representational systems of bilinguals. Other factors like the history of the learning of the second language (e.g., whether the individual matches new words and concepts in the second language to their mother tongue equivalents during learning) may also go to determine the degree of separation shown as a competent adult bilingual. It was demonstrated that university students categorized as "low" in separation benefited more on interlingual and free-recall tasks than those categorized as "high" in separation, although the two categorized groups were equally proficient in English, their second language (Opoku, 1982, 1985).

The interactive process between a first language (mother tongue) and a second language (English) was investigated on a "transfer" task among Yoruba[2]-English bilinguals at different levels of proficiency in English, their second language (Opoku, 1987). Three groups of subjects at different levels of proficiency in English participated in a study of "transfer" of learning from English to Yoruba and from Yoruba to English using translation equivalent English and Yoruba sentences. From the developmental hypothesis of separation of representational systems earlier described (Opoku, 1983), it was predicted that "transfer" from one language to the other would decrease with increasing proficiency in English and that "transfer" from Yoruba (the mother tongue) to English (the second language) would be higher than from English to Yoruba at lowers levels of proficiency in English. These predictions were derived from a hypothesis (Opoku, 1983) that English words and concepts initially derive their meanings from their Yoruba equivalents, but that with higher proficiency in English, meanings become differentiated in the two languages. The learning of Yoruba sentences was therefore expected to facilitate the learning of translation equivalent English sentences at lower levels of proficiency in English.

Similarly, the learning of English sentences was expected to facilitate the learning of translation equivalent Yoruba sentences for subjects at lower levels of proficiency in English, but the gain here was expected to be less than the gain derived from the Yoruba to English learning. This was because theoretically, the English sentences must be referred to a more developed Yoruba representational system during learning, and having already learned the Yoruba sentences should make the task easier than when the Yoruba sentences are yet to be learned. Any positive gains from Yoruba to English and from English to Yoruba were expected to be less at higher levels of proficiency in English because of the expected greater separation of representational systems and the somewhat independent functioning of the two languages.

Findings rather showed that "transfer" increased with increasing proficiency in English, and that "transfer" from English to Yoruba was higher than from Yoruba to English for all groups. However, the semantic influence of Yoruba on English seemed much greater than that of English on Yoruba and increased with proficiency in English.

While the above study demonstrated the differential influence of semantic cues in learning among bilinguals at different levels of proficiency in English, other issues were raised from the results. These issues concerned whether or not subjects at lower levels of proficiency in English could also have benefited from the semantic cues had they been required to recall the sentences verbatim, as was done in the study. Secondly, since there were no control conditions in the various groups, it is possible that the "transfer" scores recorded represented in part such "carry-over effects" as practice effects and "learning to learn"?

The major aim of this study was to answer the above questions by using more stringent controls. A secondary aim was to determine whether or not the 1987 findings could be replicated in a bilingual setting in Ghana, similar to the Yoruba-English bilingual setting in Nigeria.

Method

Subjects

A total of 320 subjects made up of primary, secondary, and university students considered to be at different levels of proficiency in English participated in the study. Eighty subjects were selected from junior secondary school (JSS 1) with just over six years formal education. Their mean age was 12.4 years (S.D. = 2.1 yrs.). Eighty subjects were selected from middle form 4 with just over nine years formal education. Their mean age was 15.0 years (S.D. = 2.3 yrs.). Eighty subjects were selected from secondary form 3 with just over twelve years formal education. Their mean age was 17.5 years (S.D. = 1.9 yrs.). Eighty subjects were first and second year students of the University of Ghana with well over sixteen years formal education. Their mean age was 21.3 years (S.D. = 2.3 yrs.). Both sexes were about equally represented in all the age groups. All subjects were native Twi[3] speakers who were exposed to English for the first time at school and spoke Twi at home. All subjects had no functional knowledge in any other language.

In the Ghanaian culture, as in many cultures in developing countries with English as the lingua franca, English is the single most important factor in education in the early school years and is used as the medium of instruction in schools. The number of years spent at school could therefore be considered a good estimate of level of proficiency in English. It was reasonably assumed that the four age groups were at different levels of proficiency in English, given the large differences between them in the number of years spent in the formal educational system. For convenience, the four age groups are referred to as Level 1 (L1), Level 2 (L2), Level 3 (L3) and Level 4 (L4) proficiency in English groups, respectively.

Materials

Three lists, each list made up of six sentences, were constructed. List 1 (LE, English list) consisted of six English sentences and was the same as the list used in the 1987 study. List 2 (LUT, unrelated Twi list) consisted of six Twi sentences that were semantically unrelated to the list 1 sentences. List 3 (LTT, Twi translations list) consisted of six Twi sentences that were translations of the list 1 sentences. A pre-test had shown that the three lists were about equally difficult to learn by equivalent age groups of subjects. The sentences of the three lists were also about equal in length (see Table 1).

Table 1

Lists of sentences used in the study

List 1: (LE, English list)

1. We shall carefully examine your case.
2. He always complains in my absence.
3. My sister's house is opposite the market.
4. She said she was dressing up.
5. She drank wine in my presence.
6. I went to his office but didn't find him in.

List 2: (LUT, unrelated Twi list)

1. Osaa yie paa wo afahye no ase.
2. Yewo nhuren fefe bi wo yen sukuu mu.
3. Ope akutu ne kwadu yie.
4. Oka kyeree abofra no se ontwen no.
5. Misiim koo afuom ansa na awia epue.
6. Me wofa wo kraman kesee bi wo ne fie.

List 3: (LTT, translations Twi list)

1. Yebeto yen bo ase ashehwe w'asem no mu.
2. Daa se minni ho a na okasakasa.
3. Me nuabaa fie ne edwa no di ahwe animu.
4. Okaa se osiesie ne ho.
5. Mekoo n'adwuma mu nanso na onni ho.

The sentences were pre-recorded on cassette tapes. One tape contained the List 1 sentences (LE) recorded over 8 trials. List 2 sentences (LUT) were also recorded over 8 trials on the same side of the tape after the List 1 recording. On the reverse side of the tape, the List 2 sentences (LUT) were recorded over 8 trials, followed by the List 1 sentences (LE), also recorded over 8 trials. A second cassette tape contained recordings over 8 trials of List 1 (LE) followed by List 3 (LTT). On the reverse side of the same tape, LTT sentences were recorded first followed by the LE sentences, both over 8 trials. There was an interval of about 2 seconds between sentence recordings in each language and an inter-trial interval of about 4 seconds. The interval between English and Twi or Twi and English recordings, as the case may be, was about 10 seconds. The order of presentation of sentences in each language was randomly mixed from trial to trial.

Design

All subjects participated in a learning task, first in one language, then in the other. For each age group, a quarter of the subjects (20) were exposed to List 1 (LE) for 8 trials and then to the unrelated Twi list (List 2, LUT), also for 8 trials. Another quarter of the subjects were exposed first to the unrelated Twi list (LUT) and then to the English list (LE). A third quarter were exposed first to LE followed by LTT. The last quarter were exposed first to LTT and then to LE. The four testing conditions for each age group were therefore as follows:

Condition 1 (LE-LUT): Learn English list; learn unrelated Twi list.
Condition 2 (LUT-LE): Learn Twi list; learn unrelated English list.
Condition 3 (LE-LTT): Learn English list; learn translations equivalent Twi list.
Condition 4 (LTT-LE): Learn Twi list; learn translations equivalent English list.

With four levels of proficiency in English (L1, L2, L3, L4), two orders of testing or language of recall (English to Twi or Twi to English), and two types of material (semantically unrelated or translations), the design was a three-way factorial design with repeated measures on language of recall.

Procedure

Subjects were randomly assigned to the various conditions. The experiment took place in an office for the Level 1, Level 2, and Level 3 subjects and in the psychological laboratory for the Level 4 subjects.

The subject sat facing two experimenters (assistants) and a tape recorder. The experiments then instructed a subject learning first in English and then in Twi as follows:

> We are going to play from this cassette tape recorder a list of six English sentences. We want you to listen attentively to the sentences as they are played and to remember them. At the end of the list, you will be given one minute to tell us (recall) as many of the sentences as you can remember in any order, but you must try to recall the sentences in their correct grammatical form. If you are unable to recall all the sentences correctly within the one minute period, we shall play the sentences a second time and ask you to recall them again in one minutes. We shall keep on doing this until you are able to correctly recall all the sentences.

The experimenters made sure that the subject understood the instructions clearly (through further instructions, clarifications, etc.) before proceeding to test the subject. At the end of each trial, the experimenters, working together, scored sentences correctly recalled by the subject on prepared record sheets. A stop watch was used to time the subject during recall. The procedure was continued for the 8 trials irrespective of whether or not the subject had learned the list before the 8th trial. At the end of the 8th trial, the subject was then instructed in Twi that the procedure was to be repeated in Twi for 6 Twi sentences. At the end of the 8th trial in Twi, the experiment was discontinued, the subject rewarded with two ball-point pens (for the Level 1, Level 2, and Level 3 subjects) or thanked for participation and promised a reward later (in the case of the Level 4 subjects). Instructions and procedure for subjects in the other conditions were the same but of course with the order reversed in the Twi first and English second conditions.

Scoring of Data

There were two scores for each subject; a score at the verbatim level of recall and a score at the semantic-support level of recall (i.e., where subject captures the meaning of a sentence but is unable to recall it verbatim). The number of errors made in learning both the English and Twi lists to the criterion of 8 trials was computed for each subject, both at the verbatim and semantic-support levels. We also computed for each subject a percentage "transfer" score from first to second learning using the formula:

$$\text{Percent "Transfer"} = \frac{(\text{Errors on 1st learn.} - \text{Errors on 2nd learn.})}{(\text{Errors on 1st learning})} \times 100$$

This measure of "transfer", of course, is a measure of relative improvement from the first to the second learning and controls for differences in learning abilities between individuals. It is therefore meaningful to compare subjects at different levels of proficiency in English and Twi on this measure (see 1987 study).

Results

Table 2 shows the means and standard deviations of the errors made by all groups of subjects at both the verbatim and semantic-support levels.

A test on first learning difficulty was performed by comparing errors on the English list (LE) between the semantically unrelated (LE-LUT) and translations equivalent (LE-LTT) conditions and on the Twi lists between the semantically unrelated (LUT-LE) and translations equivalent (LTT-LE) conditions for all groups.

Table 3 shows the results obtained from the above analysis.

Table 2

Mean number of errors committed on a learning task by 4 groups of subjects at different levels of proficiency in English (total possible maximum error value = 48)

(a): Errors at verbatim level

Level of proficiency in English (L)		Unrelated lists				Translations lists		
		LE - LUT		LUT - LE		LE - LTT		LTT - LE
L1	Mean	47.1	34.7	40.8	46.2	46.1	35.3	40.6	47.2
	S.D	2.2	8.3	7.4	2.6	3.2	8.0	7.4	1.5
L2	Mean	46.0	30.8	31.8	40.4	46.3	28.6	35.0	43.9
	S.D	4.3	8.1	8.1	9.2	1.7	7.8	8.1	8.0
L3	Mean	30.0	24.2	24.5	24.1	23.1	17.8	29.0	27.5
	S.D.	9.2	7.8	8.2	8.5	5.9	9.5	9.6	7.2
L4	Mean	25.0	20.9	25.8	22.0	27.7	22.3	29.6	20.0
	S.D.	7.3	9.4	8.8	6.4	8.0	9.8	5.0	7.8

(b): Errors at semantic-support level

Level of proficiency in English (L)		Unrelated lists				Translations lists		
		LE - LUT		LUT - LE		LE - LTT		LTT - LE
L1	Mean	39.8	16.7	16.3	35.9	38.3	18.7	21.5	38.1
	S.D.	5.0	5.9	6.7	6.0	6.0	6.0	8.8	5.3
L2	Mean	37.3	12.1	15.8	29.7	35.7	17.2	23.0	34.8
	S.D.	6.4	5.0	8.4	9.5	5.4	8.0	9.4	8.6
L3	Mean	16.1	11.3	11.4	13.7	11.6	7.2	15.0	13.2
	S.D.	9.6	5.8	4.2	7.4	5.8	4.2	6.7	6.0
L4	Mean	11.1	6.6	11.4	9.7	13.2	5.5	14.0	8.4
	S.D.	4.3	3.4	7.7	5.7	6.5	3.2	5.8	4.4

Table 3

Mean number of errors on first list for four groups of subjects at different levels of proficiency in English

Errors	Level of proficiency in English (L)		English list (LE)		Twi lists (LUT, LTT)	
			LE - LUT	LE - LTT	LUT - LE	LTT - LE
Errors at verbatim level	L1	Mean	47.1	46.1	40.8	40.6
		S.D.	2.2	3.2	7.4	7.4
		$t(38)$	1.158, n.s.		0.106, n.s.	
	L2	Mean	46.0	46.3	31.9	35.0
		S.D.	4.3	1.9	8.1	8.1
		$t(38)$	0.285, n.s.		1.218, n.s.	
	L3	Mean	30.0	23.1	24.5	29.0
		S.D.	9.2	5.9	8.2	9.6
		$t(38)$	2.823, $p<.01^*$		1.598, n.s.	
	L4	Mean	25.0	27.7	25.8	29.6
		S.D.	7.3	8.0	8.8	5.0
		$t(38)$	1.097, n.s.		1.662, n.s.	
Errors at s-s level	L1	Mean	39.8	38.3	16.3	21.5
		S.D.	5.0	6.0	6.7	8.8
		$t(38)$	0.826, n.s.		2.129, $p<.05^*$	
	L2	Mean	37.3	35.7	15.8	23.0
		S.D.	6.4	5.4	8.4	9.4
		$t(38)$	0.880, n.s.		2.581, $p<.01^*$	
	L3	Mean	16.1	11.6	11.4	15.0
		S.D.	9.6	5.8	4.2	6.7
		$t(38)$	1.793, n.s.		1.873, n.s.	
	L4	Mean	13.3	14.0	11.4	14.0
		S.D.	5.0	5.8	7.7	5.8
		$t(38)$	0.432, n.s.		1.211, n.s.	

[*]Two-tailed test

Table 4

Percentage "transfer"[*] scores for four groups of subjects at different levels of proficiency in English

	Level of proficiency in English (L)		English to Twi LE - LUT	LE - LTT	Twi to English LUT - LE	LTT - LE	Mean of level Total
"Transfer" at verb. level	L1	Mean S.D.	26.7 16.2	23.9 14.8	-20.1 42.7	-21.5 30.4	2.1
	L2	Mean S.D.	33.0 16.6	38.3 16.2	-29.4 23.0	-31.9 39.4	2.5
	L3	Mean S.D.	15.9 26.7	23.9 35.0	-8.0 49.7	5.9 75.2	
	L4	Mean S.D.	15.5 33.7	17.7 35.0	4.0 51.8	33.0 21.4	17.5

Mean Order Total   English to Twi = 24.3   Twi to English = -10.3

Mean Type Total   Unrelated = 4.7   Translations = 9.3

	Level of proficiency in English (L)		English to Twi LE - LUT	LE - LTT	Twi to English LUT - LE	LTT - LE	Mean of level Total
"Transfer" at s-s level	L1	Mean S.D.	58.5 13.6	50.9 15.0	-170.7 195.6	-113.1 112.6	-43.6
	L2	Mean S.D.	67.6 11.2	52.9 18.9	-125.7 106.4	-65.9 57.5	-17.8
	L3	Mean S.D.	18.1 45.6	36.1 48.1	-27.6 66.8	7.2 38.7	8.4
	L4	Mean S.D.	35.3 39.1	59.6 26.9	-11.2 99.4	37.5 27.9	30.3

Mean Order Total   English to Twi = 47.4   Twi to English = -58.7

Mean Type Total   Unrelated = -19.5   Translations = 8.2

[*]Percentage "Transfer" = $\dfrac{\text{(Errors on 1st learn.-Errors on 2nd learn.)}}{\text{(Errors on 1st learning)}} \times 100$

At the verbatim level, the results shows that the L3 group in the LE-LUT condition found the English list (LE) more difficult than those learning in the LE-LTT condition. At the semantic-support level, both the L1 and L2 groups found the Twi translations list (LTT) more difficult than the semantically unrelated Twi list (LUT). Thus, it appears that either complete randomization was not achieved in the study or that LUT and LE for conditions 2 and 3 respectively (see design) were not equivalent in difficulty for these groups of subjects despite efforts to achieve this through pre-tests, or that both factors contributed to the results.

Table 4 shows the "transfer" scores at both the verbatim and semantic-support levels of performance.

A 2 X 2 X 4 ANOVA was employed to analyze the "transfer" scores. For clairty of presentation, the results are summarized in Table 5.

Table 5

Summary table from 2 X 2 X 4 ANOVA on "transfer" data in Table 4

| | Level of performance | | | | | |
| Variable(s) | Verbatim | | | Semantic-support | | |
	F	df	p	F	df	p
Level of Education	3.12	3,304	<.05	14.65	3,304	<.001
Type of Material	1.28	1,304	n.s.	10.95	1,304	.001
Order of Presentation	71.38	1,304	<.001	160.49	1,304	<.001
Level X Type	0.91	3,304	n.s.	0.12	3,304	n.s.
Level X Order	12.45	3,304	<.001	24.43	3,304	<.001
Type X Order	0.14	1,304	n.s.	7.23	1,304	<.01
Level X Type X Order	1.01	3,304	n.s.	0.76	3,304	n.s.

Inspection of Table 4 reveals that subjects "transfer" more with increasing level of proficiency in English irrespective of the type of material and the order of presentation. Thus, the significant F values were obtained at both the verbatim and semantic-support levels for Level of Education (Table 5).

At the verbatim level, type of material did not affect overall performance but it affected performance at the semantic-support level, with greater "transfer" on the translations list than on the nontranslations list. Inspection of Table 4 again reveals that there was greater "transfer" when the presentation was in the order: English to Twi (E-T) than when it was in the order: Twi to English (T-E), thus accounting for the significant results obtained on this variable at both the verbatim and semantic-support levels.

The significant Level X Order interaction obtained at both the verbatim and semantic-support levels and the Type X Order interaction obtained at the semantic-support level necessitated the use of multiple comparisons. The Newman-Keuls multiple range test was employed.

Intra-level comparisons showed that performance was significantly different between the translations and the nontranslations conditions at L1 (p <.05) and at L2 (p <.05), but this was true only when "transfer" was from Twi to English. Significant differences were also obtained at both L1 and L2 on the nontranslations lists irrespective of the order of presentation, (p <.01) at both levels. These findings were true at both the verbatim and semantic-support levels. No such differences were observed however at L3 and L4. Inter-level comparisons at the verbatim level revealed that when learning was from English to Twi, there was no difference between the comparison groups at any two levels irrespective of level of education and type of material. On the other hand, significant differences were observed between L4 and L1 (p <.01), between L4 and L2 (p <.01), and between L4 and L3 (p <.05) when learning was from Twi to English. No other differences were significant.

At the semantic-support level, no differences were observed between the different groups irrespective of level of education and type of material when learning was from English to Twi. However, when learning was from Twi to English, significant differences were observed between the comparison groups when the materials were both translations and nontranslations. This was true in all cases except between L1 and L2 and between L3 and L4 on the nontranslations material, where the differences were not significant.

Discussion

For any meaningful discussion of the results from this study, it is necessary to discuss the data on first learning difficulty (Table 3) in conjunction with the results obtained on "transfer", first at the verbatim level and then at the semantic-support level.

Performance at the verbatim level

It was expected that "transfer" under the translations (experimental) conditions would be greater than "transfer" (if any) under the nontranslations (control) conditions for subjects at lower levels of proficiency in English and that this difference would progressively decrease with increasing level of proficiency in English. Our findings show that this hypothesis was not supported at the verbatim level.

It was also expected that subjects at lower levels of proficiency in English would "transfer" more than those at higher levels of proficiency, assuming that the various levels did not differ from each other on the nontranslations lists. Our findings show that while the various levels did not differ on the nontranslations lists as expected, contrary to expectation, subjects at L4 "transferred" more than subjects at lower levels of proficiency but only when learning was from Twi to English. This finding supports the prediction that any benefit derived from Twi to English order of learning would be greater than the benefit derived from English to Twi order of learning (see introduction). However, the observation that the benefit seemed to increase with increasing level of proficiency in English is contrary to prediction derived from the Opoku (1983) hypothesis.

It is interesting to observe that when learning was from English to Twi, subjects at L3 learning the nontranslations lists (LE-LUT) found the English list more difficult than those learning the translations lists (LE-LTT). (See Table 3). This finding clearly shows that "transfer" as defined in this study did involve <u>semantic transfer</u> (being aided on the second learning by semantic cues provided on the first learning), for if this was not the case, then at L3, subjects learning the nontranslations lists should have "transferred" more than those learning the translations lists. That the opposite was the case (Table 4) clearly shows that semantic transfer is an important contributor to the "transfer" data shown in Table 4, at least for subjects at L3 and L4.

Performance at the semantic-support level

At this level of performance, "transfer" under the translations lists were higher than "transfer" under the nontranslations lists only at L1 and L2, and again, when learning was from Twi to English. Inspection of Table 3 shows that at L1 and L2, subjects were expected to "transfer" more under the translations conditions than under the nontranslations conditions because of the difficulty associated with learning the nontranslation Twi list compared to the translation Twi list when learning was from Twi to English. Therefore, the significant difference observed at L1 and L2 showing greater "transfer" under the translation condition was expected even if "transfer" did not involve any semantic transfer.

Inter-level comparisons showed that when learning was from English to Twi, the hypothesis that subjects at higher levels of proficiency in English would "transfer" less than those at lower levels was not supported by the data. However, when learning was from Twi to English, subjects at higher levels of proficiency in English "transfer" more than those at lower levels, the only nonsignificant difference being the difference observed between L3 and L4. However, this finding is also confounded by the observation that a similar finding was obtained under the nontranslations conditions.

It appears then that at the semantic-support level, no firm conclusions can be drawn from the results because of the confounding factor of list learning difficulty and also the fact that it was not possible to equate performance at all levels under the nontranslations conditions.

General discussion

It is clear from the results that "transfer" as defined in this study does not involve semantic transfer alone. If semantic transfer alone was the factor contributing to the "transfer" data, then there should have been no "transfer" under the nontranslations (control) conditions. Unfortunately, such "transfer" did occur. What then does "transfer" as defined in this study involve?

In addition to semantic transfer that was operative in this study, at least at the higher levels of proficiency in English, it is evident that list learning difficulty was another important factor accounting for the "transfer" data (see discussion above under 'performance at verbatim level'). Other possible factors that might have accounted for the "transfer" scores and that may not be unrelated to list learning difficulty were practice effects and ineptitude in the second language by children at the lowest levels of proficiency (L1 and L2).

It is clear from our results that the L1 and L2 subjects in particular were more proficient in Twi than in English (see Table 2). Indeed, among these two groups of subjects, it is of interest to observe that while "transfer" was positive when learning was from English to Twi, there was failure to "transfer" (negative "transfer"?) when learning was from Twi to English. Clearly, this finding alone demonstrates the ineptitude of the children in English and it is therefore difficult to draw any conclusions from the performance of these subjects.

Semantic transfer, which this study sought to measure at the different levels of proficiency in English seems to be masked by the confounding variables enumerated above, namely: 1) list learning difficulty; 2) practice effects; and 3) ineptitude in English by subjects at lower levels of proficiency in English.

It is clear however from the "transfer" data found from Table 2 that the above confounding variables are unlikely explanations of the performance of subjects at L3 and L4. At these levels, semantic transfer seems to account for a larger proportion of the "transfer" data.

Conclusions

In this study, we have been able to demonstrate that semantic cues facilitate learning at higher levels of proficiency in a second language, but this is true only at the verbatim level of performance and when learning is from the native language (Twi) to the second language (English).

It appears that even at the highest level of proficiency in English used in this study (university level), subjects still derive considerably more benefit when the cues are provided in their mother tongue than when they are provided in English, their second language. It is of interest to observe that even with stricter controls, the 1987 findings have, in the main, been replicated in a bilingual setting similar to the Yoruba-English bilingual setting in Nigeria.

What do the above findings mean in terms of the hypothesis of bilingual representational systems formulated? It appears from the present findings and from the findings of Opoku (1987) that at the level of the sentence, the hypothesis that there is an initial fusion of bilingual representational systems with gradual separation as proficiency increases in the second language does not hold. The main reason for this is that children at lower levels of proficiency in the second language are simply not skilled enough in the second language for the hypothesis to be meaningfully tested with the learning tasks employed in the present and the 1987 study At the level of the sentence, modified or new tests are needed to validate the account of the development of representational systems of bilinguals in developing countries.   This poses a challenge to bilingual psychologists interested in these problems.

If Opoku's (1983) hypothesis is correct, then the fact that school children at lower levels of proficiency in the second language do not derive any benefit on the learning tasks means that at the sentence and perhaps prose levels of learning, such children learn by rote (without much understanding) in the second language. They do not or cannot refer concepts to the more developed mother tongue representational system because of their ineptitude in the second language.   Therefore, efforts by school teachers to teach such school children to acquire the meanings of second language concepts via the medium of the mother tongue are wasted. Perhaps this explains why school children at these levels not only find it very difficult to communicate in any intelligible manner in the second language, but also find it difficult to understand basic mathematical and scientific concepts that are taught via the medium of the second language.

We may infer from our findings that being proficient in a second language may lead to better learning of second language concepts whose direct equivalents are available in the mother tongue. At least our findings demonstrate that young bilingual school children do not derive any benefit from obvious semantic cues provided them owing mainly to their ineptitude in their second language. An implication from this for education is that developing countries needs to intensify efforts to teach the second language more effectively in the early school years if bilingual school children are to derive any benefit from semantic influences across languages.

References

Anderson, J. R. (1976). *Language, memory, and thought.* Hillsdale, NJ: Lawrence Erlbaum.

Bamgbose, A. (Ed.). (1976). *Mother tongue education: the West African experience.* London: Hodder & Stoughton.

Kintsch, W. (1974). *The representation of meaning in memory.* Hillsdale, NJ: Lawrence Erlbaum.

Kolers, P. A. (1978). On the representations of experience. In D. Gerver & W. Sinaiko (Eds.) *Language interpretation and communication.* New York: Plenum.

Kolers, P. A. & Gonzalez, E. (1980). Memory for words, synonyms and translations. *Journal of Experimental Psychology: Human Learning and Memory, 6,* 53-65.

Norman, D. A. & Rumelhart, D. E. (1975). *Explorations in cognition*. San Francisco, CA: Freeman.

Opoku, J. Y. (1982). Bilingual representational systems and interlingual transfer of learning. *Journal of Cross-Cultural Psychology*, 13(4), 470-480.

Opoku, J. Y. (1983). The learning of English as a second language and the development of the emergent bilingual representational systems. *International Journal of Psychology*, 18, 271-283.

Opoku, J. Y. (1985). Bilingual representational systems in free recall. *Psychological Reports*, 57, 847-855.

Opoku, J. Y. (1987). Second language proficiency differences in the learning of semantically-equivalent bilingual sentences. *Applied Psycholinguistics*, 8, 75-84.

Paivio, A. (1971). *Imagery and verbal processes*. New York: Holt, Rinehart & Winston.

Paivio, A. (1978). Imagery, language and semantic theory. *International Journal of Psycholinguistics*, 5(2), 31-47.

Spencer, J. (Ed.). (1971). *The English language in West Africa*. London: Longman.

Notes

1. This research was supported by a grant from the Research and Conferences Fund of the University of Ghana.

2. Yoruba is a major indigenous language spoken in Nigeria.

3. Twi is the most widely spoken indigenous language in Ghana.

Cognitive Processing in Bilinguals – R.J. Harris (Editor)
191

Lexical and Conceptual Memory in Fluent and Nonfluent Bilinguals

Judith F. Kroll
Mount Holyoke College
and
Alexandra Sholl
University of Massachusetts at Amherst

Abstract

Research on bilingual memory suggests that words in each language are stored in separate lexical systems, but that concepts are stored in a representation common to both languages. When individuals are in early phases of acquiring a second language, lexical connections appear to mediate cross-language performance. However, as second language learners acquire expertise, they begin to conceptually mediate their understanding of second language words. In this chapter we focus on the implications of this change for second language representation. We present (1) evidence that suggests that lexical connections between the two languages remain active after concept mediation is achieved, and (2) a model of bilingual representation in which cross-language connections between lexical and conceptual memory are asymmetric.

Background

A central question in past research on cognitive processes in the bilingual is whether the bilingual represents his or her two or more languages in separate or common memory systems. The literature on bilingual language processing continues to focus on this question because the empirical evidence has produced conflicting results. For example, cross-language priming experiments have typically shown that words in different languages prime each other in semantic priming tasks (Altarriba, 1990; Chen & Ng, 1989; Meyer & Ruddy, 1974; Schwanenflugel & Rey, 1986; Tzelgov & Henik, 1989) but not in repetition priming tasks (Gerard & Scarborough, 1989; Kirsner, Smith, Lockhart, King, & Jain, 1984; Scarborough, Gerard, & Cortese, 1984). The finding of transfer in semantic priming tasks has been taken as support for the common memory model, whereas the failure to find transfer in repetition priming tasks has been taken as evidence for the multiple memory model. In general, findings with tasks that emphasize surface attributes support the independent or multiple memory model, and findings with tasks that emphasize semantic or conceptual attributes support the common memory model (Durgunoglu & Roediger, 1987).

The apparently conflicting evidence can be understood if one assumes that words in different languages are represented at the surface level by independent lexical representations but at the conceptual level by a common amodal representation. A hierarchical model (Potter, 1979; Potter & Kroll, 1987; Potter, So, von Eckhardt, &

Feldman, 1984), in which amodal conceptual representations accept input from a variety of surface representations, can accommodate the evidence, by assuming that the two types of memory systems operate at different levels, enabling different types of mental functions. Thus, cross-language semantic priming occurs because the two languages access a common conceptual representation. However, repetition priming, which may be constrained by the nature of activated lexical representations, would not be observed across languages because each language corresponds to independent lexical entries.

If we assume that the hierarchical model accurately reflects the different levels of knowledge we have associated with the languages we know, we can then ask how lexical memory for second language words becomes interconnected in this representational system as a second language is acquired. Two of the alternatives that have been considered in past research are presented schematically in Figure 1. The word association model proposes that second language words are associated to first language words and that only through first language mediation, do second language words gain access to concepts. In contrast, the concept mediation model proposes that second language words directly access concepts, in the same way that it has been proposed pictures do (e.g., Potter & Faulconer, 1975).

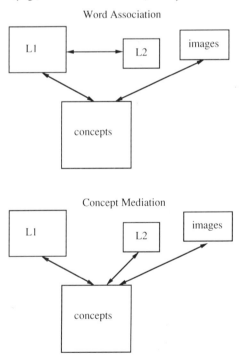

Figure 1. The Word Association and Concept Mediation models of lexical and conceptual memory in the bilingual. (Adapted from material in Potter, et al., 1984).

An initial test of these models was described by Potter et al. (1984). The logic of their study was to compare translation and picture naming, under the assumption that picture naming requires conceptual access. The two models make contrasting predictions about translation and picture naming into the second language. The word association model predicts that translation from the first language into the second should be substantially faster than naming a picture in the second language, because picture naming requires conceptual access whereas translation does not. In contrast, the concept mediation model predicts that translation and picture naming in the second language should be similar, because both require similar conceptual processing. Potter and her colleagues found that translating into the second language took about the same amount of time as naming pictures in the second language, and concluded that the pattern of results supported the concept mediation model. A surprising aspect of the results was that the same concept mediation pattern appeared to hold for all subjects, regardless of how fluent they were in the second language.

Kroll and Curley (1988) questioned the finding that all second language speakers are concept mediators regardless of their expertise. Indeed, people in early phases of second language learning often report that they are consciously aware of the first language. A reasonable alternative to the Potter et al. conclusion is that early in second language learning, individuals mediate understanding of second language words through the first language. That is, they follow the word association model. At later stages of second language learning, individuals may be able to directly understand the meaning of second language words without first language mediation. Kroll and Curley (1988) argued that past experiments may not have observed this change because the novice bilinguals tested in those studies, although far from being expert, were in fact beyond an early critical period of second language acquisition. When they compared translation and picture naming in a group of students learning German, with the group including students who had studied for less than two years, they found support for a shift from word association to concept mediation with increasing expertise. Their data are presented in a new way in Figure 2. The panel on the left is simply the time to name words and pictures in English, the native and dominant language of the subjects. These data replicate the standard word advantage in naming, and the two groups of subjects who differed only in their fluency in German, did not differ in English. The panel on the right shows the time to translate words and name pictures in the second language. The dark bars are the more fluent subjects and the striped bars are the less fluent subjects. The less fluent subjects were slower in the second language than the more fluent subjects, but the important result concerns the relative speed of translation and picture naming. For the less fluent subjects, translation times were faster than picture naming times, as the word association model predicts. For the more fluent subjects, translation and picture naming were not statistically different, as the concept mediation model predicts. These results thus supported the proposal that there is a shift during second language learning from a strategy of understanding second language words by accessing the first language, to a strategy in which concepts directly mediate second language comprehension. Chen and his colleagues have reported similar results in both cross-language Stroop tasks and in translation and picture naming tasks (Chen & Ho, 1986; Chen & Leung, 1989).

The goal of our research has been to determine whether the observed change in the processing of second language words reflects the hypothesized shift from reliance on first language words to reliance on concepts. The strategy that we have adopted is to look for evidence of conceptual processing in tasks in which context effects should be present if conceptual access has taken place. If our hypothesis about second language development is correct, then clear differences between beginning and more expert bilinguals should emerge in tasks that engage conceptual processes such that only more fluent bilinguals who conceptually mediate the second language should be influenced by the conceptual nature of the context. Thus we would expect that fluent bilinguals would be sensitive to cross-language context in priming paradigms, whereas beginning second language learners would not. And in past research that is the pattern that we have found (Kroll & Borning, 1987).

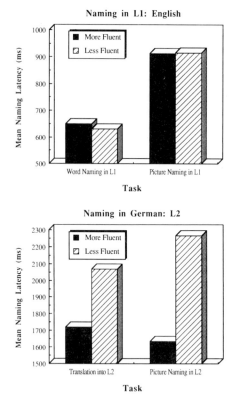

Figure 2. Data averaged from Kroll and Curley (1988). The time to name words and pictures in English and to translate words from English into German and to name pictures in German for subjects who were more and less fluent in German.

Despite the empirical support for the proposed shift from word association to concept mediation with increasing proficiency in the second language, there are two issues raised by the past research that require additional discussion. At a theoretical level, there is the question of the fate of the lexical connections once concept mediation is achieved. Do word associations between the two languages decay once an individual becomes more fluent? Or, do the initial lexical links between languages remain in place as an alternative route for processing the second language? At an empirical level, there is also a puzzling result that we have found repeatedly: the speed and accuracy of translation depends on the direction of translation. Performance is faster and more accurate to translate from the second language into the first (L2 to L1) than from the first language into the second (L1 to L2). A comparison of translation latencies for each direction of translation from a set of past studies is shown in Figure 3. These data are for subjects who were relatively fluent in their second language. The same pattern of results was found for nonfluent subjects, although they took longer than fluent subjects to perform both types of translation. The subjects in the Kroll and Curley (1988) and Kroll and Stewart (1989) studies were native English-speaking college students who were relatively fluent in German. The subjects in the Kroll and Stewart (1990) study were highly fluent Dutch-English bilinguals.

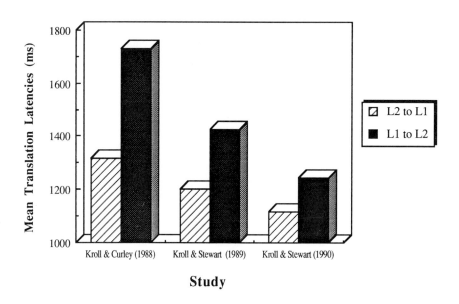

Figure 3.   A comparison of the speed of translation from L2 to L1 and L1 to L2 from three studies.   Note: The Kroll and Curley (1988) data above were from that study but did not appear in that paper.

Neither the concept mediation model nor the word association model can, in principle, account for this translation asymmetry without making additional assumptions. The two models make different predictions about the relative speed of translation compared to picture naming, but make no explicit predictions about the two directions of translation. If the longer time to translate from L1 to L2 was attributable to longer production latencies in the second language, then the difference between the two types of translation might be expected to mirror the difference between simple naming in the first and second languages. However, in the studies for which translation data is shown in Figure 3, we consistently find that the naming difference between L1 and L2 is smaller than the translation asymmetry. And because the initial recognition in naming the second language is also of a second language word, whereas initial recognition in translation is of the first language word, this comparison is likely to underestimate the translation effect relative to the naming difference.

Kroll and Stewart (1990) hypothesized that the difference in the two forms of translation reflected a difference in reliance on lexical vs conceptual mappings such that translation into L2 required concept mediation whereas translation into L1 could be accomplished by lexical mediation from L2 to L1. The observed asymmetry in translation latencies led us to propose that the strength of connections between lexical and conceptual representations differs for a bilingual's different languages primarily as a function of fluency in L2 and relative dominance of L1 to L2.[1] Specifically, lexical links from L2 to L1 are hypothesized to be stronger than lexical links from L1 to L2, but conceptual links for L1 are stronger than those for L2. Kroll and Stewart (1990) proposed a revision of the representational model of bilingual memory based on the asymmetry we have described. The revised model is shown in Figure 4.

In this chapter we examine bilingual performance in translation and semantic priming tasks to evaluate support for the proposed model. We draw on data from our own laboratory and from other recent studies to examine the hypothesized asymmetries. A critical prediction of the revised model is that translation from L1 into L2 is conceptually mediated and should therefore be more sensitive to conceptual context than translation from L2 into L1.

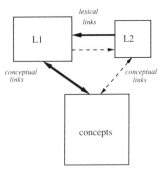

Figure 4. A revised hierarchical model of bilingual memory representation (from Kroll & Stewart, 1990).

Evidence from Translation

Kroll and Stewart (1991) compared translation and naming latencies for a group of highly fluent Dutch-English bilinguals. Subjects were asked to name or translate words in both languages in lists that were either semantically categorized or randomly mixed. The categorized lists contained words that were drawn from the same category (e.g., fruits or animals). Following the naming and translation portion of the experiment, subjects were given an incidental recall task. The translation data from that study are shown in Figure 5, where mean translation latencies are plotted as a function of the direction of translation (from L1 to L2 or from L2 to L1) and the type of list (categorized or randomized).

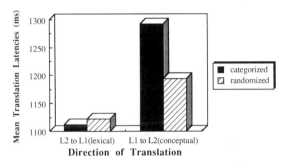

Figure 5. Mean translation latencies as a function of the direction of translation and whether the list was semantically categorized or not. Data are from highly fluent Dutch-English bilinguals.

The time to translate was significantly longer from L1 to L2 than from L2 to L1. But, most critical for the evaluation of the revised model, the semantic organization of the list had a significant effect only when subjects translated from L1 into L2. These results support the hypothesis that the translation route from L1 to L2 requires conceptual processing. The finding that categorized lists produced interference rather than facilitation in translation is similar to previous reports of category interference in Stroop-like translation tasks (La Heij, de Bruyn, Elens. Hartsuiker, Helaha, & van Schelven, 1990) and in picture naming (Kroll & Smith, 1989). Multiple access to conceptual memory may inhibit selection of a single lexical entry. Furthermore, the fact that the category structure of the list had no effect on translation from L2 to L1 supports the hypothesis that the route from L2 to L1 is mediated by lexical connections. The results are also consistent with the findings of studies that have examined tasks such as word naming that are hypothesized to be primarily lexical; word naming is not particularly sensitive to the effects of semantic priming (Lupker, 1984) or to the effects of category structure in lists (Kroll & Smith, 1989). The naming data in the Kroll and Stewart (1991) study replicated the previous results in that there were no effects of the type of list on the time to name words in either Dutch (L1) or in English (L2).

    Additional evidence to support the claim that translation from L1 to L2 is
conceptually mediated, but that translation from L2 to L1 is not, was provided by the
findings for incidental recall that followed the translation tasks in the Kroll and Stewart
(1991) study. These data are shown in Figure 6 where the mean percent recalled are
plotted as a function of the direction of translation and the type of list. The main
result was that significantly more words were recalled from the categorized list
condition than from the randomized list, but only when the direction of translation was
from L1 to L2. Although it might be argued that subjects were more aware of the
category structure in the L1 to L2 translation condition because the words appeared
in L1, recall for the same L1 words in categorized lists when the task was simple
naming was poor, and no better for categorized than randomized lists. The Kroll and
Stewart (1991) results thus suggest that the translation route from L1 to L2 specifically
engages conceptual information that influences the speed and accuracy of translation
performance and also has consequences for later tests of explicit memory.

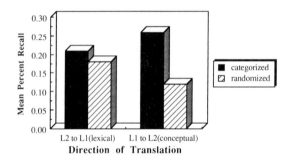

Figure 6. Mean percent incidental recall as a function of the direction of translation
and whether the list was semantically categorized or not. Data are from highly fluent
Dutch-English bilinguals.

    The revised model shown in Figure 4 can account for two important aspects of the
translation data we have described. First, the two directions of translation differ
because translation from L2 to L1 is more likely to be accomplished lexically than
translation from L1 to L2, which is more likely to engage conceptual processing. Just
as picture naming is longer than word naming (Potter & Faulconer, 1975), the more
conceptual route to translation will be longer than the lexical route. If this explanation
is correct, then the more conceptual translation (from L1 to L2) will also be more
likely to be influenced by the presence of conceptual factors, such as the category
structure of the list to be translated, and that has generally been the case in all of the
experiments in which we have compared the two forms of translation.

Evidence from Semantic Priming

Many previous studies have tested the concept mediation model of bilingual language representation by asking whether there is cross-language semantic priming. Under conditions that require rapid access to meaning to obtain priming, there should only be cross-language priming if both languages access a common conceptual memory representation. The main finding in the past literature is that semantic priming is typically found across as well as within languages for fluent bilinguals (e.g., Kirsner et al., 1984; Meyer & Ruddy, 1974; Schwanenflugel & Rey, 1986). This result is similar to cross-modal studies comparing priming between words and pictures (e.g., Kroll, 1990; Vanderwart, 1984).[2]   For both words in two languages and for pictures and words the priming data appear to support a model in which each surface form accesses a common semantic representation. However, recent studies that have carefully controlled the characteristics of the priming paradigm to optimize automatic aspects of processing (e.g., by following the suggestions of Neely, Keefe, and Ross [1989] to minimize the relatedness proportion and nonword ratio in the design of priming experiments) have reported asymmetries in the magnitude of semantic priming such that there is significant priming from L1 to L2 but less priming from L2 to L1 (Altarriba, 1990) or no priming at all from L2 to L1 (Keatley, Spinks, & de Gelder, 1990), even when the bilingual subjects are highly fluent in both languages. This asymmetry is consistent with the revised model. Especially under conditions in which there is only a brief interval or SOA between the prime and target, L1 primes will be more likely to activate conceptual relations than L2 primes. To the extent that semantic priming requires access to conceptual relations, there will only be cross-language priming when the second language is conceptually mediated.

Table 1 shows a comparison of the magnitude of cross-language semantic priming effects in those past bilingual priming studies that have included the relevant cross-language comparisons.   It is important to note that these studies varied widely in the version of the semantic priming task used, in the type of relation between primes and targets, in the language combinations of the bilingual subjects studied, and in the relative dominance of the bilinguals' two languages. Despite these differences, however, a clear pattern emerges in the comparison between the two directions of priming. In all but two cases shown in Table 1, there is a larger semantic priming effect from L1 to L2 than from L2 to L1. The two cases that fail to support the asymmetry show similar priming in both cross-language directions under conditions where the interval between the prime and target was relatively long. With a sufficiently long SOA, it may be possible to translate the L2 prime and use the stronger conceptual link with L1 to produce semantic priming.

The finding of asymmetric semantic priming, in and of itself, might be interpreted in a number of alternative ways. Even when bilingual subjects are truly bilingual, they are likely to be more dominant in L1 than in L2. When a prime is presented for a brief duration or when only a short interval separates a prime and target, it is reasonable that subjects would be able to extract more information from L1 than L2 primes.   However, taken together with the data on the effects of the direction of translation, the pattern of semantic priming results are most consistent with the interpretation that it is specifically the ease with which subjects can access conceptual representations from second language words, rather than their ability to extract information per se from second language words, that determines the magnitude of cross-language priming.

Table 1

A comparison of asymmetries in the magnitude of semantic priming for a set of bilingual priming studies that examined cross-language conditions.

Study	Language	SOA/ISI	Magnitude of Priming (ms)	
			L1 to L2	L2 to L1
Meyer & Ruddy(1974)	English/German[a]	Simultaneous	+ 143	+116
Kirsner, Smith, Lockhart, King, & Jain (1984)	French/English	2 s ISI	+ 44	+ 48
Schwanenflugel & Rey (1986)	English/Spanish	300 ms 100 ms	+ 135 + 63	+ 47 + 12
Frenck & Pynte (1987)	English/French	500 ms	+ 63	+ 51
Chen & Ng (1989)	Chinese/English	300 ms	+ 120[b]	+ 55
Keatley, Spinks, & de Gelder (1990)	Chinese/English Dutch/French	250 ms 2000 ms 200 ms	+ 38 + 13 + 20	- 6 - 8 - 1
Altarriba (1991)	English/Spanish	200 ms 1000 ms	+ 59 + 74	+ 35 + 40

[a]   The first language listed is either the native or the dominant language.
[b]   These values were estimated from published figures.

Conclusions

We have presented evidence from translation and semantic priming tasks that shows that there is an asymmetry in cross-language performance. Translation is slower and influenced by conceptual variables from L1 to L2 but not from L2 to L1. Likewise, semantic priming is greater from L1 to L2 than from L2 to L1. Taken together, the findings support the revised model of bilingual representation shown in Figure 4. Our analysis suggests that the architecture that describes the connections between a bilingual's two languages includes both lexical and conceptual links between the two languages, but that the strength of the connections differs for the two languages. Lexical links from L2 to L1 may be stronger than those from L1 to L2, particularly if second language acquisition occurs after early childhood, but conceptual links for L1 are likely to be stronger than those for L2. As greater fluency is acquired in L2, reliance on conceptual mediation between the two languages increases, although lexical connections remain active. The revised model leads to a number of interesting predictions concerning the directionality of cross-language connections that we plan to investigate in future research.

Footnotes

[1] The translation asymmetry data shown in Figure 3 were taken from three studies using bilingual samples who differed in their proficiency in using L2. Although the subjects in the Kroll and Curley (1988) and Kroll and Stewart (1989) studies were past a critical point of second language learning, they were much less fluent than the Dutch-English bilinguals in the Kroll and Stewart (1990) study, as evidenced by their strikingly long translation latencies. However, it is also clear from this comparison that L1 to L2 translation changes much more with increases in L2 fluency than L2 to L1 translation. This result is consistent with the hypothesis that it is the links between L2 and concepts that become strengthened with increasing second language proficiency. Examination of the direction-of-translation effect for nonfluent subjects in the Kroll and Curley (1988) and Kroll and Stewart (1989) studies provided additional support for this interpretation. Although nonfluent subjects are slower, overall, than fluent subjects, the difference is most dramatic for translation from L1 to L2.

[2] The results of semantic priming studies stand in marked contrast to the results of bilingual repetition priming studies in which no cross-language priming is observed (Gerard & Scarborough, 1989; Kirsner et al., 1984; Scarborough et al., 1984.) It is interesting to note that the parallel is observed with pictures and words in that pictures and the words that name them do not produce priming in repetition priming paradigms (e.g., Kroll & Potter, 1984).

Acknowledgements

This research was supported by Grant MH44246 from the National Institute of Mental Health to the first author. Portions of this material were presented at the 1990 Meeting of the Psychonomic Society and the 1991 Meeting of the American

Psychological Society. We thank Jeanette Altarriba, Thembekile Mazibuko, Caroline Sanders, and Patricia Roufca for helpful comments.

References

Altarriba, J. (1990). Constraints on interlingual facilitation effects in priming in Spanish-English bilinguals. Unpublished dissertation, Vanderbilt University.

Chen, H-C., & Ho, C. (1986). Development of Stroop interference in Chinese-English bilinguals. *Journal of Experimental Psychology: Learning, Memory, & Cognition*, 12, 397-401.

Chen, H-C., & Leung, Y-S. (1989). Patterns of lexical processing in a nonnative language. *Journal of Experimental Psychology: Learning, Memory, and Cognition*, 15, 316-325.

Chen, H-C., & Ng, M-L. (1989). Semantic facilitation and translation priming effects in Chinese-English bilinguals. *Memory & Cognition*, 17, 454-462.

Durgunoglu, A. Y., & Roediger, H. L. (1987). Test differences in accessing bilingual memory. *Journal of Memory and Language*, 26, 377-391.

Frenck, C., & Pynte, J. (1987). Semantic representation and surface forms: A look at across-language priming in bilinguals. *Journal of Psycholinguistic Research*, 16, 383-396.

Gerard, L. D., & Scarborough, D. L. (1989). Language-specific lexical access of homographs by bilinguals. *Journal of Experimental Psychology: Learning, Memory, and Cognition*, 15, 305-315.

Keatley, C., Spinks, J., & de Gelder, B. (1990). Asymmetrical semantic facilitation between languages: Evidence for separate representational systems in bilingual memory. Manuscript under review.

Kirsner, K., Smith, M. C., Lockhart, R. S., King, M. L., & Jain, M. (1984). The bilingual lexicon: Language-specific units in an integrated network. *Journal of Verbal Learning and Verbal Behavior*, 23, 519-539.

Kroll, J. F. (1990). Recognizing words and pictures in sentence contexts: A test of lexical modularity. *Journal of Experimental Psychology: Learning, Memory, and Cognition*, 16, 747-759.

Kroll, J. F., & Borning, L. (1987, November). Shifting language representations in novice bilinguals: Evidence from sentence priming. Paper presented at the Twenty-Seventh Annual Meeting of the Psychonomic Society, Seattle, WA.

Kroll, J. F., & Curley, J. (1988). Lexical memory in novice bilinguals: The role of concepts in retrieving second language words. In M. Gruneberg, P. Morris, & R. Sykes (Eds.), *Practical Aspects of Memory, Vol. 2.* London: John Wiley & Sons.

Kroll, J. F., & Potter, M. C., (1984). Recognizing words, pictures, and concepts: A comparison of lexical, object, and reality decisions. *Journal of Verbal Learning and Verbal Behavior*, 23, 39-66.

Kroll, J. F., & Smith, J. (1989, June). Naming pictures and words in categories. Poster presented at the First Annual Meeting of the American Psychological Society, Alexandria, VA.

Kroll, J. F., & Stewart, E. (1989, December). Translating from one language to another: The role of words and concepts in making the connection. Paper presented at the Meeting of the Dutch Psychonomic Society, Noordwijkerhout, The Netherlands.

Kroll, J. F., & Stewart, E. (1990, November). Concept mediation in bilingual translation. Paper presented at the 31st Annual Meeting of the Psychonomic Society, New Orleans.

Kroll, J. F., & Stewart, E. (1991). Category interference in translation and picture naming: Evidence for asymmetric connections between bilingual language representations. Unpublished manuscript, Mount Holyoke College.

La Heij, W., de Bruyn, E., Elens, E., Hartsuiker, R., Helaha, D., & van Schelven, L. (1990). Orthographic facilitation and categorical interference in a word-translation variant of the Stroop task. *Canadian Journal of Psychology*, 44, 76-83.

Lupker, S. J. (1984). Semantic priming without association: A second look. *Journal of Verbal Learning and Verbal Behavior*, 23, 709-733.

Meyer, D. E., & Ruddy, M. G. (1974, April). Bilingual word recognition: Organization and retrieval of alternative lexical codes. Paper presented at the Eastern Psychological Association Meeting, Philadelphia, PA.

Neely, J. H., Keefe, D.E., & Ross, K. L. (1989). Semantic priming in the lexical decision task: Role of prospective prime-generated expectancies and retrospective semantic matching. *Journal of Experimental Psychology: Learning, Memory, and Cognition*, 15, 1003-1019.

Potter, M. C. (1979). Mundane symbolism: The relations among objects, names, and ideas. In N. R. Smith & M. B. Franklin (Eds.), *Symbolic functioning in childhood*. Hillsdale, NJ: Erlbaum.

Potter, M. C., & Faulconer, B. A. (1975). Time to understand pictures and words. *Nature*, 253, 437-438.

Potter, M. C., & Kroll, J. F. (1987). The conceptual representation of pictures and words: A reply to Clark. *Journal of Experimental Psychology: General*, 116, 310-311.

Potter, M. C., So, K-F., von Eckhardt, B., & Feldman, L. B. (1984). Lexical and conceptual representation in beginning and more proficient bilinguals. *Journal of Verbal Learning and Verbal Behavior*, 23, 23-38.

Scarborough, D. L., Gerard, L. , & Cortese, C. (1984). Independence of lexical access in bilingual word recognition. *Journal of Verbal Learning and Verbal Behavior*, 23, 84-99.

Schwanenflugel, P. J., & Rey, M. (1986). Interlingual semantic facilitation: Evidence for a common representational system in the bilingual. *Journal of Memory and Language*, 25, 605-618.

Tzelgov, J. & Henik, A. (1989, July). The insensitivity of the semantic relatedness effect to surface differences and it implications. Paper presented at the First European Congress of Psychology, Amsterdam.

Vanderwart, M. (1984). Priming by pictures in lexical decision. *Journal of Verbal Learning and Verbal Behavior*, 23, 67-83.

Part III:

**LEXICAL ACCESS AND
WORD RECOGNITION IN BILINGUALS**

Cognitive Processing in Bilinguals – R.J. Harris (Editor)

On the Representation and Use of Language Information in Bilinguals

Jonathan Grainger
CNRS and Université René Descartes
and
Ton Dijkstra
University of Nijmegen

Abstract

The present chapter examines how the bilingual's knowledge of what language a particular word belongs to is represented in bilingual memory and how that knowledge could be used to facilitate bilingual language comprehension. Two basic hypotheses (the language tag and the language network hypotheses) are presented within the framework of bilingual versions of two different models of visual word recognition (serial search and interactive activation). It appears that the bilingual interactive activation model best accommodates some recent data on bilingual word recognition.

Introduction

Bilingual language users have knowledge concerning the particular language that each word in their working vocabulary belongs to. This knowledge is immediately and effortlessly available to the skilled bilingual. Asking a French/English bilingual what language the word FARM belongs to appears to be a ridiculously simple question. The answer arrives spontaneously and without apparent effort. This simple example, however, hides a rather complex problem; just how does this bilingual speaker realize that the word FARM is an English word?

The present chapter represents an attempt at answering that question. We wish to examine how knowledge of the language that a particular word belongs to is stored in memory and how that information can be retrieved. Related to this problem is the obviously critical question concerning how this language information intervenes (if at all) in the normal processes of language comprehension in bilinguals. Since the principal goal of the language processor is to build a semantic representation of what is heard or read, formal attributes of the linguistic information being processed that are not directly relevant to the computation of meaning can be ignored. Orthography, phonology and syntax are formal attributes that encode meaning whereas language information does not. Thus for example, knowing that a word belongs to a particular syntactic category provides some semantic information (e.g., verb-action) concerning that word whereas knowing that that word belongs to a particular language does not generally provide semantic information (an exception here is words that are homographic between languages, e.g., COIN for a French/English bilingual, although even with such interlingual homographs phonology generally provides the necessary disambiguating information).

It is nevertheless true that language information is potentially highly relevant for the bilingual speaker. Information concerning the likelihood of receiving a word in one or the other language (language context information) could be extremely useful in processing that word. If word recognition is conceived of as a search process through lexical memory, then such language context information essentially reduces the search space by half, resulting in greater processing economy. In order for language context information to be successfully used in bilingual language comprehension this external information must somehow contact the stored knowledge about language in bilingual memory (see Figure 1). We are therefore faced with a classic human information processing problem: how to get from external information to stored knowledge. The example of knowing which language a particular word belongs to in bilinguals could even be considered a paradigm case for this type of problem since it corresponds to the minimum information possible (i.e., two alternatives).

Processing language information

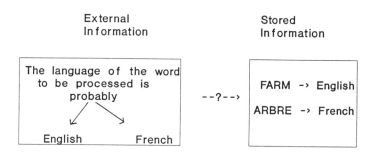

Figure 1. Bilinguals typically have external (contextual) information available concerning the likelihood of receiving words in one or the other of their languages. The problem expressed here is how such information could be matched to stored knowledge about which words belong to one language and which belong to the other language.

In the present chapter we will analyse how the knowledge of which language words belong to could be stored in bilingual memory and how such information could be used to facilitate language processing in bilinguals. We will be using as examples languages that share the same alphabet, such as English and French, and we will examine data only from visual word recognition tasks. It is in these precise circumstances that language information is the most ambiguous at sublexical levels of representation. In other words there is no information present in the letter string FIRE that allows a French/English bilingual to know that it is an English word rather than a French word without actually identifying the letter string as a word in the first place. This is clearly not the case when the word FIRE is spoken aloud since sublexical phonology does provide cues as to which language a particular speech sound belongs to. It would also not be the case when reading the word WHITE, since WH is an illegal letter combination in French. However, for the time being we will ignore the possibility of language information being represented at a sublexical level and concentrate on how this information could be represented at the lexical or supralexical levels. We will also assume that knowing that a word belongs to a language that one speaks fluently is a very different kind of knowledge compared to knowing that a word belongs to a language that one cannot speak. We suppose that the former type of knowledge is complexly intertwined with knowledge of the other aspects of that particular word and its integration as a unit within the total language system.

Two Hypotheses of Language Representation and their Expression in Models of Bilingual Word Recognition

Knowledge of which language a given word belongs to could be represented in two principal ways.
1) - The language tag hypothesis: language information is stored with each lexical representation along with orthographic, phonological, morphological and possibly syntactic information.

2) - The language network hypothesis: language information is represented in the way lexical representations are organized into two distinct lexical networks.

Readers of the bilingual literature will probably recognize the old shared/separate representations dichotomy rephrased in the above hypotheses. These hypotheses are not, however, a simple restatement of the original formulations. The shared/separate or interdependent/independent dichotomy was mainly concerned with the representation of translation equivalents in bilingual memory (Kolers, 1963; Lopez & Young, 1974). Since this early research, the problem of the representation of translation equivalents has been restated with the distinction between lexical (surface) and semantic (conceptual) representations in mind (Potter, So, VonEckardt & Feldman, 1984). It is clear that the French/English translation equivalents TREE/ARBRE may have a common semantic representation but obligatorily must have distinct orthographic representations in memory that are involved in reading these words. The question posed today concerning the types of connections between these lexical and conceptual representations (concept mediation versus word association hypotheses) is orthogonal to the problem of how language information is represented. Both the language tag and the language network hypotheses are compatible with the concept mediation and word association hypotheses of bilingual lexical organization.

One point that needs to be made clear at this point concerns the use of the term "language-specific". This concept is used to describe bilingual performance when it is observed that presentation of a word in one language does not affect later performance on its translation equivalent in the other language (Durgunoglu &

Roediger, 1987; Ransdell & Fischler, 1987). Unfortunately, many authors extend results obtained with translation equivalents to claim that bilinguals can operate without any interference from the non-target language. We will argue, however, in the present chapter that even when operating in a purely monolingual mode (i.e., when there is no overt use of the other language) lexical representations that share orthographic information with the stimulus are simultaneously activated independently of which language they belong to. This concept of an initially language-independent multiple access in bilingual word recognition is embodied in the specific models of bilingual word recognition to be described below.

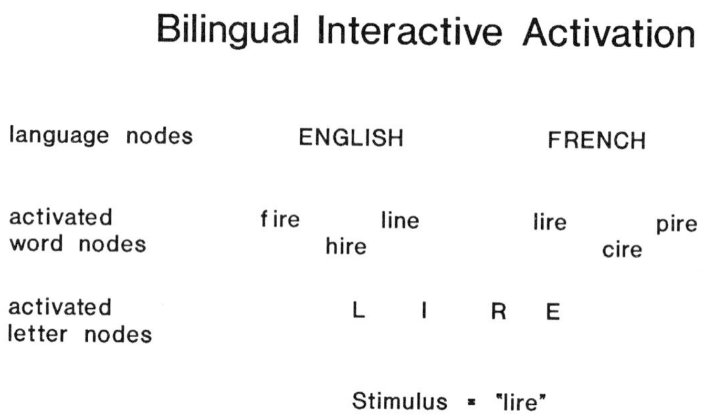

Bilingual Interactive Activation

language nodes	ENGLISH	FRENCH

activated word nodes	f ire line hire	lire pire cire

activated letter nodes	L I R E

Stimulus = "lire"

Figure 2. The BIA framework consists of three representational levels: letter, word, and language. All nodes at a given representational level are interconnected. Nodes are also connected between adjacent levels such that, for example, all English word nodes are connected to the English language node and all the French word nodes to the French language node. Some of the nodes that are activated during the processing of the word LIRE are shown in the figure.

One means of expressing the two hypotheses of language representation in a model of bilingual word recognition is to connect all lexical representations from the same language to a single node at a superior representational level (Figure 2). We will refer to these hypothetical representational units as language nodes and the model presented in Figure 2 can be considered a bilingual extension of the interactive activation model of word recognition (McClelland & Rumelhart, 1981). We will refer to this particular model as the bilingual interactive activation model or BIA, although it is best conceived of as a theoretical framework rather than as a specific model.

In the BIA framework, the language tag hypothesis of language representation is implemented in a non-interactive version of the model where the connections between word units and language nodes are unidirectional. In other words, information feeds forward from letter units to word units and on to language units but no feed-back is allowed. Thus, language node activation cannot influence word level processing in such a version of the model. In a version of BIA that implements the language network hypothesis, on the other hand, the connections between word units and language units are bidirectional and so variations in language node activation influence the activation values of word units.

Frequency ordered search

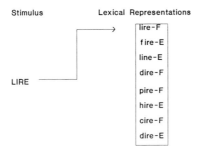

Language and frequency ordered search

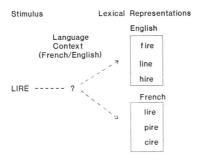

Figure 3. Two possible versions of serial search models of bilingual word recognition. In these models a serial search process operates on a set of lexical representations that are orthographically similar to the stimulus word. This search process allows the visual word recognition system to rapidly isolate the lexical representation in memory that best corresponds to sensory information extracted from the stimulus. In the upper panel search is uniquely frequency ordered whereas in the lower panel it is language and frequency ordered with language context guiding access to the appropriate language representations.

Within the framework of serial search models of visual word recognition (Forster, 1976; Paap, Newsome, McDonald, & Schvaneveldt, 1982) the distinction between the language-tag and language network hypotheses of language representation is made in terms of whether or not the search process is language-ordered or not. In classical monolingual serial search models the search process is frequency ordered to account for the pervasive effects of word frequency on word recognition performance. According to the language tag hypothesis of language representation a bilingual search model should also be frequency ordered with language information not influencing the search process. According to the language network hypothesis, on the other hand, the search process should be ordered by language first and then by frequency. In other words the search process will proceed through two sets of lexical candidates, one for each language, with frequency ranking occuring within each set.

Experimental Tests of the Models

Let us now turn to examine the alternative hypotheses about the representation of language information in bilinguals in the light of existing data on bilingual language processing. A more thorough test of these hypotheses is possible by their expression in specific models of bilingual word recognition. It is therefore the predictions of these models that will be confronted with the experimental data.

Language Decision and Lexical Decision

An interesting question, and one that is relatively easy to answer, is whether bilinguals can decide if a letter string is a word or not (independently of language) more quickly than they can decide if a given word belongs to one or the other language. In some unpublished experiments comparing language decision and lexical decision latencies in English/French bilinguals we observed that language decision latencies are on average 200 ms slower than lexical decision latencies. In these experiments the words were carefully selected so as not to contain sublexical language-specific cues (e.g., the WH in WHITE for an English/French bilingual). In the lexical decision task subjects pressed one response button when the letter string was a word, either French or English, and the other response button when the letter string was not a word. In the language decision experiment subjects were presented with the same words and responded to one language with one response button and to the other language with the other button. Obviously when comparing reaction times across these two tasks the comparisons were made for the same words responded to with the same hand.

This extremely robust and easily replicable result clearly indicates that deciding which language a word belongs to is a more difficult task than deciding whether a letter string is a word or not. Now since language decision is arguably a more natural task than lexical decision, one might have even expected the opposite result on purely intuitive grounds. It will therefore be interesting to examine how the different models of bilingual word recognition proposed above can accommodate this result. Within the BIA framework (Figure 2) subjects could perform the language decision task by setting a threshold for language node activation, responding as soon as one node reaches a criterion level of activation. Since language nodes receive input from word nodes, the rise in activation level of these language units will lag behind the rise in activation of lexical representations. This can explain why language decision takes longer than lexical decision since lexical decisions will be made on the basis of word node activation levels. On this point it is interesting to note that alphabetic decision (letter/non-letter classification) latencies are on average much shorter than lexical decision latencies (Jacobs & Grainger, 1991). The proposed explanation for this difference is analagous to the above explanation for the difference between lexical decision and language decision times: word nodes have a slower rate of rise in activation than letter nodes. Thus both an autonomous and an interactive version of BIA can account for the fact that language decision is slower than lexical decision.

Within the serial search framework, a model that embodies the language tag hypothesis of language representation has difficulty in accommodating this result. In this particular model, language information should be made available immediately after locating the correct lexical representation. This type of model therefore predicts that language decision times should be similar to lexical decision times. In a language-ordered verion of a serial search model, on the other hand, one could consider that a language decision can be made only after a word has been recognized. Recognizing the stimulus word allows the system to determine to which network that particular lexical representation belongs. In this way a language decision can only be made once the lexical representation corresponding to the stimulus word has been isolated, thus explaining why language decisions are longer than lexical decisions.

Language Context Effects on Word Recognition in Bilinguals

Numerous early studies of bilingual language comprehension demonstrated that the processing of sentences composed of words from both languages (code-mixed sentences) is harder than the processing of single language sentences (Kolers, 1966; Macnamara, 1967). More recently this basic result has received further support from research directly measuring the difficulty of individual word recognition in sentences (Soares & Grosjean, 1984).

In the processing of lists of unrelated words a similar effect of language context has been demonstrated by Grainger and Beauvillain (1987). In this experiment, lexical decision latencies (is this letter string a word, either French or English?) were longer when the lists were composed of words from both languages than when they were only composed of words from one language. More interestingly, however, it was found that the longer reaction times in the mixed lists were obtained only immediately following a word from the other language and only when the stimulus word did not contain certain language-specific orthographic patterns. Thus the word TIME took longer to recognize after the French word LIRE compared to when preceded by the English word LIFE. The word WHITE, on the other hand, remained unaffected by the language of the preceding word, a result that can be attributed to the presence of the letter sequence WH which is illegal in French.

A similar result has also been obtained using the priming paradigm where lexical decision latencies are measured to a test word that is preceded by a prime stimulus (for which no overt response is required). In these experiments the principal aim was to study interlingual and intralingual semantic priming effects, but for the present purposes we shall examine only the data obtained in the unrelated condition. A summary of these results is presented in Figure 4. The results indicate that same language primes (e.g., LIFE-HOLD) typically produce faster lexical decision latencies than different language primes (e.g., LIRE-HOLD) at both a 150 msec and a 750 msec S.O.A (stimulus onset asynchrony).

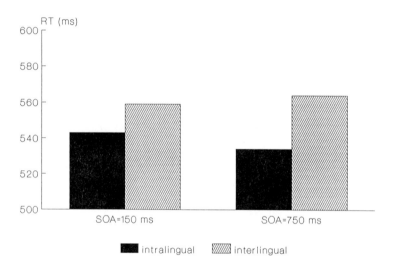

Figure 4. Language priming effects in a lexical decision task taken from Grainger and Beauvillain (1988). In the intralingual condition primes and targets are words from the same language and in the interlingual condition they are words from different languages. Prime and target words are otherwise unrelated.

Within the framework of the bilingual interactive activation model presented above, these language priming effects can be explained in terms of language node preactivation. When the prime is an English word, the "English node" will be in a heightened state of activation when the target is presented for processing. Activation then feeds back to all the English word nodes, thus facilitating their recognition compared to the situation when a different language prime is presented. An autonomous (language-tag) version of this model cannot accommodate these language priming effects.

The language-tag version of a serial search model also cannot accommodate these results. Since language information concerning a particular word is only made available once this word has been identified, language context information should not influence word recognition. The results can, however, be accommodated by a language-ordered search model by postulating that immediate language context determines which lexicon will be searched first. After recognizing an English word lexical search will automatically begin with the English candidates, thus giving rise to faster recognition times than when a different language word has just been processed. There are two major problems faced by the language-ordered search model with respect to these language priming effects. The first is that these effects, although reduced, are also obtained with very short prime presentation durations (Grainger & Beauvillain, 1988). In these conditions it is unlikely that subjects have completed prime identification before beginning to process the target and so it is unlikely that language information about the prime is available in order to guide access procedures on the target. The second point is that in the priming studies the language of the target was blocked, so subjects knew beforehand the language of the word on which they had to make a lexical decision. If this knowledge cannot guide access procedures to the correct lexical representations then the utility of such a mechanism is called into question.

Neighborhood Effects across Languages

Further evidence in favor of the bilingual interactive activation model has been recently obtained in experiments manipulating the neighborhood characteristics of words within and between languages. In experiments with monolingual subjects it has been observed that the time to recognize a written word is influenced by the characteristics of words that are orthographically similar to the stimulus (Andrews, 1989; Grainger, 1990; Grainger, O'Regan, Jacobs, & Segui, 1989; Grainger & Segui, 1990). In a model of bilingual word recognition where initial access procedures are language-independent, one would expect such orthographic neighborhood effects to extend across languages in bilingual subjects. It would therefore be interesting to know whether orthographic similarity across languages can affect word recognition performance in bilinguals.

Some preliminary experiments in this area suggest that this is the case. We have manipulated the number of orthographic neighbors (Coltheart, Davelaar, Jonasson, & Besner, 1977) of English target words in both English and French. Three categories of stimuli were defined: 1) English words with many more English than French neighbors (patriots); 2) English words with many more French than English neighbors (traitors); 3) English words with approximately the same number of neighbors in each language (neutral). None of the target words had letter clusters that are specific to English (e.g., WH, SH), and the different categories were matched for printed frequency. These English target words were tested on a group of English-French bilinguals in a lexical decision experiment with only English target words and nonwords. The results are given in Figure 5.

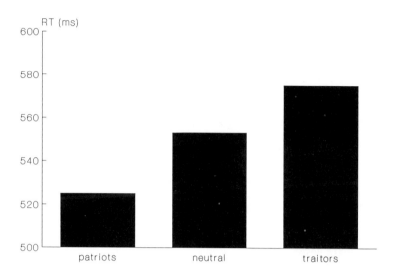

Figure 5. Effects of relative number of neighbors in two languages on bilingual subjects' performance in a monolingual lexical decision task (targets are from one language only). Patriots are words that have more neighbors in the target than the non-target language whereas traitors have more neighbors in the non-target language. Neutral words have an approximately equivalent number of neighbors in both languages.

The results add support to the hypothesis that initial access procedures in the word recognition process are language-independent in bilinguals. Even when functioning in a purely monolingual mode (monolingual lexical decision), lexical decision performance to English target words was affected by the number of French neighbors of the target relative to the number of English neighbors. Patriots were recognized more rapidly and with less errors than traitors.

With respect to the two models of bilingual word recognition presented above (language-ordered search and bilingual interactive activation), the results provide further evidence in favor of bilingual interactive activation. The language-ordered search model predicts that the number of French neighbors should not influence the recognition of English target words in monolingual lexical decision. Subjects know that they will only receive English target words and therefore search processes should be guided directly to the subset of English candidates.

These results are consistent with a model of bilingual word recognition in which each language is represented as a node with a given activation level and with reciprocal inhibition between the two language nodes. When an English-French bilingual reads an English word with more French than English neighbors (a traitor) then it is the French language node that will initially rise more rapidly in activation level since it will initially be receiving more input from the word level. Thus, in initial stages of processing the English node will be receiving inhibition from the French node, thus inhibiting the processing of the English target word.

In recent work with monolingual subjects, however, it appears that the frequency of orthographically similar words compared to the frequency of the stimulus word is an important factor in determining interference. Typically, words that are similar to a much more frequent word (e.g., BLUR similar to BLUE) are harder to recognize than words that do not have such higher frequency neighbors (Grainger et al., 1989; Grainger, 1990; Grainger & Segui, 1990). The frequency of the orthographic neighbors was not controlled in the bilingual experiments reported above, so future research should investigate neighborhood frequency effects within and between languages. The bilingual interactive activation model predicts that both the number and the frequencies of a given word's orthographic neighbors should play a role in determining the ease of recognition of this word.

Conclusions

The present chapter has attempted to examine how knowledge concerning the language a particular word belongs to is represented in bilingual memory and how this particular knowledge may be used to facilitate bilingual word recognition. The experimental results reviewed here support the network hypothesis of language representation in bilinguals. According to this hypothesis knowledge of which language a particular word belongs to is represented in the way lexical representations are organized in memory. In the particular instantiation of this hypothesis within the interactive activation framework, all lexical representations of a given language are linked together via bidirectional connections between a language node and the word level nodes. The fact that language context appears to influence word recognition in bilingual subjects adds support to this interactive model of bilingual word recognition.

One problem related to the question of language representation that was not directly addressed in the present chapter, concerns the status of between-language homographs (e.g., COIN which translates into French as CORNER). It is likely that this problem will turn out to be no different from heterophonic homographs in the same language (e.g., BOW in English). Indeed, the experimental results investigating the time-course of activation of the different readings of homographs give similar results in both monolingual (Simpson & Burgess, 1985) and bilingual (Beauvillain & Grainger, 1987) studies. It appears that both readings are activated early in processing, the degree of activation being a function of word frequency, and that in later stages of processing only the contextually appropriate reading (either in terms of semantic context or language context) remains activated, the inappropriate reading having been suppressed. This suppression can be described in terms of language nodes actively inhibiting inappropriate word-level nodes within the BIA framework.

Bilingual word recognition has proved, in the past, to be an ideal area for the application of the search metaphor of visual word recognition (Forster, 1976). Recent studies with monolingual subjects, however, have demonstrated that the activation metaphor (Morton, 1969; McClelland & Rumelhart, 1981) appears a more suitable candidate for providing coherent explanations of the observed phenomena. The present chapter indicates that the same conclusions can be drawn concerning visual word recognition in bilinguals.

The BIA framework introduced in the present chapter offers a new approach to the problem of lexical and language representation in bilingual subjects. Further work with this type of model should make it possible to provide simulations of bilingual word recognition performance and therefore a quantitative test of the predictions of various concrete implementations of the framework. It is clear that future work within this framework should also distinguish between orthographic and phonological nodes for a given word, a distinction which should prove particularly important in the processing of identical cognates in two languages (e.g., TABLE in French and English). The BIA framework directly implements a conception of bilingual word recognition according to which a given letter string will simultaneously activate all lexical representations from both languages that share letters with the stimulus. It is this simultaneous activation of lexical representations across languages in initial stages of word recognition that can account for both within and between language interference effects.

References

Andrews, S. (1989). Frequency and neighborhood effects on lexical access: Activation or search. *Journal of Experimental Psychology: Learning Memory and Cognition,* 15, 802-814.

Beauvillain, C. & Grainger, J. (1987). Accessing interlexical homographs: Some limitations of a language-selective access. *Journal of Memory and Language,* 26, 658-672.

Coltheart, M., Davelaar, E., Jonasson, J.T., & Besner, D. (1977). Access to the internal lexicon. In S. Dornic (Ed.), *Attention and Performance VI.* New York: Academic Press.

Durgunoglu, A. Y. & Roediger, H. L. (1987). Test differences in accessing bilingual memory. *Journal of Memory and Language,* 26, 377-391.

Forster, K. I. (1976). Accessing the mental lexicon. In R. J. Wales & E. W. Walker (Eds.), *New approaches to language mechanisms.* Amsterdam: North-Holland.

Grainger, J. (1990). Word frequency and neighborhood frequency effects in lexical decision and naming. *Journal of Memory and Language*, 29, 228-244.

Grainger, J. & Beauvillain, C. (1987). Language blocking and lexical access in bilinguals. *Quarterly Journal of Experimental Psychology*, 39A, 295-319.

Grainger, J. & Beauvillain, C. (1988). Associative priming in bilinguals: Some limits of interlingual facilitation effects. *Canadian Journal of Psychology*, 42, 261-273.

Grainger, J., O'Regan, J. K., Jacobs, A. M, & Segui, J. (1989). On the role of competing word units in visual word recognition: The neighborhood frequency effect. *Perception & Psychophysics,* 45, 189-195.

Grainger, J. & Segui, J. (1990). Neighborhood frequency effects in visual word recognition: A comparison of lexical decision and masked identification latencies. *Perception and Psychophysics*, 47, 191-198.

Jacobs, A. M. & Grainger, J. (1991). Automatic letter priming in an alphabetic decision task. *Perception and Psychophysics,* 49, 43-52.

Kolers, P. A. (1963). Interlingual word associations. *Journal of Verbal Learning and Verbal Behavior*, 2, 291-300.

Kolers, P. A. (1966). Reading and talking bilingually. *American Journal of Psychology,* 79, 357-376.

Lopez, M. & Young, R. K. (1974). The linguistic independence of bilinguals. *Journal of Experimental Psychology,* 102, 981-983.

Macnamara, J. (1967). The linguistic independence of bilinguals. *Journal of Verbal Learning and Verbal Behavior*, 6, 729-736.

McClelland, J. L. & Rumelhart, D. E. (1981). An interactive-activation model of context effects in letter perception, part 1: An account of basic findings. *Psychological Review*, 88, 375-405.

Morton, J. (1969). The interaction of information in word recognition. *Psychological Review,* 76, 340-354.

Paap, K. R., Newsome, S. L., McDonald, J. E., & Schvaneveldt, R. W. (1982). An activation-verification model for letter and word recognition: The word superiority effect. *Psychological Review,* 89, 573-594.

Potter, M. C., So, K. W., Von Eckhardt, B., & Feldman, L. B. (1984). Lexical and conceptual representation in beginning and proficient bilinguals. *Journal of Verbal Learning and Verbal Behavior*, 23, 23-38.

Ransdell, S. E. & Fischler, I. (1987). Memory in a monolingual mode: When are bilinguals at a disadvantage? *Journal of Memory and Language*, <u>26</u>, 392-405.

Simpson, G. B. & Burgess, C. (1985). Activation and selection processes in the recognition of ambiguous words. *Journal of Experimental Psychology: Human Perception and Performance*, <u>11</u>, 28-39.

Soares, C. & Grosjean, F. (1984). Bilinguals in a monolingual and a bilingual speech mode: The effect on lexical access. *Memory and Cognition*, <u>12</u>, 380-386.

Cognitive Processing in Bilinguals – R.J. Harris (Editor)
© *1992 Elsevier Science Publishers B.V. All rights reserved.*

Orthographic and Lexical Constraints in Bilingual Word Recognition

C. Beauvillain
CNRS and Université René Descartes

Abstract

The evidence presented in this chapter is consistent with the following conclusions.   First, lexical representation in bilinguals is governed by orthography rather than by language.   Before associating a lexical representation to a stimulus, the subset of entries will be composed from words of one or both languages as a function of orthographic properties of words.   Second, there is no language-selective access to a subset of lexical representations organized by language.

This chapter is concerned with the impact of bilingualism on lexical access function. Implicit in many theories of lexical access is the assumption that lexical memory can be distinguished from other types of memory. The contents of lexical memory traces, or entries, are assumed to specify just the linguistically relevant properties of words, and the structure of the access system is designed to meet the needs of efficient language use. If these assumptions are correct, then it is of interest to ask how the lexical entries are located in a bilingual lexicon. Our approach to the issue has been guided by the proposition that lexical representation is indifferent to bilingual experience in such a way that lexical access processes in bilinguals have a monolingual parallel.

Lexical function can be modulated by bilingual experience in a number of ways. One possibility is that language operates as a criterial feature defining a boundary between the two lexical systems.   If language defines the boundary between lexical systems, the following predictions can be made.   First, it can be predicted that words such as the English word "cover" and the French word "cuver" are recognized independently, without any interference during the perceptual analysis of the written word due to orthographic similarity between the two words. On the other hand, it can be predicted that semantically associated words from different languages as "boy" and "fille" should be processed as if they belong to independent lexical systems. Another possibility is to consider that lexical representation is indifferent to bilingual experience in such a way that orthographic or associative principles will govern interlingual as well as intralingual access function.   Such a view would be the consequence that language is not a critical feature of lexical representation and lexical access function. Third, it can be predicted that lexical access function is governed by formal description of the word that will be language independent; the information about meaning and conceptual codes that is addressed via the access process can be language-specific or not as a consequence of the retrieval demands of cognitive tasks.

Initially, the perspective of the research concerned with accessing bilingual memory has traditionally been considered in terms of a single- or a dual-code model, that is, whether bilinguals have one unified system or two independent processing systems. The single-code models assume that lexical representations and the routines to access them belong to a single conceptual memory store in which language represents one of the attributes.   Thus, McCormack (1976) addressed this question in considering the conceptual, abstract and amodal nature of lexical representations.   A language-free characterization of bilingual memory is given and a certain amount of evidence has accumulated in favour of the notion that bilinguals have two lexical systems, one for each language, which in turn are linked together via a common store of conceptual representations (Caramazza & Brones, 1979; Potter, So, Von Eckardt, & Feldman, 1984; Kirsner, Smith, Lockhart, King, & Jain, 1984).   This conception is included in dual-code models that assume separate language-specific codes but with links between coordinate concepts in the two systems.

More generally this important question concerning the nature of representation that subtends context effects in visual word recognition is linked to a current controversy in monolingual studies.   That is, what type of representation subtends context effects in conditions that exclude the use of predictive strategies?   The view that facilitation effects are conceptually mediated is opposed to the hypothesis that semantic priming is strictly intralexical and operates between associatively linked representations (Forster, 1979).   This conception has been defended by Kolers (1978, 1979) who proposes that knowledge is organized in terms of the procedures by which it is acquired and that such procedures may be language-dependent. We presented evidence suggesting that associative facilitation is mediated by lexical representation in an associative network formed by the contiguity of elements in the individual's experience.   Using a priming methodology in a lexical decision task, we observed no facilitation effects between associated words from different languages, where facilitation effects were present between associated words from the same language (Grainger & Beauvillain, 1988).

It seems clear that language-independent and language-specific patterns of data can depend on the retrieval demands of the task.   With the conceptually-driven task of free recall, language independence is generally observed.   The issue of whether bilinguals store information in one or two codes seems indeterminable because the varying retrieval demands produce different patterns of results (Durgunoglu & Roediger, 1987).

The important question addressed here is not in terms of whether or not conceptual representations are language-specific or not.   Mental representations of lexical forms are, per se, language-specific.   Information about meaning and other characteristics of words are stored in a lexicon that is addressed via an access process. What is needed is a reliable account of how bilinguals access lexical representations from their two languages.   Our review of the lexical evidence is governed by the understanding of the functional structure of the access system in terms of the encoding operations performed on the stimulus input.

Interference Effects in the Bilingual Lexicon

The question focused on here concerns the impact of bilingualism on the organization of lexical representations. How can a mental representation be located in the bilingual's lexicon during visual word recognition? We shall provide experimental evidence suggesting that bilingual word recognition is based on a stimulus-driven analysis which is indifferent to language. Thus, language should not operate as a criterial feature determining which lexical representations are initially accessed. This notion is opposite to the view that bilinguals have considerable control in the manner that they access lexical knowledge.

A first possibility is that lexical delimitation will be governed by the languages involved. The fact that bilinguals are able to function without any difficulty in only one of their languages has been interpreted as evidence of control over access to language-specific systems. The bilingual lexicon would be structured so that only one lexical system can be accessed at a time. According to this hypothesis, the bilingual's lexical system may be partitioned by language and lexical search should be selective according to which lexicon is accessed. There is a long tradition in psycholinguistic studies of bilingualism defending the claim that just one language system for comprehension can operate at a time. Studies defending this conception have shown that bilinguals are faster at comprehending unilingual passages than at comprehending multilingual passages which require switching of languages (Macnamara & Kushnir, 1971). The notion of an input switch mechanism was proposed to explain how the sensory input is directed to the appropriate processing system. According to Macnamara and Kushnir, this mechanism should operate involuntarily. When comprehension procedures in one language fail because of language alternation, the switch will automatically turn over to the other language system (Obler & Albert, 1978). Consequently, bilinguals should be unable to process words in two languages simultaneously. Switching from one language to the other takes time and imposes a load on processing because the bilingual must activate one processor while deactivating the other. Soares and Grosjean (1984) showed that in a phoneme-triggered lexical decision task bilinguals took longer to access code-switched words in a bilingual speech mode than they took to access words in a monolingual speech mode. They interpreted this result by suggesting that bilinguals search the base-language lexicon (the language of the sentence) before the other lexicon when in a code-switching speech mode. This conception succeeds in capturing the intuition that the bilingual's lexicon may be partitioned by language and that lexical search is selective according to which lexicon is accessed.

A second possibility is the bilingual lexicon is indifferent to bilingual experience in such a way that the manner in which lexical representations are discovered is language independent. Here the central hypothesis is that at some level of language processing the two lexical systems of bilinguals are activated simultaneously. The initial evidence for this comes from the presence of interlingual interference in a bilingual version of the Stroop task. Preston and Lambert (1969) reported that when English-French bilinguals were asked to name the ink colors in one language, for instance, English, they showed interference if the letters spelled a French color name that did not match the ink, though the interference was not as great as within languages. More recently, Chen and Ho (1986) replicated this result. Other data provided by picture-word interference (Ehri & Bouchard-Ryan, 1980) or by the cross-language flanker task (Guttentag, Haith, Goodman & Hauch, 1984) used the presence of between-language interference to conclude that both languages come into play simultaneously.

Another interesting result concern the interference that is observed between the two sets of phonological rules of two languages (Altenberg & Cairns, 1983). In nonword judgements in a lexical decision task, these authors have shown that the two sets of phonological rules of English and German interact in the processing of nonwords in an English lexical decision task in that the legality of the nonword in German affected nonword reaction times as much as its legality in English. Other related data reported by Lukatela, Savic, Gligorijevic, Ognjenovic, and Turvey (1978) concern the processing of ambiguous Serbo-Croatian letter strings that receive a different reading in the Roman and in the Cyrillic alphabet. They found that when subjects were induced to read these letter strings in one of the two "alphabetic modes," lexical decision latencies were affected by the fact that they could be attributed to the reading in the other alphabet. This result suggests that subjects were unable to be selective in controlling access to one set of phonological rules.

With J. Grainger (Beauvillain & Grainger, 1987), I examined the presence of such interference between the two languages of bilinguals in studying the processing of lexical forms common to English and French. Consider the word COIN read by an English-French bilingual. This word is an interlexical homograph that has a graphemic form common to French and English with two distinct pronunciations and distinct meanings in the two languages (COIN means "corner" in French). When it is presented to an English-French bilingual reader, the question is whether the language mode instructions favoring the homograph's reading in one language will lead to the selective access of one lexical system.

In these studies, the priming methodology was used to provide evidence concerning the presence or absence of a language-selective access. Evidence of an absence of selective access would be provided if subjects accessed the reading of the homograph that is inappropriate to the language mode context. Thirty homographs were embedded in a list of French context words where English-French bilingual subjects were instructed to read French context words before performing a lexical decision on English test words related to the English reading of the homographs. Selective access would be indicated if COIN presented in a list of French context words was found not to facilitate MONEY, that is, if lexical decision time to MONEY in this condition were similar to those of unrelated controls. The language mode in which bilinguals operate restricts access to the appropriate reading, that is COIN, in French, and no faciliation is expected on the processing of the test-word MONEY. Because the availability of readings may change over time, we examined this question of selective or nonselective access of interlexical homographs at 150 and 750 ms stimulus onset asynchrony (SOA). Indeed, previous research on intralingual lexical ambiguity has provided consistent evidence that multiple readings of ambiguous words are accessed at earlier SOA and that the suppression of the inappropriate reading occurred later (Swinney, 1979; see Simpson, 1984, for an overall review).

The results of this experiment showed that at the 150-ms SOA subjects could not selectively access information in one of their lexical systems according to the induced language mode, since facilitation was obtained for test words related to the inappropriate reading of the homograph context words. At the 750-ms SOA there was no evidence of such a facilitation effect. These results suggest that subjects initially do not select the reading of the homograph which is appropriate to language mode context; such a language selection should operate later. This first result suggests that there should be an initial language-independent access of interlexical homographs.

In a second experiment we tested which factors affected lexical retrieval in each of the bilingual's languages. An additional powerful test would be to examine the effects of the internal property of lexical representation as the effect of relative frequency of the alternative readings of interlexical homographs. For instance, FOUR is of a higher frequency in English than FOUR ("oven" in French), and PAIN ("bread") is of a higher frequency in French than in English. The higher and lower frequency readings of these unbalanced homographs were examined in an appropriate and inappropriate language mode at short SOA. As shown in Figure 1, the results provided strong evidence that, at short SOA, the facilitation effects observed are a function of the homograph's relative frequency independent of the language mode context. Only lexical decision times to test words related to the higher frequency reading of these homographs were facilitated relative to unrelated words. This important result that frequency rather than language determines which lexical entries are initially accessed provided additional support against a language-selective access. Lexical access of such interlexical homographs depends more on one internal property of the lexicon, the coded frequency of the different readings.

The outcome is similar where cognates (i.e. words that are graphemically and semantically identical in both languages) are considered. Caramazza and Brones (1979) tested Spanish-English bilinguals on cognates that had approximatively equal frequencies in each language. The authors observed that lexical decision times to such cognates presented in English or Spanish pure (blocked) or mixed lists were recognized as rapidly as words of the same frequency from the subjects' dominant language whatever the list context. The language context given in the experimental list did not determine which lexical entry is accessed. Note that Cristoffanini, Kirsner and Milech (1986) made similar observations in a post hoc analysis of data on nonidentical cognates (i.e., translations that share morphological relations, example: PUBLICIDAD/ PUBLICITY). Lexical decision times to such cognates which were not equivalent in frequency in the two languages were affected by the frequency of occurrence of their reading in the nontarget language. This suggests that, when morphologically related forms are considered, language does not contribute to delimitations in the bilingual lexicon (Kirsner, 1986).

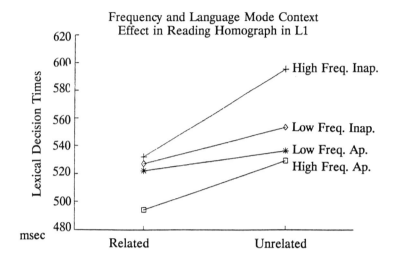

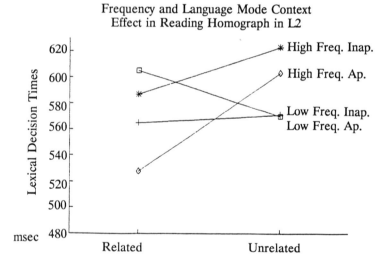

Figure 1.   Mean Lexical Decision Latencies in Milliseconds for each of the Relatedness, Frequency, and Language Mode Context Conditions at 150 ms SOA (replotted from Beauvillain & Grainger, 1987).

To summarize, there is a suggestion of frequency transfer where graphemically similar lexical forms are concerned. This effect is not limited to words that share orthographic and semantic properties. It is observed for common graphemic words that have different meanings in the two languages. The presence of a frequency ordered access of interlexical homographs suggests that the boundaries between lexical representations would be governed by orthographic properties of words. Language mode context does not affect lexical access function. The results suggest that lexical access in bilinguals is not initially language-selective.

Orthographic and Lexical Constraints

The assumption presented above was built up to account for the recognition of lexical forms common to the two languages. Given the importance of these experimental results, it is essential to enlarge the data base to the recognition of words that share orthographic sublexical units. Indeed, as assumed by many current models of word recognition, before associating a lexical representation to a stimulus, an orthographic representation of the input is used in the selection of a subset of lexical entries in the lexicon, over which a detailed search is to be made. Orthographic factors have their impact through constraints on the search set (Forster, 1976) or in the process of activation to lexical units in McClelland and Rumelhart's (1981) terms.

In the bilingual situation, we proposed the view that the lexical subsets have predetermined boundaries in which language boundaries are not represented. Whether or not language will define some boundaries between lexical entries will depend on orthographic properties of words. In the presence of language-specific orthographic cues within the word, it can be assumed that the subset of lexical entries will be restricted to one language only. However, in the absence of language-specific cues, the subset will be composed of words from both languages. The central assumption here is that in the mapping between the orthographic descriptions and the mental representations, language mode constraints cannot prevent the initial accessing of words of the non-target language.

One consequence of this assumption could be that search time in the lexicon may be decreased considerably in the presence of language-specific information in that the subset of entries to examine will be restricted to only one language. A recent study investigated this orthographic factor (Beauvillain, 1988, 1989). Language-specific and non-specific words were closely matched in frequency and equally distributed along the frequency range. If we accept the notion proposed by Forster (1976) that frequency controls the search path within a subset of lexical entries defined by orthographic similarity, the linear regression slope between the frequency of the words and the response latency should be dependent on the density of the subset of lexical entries. Because non-specific orthographic words are recognized within a subset of candidates better than specific orthographic words, response latencies should be longer than for specific words. Moreover, the linear regression slopes should be stronger for non-specific words that are selected within a subset of candidates from the two languages than for specific words for which the subset contains candidates restricted to one language only.

For an experimental evaluation of this orthographic factor, we selected two sets of 96 French words and 96 English words by using tables of bigram and trigram frequencies in English and French. Two types of words were defined according to the language-specificity of orthography. For language-specific orthographic words, bigram frequencies were higher in the target language than in the non-target language. For instance, CREAM is an English-specific word for which the sum of bigram frequencies is 138 in English and 52 in French. The non-specific orthographic words had bigram frequencies equal or approximately equal in the the two languages. For instance, for the English word TRADE, the sum of bigram frequencies is 90 in English and 96 in French. We had 48 words in each category, all words of length five letters. The two types of word lists were so constructed that for each non-specific word, there was a corresponding specific word matched in frequency. The words were distributed along the log. frequency range 0.8-3.4. In order to prevent other factors from producing spurious time differences, we carefully matched these two types of test-words for orthographic regularity within language. For English-specific words, bigram frequencies were 123 in English and 65 in French and, for English non-specific words, bigram frequencies were 118 in English and 125 in French. For French-specific words, bigram frequencies were 99 in French and 49 in English and, for French non-specific words, bigram frequencies were 124 in French and 99 in English. This bigram frequency control has the consequence that non-specific words have more orthographic neighbours than specific words that have only one language neighbour.

To address the question of whether or not lexical search in bilinguals may be initiated at different points in the lexicon as evidence of control over access to one distinct lexical system, these stimuli were embedded in two different context lists in a lexical decision task: "Pure" lists (pure English or pure French) contain words of one language only, and "mixed" lists contain words from both languages. According to a preselective search hypothesis, language blocking alters access time so that if a word is presented in the context of same language words, it will be accessed faster than if it is presented in mixed lists. Subjects were 24 bilinguals selected for their competence in English and French. They all acquired their languages very early in childhood and were ending simultaneous translation formation instruction.

The results showed that the time to recognize a word is sensitive to orthographic factors, in that lexical decision times to specific words were shorter than to non-specific words. This confirmed previous data observed in manipulating language specificity of orthographic cues within words (Grainger & Beauvillain, 1987). Note that no difference between these two types of words was observed with English or French monolingual controls. More importantly, as shown in Figure 2, the slopes of linear regression functions between lexical decision times and frequency differed between the two orthographic conditions, in the first as well as in the second language of bilinguals. Indeed, the slope of the linear regression functions was stronger for non-specific words than for specific words. This result was statistically significant both when analyzed by

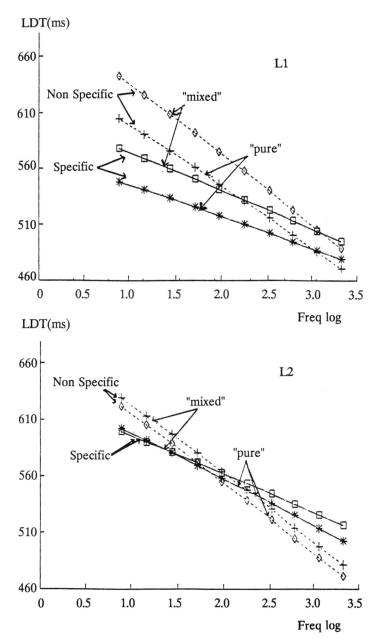

Figure 2. Effects of Frequency on Lexical Decision Times for Specific and Non-specific Words for each List Context Factor.
Top: First Language, and Bottom: Second Language of Bilinguals.

subjects and by items. This difference between the slopes of this linear regression function for the two types of words indicates that the density of the subset of lexical entries differs for the two types of words. Lexical search within a subset of non-specific words from the two languages would be longer than within a subset of specific words. This could be due to the difference in the size of the lexical subset. The size of the lexical subset would be greater for non-specific words than for specific words.

Considering the list context factor, we observed no significant effect of this factor on the response latencies. Thus, the fact that language blocking does not shorten the time to recognize a word argues against a selective search hypothesis. Indeed, a language selective search hypothesis should have predicted that lexical search can be initiated at different points in a lexicon structured by language. Such a mechanism should have produced lexical decision times shorter in the "pure" list than in the "mixed" condition. No significant difference was obtained here between "pure" and "mixed" list conditions. Note that this result differs slightly from previous data (Grainger & Beauvillain, 1987) where no pure-mixed effect was obtained for language-specific words, whereas such an effect was observed for non-specific words. This may be due to differences in the two studies in the selection of the two types of words as well as to differences between the bilingual populations. Indeed, the bilinguals in the present study were very proficient early bilinguals that were ending the Simultaneous Translation formation.

However, this interpretation of the data must be questioned, in that it could be proposed that orthographic factors could affect different aspects of the recognition process. Thus, it could be proposed that bilingual subjects actively use the presence of orthographic specificity in order to search the mental representation in the appropriate lexicon. Against this argument is the fact that the effect of orthography is not modified by the list context. Thus other data have been reported which showed that specific orthographic cues could facilitate lexical retrieval in language- mixed conditions. In a two-word lexical decision task, Kirsner, Smith, Lockhart, King and Jain (1984, Experiment 4) did not observe longer reaction times in Hindi-English mixed language word pairs than in pure-language pairs. This data differed from Meyer and Ruddy's (1974) report of longer reaction times to mixed-language pairs with English-German bilinguals. As suggested by Kirsner et al., these varying results could be attributed to the fact that German and English words do not contain distinct orthographic features, whereas English and Hindi words do.

One possibility is that the grapho-phonological recoding may produce faster recognition times for specific words that can be phonologically coded in only one language, whereas non-specific words can be coded in the two languages. Longer lexical decision times to non-specific words could be due to inappropriate phonological recoding. However, specific words did not suffer from this inappropriate phonological recoding in that they cannot be phonologically coded in both languages.

To test whether or not the difference in the lexical search time between the two types of words is due to their graphophonological recoding, a second experiment was done.   Specific and non-specific words were chosen in controlling the bigram frequencies in the two languages as in the experiment reported above.   Moreover, we selected the items in such a way that the number of candidates was the same in the two types of words.   Defining the lexical subset as the subset of words sharing all letters except one at the same position as the stimulus word, we selected non-specific French word as TORSE as belonging to a subset of English and French candidates in which the number of candidates in the two languages was the same as for the French-specific word.   For instance the French word TORSE belongs to a subset of English candidates such as HORSE, WORSE, TERSE and French candidates such as CORSE, TARSE.   This word has the same number of candidates as LIGUE that determines a subset of only French candidates (LIGNE, DIGUE, LIGUE, FIGUE, GIGUE).   These two types of specific and non-specific words were selected in such a way that words were strictly controlled in frequency and in the relative frequency of the word inside the subset of lexical entries.   Consequently, such words were matched in their frequency range within the lexical subset.   Because of the absence of an effect of the pure-mixed factor in the preceding experiment, we only tested items in the language-blocked condition.

As can be seen in Figure 3, no significant difference was observed in lexical decision times for specific and non-specific words.   Moroever, the slopes of the regression function did not significantly differ between the two types of words.   This result suggests that, for non-specific words, lexical search is not longer than for specific words.   As far as the number of candidates is the same, there is no difference between the two types of words.   If, as I have suggested from the preceding experiment, the difference between specific and non-specific words could be due to a graphophonological process that lengthens the processing time of specific words, then such a difference should have been observed here.   However, no difference was observed between the two types of words. Nothing in the data allows us to attribute the orthography effects to the phonological recoding process of words.

In summary, lexical decision times for specific and non-specific words do not differ when the number of candidates is the same.   This suggests that differences in lexical processing between these two types of words could be due to the density of the subset of candidates sharing the same orthographic cues.   The consequence of this for lexical organization is that orthography will determine lexical subsets in which language boundaries are not represented.

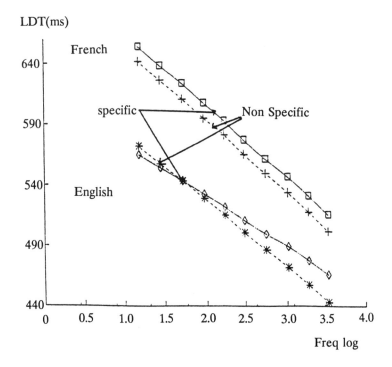

Figure 3. Effects of Frequency on Lexical Decision Times for English and French Specific and Non-specific Words.

Conclusion

The aim of this chapter was to consider the impact of bilingualism on lexical access. The results appear to support the notion that lexical representation is indifferent to bilingual experience, in which case lexical access procedures modulate interlingual as well as intralingual functions. First, the bilingual results I have summarized here strongly suggest that there is some overlap between the lexical representations of both languages. The presence of interference between the two languages suggests that subjects are initially unable to be selective in controlling access to one language system. Clearly, the lexical access of interlexical homographs depends more on internal properties of the lexicon, such as the coded frequency of the different letter strings. Second, such overlap between the two systems is shown where orthography does not specify one of the two languages. We proposed the view that the orthographic representation of words is used in the selection of a subset of lexical forms sharing orthographic properties. Language boundaries will be represented only where language-specific orthography is present within words.   The experimental evidence that orthography affects bilingual word recognition in the lexical constraints has important consequences for the understanding of the visual word recognition process. However, many questions remain, such as the precise kinds of orthographic features that are used in word recognition. Third, there is strong evidence here against a language-selective access. This evidence does not mean that language, as other properties of words, is not represented in the lexicon. It means that language does not govern the lexical access process in bilinguals.

Research into the impact of bilingualism on lexical function necessitates consideration involving individual and linguistic variation. The linguistic differences between the two languages, the order and age in which the two languages are acquired, and the amount of practice in each language may influence the lexical function in the adult bilingual. The arguments presented in this chapter have been guided by a more limited ambition concerning lexical representations; that is, an understanding of the lexical processes involved in the word recognition process with proficient bilinguals can be considered as equivalent in their two languages. Bilingual experimentation allows us to test precise factors affecting the word recognition process such as orthography, regularity, and the density of the lexical subset. Further work on the interplay between these factors will undoubtedly provide insights into word recognition.

References

Altenberg, E. P., & Cairns, H. S. (1983). The effects of phonotactic constraints on lexical processing in bilingual and monolingual subjects. *Journal of Verbal Learning and Verbal Behavior*, 22, 174-188.

Beauvillain, C. (1988). Accessing the mental lexicon with two languages. Paper presented at the Third Conference of The European Society of Cognitive Psychology, 9-12 September 1988, Cambridge.

Beauvillain, C. (1989). Traitement lexical et bilinguisme. *Le Lexique*, 8, 51-64.

Beauvillain, C., & Grainger, J. (1987). Accessing interlexical homographs: Some limitations of a language selective access. *Journal of Memory and Language*, 26, 658-672.

Caramazza, A., & Brones, I. (1979). Lexical access in bilinguals. *Bulletin of the Psychonomic Society*, 13(4), 212-214.

Chen, H.-C., & Ho, C. (1986). Development of Stroop interference in Chinese-English bilinguals. *Journal of Experimental Psychology: Learning, Memory and Cognition*, 12, 397-401.

　　　　　　　　　　　　　C. Beauvillain

Cristoffanini, P., Kirsner, K., & Milech, D. (1986). Bilingual lexical representation: The status of Spanish-English cognates. *Quarterly Journal of Experimental Psychology*, 38A, 367-393.

Durgunoglu, A., & Roediger, H. L. (1987). Test differences in accessing bilingual memory. *Journal of Memory and Language*, 26, 377-391.

Ehri, L .C. & Bouchard-Ryan, E. 1980). Performance of bilinguals in a picture-word interference task. *Journal of Psycholinguistic Research*, 9, 285-303.

Forster, K. I. (1976). Accessing the mental lexicon. In R. J. Wales and E. W. Walker (Eds.), *New approaches to language mechanisms*. Amsterdam: North-Holland.

Forster, K. I. (1979). Levels of processing and structure of the language processor. In W. E. Cooper and E. C. T. Walker (Eds), *Sentence processing*. Hillsdale, NJ: Erlbaum.

Grainger, J., & Beauvillain, C. (1987). Language blocking and lexical access in bilinguals. *Quarterly Journal of Experimental Psychology*, 39A, 295-315.

Grainger, J. & Beauvillain, C. (1988). Associative priming in bilinguals: some limits of interlingual facilitation effects. *Canadian Journal of Psychology*, 42, 261-273.

Guttentag, R. E., Haith, M. M., Goodman, G. S., & Hauch, J. (1984). Semantic processing of unattended words by bilinguals: A test of the input-switch mechanism. *Journal of Verbal Learning and Verbal Behavior*, 23, 178-188.

Kirsner, K. (1986). Lexical function: Is a bilingual account necessary? In J. Vaid (Ed.), *Language processing in bilinguals: Psycholinguistic and neuropsychological perspectives*. London: Erlbaum.

Kirsner, K., Smith, M. C., Lockhart, R. S., King, M. L. & Jain, M. (1984). The bilingual lexicon: Language-specific units in an integrated network. *Journal of Verbal Learning and Verbal Behavior*, 23, 519-539.

Kolers, P. A. (1978). On the representations of experience. In D. Gerver and W. Snaiko (Eds.), *Language interpretation and communication*. New York: Plenum.

Kolers, P. A. (1979). Reading and knowing. *Canadian Journal of Psychology*, 33, 106-117.

Lukatela, G., Savic, M., Gligorijevic, B., Ognjenovic, P., & Turvey, M. T. (1978). Bi-alphabetic lexical decision. *Language and Speech*, 21, 142-165.

Macnamara, J. & Kushnir, S. (1971). Linguistic independence of bilinguals: The input switch. *Journal of Verbal Learning and Verbal Behavior*, 10, 480-487.

McClelland, J. L., & Rumelhart, D. E. (1981). An interactive activation model of context effects in letter perception: Part I. An account of basic findings. *Psychological Review*, 88, 375-407.

McCormack, P. D. (1976). Language as attribute memory. *Canadian Journal of Psychology*, 30(4), 238-248.

Meyer, D. E., & Ruddy, M. G. (1974). Bilingual word recognition: Organization and retrieval of alternative lexical codes. Paper presented at the meeting of the Eastern Psychological Association, Philadelphia.

Obler, L., & Albert, M. (1978). A monitor system for bilingual language processing. In M. Paradis (Ed.), *Aspects of bilingualism*. Columbia, SC: Hornbeam Press.

Potter, M. C., So, K-F., Von Eckardt, B., & Feldman, L. B. (1984). Lexical and conceptual representation in beginning and proficient bilinguals. *Journal of Verbal Learning and Verbal Behavior*, 23, 23-38.

Preston, M. S., & Lambert, W. E. (1969). Interlingual interference in a bilingual version of the Stroop-word task. *Journal of Verbal Learning and Verbal Behavior*, 8, 295-301.

Simpson, G. B. (1984). Lexical ambiguity and its role in models of word recognition. *Psychological Bulletin*, 96, 316-340.

Soares, C. & Grosjean, F. (1984). Bilinguals in a monolingual and bilingual speech mode: The effect on lexical access. *Memory and Cognition*, 12, 380-386.

Swinney, D. A. (1979). Lexical access during sentence comprehension: (Re)consideration of context effects. *Journal of Verbal Learning and Verbal Behavior*, 18, 427-440.

Cognitive Processing in Bilinguals – R.J. Harris (Editor)
© *1992 Elsevier Science Publishers B.V. All rights reserved.*   237

Phonological Processing in Bilingual Word Recognition

Estelle Ann Doctor and Denise Klein
University of the Witwatersrand

Abstract

A model of bilingual word recognition is presented which is derived from current unilingual dual route and verification models. A core feature of this model is that word recognition involves obligatory grapheme-phoneme translation followed by an optional spelling check. The model is able to account for an observed interlingual homophone effect, and successfully predicts the consequences which impaired functioning of this translator would have for a bilingual who is learning to read orthographically deep and shallow languages simultaneously.

One of the aims of bilingual research has been to test models of word recognition, developed from unilingual data, in an attempt to validate, and, if possible, extend them to the bilingual lexicon. A limitation of current theories of word recognition is that most of them are based on English words and have assimilated their idiosyncrasies and peculiarities. Cross-language comparisons permit the differentiation of universal from language-specific aspects of word processing.

Theories of unilingual lexical access: Evidence for phonological recoding

Theories of unilingual lexical access have evolved from two major models of information processing. According to one, the direct access approach, orthographic characteristics of the stimulus are used to access the word's lexical entry, and phonological features are unimportant (Aaronson & Ferres, 1983; Baron, 1973; Becker, 1976, 1980; Bower, 1970; Goodman, 1969; Kleiman, 1975; Kolers, 1970; Paap, Newsome, McDonald & Schvaneveldt, 1982; and Smith, 1971). An alternative hypothesis, phonological mediation, proposes that word identification is preceded by phonological recoding of the letter string, and the resulting phonological code is used for semantic access (Gough, 1972; Rubenstein, Lewis, & Rubenstein, 1971; and Spoehr & Smith, 1973). Recent support for this model has come from Lukatela and Turvey (1990) who have shown in a series of detailed experiments that phonology is computed prelexically and automatically, and that word processing units are activated routinely by phoneme processing units. When tested on Serbo-Croatian subjects the model correctly predicted phonemic similarity effects in lexical decision and naming tasks which were independent of graphemic similarity. Phonemic similarity facilitated the naming of words and nonwords, to the same degree. Dual route models incorporate elements of direct access and phonological mediation theories: orthographic and phonological activation take place, but the debate centers on the time taken to execute the different procedures. Phonological recoding may take longer than direct word recognition but this is seldom noticed since most words can be identified directly and without phonological mediation (Allport, 1977; Coltheart, 1978; McCusker, Hillinger & Bias, 1981; Seidenberg, 1985; Seidenberg, Waters, Barnes & Tanenhaus, 1984; Waters, Seidenberg & Bruck, 1984). Computational models of reading postulate that there is parallel activation of phonological information with other representations (Seidenberg & McClelland, 1989) and that reading of words and nonwords is accomplished by the same mechanism, though the network's performance on nonwords remains controversial.

Dual route models formulated on the basis of the lexical decision paradigm offer support for phonological recoding, but only for nonwords: pseudohomophones (e.g., GRANE) are rejected more slowly than nonpseudohomophones (e.g. FRANE) in lexical decision tasks (Coltheart, Davelaar, Jonasson, & Besner, 1977; Rubenstein et al., 1971). However, this paradigm has not demonstrated phonological effects for words, and homophones have not been reported as leading to significantly less accurate or longer responses than non-homophonic words. According to dual-route theories, the effect for nonwords occurs when the phonological representation of the pseudohomophone [GRANE] activates the phonological representation of its word-pair [GRAIN], making it more difficult for the subject to reject the pseudohomophone. Whether this evidence can be taken into account in explaining word identification has been disputed (Coltheart et al., 1977; Henderson, 1982; McCusker et al., 1981), since the effects in adults, based on lexical decision making, are limited to negative responses. Phonological effects during reading of units larger than the single word have been observed during categorization-verification tasks (Meyer & Gutschera, 1975; Meyer & Ruddy, 1974), sentence verification tasks (Doctor & Coltheart, 1980) and semantic categorization tasks (Van Orden, 1987).

An alternative to dual route theory has been proposed in terms of verification models. According to this explanation, lexical entries are activated simultaneously by prelexical orthographic and phonological cues and phonological recoding is obligatory rather than optional for words (McClelland & Rumelhart, 1981; Perfetti, 1985; Van Orden, 1987). The activated phonological code is used to access the lexical entry. Before a particular entry is selected, verification takes place during a spelling check and the orthographic representation of the target is compared with the orthographic representation of a stored lexical item (Becker, 1976; 1980; Paap et al, 1982; Rubenstein et al, 1971; Schvaneveldt & McDonald, 1981). If a match is detected, word recognition occurs, if not, the next candidate is checked. The verification model differs from dual route models in one important respect: According to dual route theory, a familiar known word will bypass phonological recoding, and will be recognised directly. According to the verification model all words undergo phonological recoding and orthographic verification.

We wish to put forward an alternative model of word recognition which takes into account features of the dual route and verification models. It differs from both in that it aims specifically to describe bilingual word recognition. The model, shown in Figure 1, is based on the following assumptions:

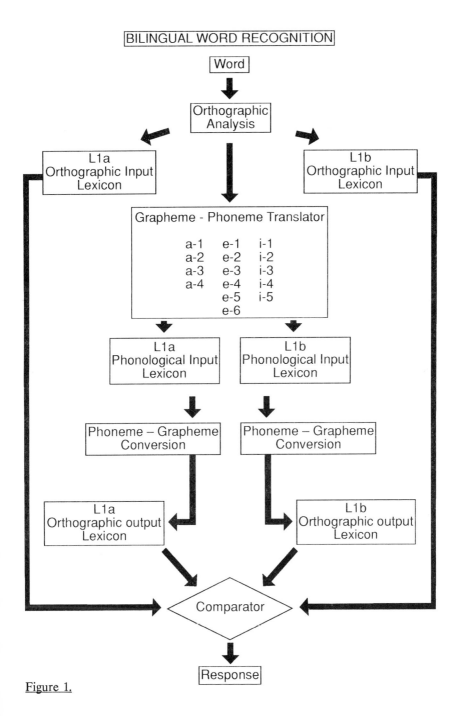

<u>Figure 1.</u>

1. A word presented for lexical decision undergoes visual analysis.

2. Each Language Specific Orthographic Input Lexicon is searched in parallel (in balanced bilinguals) for a match with the orthographic representation of the incoming stimulus (see also Gerard & Scarborough, 1989) and word frequency effects could operate. If an entry is not located in a particular Orthographic Input Lexicon further visual processing in that lexicon is inhibited.

3. At the same time the stimulus is sent in <u>parallel</u> to a Grapheme Phoneme Translator. We assume that this is prelexical and non Language Specific. It operates in parallel on all the grapheme-phoneme correspondences associated with a particular grapheme. There is likely to be only one correspondence per grapheme for shallow orthographies, while for deep orthographies there may be several. This system also allows derivation of the phonological representations of foreign words and would be prone to errors caused by choosing the wrong correspondence.

4. The output from the Grapheme Phoneme Translator is a language-independent phonological representation of the stimulus. It is used to access information in the Language Specific Phonological Input Lexicons. Once again, if an entry is not found in a particular Phonological Input Lexicon, further phonological processing in that lexicon ceases.

5. The next stage of processing is language-specific: an orthographic code is derived from the phonological entry, in much the same way as it occurs for spelling to dictation, according to language specific orthographic rules.

6. This code is used to access an entry in the Language Specific Orthographic Output Lexicon, also used for spelling. If a word match is secured, the graphic representation of this item will then be located. If not, processing is inhibited.

7. The next stage involves verification, and a comparison between the items in the Language Specific Orthographic Input and Output Lexicons.

8. If the comparison is successful, a YES decision will be made. If a mismatch is detected (pseudohomophone, misspelling), there will be an error or rechecking involving longer latencies. At least two predictions follow from this model of bilingual word recognition. Firstly, interlingual homographs (e.g. KIND) should be retrieved more quickly than other words, while there may be a phonological effect which would make decisions about interlingual homophones (e.g. LAKE and LYK in English and Afrikaans) slower and less accurate. Secondly, phonological dyslexia (Beauvois & Derouesne, 1979; Temple & Marshall, 1983) should affect both languages of the bilingual equally, and a bilingual who has difficulty reading orthographically legal nonwords derived from one language should be equally impaired in reading nonwords derived from the other language as well.

Experiment 1

In the first study we shall describe how we attempted to address the issue of how a bilingual's two languages are interconnected at the orthographic and phonological levels.

Method

Thirty-two English/Afrikaans balanced adult bilinguals were selected by their subjective rating of their bilingual proficiency and by their performance on bilingual linguistic tasks. They were presented with 640 letter strings. Half of these were real words; the remainder were nonwords. Three different types of words were presented: 80 interlingual homographs, 80 interlingual homophones and 80 words which are exclusive to each of the languages. The words were 3, 4, 5 or 6 letters long. The English words were matched with each other for frequency, regularity, part of speech and length. They were matched as closely as possible on these variables with the Afrikaans words, though all Afrikaans words are regular in their grapheme-phoneme correspondence. Half of the nonwords were pseudohomophones. Of these, half sounded like English words (e.g. GRONE) and half sounded like Afrikaans words (e.g. FLOEI). The remainder of the nonwords were derived from real English or Afrikaans words so that they looked like real words, but did not sound like real words (e.g. BEM and SUI in English and for Afrikaans). All the stimuli were displayed on the center of a CRT, slaved to an IBM PC.

Instructions were read either in English or Afrikaans, the order being counterbalanced across subjects. Subjects were instructed to decide both quickly and accurately whether each letter string which appeared in the display was a word in either of their two languages, or not, and to indicate their choice by pressing one key if the test word belonged tothe English/Afrikaans real word category and another if it was a nonword. They were told that half the items would be either real English or real Afrikaans words, and that the remainder were nonwords which resembled either an English or an Afrikaans word. Response latency and accuracy were recorded. Preceding the experiment there was a practice session consisting of examples from each category of stimuli.

Results

Words. In order to ascertain whether there were any significant differences in either response accuracy or latency depending on whether the stimuli were interlingual homographs, interlingual homophones, or words exclusive to either language, the mean number of correct responses, and the mean response latencies were calculated. These are shown in Table 1.

Table 1

Mean number of correct responses and mean response latencies calculated for words
exclusive to either language, interlingual homographs and interlingual homophones

	LATENCY (Ms)	ACCURACY (% correct)
Interlingual homographs	747	97
English only	778	89
Afrikaans only	773	91
Interlingual homophones	862	80

As expected, in balanced bilinguals, words which occur only in English or Afrikaans
did not differ from each other in either accuracy or latency. A one-way analysis of
variance confirmed that both main effects of response accuracy and latency were significant (response accuracy: $F(3,116) = 35.3$, $p< 0.01$; response latency: $F(3,116) =$
6.25, $p< 0.01$). Separate analyses were carried out using the min F' statistic (Clark,
1973) and there were significant differences for subjects (Fs) and for words (Fw)
[response accuracy: $Fs(4,431) = 8.77$, $p< 0.01$; response latency: $Fw(3,339) = 3.125$,
$p< 0.05$; response accuracy: $Fs(3,116) = 35.3$, $p< 0.01$; response latency: $Fs(3,116)$
$= 6.25$, $p< 0.01$) and for words (response accuracy: $Fw(3,316) = 11.68$, $p< 0.01$;
response latency: $Fw(3,316) = 6.25$, $p< 0.01$.) A post hoc analysis using Scheffé's test
revealed that interlingual homophones were recognized significantly more slowly and
less accurately than interlingual homographs in analyses for subjects and for words.
(Latency: Fs $(1,116) = 17.18$, $p< 0.01$; $Fw(1,158) = 11.49$, $p< 0.01$; Accuracy:
$Fs(1,60) = 11.82$, $p< 0.01$; $Fw(1,158) = 11.55$, $p< 0.05$). Interlingual homographs were
not recognized more rapidly or more accurately than words which occur only in English
or words which occur only in Afrikaans (though there was a nonsignificant trend in this
direction.)

Nonwords. No significant differences were found in response latency, but there
were significant differences in response accuracy in separate analyses for subjects and
for words $Fs(3,120) = 4.8517$, $p< 0.01$; $Fw(5,54) = 7.05$, $p< 0.01$; Min F' $(5,166) =$
2.87, $p< 0.05$). Nonwords which were pseudohomophonic with Afrikaans words were
significantly more difficult to reject (80.4% correct) than pseudohomophones and
nonpseudohomophones derived from English words (90.7% correct and 89.6% correct
respectively) in analyses for subjects and for words [$Fs(1,58) = 8.04$, $p< 0.05$;
$Fw(1,28) = 12.48$, $p< 0.01$.]

Table 2 shows the response accuracy and latency scores for nonwords compared
with the interlingual homophones.

Table 2

Response accuracy and latency scores for nonwords compared with the interlingual homophones

	LATENCY (Sec)	ACCURACY (% correct)
English Pseudohomophones	.87	90
Afrikaans Pseudohomophones	.95	80
English Nonpseudohomophones	.84	89
Afrikaans nonpseudohomophones	.86	87
Interlingual homophones	.86	80

It is evident from this table that processing time is similar for interlingual homophones and nonwords. It takes longer to respond to a nonword, and this increased latency reflects phonological processing. As with interlingual homophones, a mismatch is detected which has to be verified. A speed-accuracy tradeoff is evident for nonwords.

Particularly slower latencies and high error rates were associated with pseudohomophones derived from Afrikaans words. Because the language is orthographically regular only a small subset of letters are interchangeable, and Afrikaans words have a greater number of orthographically similar lexical neighbours than more orthographically opaque English words. Presented with a pseudohomophone such as HONT (derived from the Afrikaans word HOND), visual and phonological activation of lexical neighbours could occur. Orthographic similarity stimulates a rapid response, but accuracy is diminished. Further evidence of this emerged from an analysis in which processing of the English and Afrikaans members of the interlingual homophone pair were compared. Response times to interlingual pair members did not differ in terms of response latency, indicating that they undergo the same degree of processing. However, significantly more errors were made on the Afrikaans member of each pair (Chi-square = 24.629, df = 1, p< 0.001) because the verification procedure was less accurate for Afrikaans words.

Discussion

Let us consider how the model accounts for the results reported earlier. Firstly, we reported no differences in latency or accuracy for interlingual homographs and words specific to either language. This is difficult to explain in terms of a serial search model. If the target were a word which was exclusive to either language, the search would begin in one lexicon, probably the one containing the word accessed during the previous trial (Grainger & Beauvillain, 1987), and proceed to the other. This would lead to a significant increase in response latencies for language-specific words relative to interlingual homographs, but we found no significant difference between these stimulus types, only a slight trend in this direction. Our results are more readily explained if lexical access is assumed to be parallel. As soon as a representation in one lexicon is accessed, processing in the other may be inhibited in the case of language specific words, while the slightly quicker responses to interlingual homographs which we observed may reflect frequency effects associated with dual representation.

While the Orthographic Input Lexicons are being searched, activation of all grapheme-phoneme translation units takes place simultaneously so that a phonological entry is located in the appropriate Phonological Input Lexicon. (Bias may arise in bilinguals who are not balanced but have a dominant language.) Orthographic rules are applied which generate a code which matches an entry in the appropriate Orthographic Output Lexicon. When this is compared with the entry located in the Orthographic Input Lexicon, a YES response will be made rapidly if a match is detected.

A successful visual search process would not yield differences between targets which are interlingual homophones and other stimuli. The slow response and high error rate associated with interlingual homophones indicate that the decision is not made on the basis of the visual code alone: the phonological code is also activated. Although the visual analysis of the stimulus allows a single entry to be located in one or other of the <u>Orthographic</u> Input Lexicons, the Grapheme-Phoneme Translator gives rise to a phonological code which accesses words in both <u>Phonological</u> Input Lexicons. Both of these map onto real words in the Orthographic Output Lexicons. In the bilingual lexicon an interlingual homophone is associated with (at least) two orthographic entries and a mismatch is detected. When a comparison between the original word and the retrieved item in the Orthographic Output Lexicon is made, there is a type of Stroop effect; the orthographic analyses and the phonological analysis give rise to a conflict which can only be resolved through time-consuming and error-prone checking. An additional processing stage is initiated for interlingual homophones during which the mismatch is resolved and the response made. This is not carried out automatically, as suggested by the verification hypothesis. It need only occur when a word's phonological code activates a second orthographic code which differs from that of the target. Although Grapheme-Phoneme translation is only <u>necessary</u> for interlingual homophones, it is unlikely that the word recognition system is able to decide which stimulus is a homophone and which is not, prior to grapheme-phoneme translation. We therefore suggest that all items undergo obligatory grapheme-phoneme translation, but that a second check is only initiated if there is a mismatch.

Evidence of a visual mismatch which promotes the checking process emerged from a comparison between the graphic similarity of the interlingual homophones and response latencies associated with each. If the checking process is visual, then pairs which are orthographically distinct (e.g. EYE AAI) should be verified rapidly; others which look more similar (e.g. BRIEK BRICK) should be more difficult to verify. Using Weber's Index (Weber, 1970), we calculated the relationship between the graphic similarity of the interlingual homophone pairs, and the time taken to respond to them and found significant positive correlations between graphic similarity and response latencies for the English interlingual homophones ($\underline{r}$ = 0.44; p< 0.05) and for their Afrikaans mates ($\underline{r}$ = 0.45; $\underline{p}$< 0.05). The more similar the pairs were to each other, the more difficult the verification process and the longer the lexical decision latencies. Since Afrikaans has a shallow orthography, it contains fewer distinctive orthographic subunits than the deeper English orthography. Consequently the verification process is not as effective in Afrikaans as in English. This explains why more interlingual homophones were incorrectly rejected and why extra time was required to process pseudohomophones derived from Afrikaans words.

The second prediction to emerge from the model of bilingual word recognition relates to phonological dyslexia, so-called because the disturbance in phonological processing results in a marked deterioration in the ability to read novel words or bogus stimuli. Phonological dyslexia has predominantly been explained from a dual-route position (Kay, 1985). According to this view, the process of reading nonwords is clearly separate and dissociable from a semantically-based mechanism of reading which may be used for reading real words (e.g., Newcombe & Marshall, 1980; Shallice & Warrington, 1980). An alternative view of word recognition is that the separation of words and nonwords imposed by the dual-route model is artificial and that both words and nonwords are read by a process of activating orthographic and phonological neighbours (e.g. Marcel, 1980). The reader refers to a store of sublexical segments abstracted from known words and unknown lexical items are read by analogy. Thus, according to this model, there are no separate rules of grapheme-phoneme correspondence. According to the model of bilingual word recognition which we have proposed reading of orthographically legal nonwords derived from both languages should be equally poor if the locus of the disorder is in the language independent Grapheme-Phoneme Translator.

Experiment 2

Recently we examined a bilingual child (K.T.) of normal intelligence who experienced great difficulty learning to read and spell (Klein & Doctor, 1990). She is classified as a primary language bilingual since she acquired English and Afrikaans simultaneously, from her parents, and before the age of five years. Since the age of 8 her predominant medium of instruction has been English. The result is that she emerged with primary and secondary language competence instead of balanced bilingualism. Nevertheless, K.T's performance on two comparable language tests did not differ and she was extremely poor on both. At the time of initial testing, she was in Standard 2, aged 10 years and 2 months. At that time, and again two years later she was administered a full battery of tests based on the Coltheart (1981) battery but modified for use with bilingual children. (Full details are reported by Klein & Doctor, 1990; we shall concentrate here on aspects of her performance which pertain to the model of bilingual word recognition.)

Method and Results

K.T. was asked to read aloud separate lists of English and Afrikaans words, and orthographically legal nonwords derived from them. The stimuli were matched for frequency and ranged between 4 and 7 letters in length. The results are shown in Table 3.

Table 3

K.T.s reading of words and nonwords: Percentage correct responses

	1988		1990	
	Words	Nonwords	Words	Nonwords
English	44	34	59	31
Afrikaans	53	3	84	38

Her word reading performance was found to be similar across languages and the difference between them was not significant. Short, high frequency words were read with the most accuracy.   K.T.'s word reading is not sensitive to variations in spelling-to-sound regularity, but is subject to lexical effects. For both languages concrete words were read significantly better than abstract words, and content words were read significantly better than function words. A substantial proportion of her errors were other real words which bore some visual resemblance to the target (e.g., English: throng --> "strong"; Afrikaans: soek --> "soen"). Derivational errors in reading aloud words containing bound morphemes were also a common feature of her error responses in both languages (e.g., English: check --> "checked"; Afrikaans: mense --> "mens"). Some regularisation errors which revealedsounding-out strategies were observed, but were in the minority.

The most striking feature of K.T.'s performance was her profound difficulty reading nonwords. (See Table 3.)   K.T. could read those nonwords that had an invariant relationship in grapheme-phoneme translation but had difficulty when the relationship between graphemes and phonemes was more variable. Her nonword reading was affected by vowel complexity and only a small percentage of responses to nonwords showed readiness to make use of major correspondences. This suggests the availability of an operational channel using primitive correspondences which are inaccurate in vowel translation. The difference between correct responses to words and nonwords was significant for Afrikaans (Chi-square = 17.39, df =1, p<0.01; Fishers p<0.01) but not for English. In addition the constitution of the nonword errors differed across languages. A greater proportion of nonwords derived from English words were read as other nonwords which bore a visual similarity to the target.

Unexpectedly, K.T. performed far more poorly on nonwords derived from Afrikaans than from English, and the majority of these nonwords were misread as words.

Discussion

K.T.'s Grapheme-Phoneme Translator appeared to be underdeveloped and we considered how she had learnt to read. She may have acquired her rudimentary knowledge of English letter-sound correspondence through attending classes in which the emphasis was placed more on English than on Afrikaans. However, she was unable to apply automatically those elementary orthographic rules of English which she had been taught at school. We concluded that this tuition had not in fact helped K.T. whose reading of English words was worse than her reading of Afrikaans. She tended to rely on a visual strategy of recognizing words as wholes. Further evidence of this was that her errors on nonwords, like her errors on words, are always visually similar to the target, e.g., DRODUCT -> "drodick"; LYPHOON -> "lyphone". Similarly, her chance performance and an analysis of her error responses in tasks which do not require articulation such as the regular, irregular and nonword homophone judgement tasks and a nonword judgement task where she was required to judge whether pseudohomophones and nonpseudo-homophones sounded like real words, confirmed her struggle with phonology.

Next we considered whether there was any evidence to suggest that K.T. had been able to apply a rule-based system to her reading of Afrikaans. Such a strategy would have been particularly effective for reading Afrikaans because of its orthographic regularity. If she were able to read Afrikaans by sounding words out using the Grapheme-Phoneme Translator, she should have been able to read orthographically legal nonwords but at this she was abysmally poor. It was almost impossible for her to read nonwords derived from Afrikaans and prounounceable by the same set of rules. In addition, most of her errors made in reading Afrikaans words and nonwords were visually similar real words. In short, K.T. did not appear to us to be applying the rules of grapheme-phoneme correspondence, either in English or in Afrikaans.

Following from her poor performance on word and nonword reading, one would not expect K.T to have stable lexicons for recognising words in her different languages. We tested her on lexical decision tasks and the results confirmed uncertainty about the orthography of both English and Afrikaans (Visual Lexical Decision tasks: English 42/64 [65.6%]; Afrikaans 32/64 [50%]). K.T's visual word recognition system was poorly established for both languages.

K.T's problem may be viewed as a disturbance in the language independent Grapheme-Phoneme Translator which has retarded reading development. Seymour (1986) suggested that a primary defect in the phonological processor prevents proper mastery of correspondences between grapheme clusters and sounds during the initial acquisition of reading skill. This initial failure tends to retard the formation of an orthographic lexicon which normally proceeds on logographic lines, by discrimination between words along visual dimensions uncorrelated with sound, and with emphasis on interfacing with semantics rather than phonology. Since the earliest stages of reading do not necessarily involve the use of phonology, a phonologically impaired child might function in a similar way to all other children at the same stage. As the lexicon increases in size and too many words look alike, the child needs to develop a phonological strategy for successful reading. This was K.T's stumbling block: she persisted in using salient features of words to facilitate recognition, and was confronted with the problem of Afrikaans words which are both visually and phonologically confusable.

Since K.T. has an impaired Grapheme-Phoneme Translator, the only alternative left to her for reading is a visual strategy. Both English and Afrikaans stimuli are treated in the same way: K.T. searches for similar looking words in each lexicon. In English, the chance of using an analogy strategy successfully is greater because of the opaque orthography. The transparent orthography of Afrikaans has placed obstacles in the path of K.T.'s reading development. Afrikaans has 30 different vowel sounds corresponding to 27 different vowel symbols and 27 consonant sounds corresponding to 31 different consonant symbols. This allows greater neighbourhood effects than English where the 25 different vowel sounds are represented by 60 symbols and the 25 different consonant sounds by 44 symbols. It is possible to read visually, as children at the logographic stage and Japanese readers reading of Kanji characters demonstrate. However, such a strategy is never entirely satisfactory and K.T. could only retrieve the meaning of approximately 50% of the words to which she had some access. The Afrikaans lexicon consists of many orthographically similar items and it is more important to make use of the rules for reading. When this skill is impaired or not adequately developed, it gives rise to the production of more errors in Afrikaans than English in an English-Afrikaans bilingual.

According to our model of bilingual word recognition, any improvement in the Grapheme-Phoneme Translator should lead to improved reading. In particular, there should be a marked improvement in nonword reading. A follow-up assessment of K.T. was carried out two years after the first assessment, when she was 12, 3 years old. The results of the oral reading tests are shown in Table 3.

An oral reading test of words and nonwords again revealed that word reading was still weak in both languages and that there was no significant difference between them. Reading of nonwords remained poor. However, Afrikaans word <u>and</u> nonword reading had improved significantly over the two years, (Longitudinal assessment of Afrikaans word reading: Chi-square = 5.89, df =1, $p<0.05$; nonword reading: Chi-square = 9.65, df =1, $p<0.01$), while the improvement in English word and nonword reading was not statistically significant. This improvement in Afrikaans may indicate that K.T was making more use of Phoneme-Grapheme Translation and thus Afrikaans, because of its orthographic regularity, improved relative to English.

Conclusion

In sum, this paper has explored a model of bilingual word recognition based on obligatory phonological recoding and verification which is able to account for the interlingual homophone effect observed in lexical decisions. Models of unilingual word recognition would need to be modified to explain these findings. The case of K.T. demonstrated that impairment in the Grapheme-Phoneme Translator system, an integral part of the bilingual model, led to reading difficulties in both languages. However, if a bilingual dyslexic exhibited signs associated with surface dyslexia, such as a greater reliance on phonological recoding, then, on the basis of this model, we might expect to find differing degrees of impairment, with superior performance occurring for orthographically shallow Afrikaans relative to English. Such a case is currently being examined.

Acknowledgment Note

We thank Michel Treisman and Bepi Sartori for their invaluable contribution.

References

Aaronson, D. & Ferres, S. (1983). A model for coding lexical categories during reading. *Journal of Experimental Psychology: Human Perception and Performance*, 9, 700-725.

Allport, D. A. (1977). On knowing the meaning of words we are unable to report: the effects of visual masking. In S. Dornic (Ed.), *Attention and Performance*, VI. London: Academic Press.

Baron, J. (1973). Phonemic stage not necessary for reading. *Quarterly Journal of Experimental Psychology*, 25, 241-246.

Beauvois, M.-F. & Derouesne, J. (1979). Phonological alexia: three dissociations. *Journal of Neurology, Neurosurgery and Psychiatry*, 42, 1115-1124.

Becker, C. A. (1976). Allocation of attention during visual word recognition. *Journal of Experimental Psychology: Human Perception and Performance*, 2, 556-566.

Becker, C. A. (1980). Semantic context effects in visual word recognition: An analysis of semantic strategies. *Memory and Cognition*, 8, 489-512.

Bower, T. G. R. (1970). Reading by eye. In H. Levin and J. P. Williams (Eds.), *Basic studies on reading*. New York: Basic Books.

Clark, H. H. (1973). The language-as-fixed-effect fallacy: A critique of language statistics in psychological research. *Journal of Verbal Learning and Verbal Behavior*, 12, 335-359.

Coltheart, M. (1978). Lexical access in simple reading tasks. In G. Underwood (Ed.), *Strategies of Information Processing*. Pp. 151-216. London: Academic Press.

Coltheart, M. (1981). Disorders of reading and their implications for models of normal reading. *Visible Language*, 15, 245-286.

Coltheart, M., Davelaar, E., Jonasson, J. T. & Besner, D. (1977). Access to the internal lexicon. In S. Dornic (Ed.). *Attention and Performance VI*. Hillsdale, New Jersey: Erlbaum.

Doctor, E. A., & Coltheart, M. (1980). Phonological recoding in children's reading for meaning. *Memory and Cognition*, 8, 195-209.

Gerard, L. D. & Scarborough, D. L. (1989). Language-specific lexical access in homographs by bilinguals. *Journal of Experimental Psychology: Learning, Memory and Cognition*, 15, 305-315.

Goodman, K. (1969). Analysis of oral reading miscues: Applied psycholinguistics. *Reading Research Quarterly*, 5(1), 9-30.

Gough, P. B. (1972). One second of reading. In J.P. Kavanagh & I.G. Mattingly (Eds), *Language by ear and by eye*. Cambridge, Mass.: MIT Press.

Grainger, J., & Beauvillain, C. (1987). Language blocking and lexical access in bilinguals. *Quarterly Journal of Experimental Psychology*, 39A, 295-319.

Henderson, L. (1982). *Orthography and Word Recognition in Reading*. London: Academic Press.

Kay, J. (1985). Mechanisms of oral reading: A critical appraisal of cognitive models. In A. W. Ellis (Ed). *Progress in the Psychology of Language*, Vol 2. London: Lawrence Erlbaum Associates.

Kleiman, G. M. (1975). Speech recoding in reading. *Journal of Verbal Learning and Verbal Behavior*, 14, 323-339.

Klein, D. & Doctor, E. A. (1990). Phonological Dyslexia in an English-Afrikaans Bilingual Child. Paper presented at the 7th Annual Conference of the British Psychological Society, Cognitive Psychology Section, Leicester, England.

Kolers, P. (1970). Three stages of reading. In H. Levin & J.P. Williams (Eds.), *Basic Studies on Reading*. New York: Basic Books.

Lukatela, G. & Turvey, M. T. (1990). Phonemic similarity effects and prelexical phonology. *Memory and Cognition,* 18(2), 128-152.

Marcel, A. J. (1980). Surface dyslexia and beginning reading: A revised hypothesis of the pronunciation of print and its impairments. In M. Coltheart, K. Patterson, and J. C. Marshall (Eds). *Deep Dyslexia,* Pp. 227-258. London: Routledge and Kegan Paul.

McClelland, J. L. & Rumelhart, D. E. (1981). An interactive activation model of context effects in letter perception: Part 1. An account of basic findings. *Psychological Review,* 88, 375-407.

McCusker, L. X., Hillinger, M. L. & Bias, R. G. (1981). Phonological recoding and reading. *Psychological Bulletin,* 89, 217-245.

Meyer, D. E. & Gutschera, K. D. (1975). Orthographic versus phonemic processing of printed words. Paper presented at the Meeting of the Psychonomic Society, Denver.

Meyer, D. E. & Ruddy, M. G. (1974). Bilingual word-recognition: Organization and retrieval of alternative lexical codes. Paper presented at the meeting of the Eastern Psychological Association.

Newcombe, F. and Marshall, J. C. (1980). Transcoding and lexical stabilisation in deep dyslexia. In M. Coltheart, K. E. Patterson, and J. C. Marshall (Eds). *Deep Dyslexia.* London: Routledge and Kegan Paul.

Paap, K. R., McDonald, J. E., Schvaneveldt, R. W. & Noel, R. W. (1987). Frequency and pronounceability in visually presented naming and lexical decision tasks. In M. Coltheart (Ed), *Attention and performance XII.* Hillsdale, NJ: Erlbaum.

Paap, K. R., Newsome, S. L., McDonald, J. E., & Schvaneveldt, R. W. (1982). The activation-verification model for letter and word recognition: The word-superiority effect. *Psychological Review,* 89, 573-594.

Perfetti, C. (1985). *Reading Ability.* Oxford: Oxford University Press.

Rubenstein, H., Lewis, S. S., & Rubenstein, M. A. (1971). Evidence for phonemic recoding in visual word recognition. *Journal of Verbal Learning and Verbal Behavior,* 10, 645-657.

Schvaneveldt, R. W. & McDonald, J. E. (1981). Semantic context and the encoding of words: Evidence for two modes of stimulus analysis. *Journal of Experimental Psychology: Human Perception and Performance,* 7, 673-687.

Seidenberg, M. S. (1985). The time course of phonological code activation in two writing systems. *Cognition,* 19, 1-30.

Seidenberg, M. S. & McClelland, J. L. (1989). A distributed, developmental model of word recognition and naming. *Psychological Review,* 4, 523-568.

Seidenberg, M. S., Waters, G., Barnes, M. A. & Tanenhaus, M. K. (1984). When does irregular spelling and pronunciation influence word recognition? *Journal of Verbal learning and Verbal Behavior,* 23, 383-404.

Seymour, P. H. K. (1986). *Cognitive Analysis of Dyslexia.* London: Routledge and Kegan Paul.

Shallice, T. and Warrington, E. K. (1980). Single and multiple component central dyslexic syndromes. In M. Coltheart, K. E. Patterson and J. C. Marshall (Eds), *Deep Dyslexia.* London: Routledge and Kegan Paul.

Smith, F. (1971). *Understanding Reading: A Psycholinguistic Analysis of Reading and Learning to Read.* New York: Holt, Rinehart & Winston.

Spoehr, K. T., & Smith, E. E. (1973). The role of syllables in perceptual processing. *Cognitive Psychology,* 5, 71-89.

Temple, C. M. & Marshall, J. C. (1983). A case study of developmental phonological dyslexia. *British Journal of Psychology,* 74, 517-534.

Van Orden, G. C. (1987). A ROWS is a ROSE: Spelling, sound and reading. *Memory and Cognition,* 15, 181-198.

Waters, G. S., Seidenberg, M. S., & Bruck, M. (1984). Children's and adults' use of spelling-sound information in three reading tasks. *Memory and Cognition,* 12, 293-305.

Weber, R. M. (1970). First-graders use of grammatical context in reading. In H. Levin and J. P. Williams (Eds.) *Basic Studies on Reading.* New York: Basic Pp. 147-163.

Cognitive Processing in Bilinguals – R.J. Harris (Editor)
253

Lexical Processing in Bilingual or Multilingual Speakers

Hsuan-Chih Chen
The Chinese University of Hong Kong

This chapter is concerned with how people process words in their nonnative language. Major hypotheses about lexical representation in bilingual speakers are briefly reviewed. Two sets of studies are described and discussed. The first set includes experiments that have been carried out within a hybrid theoretical position using translation tasks. The second set of experiments used the Stroop task to explore patterns of color-naming interference in bilinguals. Several factors are identified to be important determinants in each individual set of experiments. Both sets of studies jointly indicate that the level of proficiency in a nonnative language plays a crucial role in determining lexical processing in that language.

Learning and using a nonnative language (e.g., a second or even a third language) is becoming a common experience for an in-creasing number of people, and considerable attention has been devoted to the study of cognitive processing in bilingual or multilingual speakers. In this chapter, I will attempt to focus on a small part of the larger question, which I believe is quite fundamental in the area: How do people process words in their nonnative language?

I will begin by briefly reviewing hypotheses about lexical representation in bilingual speakers. Some work that has been carried out within a theoretical framework for understanding how people process words in their nonnative language willbe described. I will review results from picture- and word-translating experiments to show that both proficiency in a nonnative language and learning strategy are important determinants for lexical processing in that language. I will then describe experiments using the Stroop color-word task to explore the pattern of color-naming interference in bilinguals and will try to identify factors that are important to the patterns of results. Implications of the results from these experiments for processing words in a nonnative language will be discussed.

Lexical representation in bilinguals

To understand lexical processing in a nonnative language, one must consider how people mentally represent words in the language. Two competing hypotheses of lexical representation have become the focus of controversy in the bilingual literature. The contrasting positions have been known as the independence vs. interdependence hypotheses or as the common-code vs. separate-code hypotheses (e.g., McCormack, 1977; Snodgrass, 1984). The interdependence hypothesis proposes that the two languages of a bilingual are stored in one single amodal system in memory. The independence hypothesis, however, postulates that the two languages are independently stored in separate memory systems. These two positions are usually presented in their extreme form and each position has received empirical support.

More recently, to resolve the interdependence vs. independence debate and to account for a variety of language-dependence and language-independence results in the literature, a third hybrid position, which has features of both, has been proposed (e.g., Potter, So, Von Eckardt, & Feldman, 1984; Snodgrass, 1984). This type of hybrid model typically holds that there is a level of representation corresponding to different perceptual forms (i.e., words in different languages and pictures).   These modality-specific, independent representations jointly share a amodal representation at an abstract, conceptual level.

The distinction between modality-specific representations and their amodal concepts has received considerable support from experimental and clinical studies with monolinguals and/orbilinguals as subjects and using verbal and/or nonverbal materials as stimuli (e.g., Chen & Ng, 1989; Besner, Smith, & MacLeod, 1990; Gerard & Scarborough, 1989; Kirsner, Smith, Lockhart, King, & Jain, 1984; Nelson, Reed, & McEvoy, 1977; Potter et al., 1984; Potter, Kroll, Yachzel, Carpenter, & Sherman, 1986; Schwartz, Marin, & Saffran, 1979; Theios & Amrhein, 1989; see Snodgrass, 1984, for a review).   In fact, the hybrid model can easily account for many language-dependence and language-independence results in the bilingual literature by taking into account factors such as task demands (e.g.,data-driven vs. conceptually driven or episodic vs. semantic) and encoding conditions (see, e.g., Grosjean, 1982; Smith, 1991; Snodgrass, 1984; for issues related to task demands and encoding conditions, see Durgunoglu & Roediger, 1987).

Picture- and word-translating results

In this section I will review some of the main results obtained in experiments with picture- and word-translating tasks which were designed to investigate whether proficient and beginning users of a nonnative language process lexical items in similar ways in the new language.   The experiments I discuss here are reported in detail elsewhere (Chen, 1990; Chen & Leung, 1989).

Two processing models: Concept mediation and word association

Two processing models generated from the hybrid position mentioned above have been proposed to describe how people process words in their nonnative language (Potter et al., 1984).   One such processing model is the concept mediation model.   This model assumes that the native and nonnative languages of abilingual operate independently so that lexical items in the two languages are not directly linked but are associated through a language-free conceptual system.   An alternative model is the word association model which assumes that words in the nonnative language are directly linked with their corresponding words in the native language rather than with their underlying concepts.   These connections are activated when a bilingual uses his/her nonnative language.

The concept mediation and the word association models were tested in our experiments by using two types of stimuli and two major tasks, following Potter et al.

(1984). All the stimuli were visually presented which included pictures of concrete objects and their corresponding words in the native language(L1). The major tasks were translating L1 words to the nonnative language (L2), and translating pictures to L2. The word association model and the concept mediation model make distinctively different predictions regarding the relative time to perform the two tasks. But, before we talk about the specific predictions generated from these two models, it is important to point out that those predictions are made on the basis of two assumptions: equal recognition times and equal semantic-access (i.e., stimulus recognition and concept retrieval) times for pictures and L1 words.   These two assumptions have been supported by the recognition threshold and the categorization data in previous studies (e.g., Chen & Leung, 1989; Potter et al., 1984).   These two models and their predictions regarding processing steps involved in the two translating tasks are shown in Figure 1.

The concept mediation model predicts that picture translating and word translating should involve similar processing procedures (i.e., started with picture/word recognition, followed by concept retrieval and retrieval of the L2 word, and ending with speaking the L2 word). Thus, the two tasks should take about the same amount of time to complete. The word association model, however, predicts that word translating should involve word recognition, retrieval of the L2 word, and speaking the word, whereas picture translating should involve picture recognition, concept retrieval, retrieval of the L1 word, retrieval of the L2 word, and speaking the word.   Because the picture translating task involves two additional steps relative to the word task, the picture task should take longer time to complete.

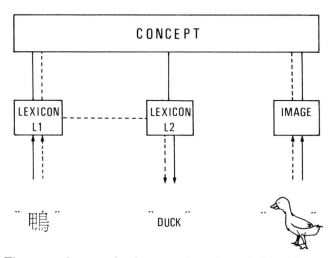

Figure 1. The processing steps in picture- and word-translating tasks, as proposed by the concept mediation model and the word association model. The solid lines indicate the steps proposed by the concept model and the broken lines indicate the steps proposed by the word model.

Beginning and proficient users of a nonnative language

In an initial study (Chen & Leung, 1989, Experiment 1), three groups of subjects were recruited, including proficient Chinese-English undergraduates (the proficient subjects), beginning Chinese-French undergraduates (i.e., the adult beginners), and beginning Chinese-English primary school students (the child beginners). All subjects were native Chinese speakers and had acquired their nonnative languages from school.

The results showed that the proficient subjects were equally efficient at picture and word translating tasks. This pattern is in line with the concept mediation model. The adult beginners were faster at word translating than picture translating. This result is consistent with the word association model. A somewhat surprising result is that the child beginners were faster at picture translating than word translating. This pattern of result is not consistent with the concept mediation model nor with the word association model. Rather, the child beginners' results seem to suggest that they might have used pictorial representations rather than L1 words as media to produce corresponding L2 responses. An alternative explanation for the results of the child beginners is that they might still have used concepts rather than pictorial representations to mediate and produce L2 responses, but the picture-to-concept link was stronger or better developed than the L1-to-concept link. This explanation, however, was ruled out by findings of a follow-up experiment (Chen & Leung, 1989, Experiment 3). This experiment used a category-matching task with pictures and L1 words to measure and compare the strengths of picture- and L1-to-concept links. Results showed that the relative times to understand a picture and an L1 word were not statistically different.

The results described above reveal clearly that the adult beginners, the child beginners, and the proficient bilinguals had distinctively different patterns of results in picture- and word-translating tasks. These results thus suggest that proficient and beginning users of a nonnative language use different ways to process words in the new language. To account for the findings of different subject groups, an intermediate hypothesis was proposed (Chen & Leung, 1989). According to this hypothesis, at the beginning stage of learning a nonnative language, the new language is operated through existing cognitive systems such as the native language or the prototypical visual image system, depending on learning strategy, but the new language gradually develops into a stage of independent operation as the learning process continues. Adult beginners of a nonnative language are likely to use the native language to acquire the new language presumably because their knowledge about the native language is sufficient enough to allow them to do so. Child beginners, on the other hand, are likely to be taught by using concrete media such as pictures or even real objects, particularly if they are learning names of concrete objects. This is probably why, in the above mentioned experiment, the adult beginners revealed a lexical mediation pattern, whereas the child beginners showed a picture mediation pattern.

The intermediate hypothesis proposes that proficiency in L2 is a major determinant in lexical processing in bilinguals. This language-proficiency proposal was tested in another experiment (Chen, 1990, Experiment 1). This was done by observing the development of patterns of lexical processing of Chinese-English bilinguals with various degrees of proficiency in their second language. Participants of this experiment were students from four grade levels (Grades 2, 4, and 6, and college) who had studied English at school for about 2, 4, 6, or over 12 years, respectively. It was found that the subjects were generally faster in translating pictures than in translating Chinese words into English. More crucially, in line with the language-proficiency proposal, the results showed that the magnitude of the picture-over-word difference systematically decreased as the subjects' proficiency in L2 increased (i.e., from about 470 msec for the second graders decreased to about 25 msec for the college students).

Nonnative language learning in an experimental setting

In the experiments summarized above, subjects of different grades were used. Note that this is not the ideal way to test the potential effects of nonnative language proficiency and learning strategy on lexical processing, because subjects of various grades not only differed in proficiency in their nonnative language, but they also varied in other aspects such as age and L1 proficiency. The optimal way to do this without confounding by subject factor would be to include subjects matched on important individual and social characteristics (e.g., age, intelligence, educational history, and native and nonnative languages) but with varied levels of proficiency in the new language and different acquisition strategies. Unfortunately, it is extremely difficult to find subjects such as these in real situations. However, it is possible to simulate the ideal case in an experimental setting. Two such experiments were thus conducted. These experiments (Chen, 1990, Experiments 2 and 3) and their main results are summarized in the following sections.

Two groups of undergraduate subjects studied a set of 20 words (i.e., names of concrete objects) in a wholly unfamiliar language, French, while proficiency in the new language and learning strategy were experimentally manipulated. The French words were paired with either corresponding L1 words (i.e., the word learning group) or corresponding pictures (i.e., the picture learning group) as study stimuli. The subjects participated in three continuous sessions. Each session included a study phase in which one set of French-picture or French-Chinese pairs were shown (the same set of stimuli was shown in each study phase) and a test phase in which the above mentioned picture- and word-translating tasks were administered (a different set of test stimuli was used in each test phase). The list of stimulus pairs was presented once in the first session, twice in the second session, and three times in the third session to ensure that a higher degree of proficiency in response to the French words could be achieved in one session relative to its previous session. The order of the pairs was randomized in each trial. During the presentation of each study pair, an experimenter read the presented French word to the subject.

In the first test session, very little learning was observed; all subjects performed very poorly in both translating tasks. The results for the second and the third test sessions are clear: The subjects responded more efficiently to the kind of learning medium used in the study trials in the second session (i.e., Chinese stimuli produced faster translating responses than did pictures for the word-learning group, whereas the reverse pattern was obtained for the picture-learning group), and as the subjects received more training in the study phase, different learning media eventually led to identical results in the third session (i.e., they could respond equally efficiently to both the training medium and the other medium type).

Note that since the subjects were tested at the end of each session with the same translating tasks, the subjects had multiple exposures to different versions of the French words in various test phases. Thus, it seems possible that this procedure of repeated testing might have contributed to the pattern of results of the third session. This possibility has been tested and ruled out in another experiment (Chen, 1990, Experiment 2). This was done by making degree of learning a between-subjects variable (subjects had either 3 or 9 study trials with a set of words in a new language). Results of this new experiment where a single-test design was adopted were highly compatible with those of the other experiment in which a repeated-test design was adopted.

Clearly, the results reviewed in the present section are not consistent with the hypothesis that beginning and proficient users of a nonnative language adopt similar strategies for processing lexical items in their new language. Rather, the findings are in line with the intermediate hypothesis, indicating that both level of proficiency in a nonnative language and strategy of learning the new language are important determinants for the pattern of lexical processing in the new language.

Stroop color-naming results

The next issue I would like to address concerns within- and between-language lexical interference in bilinguals. This issue has been traditionally studied using the Stroop color-word task (e.g., Dyer, 1971; Preston & Lambert, 1969) or Stroop-like tasks such as Picture- and symbol-word tasks (e.g., Chen & Tsoi, 1990; Magiste, 1984). For example, a Chinese-English bilingual can be asked to use English to name the inks of conflicting color words in English or in Chinese. When the subject's color naming response is slowed down by a color word in the same language relative to a neutral stimulus (e.g., a color patch), a within-language interference is demonstrated, whereas when a response is distracted by a word in the other language, a between-language interference is shown. By observing and contrasting these two types of interference, one can explore interesting and important topics such as lexical interaction between two languages and attentional processes in bilinguals.

Typical results of proficient bilinguals

Most studies using the Stroop task with proficient bilinguals as subjects find that color-naming interference is greater in the within-language condition than in the between-language condition (e.g., Chen & Ho, 1986; Dyer, 1971; Preston & Lambert, 1969; Tzelgov, Henik, & Leiser, 1990). This result indicates that proficient bilinguals can selectively concentrate on processing of words in the nonnative language even when the simultaneously presented, distracting stimuli are words in their native language. Such a result thus suggests that the proficient bilinguals can process words in the nonnative language relatively independently, without necessarily activating corresponding words in their native language. This suggestion is in line with results of other studies using a variety of semantic tasks such as translation (e.g., Chen, 1990; Chen & Leung, 1989; Potter et al., 1984), categorization (e.g., Chen, 1988), and the semantic priming paradigm with a lexical decision task (e.g., Chen & Ng, 1989; Kirsner et al., 1984; Schwanenflugel & Rey, 1986).

Results of German-Swedish bilinguals

Less typically, some studies comparing between- and within-language interference in the color-naming task with proficient bilingual subjects, especially if the orthographies of the two languages of the bilinguals are similar, have found either equivalent interference or mixed patterns of results. For example, Magiste (1984) reported an interesting study in which she recruited native German speakers whom had learned Swedish as their second language as subjects on the basis of their length of residence in Sweden. Results of this study showed that for subjects who lived in Sweden for less than two years, color names in German consistently produced greater interference than those in Swedish; for those lived there from two to seven years, color words in both languages created comparable interference; and for subjects with a lengthy stay in Sweden (i.e., more than seven years), Swedish words produced greater interference when the response was in Swedish. Magiste suggested that the pattern of interference in bilinguals was mainly determined by language proficiency (i.e., the degree of interference created by a language is determined by the level of proficiency in that language). Note that the two languages involved in Magiste's study were German and Swedish. These two languages not only belong to the same Germanic branch of the Indo-European language family, they also use the same alphabetic script. Thus, using bilinguals with highly similar languages as subjects becomes a special feature of this study.

Results of Chinese-English bilinguals

To verify the ideas that language similarity may be responsible for the results of Magiste (1984) and that language proficiency would affect the pattern of interference in bilinguals, Chen and Ho (1986) carried out a color-naming study to observe the development of between- and within-language interference of bilinguals whose first and second languages are very different. Because Chinese and English are distinctively different languages (i.e., the former belongs to the Sino-Tibetan language family and uses the logographic orthography, whereas the latter belongs to the Indo-European family and uses the alphabetic script; see Chen & Juola, 1982, for relevant discussion), Chinese-English bilinguals were used as subjects in this study. The subjects were recruited from five grade levels (Grades 2, 4, 8, and 10 and college), and they all were Chinese-dominant. These subjects had studied their second language at school for about 2, 4, 8, 10, or over 12 years (i.e., for the second, fourth, eighth, and tenth graders and college students, respectively).

The results showed that for subjects of all levels, greater within- than between-language interference was observed when the response was in the subjects' first language, Chinese (i.e., Chinese stimuli produced longer color-naming responses than did English stimuli). This result indicates that users of a nonnative language can easily resist competing stimuli in the new language when responding in their native language. However, when the response was in English, a developmental shift from greater between-language interference to greater within-language interference was found as the subjects' proficiency in English increased. Clearly, for subjects with the least knowledge of English, color names in L1, the dominant language, consistently produced greater color-naming interference than those in L2, regardless of which response language was used. For subjects with eight or more years' training in L2, despite the fact they were still dominant in L1, stimulus-response compatibility, not language dominance or language proficiency, became the main determinant for the pattern of interference. In other words, for more proficient bilinguals, in both response languages, when the stimulus language was compatible with the response language (i.e., the within-language condition), greater color-naming interference was experienced than when the stimulus and the response languages were incompatible (i.e., the between-language condition). These results indicate that the pattern of the between- and within-language interference in bilinguals is determined both by level of proficiency in the second language and stimulus-response compatibility.

Results of Arabic-Hebrew/Hebrew-Arabic bilinguals

The main results of Chen and Ho (1986) have recently been replicated by Tzelgov et al. (1990) with proficient Arabic-Hebrew and nonproficient Hebrew-Arabic bilinguals. Tzelgov et al. reported that the proficient Arabic-Hebrew revealed the typical greater within- than between-language interference, whereas the less proficient subjects showed that the pattern of interference was determined by the dominant language.   An interesting point to note is that although both Arabic and Hebrew belong to the same Afro-Asiatic language family, these two languages use different scripts.

Main determinants in the color-naming task

By comparing the results from three studies reviewed above (i.e., Chen & Ho, 1986; Magiste, 1984; Tzelgov et al., 1990), a number of interesting points regarding lexical processing and interference in bilinguals can be generated. First, a consistent finding in all three studies is that, when responding in the second language, the pattern of interference in bilinguals is systematically affected by the level of proficiency in that language. In fact, the results of the three studies imply that at an early stage of second language acquisition, users of the new language have difficulty concentrating fully on the language, presumably because their proficiency in that language is still relatively low, and they cannot resist distracting stimuli in their first language. Consequently, greater between- than within-language interference is usually found at this early stage.

However, bilinguals' ability to focus on the new language and to withstand competing stimuli in the first language gradually increases with their proficiency in the second language. Thus, an opposite pattern of results (i.e., greater within- than between-language interference) is commonly found for proficient bilinguals.

Second, the fact that findings of Tzelgov et al. (1990) are in line with those of Chen and Ho (1986) and both are different from those of Magiste (1984), indicates that orthographic similarity can affect the pattern of interference in bilinguals. It seems likely that when the orthographies of the two languages of bilinguals are relatively different, in the between-language condition, the bilinguals can more easily focus on the color-naming response in one language and resist interference from stimuli in the other language. This would thus make the between-language condition easy to respond to than the within-language condition. However, when the orthographies of the two languages are similar, as in Magiste's study, the bilinguals cannot rely on such orthographic cues to avoid interference from the stimuli in a different language. Undersuch situations, perhaps language proficiency may then become the sole determinant of the interference pattern.

One final point to note is about age of second language acquisition. This fact or has been considered by some researchers as important in second language acquisition and processing (e.g., Harley, 1986; Johnson & Newport, 1989). However, although nonproficient subjects in the study of Chen and Ho (1986) and those in Tzelgov et al. (1990) acquired their second language at different periods of age (i.e., the former group in childhood and the latter in adolescence), patterns of interference of the two groups of subjects are highly comparable. This indicates that age of acquisition may not be critical for the between- and within-language pattern of interference in bilinguals. Rather, it seems that other factors underlying age of acquisition, such as learning strategy, may be important in determining the pattern of lexical processing in bilinguals or multilinguals. This is reflected by the results reviewed above. Specifically, Chen and Leung (1989) reported that child and adult beginning users of a nonnative language showed different patterns of lexical processing. However, the responsible factor turns out to be learning strategy rather than age of acquisition, because in follow-up studies, Chen (1990) demonstrated that both the child and adult beginners' patterns of results could be replicated in an experimentally induced condition by manipulating learning strategy directly.

Summary and conclusion

In the foregoing, I have reviewed and discussed two lines of research, and have tried to show that both have implications for understanding lexical processing in a nonnative language. The first line of research using picture- and word-translating tasks has shown that level of proficiency in a nonnative language and learning strategy of the new language are two main determinants of the patterns of lexical processing in that language. The second line of research with a bilingual version of the Stroop color-naming task has similarly revealed that proficiency in a second language plays a crucial role in determining the patterns of interference, though both stimulus-response compatibility and orthographic similarity also affect the patterns.

Taken together, these two lines of research indicate that beginning and proficient users of a nonnative language process lexical items in different ways in that language. For proficient users, the nonnative language can be used relatively independently, indicating that they can directly access the meanings of words in that language. Beginning and less proficient users, however, do not seem to be able to do that. Rather, they tend to rely on their native language or other representation systems such as the prototypical visual image system to process nonnative words. The results described earlier further suggest that shifting from the dependent processing pattern in a nonnative language to the independent processing pattern seems to occur in a gradual manner rather than happening abruptly at a certain stage of nonnative language acquisition.

Acknowledgements

The preparation of this chapter was supported by a UPGC Direct Grant for Research from the Administrative, Business and Social Studies Panel, The Chinese University of Hong Kong. Some of the work described in this chapter was supported by the same grant. I would like to thank Kin-Tong Chan, Connie Ho, Yuen-Sum Leung, and Siu-Yee Mak for the valuable contribution they made to the work described here. My thanks also to Richard Harris for helpful comments on an earlier draft.

References

Besner, D., Smith, M. C., MacLeod, C. M. (1990). Visual word recognition: A dissociation of lexical and semantic processing. *Journal of Experimental Psychology: Learning, Memory and Cognition, 16*, 862-869.

Chen, H.-C. (1988). Between- and within-language repetition effects in bilinguals. *Chinese Journal of Psychology, 30*, 89-94.

Chen, H.-C. (1990). Lexical processing in a non-native language: Effects of language proficiency and learning strategy. *Memory and Cognition, 18*, 279-288.

Chen, H.-C., & Ho, C. (1986). Development of Stroop interference in Chinese-English bilinguals. *Journal of Experimenal Psychology: Learning, Memory and Cognition, 12*, 397-401.

Chen, H.-C., & Juola, J. F. (1982). Dimensions of lexical coding in Chinese and English. *Memory and Cognition, 10*, 216-224.

Chen, H.-C., & Leung, Y. S. (1989). Patterns of lexical processing in a nonnative language. *Journal of Experimental Psychology: Learning, Memory and Cognition, 15*, 316-325.

Chen, H.-C., & Ng, M.-L. (1989). Semantic facilitation and translation priming effects in Chinese-English bilinguals. *Memory and Cognition*, 17, 454-462.

Chen, H.-C., & Tsoi, K.-C. (1990). Symbol-word interference in Chinese and English. *Acta Psychologica*, 75, 123-138.

Durgunoglu, A. Y., & Roediger, H. L. (1987). Test differences in accessing bilingual memory. *Journal of Memory and Language*, 26, 377-391.

Dyer, F. N. (1971). Color-naming interference in monolinguals and bilinguals. *Journal of Verbal Learning and Verbal Behavior*, 10, 297-302.

Gerard, L. D., & Scarborough, D. L. (1989). Language-specific lexical access of homographs by bilinguals. *Journal of Experimental Psychology: Learning, Memory and Cognition*, 15, 305-315.

Grosjean, F. (1982). *Life with two languages: An introduction to bilingualism.* Cambridge, MA: Harvard University Press.

Harley, B. (1986). *Age in second language acquisition.* Clevedon, England: Multilingual Matters.

Johnson, J. S., & Newport, E. L. (1989). Critical period effects in second language learning: The influence of maturational state on the acquisition of English as a second language. *Cognitive Psychology*, 21, 60-99.

Kirsner, K., Smith, M. C., Lockhart, R. S., King, M. L., & Jain, M. (1984). The bilingual lexicon: Language specific units in an integrated network. *Journal of Verbal Learning and Verbal Behavior*, 23, 519-539.

Magiste, E. (1984). Stroop tasks and dichotic translation: The development of interference patterns in bilinguals. *Journal of Experimental Psychology: Learning, Memory and Cognition*, 10, 304-315.

McCormack, P. D. (1977). Bilingual linguistic memory: The independence-interdependence issue revisited. In P. A. Hornby (Ed.), *Bilingualism: Psychological, social, and educational implications* (pp. 57-66). New York: Academic Press.

Nelson, D. L., Reed, V. S., & McEvoy, C. L. (1977). Learning to order pictures and words: A model of sensory and semantic encoding. *Journal of Experimental Psychology: Human Learning and Memory*, 5, 485-497.

Potter, M. C., Kroll, J. F., Yachzel, B., Carpenter, E., & Sherman, J. (1986). Pictures in sentences: Understanding without words. *Journal of Experimental Psychology: General*, 115, 281-294.

Potter, M. C., So, K.-F., Von Eckardt, B., & Feldman, L. B. (1984). Lexical and conceptual representation in beginning and proficient bilinguals. *Journal of Verbal Learning and Verbal Behavior*, 23, 23-38.

Preston, M. S., & Lambert, W. E. (1969). Interlingual interference in a bilingual version of the Stroop color-word task. *Journal of Verbal Learning and Verbal Behavior*, 8, 295-301.

Schwanenflugel, P. J., & Rey, M. (1986). Interlingual semantic facilitation: Evidence for a common representational system in the bilingual lexicon. *Journal of Memory and Language*, 25, 605-618.

Schwartz, M. F., Marin, O. S. M., & Saffran, E. M. (1979). Dissociations of language functioning in dementia: A case study. *Brain and Language*, 7, 277-306.

Smith, M. C., (1991). On the recruitment of semantic information for word fragment completion: Evidence from bilingual priming. *Journal of Experimental Psychology: Learning, Memory and Cognition*, 17, 234-244.

Snodgrass, J. G. (Ed.). (1984). Concepts and their surface representations [Special issue]. *Journal of Verbal Learning and Verbal Behavior*, 23(1).

Theios, J., & Amrhein, P. C. (1989). Theoretical analysis of the cognitive processing of lexical and pictorial stimuli: Reading, naming, and visual and conceptual comparisons. *Psychological Review*, 96, 5-24.

Tzelgov, J., Henik, A., & Leiser, D. (1990). Controlling Stroop interference: Evidence from a bilingual task. *Journal of Experimental Psychology: Learning, Memory and Cognition*, 16, 760-771.

Cognitive Processing in Bilinguals – R.J. Harris (Editor)

Language as a Factor in the Identification
of Ordinary Words and Number Words

Cheryl Frenck-Mestre and Jyotsna Vaid
CNRS-Université de Provence and Texas A & M University

Abstract

What role does language play in the organization of and access to the bilingual lexicon? Two primed lexical decision experiments addressed this question, with the specific aim of comparing the salience of the language of presentation of a word when the word was a number-word (e.g. FIVE) and when it was a non-number-related word. The results of the two experiments revealed that language does not appear to be as important a feature of number words as it is for "ordinary" words of the lexicon. The findings are discussed in light of recent models of bilingual lexical access.

A considerable body of bilingual research has been devoted to determining the degree of semantic overlap between a bilingual's two languages (cf. Kirsner, Smith, Lockhart, King & Jain, 1984; Kolers & Brison, 1984; Paradis & Lebrun, 1983; Snodgrass, 1984; for reviews). Common agreement at present is that, depending upon task demands, either language-specific or language-independent results will be revealed (Snodgrass, 1984; Durgunoglu & Roediger, 1987), thus giving credibility to the notion that whereas the two languages may indeed converge at some level (semantic for example), there is a level at which the two languages are organized separately.

Less research has in fact been aimed at determining the role played by language as a factor in the organization of and access to the bilingual lexicon, independent of any semantic processing. One recent study (Cristoffanini, Kirsner, & Milech, 1986) suggested that language is not an important factor in bilingual lexical organization but rather that the lexical entries of the two languages are organized on the basis of morphology, much in the same way as has been suggested for monolinguals (Taft, 1987). This view is not, however, shared by all. In two other recent studies on the role of language in bilingual lexical access, the assumption is made that the bilingual's two languages are organized separately at the level of lexical entries, although the one study promotes a model of parallel access to the two lexicons (Grainger & Beauvillain, 1987) whereas the other supports language-selective access (Gerard & Scarborough, 1989; see also Scarborough, Gerard & Cortese, 1984).

Herein we examined the role played by language in the identification of words from the bilingual's two languages, with the specific aim of comparing the influence of the language of presentation of a word for two types of words: "number" words (e.g. seven, thirteen) and non number-related words, or "ordinary" words of the lexicon. This comparison stemmed from previous results (Vaid & Frenck, in press; Frenck & Pynte, 1987b) which suggest that the language of presentation may be a less pertinent feature of number words as compared to ordinary words.

As concerns the processing of ordinary words, a pervasive result in bilingual studies is an increase in response time whenever the bilingual must switch from one language to the other in order to process the material s/he is confronted with. In studies using visually presented sentences, overall reading time and verification time are longer when the sentence contains a language switch as compared to an otherwise equivalent monolingual sentence (Kolers, 1966; MacNamara & Kushnir, 1971). Specifically, it has been shown that the time needed to identify a target word within an auditorily presented sentence is longer if the target initiates a language switch than if it is in the same language as the sentence incorporating it (Soares & Grosjean, 1984). It should be noted, however, that the increase in processing time observed for sentences containing a language switch may in fact be due to the disruption of normal syntactic processing, depending on where the switch occurs (Chan, Chau & Hoosain, 1983). Moreover, switching languages within a sentence may be governed by very specific strategies and/or by a "bilingual syntax", familiar to the bilingual but as of yet relatively unexplored by the psychologist (Sridhar & Sridhar, 1980; but see Joshi, 1985).

This increase in processing time following a language switch is also observed regularly in studies using individual words. The overall reading time of a list of words is significantly longer when the list is "mixed" that is, when it contains words from the bilingual's two languages, than when the words are presented in a monolingual , or "pure" list (Dalrymple-Alford, 1985). Lexical decision times are also longer to target words presented in a mixed versus a pure list but, rather than an overall lengthening, results show response times to be significantly longer in the mixed list only when a given word is immediately preceded by a word from the other language (Grainger & Beauvillain, 1987). Results parallel to this are found in bilingual studies which examine the effect of semantic priming, where the prime and target word are either in the same language or in different languages. Whereas the amount of facilitation, in terms of reduced response time to the target, is often equivalent in conditions of within-language priming and across-language priming, overall response times are longer when the prime and target are presented in different languages than when the two words are in the same language (Frenck & Pynte, 1987a, 1987b; Kirsner et al., 1984; Meyer & Ruddy, 1974; but see Schwanenflugel & Rey, 1986).

In contrast to the above-mentioned results found for ordinary words, there is some evidence from two different studies that language of presentation for number words may not be a salient feature. One study (Vaid & Frenck, in press) examined incidental recall for language of presentation of spelled-out numbers, presented in one or the other of the bilingual's two languages. The results showed that correct recall was 65% overall when the bilingual had copied the numbers at initial presentation and 53% overall when the bilingual translated the numbers at the time of presentation (Vaid & Frenck, in press). These percentages are not high in themselves and are in fact substantially lower than values such as 70% to 80% observed for recall of language of presentation of ordinary words (cf. Park & Vaid, in press).

In another bilingual study (Frenck & Pynte, 1987a), a primed lexical decision task was used in which number words were used as neutral primes. Number words were chosen as neutral primes given their semantic neutrality in relation to the target words. A rather unexpected result was the apparent neutrality of number words in inducing language. Ordinary prime words significantly delayed response times to target words when the prime and target were presented in different languages (e.g. "bas" - "high") as compared to when they were in the same language (e.g. "low" - "high"). In contrast, preceding a target by a number prime word in the other language (e.g. "cinq" - "high") did not significantly increase response times as compared to when the number prime was in the same language as the target (e.g. "five" - "high").

The results obtained for number words may seem somewhat surprising if one considers the subjective reports by bilinguals which indicate a distinct language preference for performing any type of mental operation on numbers (Kolers, 1968; Vaid & Darkwah, 1991). Subjective reports are not always indicative of performance, however, and in fact no firm conclusion can be drawn from the few bilingual studies that have examined whether the language used during mental manipulation of numbers actually has an impact upon performance (Mägiste, 1982; Marsh & Maki, 1976; McClain & Huang, 1982; Tamamaki & Sridhar, 1990).

The results obtained for number words may in fact reflect something concerning the lexical organization of these words in relation to the rest of the lexicon. It may be that number words are organized along with other number symbols as a separate class, within or perhaps independent of the lexicon in general, where language may not be an important factor governing their organization. The organization of number words may well be different from that of other words of the lexicon, given the particularities of these words, notably the relatively limited number of primitives, the lack of ambiguity and the straightforward syntax governing their use (see Deloche & Seron, 1987, for a review).

We ran a set of experiments that directly compared the processing of number words and ordinary words of the lexicon. Both experiments were run with bilinguals. In both, we tested the hypothesis that the language of presentation of a word is less salient a feature when the word is a number word than when it is a non number-related word, with the underlying more general hypothesis that language per se may be less important to the lexical organization of the former than the latter type of word.

Experiment 1

Our first experiment used a primed lexical decision task to determine the effect of preceding a target by a prime in the same versus different language, when the prime was a number word and when it was an ordinary word. We expected the compatibility of prime and target word languages to influence response time to the target when the prime was an ordinary word but not when it was a number word.

Another hypothesis concerning a language compatibility effect was also tested. In the experiments previously mentioned, the effect of only one word preceding the target was examined. In the present experiment, we studied the effect of two items preceding the target, in order to demonstrate clearly that it is only the last ordinary word processed before the target which affects response time to it.

Method

Subjects. Forty skilled bilinguals, enrolled in a French university, voluntarily participated. Half were American, and had been living in France for at least 9 months, and half were French, studying to teach English who had recently lived in England for at least one year. All subjects were late bilinguals.

Materials and design. Target words were 40 non number-related nouns. These were between 3 and 6 letters long, fell in the medium or high frequency range (Trésor de la Langue Française, 1971; Thorndike & Lorge, 1944), and had dissimilar spellings in French and English (e.g. "arbre" and "tree"). No bilingual cognates were used. Forty nonwords, legal in both languages (20 derived from each language) were also used. Two prime words preceded each target. These met the same criteria as outlined for target words, but were not always non number-related nouns. Primes bore no relationship (semantic or orthographic) to the target nor between themselves. Prime one was always an ordinary word. Prime two was either an ordinary word, a number word, or a non-lexical string. Non-lexical primes were created from digrams that were frequent in English and French (Veronis, 1986; Carterrette & Jones, 1974); they were thus equally plausible in both languages while not resembling a real word in either language (e.g. "ecabe"). All 40 lexical targets were seen in each of 20 experimental conditions: 2 (prime one: within vs. across language word) X 5 (prime two: within vs. across language number, or non-lexical) X 2 (target language: English vs. French). A given subject received a different assignment of targets to conditions as determined by a Latin square design. The F values reported thus incorporate both item and subject variance in their denominators.

Apparatus and procedure. Display of stimuli and response recording were controlled by a microcomputer. Stimuli were displayed in uppercase in the center of the screen. A trial began with a fixation point, followed by a warning tone and then: (1) prime one, (2) prime two, (3) target. Each prime was displayed for 200 milliseconds (ms), followed by a 200 ms empty interval. The target remained displayed until the subject responded. The intertrial interval was 2 seconds. Each subject received a different random order of trials. Subjects were to read the primes silently and to make a lexical decision to the target (solely as a function of the lexical status of the target). Subjects responded positively with their dominant hand.

Results and Discussion

Mean response times to lexical targets are shown in Table 1. Response times and error rates were subjected to independent 2 (prime one type) x 5 (prime two type) x 2 (target language) x 2 (bilingual group) ANOVAS.

Errors. Analysis of error data revealed no significant effects. Overall accuracy was close to perfect (above 98%). Further discussion will be restricted to response time data.

<u>Response Times</u>. Our bilinguals were quicker to respond to words presented in their native language, as revealed by a significant Group X Target language interaction [$\underline{F}$(1,38) = 47.78; $\underline{p}$ < .001; Americans, 544 ms vs. 637 ms, French, 670 ms vs. 618 ms for words in English and French respectively]. Neither of these factors interacted, however, with the two factors of principal interest, Prime one type and Prime two type.

Table 1

<u>Mean response times (ms) for lexical targets as a function of prine one, prime two and language of target</u>

PRIME ONE

| Within Language | | | | | Across Language | | | | |

PRIME TWO

Target	Word W-L	A-L	Number W-L	A-L	N-L	Word W-L	A-L	Number W-L	A-L	N-L
English	580	610	593	579	618	568	628	623	620	653
French	613	664	598	606	601	616	655	638	629	655

Note: within language = same language as target, across language = language other than target's, word = non number-related, number = number-word, N-L = non-lexical, W-L = within language, A-L = across language)

There were main effects of both Prime one and Prime two types. Response times were faster when Prime one was in the same language as the target than when it was not [$\underline{F}$(1, 38) = 7.57; $\underline{p}$ < .01] and also when Prime two was in the same language as the target than when not [$\underline{F}$(4,152) = 5.72, p < .001]. An analysis of simple effects revealed however that the effect of Prime two was significant when the prime was an ordinary word ($\underline{F}$(1,38) = 15.12, $\underline{p}$<.001), but not when the prime was a number word (F < 1).

The global interaction between the factors Prime one and Prime two did not attain statistical significance ($\underline{F}$(4,152) = 2.02, $\underline{p}$ <.10). However, the expected partial interaction between these factors was significant ($\underline{F}$(1,152) = 7.49, $\underline{p}$ <.01), showing that the language of presentation of Prime one did not influence response time to the target when Prime two was an ordinary word, but that it did have a substantial effect when Prime two was a number word or a non-lexical string.

Figure 1 summarizes the results. Both of our hypotheses were supported by the obtained results. As predicted, preceding a target word by a word from another language delays identification of the target when the preceding word is an ordinary word. There is no apparent effect on response time to the target, however, when the immediately preceding word is a number word presented in another language. Hence, the language of presentation does not appear to be an important feature of number words, and certainly not to the extent that it is for ordinary words of the lexicon.

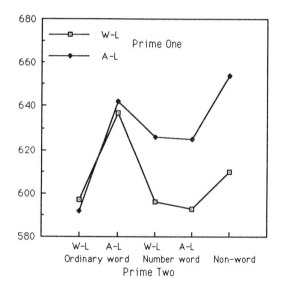

Figure 1. Lexical decision times (ms) to lexical targets as a function of Prime one (within language vs. across language prime) and Prime two (within vs. across language word, within vs. across language number, non-lexical).

Our second hypothesis was specific to the language-compatibility effect between two ordinary words. Again, as predicted, this effect was determined solely by the last ordinary word that could be identified prior to the target. Only when the second word of the sequence (prime two) was not an ordinary word of the lexicon (either a number word or a non-lexical string) did the language of the first word of the sequence (prime one) affect identification time of the target. This latter result supports our hypothesis and provides an explanation of a result found by Grainger and Beauvillain (1987). Words were identified more slowly in a mixed than in a pure language list when preceded, in the mixed list, by a word from the other language but not when preceded by a nonword. The nature of the item preceding the nonword was not reported, however, and was as likely in the mixed list to be a word from either language. The last word identified before the target may hence actually have been in the same language as the target 50% of the time in the mixed list. Thus, one would expect a delay in the mixed list about half the size of that found when the target was always preceded by a word from the other language, which is what the Grainger and Beauvillain results show.

In sum, we found a large effect of language compatibility between ordinary words which was determined by the last identified word, but no apparent effect of the language of presentation of number words.

Experiment 2

In this experiment we examined the effect of language compatibility between two words when the target itself was a number word versus an ordinary word. The primed lexical decision task was used, with the prime being either identical to the target, its translation or a neutral word.

Two hypotheses were tested. First, we expected to find a language compatibility effect between the prime and target word when the latter was an ordinary word but not when it was a number word. Second, we expected both identical and translation primes to reduce response time to the target as compared to neutral primes, for both number and non-number target words. Repeating a word in another language does not generally produce facilitation (Kirsner et al., 1984; Scarborough et al., 1984), although it has been shown to if the interval between prime and target is very short (Chen & Ng, 1989). There has been no previous comparison of identical and translation priming at very short prime-target intervals. We undertook such a comparison in this experiment.

Method

Subjects. Twenty-four proficient Spanish-English bilinguals were recruited from a southwestern university in the U.S. on the basis of their responses on a language and cultural background questionnaire. English tended to be used more often than Spanish which was mainly a conversational language. Subjects were paid for their participation.

Materials and design. Thirty-two prime-target pairs were used. Target words were between 3 and 7 letters long, of high frequency (Thorndike & Lorge A and AA frequencies), and had one unequivocal translation in Spanish which was orthographically distinct from its English equivalent. Sixteen of the targets were number words and 16 were non number-related nouns. Primes were of four types: identical to the target, translation of the target, neutral within-language, neutral across-language. The neutral primes consisted of the words "blank" and "blanco".

The combination of the factors Prime type (identical vs. translation vs. neutral within-language vs. neutral across-language) X Target language (Spanish vs English) defined 8 conditions of presentation for each type of target (number word vs. ordinary word). Two targets were seen in each condition, and each subject received a different assignment of targets to conditions as determined by a Latin square. The F values thus incorporate both subject and item variance in their denominator. To prevent subjects from noticing the relationship between prime and target words, 32 filler prime-target pairs were shown. For these pairs, there was no relationship between the two words. There were 16 within-language pairs (8 in each language) and 16 across-language pairs (8 per language). These pairs were not included in analyses. Thirty-two prime-nonword trials were employed. There were 16 primes in each language. Half the nonwords were derived from English words and half from Spanish words; the nonwords were legal in both languages.

Apparatus and procedure. Display of stimuli and response recording were controlled by a microcomputer. Stimuli were displayed in uppercase in the center of the screen. A trial began with a fixation point, followed by a prime word. The prime was displayed for 200 ms and was replaced, after a 200 ms empty interval, by the target stimulus which remained on the screen until subject's response. The intertrial interval was 2 seconds. Each subject received a different random order of trials. Subjects were to read the prime word silently and to make a lexical decision to the target. Subjects responded positively with their dominant hand.

Results and Discussion

Response times to lexical targets and error rates were subjected to independent 4 (prime type) x 2 (target language) x 2 (target type) ANOVAs.

Errors. Analysis of error rate revealed main effects of Target language [$F(1,23)$ = 6.78, $p < .05$] and of Target type [$F(1,23) = 6.48$, $p < .05$]. Fewer errors were made to words presented in English than in Spanish (1% vs. 4%), and to number words than to ordinary words (1% vs. 4%). There were no other effects related to error rate.

Response Times. Analysis of response times revealed a main effect of Target language [$F(1,23) = 20.87$, $p. < 001$], with response times being shorter to words presented in English than in Spanish (609 vs. 659 ms, respectively). There was a main effect of Prime type [$F(3,69) = 8.33$, $p < .001$]. Analysis of simple effects showed that response times were shorter when the prime was identical to the target than when it was a neutral within-language prime (600 vs. 651 ms, respectively) [$F(1,69) = 16.51$, $p < .001$], and when the prime was the translation of the target as opposed to a neutral across-language prime (617 vs. 659 ms, respectively) [$F(1,69) = 7.99$, $p < .01$].

There was a significant Prime type X Target language interaction [$F(3,69) = 5.38$, $p < .01$]. As can be seen in Figure 2, for Spanish words, repeating a word in the same language (identical prime) produced more facilitation than did repeating the word across languages (translation prime) whereas, for English target words, the amount of facilitation was not noticeably different for the two prime conditions. There was no interaction, however, between Prime type and Target type (F < 1). As is readily apparent in Figure 3, substantial facilitation was produced for both number words and for ordinary words.

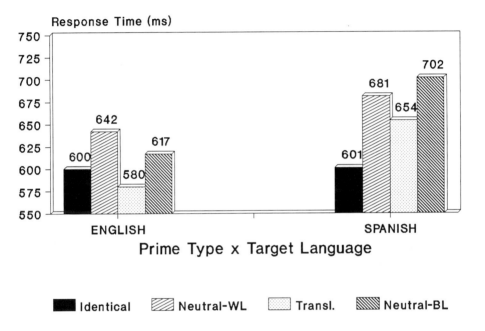

Figure 2. Mean response time (ms) to target words as a function of prime type and language of target word.

Inspection of Figure 3 also reveals the effect of language compatibility for number words and for ordinary words. The direct comparison of the two neutral prime conditions (within vs. across-language) shows that response times were virtually identical, for both types of words. That the neutral primes should not produce a language compatibility effect is to be expected, given that the prime was always the same word (either "blank" or "blanco"). The direct comparison of identical and translation priming conditions shows that for number words there is a slight increase in response time (9 ms) in the former condition and that for ordinary words there is a somewhat larger difference between the two conditions (25 ms). Although these results are in the expected direction, i.e., there appears to be a larger language compatibility effect for ordinary words than that for number words, the interaction was not reliable.

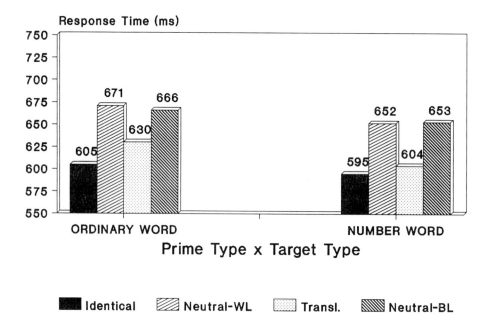

Figure 3. Mean response time (ms) to target words as a function of prime type and type of target word.

In sum, we did not obtain the expected language compatibility effects, although the results were in the predicted direction. The expected priming effects were observed, however, with there being substantial and relatively equivalent facilitation for both identity and translation priming.

General Discussion

The results of our first study show that target words are identified more slowly following the processing of a word in another language. This is true only when the preceding word is an "ordinary" word as opposed to a spelled-out number. Moreover, we found that this language-compatibility effect, for non number-related words, was determined solely by the last word identified prior to the target. These results extend those previously obtained in bilingual studies of reading and word identification. Our second experiment did not reveal the strong language compatibility effect observed for ordinary words in our first study. The difference in results between the two studies may well be linked to the differences in presentation conditions and in the relationship between the prime and target word. In the second experiment, the prime-target stimulus onset synchrony was considerably reduced and the prime bore a relationship to the target (identity or translation). Results of other studies have not shown the language-compatibility effect under similar conditions (Dalrymple-Alford, 1985; Schwanenflugel & Rey, 1986).

There is, in fact, considerable debate about the origin of the language-compatibility effect observed for non number-related words. It has been suggested, for example, that the effect is a result of differences in the strength of associative links between lexical entries (Dalrymple-Alford, 1985). In this perspective, the bilingual lexicon is organized according to morphology, or meaning, with the lexical entries for the two languages being stored within a single lexicon (see also Cristoffanini et al., 1986; Kirsner et al., 1984; Kirsner, 1986). As stipulated in the monolingual spreading-activation model (Collins & Loftus, 1975), the more related two words, the stronger the link and the shorter the semantic distance between them. In the bilingual lexicon, associative links between words would in general be stronger within the same language than across languages (with the exception of translation equivalents). As a result, the semantic distance would generally be lesser between two words from the same language than between the same two words presented in different languages, which would lead to an increase in processing time in the latter case.

While the language-compatibility effect could presumably be explained in this manner, other experimental results do not support the underlying argument that semantic distance is necessarily greater between words across languages than within a language. One suggested measure of semantic distance is the typicality of a given exemplar of a superordinate category (cf. Rosch, 1973), with the distance being greater the less typical the exemplar. Results of a recent bilingual priming study showed that the amount of facilitation produced by a category prime indeed decreased with the typicality of the target (Schwanenflugel & Rey, 1986). It is important to note that this effect was equally true within and across languages, however, and the relative amount of facilitation was roughly equivalent in the within and across-language priming conditions for all three levels of typicality. This is far from the pattern of results that would have been predicted by the hypothesis that semantic distance is even generally greater between than within languages, and as such does not lend support to the account of the language-compatibility effect in terms of a meaning-governed unitary bilingual lexicon.

Rather than interpreting the effect in terms of differences in the strength of associative links within and across languages, some researchers have interpreted the language compatibility effect in terms of pre-lexical encoding processes (Meyer & Ruddy, 1974), still within the framework of a unitary lexicon. In line with the "input-output" hypothesis (Macnamara & Kushnir, 1971), the assumption is made that the selection of languages occurs prior to lexical access, with the bilingual having to switch encoding systems in order to access a word from the other language. Switching systems would take time, which would be reflected by an increase in processing time, and could explain the language-compatibility effect. The hypothesis of language-specific lexical access has also been advanced in the framework of a language-governed bilingual lexicon, with the entries for the two languages being held in separate stores (Gerard & Scarborough, 1989; Scarborough et al., 1984).

Here again, while the idea of language-specific encoding processes and/or language-specific lexical access could explain the language-compatibility effect, it does not hold in the face of other experimental evidence. Numerous studies and experimental techniques have revealed parallel processing in the two languages. Interference from the non-pertinent language is regularly observed in bilingual versions of the Stroop paradigm, and this holds true for various language pairings (German-Swedish, Spanish-English, English-French, Chinese-English, etc.), although interference does seem to be greater the greater the visual similarity between the two languages (see Chen & Ho, 1986, for a review). Modified versions of the Stroop paradigm, such as incongruous labels within line drawings (Smith & Kirsner, 1982), and "to be ignored" words flanking a center target word (Guttentag, Haith, Goodman & Hauch, 1984) have also shown considerable influence of the non-pertinent stimuli, and equally so across languages and within the same language. That access is not restricted to only one of the bilingual's two languages is also apparent from the results of a recent bilingual priming experiment which used bilingual homographs (eg. "pain," which signifies "bread" in French) as prime words (Beauvillain & Grainger, 1987). Access to one or the other meaning of the homograph is determined by frequency and not language, with the higher frequency meaning being accessed even when the subject was instructed to read the word in the other language (see Gerard & Scarborough, 1989, for opposing results).

The account of the language-compatibility effect that is most parsimonious in the face of collective experimental evidence is that of a serial post-access checking mechanism following parallel access in the two lexicons (cf. Grainger & Beauvillain, 1987). In line with an activation-verification model of lexical access (Paap, Newsome, McDonald, & Schvaneveldt, 1982), the visual presentation of a word would activate in parallel all lexical entries at least partially compatible with the stimulus. There would then ensue a serial, frequency-ordered verification process of the activated candidates. In a bilingual situation, activation would be parallel in the two lexicons, but the verification of candidates would be performed upon the candidates of only one language at a time. Verification would normally begin in the language of the last identified word. Hence, preceding a target word by a word in the other language would lead to a delay in identification of the target, given that the target may well activate candidates in both languages, and those in the language of the last identified word, i.e. in the other language, would be verified first. This account of the language-compatibility effect indeed fits not only our data, but the majority of results found in studies of bilingual language processing. It is, moreover, reasonable to assume that the verification process would begin in the language (lexicon) of the last identified word, given that in normal situations of reading or listening, a bilingual encounters successive words in the same language.

It remains to be explained why the effect of language is apparently absent for number words of the lexicon. Various hypotheses can be forwarded. It may be that these words are organized in a lexicon specific to numerical symbols, where language is not as important a factor. It can be noted that number words are distinct from non number-related words on various accounts, which may influence lexical organization (see Deloche & Seron, 1987). There is also some clinical evidence from studies of monolingual aphasics which suggest that number-words may be represented independently of the lexicon in general. For example, it has been found that these subjects can rewrite number-words as digits, while they are unable to create a non number-related word from a sequence of letters (Deloche & Seron, 1982). Moreover, when a lexical error is made, either when transcribing a number-word from a digit or when reading a number-word out aloud, the error is almost always restricted to the number class, (e.g., "one hundred dozen" for "112", "thirteen" for fifteen", "three-quarters" for "seventy-five" (Deloche & Seron, 1982; Rinnert & Whitaker, 1973)). These observations lend support to the idea that numbers and the words designating them activate a specific part of the lexicon, if not a completely separate lexicon.

Two other accounts of the absence of a language-compatibility effect, as observed between number-words and when the target is preceded by a number-word prime, can be put forward. First, the effect may be linked to orthographic specificity. It may be that the number-words we used were in general more orthographically specific as concerns language than were the non number-related words. For example, the number-words "eight", "two", and "thirty" have orthographic patterns that are much more common in English than in Spanish or French. Inversely, the number-words "cinq", "sept" and "trois" in French are not orthographically compatible with a great number of English lexical entries; the same is true of the Spanish number-words "quatro", "siete" and "veinte," among others. Thus, when the targets were number-words, the set of candidates to be checked first in the other language (when the target was preceded by a word from the other language) would be minimal, if not nil. This would reduce, if not altogether abolish, the language-compatibility effect. Such a reduction in the language-compatibility effect has in fact been observed for ordinary words when the word is orthographically specific to one of the bilingual's two languages (Grainger & Beauvillain, 1987), or when the two languages have very distinct scripts (Kirsner et al., 1984). It should be noted however that this hypothesis does not account for the absence of the language-compatibility effect observed for ordinary-words preceded by number-words.

The absence of a language-compatibility effect for number-words as opposed to ordinary words may also be due to the fact that for number-words there is a readily available common representation across languages, i.e., the digit. It is possible that bilinguals access the digit from the number-word, thus eliminating any effect of language. For the two language pairs we employed in our experiments (French vs. English, and Spanish vs. English), this commonality of digit representation is in fact true.

Further research is necessary in order to determine which of the above-mentioned hypotheses is the best account of the language-compatibility effect. As stands, the present results provide an interesting extension of previous bilingual results concerning the role played by the language of a word in the processes which underlie its identification.

Footnotes

Portions of this research were previously presented at the 1989 annual meeting of the Psychonomics Society in Atlanta. We thank Charles Negy and Patrick von Bevill for assisting in the data collection. The second author's participation in this research was supported by a summer faculty research award at Texas A & M University.

References

Beauvillain, C. & Grainger, J. (1987). Accessing interlexical homographs: Some limitations of a language-selective access. *Journal of Memory and Language*, 26, 658-672.

Carterrette, E. C. & Jones, M. H. (1974). *Informal speech: Alphabetic and phonemic texts with statistical analyses and tables*. Berkeley: University of California Press.

Chan, M. C., Chau, H. L. & Hoosain, R. (1983). Input/output switch in bilinguals' switching. *Journal of Psycholinguistic Research*, 12, 407-416.

Chen, H. C. & Ho, C. (1986). Development of Stroop interference in Chinese-English bilinguals. *Journal of Experimental Psychology: Learning, Memory and Cognition*, 12, 397-401.

Chen, H. C. & Ng, M. L. (1989). Semantic facilitation and translation primacy effects in Chinese-English bilinguals. *Memory and Cognition*, 17(4), 454-462.

Collins, A. M. & Loftus, E. F. (1975). A spreading-activation theory of semantic processing. *Psychological Review*, 82, 407-428.

Cristoffanini, P., Kirsner, K. & Milech, D. (1986). Bilingual lexical representation: The status of Spanish-English cognates. *Quarterly Journal of Experimental Psychology*, 38A, 367-393.

Dalrymple-Alford, E. C. (1985). Language switching during bilingual reading. *British Journal of Psychology*, 76, 111-122.

Deloche, G. & Seron, X. (1982). From one to 1: An analysis of a transcoding process by means of neuropsychological data. *Cognition*, 12, 119-149.

Deloche, G. & Seron, X. (1987). Numerical transcoding: A general production model. In G. Deloche & X. Seron (Eds.), *Mathematical disabilities: A cognitive neuropsychological perspective*. London: Lawrence Erlbaum Associates.

Durgunoglu, A. Y. & Roediger, H. L. (1987). Test differences in accessing bilingual memory. *Journal of Memory and Language*, 26, 377-391.

Frenck, C. & Pynte, J. (1987a). Parafoveal preprocessing in bilinguals. In J. K. O'Regan & A. Levy-Schoen (Eds.), *Eye Movements: From physiology to cognition*. Amsterdam: Elsevier.

Frenck, C. & Pynte, J. (1987b). Semantic representation and surface forms: A look at across-language priming in bilinguals. *Journal of Psycholinguistic Research*, 16, 383-395.

Gerard, L. D. & Scarborough, D. L. (1989). Language-specific lexical access of homographs by bilinguals. *Journal of Experimental Psychology: Learning, Memory and Cognition*, 15, 305-315.

Grainger, J. & Beauvillain, C. (1987). Language blocking and lexical access in bilinguals. *Quarterly Journal of Experimental Psychology*, 39A, 295-319.

Guttentag, R., Haith, M., Goodman, G., & Hauch, J. (1984). Semantic processing of unattended words by bilinguals: A test of the input switch mechanism. *Journal of Verbal Learning and Verbal Behavior*, 23, 178-188.

Joshi, A. K. (1985). Processing of sentences with intrasentential code switching. In D. R. Dowty, L. Karttunen & A. M. Zwicky (Eds.), *Natural language parsing: Psychological, computational and theoretical perspectives*. Cambridge: Cambridge University Press.

Kirsner, K. (1986). Lexical function: Is a bilingual account necessary? In J. Vaid (Ed.), *Language processing in bilinguals: Psycholinguistic and neuropsychological perspectives*. Hillsdale, NJ: Lawrence Erlbaum Associates.

Kirsner, K., Smith, M. C., Lockhart, R. S., King, M. L. & Jain, M. (1984). The bilingual lexicon: Language specific units in an integrated network. *Journal of Verbal Learning and Verbal Behavior*, 23, 519-539.

Kolers, P. A. (1966). Reading and talking bilingually. *American Journal of Psychology*, 79, 357-376.

Kolers, P. A. (1968). Bilingualism and information processing. *Scientific American*, 218, 78-86.

Kolers, P. A. & Brison, M. (1984). Commentary: On pictures, words and their mental representation. *Journal of Verbal Learning and Verbal Behavior*, 23, 105-113.

Macnamara, J. & Kushnir, S. L. (1971). Linguistic independence of bilinguals: The input switch. *Journal of Verbal Learning and Verbal Behavior*, 10, 480-487.

Mägiste, E. (1982). The importance of language strategy in simple arithmetic. *Educational Psychology*, 2, 159-166.

Marsh, L. G., & Maki, R. (1976). Efficiency of arithmetic operations in bilinguals as a function of language. *Memory and Cognition*, 4, 459-464.

McClain, L. & Huang, J. S. (1982). Speed of simple arithmetic in bilinguals. *Memory and Cognition*, 10, 591-596.

Meyer, D. E. & Ruddy, M. G. (1974). Bilingual word recognition: Organization and retrieval of alternate lexical codes. Paper presented at the meeting of the Eastern Psychological Association, Philadelphia.

Paap, K. R., Newsome, S. L., McDonald, J. E. & Schvaneveldt, R. W. (1982). An activation-verification model for letter and word recognition: The word superiority effect. *Psychological Review*, 89, 573-594.

Paradis, M. & Lebrun, Y. (1983). La neurolinguistique du bilinguisme: Représentation et traitement de deux langages dans un même cerveau. *Langages*, 72, 7-13.

Park, K. & Vaid, J. (in press). Lexical representation of script variation: Evidence from Korean biscriptals. In I. Taylor and D. Olson (Eds.), *Scripts and literacy*. Cambridge: Cambridge Univeristy Press.

Rinnert, C. & Whitaker, H. A. (1973). Semantic confusions by aphasic patients. *Cortex*, 9, 56-81.

Rosch, E. (1973). Natural categories. *Cognitive Psychology*, 4, 328-350.

Scarborough, D. L., Gerard, L. & Cortese, C. (1984). Independence of lexical access in bilingual word recognition. *Journal of Verbal Learning and Verbal Behavior*, 23, 84-89.

Schwanenflugel, P. J. & Rey, M. (1986). Interlingual semantic facilitation: Evidence for a common representation system in the bilingual lexicon. *Journal of Memory and Language*, 25, 605-618.

Smith, M. C., & Kirsner, K. (1982). Language and orthography as irrelevant features in color-word and picture-word Stroop interference. *Quarterly Journal of Experimental Psychology*, 34A, 153-170.

Snodgrass, J. G. (1984). Concepts and their surface representations. *Journal of Verbal Learning and Verbal Behavior*, 23, 3-22.

Soares, C. & Grosjean, F. (1984). Bilinguals in a monolingual and bilingual speech mode: The effect on lexical access. *Memory and Cognition*, 12, 380-386.

Sridhar, S. N. & Sridhar, K. K. (1980). The syntax and psycholinguistics of bilingual code-mixing. *Canadian Journal of Psychology*, 34, 407-416.

Taft, M. (1987). Morphographic processing: The BOSS reemerges. In M. Coltheart (Ed.). *Attention and performance XII: The psychology of reading*. Hillsdale, NJ: Lawrence Erlbaum Associates.

Tamamaki, K. & Sridhar, S. N. (1990). Relative efficiency of bilinguals' arithmetic operations in their two languages as a function of language use. Unpublished manuscript, State University of New York at Stony Brook.

Thorndike, E. L. & Lorge, L. (1944). *The teacher's wordbook of 30,000 words*. NY: Teachers College, Columbia University.

Trésor de la Langue Française (1971). *Dictionnaire des fréquences*. Paris, Klinckseick.

Vaid, J. & Darkwah, A. (1991). Language preference for mental calculations: Survey data. Texas A & M University. In preparation.

Vaid, J. & Frenck, C. (in press). Incidental memory for format of presentation of number stimuli: Evidence from monolinguals and bilinguals. *Brain and Cognition.*

Veronis, J. (1986). Etude quantitative sur le système graphique et phonographique du français. *Cahiers de Psychologie Cognitive*, 6, 501-531.

Cognitive Processing in Bilinguals – R.J. Harris (Editor)
© *1992 Elsevier Science Publishers B.V. All rights reserved.*

Word Recognition in Second-language Reading

Helena-Fivi Chitiri, Yilin Sun, Dale M. Willows
Ontario Institute for Studies in Education
and
Insup Taylor
University of Toronto

Abstract

The present chapter addresses L2 word recognition in relation to both the writing scripts' characteristics and learners' reading proficiency. In addition to a literature review, it presents two studies that examined these issues. The first study on the reading of English-Greek bilinguals indicated that word recognition differs between languages depending upon the language and writing system characteristics. The second study on reading in Chinese as a second language also indicated, however, the ability of bilinguals to respond to these characteristics depends upon their level of reading proficiency in each language. The nature of L2 word recognition processes was closely related to learner's reading experience and reading proficiency in the L2. Therefore, reading proficiency seems to be a better indication of reading skill rather than the level of general language proficiency used in most L2 reading studies.

The ability to read is fundamental to our literate society. The importance of reading, however, is not limited to functioning in one's mother tongue but is becoming increasingly important in second language practice as well. Indeed, it would seem that for many people the opportunities to read their second language outweigh the opportunities to speak it. Yet, despite the importance of reading in a second language, little research has been done in this area. Moreover, this existing research suffers from methodological inadequacy (Bernhardt & Everson, 1988). Reading processes, in whatever language/script, involve several subskills, such as recognizing words in a text, organizing them into larger syntactic units, and extracting a message of the text (e.g., Taylor & Taylor, 1983, p. 393). In this chapter we will focus on one of these subskills, word recognition. Specifically, we will examine word recognition in a second language (L2) in relation to learners' sensitivity to the characteristics of the script, or orthography, of the L2.

Previous research has found a link between word recognition and general proficiency in a second language. This finding, however, is based mainly on studies that have examined the reading of English as a second language. Until recently this restriction to one language could be justified by the fact that little was known about reading in other languages except English. In addition, the prevailing idea about the reading process was that it is very similar regardless of orthographies (Goodman, 1976; Gray, 1956). More recent studies on word recognition in different writing systems among monolinguals have produced results that challenge the above assumptions. Specifically, these studies suggest that the writing system does indeed have an impact on word recognition (Frost, Katz, & Bentin, 1987). In second language reading, this idea is further supported by the finding that beginning L2 readers transfer word recognition patterns from their first language into their second language (Brown & Haynes, 1985; Koda, 1988). Very little is known, however, about the impact of the writing system among L2 readers of intermediate and more advanced reading level.

The present chapter will address L2 word recognition in relation to both the script's characteristics and learners' reading proficiency. In addition to reviewing studies that have addressed these issues, the chapter will also present in detail two studies: One which examined the reading behavior in both the L1 and L2 of Greek adolescents who were advanced learners of English, and another which studied word recognition of English-speaking learners of Chinese of different proficiency levels. Our intention is to show that in order for L2 readers to acquire native-like reading fluency they must be sensitive to the characteristics of the L2 script which differ from those of the L1, and, moreover, that this process is related to the amount of the learners' reading experience in L2.

The chapter is organized in two parts, beginning with a review of studies that have examined word recognition in relation to the characteristics of the orthography and the reading proficiency of second language learners.

Word Recognition in Relation to the Characteristics of the Orthography

Until recently the predominant view of the reading process was that it was very similar across languages and orthographies (Goodman, 1976). This notion applied to reading comprehension as well as word recognition. In an older study it was found, for example, that readers' eye movements across different scripts were in fact very similar (Gray, 1956). Contrary to this view, however, an increasing number of recent studies indicate that the orthography does indeed have an impact on readers' word recognition.

Studies that have examined the role of the orthography have focused mainly on the relationship between letter and sound. Specifically, they have asked whether orthographies that represent the sounds of the language in a direct and consistent way encourage their readers to rely more on the phonological code than do orthographies where pronunciation is represented in a less consistent way. This assumption, which has been termed the *orthographic depth hypothesis*, has found support in several studies. Research comparing word recognition in English and Serbo-Croatian has found, for example, that Serbo-Croatian readers rely primarily on the phonological code for word recognition while English readers do not (Frost & Katz, 1989; Feldman & Turvey, 1983; Turvey, Feldman, & Lukatela, 1984). This pattern is consistent with the Serbo-Croatian script which represents sound in a direct way in contrast to English where sound is often represented in an indirect way. The lack of dependency on the phonological code is even more pronounced in scripts that represent sound in a very ambiguous way as in the case of Hebrew in its unvowelized form (Frost, Katz, & Bentin, 1987).

In addition to the impact of the orthography on reading, some studies have suggested that readers are influenced by the syntactic characteristics of their languages. For example, some studies have indicated that, unlike English, function words are attended to more than content words in inflected languages like Spanish and German (Bernhardt, 1986; Clarke, 1979).

While the above studies have examined word recognition among monolinguals, the question arises whether similar differences between languages would be also apparent among bilinguals. A controversy surrounds the issue of how bilinguals operate in their two languages: Some theorists suggest that bilinguals operate through the same memory store, while others suggest that bilinguals operate through different memory stores. More recently, however, a study on bilingual functioning suggests that bilinguals can perform in either way depending upon the nature of the task (Durgunoglu & Roediger, 1987). Specifically, tasks stressing the surface representation of language (e.g., unscrambling a word, matching sounds) depend on the use of language-specific behavior, while tasks stressing the underlying form of words like word classification and free recall are not influenced by the language of the task. This distinction of bilingual behavior as dependent on the nature of the task as well as types of material has also been advocated by the model of bilingual memory proposed by Taylor and Taylor (1990).

Since word recognition deals with the written representation of language, one would expect that bilingual readers would show language-specific behaviours when reading in either of their languages. The existing research on this issue, however, is very limited and the only study that has adequately addressed this issue was Segalowitz and Hebert (1990). In this study French-English bilinguals with a balanced knowledge of both languages were given words that were homophones and sentences that included homophones. Readers' responses to the homophones differed considerably between the two languages: In English, readers took longer and made more mistakes, while in French the presence of homophones did not affect performance. This difference in performance is consistent with the degree of letter-to-sound correspondence of the two orthographies: French has a more consistent relationship between letters and sounds than English does, allowing its readers to generate quickly and easily a reliable code both for words and for nonwords.

The impact of script characteristics in the word recognition of bilinguals has been studied more extensively in relation to the effect that the L1 writing system has on the L2. These studies have found that the more similar the two writing systems are, the easier it is for L2 learners to adapt to the characteristics of their L2 script. Thus, beginning English learners of Arabic and Spanish background have less difficulty in discriminating between words and nonwords and sounding out homophones in English as compared to learners of Japanese background (Brown & Haynes, 1985; Koda, 1988). This difference in behavior was attributed to the fact that while Spanish and

Arabic are alphabetic orthographies, relying on letter-sound representations, the Japanese Kanji is a logography in which a character stands for a whole morpheme.

The discrepancy between the L1 and L2 scripts can have an effect on advanced L2 readers as well. For example, in a study comparing skilled L2 readers of German and Chinese, the eye movements of German readers resembled those of native readers while those of the Chinese learners did not (Bernhardt & Everson, 1988). Since both groups of learners had English as their mother tongue, the difference in behavior was attributed to the larger discrepancy between the scripts of English and Chinese as compared to English and German.

Word Recognition and the Level of Proficiency in Second Language

L2 readers show sensitivity to the characteristics of their L2 script but this sensitivity must be developed. As with learning to speak the language, readers go through different stages of development, gradually approaching the patterns of native readers. What is important to keep in mind, however, is that reading fluency is dependent upon specific reading experience and as a result it can differ from general language proficiency. This distinction between these two kinds of proficiency is important and has been often overlooked in research on second language reading.

Studies on L2 word recognition have shown that there is a strong link between reading behavior and general proficiency in the second language. Specifically, with increasing proficiency there is a progressive change of attention from predominantly graphic to syntactic and semantic processing (Cziko, 1978, 1980; Hatch, Polin, & Part, 1974). In a study comparing the oral miscues of intermediate and advanced learners of French to those of native speakers, Cziko (1980) found that intermediate learners made many more graphically similar miscues than did the other two groups. In addition, intermediate learners did not show the same degree of sensitivity to syntactic and semantic constraints of the text as did the advanced French learners and the native speakers. This progressive change of reading behavior was also validated in an eye movement study of proficient and less proficient learners of German (Bernhardt, 1986). In this study less proficient learners fixated more frequently and for longer intervals as compared to both native readers and proficient L2 learners.

Deviations from native readers' behavior are not limited to beginning and intermediate L2 learners. When learners' reading proficiency level is controlled, even the word recognition processes of L2 learners with a high level of general language proficiency can differ from those of native readers. This finding is not surprising considering the complexity of word recognition. Indeed, proficient L2 speakers with slower reading rates in their L2 have been found to be deficient in the use of several of the information sources contributing to word recognition. Specifically, they are less able to respond to the orthographic conventions of their L2 (Favreau, Komoda, & Segalowitz, 1980), they are less efficient in using semantic information when making lexical decisions (Favreau & Segalowitz, 1983), and they are affected more by the presence of semantically inappropriate homophones (Segalowitz & Hebert, 1990).

The discrepancy between the behavior of advanced L2 readers and native readers should not be interpreted in terms of ignorance but rather in terms of insufficient automatization of the appropriate processes. This interpretation seems to be confirmed by Favreau et al.'s (1980) finding: When bilinguals who scored at least 70% on listening and reading comprehension in both their languages but who had slower reading rates in their second language were given more time, they were able to correctly respond to the orthographic conventions of their L2 script. The automatization of word recognition patterns in the second language, however, seems to be dependent upon the amount of exposure to second language reading: Differences between L2 and native readers' behavior were observed even among L2 readers with as small a discrepancy in reading rate as 10% between their two languages (Favreau & Segalowitz, 1983).

It would seem, therefore, that while L2 readers can satisfactorily meet the requirements of reading material in their second language, they can achieve native-like proficiency only with considerable experience. This reading experience is needed to automatize and successfully integrate the different subskills involved in word recognition. The following study, presented in more detail in Chitiri (1991), further illustrates the discrepancy that can exist between general language proficiency and reading proficiency in the second language. It does so by examining the word recognition patterns of Greek-English bilinguals who are advanced learners of English and comparing these patterns to those of English monolingual readers. In order to provide a better understanding of bilingual processes, the study also examined word recognition in bilinguals' mother tongue.

Bilingual Word Recognition in Two Alphabetic Orthographies

This study examined the effect of language and orthographic system characteristics on bilingual word recognition processes in English and Greek. Both languages belong to the Indo-European language family and use alphabets. English uses the Roman alphabet and has an orthography whose letter-sound correspondence is irregular and complex. Greek, on the other hand, uses the Greek alphabet and its orthography is quite regular and consistent in representing the sounds of the language.

Participants in this study were Greek adolescents, who were advanced learners of English. In order to provide an objective assessment of subjects' proficiency and also to allow for a comparison of general language and specific reading performance, subjects were administered two pretest measures in each language: (a) a written test of syntactic knowledge (Geva & Ryan, 1986); and (b) a test of oral reading proficiency, the Gray Oral Test-Revised (Wiederholt & Bryant, 1986).

The actual study examined word recognition in relation to two issues: first, the impact of the degree of letter-to-sound correspondence of the orthography; and second, the influence of a language's syntactic nature. To study the nature of the orthography, readers' responses to two phonologically defined factors, syllable and stress, were compared between English and Greek. Because of the strong letter-to-sound correspondence of Greek, it was hypothesized that in this language the examined factors would play a stronger role than in English, where the relationship between spelling and pronunciation is not always consistent.

To determine the influence of syntax on word recognition, the study examined readers' sensitivity to the different role of inflections in the two languages. In Greek, inflections convey information about the gender, number, and case of nouns and their modifiers as well as specify the person and tense of verbs. In English, inflections are very few and have a limited function. The role of syntax on word recognition was studied in relation to the processing of content and function words, some of which are inflected in Greek, and the processing of content word endings, all of which are inflected in Greek. Here again it was hypothesized that, because of the inflected nature of Greek, readers would be more attentive to inflected function words and content word endings than they would be in English.

The roles of the orthography and syntax were examined in relation to the word recognition of a specific number of content words, which were equated in terms of length and frequency across languages, and a similar number of function words. These words were embedded in continuous text that was similar across the two languages. The method used to study the nature of word recognition processes was letter cancellation (Corcoran, 1966; Healy, 1980; Healy, Conboy, & Drewnowski, 1987). In this method, which is supposed to reflect underlying reading processes, readers are asked to cross out a specific letter while reading for meaning.

The results from monolinguals confirmed our predictions. Reflecting the consistent letter-to-sound correspondence of the Greek orthography, the monolingual Greek readers attended to syllable and stress more than the monolingual English readers. Similarly, in accordance with the inflected nature of Greek, Greek readers attended more to inflected function words and to content word endings. In English, by contrast, readers paid less attention to function words and to content word endings.

Bilingual performance differed between the two languages, suggesting that bilinguals did not operate through the same code for both languages but through separate codes. Specifically, they showed sensitivity to the orthographic and syntactic characteristics of each language. Though their behavior was identical to that of monolinguals in Greek, it differed from that of English-speaking monolinguals.

This discrepancy between monolingual and bilingual behavior in English was found in both issues studied. Concerning the processing of phonological information, the reading patterns of bilinguals, even though not contrary to those of English monolinguals, were not completely consistent with them. Bilinguals in English showed more pronounced stress effects and a complete absence of syllabic effects. (English-speaking monolinguals likewise did not show any syllabic effects but they discriminated between two- and three-syllable words.) When processing syntactic information, bilinguals differed from monolinguals most clearly in the processing of content and function words. In this case, when reading English, bilinguals did not differentiate at all between the two word classes, unlike monolinguals, who attended more to content words.

This discrepancy from monolingual behavior in L2 suggests that these learners, despite high levels of language proficiency, still have not attained native-like reading proficiency. This distinction between general language and reading proficiency was found also in students' performance on the two pretest measures assessing syntactic knowledge and oral reading proficiency administered at the outset of the study. In this case, while bilinguals performed similarly in the two languages on the test of syntactic knowledge, their oral reading differed substantially between English and Greek: In English they took considerably longer to read and made more errors.

Seen from this perspective, bilinguals' discrepancy from the monolingual patterns in their L2 (English) should not be attributed primarily to poor language knowledge but instead to their still developing reading skill. This point was especially obvious in the processing of syntactic information. As already mentioned, bilingual readers did not differentiate at all between content words and function words in English, showing a behavior akin to that of unskilled readers (Hatch et al., 1974). What accounts for this failure to distinguish between the two word classes could not be based on students' syntactic knowledge concerning the less important role of function words in English. It would seem, rather that it is based on the difficulty of integrating syntactic information while reading (LaBerge & Samuels, 1974; Samuels & Kamil, 1984). Alternatively, it is also possible that their behaviour reflected transfer of usual Greek reading patterns where inflected function words are attended to the same degree as content words.

The importance of reading proficiency for the acquisition of native-like skill in word recognition is pursued further in the following section which examined the word recognition processes of second-language readers of a logographic orthography, Chinese.

Second Language Reading in a Logographic Orthography

In comparison to alphabetic orthographies, little research has been done on reading a logographic orthography as a second language. What we do know about word recognition in logographic systems comes primarily from studies in Chinese as a first language. The present study, reported by Sun (1991), deals with Chinese and examines the word recognition of native and non-native speakers of different proficiency levels.

The Chinese script is made up of characters each of which represents a morpheme, the smallest meaningful unit. For example, the character "+" /shi/ which resembles the *plus* sign, represents the morpheme *ten*. Chinese characters are suited to represent the Chinese language, which consists mainly of monosyllabic, non-inflected morphemes (Leong, 1973, 1986; Taylor & Taylor, 1983). A Chinese character, though it represents sound, (which is always one syllable) as well as the meaning of a morpheme, happens to be better at representing the meaning. Indeed, a character represents primarily the meaning and only secondarily the sound of the morpheme.

Studies on Chinese as a first language have examined whether the lack of symbol-to-sound mapping in Chinese encourages readers to rely more heavily on visual discrimination and rote memorization strategies. The results obtained, however, have not been unanimous. Some studies indicated that for native readers of Chinese, phonological representation of words in short-term memory exists much the same as it exists for native readers of alphabetic systems (Chu-Chang & Loritz, 1977; Cheng & Shih, 1988; Hayes, 1988; Seidenberg, 1985; Tzeng, Hung & Wang, 1977). Other researchers, however, have shown a high degree of visual encoding strategies in Chinese (Chen & Juola, 1982; Chen, Yung, & Ng, 1988; Peng, Guo, & Zhang, 1985). Finally, still other researchers suggest that Chinese characters invoke meaning much faster than do words in an alphabetic language (Biederman & Tsao, 1979; Hoosain & Osgood, 1983; Treiman, Baron, & Luk, 1981). There has been also experimental evidence to suggest that native Chinese readers utilize all three types of information in word processing. However, it is not clear whether or not non-native readers of Chinese use the same information processing strategies as native Chinese, nor is it clear whether strategies depend primarily on the nature of a task. The answers to these questions would help researchers understand the second language reading process in a non-alphabetic language system.

The only published study concerning the reading of Chinese as a L2 is one conducted by Hayes (1987). Hayes studied word encoding processes in two groups of Chinese readers: a native group and a proficient non-native group. His research included two experiments, the first dealing with context-free word recognition and the second with context-embedded word recognition. In the first experiment, subjects viewed a Chinese character on a slide and had to recognize it among a number of related or unrelated characters. Related characters or distractors bore graphic, phonological, and semantic similarity to the actual characters. If subjects made predominantly graphic errors, they were using a graphic (visual) encoding strategy. Similar conclusions could be drawn with respect to phonological and semantic errors. In the second task, context-embedded word recognition, subjects had to decide upon the validity of the presented statements. Some of the sentences included a graphic, phonological, or a semantic distractor while others did not.

Hayes concluded that on context-free word recognition native readers relied primarily on a phonological strategy while non-natives depended on a mixture of phonological and graphic processing. In contextual word recognition, both groups relied more heavily on visual processing, but they also made some use of phonological and semantic processing. However, the overreliance on visual processing was not of similar magnitude between the two groups but was more pronounced among non-native speakers. Since Hayes did not control the students' reading proficiency level, it is not easy to explain whether these differences in the patterns of the L2 were caused by insufficient proficiency or transfer of L1 behavior. Furthermore, there are problems with his methodology, especially in his context-free word recognition:

possible memory confounding, the limited number of trials, and the lack of control of stimuli for printed word frequency and orthographic structure complexity (number of strokes per character).

Recently, Sun (1991) investigated word recognition processes both with and without context using procedures designed to overcome the methodological shortcomings of Hayes' research. Her subjects were native speakers of Chinese (L1NP), non-native high proficiency readers (L2HP) and intermediate readers (L2IP). All subjects were given screening measures to assess their reading proficiency.

The study consisted of two experimental tasks on the computer. The first task, context-free word recognition, involved Chinese characters which varied in printed frequency and stroke complexity. In this task students were presented with two items separated by a brief interval and had to decide whether the second item (test item) was the same as the one presented first (target item). For 50% of the trials the second item (test item) was a real Chinese word that resembled the target item either graphically, phonologically, or semantically. In the second task, context-embedded word recognition, subjects were presented with sentences and had to decide upon the validity of a sentence. In 50% of the presented sentences one word had been replaced by another Chinese word that resembled the target either graphically, phonologically, or semantically, rendering the sentence anomalous. In both tasks only one type of distractor (foil) was tested on each different trial when the test item was not the same as the target.

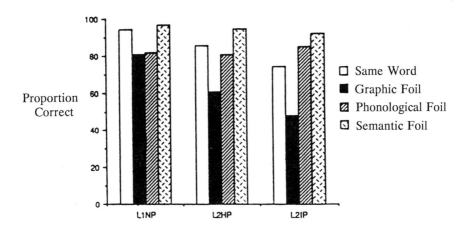

Figure 1: Context-free word recognition for same and different trials.

As shown in Figure 1, the results of context-free word recognition revealed a clear pattern. Regarding the recognition of the same target, accuracy in context-free word recognition improved with increasing skill, such that L1 readers did better than the experienced L2 readers, who in turn outperformed the less skilled L2 readers (L1NP > L2HP> L2IP). Differences in the performance of the three groups were also apparent when the test item differed from the target item. In this case the observed differences related mainly to the processing of graphic foils since the three groups were equally accurate at detecting phonological and semantic discrepancies. On the processing of graphic foils, accuracy improved with increasing reading skill (L1NP > L2HP > L2IP), suggesting that less proficient readers have not yet automatized the processing of visual information. That is, when presented with two graphically similar trials, less proficient L2 readers were simply confused and unable to discriminate the minor visual differences between characters. The three groups differed not only in accuracy but also in speed, with the most experienced readers responding more quickly than the L2 groups under all conditions.

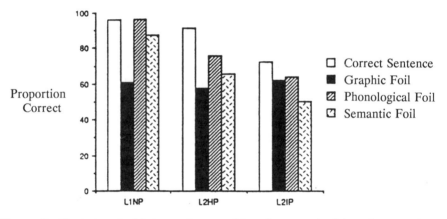

Figure 2: Context-embedded word recognition for meaningful and anomalous sentences.

Differences in the word recognition processes of the three groups were also observed in the sentence verification task (see Figure 2). Here again, the most experienced readers were more accurate in judging correct sentences as compared to the less proficient ones (L1NP > L2HP > L2IP). The three groups also differed in their processing of anomalous sentences, especially when the sentences included phonological and semantic foils. In these instances, the accuracy rate increased with increasing skill (L1NP > L2HP > L2IP). Less proficient readers were severely confused by the presence of homophones and semantically related items as compared to the other two groups. The native speakers and the advanced second language readers, on the other hand, did poorly when processing anomalous sentences containing graphic foils, implying that their attention was focused more on higher level processes referring to meaning. The three groups also differed in the time measures which included reading time and decision time. The processing time for more experienced readers was significantly faster than for less proficient readers (L1NP > L2HP > L2IP).

The findings of the native readers in this study suggest that first language reading in Chinese is an integrated information processing activity. At the same time, because of the highly complicated nature of Chinese characters, native readers seem to be very efficient in processing graphic information as shown in their performance on context-free word recognition. In contrast to native readers, second-language readers, even good readers, made more task-related errors. Because of the consistent pattern of L1NP > L2HP > L2IP under all conditions, the differences between first and second language readers and between proficient and less proficient second language readers may in fact lie in their discrepancy in reading proficiency.

Summary and Conclusions

The present chapter addressed L2 word recognition in relation to both the scripts' characteristics and the learners' reading proficiency. In addition to a literature review, it presented two studies that examined these issues. The first study on the reading of English-Greek bilinguals indicated that word recognition differs between languages depending upon the language and writing system characteristics. The second study on reading in Chinese as a second language also indicated, however, that the ability of bilinguals to respond to these characteristics depends upon their level of reading proficiency in each language. It is obvious, from the literature review and the present studies, that the nature of L2 word recognition processes is closely related to the learner's reading experience and reading proficiency in the L2. Therefore, reading proficiency seems to be a better indication of reading skill than the level of general language proficiency used in most L2 reading studies to date. Indeed, it seems that if future research is to provide a better understanding of L2 reading processes, it must differentiate between reading and language proficiency.

References

Bernhardt, E. B. (1986). Cognitive processes in L2: An examination of reading behaviours. In J. Lantolf, & A. Labarca (Eds.), *Second language acquisition in the classroom setting.* Norwood, NJ: Ablex.

Bernhardt, E. B., & Everson, M. E. (1988, December). Second language reading: A cognitive perspective. Paper presented at a meeting of the National Reading Conference, Tucson, AZ.

Biederman, I., & Tsao, Y. (1979). On processing Chinese ideographs and English words: Some implications from Stroop-Test Results. *Cognitive Psychology*, 11, 125-132.

Brown, T. L., & Haynes, M. (1985). Literacy background and reading development in a second language. In T. H. Carr (Ed.), *The development of reading skill*. San Francisco: Jossey-Bass.

Chen, H.C., & Juola, J. (1982). Dimensions of lexical coding in Chinese and English. *Memory & Cognition*, 10 216-224.

Chen, M. J., Yung, Y. F., & Ng, T. W. (1988). The effect of context on perception of Chinese characters. In I. M. Liu, H. C. Chen, & M. J. Chen (Eds.) *Cognitive aspects of the Chinese language, Vol. 1*. Hong Kong: Asian Research Service, Pp. 27-39.

Cheng, C. M., & Shih, S. I. (1988). The nature of lexical access in Chinese: Evidence from experiments on visual and phonological priming in lexical judgement. In I. M. Liu, H. C. Chen, & M. J. Chen (Eds.), *Cognitive aspects of the Chinese language, Vol. 1*. Hong Kong: Asian Research Service, Pp. 1-14.

Chitiri, H. F. (1991). *The influence of language and writing system characteristics on the reading process*. Unpublished Ph.D. dissertation. University of Toronto.

Chu-Chang, M., & Loritz, D. J. (1977). Even Chinese ideographs are phonologically encoded in short-term memory. *Language Learning*, 27, 341-352.

Clarke, M. A. (1979). Reading in Spanish and English: Evidence from adult ESL students. *Language Learning*, 29, 121-150.

Corcoran, D. W. J. (1966). An acoustic factor in letter cancellation. *Nature*, 210, 658.

Cziko, G. A. (1978). Differences in first and second language reading: The use of syntactic, semantic and discourse constraints. *Canadian Modern Language Review*, 34, 473-489.

Cziko, G. A. (1980). Language competence and reading strategies: A comparison of first and second language oral reading errors. *Language Learning*, 30, 101-116.

Durgunoglu, A. Y., & Roediger, H. L. (1987). Test differences in accessing bilingual memory. *Journal of Memory and Language*, 26, 377-391.

Favreau, M., Komoda, M. K., & Segalowitz, N. (1980). Implications of the word superiority effect in skilled bilinguals. *Canadian Journal of Psychology*, 34, 370-380.

Favreau, M., & Segalowitz, N. S. (1983). Automatic and controlled processes in the first-and second language reading of fluent bilinguals. *Memory and Cognition*, 11, 565-574.

Feldman, L. B., & Turvey, M. T. (1983). Word recognition in Serbo-Croatian is phonologically analytic. *Journal of Experimental Psychology: Human Perception and Performance, 9*, 414-420.

Frost, R., Katz, L., & Bentin, S. (1987). Strategies for visual word recognition and orthographic depth: A multilingual comparison. *Journal of Experimental Psychology: Human Perception and Performance*, 13, 104-115.

Frost, R., & Katz, L. (1989). Orthographic depth and the interaction of visual and auditory processing in word recognition. *Memory & Cognition*, 17, 302-310.

Geva, E., & Ryan, E. B. (1987, June). Linguistic and memory correlates of academic skill in first and second language. Paper presented at a meeting of the Canadian Psychological Association, Vancouver, BC.

Goodman, K. S. (1976). Reading: A psycholinguistic guessing game. In H. Singer & R. Ruddell (Eds.), *Theoretical models and processes of reading* (2nd ed.). Newark, DE: International Reading Association.

Gray, W. S. (1956). *The teaching of reading and writing: An international survey.* Paris: UNESCO.

Hatch, E., Polin, P., & Part, S. (1974). Acoustic scanning and syntactic processing. Three experiments-First and second language learners. *Journal of Reading Behavior*, 1974, 275-285.

Hayes, E. B. (1987). An investigation of the amount of phonological encoding vs. visual processing strategies employed by advanced American readers of Chinese Mandarin and native Chinese readers. Unpublished Ph. D. dissertation, Ohio State University.

Hayes, E. B. (1988). Encoding strategies used by native and non-native readers of Chinese Mandarin. *The Modern Language Journal*, 72, 188-195.

Healy, A. F. (1980). Proofreading errors on the word *the*: New evidence on reading units. *Journal of Experimental Psychology: Human Perception and Performance*, 6, 403-409.

Healy, A. F., Conboy, G. L., & Drewnowski, A. (1987). Characterizing the processing of units of reading. In B. K. Britton & S. M. Glynn (Eds.), *Executive control processes in reading*. Hillsdale, NJ: Erlbaum.

Hoosain, R., & Osgood, C. E. (1983). Processing times for Chinese and English words. *Perception and Psychophysics*, 34, 573-577.

Just, M. A., & Carpenter, P. A. (1987). *The psychology of reading and writing*. Boston: Allyn and Bacon.

Koda, K. (1988). Cognitive processes in second language reading: Transfer of L1 reading skills and strategies. *Second Language Research*, 4, 133-156.

LaBerge, D., & Samuels, S. J. (1974). Toward a theory of automatic information processing in reading. *Cognitive Psychology*, 6, 293-323.

Leong, C. K. (1973). Hong Kong. In J. Downing (Ed.) *Comparative reading: Cross-national studies of behavior and processes in reading and writing*. New York: Macmillan.

Leong, C. K. (1986). Reading and writing disorders in Chinese-Some theoretical issues. In H. S. R. Kao and R. Hoosain (Eds.) *Psychological studies of the Chinese language*. Hong Kong: The Chinese Language Society of Hong Kong.

Peng, D. L., Guo, D. J., & Zhang, S. L. (1985). The retrieval of information of Chinese characters in making similarity judgement under recognition condition. *Acta Psychologica Sinica*, 3, 227-234.

Samuels, S. J., & Kamil, M. (1984). Models of the reading process. In P. D. Pearson (Ed.), *Handbook of reading research*. New York: Longman.

Segalowitz, N., & Hebert, M. (1990). Phonological recoding in the first and second language reading of skilled bilinguals. *Language Learning*, 40, 503-538.

Seidenberg, M. S. (1985). The time course of phonological code activation in two writing systems. *Cognition*, 19, 1-30.

Sun, Y. L. (1991, July). Word recognition processes of second language readers of Chinese. Paper presented at the International Conference on Second Language Acquisition in the Chinese Context, Hong Kong.

Taylor, I., & Taylor, M. M. (1983). *The psychology of reading*. New York: Academic Press.

Taylor, I., & Taylor, M. M. (1990). *Psycholinguistics*. Englewood Cliffs, NJ: Prentice Hall.

Treiman, R. A., Baron, J., & Luk, K. (1981). Speech recoding in silent reading: A comparison of Chinese and English. *Journal of Chinese Linguistics*, 9, 116-125.

Turvey, M. T., Feldman, L.B., & Lukatela, G.   (1984).   The Serbo-Croatian orthography constrains the reader to a phonologically analytic strategy. In L. Henderson (Ed.), *Orthographies and reading*. London: Lawrence Erlbaum Associates.

Tzeng, O. J. L., Hung, D., & Wang, W. S. Y. (1977). Speech recoding in reading Chinese characters. *Journal of Experimental Psychology: Human Learning and Memory*, 3, 621-630.

Wiederholt, J. L., & Bryant, B. R. (1986). *Gray Oral Reading Test-Revised (GORT-R)*. Austin, TX: Pro-Ed.

Cognitive Processing in Bilinguals – *R.J. Harris (Editor)*
© *1992 Elsevier Science Publishers B.V. All rights reserved.*

A Functional View of Bilingual Lexicosemantic Organization

Marianne C. Votaw
University of Virginia

This model focuses on individual differences in constraints on language choice. Bilinguals may live among speakers of only one of their languages, or with bilinguals who share the same two languages. In the former (constrained) case, the constraints on language choice result in a more language-dependent organization than the latter (unconstrained). Changes in reaction-time used to explore this organization can be contaminated by these individual differences. RTs to targets belonging to an unexpected language are slowed for constrained bilinguals, but unconstrained bilinguals form no language expectations from context. Violated expectations yield both a lack of visible associations across languages and extra time to process stimuli following a change in language, for constrained bilinguals only. Therefore, investigations of bilingual lexicosemantic networks must consider the role of language for the subjects.

This chapter will present a functional view of how the meanings of words are represented in bilingual lexicosemantic networks. Although there are several theories about the role of the language in organizing such networks, most of these investigate "the" bilingual lexicon. This chapter will show that these investigations often ignore crucial individual differences among bilinguals. To this end, the first part of this chapter will explore the role of language choice in bilingualism, and will illustrate the critical difference between bilinguals: the importance of language choice to their ability to communicate. The next section will sketch the major paradigms for exploring the organization of lexicosemantic networks within an activation model of lexical access, including the assumptions underlying network models of lexicosemantic storage. The rest of this chapter will then review reaction-time investigations into bilingual lexicosemantic organization, some of which seem to indicate that meanings are represented according to the language in which words occur, while others support a language-independent organization. Individual differences between the samples under study will be used to help explain these contradictions. This functional reinterpretation will show that individual differences in the role of language choice to the ability to communicate result in differences in the role of language in organizing individual bilinguals' lexicosemantic networks.

Bilingualism: Overview

Bilingualism is defined here as having a choice of two available languages for conversation. *Fluent* bilinguals are equally comfortable in each language, although even in the best case fluency is rarely balanced across all conversational domains (Baetens Beardsmore, 1986). Given fluent bilingualism, the critical difference in bilingual language function is in the importance of language choice. As this variable stems from sociolinguistic and psychological pressures, it will be examined in terms of *constraint*. Half of the world is monolingual, and *mutual* bilinguals, defined as bilinguals who share the same two languages, are also relatively rare (Heller, 1988). Therefore, language choice is often constrained to only one communicable language. This constraint is externally imposed when only one language is *feasible* for communication, defined as when the other language could not be understood (Hymes, 1972). Internally-imposed *restraint* from a preference for one language can also be strong even among mutual bilinguals, either from topic- or individual-centered fluency differences. Also, bilingual cultures reward various degrees of restraint in their members (Baetens Beardsmore, 1986; Heller, 1988). For example, most Catalans avoid using Castillian Spanish although they understand it, whereas many Hispanic

Americans prefer Spanglish to either English or Spanish (Lipski, 1985; Zaraus, 1980). In that case, restraint reflects each language's *appropriateness*, defined as its fit to the social situation (Hymes, 1972).

The importance language choice is thus determined by the context in which bilinguals communicate. Ferguson's term *diglossia* for context-dependency of choice of style within one language, i.e. informal vs. formal speech, has been adopted into literature on bilingualism to reflect context-dependency of language choice (Heller, 1988; Paradis, 1987). However, the constraints on each individual language may not be complementary: Although one language (L_i) might be constrained to certain contexts, the other (L_j) might be appropriate in all contexts. In that case, the individual could be considered diglossic as choice of L_i depends on context, but then the lack of constraint on L_j would not be evident. Asymmetry in context-dependency would, however, be clear if constraint were considered for each language independently.

Paradigmatic Assumptions and Concerns

Studies of bilingualism, as in monolingual research, make use of a network metaphor for lexicosemantic storage, where the meanings of words are represented at *nodes* interconnected by associations between the meanings being represented (e.g., Abbott & Black, 1986; Anderson, 1983). *Lexical access*, the process of reaching the meaning, is thus hypothesized as activating the node representing that meaning (Collins & Quillian, 1970). Therefore, most studies of network organization use reaction-time (RT) paradigms: words whose meanings are accessed more quickly are represented at more active nodes. Lexical access, furthermore, is performed in two major stages: prelexical and matching. Prelexical processing uses orthographic information to find the root (Downie, Milech & Kirsner, 1985; Stemberger & MacWhinney, 1986; Taft & Forster, 1975). Matching compares this root to the set of stored representations of core meanings (Becker, 1980; Collins & Quillian, 1970; Morton, 1980). That is, the network is searched until the node representing that root is found. Matching occurs in the same manner for all words; in lexical decision tasks, an exhaustive search is made for *pseudowords*, defined as orthographically legal and pronounceable stimuli which have no representation to match. This results in longer RTs compared to words (Balota & Chumbley, 1983).

The degree of association between nodes is quantified by changes in RT. *Priming* is defined as a reduction in RT to a particular word (the *target*) following a particular prior word (the *prime*), compared to RT when that target is preceded by a neutral stimulus. This facilitation occurs through an automatic spread of activation from the node representing the prime (Meyer, Schvaneveldt, & Ruddy, 1975; Neely, 1977). Lexical access to related words is then speeded because those representations have already been activated because of their proximity to the prime. As the degree of activation is seen as fading with distance as it spreads through the network, the amount of priming defines the closeness of the relationship (Ashcraft, 1976; de Groot, 1983).

Activation also decreases with delay between the appearances of prime and target (Stimulus Onset Asynchrony, or *SOA*). Longer SOAs, furthermore, allow effortful processing about the prime, whereas RTs at short SOAs reflect automatic spreading activation (Neely, 1977; Posner & Snyder, 1975). Thus at SOAs between prime and target of 50 msecs or less, all associations to ambiguous targets are activated, even those related to context-inappropriate meanings (Swinney, 1979). At slightly longer delays only access to context-appropriate associations is facilitated. Thus context effects on targets require some delay after presentation of the prime.

Slightly longer SOAs, 150 msecs or more (LaBerge, Van Gelder & Yellot, 1970; Neely, 1977; Posner & Snyder, 1975), also allow the formation of expectations about the upcoming target, which shorter SOAs minimize. With time to form these expectations, recognition of targets in unexpected relationships to the prime is slowed. This increase in RT compared to targets following a neutral stimulus defines *inhibition*. Expectations about upcoming targets can be generated either by the prime or by the experimenter's instructions (Neely, 1977). In either case, targets which violate these expectations are more difficult to access than baseline (Balota & Chumbley, 1984; Lorch, Balota, & Stamm, 1986), even if there is a semantic relationship between prime and target (Neely, 1977; Favreau & Segalowitz, 1983). In addition to processing differences, paradigms using short SOAs generally require responses only to targets, with primes being presented but not requiring a response, i.e. 2-word lexical decision. Longer SOAs allow subjects to respond to every stimulus.

Inhibition from unexpected targets has been shown not to be attributable to a more difficult lexical access. Post-lexical processing is involved, notably the word/not-word decision stage in lexical decision: naming and category-verification tasks do not show the same increases in RT for unexpected targets (Lorch, Balota, & Stamm, 1986). More frequent words are also recognized more quickly in lexical decision, in contrast to category-verification and naming (Balota & Chumbley, 1983). Therefore, although frequency and expectations impact subjects' ability to call a stimulus a word, these effects may not reflect speed of lexical access.

Research in bilingualism is primarily concerned with the role of language in the organization of the lexicosemantic network. This question is often phrased as a choice between two possible types of organizations: in the *compound* bilingual lexicosemantic network, nodes are related through associations between language-independent meanings, and there is no organization according to the language to which individual words belong (McCormick, 1977). The opposing view is of a language-dependent network, where concepts are organized into two *coordinate* lexicosemantic systems, one per language (Kolers, 1979), and associations are only within each system. Intermediate theories assume *dual-coding*, where both language-independent meanings and language-dependent words are represented (Potter, So, Von Eckardt & Feldman, 1984). In these views, associations are either directly between the words (word association), or indirectly through the underlying meanings (concept mediation; Potter et al., 1984).

Most of this research compares changes in RT when prime and target are in different languages, termed here *trans-priming*, to changes when both words are in the same language, called here *cis-priming*. Borrowing "cis-" (same side) and "trans-" (other side) from organic chemistry avoids the terms "inter-" and "intralingual" priming, which are easily confused as they are highly similar. The role of the language to which the words belong in organizing representations of their *referents*, i.e. the concepts to which the words refer, is most cleanly addressed in trans-priming studies if the two languages share a writing system. Independent manipulations of similarities between semantic referents and lexical forms of prime and target are possible (see Table 1). Investigations of trans-priming between languages which do not share orthography (e.g., Kirsner, Smith, Lockheart, King & Jain, 1984, Exp. 4, with English and Hindi; Potter et al., 1984, Exp. 1, with English and Chinese) cannot address the effects of lexical similarity as no forms across languages are visually related. Auditory presentations (e.g., Soares & Grosjean, 1984) also preclude manipulations of lexical similarity as pronunciations differ across languages, even if the visual form is identical.

These stimuli, furthermore, vary in their degree of experimental controllability: TEs, Same-IHs, Unrelated-IHs and Unrelated-Pairs are more rigidly controllable than are the intermediate (related in referent or cognate in form) pairs. These intermediate stimuli can also vary in their degree of similarity. For example, the Eucognates INDEPENDENCE (English) and INDEPENDANCE (French) are visually more similar than are the Eucognates STAR (English) and ESTRELLA (Spanish), which last is more similar to the French Eucognate ETOILE. STAR and ETOILE don't even look related.

Similar variations in shared meaning are possible. However, stimulus-type boundaries according to referent are fuzzy, because what a word means to a particular language-user is not as definable as the letters which compose that word's written form. In addition, TEs may not really be "equivalent" for many bilinguals. For instance, certain bilinguals do not give the same associations to TEs (e.g., Tyson, Doctor & Mentis, 1988). However, if the two words are given as translations of each other in reputable dictionaries, they are considered to mean the "same" thing for the purposes of these experiments. The possibility that associations between concepts are different depending on the lexical form used to convey those concepts can be minimized in lexical decision by using category-exemplar pairs: no matter what language is used, a DESK is FURNITURE and an APPLE is a FRUIT.

Table 1: Glossary and examples of trans-priming stimulus pairs.

	<------% Shared Meaning------>		
	Maximal (Same referent)	Intermediate (Related referents)	Minimal (Unrelated referents)
% Shared Form:			
Maximal: (Interlexical Homographs: IHs)	*Same-IHs*	*Related-IHs*	*Unrelated-IHs*
Examples:	SILENCE (Eng., Fr.)	COSTUME (Fr. "3pc. suit")	MOST (Hungarian "now")
Intermediate: (Cognate forms)	*Eucognates*	*Related Cognates*	*Pseudocognates*
Examples:	CAT (Eng.) GATO (Sp. "cat")	LIBRARY (Eng.) LIBRAIRIE (Fr. "bookstore")	GRIP (Eng.) GRIPPE (Fr. "'flu")
Minimal: (Unrelated forms)	*Translation Equivalents (TEs)*	*Related-Pairs*	*Unrelated-Pairs*
Examples:	DOG (Eng.) CHIEN (Fr.)	DOG (Eng.) GATO (Sp. "cat")	DOG (Eng.) LIBRAIRIE (Fr. "bookstore")

Note: Eng. = English, Fr. = French, Sp. = Spanish.

Years of research by many investigators have yet to determine the organization of "the" bilingual lexicosemantic network, and all of the various theories have found empirical support. However, these examinations do not often consider the function of language in the type of bilingualism being investigated, although age of acquisition of the second language is often controlled. Thus, contradictions in the literature may be caused by ignored individual differences between the various bilinguals selected. In a functional perspective, furthermore, neither representation nor organization occur in a vacuum: what will be represented is whatever the language-user needs to communicate, and these representations will be organized according to the individual's experiences with those concepts.

Therefore, the way in which words actually are used in communication should impact on the way in which their representations are organized. When language choice is constrained, both the language chosen and the semantic information are critical to communication. In unconstrained bilingualism, language choice is not nearly as important as is the concept to be communicated. Therefore, the importance of language choice should affect the role of language in organizating any bilingual's lexicosemantic network. Language would also provide a more coherent context in constrained bilingualism, where context habitually determines the language, than in unconstrained bilingualism where language choice is not context-dependent. Therefore, assessment of language usage is necessary for functional interpretations of any study. Unconstrained bilingualism is certainly less common, but a global assumption of constraint in usage would be unwise. Sociolinguistic information about the area from which subjects were recruited helps, but bilinguals in constraining cultures may have found mutually-bilingual niches, and those from bilingual societies may prefer to use one language at a time. In addition, even when language choice in conversation is unrestrained, the majority of written works are in only one language. Bilingual authors rarely alternate languages within sentences, bilingual schools' textbooks are in one language or the other, bilingual communities publish newspapers in each language but do not generally use both languages within the same article. Most of these paradigms present visual stimuli, so investigations of even the most unconstrained bilingualism may show some small effects of constraint from habitual reading patterns. This problem would be minimized with auditory presentation of stimuli.

Constraint also affects the importance of separating alternate forms for the same referent: Constrained bilinguals must select words according to context language, while unconstrained bilinguals could select either alternative. The importance of that separation, furthermore, depends on the similarity between these alternate forms: Choose the wrong TE when in a constrained conversation, and you will lose your audience. That risk is lessened if the alternative form is cognate, and even less from choosing the wrong Same-IH. Thus in constrained bilingualism, the degree to which representations are separated by the language in which the word occurs should depend on the disparity between the lexical forms. This comparison is not relevant for forms which do not share a referent, nor would such a difference be expected for unconstrained bilinguals.

Individual differences in usage would not only affect the actual organization of the network, but could also affect RT data in such a way as to lead to erroneous interpretations about associations. First, habitual constraints in language choice create expectations as to which language will be used in any familiar context. One could expect, for example, to speak English at home and French at school. Bilinguals without such constraints would not expect only one language to be used per context; if these individuals habitually alternate languages, language expectations would be entirely absent. In new situations, constrained bilinguals would expect that the language initially chosen would continue to be used; unconstrained bilinguals, in contrast, would not form same-language expectations, especially if they habitually alternate languages in conversation. These expectations could also be asymmetrical if L_i is habitually constrained to certain contexts but not L_j Then, initial use of L_i would lead subjects to expect more L_i, while use of L_j would not predict the language of the next word. For instance, either French or English could be used at home but only French at school.

Expectations can create artifacts in RT research because the closeness of relationships between nodes is empirically defined by the amount of priming. However, changes in RT at longer SOAs are known to be affected by expectations about the upcoming target. For constrained bilinguals, these expectations would include the language to which the target should belong. RTs to targets which violate these language expectations would then be increased, possibly eliminating any facilitation from semantic associations between prime and target which do, nonetheless, exist in the network. This lack of facilitation, however, would be interpreted as showing that there are no such cross-language associations if language expectations are not considered by the researcher. Specific instructions that prime and target will be in different languages would increase the possibility that any facilitation attributable to spreading activation between related nodes could be seen, as the language change would then be expected. Unconstrained bilinguals are less likely to have expectations as to the language of any upcoming word, although their semantic expectations should be the same. Language expectations would be weakest for bilinguals whose conversations habitually alternate languages. Therefore, unconstrained bilingual subjects should not show inhibition after a change in language, even without warning, as they would form no same-language expectations even if given the time.

The inhibitory effect of language change for constrained bilinguals could be interpreted as evidence for a *switch* mechanism as postulated by Kolers (1966), Macnamara and Kushnir (1971) and others. Also, it may yield an *alternation deficit*, defined as an increase in RT to words in either language when both are used within the same task, compared to monolingual conditions (e.g., Meyer & Ruddy, 1974). In addition, asymmetrical constraints could lead bilinguals only to show such inhibitory effects when the prime is in the language generally constrained, as that predicts a same-language target, while primes in the other, usually unconstrained language might create no language-specific expectations.

Uncertainty about the type of bilingualism under investigation is not the only difficulty in interpreting evidence from bilingual priming paradigms. The most common baseline against which changes in RT are measured is RT to words presented after a neutral stimulus (e.g., Caramazza & Brones, 1980). However, no wordlike stimulus is neutral in terms of its language. Common "neutral" primes include the word "BLANK" or stimuli such as "XXXXX" or "OOOO." In the first example, the "neutral" stimulus is squarely in English; the latter stimuli are also differently pronounced if "read" in different languages, and are therefore not controllably neutral. Any of these could give an habitually-constrained bilingual expectations as to the language of the upcoming target. Therefore, targets following unrelated words in the other language would be a better baseline for trans-priming studies as they control for language expectations.

It is also possible that stimuli violate language expectations proportionally to the difference in form between shared-referent alternatives, as a form similar to the one expected would be less suprising than an entirely unrelated form. In this case, presentation of a TE in the unexpected language would be more inhibiting to RTs than presentation of the "other" Eucognate. Same-IHs may not violate language expectations at all in visual presentations, as the form is the same as in the expected language. Expectation effects, however, would only be present in paradigms using longer SOAs where expectations and context information are given time to be processed. If this interaction between lexical similarity and degree of trans-priming is still present at a short SOA, any increase in a deficit in trans-priming with greater lexical disparity would be truly reflective of a greater separation of TEs than of stimuli more similar in form.

Furthermore, self-reported measures of fluency are not reliable: many subjects who consider themselves equally fluent show by their RT data that this is not the case. Fluency has strong effects on spreading activation: Frenck and Pynte (1987) examined cis- and trans-priming using TEs in lexical decision with sequential bilinguals, half fluent and half not. Although primes were always in French in one block and always in English in another, targets could be in any language, and subjects were given no instructions as to the language of any stimulus. For the nonfluent bilinguals, trans-priming only occurred when the prime was in the dominant language. There was no such asymmetry for the fluent bilinguals. As age of acquisition was confounded with balance in this study, in that age of acquisition of L_2 was later for the nonfluent subjects though all were sequential bilinguals, the asymmetry attributed to fluency may be a function of age of acquisition of L_2. However, other research with "repetition" priming in nonfluent bilinguals using TEs and long SOAs (Kirsner et al., 1984, Exps. 2, 3 & 5) has shown that activation spreads only out of fluent languages. Thus, the later age of acquisition is not likely to underlie the asymmetry found by Frenck and Pynte (1987).

In contrast, Grainger and Beauvillian (1988, Exps. 1 & 2) using semantic rather than repetition trans-priming found facilitation only when the target was in the dominant language of nonfluent bilinguals in a 2-word lexical decision task. However, this only occurred at the 750-msec SOA; there was no trans-priming in either direction at a 150-msec SOA, indicating that trans-priming involved effortful processing rather than automatic spreading activation. Grainger and Beauvillian also instructed their subjects to expect the language change; Frenck and Pynte (1987), as well as Kirsner et al. (1984, Exps. 2, 3 & 5) did not. It therefore seems that with specific instructions to expect a change in language, effortful activation of putative related targets is easier in a better-known language, leading to facilitation for targets only in that dominant language. This finding was also independent of both of age and method of acquisition of L_2, as these varied between experiments 1 and 2 (Grainger & Beauvillian, 1988).

Thus, fluency differences affects the spread of activation across languages in more ways than one. Furthermore, speed of reading even for fluent bilinguals also needs to be assessed: Favreau and Segalowitz (1983) compared cis-priming to expected and unexpected targets in lexical decision at a 200- and a 1150-msec SOA with fluent bilinguals, half of whom who read their second language significantly more slowly. Subjects were specifically instructed to expect a related target in some conditions, and unrelated target in others, with relationship determined by membership in a common category (e.g., CARROT was related to POTATO but not to ROBIN). These associations were carefully normed to ensure the same relationship in both languages. In Expect-Unrelated conditions, subjects were trained as to which unrelated category to expect. Thus, in all conditions subjects could form semantic expectations given the time, but the expected category was not always semantically related. SOA and Expectancy factors were blocked so that instructions could be clear for each condition and to allow within-subjects comparisons. In all conditions both related and unrelated targets were presented, providing a clear separation of expectation effects from effects of semantic relatedness.

Results revealed little difference between reading-balanced and other bilinguals in their first or reading-dominant language, regardless of expectations or SOA. At the longer SOA, both groups showed facilitation for expected targets and inhibition for unexpected ones, regardless of semantic relationship. This is the exact pattern seen for monolinguals (Neely, 1977). At the shorter SOA, both groups were faster for expected targets in both languages, significantly so if those targets were also related. Furthermore, related but unexpected targets showed significant facilitation for both groups in L_1 at the shorter SOA; however, only the balanced-reading group also showed that effect in L_2. Thus, activation did not spread automatically from related primes within a less-quickly read language when instructions were to expect an unrelated target, although it did when instructions were to expect related words. This shows an effect of instructions at a short SOA, which indicates that 200 msecs is not short enough for effortful processing to be prohibited. Indeed, other research tends to show that at SOAs of greater than 150 msecs, non-automatic processes can be used (e.g., LaBerge et al., 1970; Lorch, Balota & Stamm, 1986; Neely, 1977).

Thus in languages more slowly read, fairly short SOAs do not reveal automatic spreading activation counter to instructions, whereas in languages read more quickly, such a spread is evident regardless of SOA. At longer SOAs, there was no difference in direction or significance of effects between these groups of bilinguals. However, a reexamination of effect sizes across groups within each condition reveals that reading-balanced bilinguals show greater changes in RT, whether facilitory or inhibitory, especially in L_2. Differences of less than 5 msecs were disregarded; of the 13 remaining comparisons, 11 were greater for the balanced readers (a significant proportion; $p < .05$ by sign test). All comparisons within L_2 favored the balanced readers (7 out of 7; $p < .05$). Thus the major effect of a slower reading speed despite fluency is a reduction in magnitude of any changes in RT, whether facilitory or inhibitory, and this reduction is especially clear in the less-well read language.

This study shows that bilinguals are just as capable as are monolinguals of using experimenter instructions to set up categorical semantic expectations. What is not demonstrated here is whether bilinguals habituated to expect only one language per context can use specific instructions to expect a change in language: this was not a trans-priming investigation, and these subjects were likely to be unconstrained in language choice. Furthermore, even if auditory-vocal fluency and reading comprehension are equal, slower reading in one language can lead to diminished effects, especially within that language; it is therefore likely that reading-imbalances also affect trans-priming patterns, which Favreau and Segalowitz (1983) were not examining. The spread of activation from primes in a less-quickly read language to any target, whether in the same language or not, would be expected to be diminished. These asymmetries in trans-priming attributable to fluency or reading speed indicate a need to analyze results separately by language in any trans-priming investigation where subjects are faster in one language. Deficits in trans- compared to cis-priming may stem from difficulties in spreading activation attributable to lack of fluency or slow reading ability, rather than from a lack of associations across languages.

Literature Revisited

Because of these subject-centered and paradigmatic concerns, this review will reexamine the literature on trans-priming patterns with visual presentations and shared orthography, focussing on fluent bilingualism. The most likely function of language for the subjects of each investigation will be determined by data provided by the authors, incorporating any available sociolinguistic information about the geographical area. In the absence of specific mention, subjects will be assumed to have been recruited from the school with which the first author is affiliated. Particular attention will be paid to differences in patterns at long and short SOAs for constrained bilinguals, to separate artifactual effects of expectations from measures of network organization shown by automatic spreading activation. This first section will focus on investigations with subjects likely to function under great constraints on both languages. These participants specifically reported using both languages commonly but in distinct contexts, as L_i at home, around the neighborhood, or with speakers of the "foreign" language, and L_j at work, school or with speakers of the national language. Asymmetrical constraints are possible because choice of the national language may be less constrained.

Gerard and Scarborough (1989) investigated "repetition" priming in mono- and bilinguals in lexical decision tasks conducted in two phases. Words were TEs (repetition of referent alone), Same-IHs (repetition of both referent and form), Unrelated-IHs (repetition of form alone) and Unrelated-Pairs (neither form nor referent repeated). Frequencies of these pairs in each language were comparable except for the Unrelated-IHs, half of which had higher-frequency readings in one language. Pseudowords were derived from real words of each stimulus type in the target language. Availability of mutual bilinguals and the frequency of alternating speech (Spanglish) were not reported, though Spanglish is known to be common in that area (Lipski, 1985). It is therefore possible that choice of English was less constrained than choice of Spanish, despite specific mention that these languages were used for different purposes.

Subjects were told that their vocabulary was being tested in only one language in each phase, and a long SOA was used between subsequent stimuli. Delays between first and second presentations of "repetitions" were also long, even when stimuli were repeated within sessions. No stimuli were presented which could not be read in the target language, although some stimuli also had meanings if read in the nontarget language. Thus the language-expectations, which would be strong in this sample and maximized by the design, would never have been violated by orthography. In the second session, the language being tested was changed for the bilingual subjects.

Gerard and Scarborough found that while repeating the same form resulted in facilitation, there was no effect at all of repeating the referent: Same- and Unrelated-IHs showed the same degree of facilitation compared to Unrelated-Pairs, even though they were later embedded in contexts specifying the other language. This indicates an effect of familiarity of form rather than residual activation of the words' meaning, an interpretation strengthened by the finding that TEs showed no facilitation at all. Furthermore, frequency effects were related to the reading in the context-appropriate language for the nonbalanced Unrelated-IHs: if the higher-frequency reading was in the nontarget language, the stimuli were recognized as low-frequency words, which was true in the target language. Better reading ability in English was also confirmed for the bilingual subjects by the RT data. That finding, together with the likelihood of asymmetrical constraints, indicates a need for language-specific analyses.

Facilitation attributable to familiarity with form rather than to residual activation replicates earlier studies with similarly-constrained subjects, also making lexical decisions in only one target language per session (Scarborough, Gerard & Cortese, 1984, Exps. 1, 2). Words in those studies were TEs or Unrelated-Pairs, not cognates or homographs, and were again "repeated" across sessions. Pseudowords were derived from nonstimulus words without cognate or homographic translations, and in Exp. 1 only they were language-appropriate. Thus, pseudoword orthography would not violate language expectations. Subjects were again instructed to expect a particular language, and given time to maximize both the processing of context information and the formation of expectations for upcoming targets. Again, stimuli were repeated both within and across sessions, and target language was changed in the second phase for half the bilingual subjects.

Scarborough et al. (1984, Exp. 1) found repetition effects and frequency effects within the first session, and the repetition effect was stronger for stimuli recognized more slowly on first presentation (low-frequency words in any language, and Spanish words when Spanish was the target language). This confirms that these subjects were also English-Reading dominant. Repetition across sessions only facilitated recognition of stimuli exactly repeated, i.e. re-presented in the same language. This effect was also stronger for low-frequency words, which had been more slowly recognized upon first presentation. There was no facilitation for TEs, that is for the bilinguals whose target language was changed, not even for low-frequency words. Again, repeating the form but not the referent facilitated later recognition, although there is a slight possibility that individual differences were confounded with the change in target language; this would be a stronger result had that comparison been made within-subjects.

These two studies indicate that constrained bilinguals, under specific instructions to expect and respond only in one language per session, are only faster at recognizing "repeated" stimuli if they had previously recognized that form. When the expected language is changed across sessions, previous access to the same referent did not facilitate later recognition of unrelated forms. The lack of facilitation for "repeated" TEs is not attributable to violated expectations in this design. Therefore, the results of both these studies imply that a referent accessed through L_i may not represent the same concept as that accessed through L_j for highly-constrained bilinguals. These results could also show that the expectation of a particular language results in inhibition of entire system for processing the other language. This interpretation involves distinct language systems for constrained binguas, as specified by the coordinate theory of lexicosemantic organization. Unconstrained bilinguals should not evolve separate language systems as language usage is not separated by contextual constraints. Therefore, this experiment needs to be replicated in unconstrained bilingualism.

In this coordinate view, homographic forms can be processed though either system, and so their repetitions are more quickly recognized even though a different system is doing the processing. Activation of representations accessed through L_i, however, is eliminated by the instructions to expect L_j in the later session. Thus, when TEs of L_i words are presented, there is no facilitation because there was no previous processing on that form. Same-IHs have no advantage over Unrelated-IHs as residual activation of the meaning accessed through one language has been eliminated by expectations of the other language. In this interpretation, it is possible that the meaning(s) accessed though the different systems be distinct even though the alternate forms of both Same-IHs and TEs are dictionary equivalents. The two meanings would still be semantically related, but semantic priming is not robust enough to appear under these conditions of long delay and many intervening trials (e.g., deGroot, 1983).

In Exp. 2 (Scarborough et al., 1984), the stimuli were again either TEs, Unrelated-Pairs or pseudowords derived from those word-types, and the subjects again were instructed to expect only one language per session. In contrast to Exp. 1, stimuli in this study included words from the nontarget language in "Mixed" conditions, and pseudowords derived from words in the nontarget language in "Pure" conditions. Language expectations could therefore have been violated by presentation of stimuli orthographically illegal in the target language in both Mixed and Pure conditions, compared between-subjects. Half of all stimuli were repeated within, but not across, sessions, still with a long delay between repetitions and a long SOA between subsequent stimuli. Both condition types were run in each target language, changed across sessions.

Frequency effects were found, but as all words had similar frequencies in both languages it cannot be determined if frequency in the nontarget language had any effect. Such an effect would not be predicted for these subjects, in keeping with Gerard and Scarborough (1989). Bilinguals were slower to reject pseudowords in the target language than were monolinguals, which would indicate that bilinguals' exhaustive search was through a larger set of stored representations. Furthermore, responses to Mixed lists were slowed compared to Pure lists, showing an alternation deficit from the inclusion of words, not just orthography, from the nontarget language. However, this was true for the monolingual subjects as well as for the bilinguals. Therefore, unless the monolingual subjects had more knowledge of Spanish than thought, this alternation deficit cannot be attributed to violations of expectations from presentation of nontarget-language words. Furthermore, bilinguals rejected words and pseudowords from the nontarget language more quickly than pseudowords from the target language. This indicates that no search was made when orthographical information specified that a stimulus could not be a word in the target language. Orthography is processed prior to lexical access (Taft & Forster, 1975), and thus nontarget orthography enabled a quick rejection. Comparisons of Yes and No responses are hampered in this design by confounding with handedness. However, No responses were always made with the nondominant hand, and thus should be slower than Yes answers. Therefore, the finding that words from the nontarget language were rejected (No response) more quickly than target-language words were recognized (Yes response) is a good indication that these nontarget words were rejected before the network was searched for their representation.

Repetition also speeded responses to words in the target language more than to words in the nontarget language or to pseudowords of either type, also showing that no search phase followed presentation of orthographically-inappropriate stimuli. There was no repetition priming even *within* the inappropriate language, compared to the baseline familiarity effect seen for repeated pseudowords. Therefore, it seems that subjects rejected nontarget-language words as soon as the illegality in orthography was perceived, despite the fact that reading is overlearned. Lexical access was not performed in the unexpected language, and so later recognition of that same form was not speeded any more than recognition of familiar pseudowords. However, lexical access in the target language had been completed, and so recognition of repetitions was facilitated by residual activation of the meaning in addition to familiarity with the form.

Scarborough et al. (1984) investigated the possibility that facilitation of No responses to nontarget-language stimuli was based on orthographic information. That interpretation was then rejected when different bilinguals had difficulty in determining the language from which pseudowords had been derived. However, it is possible that the particular bilinguals making that later discrimination were less constrained than the subjects in the earlier lexical decision task, and that differences between languages therefore were not as contextually relevent to that later sample. It is also possible that some information can be used in lexical decision even though it is not available for conscious use. Furthermore, there is converging evidence that orthographic information is used in lexical decision by constrained bilinguals: Grainger and Beauvillian (1987, Exp. 2) demonstrated that the presence of language-specific orthography, as -GHT ending an English word or -IOUX a French word, speeds RTs in lexical decision for constrained bilinguals. The stimuli presented by Scarborough et al. were not carefully controlled for absence of orthographical language markers as were the stimuli chosen by Grainger and Beauvillian (1987, Exp. 1), so the possibility definitely exists that there was such language-specific orthography available to the subjects.

Grainger and Beauvillian, however, also found that such language-specific orthographical information eliminated the alternation deficit for habitually-constrained bilinguals (1987, Exp. 2), while Scarborough et al. (1984) did find such a deficit. However, that deficit was also present for monolingual subjects in Scarborough et al.'s study, and only if the language-inappropriate stimuli were real words rather than pseudowords. Moreover, subjects in Scarborough et al.'s investigation were instructed to expect only the target language; the deficit appeared for monolinguals as well when words in the nontarget language were presented unexpectedly. These unexpected words would also require a No response, made with the nondominant hand for all subjects. Grainger and Beauvillian, in contrast, gave subjects no instructions as to language, and words in both languages were presented and required Yes responses.

Therefore, there is a strong likelihood that the alternation deficit for constrained bilinguals is an effect of violating same-language expectations, and that providing information which specifies the "other" language early in the process of lexical access reduces the surprise effect. This would then eliminate the alternation deficit unless other sources of interference arise, such as stimuli which contradict specific experimenter instructions. However, the discrepancy in response demands between these two investigations, and especially the finding that monolingual subjects showed the same deficit even though they should not have known the unexpected words, indicates a need for further research into orthographic legality, expectations, and the alternation deficit.

Grainger and Beauvillian's (1987, Exps. 1, 2) investigation of the alternation deficit in lexical decision used a long SOA (about 1000 msecs) with no instructions as to language. This design therefore maximized the formation of language expectations from one word to the next. Furthermore, the subjects specifically reported using English at work and French at home in Exp. 1, though faster RTs in French confirm a likelihood of French-Reading dominance. In Exp. 2, however, subjects were recruited from bilingual high schools in France, and thus in at least school contexts had less constraint on either language. Furthermore, RTs indicated better speed in English for those high-schoolers, implying English-Reading dominance and increasing the likelihood of constraint on the choice of French for that sample. Both samples are thus considered to be constrained, although more conformity across samples or within-subject comparisons would be needed in replications of this research.

In the absence of language-specifying orthography in the targets, RTs were slowed after a word in the other language, compared to after a pseudoword or a word in the same language. Violated language expectations can account for this pattern, as two words can be either in the same language or not, but pseudowords are not in either language. Thus, the pseudowords did not create same-language expectations, but words did. However, these were not violated by a word in the same, expected language. This interpretation would be confirmed by separate analyses of RTs by language, as constraint was likely to be stronger for English in this sample. French targets would then show more of an alternation deficit than would English targets, as a prior word in English would create greater same-language expectations than one in French.

In Exp. 2, orthographical information in the targets eliminated the alternation deficit. The reduction in constraint on French in this sample compared to that in Exp. 1 should have most strongly affected expectations to English targets following words in French, again requiring separate analyses by language. This lack of alternation deficit, furthermore, is not attributable to the decrease in constraint in school contexts for these later subjects: RTs to language-specified words were globally faster than to words without such information, a within-subjects comparison. Also, these latter subjects did show an alternation deficit when the targets were not orthographically language-specific. Therefore, having language specified orthographically, i.e. early in processing (Taft & Forster, 1975) speeds word recognition. Furthermore, information available prior to lexical access that a stimulus is in an unexpected language eliminates the inhibition from violating that expectation. What is so interesting about that finding is that inhibition has been shown to arise post-lexically (Lorch, Balota & Stamm, 1986), in the stage where the decision is made to call the stimulus a word. Thus, specifying an unexpected language prelexically seems to circumvent post-lexical effects of violated expectations. Therefore, prelexical information that the "other" language is being used serves the same purpose as instructions to expect the change in language. However, the lack of evident inhibition may possibly be an artifact of the speedier recognition of the language-specified words. In either case, these results demonstrate that the alternation deficit could easily be an effect of violated expectations in constrained bilingualism in the absence of information specifying the change in language.

In sum, Gerard and colleagues' results demonstrate that bilinguals habituated to functioning under strong contextual constraints can effectively respond as monolinguals in tasks with specific instructions to expect one language and enough time to maximize processing of contextual information. These individuals can use orthographical information to do so, to the point of avoiding lexical access completely in unexpected languages. Grainger and Beauvillian also showed that orthographical information speeds RTs and can be used by constrained bilinguals to circumvent the surprise effect of an unexpected language change. However, confirmation of the role of expectations in these effects is still needed. Decreasing SOA to prohibit effortful processing would not be convenient in these paradigms as lexical decisions were required for all stimuli, and stimuli would still be repeated following a long delay. Replication with bilinguals who report no such constraints would therefore be a better test of this functional interpretation.

Habitually unconstrained bilinguals are predicted to show a greater "repetition" priming for Same-IHs than for Unrelated-IHs when only one target language is used per session, as these bilinguals should be incapable of inhibiting lexical access based on orthographical illegality. Their lack of language expectations would then lead either to a tendency to respond positively to words in the non-target language, or to Stroop-type interference and greatly increased RTs in rejecting these words. Scarborough et al.'s (1984) paradigm would also need to allow unconfounded comparisons of Yes and No responses by counterbalancing the hand used to make the responses across subjects. Furthermore, unconstrained bilinguals should show no alternation deficit even in the absence of language-specific orthography, as they would have no strong language expectations to violate. In fact, these bilinguals would probably not use orthographical information, as specifying language confers no functional advantage to unconstrained communication. Language-specific orthography might therefore provide no advantage in word recognition for unconstrained bilinguals, as Grainger and Beauvillian found (1987, Exp. 2) in constrained bilingualism.

So far, these investigations have supported functionalist interpretations of results obtained from bilinguals habituated to functioning under great constraints on both languages. This next section will examine investigations with subjects still likely to have great constraint on choice of at least one language by virtue of selection from monolingual schools in monolingual communities in monolingual nations, but who do not report that different languages were used in different contexts. Beauvillian and Grainger (1987, Exp. 1) in a 2-word lexical decision task at either a 150- or a 750-msec SOA, varied between subjects, gave specific instructions to expect primes to be in French and targets either to be in English or not to be words at all. Thus even though the subjects were habitually constrained in language choice, the instructions would allow subjects to expect the change in language. The pseudowords were derived from nonhomographic English words, so no orthographically illegal stimuli were presented.

Primes included, unbeknownst to the subjects at least initially, Unrelated-IHs where the reading in each language was equally frequent. These were embedded in language-specific nonhomographic blocks, and repeated across blocks such that they were presented once embedded in each language context. Targets could be semantically related or unrelated to the language-inappropriate meaning, as defined by language context. No targets were related to the language-appropriate reading of the Unrelated-IHs, so any facilitation would indicate trans-priming. Semantic priming was then calculated relative to "repetition" priming. However, what was repeated was the lexical form, as it later specified a different referent

Findings indicated no overall differences in RT according to SOA. Therefore, these constrained bilinguals could use the instructions to expect the change in language, or an alternation deficit would have appeared at the longer SOA. There was also no overall priming, however. Specific analyses by SOA revealed insignificant facilitation at the short SOA, and insignificant inhibition at the long SOA. Further analyses indicated that trans-priming did occur, but only for first presentations at the shorter SOA. There was no trans-priming even of first presentations at the longer SOA, which should not be an artifact of language expectations in this design. Thus, these findings indicate that initially, there was an automatic access of all meanings of these ambiguous stimuli, and this activation spread to meanings related both appropriately or inappropriately to the context. However, with extra time to process context information, access to inappropriately-related words was no longer facilitated. Therefore, once context information has time to be processed, there is effortful inhibition of the inappropriate meanings which had, initially, been automatically accessed. As context here is determined by language, this yields facilitation only of meanings related to the context-appropriate meaning of these Unrelated-IHs. This parallels monolingual findings on ambiguity (e.g., Swinney, 1979).

In addition, Grainger and Beauvillian's (1987) results that trans-priming only occurred at the shorter SOA seem in direct opposition to their 1988 findings, where trans-priming only occurred at the longer SOA. However, the critical stimuli in 1987 were Unrelated-IHs, and repetition of form but not meaning was studied as the second presentation was in a context specifying the "other" referent. The 1987 study demonstrated that initial lexical access from Unrelated-IHs is not dependent on the language specified by context until context information has time to be processed. Thus, there was no facilitation at the longer SOA or for second presentations, now embedded in "other-language" contexts. In the 1988 investigation, in contrast, semantic trans-priming was found to require a greater delay between prime and target. However, nonfluent bilinguals participated in 1988, leading to difficulty in effortful activation of putative targets in the less-fluent language.

In addition, the RT data show that the 1988 subjects were not faster with related pairs at the longer SOA compared to RTs to any stimuli at the shorter SOA. Rather, the Unrelated-Pairs at the longer SOA were recognized more slowly than were words in any other condition. In fact, RTs to related pairs were identical to the millisecond in the two SOA conditions. "Facilitation" was seen at the long SOA because with the shorter delay, not enough processing about the prime was possible for the subjects to form semantic expectations. Thus for unrelated targets, RTs were only slowed at the longer SOA. Therefore, the 1988 finding that trans-priming only seemed to occur at the longer SOA may stem from violated semantic expectations once these had time to arise.

In addition, the magnitude of the delay before context takes effect indicates a need to replicate monolingual work on disambiguation with bilinguals. Context may require a longer processing time for disambiguation for bilinguals, more than 150 msecs, than for monolinguals where 50 msecs is sufficient. With Unrelated-IHs, furthermore, it is the language of the word which is ambiguous, rather than the meaning of the word within a language. It is therefore also possible that disambiguation of language takes more time than clarification of the referent. This could be examined through comparing ambiguous words without language ambiguity (e.g., REFUSE), with Unrelated-IHs. However, Swinney's paradigm involved embedding the ambiguous prime in an auditorily-presented disambiguating sentence as the subject made lexical decisions to visually-presented targets. Spoken Unrelated-IHs are no longer ambiguous, in contrast to their written form; therefore, that particular design would require alteration to investigate bilingual disambiguation by language. Requiring lexical decision to auditorily-presented targets as subjects read disambiguating sentences containing the Unrelated-IH primes would be possible, but would then need replication in monolinguals.

In addition to semantic facilitation, Beauvillian and Grainger (1987, Exp. 1) also found "repetition" trans-priming, which with these stimuli is indicative of facilitation from familiarity with the visual form, replicating Scarborough et al. (1984) as well as Gerard and Scarborough (1989). Subjects were faster at recognizing repetitions, even though the repeated Unrelated-IHs were now embedded in a context specifying a distinct meaning. This familiarity effect also replicates previous findings by the same authors (Beauvillian & Grainger, 1986), in which similar subjects to the 1987 sample were induced to "read" Same-IHs in one particular language in the same paradigm. Blocking by language would eliminate violations of the language expectations these subjects would be likely to have. In fact, the magnitude of facilitation when those Same-IHs were repeated after a long delay was the same whether the later lists provided a context specifying the same or the other language.

The authors interpreted that result as indicating that subjects failed to access only the language-appropriate reading of the Same-IHs, which is similar to their 1987 interpretation. However, the reading of Same-IHs is unambiguous, so there is no language-inappropriate meaning as there is with Unrelated-IHs. That finding does indicate an equivalence in the concepts accessed by Same-IHs through the different languages for those constrained bilinguals. Therefore, the immediate facilitation of words inappropriately-related to Unrelated-IHs (1987, Exp. 1) but not the repetition priming for Same-IHs (1986) shows that both meanings were accessed despite the clarifying context. As subjects in both studies were constrained in language choice, they should have been able to use context to determine language. Therefore, these findings demonstrate that for constrained bilinguals, lexical access from language-ambiguous forms is not initially language-dependent. However, given time to process contextual information, bilinguals habituated to contextual constraints show effortful inhibition of contextually-inappropriate meanings.

In Exp. 2 (1987), Beauvillian and Grainger used 2-word lexical decision at a 150-msec SOA to examine semantic cis- and trans-priming. As in Exp. 1, primes included Unrelated-IHs, but now the different meanings had measurably different frequencies. The subjects in Exp. 2 were less habitually-constrained in school contexts than were those in Exp. 1, but the subjects in Exp. 2 were specifically instructed as to the language in which to expect both primes and targets. Therefore, the variation in constraint between samples was not likely to have affected these findings. The short SOA, in any case, should not allow expectations about the target to form. The Unrelated-IHs were embedded in a single-language context in the same manner as previously-described experiments by these authors; however, context information also requires a longer SOA to be fully processed, although this design was intended to disambiguate the Unrelated-IHs. In fact, Beauvillian and Grainger found that only associations to the higher-frequency reading were facilitated, regardless of the language in which subjects had been induced to read the primes.

This frequency effect argues that the presentation of a particular lexical form will initially, before context effects arise, activate all meanings for that form in language-independent fashion. This finding parallels these authors' findings from Exp. 1 as well as their 1986 results. However, it counters Gerard and Scarborough's (1989) findings of language-appropriate frequency effects, but those latter results were obtained at a long SOA. Thus, these studies indicate that before context information is processed, frequency effects and lexical access from language-ambiguous stimuli are both language-independent. In contrast, once time is given for effortful processing about the language context surrounding the prime, frequency effects and access to the meaning of (now disambiguated) ambiguous stimuli are both language-appropriate.

These studies with constrained bilinguals can all be interpreted as indicating effects of violated expectations, predicted by a functionalist perspective. Kirsner et al. (1984, Exp. 1) also support this functional view of bilingualism. Professional translators, who could be expected to encounter both languages in their job but not otherwise, participated in a lexical decision task with a long SOA without instructions to expect a language change. This design therefore maximized the formation of language expectations. The authors found a repetition effect within languages, but no facilitation for later-presented TEs. Therefore, previous activation of a word's meaning did not facilitate recognition of that word's TE presented in an unexpected language, similar to Gerard and Scarborough (1989) and Scarborough et al. (1984), even though Kirsner et al.'s subjects were trained to provide translations. This indicates that habitual conversational constraints had more of an impact on language expectations than did the subjects' professional training. Furthermore, the texts these individuals translate would be all in one language, and that reading experience could enhance same-language expectations for visual input. They would not encounter both languages in most conversational contexts as they were not interpreters, and did not have a supporting mutual bilingual community. For these particular subjects, this finding is less likely to indicate that the meanings were not equivalent when accessed through different languages, as Scarborough et al.'s (1984) results might have shown: Kirsner et al.'s subjects were trained by their profession to treat TEs as equivalent. Thus, the simpler interpretation is that these constrained bilinguals formed same-language expectations, and that the inhibition from violations of these expectations countered any facilitory effects of residual activation of repeated referents.

These studies of constrained bilingualism, taken together, support a functional model of lexical access and lexicosemantic organization in bilingualism. Grainger and Beauvilian have demonstrated that bilinguals who habitually function under constraints in language choice, even if those constraints are lifted in limited contexts, show an immediate language-independent lexical access to all meanings by presentations of language-ambiguous lexical forms. However, once time is given for context information to specify the language surrounding that lexical form, language-inappropriate meanings are effortfully inhibited. This inhibition of representations according to language context defines a language-dependent organization of the network: some representations are language-appropriate, others are not. In the second 1988 investigation by those authors, furthermore, constrained but nonfluent bilinguals showed an initial automatic spread of activation which was language-specific despite specific instructions to expect a change in language. This is evidence for a language-dependent lexicosemantic organization in constrained bilingualism, at least for nonfluent bilinguals. To confirm this functionalist interpretation, Grainger and Beauvillian's 1988 research needs replication with fluent bilinguals, and all these studies require replication with unconstrained, preferably habitually-alternating, bilinguals.

Another prediction of a functional model is that the degree of separation of alternate forms for the same referent be proportional to the difference in those forms: It is more important to select the correct TE than the corrrect Same-IH in constrained conversations. One investigation of this effect of lexical similarity was provided by Cristoffanini, Kirsner and Milech (1986, Exp. 1). A naming task was followed by a long-SOA lexical decision task to examine "repetition" priming (relative to exact repetitions) following a long delay of TEs, Eucognates varying in degree of lexical similarity, and Same-IHs. However, the example of distantly-related Eucognates, CALUMNIA/CALAMITY, raises doubts about their stimuli, as CALUMNIA is the Eucognate of CALUMNY, which is semantically unrelated to calamity (Spanish CALAMIDAD, a regular -DAD/-ITY translation; Smith, 1982). Subjects were recruited from an area without a supporting mutually-bilingual culture, and were likely to be sequential bilinguals as "their use of the languages extended to at least 5 years" while the subjects were over 30, on average. Thus, they may have acquired English because of immigration to Australia, and therefore in a separate context from Spanish, increasing contextual constraints on each language.

The initial naming phase was blocked by language, eliminating violations of same-language expectations, and the only error was, rarely, reading the Same-IHs in the "other" language. That indicates that language blocking was almost entirely effective, and "mis"pronunciation of Same-IHs would not activate a different referent anyway. In the later lexical decision phase, the subjects were only presented with English words and pseudowords orthographically legal in English, and were instructed that these stimuli were either English words or not words at all. Thus, there was no unexpected language change. Cristoffanini et al. found facilitation for repeated referents, regardless of the language in which that referent had been originally presented, as long as there was some overlap in visual form: TEs alone showed no trans-priming. This follows the functional predictions of greater separation for TEs, as only a TE is truly unfeasible to communication when the wrong one is selected. Functionalism is further supported by the finding that RTs were fastest to

Same-IHs, intermediate to the Eucognates, and slowest with the TEs. Also in keeping with functionalist predictions, the magnitude of trans-priming was also proportional to the regularity of change between the cognate forms. However, regularity is not a direct measure of similarity: the irregular forms could have 1, 2 or 3 letters different. Thus, some of the authors' comparisons across classes may not strictly relate to effects of similarity in form.

Comparing the -TION/-CION and the -DAD/-ITY regular Eucognates alone, however, does directly illustrate effects of lexical similarity while holding regularity constant. In this comparison, the greater the lexical similarity, the greater the degree of relative trans-priming, exactly as functionalism would predict. This interaction cannot be attributed in this design to a greater violation of expectations by more dissimilar alternate forms. The -TION/-CION Eucognates showed more relative trans-priming than the Same-IHs, but these closest-Eucognates were also longer on average than the other stimuli, leading to slower reading times. RTs to New stimuli in that class were the longest reported, so the advantage of Eucognates over Same-IHs in this instance does not weaken the functional interpretation. There is a definite interaction between the importance of contextual separation of alternate forms in communication, and the degree of relative trans-priming between these forms, in a paradigm where language expectations would not affect RTs.

Frequency information for the Spanish words was not provided in the Methods section, although frequencies were low for the English stimuli. However, later analyses compared English word-pairs with similar frequencies to their cognate translations which had markedly different frequencies in Spanish. The fact that such comparisons were possible, unfortunately, indicates that word frequencies could have been different in English and Spanish. As this was a lexical decision task, frequency effects are expected, and these may have interacted with the other RT data. However, this later frequency analysis concentrated on cognates being presented for the first time, as frequency effects are minimized in primed stimuli (Scarborough, Cortese & Scarborough, 1977). Interestingly, lexical decision to the English Eucognates was predicted by the frequency of the Spanish translations, not of the English words actually being presented. Furthermore, choice of Spanish was likely to be more constrained for these subject. Thus, if there is a lexical relation between words in a bilingual's two languages, frequency differences in one language, even a more-constrained one, can affect RTs to words in the other language. Whether this is also the case for TEs remains to be seen. This could present serious interpretation problems for studies where frequency is only assessed or controlled in one language, which is unfortunately not uncommon as norms are so much more available in English (compare the recency of Kucera & Francis' 1982 norms with the commonly-used Julliand & Chang-Rodriguez, 1964).

However, this language-independent frequency effect at a long SOA, when language context should have been fully processed, seems to counter findings with nonbalanced Unrelated-IHs: Beauvillian and Grainger (1987) found language-appropriate frequency effects at a long SOA, whereas Gerard and Scarborough (1989) found language-independent frequency effects at a short SOA. Thus, lexical access from language-ambiguous forms where the different meanings have different frequencies is language-independent at short SOAs, and language-dependent at long SOAs. This is a context effect: whether all meanings are activated or only the language-appropriate one depends on processing time. In contrast, Cristoffanini et al.'s (1986) stimuli were not Unrelated-IHs, but Eucognates with different frequencies in the two languages. In this case there was one meaning which could be accessed through a choice of forms, rather than a choice of meanings from one form. Thus Cristoffanini et al.'s (1986) results indicate that the frequency of access to the words' meanings, not the frequency of presentation of their visual forms, determines how easily a stimulus is called a word. This indicates a possible need to reformulate the basis of frequency effects among monolinguals: it may not be how often a visual form is seen, but how often a particular referent is accessed, which underlies the frequency effect.

These investigations clearly support a functionalist interpretation of the role of language in bilingual networks. This next section will focus on studies with participants likely to have little constraint in language choice. These subjects were recruited from large bilingual communities within monolingual nations. Asymmetries are thus still possible as choice of the national language is less likely to be constrained. Caramazza and Brones (1979) examined lexical decision times in the absence of repetition or semantic priming at a long SOA using Same-IHs and other words which were not homographic. This design would maximize expectation and context effects. Whether the non-IHs had cognate translations was not specified, and RTs showed that these bilinguals were slower at reading their second language. Pseudowords were constructed to be English-seeming or Spanish-seeming, as appropriate to the condition. However, Spanish pseudowords can almost always be pronounced in English, whereas the reverse is not necessarily true.

The three conditions were Spanish words and pseudowords only, English words and pseudowords only, or Spanish and English words and pseudowords ("Mixed"). In the monolingual conditions, Same-IHs could be "read" in the nontarget language, but such other-language readings would not affect the meaning of the word. Mixed conditions had no target language. Comparisons of RTs between each monolingual condition and the Mixed conditions revealed no alternation deficit for either language, despite random stimulus order in Mixed conditions and a long SOA. Thus for these unconstrained bilinguals, language changes without warning did not increase RTs, even though time to process context information and form language expectations was allowed. This confirms that these unconstrained bilinguals did not form same-language expectations.

Caramazza and Brones (1979) also found a difference between whether the Same-IHs were presented embedded in a monolingual context specifying the subjects' more- or less-quickly read language, defined by the RT data. In the Reading-dominant condition, Same-IHs were recognized as quickly as other words, and both were recognized more quickly than pseudowords were rejected. However, in the slower-read language condition, Same-IHs were recognized more quickly than other words, which were still recognized more quickly then pseudowords were rejected. The slower No responses cannot be attributed to slower responses with nondominant hands, as response hands were counterbalanced. Therefore, the ability to read a stimulus in the language more-quickly read (L_1) confers an advantage over other words in L_2, while readability in the less-well read language does not confer the same advantage for L_1. In the monolingual conditions, English nonhomographs were recognized more slowly than Spanish nonhomographs, which did not differ from Same-IHs embedded in either language context. Thus, subjects were slow at recognizing stimuli which could not be read in their Reading-dominant language. This again reconfirms the need to assess, rather than ask for self-report, the degree of fluency and the speed of reading in each language. Even when functioning in a context specifying the less-well read language, these unconstrained bilinguals could use readability in their more-quickly read language to aid their response times to Same-IHs. These findings need replication with reading-balanced bilinguals to confirm this interpretation. Beauvillian and Grainger's (1986) results might also be reanalyzed to see if constrained bilinguals, who are habituated to limiting themselves to the language appropriate to the context, also show facilitation from readability in an inappropriate language.

In a later investigation with similarly-unconstrained bilinguals, Caramazza and Brones (1980) used category-verification at a 2000-msec (Exp. 1) and a 0-msec (Exp. 2) SOA. The paradigm in Exp. 1, where the long SOA would have permitted expectations to form, would have maximized such expectations by randomizing order of presentation. However, inhibition from violated expectations has been found not to occur in category-verification (Lorch, Balota & Stamm, 1986), so the finding that at both SOAs trans-priming was as robust as cis-priming does not confirm that these subjects formed no language expectations. It does indicate that the organization of meanings within these unconstrained bilinguals' lexicosemantic network is language-independent, at least for category-exemplar associations. The degree of facilitation did not differ depending on whether the related meanings were accessed through the same language or not.

The strength of cross-language associations would not be expected to differ according to the lexical similarity of prime and target assuming shared referents in these unconstrained subjects. However, whether that effect actually was absent cannot be addressed by Caramazza and Brones' (1980) findings as the authors do not specify whether their stimuli were controlled for relatedness of form. The examples given indicate that they used TEs, but one of the category names has cognate forms in Spanish (FRUTA) and English (FRUIT), and the names of many fruits and vegetables, as well as some items of furniture, are cognate in Spanish and English. It is predicted that TEs would not show different effects from Eucognates, if there were any among the targets, as these subjects were habitually unconstrained in language choice.

Category-exemplar associations were also investigated by Schwanenflugel and Rey (1986) in a 2-word lexical decision task, where inhibitory effects would be seen if expectations were formed and violated. The authors also included detailed usage information for their subjects, indicating that these were nearly completely unconstrained bilinguals: they used English and Spanish equally often, were recruited from an area with a large mutually-bilingual population, and habitually alternated languages within utterances. Stimuli combined TEs and Eucognates but avoided IHs, and used a 100- and a 300-msec SOA, unfortunately compared between subjects. Random order of stimuli would maximize expectation effects, and the "neutral" prime in this study was either the word "READY" or the Spanish equivalent "LISTO." These primes therefore ensured that language expectations, if there were any, were the same for primed and unprimed stimuli.

Fulfilling functionalist predictions, trans-priming was found to be as robust as cis-priming at both SOAs, similar to Caramazza and Brones (1980). In Schwanenflugel and Rey's paradigm, however, inhibition would have been seen had there been violated expectations. Further support for the functionalist perspective is seen in the lack of any alternation deficit, even at the longer SOA. These findings, therefore, show that these unconstrained bilinguals did not form same- language expectations even if given the time, and showed no evidence of a language-dependent organization of their lexicosemantic network. Again, however, category-exemplar associations are the least likely to differ across languages, as membership in a category is not defined by language. The research reviewed in this last section, therefore, indicates most cleanly that unconstrained bilinguals show no inhibitory effects of unexpected language change, even at longer SOAs, even in the absence of instructions to expect a change in language. This is exactly what functionalism would predict, especially as research with constrained bilinguals has demonstrated such effects. The scarcity of research into habitually-unconstrained bilingualism, furthermore, parallels the preponderance of constraint among bilinguals (Baetens Beardsmore, 1986; Grosjean, 1982; Heller, 1988).

Conclusions

In conclusion, there is a substantial body of evidence that investigations into the organization of bilingual lexicosemantic networks need to consider the particular bilinguals being examined. First, nonfluent bilinguals show automatic spreading activation only from primes in their dominant language (Frenck & Pynte, 1987; Kirsner et al., 1984). Nonfluent bilingualism also results in effortful activation only of targets in the dominant language (Beauvillian & Grainger, 1988). Fluent bilinguals with different reading abilities show a less-robust spread of activation within either language, which is especially marked in their less quickly-read language (Favreau & Segalowitz, 1983). Therefore, self-reported measures need to be supplemented with actual assessment both of fluency and of reading ability in both languages.

Furthermore, if language choice is critical to communication, language suffices to determine a coherent context (Grainger & Beauvillian, 1987; Gerard & Scarborough, 1989). These context effects are so strong in constrained bilingualism that lexical access to language-inappropriate words can be entirely avoided, despite the overlearning of reading (Scarborough et al., 1984). It is still unknown whether unconstrained bilinguals fail to delimit context according to language, or whether unconstrained bilinguals are capable of failing to access the meaning of contextually-inappropriate words.

The contextual separation of languages for constrained bilinguals also interacts with orthographic disparity between forms for the same referent, in keeping with conversational constraints (Cristoffanini et al., 1986): TEs are kept more separate than are Eucognates, which are in turn more separate than Same-IHs. Whether such separation is reduced in unconstrained bilingualism where functional separation is eliminated, even for TEs, still needs to be shown. Constrained bilinguals are also capable of using orthographic information which specifies language to speed recognition of words, to circumvent inhibition from an unexpected language change, and to avoid accessing language-inappropriate stimuli (Grainger & Beauvillian, 1987; Scarborough et al., 1984). In unconstrained bilingualism, the unimportance of language choice should eliminate these effects, but empirical verification of that prediction is still needed.

There is also evidence that lexical access of language-ambiguous forms is initially language-independent, even for constrained bilinguals. With time to process context information, inappropriate meanings are inhibited in constrained bilingualism (Beauvillian & Grainger, 1987; Gerard & Scarborough, 1989). This parallels monolingual disambiguation by meaning, which however requires less extra processing time than does disambiguation by language for bilinguals. Whether this is also the case for unconstrained bilingualism still requires experimental confirmation; unconstrained bilinguals may not disambiguate according to language, as for those bilinguals language habitually does not delineate a specific context. Frequency effects (Beauvillian & Grainger, 1987; Gerard & Scarborough, 1989; Kirsner et al., 1984) also indicate that constrained bilinguals use language to determine context, and show frequency-related lexical access of ambiguous forms only if given the time to process context information. Nonambiguous stimuli, furthermore, indicate that greater frequency of lexical access, rather than of form presentation, speeds lexical decision times. This finding in particular indicates a need to reconsider interpretations of frequency effects in monolinguals.

Data certainly show that constrained bilinguals form expectations as to the language of upcoming targets; these expectation are highly similar to semantic categorical expectations (Beauvillian & Grainger, 1987; Favreau & Segalowitz, 1983). For constrained bilinguals, language membership can therefore be considered as forming a supraordinate category, allowing global inhibition of targets belonging to the "other" category when expectations are given time to form. Specific instructions to expect the other language thus have similar effects as instructions to expect an unrelated semantic category (Beauvillian & Grainger, 1987). This categorization according to language may be the basis for the language-dependency of lexicosemantic organization in constrained bilingualism. Unconstrained bilinguals show no differences in category-exemplar associations within- and across-languages (Caramazza & Brones, 1980), nor do they form same-language expectations even if given the time (Schwanenflugel & Rey, 1986). Confirmation that unconstrained bilinguals fail to show other indications of language-dependent organization still requires research. In sum, these differences between constrained and unconstrained bilinguals, taken together, indicate that great care must be taken in interpreting RT evidence in priming paradigms. Not only does language usage impact on lexicosemantic organization, but inhibition from violated language expectations must be separated from actual distance in the networks.

References

Abbot, V., & Black, J. B. (1986). Goal-related inferences in comprehension. In Galambos, J. A., Abelson, R. P. and Black, J. B. (Eds.) *Knowledge structures* (pp. 123-142). Hillsdale, NJ: Lawrence Erlbaum Associates.

Anderson, J. R. (1983). *The architecture of cognition.* Cambridge, MA: Harvard University Press.

Ashcraft, M. H. (1976). Priming and property dominance effects in semantic memory. *Memory & Cognition*, 4, 490-500.

Baetens Beardsmore, H. (1986). *Bilingualism: Basic principles* (2nd. Ed.). London: Multilingual Matters, Ltd.

Balota, D. A., & Chumbley, J. I. (1983). Are lexical decisions a good measure of lexical access? The role of word frequency in the neglected decision stage. *Journal of Experimental Psychology: Human Perception and Performance*, 10(3), 340-357.

Beauvillain, C., & Grainger, J. (1986). Procédures d'accès au lexique chez le bilingue. In Caverni, J. P., Bonnet, C., and Codol, J. P. (Eds). "Hommage à Georges Noizet: Jugement et langage". *Bulletin de Psychologie*, Special Edition.

Beauvillain, C., & Grainger, J. (1987). Accessing interlexical homographs: Some limitations of a language-selective access. *Journal of Memory and Language*, 26, 658-672.

Becker, C. A. (1980). Semantic context effects in visual word recognition: An analysis of semantic strategies. *Memory & Cognition*, 8, 493-512.

Caramazza, A., & Brones, E. (1979). Lexical access in bilinguals. *Bulletin of the Psychonomic Society*, 13, 212-214.

Caramazza, A., & Brones, E. (1980). Semantic classification by bilinguals. *Canadian Journal of Psychology*, 34, 77-81.

Collins, A. M., & Quillian, M. R. (1970). Facilitating retrieval from semantic memory: The effect of repeating part of an inference. *Acta Psychologica*, 33, 304-314.

Cristoffanini, P., Kirsner, K., & Milech, D. (1986). Bilingual lexical representation: The status of English-Spanish cognates. *Quarterly Journal of Experimental Psychology*, 31A, 367-393.

deGroot, A. M. B. (1983). The range of automatic spreading activation in word priming. *Journal of Verbal Learning and Verbal Behavior*, 22, 417-436.

Downie, R., Milech, D., & Kirsner, K. (1985). Unit definition in the mental lexicon. *Australian Journal of Psychology*, 37, 141-155.

Favreau, M., & Segalowitz, N. S. (1983). Automatic and controlled processes in the first- and second-language reading of fluent bilinguals. *Memory & Cognition*, 11, 565-574.

Frenck, C., & Pynte, J. (1984). Semantic representation and surface forms: A look at across-language priming in bilinguals. *Journal of Psycholinguistic Research*, 16, 383-396.

Gerard, L., & Scarborough, D. L. (1989). Language-specific lexical access of homographs by bilinguals. *Journal of Experimental Psychology: Learning, Memory and Cognition*, 15, 305-315.

Grainger, J., & Beauvillain, C. (1987). Language blocking and lexical access in bilinguals. *Quarterly Journal of Experimental Psychology*, 39A, 295-319.

Grainger, J., & Beauvillian, C. (1988). Associative priming in bilinguals: Some limits of interlingual facilitation effects. *Canadian Journal of Psychology*, 42, 261-273.

Heller, M. (Ed.), (1988). *Codeswitching: Anthropological and sociolinguistic perspectives.* Berlin, New York: Mouton de Gruyter.

Hymes, D. (1972). On communicative competence. In Pride, J. B. and Holmes, J. (Eds.), *Sociolinguistics* (pp. 269-293). Harmondsworth: Penguin.

Julliand, A., & Chang-Rodriguez, E. (1964). *Frequency dictionary of Spanish words.* The Hague: Mouton de Gruyter.

Kirsner, K., Smith, M. C., Lockhart, R. S., King, M. L., & Jain, M. (1984). the bilingual lexicon: Language-specific units in an integrated network. *Journal of Verbal Learning and Verbal Behavior*, 23, 519-539.

Kolers, P. A. (1966). Reading and talking bilingually. *American Journal of Psychology*, 79, 357-376.

Kolers, P. A. (1979). Reading and knowing. *Canadian Journal of Psychology*, 33, 106-117.

Kucera, H., & Francis, W. N. (1982). *Frequency analysis of English word usage: Grammar and lexicon.* Boston: Houghton-Mifflin.

LaBerge, D., Van Gelder, P., & Yellot, J. I. (1970). A cuing technique in choice reaction time. *Perception and Psychophysics*, 7, 57-62.

Lipski, J. M. (1985). Linguistic aspects of Spanish-English language switching. *Special Studies #25*, Center for Latin American Studies, Arizona State University.

Lorch, R. F., Balota, D. A., & Stamm, E. C. (1986). Locus of inhibitory effects in the priming of lexical decisions: Pre- or post-lexical access? *Memory & Cognition*, 14, 95-103.

Macnamara, J., & Kushnir, S. L. (1971). Linguistic independence of bilinguals: The input switch. *Journal of Verbal Learning and Verbal Behavior*, 10, 480-487.

McCormick, P. D. (1977). Bilingual linguistic memory: The independence-interdependence issue revisited. In P. A. Hornby (Ed.), *Bilingualism: Psychological, social and educational implications* (pp. 57-66). New York: Academic Press.

Meyer, D. E., & Ruddy, M. G. (April, 1974). Bilingual word recognition: Organization and retrieval of alternate lexical codes. Paper presented at the meeting of the Eastern Psychological Association, Philadelphia.

Meyer, D. E., Schvaneveldt, R. W., & Ruddy, M. G. (1975). Loci of contextual effects on visual word recognition. In Rabbitt, P. M. A. and Dornic, S. (Eds.), *Attention and performance V* (pp. 98-118). London: Academic Press.

Morton, J. (1980). The logogen model and orthographic structure. In Frith, U. (Ed.), *Cognitive processes in spelling.* London: Academic Press.

Neely, J. H. (1977). Semantic priming and retrieval from lexical memory: Roles of inhibitionless spreading activation and limited-capacity attention. *Journal of Experimental Psychology: General*, 106, 226-254.

Paradis, M. (1987). *The assessment of bilingual aphasia.* Hillsdale, NJ: Lawrence Erlbaum Associates.

Posner, M. I., & Snyder, C. R. R. (1975). Facilitation and inhibition in the processing of signals. In Rabbit, P. M. A. and Dornic, S. (Eds.), *Attention and performance V* (pp. 669-682). London: Academic Press.

Potter, M. C., So, K., Von Eckardt, B., & Feldman, L. B. (1984). Lexical and conceptual representation in beginning and proficient bilinguals. *Journal of Verbal Learning and Verbal Behavior*, 23, 23-38.

Scarborough, D. L., Cortese, C., & Scarborough, H. S. (1977). Frequency and repetition effects in lexical memory. *Journal of Experimental Psychology: Human Perception and Performance*, 3, 1-17.

Scarborough, D. L., Gerard, L., & Cortese, C. (1984). Independence of lexical access in bilingual word recognition. *Journal of Verbal Learning and Verbal Behavior*, 23, 84-99.

Schwanenflugel, P. J., & Rey, M. (1986). Interlingual semantic facilitation: Evidence for a common representational system in the bilingual lexicon. *Journal of Memory and Language*, 25, 605-618.

Smith, C. (1982). *Collins Spanish Dictionary*. London, Glasgow: Collins.

Soares, C., & Grosjean, F. (1984). Bilinguals in a monolingual and bilingual speech mode: The effect on lexical access. *Memory & Cognition*, 12, 380-386.

Stemberger, J. P., & MacWhinney, B. (1986). Frequency and the lexical storage of regularly inflected forms. *Memory & Cognition*, 14, 17-26.

Swinney, D. A. (1979). Lexical access during sentence comprehension: (Re)-consideration of context effects. *Journal of Verbal Learning and Verbal Behavior*, 18, 645-659.

Taft, M., & Forster, K. I. (1975). Lexical storage and retrieval of prefixed words. *Journal of Verbal Learning and Verbal Behavior*, 14, 638-647.

Tyson, G. A., Doctor, E. A., & Mentis, M. (1988). A psycholinguistic perspective on bilinguals' discrepant questionnaire responses. *Journal of Cross-Cultural Psychology*, 19, 413-426.

Zaraus, J. M. S. C. (1980). La problematica del bilinguismo en el estado Español: Jordanas del bilinguismo. I. C. E., Universidad del Pais Vasco, Lejona, Vizcaya, España.

Part IV:

**THE ROLE OF SYNTAX IN
BILINGUAL COGNITIVE PROCESSING**

Cognitive Processing in Bilinguals – R.J. Harris (Editor)
© 1992 Elsevier Science Publishers B.V. All rights reserved.

Changes in Sentence Processing as Second Language Proficiency Increases

Janet L. McDonald   L. Kathy Heilenman
Louisiana State University   University of Iowa

Due to differences between the grammars of English and French, native speakers of these languages rely differently on the cues of word order, verb agreement and noun animacy in assigning the actor role. In this chapter we examine how native English speakers gain mastery over appropriate French strategies with increasing second language proficiency. The time course of this mastery includes initial abandonment of English word order strategies followed by later development of appropriate French word order strategies, and even later strengthening of an appropriate verb agreement strategy. We show how this sequence of development is tied to the properties of French input these learners receive.

One of the tasks involved in sentence comprehension is the use of surface form cues to assign underlying function. This is, however, not a straight-forward task. As noted in the tenets of the Competition Model (Bates & MacWhinney, 1982; 1987; 1989), the mapping between form and function is not one-to-one; rather it is many-to-many. For example, a function such as the actor role (i.e., who or what performs the action of the verb) can be marked by such devices as word order, verb agreement, case inflection, noun animacy, and prosodic stress. A form, such as word order, can mark the functions of subject, actor and given information. (Note that as a result of this many-to-many mapping, many functions have substantial overlap—i.e., the grammatical role of subject and the more semantic role of actor are often marked by the same cues, and although the roles are not identical, they do have a high degree of overlap in many languages.)

The Competition Model claims that the degree to which native speakers will rely on various surface cues to assign an underlying function is tied to the form-to-function mapping in a language. Since different languages have different form-to-function mappings, different patterns of cue usage should occur across languages. This indeed turns out to be the case. For example, when asked to determine the actor in sentences containing various combinations of the cues of word order, verb agreement and noun animacy, native English speakers rely most strongly on word order, native Italian speakers on verb agreement, and native German speakers on a combination of agreement and animacy (MacWhinney, Bates & Kliegl, 1984). These differences in cue usage directly reflect the utility or validity of these cues in marking the actor role in these languages.

Due to these cross-linguistic differences in form-to-function mappings, one of the problems facing a second language learner is the acquisition of the mapping appropriate to the new language. Previous research on second language learners within the Competition Model framework has found a range of results from the transfer and usage of first language strategies in the second language, through the usage of a set of strategies intermediate between those appropriate to the two languages, to the successful adoption of strategies appropriate to the new language (Bates & MacWhinney, 1981; Gass, 1987; Harrington, 1987; Heilenman & McDonald, 1991; Kilborn & Cooreman, 1987; Kilborn, 1989; Kilborn & Ito, 1989; McDonald, 1987; McDonald & Heilenman, in press; Sasaki, 1991; Wulfeck, Juarez, Bates, & Kilborn, 1986). Indeed, as second language proficiency increases, speakers may progress through these stages. However, since no standard measure of second language mastery has been administered to subjects across studies, it is generally not possible to correlate strategy use and second language proficiency. The few research projects that have looked cross-sectionally at second language learners of various degrees of fluency have found that with increasing exposure, second language learners' cue usage becomes more target-like, although their performance may still be distinguishable from that of native speakers (McDonald, 1987; Kilborn, 1987; Kilborn & Ito, 1989).

The use of a cross-sectional design makes it possible to see how strongly first language strategies are transferred to the second language, as well as the order in which the various cues important to the second language are mastered. In the following experiment, we examine the learning curve for native speakers of English learning French in college starting at a beginning level. We examine their use of the cues of word order, verb agreement and noun animacy for assigning the actor role. Before turning to the experiment, we give a brief description of these cues as they are used in English and French. Included after each description are the results of previous research indicating how native speakers of each language use these cues to assign the actor role.

English cues. Standard word order in English is SVO. All clauses of the NVN pattern are interpreted as SVO; an OVS interpretation is not possible. For relative clauses or wh-questions of the NNV pattern, the usual interpretation is OSV, although an SOV interpretation occasionally occurs in poetry. The VNN pattern is very rare in English, occurring mainly in imperatives (Clean your room, Bob) and is interpreted as VOS. Thus, the first noun is always the subject in NVN sequences, and the second noun is the subject in NNV and VNN sequences.

In English, verbs must agree with their subjects in person and number. However, for verbs other than copulas and auxiliaries, all forms except the third person singular are identical; even this distinction is lost in other than the present tense. Thus, verb agreement is generally not very informative. Finally, although the subject or actor role contains no animacy restrictions in English, a large portion of actors tend to be animate in English. (For a more detailed discussion of these cues in English, see MacWhinney, Bates and Kliegl (1984)).

These facts about English grammar are reflected in native English speakers' use of these cues in the interpretation of English sentences. As shown in MacWhinney, Bates and Kliegl (1984) and replicated in many other studies, native English speakers overwhelmingly use word order as a cue to sentence interpretation, choosing the first noun as actor in NVN sequences, and the second noun as actor in NNV and VNN sequences. Although both agreement and animacy are used in interpretation, they account for very little of the variance in choice behavior.

French cues. Standard word order in French is SVO, although variations in this order are permitted with the use of case marked pronouns or interrogatives. For example, NVN sequences may also have an OVS interpretation, as in interrogatives (Que voit l'homme? 'What (objective case) sees the man?') or relative clauses (La table que voit l'homme est verte 'The table that (objective case) sees the man is green'). For NNV sequences, both SOV and OSV interpretations are possible. SOV is the required order when non-subject clitic pronouns occur in a sentence (e. g., Il la voit 'He (nominative case) it (objective case) sees'), and OSV is possible in questions (Qu'est-ce que l'homme voit? 'What is it that (objective case) the man sees?') or relatives (La table que l'homme voit est verte 'The table that (objective case) the man sees is green'). VNN sequences are infrequent, but both VSO and VOS interpretations are possible. VSO occurs in inverted questions (Voit-il la table? 'Sees he (nominative case) the table?'), but VOS can occur in commands (Regarde la table, mon petit 'Look at the table, my little one'). In addition, the ability to dislocate full nouns when clitic copies are used can result in all possible word orders for a declarative sentence (Trévise, 1986). When such clitic copies are involved, the subject is the element most often dislocated, both to the left and to the right (Ashby, 1988; Barnes, 1985). In cases of non-standard word orders, it is generally the case inflection of the interrogative, relative pronoun or clitic pronoun that determines role assignment.

In French, verbs must agree with their subjects in person and number. While verb morphology in French is richer than in English, most verbs have identically pronounced forms for first, second and third person singular, and often third person plural as well. (While some of these forms are distinct in written French, these distinctions are lost in the oral form.) Although actors in French may be either animate or inanimate, text counts show that they are disproportionally animate nouns (McDonald & Heilenman, in press). (For a more complete discussion of these cues in French, see Kail (1989) or McDonald & Heilenman (in press)).

Previous research with native French speakers has shown that adult speakers use verb agreement more strongly than word order (Kail, 1989; Kail & Charvillat, 1988; McDonald & Heilenman, in press), and also use noun animacy more strongly than word order (Kail, 1989; Kail & Charvillat, 1986; McDonald & Heilenman, in press).[1] Depending on the type of stimuli used, word order may or may not have a significant influence on performance. For stimuli without case marked clitics, native French speakers tend to show a first noun preference for NVN word orders (although this is considerably weaker than that shown in English), a slight first noun preference for NNV sequences, and neutral performance on VNN sequences (Kail, 1989; Kail & Charvillat, 1986).

Thus, previous research documents differences in cue usage by native speakers of English and French. For native English speakers, word order is the most important cue to sentence interpretation. Native English speakers exhibit a first noun preference for NVN sequences, and a second noun preference for NNV and VNN sequences. For native French speakers, verb agreement and noun animacy are more important cues than word order. When in the absence of other cues French speakers do use word order, their use of an SVO interpretation is weaker than that of native English speakers, and they show a slight first noun preference on NNV patterns and neutral behavior on VNN patterns. Thus, native English speakers learning French must, in general, increase their reliance on verb agreement and noun animacy so that they are stronger than word order. Such learners must also somewhat weaken their first noun preference for NVN strings, change their second noun preferences in NNV strings to a first noun preference, and nullify their second noun preference in VNN strings. The following experiment explores if English speakers make such modifications in their comprehension of French, and if so, the order in which these changes occur.

Method

Subjects. Four groups of native English speakers currently enrolled in university level French courses took part in the experiment. These included 46 students in first semester French (Group 1), 45 students in second semester French (Group 2), 25 students in third semester French (Group 3), and 7 students in or beyond fourth semester French (Group 4). None of the second language learners had had a significant experience with languages other than English or French either inside or outside of the classroom, and none had been in a French speaking country for more than a total of three weeks. In addition to the four second language groups, two native speaking control groups were included in the experiment. These groups were made up of 18 native English speakers who had had no foreign language immersion experience, and 8 native French speakers. While the second language learners judged sentences in their second language, the native language groups judged sentences in their native language.

---

[1]Although not tested in the current experiment, when case inflection information is present, particularly when both subject and object clitics are present, native speakers make very strong use of these cues (Heilenman & McDonald, 1991; McDonald & Heilenman, in press).

Stimuli. In experiments designed to test strength of cue usage within the Competition Model paradigm, it is necessary to completely cross all levels of a cue with all levels of the other cues—it is particularly easy to see the relative importance of cues on sentences where they conflict. Although this complete crossing often yields ungrammatical sentences, previous research has shown that grammatical and ungrammatical sentences are judged using similar strategies (MacWhinney, Pleh & Bates, 1985). Accordingly, the stimuli for this experiment were devised by completely crossing three levels of word order (NVN, NNV and VNN), three levels of verb agreement (VA0—verb agrees with both nouns, VA1—verb agrees only with the first noun, and VA2—verb agrees only with the second noun), and four levels of noun animacy (AA—first and second noun animate, AI—first noun animate, second noun inanimate, IA—first noun inanimate, second noun animate, and II—both nouns inanimate). This complete crossing yielded 36 different sentence types. Two examples of each type were formed, one version with a singular first noun, and one with a plural first noun yielding a total of 72 test sentences. An additional four warm-up sentences with similar characteristics to the test sentences were also formed.

Vocabulary was selected from a pool of 12 animate nouns (*l'homme,* 'the man', *le monsieur* 'the gentleman', *le frère* 'the brother', *le cow-boy* 'the cowboy', *le garçon* 'the boy', *le papa* 'the father', *la femme* 'the woman', *la dame* 'the lady', *la soeur* 'the sister', *la princesse* 'the princess', *la fille* 'the girl', *la maman* 'the mother') and 12 inanimate nouns (*le chapeau* 'the hat', *le cahier* 'the notebook', *le livre* 'the book', *le sac* 'the bag', *le vélo* 'the bicycle', *le crayon* 'the pencil', *la chaussure* 'the shoe', *la valise* 'the suitcase', *la cassette* 'the cassette', *la table* 'the table', *la chaise* 'the chair', *la lampe* 'the lamp') and three causative verbs (*faire bouger* 'to make move', *faire tomber* 'to make fall', *faire tourner* 'to make turn'). These causative verbs were chosen because a distinction between third person singular and plural is clearly detectable with the verb *faire* (third person singular: *fait*; third person plural: *font*). Vocabulary items were assigned to sentence slots randomly, with the restriction that the same noun could not occur twice in the same sentence.

The test sentences were randomized, and a native speaker of French recorded each sentence followed by a short pause. An equivalent tape was made in English by a native English speaker. All sentences were spoken with a similar flat intonation contour.

Procedure. After filling out a form about their language background, the second language learners listened to a tape containing a list of the French vocabulary that would be used in the experiment along with their English translations. If they were unfamiliar with an item they were allowed to write down its translation and study this before proceeding to the main part of the experiment. Although care was taken to choose simple vocabulary, this vocabulary presentation insured that all subjects would be familiar with the words.

For the sentence comprehension portion of the experiment, all subjects were told that they would be listening to some simple sentences and that they were to choose the noun in each sentence that performed the action of the verb. It was stressed that some of the sentences might sound odd and that there were no right or wrong answers in the task. Rather, it was their first impression of the meaning of the sentence which was of interest. Subjects were provided with answer sheets that listed the two nouns contained in each sentence and were instructed to circle the noun that was the actor in each sentence. Subjects then listened to the tape and marked their answer for each sentence immediately after hearing it. Subjects could extend the time after each sentence by pushing the pause button; however, they were not allowed to hear any sentence more than once.

Results

<u>Native English speakers.</u> The native English speakers made strong use of the word order cue (F(2,34)=56.9, p<.001), choosing the first noun 88% of the time in NVN strings, 20% of the time on NNV strings and 26% of the time on VNN strings. They also made significant use of verb agreement (F(2,34)=12.0, p<.001), choosing the first noun 44% of the time when agreement was not informative, 56% of the time when agreement favored the first noun, and only 33% of the time when agreement favored the second noun. Noun animacy also significantly influenced choice behavior (F(3,51)=6.9, p<.001), with subjects choosing the first noun 44% of the time when both nouns were animate, 55% of the time when only the first noun was animate, 37% of the time when only the second noun was animate, and 46% of the time when neither noun was animate. Word order was by far the most influential cue for native English speakers: it accounted for 47% of the variance in choice behavior, while agreement accounted for only 4%, and noun animacy for 2%.

Word order interacted with verb agreement (F(4,68)=4.1, p<.01) due to ceiling and floor effects (i..e., first noun choice was so high for the NVN word order, that adding an agreement cue favoring the first noun could not increase its choice significantly. Likewise, the choice of the second noun was so high in the NNV word order that adding an agreement cue favoring the second noun could not increase its choice significantly.) An interaction between word order and noun animacy (F(6,102)=2.3, p<.05) was also caused by similar ceiling and floor effects.

Thus, the results for the native English speakers agree with previous findings. Word order is the dominant cue in English, with native speakers showing a first noun preference on NVN strings and second noun preference on NNV and VNN strings.

<u>Native French speakers.</u> The native French speakers made significant use of word order (F(2,14)=10.5, p<.01), choosing the first noun 73% of the time in the NVN order, 53% of the time in the NNV order, and only 36% of the time in the VNN order. Verb agreement also significantly influenced choice behavior (F(2,14)=47.5, p<.001), with subjects choosing the first noun 59% of the time when agreement was not informative, 88% of the time when it favored the first noun, and 15% of the time when it favored the second noun. Noun animacy was also used as a cue for assigning the actor role (F(3,21)=15.2, p<.001), with the first noun being picked 57% of the time when both nouns were animate, 67% of the time when only the first noun was animate, 37% of the time when only the second noun was animate, and 55% of the time when both nouns were inanimate. All two way interactions and the three way interaction were also significant due to ceiling and floor effects. Verb agreement was the strongest cue for native French speakers, accounting for 44% of the variance, followed by word order with 11% of the variance, and noun animacy with 6%.

The performance of the native French speakers confirms some trends found in previous research. For example, verb agreement was again shown to be a strong cue to the actor role. However, their performance also differs from past results. Unlike previous results, word order in the current experiment accounted for more variance than did noun animacy. Word order preferences also differed somewhat from past research—in this experiment native speakers manifested a second noun rather than neutral preference for VNN sequences. Although VNN strings are infrequent in French, we speculate that this second noun preference may arise from sentences where the subject has been dislocated to the right (*Il voit la table l'homme* 'He sees the table the man').

<u>Second language learners of French.</u> All four groups of French learners made significant use of word order (Group 1: F(2,90)=32.3, p<.001; Group 2: F(2,88)=25.7, p<.001; Group 3: F(2,48)=24.8, p<.001; Group 4: F(2,12)=11.5, p<.01). However, their pattern of preference changed from that of native English speakers. As shown in Figure 1, even the first group of

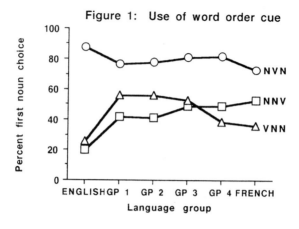

Figure 1: Use of word order cue

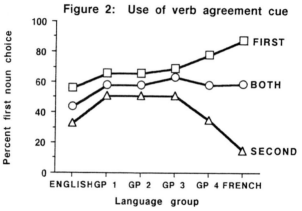

Figure 2: Use of verb agreement cue

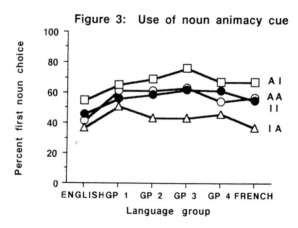

Figure 3: Use of noun animacy cue

learners slightly decreased the strength of their first noun choice on NVN strings, strongly weakened their second noun preference on NNV strings and converted from a second noun to a slight first noun preference for VNN strings. All four groups of second language learners differ from the native English speakers in their use of word order cues (Group 1: F(2,124)=13.1, p<.001; Group 2: F(2,122)=10.2, p<.001; Group 3: F(2,82)=11.6, p<.001; Group 4: F(2,46)=3.6, p<.05). It is not until the most advanced group, Group 4, that a second noun preference on VNN strings re-emerges. Only at this point does word order usage become clearly indistinguishable from native French speakers (Group 1: F(2,104)=3.8, p<.05; Group 2: F(2,102)=3.4, p<.05; Group 3: F(2,62)=2.4, p<.10; Group 4: F(2,26)=.6, n.s.).

All groups of French learners also made significant use of verb agreement cues (Group 1: F(2,90)=9.0, p<.001; Group 2: F(2,88)=8.9, p<.001; Group 3: F(2,48)=7.5, p<.01; Group 4: F(2,12)=11.3, p<.01). However, as shown in Figure 2, it is not until the fourth group of learners that verb agreement starts to increase in usage, although its overall use here is only marginally stronger than the native English speakers (F(2,46)=2.4, p=.10). Verb agreement comes into play for this fourth group more strongly on the non-canonical than canonical word orders, as shown by an interaction between group, word order and verb agreement (F(4,92)=3.5, p<.05). Even though this last group has increased their use of verb agreement, all second language groups fail to use this cue at the native speaker level (Group 1: F(2,104)=19.7, p<.001; Group 2: F(2,102)=19.7, p<.001; Group 3: F(2,62)=17.0, p<.001; Group 4: F(2,26)=3.4, p<.05).

The use of the noun animacy cue does not change to any great extent across the groups of French learners. As shown in Figure 3, because the native English and native French groups do not differ dramatically in their use of the animacy cue, there is no reason for the learners to alter their dependence on it. None of the second language groups differ from either of the native speaker groups, except that group 3 shows a slightly stronger use of animacy than does the native English speaker group (F(3,123)=3.8, p<.05).

Discussion

The above results give the following picture of the time course of cue mastery by native English speakers learning French: The first change, which occurs quite early in the learning process, is an abandonment of English word order strategies, particularly in the non-canonical orders—the second noun preference on NNV is weakened, and the second noun preference on VNN strings is replaced by a slight VSO preference. After considerable exposure, in this case, at or after the fourth semester of French, the interpretation of VNN strings reverts back to VOS, and the word order preferences manifested by the second language learners become indistinguishable from that of native French speakers.[2] Finally, in the last group of learners tested, there is evidence that the verb agreement cue is beginning to be used more strongly. Thus, the onset of mastery of the verb agreement cue is later than that of word order. (Native English speakers can master the verb agreement cue—very advanced English/French bilinguals

---

[2]Note in the present data that after word order strategies were judged to be ineffective, subjects did not develop a sudden reliance on noun animacy. This contrasts with the results of Gass (1987) for Italian, and Sasaki (1991) and Kilborn and Ito (1989) for Japanese, who find that their subjects do develop strong animacy strategies. Thus, when a syntactic strategy is found to fail, it is not necessarily the case that learners turn towards an easily adoptable semantic strategy. It may depend on how useful such a semantic strategy is for interpreting the new language.

use this cue at levels indistinguishable from native speakers (McDonald & Heilenman, in press)).

Can the order in which first language cues are dropped and second language cues mastered be predicted by the input learners are receiving? The rapid change of reliance on word order strategies may have to do with the number of errors such strategies would cause the second language learner to make. (See McDonald (1986; 1989) for a detailed explanation of cue acquisition based on a learning-on-error model.) Accordingly, we examined the kinds of sequences that occur in the speech of native French speakers. Two corpora of spoken French were examined—the first a transcription of a native French speaker teaching a first-semester French class, and the second a series of three conversations involving native French speakers (Cosnier & Kerbrat-Orecchioni, 1987). We abstracted all sequences involving a verb, subject and direct object from these corpora, noted their word order and which noun was the actor. If the strict word order strategies of English are used to assign the actor role to these French sequences, there would be misinterpretations on 20% of the sequences uttered by the teacher and 29% of those in the conversations among natives. Given this large error rate, it would be reasonable to expect that speakers would note the inappropriateness of their English word order strategies and decrease their reliance on them.

The word order preferences for NVN, NNV and VNN strings may be adjusted according to the frequency with which the two possible interpretations of each pattern is heard. For example, although the teacher used both SVO and OVS interpretations of the NVN word order, the SVO interpretation was four times as frequent. Thus, the presence of OVS interpretations would cause learners to lower their preference for a SVO interpretation over that which they manifest in English, but the preponderance of an SVO interpretation would still cause them to favor a first noun strategy. Similarly, beginning learners hear both OSV and SOV interpretations of NNV word order. In the teacher corpus, however, there were many more OSV than SOV interpretations, due to the preponderance of questions of the form Qu'est-ce que-Subject-Verb? ('What is it that-Subject-Verb?'). The presence of the SOV interpretation would cause subjects to weaken their second noun preference for these strings as compared to that which they show in English, but the higher frequency of OSV to SOV interpretations would cause students to weakly favor this interpretation. It should be noted that questions were relatively infrequent in the native speaker corpus, where there were about twice as many SOV as OSV interpretations of NNV strings. Thus, as learners advance in their knowledge of French, and the type of speech that gets addressed to them becomes more native like, the percentage of OSV interpretations they hear may decline, and they may correspondingly lose their slight OSV preference for NNV strings. Finally, consider the interpretation of VNN strings. Beginning learners immediately drop their second noun preference for these strings, even though native French speakers showed a second noun strategy on these strings. This second noun preference did not emerge again until the fourth semester. One reason for the initial loss of this preference may be the very low incidence of VNN sequences in French. In the native speaker spoken corpus, none of the 204 strings followed this pattern. In the teacher talk corpus, two of the 125 sentences had this form, but both had a VSO interpretation (Alors à quelle heure faites-vous ça? 'Then at what time do you that?; A quelle heure regardes-tu la télévision? 'At what time watch you television?') Thus, the very small amount of input learners get contradicts their English preferences, and this may result in the loss of this bias.

The late increase of strength in the verb agreement cue may also be a property of the French input. As previously noted, many of the spoken forms of French verbs are indistinguishable from one another. Indeed, in the teacher talk corpus, only 43% of the utterances had useful verb agreement cues. (This figure declines to 21% if speakers are not aware of the tense of the discourse.) Interestingly, native French-speaking children initially show weaker use of verb agreement than word order cues (Kail, 1989; Kail & Charvillat, 1988). Thus, while verb agreement is an important cue in French, its lack of general availability seems to delay its use as a strong cue in both first and second language learners.

The rapid loss of English word order strategies manifested by the beginning French learners in this paper confirms a trend in the literature. That is, it appears that in general English word order strategies are quickly abandoned when the second language has a freer word order. For example, Gass (1987) investigated the use of word order and noun animacy cues in native English speakers learning Italian. Unlike English, Italian has much freer word order, and uses animacy as well as other devices as stronger cues to sentence interpretation. The word order biases shown by native speakers of Italian are different from those found for native speakers of English—i.e., moderate first noun preferences in NVN and NNV strings and neutral performance on VNN strings (Bates, McNew, MacWhinney, Devescovi & Smith, 1982). Gass (1987) found that learners who were acquiring Italian in a natural environment had somewhat weakened their strong first noun bias for NVN strings, had shifted from a second noun bias to a first noun bias in NNV strings, and had neutralized their second noun bias in VNN strings. Thus, these intermediate-level learners had successfully altered their word order biases to bring them in line with Italian. They were also using animacy cues more strongly than word order in determining the actor in Italian sentences.

English word order strategies are also quickly lost when English speakers learn Japanese (Sasaki, 1991; Kilborn & Ito, 1989). In Japanese, the only legal strings are those with verb final, and the most common interpretation of an NNV string is SOV. In Sasaki's (1991) native speaking Japanese group, a slight first noun preference was manifested over all word orders. Native English speakers learning Japanese essentially correctly neutralized all their word order biases and depended on animacy to determine the actor role (Sasaki, 1991). These results contrast somewhat to those of Kilborn and Ito (1989), who found moderate first noun preferences in native Japanese speakers, the strongest of which was in the NNV word order. Their English/Japanese bilingual subjects showed appropriate weakening of the first noun bias for NVN sentences and neutralized the second noun preference for VNN strings, although they did not show the first noun bias of the native Japanese group. However, for NNV strings, the bilingual speakers chose the first noun as actor more strongly than did the native speakers. Kilborn and Ito (1989) hypothesized that English speakers, who may be more sensitive to word order in general because of its strong use in English, may use a meta-strategy of paying attention to word order, and this causes them to develop word order biases that are stronger than native speakers. In any case, in both Sasaki's (1991) and Kilborn & Ito's (1989) studies, English speakers lost or altered their English word order preferences.

This rapid loss of incorrect English word order strategies was also noted in a study of English speakers learning Dutch (McDonald, 1987). Among other things, these subjects were tested on their interpretation of relative clauses of the NNV ordering. While in English the preferred interpretation of such strings is OSV, in Dutch it is SOV. English/Dutch bilinguals quickly dropped their second noun preference, and although not significant, showed a growing tendency with increasing Dutch exposure for a first noun preference.

Thus, we see a general pattern of loss of English word order strategies for use in other languages. We speculate that this quick abandonment of English word order preferences has to do with the number of errors such strategies cause in the new language. For example, English word order strategies would cause errors on OVS, SOV and VSO grammatical strings in Italian, SOV strings in Japanese and SOV relative clauses in Dutch. Given that these strings are relatively frequent in these languages, learners should note the lack of usefulness of English strategies for their second language.

Given that English speakers quickly alter word order preferences when interpreting other languages, what happens when speakers of other languages learn English? An interesting asymmetry exists between the ease with which native English speakers lose their word order strategies for interpreting other languages and the difficulty speakers of other languages have in losing their non-word order strategies when interpreting English. For example, when speakers of languages where animacy is an important cue learn English, they tend to maintain their dominant use of animacy. This is not to say there is no adjustment of word order preferences in the direction of English strategies, but that animacy still tends to dominate word order. This dominant use of animacy was true for Italian speakers learning English (Gass, 1987), as well as for Japanese speakers learning English (Harrington, 1987; Kilborn & Ito, 1989). This failure to lose first language strategies for the interpretation of English may be tied to the low number of errors such strategies cause for understanding English sentences. To test this hypothesis, we applied an animacy strategy to 100 English sentences taken from a conversation between two native speakers (Craig & Tracy, 1983). The animacy strategy alone assigned the actor role correctly on 81% of these sentences, incorrectly on 1% and at chance level on 18%, yielding an overall error rate of 10%. However, even in languages where animacy is a more important cue than word order, there are word order biases for the interpretation of sentences without an animacy contrast. If the bias is, as it is in most cases, SVO, then the above error rate falls to 1%. Thus, the use of an animacy strategy in conjunction with a weaker SVO strategy would yield a very low error rate on English sentences. Given this low error rate, beginning learners would have only minimal cause to abandon their first language strategies when processing English.

In general, then, if second language learners are influenced by the errors their first language strategies cause in second language interpretation, they should quickly abandon strategies that yield a high error rate, but maintain, or abandon more slowly those that yield a low error rate. Such a learning-on-error model predicts rapid loss of English word order strategies for processing languages with freer word order, and slower loss of first language animacy strategies when processing English.

Summary. Bilinguals appear to be able to make adjustments in their cue usage toward the strategies appropriate in their second language. These modifications take place over time, however. As shown by the current research, these modifications may involve first abandoning inappropriate first language strategies that yield a high error rate when used to interpret second language strings. With increasing exposure, learners develop strategies appropriate to the second language based on the utility of these cues in the language samples to which they are exposed.

References

Ashby, W. J. (1988). The syntax, pragmatics and sociolinguistics of left- and right-dislocations in French. *Lingua, 75,* 203-229.

Barnes, B. K. (1985). *The pragmatics of left detachment in spoken standard French.* Amsterdam: John Benjamins.

Bates, E., & MacWhinney, B. (1981). Second language acquisition from a functionalist perspective: Pragmatic, semantic and perceptual strategies. In H. Winitz (Ed.), *Annals of the New York Academy of Sciences conference on native and foreign language acquisition.* New York: New York Academy of Sciences.

Bates, E., & MacWhinney, B. (1982). Functionalist approaches to grammar. In E. Wanner & L. R. Gleitman (Eds.), *Language acquisition: The state of the art.* Cambridge: Cambridge University Press.

Bates, E., & MacWhinney, B. (1987). Competition, variation and language learning. In B. MacWhinney (Ed.), *Mechanisms of language acquisition.* Hillsdale, NJ: Lawrence Erlbaum.

Bates, E., & MacWhinney, B. (1989). Functionalism and the Competition Model. In B. MacWhinney & E. Bates (Eds.), *The crosslinguistic study of sentence processing.* Cambridge: Cambridge University Press.

Bates, E., McNew, S., MacWhinney, B., Devescovi, A., & Smith, S. (1982). Functional constraints on sentence processing: A cross-linguistic study. *Cognition, 11,* 245-299.

Cosnier, J., & Kerbrat-Orecchioni, C. (1987). *Décrire la conversation.* Lyon: Presses Universitaires de Lyon.

Craig, R. T., & Tracy, K. (1983). *Conversational Coherence.* Beverly Hills: Sage Publications.

Gass, S. M. (1987). The resolution of conflicts among competing systems: A bidirectional perspective. *Applied Psycholinguistics, 8,* 329-350.

Harrington, M. (1987). Processing transfer: Language-specific processing strategies as a source of interlanguage variation. *Applied Psycholinguistics, 8,* 351-378.

Heilenman, L. K., & McDonald, J. L. (1991). The acquisition of clitics by classroom second language learners of French. Unpublished manuscript.

Kail, M. (1989). Cue validity, cue cost, and processing types in sentence comprehension in French and Spanish. In B. MacWhinney & E. Bates (Eds.), *The crosslinguistic study of sentence processing.* Cambridge: Cambridge University Press.

Kail, M., & Charvillat, A. (1986). Linguistic cues in sentence processing in French children and adults from a crosslinguistic perspective. In I. Kurcz, G. Shugar & J. Danks (Eds.), *Knowledge and language.* Amsterdam: North-Holland.

Kail, M., & Charvillat, A. (1988). Local and topological processing in sentence comprehension by French and Spanish children. *Journal of Child Language, 15,* 637-662.

Kilborn, K. (1987). *Sentence processing in a second language: Seeking a performance definition of fluency.* Unpublished Ph.D. dissertation, University of California, San Diego.

Kilborn, K. (1989). Sentence processing in a second language: The timing of transfer. *Language & Speech, 32 ,* 1-23.

Kilborn, K. & Cooreman, A. (1987). Sentence interpretation strategies in adult Dutch-English bilinguals. *Applied Psycholinguistics, 8,* 415-431.

Kilborn, K., & Ito, T. (1989). Sentence processing strategies in adult bilinguals. In B. MacWhinney & E. Bates (Eds.), *The crosslinguistic study of sentence processing.* Cambridge: Cambridge University Press.

MacWhinney, B., Bates, E. & Kliegl, R. (1984). Cue validity and sentence interpretation in English, German and Italian. *Journal of Verbal Learning and Verbal Behavior, 23,* 127-150.

MacWhinney, B., Pleh, C., & Bates, E. (1985). The development of sentence interpretation in Hungarian. Cognitive Psychology, 17, 178-209.

McDonald, J. L. (1986). The development of sentence comprehension strategies in English and Dutch. Journal of Experimental Child Psychology, 41, 317-335.

McDonald, J. L. (1987). Sentence interpretation in bilingual speakers of English and Dutch. Applied Psycholinguistics, 8, 379-413.

McDonald, J. L. (1989). The acquisition of cue-category mappings. In B. MacWhinney & E. Bates (Eds.), The crosslinguistic study of sentence processing. Cambridge: Cambridge University Press.

McDonald, J. L. & Heilenman, L. K. (in press). Determinants of cue strength in adult first and second language speakers of French. Applied Psycholinguistics.

Sasaki, Y. (1991). English and Japanese interlanguage comprehension strategies—An analysis based on the Competition Model. Applied Psycholinguistics, 12, 47-73.

Trévise, A. (1986). Is it transferable, topicalization? In E. Kellerman & M. Sharwood Smith (Eds.), Crosslinguistic influence in second language acquisition. New York: Pergamon Press.

Wulfeck, B. B., Juarez, L., Bates, E. A., & Kilborn, K. (1986). Sentence interpretation strategies in healthy and aphasic bilingual adults. In J. Vaid (Ed.), Language processing in bilinguals: Psycholinguistic and neuropsychological perspectives. Hillsdale, NJ: Lawrence Erlbaum.

On-line Integration of Grammatical Information in a Second Language

Kerry Kilborn
Max Planck Institut für Psycholinguistik

Abstract

This chapter examines whether performance differences between native and advanced non-native speakers of English can be accounted for in terms of cognitive factors affecting the temporal integration of different types of grammatical information during on-line comprehension. This question is approached from a dual vantage point. First, L1 and L2 speakers of English are compared on a language processing task specifically designed to tap into the temporal course of integration during on-line sentence comprehension. Second, a group of L1 speakers perform the same task in their native language under "noisy" conditions (a partial auditory mask). This approach is an attempt to simulate non-native performance in native speakers, with the aim of gaining insight into the contribution of non-linguistic, cognitive factors to language use under less-than-ideal conditions. Both L2 speakers and L1-under-noise subjects display a marked failure to integrate syntactic with semantic information as rapidly as L1 speakers under normal listening conditions. The striking similarity in performance by L2 and L1-under-noise groups does not prove that the same processing mechanism is responsible. However, the results do suggest that a complete understanding of the performance side of becoming fluent in a second language will have to include a consideration of general cognitive aspects of language use.

Introduction

Language understanding is a behavior which takes place in real time. For normal comprehension to occur, a listener must compute structural as well as meaning-based information and relate the ongoing analyses of these two global information sources in language to each other quickly and efficiently. For fluent comprehension in a second language to occur, the L2 learner must access the appropriate syntactic and semantic information at the moment it is needed, and carry out the integration process without significant delay. Many factors can contribute to a lack of fluent processing. These include increased overall processing difficulty ("cognitive load"), inappropriate allocation of attention to grammatical information sources, and L1 influence on processing, to name just a few.

The question addressed in this chapter is whether performance (i.e., broadly, fluency) differences between native and advanced non-native speakers of English can be accounted for in terms of differences in the time course of integrating different types of grammatical information as it unfolds in real time. This question is approached from a dual vantage point. First, L1 and L2 speakers of English are compared on a language processing task specifically designed to tap into the temporal course of integration during on-line sentence comprehension. This portion of the study allows us to observe directly whether there are qualitative and/or quantitative differences in on-line processing between native and non-native speakers of a language. Second, a group of L1 speakers performs the same task in their native language under "noisy" conditions (a partial auditory mask). This approach, which makes the processing task perceptually more difficult, is an example of what Norman and Bobrow (1975) have called "data-limited processes," which are processes that operate as best they can on an impoverished input. This is an attempt to simulate non-native performance in native speakers, with the aim of gaining insight into the contribution of non-linguistic, cognitive factors to language use under less-than-ideal conditions.

Marslen-Wilson and Tyler (1980), in research based on their Cohort Model of auditory word recognition, have demonstrated that different grammatical information sources "communicate" with one another interactively, allowing words to be recognized on the basis of this integration before enough acoustic-phonetic input has been received to permit recognition on that basis alone. Following Marslen-Wilson and Tyler, the research presented here involves a simple word monitoring task. In this task, subjects listen for pre-specified words in three different types of sentence contexts: Normal, Syntactic and Random. These different contexts or prose types provide varying degrees of information that subjects may use during on-line processing. Normal sentences provide both semantic and syntactic information; in Syntactic sentences only structural information is present; and in Random sentences neither semantic nor syntactic information is available. By gradually stripping away different sources of information and holding the processing task otherwise constant, we can begin to build a picture of the contribution made by each type of information during real-time sentence processing.

One question we may ask about L2 speakers is whether they are able to integrate different types of grammatical information in real time in the same manner as L1 speakers. There are at least three possible outcomes, which we will discuss in turn. One possibility is that different information sources are integrated by L2 speakers in fundamentally the same way as by L1 speakers. If this is true, then we would predict that, while responses by L2 speakers may be somewhat slower overall, this difference would be observed in equal proportions in all conditions (i.e., on-line demands would affect different components of language to the same extent). In other words, there may be a main effect of language group, but no interaction of group by prose type, indicating similar on-line facilitation of processing by different information sources.

A second possibility is that L2 speakers use a qualitatively different processing strategy than L1 speakers. For example, an L2 speaker may initially develop a strategy that avoids the "hard" part of L2 processing--interpreting syntactic relations quickly and accurately--by placing an inordinately heavy dependence on meaning relations and other contextual information in comprehension (see Gass, 1986, 1989). While this does not mean that the learner cannot (eventually) master the broad spectrum of L2 syntactic information, the combined processing load may create time pressures under normal processing that the L2 speaker meets by attending to the part of the input that is easiest to decode quickly. Such a strategy may become refined with practice, to the extent that for all practical purposes L2 processing is as efficient and as effortless as for native speakers. However, the underlying representational structures that support this processing would in this case be qualitatively different from those in L1 speakers, leading to differences in performance on the word monitoring task in this experiment. Specifically, we would predict that in sentences with normal semantic relations, L2 speakers ought to perform at or near native speaker levels. Performance will diverge most when no meaning is available: removing semantic information will "hurt" L2 speakers relatively more than L1 speakers. In other words, if real-time processing in L2 does not benefit from syntactic structure in the same way as L1, then the presence of that structure will not facilitate word monitoring latencies relative to random word strings, and we will observe both a main effect of language group and a group by prose type interaction with the largest difference on Syntactic sentences.

A third possible outcome is suggested directly by the Cohort model. The Cohort model explains the facilitation in word monitoring latency produced by syntactic information over random word lists, and in turn by syntactic plus semantic information over syntactic information alone, in terms of communication between different levels of the processor. The contributions from different information sources (e.g., syntax, semantics) are assessed continually during processing, providing an integrated parse of incoming material as completely and rapidly as possible. For L2 speakers, this on-line computation may indeed take place, but its success may be a matter of degree. It may depend, for example, on the perceptibility of the input (level of signal versus noise), on the amount of supporting context available, on the linguistic and conceptual complexity of the message, and the rate at which the message is delivered. In this experiment, these factors are held more or less constant. If L2 speakers are less adept at performing the on-line computations necessary to quickly and efficiently integrate information from different sources under these conditions, then we ought to obtain a group by prose type interaction of the following sort: No difference will be observed between L1 and L2 speakers on Random and Syntactic prose sentences, but response latencies on Normal sentences should be facilitated less for L2 speakers than for L1 speakers. This finding would indicate that, rather than specific difficulty with particular L2 processing components, it is the integration of those components that presents problems for the L2 speaker.

Word Recognition under Noise

One of the ways automatic behaviors have been studied is to see how performance changes when the task in question is made more difficult (see Posner & Boies, 1971; Shallice, 1988; Kilborn, in press). In the current experiment, we investigate how automaticity in processing may break down by having monolingual subjects perform the word monitoring task under "noise" conditions. The noise in this case (pink noise played simultaneously with stimulus sentences) is intended to degrade the input to a point at which the task can still be performed but is uniformly more difficult, allowing us to see which components of language that contribute to performance on this task are most susceptible to stress (Broadbent, 1982).

While the question of automaticity in language processing is interesting in its own right, it may also have relevance to the development of fluency in a second language. One reason for including the stress condition in this experiment is to see whether any differences between L1 and L2 speakers can be accounted for in terms of sheer increased difficulty in extracting information from a noisy signal. In other words, the noise condition may allow us to simulate (some level of) L2 performance in L1 speakers. If similar patterns obtain between stressed L1 speakers and L2 speakers, we may conclude that a similar problem is faced by the L2 speaker. There is one important difference, however. Difficulty in processing by L2 speakers is not due directly to a degradation of bottom-up information. Rather, the limiting factor for L2 speakers is likely to be a lack of immediate, on-line control over relevant top-down information. This is an example of what Norman and Bobrow (1975) refer to as a "resource-limited process."

Experimental Studies of On-line Integration

Three groups participated in this experiment. These included one group of 20 monolingual English speakers who received all stimuli under normal conditions, a second group of 20 subjects who received all stimuli under masked conditions, and a group of 15 German-English bilingual subjects (native German-speaking instructors in German language and literature at the University of California, San Diego USA).

Design and Materials

Three blocks of 40 sentences were constructed in each language. **Normal** sentences maintain syntactic and semantic relations as usual. **Syntactic** sentences were constructed by replacing open class (content) words in the Normal sentences with pseudo-randomly selected words of the same form class (i.e., nouns replace nouns, verbs replace verbs, etc), matched for length and frequency. Thus, Syntactic sentences have intact structural relations, and are of the same length and complexity as Normal sentences, but have no plausible semantic interpretation. **Random** sentences were constructed by first making an additional set of Syntactic strings, then randomizing the order of words within each sentence while keeping the target position constant. Random sentences thus maintain neither semantic nor syntactic relations, but do contain the same proportion of content and function words as Normal and Syntactic sentences. All sentences were 9 to 12 words. Half of the targets occurred in **early** positions (the first half of the sentence), and half in **late** positions (second half). Sample materials appears below:

Prose Type	Visual Target	Auditory Sentence
Normal	*RULES*	Playing hockey without observing the **rules** is extremely dangerous.
Syntactic	*TRAIN*	Checking gravel without walking the **train** is perfectly yellow.
Random	*TRIP*	Is ducks without securely the tired **trip** blocking illegal.

Procedure

Subjects were tested individually. In a testing session, subjects were seated before a CRT screen, on which the target word was presented 2 seconds before the onset of an auditory sentence. A microcomputer randomly selected a digitized sentence from the appropriate set and played it via headphones to the subject. Subjects were instructed to read the target word, then to listen carefully to the following sentence and to press a response button as quickly as possible when the target word was detected. For the "stressed" control group, the procedure was identical except that the stimulus sentences were partially masked by pink noise.

Results

Mean reaction times were entered as data into an analysis of variance in a 4-way design with Subjects and Groups as between-subject factors, and Sentence Type and Position as within-subject factors. The main findings are listed in Table 1.

Monolingual English controls. We turn first to the performance of monolingual English speakers. The fastest responses were to target words in Normal sentences (230 msec), next fastest to words in Syntactic sentences (304 msec), and slowest to words in Random sentences (341 msec). The main effect of Sentence Type was significant, $\underline{F}(2,148) = 23.6$, $\underline{p}<0.01$. Scheffé confidence intervals were calculated around the mean of each Sentence Type, revealing significant differences at the $p<0.01$ level between each condition. Subjects also responded faster to words in the second half of all sentences (275 msec) than to words in the first half (309 msec), $F(1,133) = 6.6$, $p<0.05$. This was true for each of the prose conditions.

Table 1

Mean reaction times in word monitoring task

	English L1 speakers		German-English bilinguals	
Prose Type	Clean	Noise	German (L1)	English (L2)
Normal	230	322	221	292
Syntactic	304	361	264	317
Random	341	393	342	354

These findings essentially replicate similar results reported by Marslen-Wilson and Tyler (1980). The pattern that emerges from the findings with English L1 speakers suggests that, not only is syntactic and semantic information utilized very rapidly during sentence comprehension, but that these information sources interact in ways that aid rapid integration of the incoming signal, allowing listeners to arrive at word recognition more quickly when both meaning and structure are present than when only structure is available. It is interesting to note that the mean response latency in normal sentences--230 milliseconds--corresponds to roughly two phonemes in normal speech. In most words, the "uniqueness point"--the point at which a word can be uniquely identified based on the acoustic information available--occurs later than this (Marslen-Wilson, 1987; Zwitserlood, 1989). This lends support to the notion that sentence comprehension depends on a rapid, interactive integration process in which global information sources contribute to lexical access.

German-English bilingual subjects. The reaction time data from the bilingual subjects are analyzed in two ways. First, we compare between subjects in English -- performance in English as L1 versus English as L2. Next, we compare performance in English (L2) and German (L1) within the bilingual group alone, treating language as a within-subject factor.

For the English as L1 versus English as L2 between-groups analysis, the group (monolingual versus bilingual) X prose type (Normal, Syntactic, Random) interaction was significant at $F(2,66) = 10.7$, $p<0.001$. A Scheffé test showed that the source of this interaction is in the difference between L1 and L2 groups in the Normal condition: responses by bilingual subjects (292 msec) were significantly slower than those by monolingual English speakers (230 msec). Group differences within the Syntactic and Random conditions were not significant. This points to some important differences in the on-line processing characteristics of non-native speakers; we will return to these findings shortly.

For the *German as L1 versus English as L2 within-subjects analysis,* the language (German versus English) X prose type (Normal, Syntactic, Random) interaction was significant at $\underline{F}(2,28) = 7.7$, $\underline{p}<0.002$. In German, subjects were fastest in Normal prose (221 msec), next fastest in Syntactic prose (264 msec) and slowest in Random prose (341 msec). In English, there was a trend in the same direction, but responses to targets in Normal prose (292 msec) were not significantly faster than to targets in Syntactic prose (316 msec). However, responses in both Normal and Syntactic prose conditions were significantly faster than in English Random sentences (354 msec).

<u>Simulating non-native performance: Sentence processing by monolinguals under noise.</u> A second group of 18 monolingual English speakers performed the word monitoring task with the addition of a partial mask ("pink noise"). The aim here was to provide a mask which made the task noticeably more difficult but not impossible to perform. Pilot subjects who performed both "clean" and "noise" versions of the tasks reported that the masked tasks did require a higher level of effort and concentration. In the current experiment, the group factor was treated as a between-subjects variable in a 2 (group: "clean" versus "noise") x 2 (position) x 3 (prose type) ANOVA.

The main effect of group in the auditory modality was significant, $\underline{F}(1,36) = 20.3$, $\underline{p}<0.001$. This indicates simply that mean response time was faster under clean conditions (292 msec overall) than under noise (359 msec). The group x prose type interaction was also significant at $\underline{F}(2,72) = 8.6$, $\underline{p}<0.001$. The presence of noise in the signal had a greater effect on monitoring times in Normal than in Syntactic or Random sentences. This finding suggests that the temporal course of integrating grammatical information during on-line processing is disrupted by a condition which limits the accessibility of "time-sensitive material" to the processing system. The implications of this for non-native language performance are discussed in more detail below.

Discussion

There were three different types of sentence contexts in which target words appeared: Normal, Syntactic, and Random. These different contexts provide different degrees of information that subjects may use during on-line processing. Normal sentences provide both semantic information and syntactic information; in Syntactic sentences only structural information is present; and in Random sentences neither semantic nor syntactic is available. By gradually stripping away different sources of information and holding the processing task otherwise constant, we can begin to build a picture of the contribution made by each type of information during real-time sentence processing. As we have seen, word monitoring times in English L1 speakers are fastest in Normal sentences, intermediate in Syntactic sentences, and slowest in Random sentences. This pattern of facilitation across prose types suggests that not only are syntactic and semantic information utilized very rapidly during sentence comprehension, but that these information sources interact in ways that aid rapid integration of the incoming signal, allowing listeners to arrive at word recognition decisions more quickly when both meaning and structure are present than when only structure is available.

The findings from the monolingual English speakers in the auditory modality are largely a replication of similar results found by Marslen-Wilson and Tyler (1980). In this experiment, we extended the findings to native speakers of German. A similar pattern of results was obtained in German as L1, which suggests that the experimental paradigm used here is generalizable to processing in different languages.

On-line processing in L2: failure to integrate. Three predictions were made regarding real-time word monitoring in L2 speakers. The first prediction was that L2 speakers do not differ qualitatively from L1 speakers in the way in which they integrate information from different sources. The second prediction was that particular components (e.g., syntax) in L2 may be more difficult to deal with than others (e.g., word meanings). The third prediction was that, in contrast with native speakers, non-native speakers would lack facility in the rapid integration of different types of information used during on-line processing.

The evidence here clearly supports the third prediction. Specifically, we observed that in English, word recognition latency in L2 speakers was facilitated in the Syntactic prose condition over the Random prose condition. This was also the case with English L1 speakers, showing that performance by native and non-native speakers alike benefited from the presence of structural information. However, unlike native English speakers, performance by the L2 subjects did not improve further when structure and meaning were both present. As far as possible, extraneous factors (context, rate of presentation, volume, etc.) were held constant; to the extent that such factors did not impinge on this task, we were able to obtain a relatively "pure" measure of the ability to integrate the types of information present. It is precisely this integration--or more precisely, the lack of it within the interval during which word recognition occurs--that characterized the on-line processing in English as L2. We will return to the "failure-to-integrate" phenomenon below.

Strategies in on-line processing. The Cohort Model postulates that syntactic, semantic, and lexical information are extracted from a signal simultaneously, and that these different informational components are integrated on-line. In the case of a non-native speaker, we may ask whether and to what extent lexical, structural, and interpretive knowledge sources based in different languages communicate or interact during processing.

One way to consider this issue is suggested by another psycholinguistic model of language performance, the Competition Model (MacWhinney & Bates, 1987, 1989; MacWhinney, 1987; this volume). Briefly, the Competition Model derives from an account of the functional aspects of mapping linguistic forms to underlying meaning. The sources of information a listener uses to decide which function is meant to be expressed by a given form are referred to as "cues." Cues are particular instances of form-function mappings, and are assigned weights within the model according to their statistical distributions in the language. Thus, the usefulness--and relative weight--of a given cue is determined by a combination of factors, including how reliable a cue is, i.e., whether it always maps the same form(s) to the same function(s), and how often the cue is available (e.g., animacy may be heavily depended upon when a distinction is present, as in "The boy broke the window," but not in "The ball broke the window").

The Competition Model suggests four hypotheses regarding the ways in which language processing strategies may interact in individuals who speak more than one language: (1) L1 strategies may be applied to both languages; (2) L1 and L2 strategies are applied correctly in the appropriate situations; (3) L2 strategies may eventually become dominate, supplanting L1 strategies; and (4) L2 strategies may join L1 strategies in forming an amalgam that is used for both languages. A number of processing studies with bilinguals have shown that various forms of transfer do occur; thus far, these differences have not been related to years of experience or other obvious factors, suggesting that differences in bilingual processing styles may play an important role (Bates & MacWhinney, 1981; Harrington, 1987; Kilborn & Cooreman, 1987; Kilborn, 1989; Kilborn & Ito, 1989; Wulfeck, Bates, Juarez, & Kilborn, 1986).

Given the findings that L1 cues sometimes invade into L2 processing, we may ask what implications this has for the on-line interactive processing of information in L2 sentences. For example, when the first and second language systems--lexical, structural, interpretive, etc.--are at variance with one another, attempting to adapt L1 circuitry to handle L2 input may cause difficulties for rapid, efficient on-line processing. The ways these differences manifest themselves during on-line processing may vary depending on the current stage of L2 acquisition and the way in which different cues interact across languages. In terms of the four hypotheses outlined above, we may observe any of the following situations in an on-line processing context.

If L1 strategies are applied to both languages (Hypothesis 1), the non-native speaker may find that cues which carry much of the processing load in L1 actually interfere with the integration of L2 information sources. For example, German, due to the presence of explicit case and agreement markers, allows much more word order variation than English, which has a relatively impoverished morphological system. A native German speaker may attempt to assign thematic roles in English on the basis of the few morphological cues that are present, ignoring the normally dominant cue of word order in English. In on-line processing, this strategy may lead the L2 speaker to misassign subject and object roles, or to refrain from making any assignment until other information has been received. In either case, the on-line, interactive nature of processing will have been disrupted due to the application of L1 strategies to L2 processing.

Another possibility is that L2 strategies are applied appropriately, without direct or indirect interference from L1 (Hypothesis 2). In this case, we would expect the integration of different information sources in L2 by non-native speakers to parallel that by native speakers. While this appears to place us in the rather uncomfortable position of predicting no differences, we may view this in another way. In principle, we may define fluency as achieving native-like proficiency in L2. In other words, such parallel performance in on-line processing represents an endpoint in the development of proficiency in L2. However, even native speakers do not perform uniformly in most behavioral tasks; it would not be unreasonable to expect an even broader range of performance by L2 speakers depending on their stage of acquisition. Rather than presenting a problem, the potential for stratification of L2 speakers on different dimensions of on-line L2 processing offers a rich and detailed picture of the routes different learners may take to fluency.

The third hypothesis, that L2 strategies are not only applied to L2 but may come to dominate even in L1 processing, suggests a rather different set of questions. To return to the example from German and English, this hypothesis predicts that the native German speaker would not only apply L2 (English) processing strategies (e.g., use of word order cues rather than case marking and agreement morphology) correctly in L2, but that this strategy would carry over into German as well. If this were true, then we would expect a kind of reverse disruption in the on-line processing of L1 (German) to occur (e.g., thematic roles may be assigned on the basis of an L2-appropriate strategy, in this instance word order, creating conflicts when L1 cues point to different assignments). Many L2 learners have short-term confusion in L1 upon returning to L1 use after extensive exposure to and use of L2. The possibility that L2 acquisition may have a profound impact on the status of the learner's L1 is a topic which has only recently received serious attention (Odlin, 1989).

The fourth hypothesis holds that strategies from both L1 and L2 may become fused into a single amalgamated system that is applied to processing in both languages. In terms of on-line, interactive processing, this predicts that sentence processing in bilinguals may differ qualitatively from that in monolinguals of both languages, but that on-line patterns would be identical across languages within an individual.

These possibilities are not mutually exclusive. Each may be characteristic of different stages on a continuum from novice to advanced L2 speaker. Furthermore, individual speakers may differ in the extent to which transfer does and does not occur. This underscores the notion that there may be many, perhaps parallel, routes to fluency: Any model of L2 acquisition must be sufficiently general to capture this flexibility. Taken together, the different psycholinguistic paradigms used to investigate language processing which we have discussed here suggest a number of factors which could contribute to a general model of L2 acquisition: The notion of differential activation levels, resulting from an overlap between sensory and contextual information, as well as structural or functional overlap between a bilingual's two languages, may contribute to our understanding of the process of becoming fluent in a second language.

Word monitoring made difficult: breaking into automaticity. When non-native English speakers performed the word monitoring task under normal conditions, we observed a deviation from the monolingual pattern for normal, syntactic, and random prose. Bilinguals were not simply slow overall; rather, they were specifically much slower than monolinguals in the integration of semantic and structural information (i.e., the difference between monolinguals and bilinguals was greatest in the normal prose condition).

The pattern of results from monolinguals performing an on-line processing task under noise was strikingly similar in several regards to the performance of non-native speakers in English. Of course, this failure-to-integrate effect may have quite different explanations in bilinguals than in normals-under-stress. However, it would naturally be more satisfying from a theoretical point of view if a single explanation could be made to account for all the data, and even more so if that explanation were founded on current psycholinguistic theory.

One such explanation favors the view of processing espoused by Fodor (1983), Forster (1981), Seidenberg (1985), and others, namely the view that processing is essentially modular. The interpretation of our findings from this perspective would be that semantic and syntactic information are computed separately in the earliest stages and then fed into an "integrating device." Skilled monolinguals can do this very fast; non-native speakers and monolinguals under noise cannot.

While this interpretation cannot be ruled out, there are other possible explanations which do not involve assumptions of modularity in the processing system. There is clear evidence for transfer of L2 cues into L1 sentence processing (Gass, 1989; McDonald, 1984). Kilborn (1989) found that native German speakers depended on morphological and semantic cues in English, cues which English monolinguals typically do not use. One reason monolingual English speakers may not depend heavily on these cues is that they are often unavailable, or when they are present, they are unreliable as cues to sentence meaning. However, if an L2 subject is generally predisposed to attend to such cues (whether due to unconscious transfer from L1 or conscious rule use), he/she is likely to do so whenever L2 input must be processed, including in the on-line environment of the word monitoring task. In effect, by applying L1 cue weightings to L2 cues, the L2 speaker is paying attention to the wrong grammar; this is a distinct disadvantage when rapid, efficient integration of semantic and syntactic information in L2 is required.

One important question that remains, however, is why monolinguals under noise, who presumably keep the same cue weights, resemble bilinguals in L2? The language processing mechanism is characterized by the Competition Model as depending implicitly on the distributional features within a language. The findings from a number of studies that L2 speakers gradually shift reliance from L1-appropriate cue settings to L2-appropriate settings demonstrate that another feature of the system is adaptability. It may be that, under less than optimal processing conditions, certain constraints are relaxed and others imposed when the cost-benefit ratio among available processing cues changes. Since processing conditions vary in everyday language, the processor must possess considerable flexibility in some form; one way this may be manifested is in the ability to realign cue weights according to current processing needs. This provides at least one alternative explanation for the similar patterns observed in bilinguals and normals-under-stress on the word monitoring task: If cue weights shift under noise conditions, integration of semantic and syntactic information may suffer in monolinguals much in the same way as in bilinguals.

Yet a third possibility is suggested by a "cohort" (some would argue successor) of the Cohort Model, namely the Trace Model (McClelland & Elman, 1986). The Trace Model postulates a distinctly non-modular processor that does not assume a moment of bottom-up priority, as does the Cohort Model. In Trace the timing of parallel upward and downward flow of information between the form, word, and meaning levels of the processor is critical. Integration could be hampered under noise conditions because the timing of the interaction between different levels in the processor would be affected. This account could be distinguished from a modular view, in which different levels are not permitted to communicate as they are in the Trace Model, in experiments in which the amount of contextual support--i.e., biasing lead-in context--is varied under noise. The Trace Model would predict that the heavier meaning component would alter the timing of form-word-meaning interactions, and hence improve on-line integration, while a modular view would not allow meaning to play a role in resolving structure or vice-versa.

Conclusion

The on-line processing results from monolingual English speakers and from native German speakers in German indicate that structural information can be independently utilized to aid in word recognition. When both semantic and syntactic features are present, responses are faster yet, reflecting the rapid integration of these two global linguistic information sources. The performance of native German speakers in English as L2 showed that they benefited from structural information in their second language in both semantically intact and anomalous sentences. However, non-native speakers gained no additional facilitation from the availability of meaning in normal sentences, indicating a lack of integration.

The findings from monolinguals who performed the word monitoring task under noise conditions suggest that a global reduction in processing capacity can selectively affect some aspects of on-line processing. In the current study, it was not syntactic information per se which was put "at risk" by the noise manipulation. Rather, the lack of facilitation in Normal sentences relative to Syntactic sentences was due to an induced failure to integrate. The similar patterns of performance observed in the L1-under-noise group and the L2 speakers do not prove that the same mechanism is responsible. However, they do suggest that a complete understanding of the performance side of becoming fluent in a second language will have to include a consideration of general cognitive aspects of language use.

The study of bilingualism has long had an applied flavor which has made it somewhat suspect as a topic for "hard" research. This no doubt lies rooted to a large degree in a scientific culture that is itself unusually monolingual, "unusually" because monolingualism is not characteristic of most of the world's inhabitants. Virtually all extant models of language use have been developed in a monolingual context. Such models are clearly not sufficient to account for bilingual language use. Ultimately, any model of language processing should be able to account for both bilingual as well as monolingual language performance.

References

Bates, E., & MacWhinney, B. (1981). Second language acquisition from a functionalist perspective: Pragmatic, semantic and perceptual strategies. In H. Winitz (Ed.), *Annals of the New York Academy of Science Conference on Native and Foreign Language Acquisition*, Pp.190-214. New York: New York Academy of Sciences.

Bates, E., & MacWhinney, B. (1987). Competition, variation and language learning. In B. MacWhinney (Ed.), *Mechanisms of language acquisition*, Pp. 157-193. Hillsdale, NJ: Erlbaum.

Bates, E., & MacWhinney, B. (1989). Functionalism and the Competition Model. In B. MacWhinney and E. Bates (Eds.) *The crosslinguistic study of sentence processing*. New York: Cambridge University Press.

Broadbent, D. E. (1982). Task combination and selective intake of information. *Acta Psychologica, 50*, 253-290.

Fodor, J. (1983). *The modularity of mind*. Cambridge, MA: MIT Press.

Forster, K. I. (1981). Priming and the effects of sentence and lexical contexts on naming time: Evidence for autonomous lexical processing. *Quarterly Journal of Experimental Psychology, 33*, 465-496.

Gass, S. (1986). An interactionist approach to L2 sentence interpretation. *Studies in Second Language Acquisition, 8*(1), 19-37.

Gass, S. (1989). How do learners resolve linguistic conflicts? In S. Gass and J. Schachter (Eds.), *Linguistic perspectives on second language acquisition*. New York: Cambridge University Press.

Harrington, M. (1987). Processing transfer: Language-specific processing strategies as a source of interlanguage variation. *Applied Psycholinguistics, 8*, 351-378.

Kilborn, K. (1989). Sentence processing in a second language: The timing of tranfer. *Language and Speech, 32*(1), 1-23.

Kilborn, K. (in press). Selective impairment of grammatical morphology due to induced stress in normal listeners: Implications for aphasia. *Brain and Language*.

Kilborn, K., & Cooreman, A. (1987). Sentence interpretation strategies in Dutch-English bilinguals. *Applied Psycholinguistics*, 8, 415-431.

Kilborn, K., & Ito, T. (1989). Sentence processing strategies in adult bilinguals: Mechanisms of second language acquisition. In B. MacWhinney and E. Bates (Eds.) *The crosslinguistic study of sentence processing*. New York: Cambridge University Press.

MacWhinney, B. (1987). Applying the Competition Model to bilingualism. *Applied Psycholinguistics*, 8, 315-326.

Marslen-Wilson, W. D. (1987). Functional parallelism in spoken word-recognition. *Cognition*, 25, 71-102.

Marslen-Wilson, W. D., & Tyler, L. K. (1980). The temporal structure of spoken language understanding. *Cognition*, 8, 1-71.

McClelland, J. L., & Elman, J. L. (1986). Interactive processes in speech perception: The Trace Model. In D. E. Rumelhart and J. L. McClelland (Eds.), *Parallel distributed processing*. Cambridge: MIT Press.

McDonald, J. (1984). The mapping of semantic and syntactic processing by first and second language learners of English, Dutch, and German. Doctoral dissertation, Carnegie-Mellon University.

Norman, D. A., & Bobrow, D. G. (1975). On data-limited and resource-limited processes. *Cognitive Psychology*, 7, 44-64.

Odlin, T. (1989). *Language transfer: Crosslinguistic influence in language learning*. Cambridge: Cambridge University Press.

Posner, M. I., & Boies, S. J. (1971). Components of attention. *Psychological Review*, 78, 391-408.

Shallice, T. (1988). *From neuropsychology to mental structure*. New York: Cambridge University Press.

Seidenberg, M. (1985). Constraining models of word recognition. *Cognition*, 20, 169-190.

Wulfeck, B., Bates, E., Juarez, L., & Kilborn, K. (1986). Sentence interpretation strategies in healthy and aphasic bilingual adults. In J. Vaid (Ed.), *Language processing in bilinguals: Psycholinguistic and neuropsychological perspectives*. Hillsdale, NJ: Lawrence Erlbaum.

Zwitserlood, P. (1989). The locus of the effects of sentential-semantic context in spoken-word processing. *Cognition*, 32, 25-64.

Cognitive Processing in Bilinguals – R.J. Harris (Editor)
© *1992 Elsevier Science Publishers B.V. All rights reserved.*

Non-native Features of Near-native Speakers:
On the Ultimate Attainment of Childhood L2 Learners

Kenneth Hyltenstam
Stockholm University

Abstract

Oral and written second language data from two groups of adolescent bilingual speakers (L1 Finnish/L2 Swedish, L1 Spanish/L2 Swedish respectively) were analyzed and compared to equivalent data from a group of matched monolingual speakers of Swedish. Each group comprised 12 subjects, all of whom were students at upper secondary school level. The bilingual speakers were judged by their teachers to speak Swedish without any noticeable foreign accent in everyday oral conversation. They had all started their second language acquisition before puberty, some at pre-school age (< 6) and some at school-age (> 7). The bilingual and monolingual speakers had earlier been shown not to differ significantly on measures designed to tap language proficiency in cognitively demanding linguistic tasks (Hyltenstam & Stroud, in preparation). On measures of lexical/grammatical accuracy and appropriateness, however, the topic of the present analysis, there were clear differences between bilingual and monolingual speakers of Swedish. The results in the present paper are presented against the background of the notions of completeness and fossilization. The issue of competence vs. control is also addressed. Furthermore, the relationship between ultimate attainment and age of onset of second language acquisition is treated in some detail.

On Ultimate Attainment

Although the last decade's research on second language acquisition has pointed to many parallels between first and second language acquisition, notably in the area of structural development, there are certainly also differences between the two acquisitional types. The most obvious difference is that second language acquisition often--presumably in the majority of cases--leads to a state of ultimate attainment which is unlike that of native speakers of the target language. This can be seen most clearly when the ultimate attainment of **adult** second language learners is compared with that of first language learners. Recently, however, the question has been raised whether **childhood** second language acquisition may not also lead to a different state of ultimate attainment.

To be sure, there is a continuum of nativeness in the outcomes of second language acquisition. This applies to both adults and children. We know from informal observation, however, that the distribution of degree of nativeness is different among child and adult second language learners. A reasonable hypothesis about this distribution is illustrated in Figure 1.

FAR FROM   CLOSE TO
NATIVE   NATIVE

children:

    _ _ _ _ _ _ _ _ _ _ _ _ _____

adults:

    _____ _ _ _ _ _ _ _

Figure 1: Hypothesized distribution of ultimate attainments of child and adult second language learners.

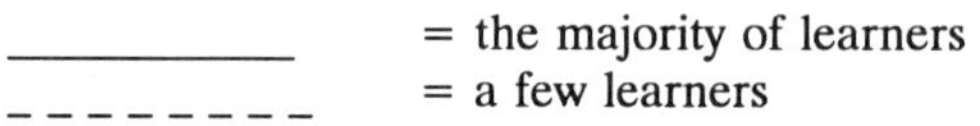

    _____   = the majority of learners
    _ _ _ _ _ _ _ _   = a few learners

The individual variation in each group may have a number of social, psychological or cognitive causes (see Schumann, 1978, for an inventory). Interesting neuropsychologial issues pertaining to some of the individual variation are discussed in Novoa, Obler & Fein (1988) and, particularly for child learners, in Humes-Bartlo (1989). The topic of individual variation will not, however, be dealt with further in this article.

Among the specific features claimed to characterize the ultimate attainment of second language learning, only three will be discussed here, namely **lack of completeness** (Schachter, 1988), **fossilization** (Schachter, 1988; Selinker, 1972; Yorio, 1985), and overloaded language processing resources resulting in momentary **control failures** (Dornic, 1978). Other characteristic features comprise lack of clear (Schachter, Tyson & Diffley, 1976) or uniform (Coppieters, 1987) grammatical intuitions and specific receptive difficulties with disturbed or distorted speech signals (Bergman, 1980).

Lack of Completeness

One might claim with Schachter (1988, p. 225) that "completeness is clearly not a property of the grammar of most adult second language learners, and may not be a property of the grammar of any adult second language learner." Schachter, who specifically discusses adult learners, points to the notion of **completeness** as being one of the main features distinguishing native and non-native language proficiency. This notion is applied to capture a "state of subconsciously knowing the rules that form the syntactic, phonological, and semantic patterns of the language" perfectly, i.e. to a degree where the speaker is indistinguishable from native speakers of the language. This means that native speakers have a complete mastery of the rules of their language, even though some may have "greater verbal facility" than others. Adult second language learners generally do not reach this stage of complete mastery.

Fossilization

A related but different phenomenon, which Schachter (1988) also refers to as a distinguishing feature, is that of **fossilization**. Using the term in the sense, in which it was introduced by Selinker (1972), i.e. "the regular reappearance or re-emergence in IL [interlanguage] productive performance of linguistic structures which were thought to be eradicated", Schachter (1988, pp. 238ff.) notes that fossilization can be observed in the ultimate attainment of adult second language learners, but not in that of first language learners. The notion of fossilization is itself, however, a tricky one in many ways. As mentioned by Yorio (1985), for example, a more common sense of the term than the one Selinker originally defined, associates fossilization with **permanent errors** (Yorio, 1985, p. 14). Even though one might intuitively feel that fossilization in this sense does exist, the notion poses problems as a scientific tool, as there seems to be no methodology available that can be used to verify or falsify the permanence of a linguistic structure in a speaker.

Control Failure

The phenomenon which Selinker (1972) called fossilization, "the re-emergence of structures that were thought to be eradicated", might be labelled **control failures** by other researchers. Yorio (1985, p. 9) notes that "there are several cases where the same expression or pattern is used correctly in one place and incorrectly in another" and that the learner's "control of the grammar fails him", even though he may have mastered the relevant structure in principle. This fact may be interpreted within a model of language processing that recognizes that the use of a second language, even at the stage of ultimate attainment, may consume more processing capacity due to the fact that more controlled processing is required than in the case of first language processing (McLaughlin, 1980). This would explain why language processing in second language speakers is more sensitive to various kinds of stress, resulting in a larger frequency of slips or other error types (Dornic, 1978).

Competence vs. Control

Relating the issues of **lack of completeness** and **fossilization** to the distinction of **competence/performance** or **competence/control**, the following emerges: Lack of completeness is a phenomenon that characterizes the competence of a second language learner. The learner has not acquired the actual aspects of the second language and may operate with "primitive versions of several subsystems ... and sometimes without certain subsystems entirely" (Schachter, 1988, p. 224). The second sense of fossilization in which the notion is associated with permanent errors must also be seen as a competence phenomenon. The learner has permanently incorporated erroneous structures in his second language system. If we take fossilization in its original sense, that of re-emerging errors, it is clearly a feature of performance, i.e. the result of control problems. As noted by Selinker (1972), fossilization manifests itself "when the learner's attention is focused upon new and difficult intellectual subject matter or when he is in a state of or other excitement, and strangely enough, sometimes when he is in a state of extreme relaxation".

Child Second Language Learners

So far, we have focused on the distinction between adult second language acquisition and first language acquisition. The assumption behind many studies that address the question of ultimate attainment is that second language acquisition in childhood is parallel to first language acquisition with respect to ultimate attainment. The general view up until the late 1970s was that an age of onset (AO) of second language acquisition below puberty would lead to a native-like ultimate attainment. This assumption has been questioned during the last decade, on the basis of both research results and practical observations. Reviewing the literature, Long (1990) claims that the ultimate attainment of second language acquisition can be distinguished from that of first language acquisition even when AO is considerably below puberty: ".. starting after age 6 appears to make it impossible for many learners (and after age 12 for the remainder) to achieve native-like competence in phonology; starting later than the early teens, more precisely after age 15, seems to create the same problems in morphology and syntax. Preliminary results suggest that similar generalizations will eventually be found to hold for lexis and collocation, and for certain discourse and pragmatic abilities" (p. 274). The explanation Long advocates for this is the existence of a neuropsychologically determined period in early childhood, when the child is sensitive to language acquisition, i.e. there are **maturational constraints** that determine when the human being is ready to acquire the various aspects of language. If language is not acquired during the sensitive periods, the learner will have to utilize strategies different to those employed by first language learners.

Present Study

Against the background presented here, the following questions were addressed in this investigation:

1. Are there measurable structural differences in ultimate attainment resulting from first and second language acquisition, even when the second language has been acquired in childhood and when the second language learner is perceived as native-like in the target language?

2. What is the role of age of onset in determining the degree of nativeness in the second language learner's ultimate attainment?

3. Can any potential differences be interpreted as competence or control based, i.e. how do the notions of lack of completeness, fossilization and control failures apply to such differences?

Method

<u>Subjects</u>

In comparing the characteristics of the ultimate attainment of second language acquisition in childhood, the methodology chosen here was to select highly proficient second language speakers, or, indeed, second language speakers who could be taken for natives, and to analyze the differences between this group and a group of matched native speakers. Thus, a total of 24 adolescent bilinguals (17-18 years of age), who were second language speakers of Swedish and who had started their SL learning before puberty (in one case during puberty), were chosen for this investigation. Half of these bilingual subjects were first language speakers of Finnish; the other half had Spanish as their first language. The monolingual group comprised 12 native speakers of Swedish. The three groups will be referred to as Fi, Sp and Sw respectively below.

Two criteria were used for selection of the bilingual subjects: First, they were to sound like native speakers of Swedish in everyday, oral interactional language use, i.e. they should not be immediately identifiable as non-native speakers in their manifestation of phonology, grammar and/or lexicon. Second, they were to be active bilinguals, i.e. both their languages, Swedish and Finnish or Swedish and Spanish respectively, were to be used on a regular basis.

Average grades and tracks at school and parental SES were used as matching factors. As regards grades, students representing the whole continuum from a high of 5 to a low of 2 were included in each of the three groups. (Students with an <u>average</u> 1, which is the lowest grade, do not exist at this level.) The students' grades in the Swedish language were not used as a matching factor; interestingly, however, the three groups turned out to differ in this respect: The Finnish group had an average of 3.7, the Spanish 3.1, and the monolingual Swedish group 2.8! Parental SES, which was graded from 1 to 3, was based solely on occupation.

Furthermore, the bilingual subjects were chosen so as to represent different AO for their second language, even though the two groups could not be matched on this factor for practical reasons: 16 had an AO at or below age 6 (the early group), while 8 had started to acquire Swedish at or above age 7 (the late group). In the Finnish group only one subject was a late starter, while in the Spanish group this was the case for 7 subjects. Parenthetically, this fact is a reflection of the different immigration histories in Sweden of the two ethnic groups: the peak in immigration from Finland occurred in the 1960s and early 1970s, while immigration from Latin America has been large throughout the 1970s and 1980s.

The teachers of the students assisted in the selection of subjects according to our criteria. The teachers also provided some of the background information about the subjects (in particular information about grades). Additional background information was collected through a written questionnaire administered to the students.

Table 1 gives a summary of the background characteristics of the three groups of subjects.

Table 1: Background factors for bilingual and monolingual subjects.

	Bilinguals		Monolinguals
	Fi (n=12)	Sp (n=12)	Sw (n=12)
SES	2.1	2.0	2.1
average grades	3.1	3.3	3.3
Swedish grades	3.7	3.1	2.7
AO < 6	n=11	n=5	
AO > 7	n=1	n=7	

Fi = Finnish group
Sp = Spanish group
Sw = Swedish group
SES = socio-economic status
AO = age of second language acquisition onset

Data and Procedure

The subjects were administered both oral and written tasks. Swedish data were elicited from all subjects. Although the focus in this investigation was on the bilingual subjects' second language, Swedish, oral Finnish and Spanish data, parallel to the Swedish data, were also elicited. The oral tasks in each language comprised retellings of four prepared texts, two of which the subjects heard recorded on tape and two of which they read. Different texts were used for Swedish and for Finnish/Spanish, but efforts were made to make them parallel in length and construction, as well as in general degree of difficulty.

Two of the texts (1 oral and 1 written) were structurally and mnemotechnically simple - they were fables - but contained referential difficulties. The other two were rich in content, long and more loosely structured. The degree of difficulty of the task was also kept high by the fact that the subjects could listen to or read each text once only.[1] The retellings were done to a native speaker of each language, who gave positive feedback but provided no comments as to form or content. The retellings were recorded on audiotape.   In most cases, data from the bilingual subjects were collected in both languages on the same day. Approximately half of the subjects performed the task in Swedish first, while the other half completed the Finnish or Spanish task first.

The written task consisted of composition writing about a section of Charlie Chaplin's silent film **Modern Times,** which had been shown to the subjects beforehand. The subjects were asked to describe and comment upon what they had seen. There was no time limit for the completion of this task, but it was made clear that the task could generally be finished in one and a half hours or less.

Analysis

The oral data were transcribed in normal orthography. Both the oral and written data were then subjected to several different analyses (see Hyltenstam & Stroud, in preparation). Relevant to the discussion in the present paper, an analysis of lexical and grammatical errors was undertaken. In this analysis, all types of "deviations" from the native norm were identified by the present investigator, i.e. both mere slips or other performance errors and errors that presumably mirror lack of competence in a certain area were noted. This was motivated by the intention to tap not just competence failures, but also error types that could be the result of control problems. Furthermore, in many cases it was impossible to find distinguishing criteria for the two categories.

Some of the errors observed could be given a straightforward transfer interpretation, while others could be seen as overgeneralizations or other simplifications. In the present analysis, however, an interpretation of the causes of the errors along these lines is of little interest and will not be discussed further.

Results

Quantification of the Data

The results will be presented at the group level rather than for individuals. Individual patterns will be commented upon whenever appropriate. In order to make the data from the three groups of subjects comparable, the amount of data from each group was measured by calculating the number of words. The number of words produced in the written and oral data respectively by the three groups is shown in Table 2.

Table 2: Amount of data measured on number of words produced

	Written data	Oral data
Finnish	5037	7168
Spanish	5157	7137
Swedish	4346	7887

As can be seen, the amount of data from the two bilingual groups is very similar, while the Swedish group produced fewer words than the other groups in the writing task and more in the oral tasks. Due to internal variability, however, these differences between any of the pairs are non-significant (t-test).

Table 3 displays the number of lexical and grammatical errors per 100 running words that were found in the data from each group.

Table 3: Number of errors per 100 running words

	Written data		Oral data	
	Lex	Gram	Lex	Gram
Finnish	0.8	0.6	0.4	0.3
Spanish	1.3	0.9	0.4	1.0
Swedish	0.4	0.4	0.2	0.1

Although the frequency of errors is very low in all groups, the bilingual groups produce from twice as many (the Finnish group) to approximately three times as many (the Spanish group) errors as the Swedish group. The difference between each of the bilingual groups and the monolingual group is statistically significant (Finnish-Swedish: t = 2.28, p<.025; Spanish- Swedish: t = 2.32, p<.025), while the difference between the two bilingual groups is non-significant (t = 1.26). This difference between bilinguals and monolinguals on aspects of linguistic form is the more remarkable, if one considers that the bilingual subjects performed at the same level as the monolinguals on linguistic aspects of decontextualized language use (varied and specific lexicon, degree of syntactic complexity and variation; see Hyltenstam & Stroud, in preparation).

There was considerable variation between subjects within the groups with respect to how many errors they produced. The heterogeneity is, as one might suspect, larger within the bilingual groups than in the monolingual group. The distribution of errors among subjects is shown in Table 4. As Table 4 shows, only single subjects have more than 5 errors in any error category, and none of the monolingual subjects are found here.

We have already mentioned that the number of errors is extremely low both in the bilingual and in the monolingual subjects. Had this not been the case, the bilinguals would, of course, not have been considered native-like. In order to illustrate how few errors are actually made, one might look at the distribution of grammatical errors in different categories. This is displayed in Table 5.

Table 4: Number of subjects producing errors in given intervals

Number of errors	Finnish				Spanish				Swedish			
	Written		Oral		Written		Oral		Written		Oral	
	Lex	Gram	Lex	Gram	Lex	Gram	Lex	Gram	Lex	Gram	Lex	Gram
0	3	3	3	3	0	3	1	2	6	6	1	6
1-5	6	8	8	8	8	7	10	5	6	6	11	6
6-10	2	0	1	1	3	1	1	3	0	0	0	0
> 10	1	0	0	0	1	1	0	2	0	0	0	0

As can be seen from Table 5, the highest frequency of errors falls within the category of NP. In the written data, there were in total 1582 NPs in the Finnish group, 11 of which contained an error. In the Spanish group the figures were 1604 NPs, 23 of which were erroneous, and in the Swedish group 1656 NPs were produced with 6 errors.

Table 5: Distribution of grammatical errors in various categories in written (W) and oral (O) data

		NP	V	Pron	Advb	W-ord	Del	Other	Total
Finnish	W	11	4	2	1	4	3	5	30
	O	11	3	4	0	2	3	1	24
Spanish	W	23	4	5	5	3	4	4	48
	O	46	6	3	0	5	9	3	72
Swedish	W	6	0	2	2	0	2	5	17
	O	5	0	0	0	0	3	3	11

Looking now at the distribution of errors in relation to AO, we get the result displayed in Figure 2.

Total number of errors

Figure 2: Distribution of errors among 24 second language learners of Swedish with AO < age 6 (#) and > age 7 (*), respectively, compared to first language learners (o).

Although the number of subjects is very small, there is an interesting and suggestive pattern in Figure 2. Between the first language learners and the late second language learners (with AO > 7) there is a complementary distribution. No one in the first language learner group has more than ten errors, while no one in the late second language learner group has less than 13 errors. The early second language learner group (with AO < 6) overlaps with both the other groups. Some learners have a low error frequency in the range of what is found among the first language learners; others produce as many errors as the late second language learners.

Qualitative Description of the Data

If we look at the quality of the errors, there are several points to be made (see Hyltenstam, 1988a and 1988b, for a more extensive discussion). The lexical errors involve single lexical units and lexical phrases in like proportions and comprise both formal and semantic aspects of the unit. A lexical phrase is a cover term for idioms, other set phrases, and word constellations that are determined by language specific sub-categorization rules and selection restrictions. What is particularly salient among the bilingual groups are the many examples of forms that are **close approximations** to the target form (cf. the notion of **malapropism**, Clark & Clark, 1977, pp. 287ff.) Some examples of this are (1) (from a Spanish subject's written data), (2) (Finnish subject, written data), and (3) (Spanish subject, written data).

(1)   majskorv (= majskolv)
      'corn-sausage (= corn-cob)'

(2)   den fungerar nog inte på längden
            (= i längden)
      'it probably will not work lengthwise'
                  '(= in the long run)'

(3) <u>mellan</u> chefen ser det
     (= medan)
     '<u>between</u> the boss sees it'
     '(= while)'

As seen in (3) these approximations sometimes involve basic vocabulary. In many cases the erroneous forms produced represent existing, sometimes quite frequent, lexical items.

Approximations of this kind also occur among the monolingual speakers. The difference is, firstly, that they are much less frequent in this group - we found 59 in the Finnish group, 70 in the Spanish group as against 21 in the Swedish group - and, secondly, that they never involve frequent everyday words.

Another type of lexical error involves a **contamination,** i.e. a lexical form where elements from two or more target forms have been combined. Example (4) from a Finnish subject (oral data) exemplifies this type.

(4) man <u>beräknar med</u> att ...
          (=räknar med, beräknar)
     'one <u>reckons on</u> that ...'
        '(= reckons, counts on (= estimates))'

What is interesting is that this type of lexical error does not distinguish the groups in the same way that the approximations did. The Finnish group had 12, the Spanish 12, and the Swedish group 14 such contaminations. It should be added here, that in some cases it is difficult to make a clear distinction between the categories of approximation and contamination. Without doubt, however, the actual proportions between the categories and their distribution in the bilingual and monolingual groups respectively are mirrored in the figures given above.

In the realm of grammar, the bilingual subjects produced error types typically found in much less advanced second language speakers, for example gender agreement errors in the indefinite and definite articles as in (5),

(5) <u>den</u> löpande bandet
     (= det)
     'the assembly line'

article deletion as in (6),

(6)   med _ stor brädlast
      (= en)
      'with _ big cargo of timber'
      '(= a)'

errors in choice of reflexive vs. non-reflexive possessive pronoun as in (7),

(7)   ... mat som sina fruar kanske lagat till
      (= deras)
      '... food which their /REFLEXIVE/ wives perhaps have made'
      '(= their /NON-REFLEXIVE/)'

and errors of word order involving placement of sentence adverbials as in (8)

(8)   han troligen blir bortförd
      (= blir troligen)
      'he gets probably taken away'

or violating the verb second constraint in Swedish main clauses as in (9).

(9)   senare på eftermiddagen han som blev försökskanin började ...
      (=började han som blev försökskanin ...)
      'later in the afternoon he who became a guinea-pig started ...'

Some of these types, even if they can be considered typical second language errors, are also found among the monolingual Swedish subjects. In (10), for example, we find an erroneous choice of reflexive possessive pronoun.

(10) Charlie Chaplin och sina kamrater stämplar in
      (=hans)
      'Charlie Chaplin and his /REFLEXIVE/ companions clock in'
      (= his /NON-REFLEXIVE/)

Example (10) is interesting, since it may mirror the possibility that the distinction between the reflexive and non-reflexive possessive pronoun is not as clear-cut in "unedited" Swedish as grammatical descriptions of the language sometimes indicate.

As seen in Table 5 above, the grammatical errors in the Swedish group were very few. As in the bilingual groups, most errors concern the NP. The extremely low frequency of errors in the oral mode is a salient fact. Indeed, most grammatical errors in the monolingual group can be interpreted as clear slips or a result of the students' not being able to handle the language without grammatical deviances in the literate mode.

Discussion

The exploratory nature of this research, and the small number of subjects studied make definite answers to the questions raised above impossible. We are, however, in a position to propose a number of more specific hypotheses, which would be testable in a larger study.

The first hypothesis we would like to sustain then, is that second language acquisition, not only among adults, but also when it takes place in childhood (see below) can, under certain conditions, result in an ultimate level of attainment which is different in terms of error frequency from that of first language speakers of the same language. In the present study the near-native second language speakers as a group were significantly different from the first language speakers with regard to the total amount of errors. Looking at the quality of the errors in the two groups, we see that lexical and grammatical structures are treated differently.

In the lexicon there is no single type of error which can be referred solely to bilingual or monolingual speakers. It is, rather, the frequency of certain error types that is the salient distinguishing characteristic. In particular, what we have called **approximations** in our typology are much more common among the bilingual subjects than among the monolingual ones. Furthermore, these approximations sometimes involve high frequency vocabulary, something that we do not find among the monolinguals.

Among the grammatical errors one can note a difference between the second language speakers and first language speakers both in terms of quantity and quality. In our data, there are a number of "second language errors" which do not occur at all in the monolingual group, for example word order errors and certain errors in verb forms (including those involving tense distinctions). One must, however, interpret these results with caution. Some types of errors not found in the present data from monolinguals might turn up in a larger data base.

The hypothesis suggested by Long (1990) and others of a correlation between age of onset of the second language and level of ultimate attainment is in part supported by our results. Recall our findings that the late (> 7) and the early (< 6) AO group differed substantially when compared with the monolingual group: All the individual subjects in the late AO group had an error frequency well above that exhibited by any single subject in the monolingual group, i.e. the subjects in the two groups were in complementary distribution. The early AO bilingual group, on the other hand, was more heterogeneous and overlapped both with the monolingual group and with the late AO group.

Our results generally corroborate the hypothesis proposed by Long and others on the relationship between AO and ultimate attainment. The age of 6 or 7 does seem to be an important period in distinguishing between near-native and native-like ultimate attainment. The results, in particular, support the idea that acquisition after the age of 7 does not only hinder native-like attainment of phonology, which the studies reviewed by Long (1990) clearly lent support to, but may also lead to non-completeness and to the promotion of fossilization in the realm of grammar and lexicon, something that Long on the basis of his material cautiously referred to the early teens.

Importantly, however, the relationship between AO and ultimate attainment is not a straightforward one, as suggested by our results from the early AO group. If AO is below age 6, individual differences among second language learners (in their social situation and psychological and cognitive profiles) may determine whether the ultimate attainment will be completely native-like or not. More specifically, it may be suggested that AO interacts with frequency and intensity of language use. This may apply to both first and second language acquisition. Although we do not, unfortunately, have information on our subjects' second language use patterns during the early years, there is some suggestive evidence on this point from their first language use. If we look at the first language data from our bilingual subjects, we find that an early AO may be a necessary although not sufficient requirement for native-like ultimate attainment. These data suggest that in the majority of cases it is the first language which is the weaker one, which is of course in line with what should be expected as an effect of the limited opportunities for using the minority language. One of the ways in which this manifests itself is that the subjects produce a higher frequency of errors in their first language[2] than in their second one. In other words, the fact that the first language has been acquired at the "right" age does not seem to have been sufficient to ensure a native-like ultimate attainment.

Now, are the errors observed in our data competence or control based? If interpreted as competence based, the errors reflect the fact that certain units, distinctions and subsystems have not been acquired, i.e. they would manifest a lack of completeness (Schachter, 1988). Alternatively, but still interpreted as competence related, they could be seen as permanent errors, i.e. as features of fossilization in Yorio's (1985) sense. If viewed as a reflection of control problems, the errors would best be interpreted as features of fossilization in the Selinker (1972) sense.

What evidence is there for one or the other interpretation? First, we might suggest as a hypothesis that second language speakers with a near-native level of ultimate attainment produce errors of both types, i.e. both competence based and control based errors, in higher proportions than native speakers. Trying to classify each error in one or the other category is of course very difficult, and in many cases impossible. However, it is clear that many, probably the majority, of the grammatical errors are not competence based, since the individual speakers who produce a certain type of error manifest the same structural phenomenon without any error in almost all other instances. The only exception to this in our data may be the bilingual Spanish/Swedish speaking boy who produced the reflexive form of the possessive pronoun in two instances where the context required a non-reflexive form (for one example, see (7) above). In the data from this subject, there were 6 further occurrences of possessive pronouns, all of which were found in reflexive contexts. This means that this particular speaker did not show any evidence of making the distinction between reflexive and non-reflexive forms whatsoever.[3] On the other hand, it would be premature to conclude from this small data base that he does not grasp the distinction at all.

In the realm of lexical errors, it seems more reasonable to believe that a fair number of the errors are indeed competence based, i.e. that the phonological form or the semantic content is represented in the speaker's mental lexicon in a way different from what is typically found in native speakers. Again, however, it is impossible to know for each individual case which interpretation is more correct. The following examples taken from another data source may illustrate the problem. The examples were produced by an adult 27-year-old second language near-native speaker of Swedish, who at the age of 7 was adopted from Germany by a Swedish family. He was communicating with a native Swede, who in some cases requested clarification on non-native vocabulary (NNS = near-native speaker; NS = native speaker):

(11) NNS: Då får man ju lägga sitt liv på spel.
          (= sätta)
         'Then you must lay your life at stake.
          (= put)

    NS: Vad sa du?
       'What did you say?'

    NNS: Sätta sitt liv på spel.
       'Put your life at stake.'

(12) NNS: Det är skönt att komma hem till ett varmt och boningsfullt hus.
         (non-existing word, possibly made up of ombonad, 'warm and cozy' and
         -full, '-ful')
         'It is nice to come home to a warm and cozyful house.
             (= cozy)

    NS: Vad sa du?
       'What did you say?

    NNS: Det är skönt att komma hem till ett varmt hus.

'It is nice to get home to a warm house.'

NS: Du sa visst nåt mer?
       'I think you said something else?'

NNS: Varmt och trevligt hus.
       'Warm and nice house.'

It is obvious from example (11) that a form which was produced erroneously may still be represented correctly in the mental lexicon of the speaker, but difficult to access. After additional lexical searching, the speaker finds the correct form in this case. In (12), on the other hand, the form ombonad, 'warm and cozy', is not retrieved. The speaker gives up and choses the more frequent word trevlig, 'nice', as an alternative.

These examples support the idea that the second language speaker exercises less control in manifesting his/her lexical knowledge. This may lead to what we observe in the present data, namely choice of either existing or non-existing forms that are approximations of the target form and to contaminations of two or more expressions. It is difficult and to some extent meaningless to draw a clear distinction between competence and control phenomena (see for example Bailey, 1973), since the representation of linguistic knowledge must involve both aspects. Features of linguistic structure, most clearly within the speakers competence are those the speaker most easily can control in language processing.

To conclude, it should be pointed out that while the results of the present investigation are interesting and suggestive, the study clearly has an exploratory character. Since the differences between near-native and native speakers are so small and generally difficult to detect in normal communication, they need to be investigated in large amounts of data from many subjects where quantification of structural types can make the differences more salient than we were able to in the present research.

Acknowledgments

I would like to thank Christopher Stroud for valuable comments on both content and style of an earlier draft of this paper. I am also indebted to Pirkko Bergman, Kari Kuusisto, Alli Risberg, and Lars Sjödin, who collected and transcribed the data.

Footnotes

1. The reason tasks were chosen that placed heavy cognitive demands on the subjects was that we also wanted to compare how bilingual and monolingual subjects reacted in a situation where decontextualized language use was necessary (see Hyltenstam & Stroud, in preparation; Hyltenstam, 1988b).

2. Figures for the error frequencies in the subjects' first languages are not stated here, because even though the errors have been calculated, the figures have so far not been checked. There are also certain problems with comparability between the languages involved which have to be solved. See Hyltenstam & Stroud (in preparation). The over-all statement made in the text ought not to be too far off the mark, however.

3. The choice of the reflexive form in Swedish may be determined by the greater formal similarity between Spanish su; sus, ('his/her; their') and Swedish reflexive sin/sitt; sina than between the Spanish pronouns and the Swedish non-reflexive ones hans/hennes; deras.

References

Bailey, C.-J. N. (1973). *Variation and linguistic theory.* Arlington, VA: Center for Applied Linguistics.

Bergman, M. (1980). *Aging and the perception of speech.* Baltimore: University Park Press.

Clark, H. H. & Clark, E. V. (1977). *Psychology and language. An introduction to psycholinguistics.* New York: Harcourt Brace Jovanovich.

Coppieters, R. (1987). Competence differences between native and fluent non-native speakers. *Language, 63,* 544-573.

Dornic, S. (1978). The bilingual's performance: Language dominance, stress, and individual differences. In D. Gerver & H.W. Sinaiko (Eds.) *Language, interpretation, and communication.* New York: Plenum Press.

Humes-Bartlo, M. (1989). Variation in children's ability to learn second languages. In K. Hyltenstam & L.K. Obler (Eds.) *Bilingualism across the lifespan: Aspects of acquisition, maturity, and loss.* Cambridge: Cambridge University Press.

Hyltenstam, K. (1988a). Lexical characteristics of near-native second-language learners of Swedish. *Journal of Multilingual and Multicultural Development*, 9, 67-84.

Hyltenstam, K. (1988b) Att tala svenska som en infödd - eller nästan. [Speaking Swedish like a native - or close to]. In K. Hyltenstam & I. Lindberg (Eds.) *Första symposiet om svenska som andraspråk. Volym I: Föredrag om språk, språkinlärning och interaktion*. Stockholm: Centrum för tvåspråkighetsforskning.

Hyltenstam, K. & Stroud, C. (in preparation) Svenskan hos tvåspråkiga gymnasieelever. [The Swedish of bilingual upper secondary school students]. Stockholm: Centrum för tvåspråkighetsforskning.

Long, M. H. (1990). Maturational constraints on language development. *Studies in Second Language Acquisition*, 12, 251-285.

McLaughlin, B. (1980). Theory and research in second-language learning: An emerging paradigm. *Language Learning*, 30, 331-350.

Novoa, L., Obler, L. K. & Fein, D. (1988). A neuropsychological approach to talented second language acquisition. A case study. In L.K. Obler & D.A. Fein (Eds.) *The exceptional brain*. New York: Guilford.

Schachter, J. (1988). Second language acquisition and its relation to universal grammar. *Applied Linguistics*, 9, 219-235.

Schachter, J., Tyson, A., & Diffley, F. (1976). Learner intuitions of grammaticality. *Language Learning*, 26, 67-76.

Schumann, J. H. (1978). Social and psychological factors in second language acquisition. In J. C. Richards (Ed.) *Understanding second and foreign language learning. Issues and approaches*. Rowley, Mass.: Newbury House.

Selinker, L. (1972). Interlanguage. *IRAL*, 10, 209-231.

Yorio, C. A. (1985). Fossilization. Paper presented at the Applied Linguistics Winter Conference (New York, Jan. 19, 1985).

Part V:

LANGUAGE TRANSFER AND
CODE-SWITCHING IN BILINGUALS

Cognitive Processing in Bilinguals – R.J. Harris (Editor)

Transfer and Competition in Second Language Learning

Brian MacWhinney

Carnegie Mellon University

Abstract

Recent work has explored the application of the Competition Model (MacWhinney & Bates, 1989) to the study of second language acquisition. In making this extension, it is important to distinguish between transfer from L1 and direct learning of L2. Both processes can be analyzed in terms of the constructs of cue reliability, cue cost, and form-function mappings. The model predicts certain typical varieties of transfer during the process of phonological, syntactic, and lexical learning. In the attempt to maximize the transfer of L1 structures the learner uses a variety of complex learning strategies. In areas where transfer is poorly supported, the learner acquires L2 structures directly. Cue reliability and cue cost estimates can also be used to characterize the direct acquisition of L2 structures.

Psycholinguists come in two types. There are those who study adults and those who study children. The psycholinguists who study children care about "acquisition" and the psycholinguists who study adults care about "processing." Until recently, these two groups have acted much as separate "modules." This separation is most unfortunate, since we know that acquisition influences processing and that processing influences acquisition. Fortunately, the study of second language acquistion provides a way to dissolve the barriers between these modules. Adult second language learners and adult bilinguals make excellent experimental subjects. Unlike children (Friederici, 1983; Tyler & Marslen-Wilson, 1981), adults can read printed words on a computer screen and make quick and well-controlled judgments in reaction time experiments. Because it is relatively easy to acquire data on language processing in adult second language learners and bilinguals, we can use this population to broaden our understanding of the changes in language processing that occur during language acquisition (Kilborn, 1989).

The study of adult second language learning also allows us to correct another limitation in the scope of adult psycholinguistics. Virtually all of the current edifice of adult psycholinguistics is built upon data derived from the study of language processing in English-speaking college freshmen. This anglocentric bias is bound to lead to a misleading view of the language-making capacity. Child language researchers have already begun to escape from this bias. The ground-breaking crosslinguistic developmental research of Slobin (1985) and his colleagues has vastly expanded our understanding of what it means to acquire a human language.

Adult psycholinguistics has only recently begun to escape from its anglocentric straight-jacket. Within the context of a model of sentence processing called the Competition Model, MacWhinney and Bates (1989) have opened the doors of psycholinguistics to a wider array of crosslinguistic data, including adult sentence processing, language in aphasia, and second language learning. Although the Competition Model (Bates & MacWhinney, 1982) was not originally based on data from second language acquisition, its crosslinguistic developmental orientation seems to make it well-suited for use in this area too. At the same time, it is clear that data on the learning of foreign languages can play an important role in the testing and elaboration of the Competition Model.

Form-Function Mappings

The fundamental idea underlying the Competition Model is simple and rather traditional. The model takes as its starting point the Saussurean vision of the linguistic sign as a set of mappings between forms and functions. *Forms are the external phonological and word order patterns that are used in words and syntactic constructions.* *Functions* are the communicative intentions or meanings that underlie language usage. In the Competition Model, each lexical item or syntactic construction can be understood as a form-to-function mapping. Take the word "bat" as an example. The functions for this word involve the expression of the various semantic properties of the animal, along with its visual and auditory images. The form of the word is the set of phonological cues contained in the sound sequence /bAt/. On the syntactic level, a similar relation holds. Structures such as preverbal positioning or verb agreement marking are treated as forms. These forms are mapped to functions such as agency, topicality, perspective, first mover, causer, volitional agent, and so on.

In addition to the *correlations* between particular subsets of forms and subsets of functions, there are also correlations within the overall set of functions and within the overall set of forms. We can call these function-function correlations and form-form correlations. On the functional level, it is generally true that topics can also be animate, definite, given, and so on. These correlations are reflections of certain real correlations between properties of the world in which we live. Because the functions we choose to talk about are so highly correlated in real life, the forms we use to talk about these functions also become highly correlated. This makes it so that no single form expresses any single function and the relation between forms and functions is both fluid and robust. There are also important correlations on the level of forms. For example, words that take the article "the" also are capable of taking the plural suffix.

We speak of these various mappings as correlations because we know that all categories are imperfect and subject to category leakage (MacWhinney, 1989). For example, the correlation between preverbal positioning and agency in English breaks down in the passive and the imperative. Similarly, the correlation between plural marking and semantic plurality breaks down with words like "pants" or "faculty."

Cues and Cue-Validity

Our analysis so far has kept close to the basic Saussurean concept of a form-function mapping. To recast this thinking in terms of a processing model, we will have to adapt some of the terminology. Instead of forms, we can talk about the "cues" used by the listener to facilitate the activation of alternative functions or "competing construals." For example, the individual phonological segments in the word "bat" can each be viewed as cues to activation of the meaning underlying "bat." The cues in the first two segments would also activate words like "bad" and "bag" and so on. For a fuller discussion of the ways in which cue match can facilitate activation see MacWhinney and Anderson (1986). Note, however, that the equation of "cue" with "form" holds only for comprehension. When we switch to thinking about sentence production, we need to think of the underlying functions as cues, and the actual forms being selected as "competing forms." This use of the term "cues" allows us to draw parallels between processing and acquisition in comprehension and production. In both processes, the activation of certain cues as inputs is what leads to the final selection between competing outputs.

Most of the work on the Competition Model has focused on sentence comprehension. The interaction of cues such as preverbal positioning, animacy, case-marking, and subject-verb agreement has been modelled mathematically in the Competition Model using maximum likelihood techniques (McDonald & MacWhinney, 1989). The data modelled in these studies come from experiments with real subjects in many languages and at many age levels using sentences in which the various cues are placed into "competition" with each other in an orthogonalized ANOVA design. The maximum likelihood techniques make it possible to estimate the *cue strengths* of particular cues. For example, in our studies of sentence processing in English, Italian, German, French, and Hungarian, we have been able to estimate the relative strengths of preverbal positioning, subject-verb agreement, and animacy as cues to the function of "agency." We have found that, in English, the preverbal positioning cue is extremely strong and that the agreement and animacy cues are only of any importance at all when there is no preverbal noun, as in VNN sentences. In Italian, on the other hand, the agreement cue is far stronger than the word order cue. Although both English and Italian are described as SVO languages, the actual strengths of the basic cues to sentence interpretation in these two languages are radically different.

Perhaps the most important empirical claim of the Competition Model is that cue strength in the adult native speaker is directly proportional to *cue validity*. What is crucial about this claim is that our cue validity measures are taken from actual text counts based on spoken or written discourse, whereas our cue strength measures are derived from experiments. This way of understanding the relation between the learner and the environment avoids the circularities often found in mathematical modelling in psychology. The idea is that, during language learning, children come to appreciate the relative order of cues in their language and to tune their cognitive systems so that they correctly mirror the environment. At first, the child picks up cues on the basis of their *overall availability*. At this early period, English-speaking children are already paying more attention to word order than are their Italian counterparts. And Hungarian-learning children are making more use of case marking than are their German counterparts. Within a single language, if there are two ways to mark a given function, the child will first start to use the one that is more frequent. For example, in Hebrew, the child will first use the inflectional reflexive, because it is more common. Only later will the child pick up the periphrastic reflexive (Sokolov, 1989). In this early period, the child will also be strongly influenced by *cue detectability*, since it is difficult to pick up cues that are hard to perceive. For example, the Turkish child picks up accusative marking earlier than the Hungarian child (MacWhinney, Pléh, & Bates, 1985), largely because of the clearer phonological status of the Turkish accusative suffix.

As development proceeds, the learner adjusts cue strengths to be more and more in tune with the *reliability* of cues, rather than simply their overall availability. In particular, the learner wants to know which cue to bet on when there is a head-to-head conflict between cues. For example, the preverbal positioning cue is highly available and fairly reliable, but when it comes into direct conflict with the case-marking cue on personal pronouns, the case-marking cue always wins. In the end, it is this *conflict reliability* which determines the final strength value of the cue in the language. Often, a completely adult-like set of cue strengths will not be acquired until about age 12 (McDonald, 1989).

There are aspects of language for which the simple correlation between cue strength and cue validity tends to break down. These exceptions to the basic rule occur whenever a cue places a particular strain on the processing mechanism. For example, we have found that young Italian children take a long time learning to make use of the highly reliable cue of subject-verb agreement (Devescovi, D'Amico, Smith, Mimica, & Bates, 1990). The problem seems to be that the variable word order of Italian requires the listener to process long-distance dependencies between separate words. By way of contrast, the marking of case in Hungarian only requires the listener to detect the presence of an accusative marker placed directly on the noun. Another set of divergences from simple cue validity occurs in relative clause processing where the piling up of nouns without verbs in an SOV language like Hungarian (MacWhinney & Pléh, 1988) can lead to delays in processing. The Competition Model refers to these various processing factors as *cue costs*. We do not consider cue costs as noise factors to be swept under the theoretical rug. On the contrary, they provide us with important glimpses into those aspects of the language processor which determine language universals.

Transfer

The role of transfer in second language learning has been debated for decades. Empiricists have always emphasized the extent to which learners attempt to acquire L2 by generalization from L1. Intuitive accounts have focused on accents and culturally-specific learner styles as evidence of influences of L1 upon L2. The descriptivist-structuralist approach (Lado, 1957; 1971) looked at transfer as a way of supporting the usefulness of comparative analysis as a basis for language pedagogy. When research showed that many of the predictions of comparative analysis were only weakly supported, this also cast doubt on the role of transfer in language learning. In the early 1970s the established wisdom was that the predictions of contrastive analysis for second language learning were largely incorrect and that transfer played little role in second language learning. In hindsight, these failures to support contrastive analysis could just as well have been attributed to problems with the linguistic model and to limitations in the behaviorist framework, rather than to the process of transfer itself.

With the demise of behaviorism (Chomsky, 1959; Skinner, 1957) the theory of transfer was banished to the behaviorist dungeon. While it languished there, theorists treated L2 acquisition as a replay of the basic process of L1 acquisition (Dulay & Burt, 1974a; 1974b). However, this research program also ran into trouble (Huebner, 1983; Rosansky, 1976). Slowly, researchers began to realize that both transfer and direct acquisition of L2 had to figure as important components in an adequate account of second language learning (Dechert & Raupach, 1989; Gass & Selinker, 1983; Kellerman & Sharwood Smith, 1986; Odlin, 1989; Ringbom, 1987). But exactly how should this be done? The psychological theory of transfer has now been reformulated within the richer framework of problem-solving theory (Singley & Anderson, 1989) and analogical theory (Rumelhart & McClelland, 1986; Vosniadou & Ortony, 1989). However, these newer cognitive models have not yet been brought to bear on the problems of second language acquisition. In this section, I wish to explore some of the ways in which the Competition Model can be used to understand aspects of positive and negative transfer in the early stages of second language learning.

Phonology

How can we conceptualize transfer within the framework of the Competition Model? The easiest place to begin is with phonological transfer. Dickerson (1987), Flege (1987) and others have shown that a great deal of phonological learning within L2 relies upon the structures and units of L1. Within the Competition Model framework, we can view this transfer as involving the accretion of new lexical items based on an old set of phonological units. The crucial idea here is that the brain provides the language learner with neural substrate (Damasio, 1981) that tends to facilitate the "fast mapping" (Carey, 1978) of new lexical items. Lexical items can be viewed as largely arbitrary (Saussure, 1966) associations of phonological forms to semantic functions. However, the system for coordinating phonological units is much more tightly integrated and less easily changed. Because of this, new words are constructed by simply devising new associations between old semantic units and old phonological units.

MacWhinney (1990) proposed a Competition Model view of phonology based on a connectionist network. This network learns to auto-associate a set of auditory units to a set of articulatory units. Presumably, these associations are built up and solidified during the first two years of life. Of course, we know that not all articulatory patterns are learned with equal ease. Phonological processes (Stampe, 1973) force certain patterns to have a higher cue cost. However, as the system matures, the strength of the various cues comes to approximate their true validity in the language. When language learners begin acquiring vocabulary in L2, they simply treat these as additional words of L1 composed of sounds that match most closely to auditory and articulatory items already in their repertoires. Odlin (1989) reviews dozens of studies which illustrate transfer of this type in both segmental and supersegmental phonology. In some cases, this transfer is fairly successful and goes unnoticed. For example, the places of articulation of nasal consonants are often similar between languages and even stop consonants often have similarities. However, the exact amounts of voicing of stop consonants or the exact forms of articulation for vowels seldom transfer without producing some accent. Some of the negative transfer also affects audition, where Chinese speakers may confuse "rice" and "lice," because of the absence of the /r/-/l/ distinction in Chinese.

The Competition Model does not assume that all L2 phonological learning is based on transfer. There are two additional factors which determine the shape of the learner's system: cue costs and L2 generalizations (Gass & Selinker, 1983). Cue costs express language universal phonological processes such as devoicing, vowel harmony, and other neutralizations (Major, 1987). These processes can be expressed in terms of universal markedness theory. However, their real basis surely lies in the mechanisms of auditory and articulatory processing. In the early stages of L2 acquisition, L2 generalization plays only a minor role. However, as learning progresses, the L2 phonological auto-associative net begins to have a structure that is at least partially independent of the L1 net. As that network grows, we see the emergence of phonological overgeneralizations that match in part those exhibited by L1 learners.

How can we predict which of these three factors will be operative in a given stage of L2 phonological learning? The Competition Model prediction is that L2 learning will begin with massive transfer from L1 within the limitations set by cue costs or phonological processes. Here we expect some individual differences. Learners who have a richer array of auditory and articulatory patterns in L1 will be able to transfer somewhat more fine-grained patterns and show somewhat less negative transfer. These same speakers will also have succeeded more fully in overcoming cue cost limitations in L1. When they come to L2, they will also be able to overcome cue cost limitations. When L1 is close to L2, transfer will also be more clearly positive.

After a period of initial massive transfer from L1 to L2, we expect to see a long period in which the system tries to deal with the fact that its articulatory output does not correctly match the L2 target. Learning at this stage is promoted most strongly by correct registration of the phonology of the L2 target lexical items. If the target forms are passed through an L1 filter, the learner will never be able to detect a mismatch (MacWhinney, 1978) between one's own forms and the correct target forms. Without the detection of error, the L2 auto-associative network will not develop. Learners must be encouraged to perceive the mismatch between their output forms and the correct input forms. It would seem that the best way to bring this about would be through a process in which learners attempt to match their own productions to computer-controlled digitized speech. Such a procedure should be particularly helpful in acquiring intonational contrasts.

Lexical Items

During the initial stages, much of the work of second language learning involves lexical acquisition. As we noted above, the organization of language within the brain promotes the relatively easy acquisition of new mappings between sounds and meanings. However, these mappings typically reuse old phonological units and old semantic units. In terms of semantic representations, there is a fairly massive conceptual transfer from L1 to L2. Consider the learning of the Spanish word **mesa** by an English speaker. The speaker has already acquired a set of function-function correlations between the various meanings underlying the concept of "table." On the phonological level, the learner maps the sounds of **mesa** onto already existing English segmental units. The only new learning that has to occur is in the mapping between the new sound string and the old meaning set. In this case, the transfer of old units and correlations is essentially positive. Of course, the actual phonological units used to represent **mesa** will be English-based, but the learner is able to use this simple transfer process to express a meaning easily and with a minimum of new learning. For common concrete nouns like **table** and **salt**, the process of lexical learning may proceed with minimal error. However, abstract nouns, verbs, and adjectives may have subtle meanings that will have to be relearned in L2 (Ijaz, 1986).

Kroll and Stewart (1990) have shown that the transfer of old meanings to new lexical items in beginning L2 learners actually involves a mapping that goes through old L1 units. This makes sense when one realizes that, unlike the phonology, the meaning underlying a new word in L2 is not initially being restructured. Rather, the concept underlying **table** is taken as a whole and mapped to the new sound /mesa/. Of course, this leaves the learner with two phonological forms for "table." There is little danger that /mesa/ will intrude upon English. What the learner has establish is a set of associations between the new Spanish words that guarantees that they will be activated together when speaking Spanish as L2.

Automatization

So far, all of the strategies we have discussed involve ways of structuring the mapping between an L2 phonological string and an L1 conceptual or semantic representation. The mappings produced by these transfer strategies are not as direct as the corresponding native language mappings, because they use both L1 and L2 representations. Over time, learners will attempt to restructure their representations so that true L2 phonological forms are mapped directly onto true L2 semantic forms. Instead of accessing the word **mesa** through the English word **table** (Kroll & Stewart, 1990), the learner will access **mesa** directly. Increasing the speed of access involves processes which cognitive psychologists generally refer to as "automatization." However, in the case of L2 acquisition, one needs to differentiate two ways in which automatization can be achieved. These are "proceduralization" and "compilation" (MacWhinney & Anderson, 1986). Proceduralization leads to the smoother and faster L2 functioning without major reorganization. Compilation, on the other hand, attempts to restructure processing so that processing goes directly from meaning to sound within L2. In many learners, these two forces work against each other. If a particular mapping using L1 transfer to L2 becomes highly proceduralized or automated, it becomes difficult to restructure it. In such cases, learners can end up blocking the "recompilation" of their processing system into more native-like systems.

Syntax through Translation

    The basic lexical strategy we have been examining can also be applied to syntactic learning. Using a *one-to-one* lexical mapping strategy, we find learners producing sentences such as, "*Ich wurde möchte zu gehen in das Geschäft," which derives apparently by word-for-word conversion from the English sentence, "I would like to go into the store." Or, to take an example from an English speaker's early Spanish, we find, "Yo soy hablando," derived from English "I am speaking." The corresponding German learner form would be "*Ich bin sprechen."

    What happens when a simple type of transfer is blocked? When this occurs, the learner utilizes a secondary path of transfer to go around the barrier. For example, when confronted with the failure of one-to-one mapping, the learner can attempt a *many-to-one* mapping. For example, one can translate the German word "möchte" by the English phrase "would like to." At this point, his translation of "I would like to go into the store" would be "*Ich möchte gehen in das Geschäft." In general, we can view transfer not as a simple uniform process, but as a general approach to language learning in which the learner is exploring all possible *paths of transfer*. When a particular path of transfer is blocked, the learner explores another path. When all transfer paths are blocked, the learner either gives up or waits for new information. According to this account, the beginning learner always attempts to construct an L1-based interpretation of L2 structures.

    The reader may object that any reasonable approach to L2 learning will keep the learner from even attempting simple lexical translation schemes of the type discussed here. The whole point of functional language training is to avoid simple translation and to have the student thinking and speaking directly in L2 from the beginning. However, the analysis I am offerring is not in disagreement with this position. The Competition Model holds that these simple mappings can be corrected without requiring that the learner produce errors overtly. As MacWhinney (1978) and Berwick (1987) have noted, errors in syntactic processing can often be corrected on the basis of data derived from "failure to parse." If the comprehension system is unable to find a one-to-one map from German "möchte" to a single English lexical item, it can still attempt a many-to-one mapping. The learner simply realizes that the input form "möchte" maps onto the string "would like to." In general, learners will either discover such mappings for themselves or perhaps acquire them from the textbook. In this way, many of the most obvious transfer errors will never actually occur in production.

This is particularly true if the classroom emphasis is on listening to L2 forms and the learner is not required to produce forms which he or she does not control (Klein & Perdue, 1989).

The learner's lexical transfer strategies need not stop with one-to-one and many-to-one mappings. There are several additional strategies that can be used that still depend on a mapping from L2 to L1. These strategies are more abstract and less general than the simple strategies of one-to-one and many-to-one mapping. For that reason, we would expect that structures that require these elaborate remappings would be relatively more difficult to acquire. In *discontinuous mapping*, the learner picks up new lexical items that have discontinuous mappings onto L2 forms and vice versa. Here, again, it is the initial "failure to parse" that leads the learner to invoke the strategy. For example, the German word **keinen** can be mapped onto the English sequence "not .... a ..." This will allow the learner to formulate the English sentence "He has not seen a man" as the German sentence "Er hat keinen Mann gesehen." Yet another strategy involves the *analysis* of pieces of L2 words. Using this strategy, the learner can identify the Spanish conditional suffix /ri/ with the English word "would." Thus, the Spanish phrase "habría visto" can be analyzed in English as "have-would-I seen." At the same time, the learner can parse new strings such as "hablaría" or "comerían" always by pulling out the /ri/ from the surrounding material. This strategy is more analytic than a simple one-to-many mapping.

Cue-based Syntax

The various simple translation schemes discussed above can provide a beginning learner with a large initial vocabulary and some communicative abilities. Because the adult learner is already a competent member of one society, it is often possible to take these transfer-based abilities and achieve some level of communication. It is remarkable how much of L2 an adult learner can control without really dealing with L2 on its own terms. However, there are still higher levels on which the learner can transfer cues from L1. One of these higher levels involves the transfer of the overall weights of cues to syntactic roles in sentence comprehension.

Within the Competition Model (MacWhinney, 1987b), syntactic learning involves the formation and restructuring of the argument frames of particular lexical items, as well as the generalization of these frames across groups of lexical items. Some aspects of L1-to-L2 transfer involve the argument frames of particular lexical items. In general, when a new L2 word is learned, the complete argument frame of the L1 analog is transferred. In some cases, no error will result. However, for most closed class lexical items, there will be problems. For example, French and Spanish locative prepositions do not code directionality, whereas their English equivalents do. Direct translation of the English word **into** as French **en** will lead to errors such as the French sentence "*Je suis allé en le magasin" for "Je suis entré dans le magasin" on the basis of English "I went in the store." In French, the verb that expresses the motion must also express the nature of goal. The correction of these mismappings involves more than simply lexical learning. It requires that the learner to restructure argument frames (MacWhinney, 1987b) for each new closed class lexical item and for many new verbs. This *frame restructuring* requires the learner to make a clear distinction between the L1 analog and the L2 form, thereby exerting a pressure toward the separation of the two languages.

Other forms of syntactic learning involve general patterns across constituents. Within the Competition Model, these general patterns are viewed as emerging from networks that correlate the semantics of lexical items to particular argument frames. Not all patterns are fully predictable from simple semantic patterns. However, the connectionist networks used in the Competition Model can handle the "abduction" of form classes from semantic-syntactic correspondences. Just as the learner transfers individual lexical frames from L1 to L2, so the learner can also transfer general patterns. For example, the English learner of Spanish initially assumes that the adjective precedes the noun. However, this rule is immediately subjected to massive negative evidence, as soon as the learner begins to hear Spanish noun phrases. At first, the learner may attempt to handle this through a process of *shuffling* in which a constituent is moved from its normal position to another position in the sentence. This strategy is used when formulating "Ella es una niña bonita" on the basis of "She is a pretty girl." The shuffling strategy allows the learner to preserve the basic lexical transfer strategy. Shuffling can also reorder major constituents. Initially, the Spanish learner of English uses Spanish-based patterns to produce "*Come here all my friends" on the basis of Spanish "Vienen aquí todos mis amigos." However, the learner soon realizes that English requires the subject to precede the verb. These shuffling strategies are only crutches along the pathway toward real control of L2 syntactic patterns. Eventually, the learner is able to use a syntactic network in L2 to order constituents directly without reference to L1 patterns and without shuffling.

The learner also has to pick up patterns of *omission* and *agreement* marking through initial reference to L1 structures. For example, the English learner of Spanish may initially say "Yo tengo un libro" for "I have a book." This use of the personal pronoun "yo" is not an error, but it implies some pragmatic contrast. At first, the learner must overtly delete the subject pronoun. Over time, he drops his reliance on the omission strategy as a way of correcting L1 transfer errors and directly produces sentences with pronouns omitted.

Generalized Cues

So far we have treated syntactic cues as primarily lexically-based. However, because there are so many words in many of the important syntactic classes, it is usually easier to think of these cues as general across word types. For example, it is a quite general fact across the thousands of transitive verbs in English that the noun preceding the verb is the subject and the noun following the verb is the object. This is a general cue to sentence processing in English, but these same cues will not work for an SOV language like Turkish. However, when acquiring a new language, learners are often in a position where they have to rely on these old cues.

There are now eight Competition Model studies that investigate the transfer of general L1 sentence processing cues to L2. Beginning with a study of German-English and Italian-English bilinguals (Bates & MacWhinney, 1981), we have found repeatedly that L2 learners have what we have come to refer to as a "syntactic processing accent." This research is summarized in a special issue of the journal *Applied Psycholinguistics* in 1987 (Gass, 1987; Harrington, 1987; Kilborn & Cooreman, 1987; MacWhinney, 1987a; McDonald, 1987) and in Kilborn and Ito (1989). More recent studies (Kilborn, 1989; McDonald & Heilenman, 1989; Sasaki, 1991; Takehiko, Tahara, & Park, 1989) have extended and supported the earlier findings. To give an example of a typical finding, we observed that Germans listening to English NNV sequences assume that the first noun is the subject, whereas English monolinguals assume exactly the opposite. Similarly, Italians learning English pay attention to agreement cues and place little reliance on the preverbal positioning cue, whereas English monolinguals do exactly the opposite. This type of L1 to L2 transfer of cue strengths is exactly the pattern that would be predicted by the Competition Model.

McDonald and MacWhinney (1989) and McDonald and Heilenman (1989) have constructed mathematical models of the cue strength interactions in our experiments with bilinguals and L2 learners and found that the strength of cues at various points in learning are well-predicted by the various cue validity measures in the Competition Model. In general, the results to date have supported the Competition Model. There are two areas in which the simplest predictions of a model based only on transfer driven by cue validity have not been supported. Gass (1987) suggested that the semantic cue of animacy seems to have a certain universal prepotency in both L1 and L2 learning. Within the Competition Model framework presented earlier, we can think of the prepotency of the animacy cue as involving a particularly low cue cost. In particular, Gass found that English learners of Italian are quick to drop their strong dependency on the preverbal positioning cue of English and pick up the reliance on animacy as a cue to subject that we find in monolingual Italians. A variety of additional evidence suggests that animacy may have the kind of prepotency suggested by Gass, although further work will be needed to understand the exact nature and size of this effect.

Another challenge to the Competition Model in its simplest form is the finding by Kilborn and Ito (1989) that English learners of Japanese attempt to make rigid use of SOV order as a cue to sentence interpretation, much as they have made rigid use of SVO order in English. Indeed these English-speakers relied much more on SOV than native speakers of Japanese. Of course, the system of case-marking in Japanese has aspects that may be difficult for learners and this may have led to a tendency to rely most heavily on the simplest cue, even though its actual cue validity is comparatively lower. But the point is that English speakers seem to be particularly interested in trying to find some cue that will look maximally like the preverbal positioning cue they have come to know and love in their native language. In other words, they seem to be exploring a secondary *path of transfer* that looks for something close to their major L1 cue, since it is clear that the exact preverbal cue of L1 is not used in Japanese.

Functional Restructuring

So far, we have assumed that L2 acquisition involves an absolute minimum of functional restructuring. However, there is good reason to believe that, after the earliest stages, L2 learners are spending a great deal of time creating a new set of conceptual categories. Many of these new categories are lexical. If two words in L1 map onto a single word in L2, the basic transfer process is unimpeded. It is easy for a Spanish speaker to take the L2 English form **know** and map it onto the meanings underlying **saber** and **conocer** (Stockwell, Bowen, & Martin, 1965). What is difficult is for the L1 English speaker to acquire this new distinction when learning Spanish. In order to correctly control this distinction, the learner must restructure the concept underlying **know** into two new related structures.

Functional restructuring also occurs on the level of grammatical categories. A prime example of this type of restructuring might be the foreigner's attempts to pick up the category structure underlying the two major verbal conjugations of Hungarian. The intransitive conjugation is used not only when the verb is intransitive, but also when the direct object is modified by an indefinite article or by no article at all, when it is in the first or second person, when the head of the relative clause is the object within the relative clause, when the direct object is quantified by words like "each," "no," and so on. For example, the "intransitive" conjugation is used when a Hungarian says "John runs," "John eats an apple," "John eats your apple," and "John eats no apple." On the other hand, the transitive conjugation is used when the object is definite, when it is modified by a third person possessive suffix, when it is possessed by a third person nominal phrase, and so on. Thus, the "transitive" or "definite" conjugation is used when the Hungarian wants to say "John eats the apple" or "John eats Bill's apple." There are some 13 conditions which, taken together, control the choice between the transitive and intransitive conjugations (MacWhinney, 1989). There is no single principle that can be used to group this 13 conditions. Instead, both transitivity, definiteness, and referential disambiguation all figure in as factors in making this choice. This way of grouping together aspects of transitivity, definiteness, and possession is extremely foreign to most non-Hungarians. Not surprisingly, L2 learners of Hungarian have a terrible time marking this distinction; errors in choice of the conjugation of the verb are the surest syntactic cue that the learner is not a native Hungarian.

In order to acquire this new category, the L2 learner begins by attempting to transfer from L1. To some degree this can work. The learner attempts to identify the intransitive with the English intransitive. However, the fact that many sentences with objects also take the intransitive if the objects are somehow "indefinite" tends to block the simple application of this conceptual structure. In the end, no simple transfer will succeed and the learner must resign oneself to picking up the pieces of this new category one by one and welding them together into a connected system. Here is an area where attempts at linguistic analysis on the learner's part only make matters worse. If the learner had proceeded like a Hungarian child (MacWhinney, 1974), he would have learned the conjugations by generalizing from a few key collocations and phrases. The adult needs to amplify this case-based approach to learning with a way of focusing on contrastive structures in which cues are competing. For the adult, such focusing on particularly difficult parts of a grammatical system will increase the efficiency of acquisition.

In many cases, the transfer of syntactic patterns from L1 to L2 is structurally correct, but pragmatically inaccurate. For example, Trevise (1986) observes that French speakers make excessive use of topicalization structures in English in the form of structures corresponding to left-dislocation, right-dislocations, and "c'est .. que" in French. Although these structures are all permissible in English, the actual conditions on their usage are far more restrictive than in French. Similarly, Seliger (1989) notes that Hebrew learners of English tend to systematically underuse the passive. He attributes this underusage to the relatively tighter, genre-dependent conditions on the use of the passive in Hebrew. In general, it is clear that simple transfer of an L1 structure to L2 is not sufficient to guarantee correct usage, since both underutilization and overutilization can occur until the full conditions governing the use of a construction in L2 are learned.

Fossilization and the Critical Period

In his seminal analysis of the biological bases of language, Lenneberg (1967) argued for a critical period for language acquisition. It is clear that, past a certain age, at least some aspects of a second language become more and more difficult to acquire. The most obvious problems are in the area of phonological learning. If the learner has not been exposed to a wide variety of phonological contrasts before puberty (Oyama, 1976), the decreased plasticity of the brain can make it progressively more difficult to acquire new articulatory patterns, since these patterns will be driven by the ability to code auditory contrasts. There are apparently important individual differences in the nature of early experiences and the extent to which they leave some residual plasticity for later learning, since some adults are able to pick up second languages with only some difficulty and others find full acquisition of L2 virtually impossible.

How does the Competition Model account for these apparent problems in later acquisition? The basic account is that increased automatization of the L1 system makes the addition of new auditory, articulatory, and semantic contrasts progressively more difficult. The more automatized a system becomes, the less it is available for restructuring. It may be this automatization that is the root cause of "fossilization." Even learners who are continually being exposed to large amounts of high quality L2 input may fail to shake off certain fossilized errors.

There is a second important difference between L1 and L2 learning that tends to support fossilization. This is the fact that L2 learning relies on a massive amount of top-down constructive processing. The L2 learner can often pull one or two words out of a conversation and understand fully what is being discussed. This form of processing is not available to the child. Unfortunately, constructive processing of this type tends to bypass some of the basic processes of lexical analysis and acquisition which may be crucial for acquisition of full native-like control of the language (Johnson & Newport, 1989).

Yet a third factor supporting fossilization can be the diminished pool of perceived error facing the language learner. The L2 learner who is able to maximize top-down comprehension processes and who is able to utilize simple transfer processes to acquire a moderate ability to produce sentences may arrive in a position where the remaining amount of error easily detectable in one's own productions is insufficient to force a full reorganization of one's decidedly non-native system. To make further progress, the learner would have to refocus attention on the details of phonological form and argument structure, rather than on the actual process of communication. Even if errors are detected, the actual reorganization of the system to decrease particular errors will run against the strength of already automated procedures. Unless the learner diverts attention to these secondary concerns, one's control of L2 will tend to fossilize.

Instruction and the Competition Model

The issue of pedagogical approaches to second language learning is one which has both theoretical and practical importance. If a pedagogical approach can be grounded on psycholinguistic data, it may be possible to elaborate both practice and theory in tandem. From the previous discussion, it would appear that the Competition Model would be most in accord with the following pedagogical principles:

1. Language should be learned in context with maximal experiential grounding.

2. Early instruction should use simple, frequent forms.

3. Early training should focus on the restructuring of the *phonological* system in the context of computer-controlled exercises encouraging the learners to match their own productions to clear L2 samples.

4. Neither grammar nor phonology should be taught apart from particular lexical forms. Phonological training and grammatical instruction should be done in the context of the acquisition of new lexical items in simple syntactic frames.

5. Since *transfer* is inevitable, instruction should be designed to maximize the positive effects of transfer and minimize the negative effects.

6. Early in learning, there is an important role of *rote* acquisition of forms. Later in learning, such rote learning should be deemphasized.

7. Ideally, new *lexical* items should be acquired in the context of syntactic groupings which fully display their alternative argument frames. Implementation of a Hyper Text system for lexical frames can allow the student to learn syntax in terms of operations on particular lexical groups. The instructional process does not need to specifically teach transfer or remapping strategies, since students will

automatically apply them. However, errors produced by the transfer of L1 lexical frames need to be clearly presented in terms of HypterText systems.

8. Inevitably, the simplest transfer strategies will produce errors. However, it is better to focus on allowing the student to first deal with difficult materials in comprehension, rather than attempting, initially, to generate, detect, and correct errors in production.

9. As the student advances, the goal of instruction should be to progressively sharpen attention to those aspects of language which had previously been ignored and where the student is likely to make the largest numbers of errors. This can be done most effectively by increasing emphasis on *error detection* and *error correction* in later stages of L2 learning to prevent the fossilization of forms and mappings. This type of training should focus on *functional restructuring*.

A complete instructional system should include tools that facilitate error detection and provide the learner with specific instruction designed to correct each error type. In accord with the Competition Model, error-driven instruction should focus on the presentation and elaboration of the L2 pattern that should compete with the learner error. For example, ifthe learner produces a gender error in German in a particular case, there should be instruction to correct this error that illustrates the particular form in the context of others that are phonologically similar and which have the same gender (MacWhinney, Leinbach, Taraban, & McDonald, 1989).

The generation of errors and the use of tools for correcting these errors can provide us a way of gaining new psycholinguistic data on learner strategies and the relative efficacy of different instructional methods. The current top priority for research in foreign language learning should be the acquisition of new empirical data of this type. Using structured methods such as fill in the blanks, matching, question-and-answer, dictionary exercises, translation, error detection, and multiple choice, we can elicit similar responses in a group of learners who can be tracked within the program. It will then be possible to conduct psycholinguistic experiments within the context of the tutoring system itself. These data will allow us to elaborate increasingly refined models of the learner and will also facilitate development of the Competition Model for second language learning.

Summary

Research within the context of the Competition Model is now focusing increasingly on L2 acquisition. The model views L2 learning as a process of cue acquisition which relies initially on transfer from L1 to L2. Cues with the strongest strength have the strongest transfer, although there is fairly general transfer across particular well-worn paths, such as the path with allows the transfer of the meanings underlying L1 words to L2 words. In some cases simple transfer is blocked and the learner develops a set of strategies to get around this blockage by postulating more complex remappings from L1 to L2.

The learner's attempt to proceduralize the mappings from L1 to L2 runs counter to attempts to restructure the L2 to avoid reliance on L1. In order to prevent fossilization and to facilitate functional restructuring, it is important to expose the learner to precisely those structures that differentiate true L2 strategies from transferred L1 strategies. Because transfer is inevitable, there is no sense trying to defeat it. Instead, emphasis should be placed on moving the learner through the period of transfer into a period of functional restructuring.

References

Bates, E., & MacWhinney, B. (1981). Second language acquisition from a functionalist perspective: Pragmatic, semantic and perceptual strategies. In H. Winitz (Ed.), *Annals of the New York Academy of Sciences conference on native and foreign language acquisition.* New York: New York Academy of Sciences.

Bates, E., & MacWhinney, B. (1982). Functionalist approaches to grammar. In E. Wanner & L. Gleitman (Ed.), *Language acquisition: The state of the art.* New York: Cambridge University Press.

Berwick, R. (1987). Parsability and learnability. In B. MacWhinney (Ed.), *Mechanisms of language acquisition.* Hillsdale, NJ: Lawrence Erlbaum.

Carey, S. (1978). The child as word learner. In J. B. M. Halle & G. Miller (Eds.), *Linguistic theory and psychological reality.* Cambridge, MA: The MIT Press.

Chomsky, N. (1959). Review of Skinner's *Verbal Behavior. Language,* 35, 26-58.

Damasio, H. (1981). Cerebral localization of the aphasias. In M. T. Sarno (Ed.), *Acquired Aphasia.* New York: Academic Press.

Dechert, H., & Raupach, M. (Ed.). (1989). *Transfer in language production.* Norwood, NJ: Ablex.

Devescovi, A., D'Amico, S., Smith, S., Mimica, I., & Bates, E. (1990). *The development of sentence comprehension in Italian and Serbo-Croatian: Local versus distributed cues.* Unpublished manuscript.

Dickerson, W. (Ed.). (1987). Explicit rules and the developing interlanguage phonology. In A. James & J. Leather (Eds.) *Sound patterns in second language acquisition.* Dordrecht: Foris Publications.

Dulay, H., & Burt, M. (1974a). Natural sequences in child second language acquisition. Language learning, 24, 37-53.

Dulay, H., & Burt, M. (1974b). A new perspective on the creative construction process in child second language acquisition. Language Learning, 24, 253-278.

Flege, J. (1987). Effects of equivalence classification on the production of foreign language. In A. James & J. Leather (Eds.) *Sound patterns in second language acquisition*. Dordrecht: Foris Publications.

Friederici, A. (1983). Children's sensitivity to functions words during sentence comprehension. *Linguistics*, 21, 717-739.

Gass, S. (1987). The resolution of conflicts among competing systems: A bidirectional perspective. *Applied Psycholinguistics*, 8, 329-350.

Gass, S., & Selinker, L. (Eds.). (1983). *Language transfer in language learning*. Rowley MA: Newbury.

Harrington, M. (1987). Processing transfer: language-specific strategies as a source of interlanguage variation. *Applied Psycholinguistics*, 8, 351-378.

Huebner, T. (1983). *A longitudinal analysis of the acquisition of English*. Ann Arbor: Karoma.

Ijaz, H. (1986). Linguistic and cognitive determinants of lexical acquisition in a second language. *Language Learning*, 36, 401-451.

Johnson, J., & Newport, E. (1989). Critical period effects in second language learning: the influence of maturational state on the acquisition of English as a second language. *Cognitive Psychology*, 21, 60-99.

Kellerman, E., & Sharwood Smith, M. (Eds.). (1986). *Crosslinguistic influence in second language acquisition*. New York: Pergamon Press.

Kilborn, K. (1989). Sentence processing in a second language: The timing of transfer. *Language and Speech*, 32, 1-23.

Kilborn, K., & Cooreman, A. (1987). Sentence interpretation strategies in adult Dutch-English bilinguals. *Applied Psycholinguistics*, 8, 415-431.

Kilborn, K., & Ito, T. (1989). Sentence processing in Japanese-English and Dutch-English bilinguals. In B. MacWhinney, & E. Bates (Eds.), *The crosslinguistic study of sentence processing*. New York: Cambridge University Press.

Klein, W., & Perdue, C. (1989). The learner's problem of arranging words. In B. MacWhinney, & E. Bates (Eds.), *The crosslinguistic study of sentence processing*. New York: Cambridge University Press.

Kroll, J., & Stewart, E. (1990, November). *Concept mediation in bilingual translation*. Paper presented at Psychonomic Society meeting, New Orleans.

Lado, R. (1957). *Linguistics across cultures*. Ann Arbor: University of Michigan Press.

Lado, R. (1971). Second-language teaching. In C. E. Reed (Ed.), *The learning of language*. New York: Appleton-Century-Crofts.

Lenneberg, E. H. (1967). *Biological foundations of language*. New York: Wiley.

MacWhinney, B. (1974). *How Hungarian children learn to speak*. Unpublished doctoral dissertation, University of California, Berkeley.

MacWhinney, B. (1978). The acquisition of morphophonology. *Monographs of the Society for Research in Child Development*, 43, Whole no. 1.

MacWhinney, B. (1987a). Applying the competition model to bilingualism. *Applied Psycholinguistics*, 8, 315-327.

MacWhinney, B. (1987b). The competition model. In B. MacWhinney (Ed.), *Mechanisms of language acquisition*. Hillsdale, NJ: Lawrence Erlbaum.

MacWhinney, B. (1989). Competition and lexical categorization. In R. Corrigan, F. Eckman, & M. Noonan (Eds.), *Linguistic categorization*. New York: Benjamins.

MacWhinney, B. (1990). Connectionism as a framework for language acquisition theory. In J. Miller (Ed.), *Progress in research on child language disorders*. Austin, TX: Pro-Ed.

MacWhinney, B., & Anderson, J. (1986). The acquisition of grammar. In I. Gopnik & M. Gopnik (Eds.), *From models to modules*. Norwood, NJ: Ablex.

MacWhinney, B., & Bates, E. (Eds.). (1989). *The crosslinguistic study of sentence processing*. New York: Cambridge University Press.

MacWhinney, B., Leinbach, J., Taraban, R., & McDonald, J. (1989). Language learning: Cues or rules? *Journal of Memory and Language*, 29, 255-277.

MacWhinney, B., & Pléh, C. (1988). The processing of restrictive relative clauses in Hungarian, *Cognition*, 29, 95-141.

MacWhinney, B., Pléh, C., & Bates, E. (1985). The development of sentence interpretation in Hungarian, *Cognitive Psychology*, 17, 178-209.

Major, R. (1987). The natural phonology of second language acquisition. In A. James, & J. Leather (Eds.), *Sound patterns in second language acquisition*. Dordrecht: Foris Publications.

McDonald, J. (1987). Sentence interpretation in bilingual speakers of English and Dutch. *Applied Psycholinguistics*, 8, 379-413.

McDonald, J. (1989). The acquisition of cue-category mappings. In B. MacWhinney & E. Bates (Eds.), *The crosslinguistic study of language processing*. New York: Cambridge University Press.

McDonald, J., & Heilenman, K. (1989). *Determinants of cue strength in adult first and second language speakers of French.* Unpublished manuscript, Louisiana State University.

McDonald, J., & MacWhinney, B. (1989). Maximum likelihood models for sentence processing research. In B. MacWhinney, & E. Bates (Eds.), *The crosslinguistic study of sentence processing*. New York: Cambridge University Press.

Odlin, T. (1989). *Language transfer: Cross-linguistic influence in language learning.* New York: Cambridge University Press.

Oyama, S. (1976). A sensitive period for the acquisition of a nonnative phonological system. *Journal of Psycholinguistic Research*, 5, 261-283.

Ringbom, H. (1987). *The role of the first language in foreign language learning.* Clevedon: Multilingual Matters.

Rosansky, E. (1976). Methods and morphemes in second language acquisition research. *Stanford Papers And Reports on Child Language Development*, 12, 199-211.

Rumelhart, D., & McClelland, J. (1986). *Parallel distributed processing.* Cambridge, MA: MIT Press.

Sasaki, Y. (1991). Development of English and Japanese interlanguage processing: An analysis based on the competition model. *Applied Psycholinguistics*, 12, 47-73.

Saussure, F. de. (1966). *Course in general linguistics.* New York: McGraw-Hill.

Seliger, H. (1989). Semantic transfer constraints on the production of English passive by Hebrew-English bilinguals. In H. Dechert & M. Raupach (Eds.), *Transfer in language production*. Norwood, NJ: Ablex.

Singley, K., & Anderson, J. (1989). *The transfer of cognitive skills.* Cambridge, MA: Harvard University Press.

Skinner, B. F. (1957). *Verbal behavior.* New York: Appleton-Century-Crofts.

Slobin, D. (1985). *The crosslinguistic study of language acquisition*. Hillsdale, NJ: Lawrence Erlbaum.

Sokolov, J. (1989). The development of role assignment in Hebrew. In B. MacWhinney & E. Bates (Eds.), *The crosslinguistic study of sentence processing*. New York: Cambridge University Press.

Stampe, D. (1973). *A dissertation on natural phonology*. Chicago: University of Chicago Press.

Stockwell, R., Bowen, J., & Martin, J. (1965). *The grammatical structures of English and Spanish*. Chicago: University of Chicago Press.

Takehiko, I., Tahara, T., & Park, W. (1989). Developmental psycholinguistic comparison between Japanese and Korean, and within Japanese. In F. Peng (Ed.), *Language in the individual and the society*. Hiroshima: Bunka-Hyoron.

Trévise, A. (1986). Is it transferable, topicalization? In K. Kellerman & M. Sharwood Smith (Eds.), *Crosslinguistic influence in second language acquisition*. New York: Pergamon.

Tyler, L. (1983). The development of discourse mapping processes: the on-line interpretation of anaphoric expressions. *Cognition*, 13, 309-341.

Tyler, L., & Marslen-Wilson, W. (1981). Children's processing of spoken language. *Journal of Verbal Learning and Verbal Behavior*, 20, 400-416.

Vosniadou, S., & Ortony, A. (Eds.). (1989). *Similarity and analogical reasoning*. New York: Cambridge University Press.

Cognitive Processing in Bilinguals – R.J. Harris (Editor)
© *1992 Elsevier Science Publishers B.V. All rights reserved.*

An Overview of Cross-language Transfer in Bilingual Reading

Aydin Y. Durgunoğlu and Barbara J. Hancin
University of Illinois at Urbana-Champaign

Abstract

The focus of this chapter is on the influence of first-language knowledge, strategies and processes on reading in a second language, that is, on cross-language transfer. We identify major subcomponents of the reading process and review research that examines the influence of the first language within those subcomponents.

The domain of second language reading is a rich source for insights into bilingual cognitive processing. Reading entails the utilization of linguistic and metalinguistic knowledge in order to comprehend the meaning of written symbols. When bilinguals are reading in their second language (L2), they usually bring a wealth of knowledge, strategies and processes from their first language (L1). The question addressed in this chapter is how and when the L1 influences L2 reading, that is, cross-language transfer. We believe this topic is important for several reasons. At a theoretical level, what transfers across languages can give researchers an indication of the type of structure imposed by bilinguals on their L1 (Kellerman, 1986), because unless the bilinguals have an (implicit) awareness of the linguistic structure in their native language, they cannot impose this structure on the L2 processing.

At the applied level, understanding the nature of cross-language transfer in reading can enable us to predict not only the conditions under which a bilingual will have difficulty when processing L2, i.e., negative transfer, but also the conditions under which a bilingual will show facilitation, i.e., positive transfer. This information can help to structure instruction so it can build upon the strengths bilinguals already have in their L1. In this chapter, we review evidence of cross-language transfer in different subcomponents of the reading process. Our intention is to summarize what we already know and indicate areas that need to be investigated more thoroughly.

A Brief History

One of the earliest models on cross-language influence was developed by Lado (1957). In what is known as the Contrastive Analysis (CA) approach, L2 acquisition was considered to be highly influenced by the characteristics of L1. Hence, detailed, descriptive analyses of the structures in both the L1 and the L2 of a bilingual were recommended. Whereas structures similar in the two languages were assumed to facilitate acquisition, structures different in the two languages were assumed to slow acquisition. CA developed at a time when behaviorist views dominated psychology and education. Transfer was usually interpreted as L1 habits interfering with acquisition of the L2 structures. Although Lado was interested in comparing not only grammatical and phonological constructs in the two languages of a bilingual, but also distribution of forms and meanings and culture, CA was basically used most frequently for comparing the linguistic features of the two languages (see McKay & Wong, 1988; Robinett & Schacter, 1983, for examples).

As major theoretical shifts occurred in linguistics and psychology (e.g., Chomsky, 1959), researchers began to focus more on universals of language acquisition rather than on differences among languages. An alternative hypothesis to CA, namely, L1=L2 or identity hypothesis was proposed (Dulay & Burt, 1974; Dulay, Burt & Krashen, 1982). The analysis of the kind of errors produced in the second-language speech of bilinguals seemed to indicate that the errors followed a pattern similar to that of monolingual children acquiring their L1. These data were taken to imply a universal developmental sequence in language acquisition. The identity hypothesis claimed that second-language learners actively organize the new language that they hear and make generalizations about its structures, just like children learning their L1. Within this framework, the role of L1 and cross-language transfer was assumed to be limited or unimportant. For example, Bailey, Madden & Krashen (1974) observed that the ordering of the accuracies of producing 8 grammatical morphemes (such as present progressive -ing, plural -s) in English speech was similar for second language learners from different language backgrounds.

As Odlin (1989) summarized, the reaction to CA, and the popularity of the L1=L2 universalist hypothesis diverted attention away from the issue of cross-language transfer. However, logically, rejecting CA as a methodology did not necessarily imply that transfer does not occur across languages of a bilingual. Most of the research on the L1=L2 hypothesis was on inflectional morphology and syntax. Although these areas could be exhibiting the operation of universal linguistic principles to a large extent, other areas, such as vocabulary development, phonology, and metacognitive strategies, could exhibit the influence of L1 knowledge and strategies on L2 processing. Consequently, researchers once again began to focus on the influence of the L1 and the cross-language transfer issue was resurrected in the 1980's (see Gass & Selinker, 1983; Kellerman & Sharwood Smith, 1986; Odlin, 1989; Ringbom, 1987). The current focus on cross-language transfer, however, is different from the CA tradition. Some researchers have even suggested using terms like **crosslinguistic influence** (Sharwood Smith & Kellerman, 1986) or **the role of mother tongue** (Corder, 1983) in order to overcome the behaviorist connotations of the term **transfer.**

Differing from the CA approach, current studies indicate that formal structural similarity is not enough for transfer to occur (Sharwood Smith & Kellerman, 1983). The second-language learners need to be aware of the parallels between their L1 and L2. This can sometimes lead to drawing parallels even when there are none in the formal structures of the languages. In other words, it is not the formal linguistic typology, but psychotypology (Kellerman, 1986), a learner's <u>perception</u> of similarities between the two languages, which is important. Current cross-language transfer research also differs from the research three decades ago because now the role of language universals is acknowledged and integrated into models (see Bley-Vroman, 1986; Corder, 1983; Gass, 1986 for examples).

Cross-language Transfer in Reading

As this brief historical sketch suggests, most of the cross-language transfer research has been carried out on acquisition and production of L2 structures and relatively little work has been done on cross-language transfer in bilingual reading. Although some of the previous transfer research is very relevant for reading, it does not address all the possible loci of transfer. Even researchers who <u>do</u> study cross-language transfer in reading usually focus on transfer of background knowledge or metacognitive strategies, but not on the initial word recognition stages. There are several reasons why cross-language transfer in initial word recognition stages of reading has not been studied as vigorously: First, there is an overreliance on top-down, psycholinguistic-guessing-game models in the fields of L2 reading (Carrell & Eisterhold, 1983). These top-down models assume that visual processing plays a limited role in reading because reading proceeds by forming hypotheses about upcoming words and minimally sampling the visual information on the page. Such a view of reading has not been supported by the L1 reading research in the last decade (see Rayner & Pollatsek, 1989; Stanovich, 1980; 1986, for reviews), and yet most of the L2 reading research is based on that model. Consequently, in L2 reading, background knowledge that should enable a reader to make predictions is investigated much more often than visual processing (Weber, 1991). Cross-language transfer research follows this trend as well.

Another difficulty for studying cross-language transfer in reading is due to the nature of the reading process. Most children acquire language with little or no difficulty, but the acquisition of reading requires more effort and instruction. Although there is some overlap, comprehension of speech is different from comprehension of written texts (for reviews, see Horowitz & Samuels, 1987). When investigating the effects of L1 on L2 acquisition, often the L1 knowledge is assumed to be well-developed and it usually is. Such an assumption is not necessarily true in L2 reading research.   L1 reading may be at different levels of proficiency across different bilinguals. Hence, there is a controversy about what transfers in bilingual reading. If there is a weakness in L2 reading, is it a language problem or a reading problem (Alderson, 1984)?   Some researchers claim that reading is a universal process (cf. Goodman, 1970) and hence should be similar across languages. Hence, it is expected that reading abilities will transfer across languages. Individuals proficient in their L1 reading will also be proficient in their L2 reading.   On the other hand, some researchers claim that reading problems in the L2 are largely due to inadequate knowledge of the L2 because it is assumed that a reader may not have enough linguistic proficiency in order to pick up correct cues from the text to make correct guesses and predictions.   Finally, there are other researchers who claim a middle ground.   According to this group, the skills and knowledge from the L1 can transfer to L2 reading, but only when the reader has a certain level of linguistic proficiency in the L2 (for an overview, see Alderson, 1984).   Although it is couched within an outdated top-down view of reading, this controversy is still useful in pointing out that when considering the influence of the L1 on L2 reading, variables such as L2 linguistic proficiency as well as L1 <u>and</u> L2 reading proficiency are crucial.   As Hornberger (1990) noted, for a child in a bilingual education program, L2 literacy is built on

A.Y. Durgunoğlu and B.J. Hancin

minimal reading proficiency in the L1, whereas for a university student learning a foreign language, L2 literacy is built on a highly developed L1 reading proficiency. In sum, what transfers from the L1 to L2 reading may depend on how developed L1 reading proficiency is.

Components of the Reading Process

In this paper, we will focus on different components of the reading process in order to identify the loci and nature of cross-language transfer. Some of the components are, in reality, highly interactive and integrated; however, we agree with Carr and his colleagues (see Carr & Levy, 1990) and Rayner and Pollatsek (1989) that although it is important to put all the information together to have an overall model of the reading process, it is likely that "the greatest advances in understanding reading will come through researchers working on each subcomponent process...As we understand each of the component processes in reading better, we will be able to put them together to understand 'the big picture'" (Rayner & Pollatsek, 1989, p. 478-79).

Reading can be thought of as a combination of several subcomponent processes. To give a generic overview, orthographic processing refers to translating written symbols to a visual code and activating the meaning of that visual code. Phonological processing refers to translating visual information to a phonological code and activating its meaning. As individual words are recognized, clusters of them are assumed to be kept in working memory for assigning syntactic functions, and later, with the help of background knowledge, the activated meanings are integrated into the ongoing text representation. During the whole process, metacognitive processes guide attention and warn the reader if any misunderstanding or a conflict with the background knowledge or current text representation occurs. We will now look at each of these components for possible cross-language transfer effects.

Orthographic and Phonological Processing

Orthographic processing requires different sets of knowledge and strategies. One basic subcomponent is the knowledge of individual symbols and their identities. For example, an English speaker learning to read in Arabic or Greek needs to memorize the alphabet, the symbols and their referents. At a more metalinguistic level, beginning readers need to understand what is represented by each orthographic symbol. In alphabetic languages, letters usually represent sounds or phonemes, whereas in languages such as Japanese or Chinese, the symbols may refer to syllables, morphemes or words. Another component of orthographic processing is awareness of common orthographic patterns in alphabetic languages. For example, in English, **u** is the most likely letter to follow an initial **q**, but not an initial **i**. Research with monolinguals shows that although they may not easily verbalize this knowledge, skilled readers are very sensitive to common letter combinations in their written language (Henderson & Chard, 1980). In making word/nonword decisions on letter strings, if the overall test list contains random letter strings (e.g., RYGJIK), rather than word-like nonwords (e,g,. GUITAS) mixed in with words, readers use different strategies. With random letter strings in a list, the word/nonword decisions can be based on orthographic information rather than on the meaning of the words (Seidenberg, 1985). If, however, the test list contains word-like nonwords, with common orthographic patterns, then a semantic analysis is necessary to distinguish between words and nonwords (C.T. James, 1975). Awareness of such redundancies in letter sequences that facilitates word recognition usually develops as a result of experience rather than as a result of knowing the rules.

Favreau, Komoda and Segalowitz (1980) found that the efficient usage of orthographic redundancies in a language differed in the two languages of a bilingual. They used a word superiority effect paradigm to investigate the influence of orthographic redundancies. Native speakers of English who were also fluent in French, first briefly saw a word (e.g., WORK), an anagram (e.g., ORWK) or a single letter (e.g., K). After the offset of the item, two letters were presented above and below the location where the critical letter occurred and the subjects were asked to choose the letter that actually appeared in the stimulus just presented. The usual finding in this type of experiments is that letters of the words are identified more accurately than the letters of anagrams or even better than single letters. This is called the word superiority effect because the orthographic redundancy found in words seems to facilitate the identification of its component letters.

Favreau and her colleagues found that with English materials and instructions, regular word superiority effect appeared. However, when the task and materials were in French, no word superiority effect was found. All three conditions led to the same level of accuracy. In a second experiment, the mean duration of French materials was longer than that of English materials. With differing mean durations, both French and English materials yielded significant word superiority effects. In sum, the fluent bilingual subjects were able to use the orthographic redundancies in their L2 to facilitate the processing of individual letters when they had sufficient processing time.

Finally, orthographic knowledge also involves mapping of symbols to the speech code. In languages such as Turkish and Serbo-Croatian that have "shallow" orthographies, the correspondence between a letter and its sound is very transparent. For example in all of the following Turkish words the letter **a** is pronounced as "ah", ALTIN, KALEM, BORA. Contrast it with the pronunciation of **a** in the following English words, ANT, GAVE, CAR.

In English, some words have spelling patterns that are always pronounced the same way, just like the orthographic-phonological regularity in "shallow" orthographies. These are usually called regular or consistent words (Seidenberg, 1985, 1989; Jared, McRae & Seidenberg, 1990). For example, the ending (or more technically, the rime) **-est** is always pronounced the same way in different words such as BEST, NEST, REST. Some researchers assume that these regular words are pronounced using regular spelling-to-sound correspondence rules. In other words, the phonological translation of a visually presented word is used to activate its meaning. This is called indirect access to meaning or phonological mediation.

In English there are also inconsistent words. Such words have different pronunciations although the spelling pattern in their word family is the same. For example, the words MINT and PINT are classified as inconsistent because although their spelling patterns have the common rime -**int**, they are pronounced differently. (PINT is also called an exception word because its pronunciation differs from that of the whole family, MINT, HINT, TINT, LINT). Trying to pronounce exception words PINT and HAVE using spelling-to-sound correspondence rules will lead to errors. Hence, some theorists propose a second route which involves accessing the meaning of a word directly using visual-orthographic information--with no phonological mediation--and later "looking up" its pronunciation from the lexicon (see Carr & Pollatsek, 1985; McCusker, Hillinger & Bias, 1981; **Brain and Behavioral Sciences**, 1985 for reviews).

More recently, Seidenberg and McClelland (1989, see also Seidenberg, 1985) have proposed that orthographic and phonological processing are not two independent routes, but rather parallel components of the same interactive processing system. In their connectionist model, spelling and pronunciation of a word are represented by patterns of activation across units encoding orthographic and phonological information. It must be emphasized that these units are the same for all words and nonwords. What changes is the pattern of activation across these units for different items. The weights of the connections between orthographic and phonological units get adjusted with experience and constitute the knowledge of the spelling to sound correspondences. For both regular and exception words, as well as nonwords, the frequency of experiences with the item itself and with its similarly-spelled neighbors determine the naming performance (Seidenberg, 1989; Seidenberg & McClelland, 1989; Jared, McRae & Seidenberg, 1990). To summarize, in this model, the processing of a written word activates in parallel, both phonological and meaning information, but phonological activation is slower because it depends on input from orthographic processing. This assumption implies that phonological information should be effective only under difficult conditions with relatively long response latencies, such as when words have unfamiliar spelling patterns or readers are inexperienced in recognizing spelling patterns, in sum, when orthographic processing is inefficient in activating meaning.

Different orthographies. A natural extension of the discussion on the role of phonology in word recognition is what happens in languages with different orthographic systems. Because orthographies differ in the extent to which they encode phonological information, some researchers have suggested that differences among orthographies may influence the way in which they are processed. Writing systems with shallow orthographies, such as Serbo-Croatian, with its very regular spelling to sound correspondences, may encourage phonologically mediated word recognition based on spelling-to-sound conversion rules (Feldman & Turvey, 1983; Katz & Feldman, 1983). In a language like Hebrew, however, with a "deeper" orthography, phonological mediation may not be very feasible (Bentin, Bargai & Katz, 1984; Frost, Katz & Bentin, 1987) because, in Hebrew, phonological information is represented much more indirectly in text. For example, adult readers usually see texts written only in consonants, with vowel dots omitted. Hence, a single consonant string may refer to different words when different vowels are added. Frost et al. (1987) compared naming latencies to high and low frequency words and to nonwords in Serbo-Croatian, English and Hebrew. They found that, overall, the difference between the pronunciation latencies of nonwords and high frequency words was only 56 ms in Serbo-Croatian, whereas in English this difference increased to 101 ms and in Hebrew, the difference was 157 ms. That is, the wordness or lexicality of an item made less of a difference in Serbo-Croatian as compared to English or Hebrew, indicating that Serbo-Croatian items tended to be pronounced as letter strings with little effect of their lexical status.

Seidenberg (1985; 1989; 1990) argues that any writing system incorporates both phonological and orthographic processing. The regularities in the orthographic system, such as those between spelling-to-sound correspondences, will be established depending on prior experience with the words and their neighbors regardless of the nature of the writing system. However with a shallow orthography, it might be possible to get these regularities established much earlier and more efficiently. Consequently, in a language such as Serbo-Croatian, it is likely that a phonological mediation to meaning is more efficient than direct orthographic processing to meaning. Moreover, this model predicts that high frequency words should be recognized rapidly on a visual basis regardless of the deepness of orthography because of extensive exposure to that item that strengthened its correct pronunciation. Any differences as a function of the writing system should only appear for low frequency items. In sum, he suggests that it is erroneous to conclude that word recognition in different orthographies exhibit different types of processing.

Transfer of orthographic-phonological information.   Bilinguals usually have extensive experience with the orthographic patterns in their L1. Based on the connectionist model described above, these patterns might be active even when reading in a second language and hence yield the effects of orthographic redundancies in L1 on L2 processing. This awareness of orthographic constraints has been studied with German-English bilinguals (Altenberg & Cairns, 1983). In an English lexical decision task, monolingual and bilingual subjects saw words that were orthographically legal in both English and German (e.g., FLAG) or in English but not in German (e.g., TWIN). For the monolinguals, the response times to these two types of words were equivalent. In contrast, bilinguals were faster on words that were legal only in English. These results indicate that orthographic constraints in both languages affected performance of bilinguals even though the task was in English.

Nas (1983) also reported the influence of L1 orthography and phonology on the English lexical decisions of Dutch-English bilinguals. In that study, the test list included English high frequency words, English-like nonwords (e.g., PRUSK) and pseudohomophones. The pseudohomophones were nonwords (e.g., SNAY) that were pronounced like a real Dutch word (e.g., SNEE). The lexical decision latencies to pseudohomophones were significantly longer compared to nonwords that did not sound like Dutch words. Hence, although no Dutch words were included in the test list, it was harder to reject nonwords that sounded like Dutch words.

In contrast, Scarborough, Gerard and Cortese (1984) did not find effects of the other language of a bilingual in their experiment. In that study with Spanish and English bilinguals, the test lists contained words in the target language (both high and low frequency) and nonwords based on the orthography of the target language. More interestingly, the test lists also contained either words from the nontarget language (both high and low frequency) or nonwords based on the orthography of the nontarget language. For example, if the target language was Spanish, the test list included **mesa** (meaning table), **narin** (nonword) and **city** (word in the nontarget language) or **trenty** (nonword based on the nontarget language orthography). In addition, half of these three types of items were repeated. The data indicated that bilinguals were treating the words in their second language as if they were nonwords. For example, nontarget-language words showed no effects of frequency, and they showed repetition effects comparable to those of nonwords rather than those of words.

The discrepant results of these studies indicate that cross-language transfer cannot be defined in absolute terms because it depends on the experimental context and materials. Supporting this conjecture is a study by Grainger & Beauvillain (1987). These researchers showed that mixing languages in a test list slowed lexical decisions only on words with similar orthographies in the two languages compared to those in a test list with unmixed languages. Words with distinct spelling patterns in the two languages were not affected by mixing of the languages.

The overlap in spelling patterns is at the maximum for interlexical homographs (e.g., the word PAIN meaning bread in French). Beauvillain and Grainger (1987) investigated whether a word like **pain** facilitated the processing of the related words in the two languages, **ache** or **beurre** (meaning butter). Their data indicated that frequency rather than language determined the facilitation of related meaning. **Pain** with its low frequency reading in English but high frequency reading in French, facilitated the processing of **beurre,** but not that of **ache,** although **pain** was read as an English word. When a word like **four** with a low frequency reading (meaning oven) in French but a high frequency reading in English was presented, it facilitated the processing of **five** even when it was presented as a French word. These results indicate that when a word with a common spelling pattern in two languages is presented, it facilitates processing of its most common associate even across languages.

The effects of L1 orthography on L2 tasks have not been systematically investigated in particular with beginning readers. It needs to be tested if readers recognize L2 words with familiar L1 patterns more rapidly in silent reading even though phonologically they may not be similar. Conversely, if the spelling patterns in a reader's L1 is dissimilar to the spelling patterns in L2, does it cause difficulties (Barnitz, 1985)?

In oral language production and in reading out loud, the effects of L1 on L2 pronunciations was studied extensively in earlier CA studies. An example is Portuguese speakers pronouncing an English word beginning with an 'r'. Though the flapped 'r' exists in Portuguese, it is pronounced as [x] in syllable-initial position after a consonant or word initially, that is after a (hard stop), leading to pronunciations such as [xaet] (like hat) for 'rat' and [xol] (like hole) for 'roll'. Though beneficial for the data they provide, these earlier studies were descriptive in nature and did not have the predictive power to determine a priori when L2 pronunciations would be affected by the L1. Currently, we are working on a computational model of an L2 phonology (cf. Dell & Juliano, 1991), in which the words in the L2 are filtered through the L1 phonology. How the nature and frequency of phonological units (features, syllable structures) available in L1 constrain the L2 pronunciations are of interest. By comparing the pronunciations predicted by the model with actual L2 phonetic transcriptions, we hope to identify what aspects of the L1 phonology are imposed on the L2, thus marking the L2 pronunciation and perhaps inhibiting comprehension and communication.

Morphological Processing

Another variable that may affect cross-language transfer is the morphemic complexity of the words. In some Indo-European languages, there is a systematic relationship between corresponding morphological suffixes across languages. For example, compare these English and Spanish word pairs: organiza<u>tion</u> and organiza<u>ción</u>; <u>re</u>juvenate and <u>re</u>juvencer; rapid<u>ly</u> and rapida<u>mente</u>. It is likely that with no or minimum instruction, proficient L1 readers can map these suffixes with their corresponding forms in L2, e.g., "tion" and "ción" are parallel and they turn a verb like "organize" into a noun in both languages. In order to investigate if such knowledge in the L1 can transfer to L2, one needs to consider if the reader is sensitive to these morphological structures in the L1 (Tyler & Nagy, 1989), and, if the answer is yes, does the reader apply this knowledge to recognize L2 words? Some observational data indicated that speakers of Indo-European languages, such as Spanish, were indeed more sensitive to English morphology and word stems in their speech (Saville-Troike, 1984).

In a recent pilot study, we compared the performance of adult Korean- and Spanish-speakers on tasks involving morphologically complex English words. These two language backgrounds were of interest because Spanish and English share many cognates and they both have a relatively weak morphological system in terms of word formation. In contrast, Korean and English do not share cognates and Korean has a rich morphological system, with words easily broken down into morphological templates. In one task, these beginning bilinguals from different language backgrounds completed the letters missing from the stem or the suffix of a word (morpheme-completion test). In another task, they circled derivationally complex words that they thought were **possible** English words (wordness judgment test). In both tasks there were four types of words: both the stem and suffix were cognates in Spanish and in English, either the stem or the suffix was a cognate or neither was a cognate.

Overall, both groups had comparable levels of performance on the two tasks, that is, the main effect of L1 background was not significant. However, when the cognate status was taken into consideration, L1 background made a difference. The data in the morpheme-completion test yielded a significant language background by stem cognate status interaction. Spanish-, but not Korean-speakers, completed cognate stems more accurately than noncognate stems. Likewise, Spanish-speakers were more accurate in completing cognate than noncognate suffixes, whereas Korean-speakers were more accurate on noncognate suffixes. On the wordness judgment test, both groups circled as well-formed, words with cognate stems more often than words with noncognate stems. However, the difference between cognate and noncognate circling performance was smaller in the Korean group as compared to the Spanish group. These data provide us with the preliminary evidence that in identifying morphologically complex words, Spanish-speakers do rely on the overlap between English and their L1.

Meaning Activation

One of the most rigorously investigated areas is how bilinguals represent the meaning of words in their two languages (for example, see Chen & Leung, 1989; Chen & Ng, 1989; Cristoffanini, Kirsner & Milech, 1986; Gerard & Scarborough, 1989; Kirsner, Smith, Lockhart, King & Jain, 1984; Potter, So, Von Eckardt & Feldman, 1984; Scarborough, Gerard & Cortese, 1984, also the chapters on lexical access in this book). This research area has implications for the transfer issue because, depending on the associations between different concepts in the two languages, conceptual information in the L1 may affect the activation of word meanings in the L2. In one comprehensive study, de Groot and Nas (1991) carried out several lexical decision experiments with bilinguals proficient in both L1 and L2. Their data indicated that such fluent bilinguals seem to have a highly interconnected network of translation equivalents in the two languages (e.g., **girl** in English and **meisje** in Dutch). The interlanguage associations were even stronger with cognates (e.g., **grond** in Dutch and **ground** in English). In terms of transfer, presenting a semantically related word (e.g., **kalf**) or a translation (e.g., **koe**) in one language helped in the semantic processing of the target word (e.g., **cow**) in another language. There are two caveats, however. First, on some tasks that require subjects to use orthographic information more than semantic information, or on tasks that do not require subjects to intermix languages, bilinguals seem to have separate, independent semantic representations (Durgunoğlu & Roediger, 1987; Scarborough et al., 1984). Also, the connections between the two languages of a bilingual may have different properties depending on the age, proficiency in L2 and the nature of L2 education (Chen, 1990; Chen & Leung, 1989).

Recently we (Nagy, Garcia, Durgunoğlu & Hancin, 1991) have observed how awareness and knowledge of cognates affects reading comprehension. The question was, if fourth, fifth and sixth grade Spanish-English bilingual students know the Spanish cognates (e.g., **animal, familia, transportar**), will this knowledge help in understanding the same words in the English passages and increase their overall level of comprehension? To answer this question, we first used English and Spanish checklists to determine whether the students knew these cognates in either of the two languages. Then we gave them English passages containing these cognates and asked multiple choice comprehension questions targeting these cognates. Finally we also asked about their explicit awareness of cognates by asking them to circle any cognates that they noticed in the clean copies of reading passages. A multiple regression analysis was carried out with comprehension test performance as the dependent variable and the performance on checklist and circling tests along with their interactions as independent variables. In predicting performance on the comprehension test, even after the reported knowledge of the English word itself was taken into consideration, knowledge of the word in Spanish along with awareness of that word as a cognate were significant predictors of performance. Hence, these data indicate that even for intermediate bilingual readers, there is some cross-language transfer that helps in comprehending cognate English words and the text. However, just knowing the word in Spanish is not enough to understand its cognate in English. What is also needed is an awareness that a word is possibly a cognate.

<u>Syntactic Processing</u>

Some of the richest data in second language acquisition come from studies on syntactic transfer. In this line of studies, researchers usually take a linguistic parameter and compare the syntactic processing of groups of bilinguals who have similar or different parameter settings in their L1. For example, White (1989) focused on the adjacency condition. In English, there is a strict adjacency requirement. Nothing can intervene between a verb and its direct object, unless under some very narrow conditions. Hence, in English, "Mary ate her dinner quickly" is grammatical, whereas "Mary ate quickly her dinner" is not. French, in contrast, has a more flexible adjacency requirement. In White's study, native speakers as well as L2 learners made grammaticality judgments on sentences in which the position of the direct object relative to the verb was manipulated. French sentences that violated the English adjacency requirement were judged as ungrammatical by more English speakers learning French than by native French speakers, 70% versus 40%, respectively, hence reflecting the relative rigidity of the English adjacency condition. In contrast, English sentences that violated the adjacency condition were judged as grammatical by more French speakers learning English than by native English speakers, 46% versus 10%. In short, the salient grammatical parameter setting in L1 was transferred to L2.

Most of the research on bilingual syntactic processing has been carried out in the field of second language acquisition, focusing on how grammatical knowledge in L1 affects acquiring parallel or divergent constructs in L2 (for reviews see Madrid & Garcia, 1985; McLaughlin, 1984). The critical question is whether the syntactic structures from the L1 imposed on L2 processing also affect reading comprehension. MacWhinney and Bates (1987) have shown that the way in which individuals interpret a noun as the agent of the sentence that they have heard depends on several factors, such as the rigidity of word order in a language, the importance of animacy cues, and morphological markers. Moreover, the system of cues in L1 is sometimes applied to the processing of L2 sentences (Kilborn & Ito, 1989). Because cross-language transfer can affect how nouns are assigned a syntactic function, we can infer that this will affect the overall comprehension through the kind of text representation that is created.

For monolinguals reading in English (or in Dutch, see Frazier, 1987), several simple principles (e.g., minimal attachment principle) have been proposed to explain how groups of words in working memory are assigned to their syntactic constituents. For example, the minimal attachment principle states that when reading the sentence "the lawyer heard the story", the tendency is to interpret the second noun as the direct object which can lead to errors with sentences such as "The lawyer heard the story was true". Contrastive analyses across readers from different L1 backgrounds are needed to examine how these principles apply to L2 readers. For example, in Turkish, the direct object is always specified by the inflection -i on the noun, rather than by the word order as in English (Slobin & Bever, 1982). For a Turkish speaker, the tendency to interpret the second noun as an object might be much weaker, because in that bilingual's L1, the inflection, rather than word order, specifies the direct object of the verb. Some support for this idea comes from studies by Danks and his colleagues in Polish (in Danks & End, 1987). When reading passages with syntactic violations (e.g., **injury** replacing **injured**) aloud, monolingual English speakers restored most of the violations quite easily. However, when the same experiment was carried out with Polish speakers and in Polish, there were few restorations. Danks and End suggest that because Polish marks syntactic structure primarily with inflectional endings, distortions in the suffixes were much more salient for Polish readers as compared to American readers. Polish readers were more disrupted by any violations in the word endings. Although how L1 syntactic structures are imposed on L2 processing has been extensively studied for production and acquisition of another language, more research needs to focus on cross-language transfer of syntactic processing in L2 reading.

Background Knowledge

As words are parsed by the syntactic processor, they need to be integrated into the continuously-updated representation of the text. For both monolingual and bilingual readers, one of the most important components of reading comprehension is integrating the material that is read into the text representation. Background knowledge and cultural schemas play an important role in this process. The effects of background and world knowledge affecting L2 reading are very well-documented (Carrell & Eisterhold, 1983; M.O. James, 1987; Steffensen, 1987). If the L2 readers have the general cultural framework assumed by the writer, then they can easily comprehend a text and make the necessary inferences. Their performance on recall or comprehension tests are not worse than those of monolinguals (Aron, 1986; Connor, 1984). On the other hand, if they do not have adequate background knowledge, they may distort the text by trying to fit the textual information to their preexisting knowledge structures or have trouble comprehending the text (Steffensen & Joag-Dev, 1984; Steffensen, Joag-Dev & Anderson, 1979). For example, the influence of L1 culture and knowledge affecting L2 reading comprehension can be seen in the protocols of an Indian subject recalling details of an American wedding ceremony and interpreting the bride wearing a family heirloom as the wedding dress being old (Steffensen, et al., 1979). In short, because some of the background knowledge in the L1 does not match the background knowledge necessary to interpret an L2 text, some comprehension problems can occur. Hence, cross-language transfer of background knowledge and cultural schemata is of major concern for L2 pedagogy.

Metacognitive and Metalinguistic Awareness

As reading progresses, self-monitoring of text understanding becomes essential. According to Baker and Brown (1984), skilled readers have a so-called metacognitive awareness of the reading process. Skilled readers have knowledge about their own cognitive resources and what skills are needed to perform the kind of reading task at hand. They also continuously monitor their understanding of the text and take strategic actions, such as rereading, if comprehension is faulty. Recent studies have begun to show the transfer of metacognitive strategies across languages. Hague and Olejnik (1989) reported that awareness of the text structure that can aid comprehension, transfers across languages. Block (1986) noted the similarity of strategies for comprehension of an English text, regardless of the readers' language background.

Currently, another term "metalinguistic awareness" is used to refer more specifically to the developing notions of beginning readers that underlie literacy acquisition (for reviews, see Clay, 1979; Mason & Allen, 1986; Yaden, 1986). One area of metalinguistic awareness research focuses upon young children's notions of purposes and processes of literacy acts, such as why people read or write and conventions of printed language, such as word boundaries or punctuation.

Another type of metalinguistic awareness is understanding the structural properties of spoken and written language. Researchers have shown that bilingual children, by necessity, learn that words are arbitrary labels for concepts. A writing instrument can be called "pencil" in one language and "kalem" in another. Consequently, bilingual children seem to develop the concept of word earlier and can distinguish between a word's form and meaning (Ben-Zeev, 1977; Bialystok, 1987, 1991; Ianco-Worrall, 1972).

In beginning monolingual readers, one of the best predictors of reading acquisition is another type of metalinguistic awareness. This so-called "phonemic awareness" refers to a beginning reader being aware that words in the spoken language consist of smaller parts, phonemes. For example, the word **top** consists of the phonemes, /t/, /o/, /p/. If beginning readers have the sensitivity to the small components of a word in their spoken language, they seem to have less difficulty in mapping the letters to sound when learning to read an alphabetic language, in short, understanding the alphabetic principle. The role of phonemic awareness in reading acquisition is a widely researched topic with monolingual children (Goswami & Bryant, 1990; Tunmer & Nesdale, 1985; Wagner & Torgeson, 1987; Yopp, 1988).

In a recent study we looked at cross-language transfer of L1 phonemic awareness and its effects on L2 word recognition (Durgunoğlu, Nagy & Hancin, 1991). First, we determined the <u>Spanish</u> phonemic awareness levels of Spanish-English bilingual children in kindergarten and first grade. We used a battery of phonemic awareness tests that included segmenting, blending and matching tasks. The children segmented words into component phonemes, syllables or onset-rimes. For example when the experimenter said the word **nos**, children segmented it into phonemes, **n-o-s**. Conversely, the children blended the sounds given by the experimenter to identify a Spanish word. In the matching test, out of three words, they identified the one that matched the initial sound(s) of a target word, e.g., if the target word was **coche**, they selected the matching word from the set **carta dedo misa**. We also determined both Spanish and English oral proficiency of the children. Next, we observed how the level of phonemic awareness in Spanish predicted performance on learning to read unfamiliar English-like pseudowords and reading English words. The English word and pseudoword recognition were the dependent variables in the multiple regression equation. The data indicated that 81% of the variance in English word recognition and 72% of the variance in pseudoword identification could be explained by only two variables: Spanish phonemic awareness and Spanish word recognition levels. More interestingly, English oral proficiency was not a significant predictor on English word recognition tests. These data strongly suggest that phonemic awareness in L1 can transfer and predict L2 word recognition of beginning bilingual readers.

Conclusions

As this overview of cross-language transfer research indicates, most of the current research in crosslinguistic influence is carried out in the area of second language acquisition, especially in acquisition of syntactic constructs. More research on the effects of L1 on L2 reading is needed especially in the initial word recognition stages. In order to systematically study cross-language transfer in L2 reading, we proposed an approach based on a component skills analysis (cf. Carr & Levy, 1990). Isolating the components of the reading process and investigating the nature of cross-language transfer within each component is essential for us to truly understand cross-language transfer in L2, particularly, and bilingual cognitive processing, generally.

Author note

Preparation of this chapter was supported in part by a grant from the Mellon Foundation and by the Office of Educational Research and Improvement under Cooperative Agreement No. G0087-C1001-90 with the Reading Research and Education Center. The publication does not necessarily reflect the views of the agencies supporting the research.

References

Alderson, J. C. (1984). Reading in a foreign language: a reading problem or a language problem? In J. C. Alderson & A. H. Urquhart (Eds.). *Reading in a foreign language.* (pp.1-24). London: Longman.

Altenberg, E. P. & Cairns, H. S. (1983). The effects of phonotactic constraints in lexical processing in bilingual and monolingual subjects. *Journal of Verbal Learning and Verbal Behavior*, 22, 174-188.

Aron, H. (1986). The influence of background knowledge on memory for reading passages by native and nonnative speakers. *TESOL Quarterly*, 20, 136-140.

Bailey, N., Madden, C., & Krashen, S. (1974). Is there a "natural sequence" in adult second language learning? *Language Learning*, 24, 235-243.

Baker, L., & Brown, A. L. (1984). Metacognitive skills and reading. In P. D. Pearson, R. Barr, M. L. Kamil, & P. Mosenthal (Eds.). *Handbook of reading research* (pp. 353-395). New York: Longman.

Barnitz, J. G. (1985). *Reading development of nonnative speakers of English.* Orlando, FL: Harcourt Brace Jovanovich, Inc.

Beauvillain, C., & Grainger, J. (1987). Accessing interlexical homographs: Some limitations of a language-selective access. *Journal of Memory and Language*, 26, 658-672.

Ben-Zeev, S. (1977). The influence of bilingualism on cognitive strategy and cognitive development. *Child Development*, 48, 1009-1018.

Bentin, S., Bargai, N., & Katz, L. (1984). Orthographic and phonemic coding for lexical access: Evidence from Hebrew. *Journal of Experimental Psychology: Learning, Memory, and Cognition*, 10, 353-368.

Bialystok, E. (1987). Words as things. Development of word concept by bilingual children. *Studies in Second Language Acquisition*, 9, 133-140.

Bialystok, E. (1991). Metalinguistic dimensions of bilingual language proficiency. In E. Bialystok (Ed.). *Language processing in bilingual children.* (pp. 113-140). Cambridge: Cambridge University Press.

Bley-Vroman, R. (1986). What is the logical problem of foreign language learning? In S. M. Gass & J. Schacter (Eds.). *Linguistic perspectives on second language acquisition.* (pp. 41-68). Cambridge, Cambridge University Press.

Block, E. (1986). The comprehension strategies of second language readers. *TESOL Quarterly*, 20, 463-494.

Carr, T. H. & Levy, B. A. (Eds.) (1990). *Reading and its development.* New York: Academic Press.

Carr, T. H. & Pollatsek, S. (1985). Recognizing printed words: A look at current models. In D. Besner, T. G. Waller and G. E. Mackinnon. *Reading Research, Vol. 5* (pp. 1-82). Orlando, FL: Academic Press.

Carrell, P. L., & Eisterhold, J. C. (1983). Schema theory and ESL reading. *TESOL Quarterly*, 17, 553-573.

Chen, H-C. (1990). Lexical processing in a nonnative language: Effects of language proficiency and learning strategy. *Memory and Cognition*, 18, 279-288.

Chen, H-C., & Leung, L. Y-S. (1989). Patterns of lexical processing in a nonnative language. *Journal of Experimental Psychology: Learning, Memory, and Cognition*, 15, 316-325.

Chen, H-C., & Ng, M-L. (1989). Semantic facilitation and translation priming effects in Chinese-English bilinguals. *Memory and Cognition*, 17, 454-462.

Chomsky, N. (1959). A review of B. F. Skinner's Verbal Behavior. *Language*, 35, 26-58.

Clay, M. (1979). *The early detection of reading difficulties*. Auckland, NZ: Heinemann.

Connor, U. (1984). Recall of text: Differences between first and second language readers. *TESOL Quarterly*, 18, 239-256.

Corder, S. P. (1983). A role for mother tongue. In S. M. Gass & L. Selinker (Eds.). *Language transfer in language learning.* (pp. 85-97). Rowley, MA: Newbury House.

Cristoffanini, P., Kirsner, K., & Milech, D. (1986). Bilingual lexical representation: The status of Spanish-English cognates. *Quarterly Journal of Experimental Psychology,* 38A, 367-393.

Danks, J. H. & End, L. J. (1987). Processing strategies for reading and listening. In R. Horowitz & S. J. Samuels (Eds.) *Comprehending oral and written language.* (pp. 271-294). New York: Academic Press.

de Groot, A. M. B. & Nas, G. L. J. (1991). Lexical representation of cognates and noncognates in compound bilinguals. *Journal of Memory and Language*, 30, 90-123.

Dell, G. & C. Juliano (1991). *Connectionist approaches to the production of words.* (Tech. Rep. No. CS-91-05). Champaign: University of Illinois, Beckman Institute.

Dulay, H., & Burt, M. (1974). Natural sequences in child second language acquisition. *Language Learning*, 24, 37-53.

Dulay, H., Burt, M., & Krashen, S. (1982). *Language Two*. Oxford: Oxford University Press.

Durgunoğlu, A. Y., Nagy, W. E., & Hancin, B. J. (1991). *Cross-language transfer of phonemic awareness*. (Tech. Rep. 541). Champaign: University of Illinois, Center for the Study of Reading.

Durgunoğlu, A. & Roediger, H. (1987). Test differences in accessing bilingual memory. *Journal of Memory and Language*, 26, 377-391.

Favreau, M., Komoda, M. K., & Segalowitz, N. (1980). Second-language reading: Implications of the word-superiority effect in skilled bilinguals. *Canadian Journal of Psychology*, 34, 370-380.

Feldman, L. B. & Turvey, M. T. (1983). Word recognition in Serbo-Croatian is phonologically analytic. *Journal of Experimental Psychology: Human Perception and Performance*, 9, 288-298.

Frazier, L. (1987). Sentence processing: A tutorial review. In M. Coltheart (Ed.). *Attention and performance XII*. (pp. 554-586) Hillsdale, NJ: Erlbaum.

Frost, R., Katz, L., & Bentin, S. (1987). Strategies for visual word recognition and orthographic depth: A multilingual comparison. *Journal of Experimental Psychology: Human Perception and Performance*, 13, 104-115.

Gass, S. M. (1986). How do learners resolve linguistic conflicts? In S. M. Gass & J. Schacter (Eds). *Linguistic perspectives on second language acquisition* (pp. 183-202). Cambridge, UK: Cambridge University Press.

Gass, S. & Selinker, L. (1983). *Language transfer in language learning*. Rowley, MA: Newbury House, Inc.

Gerard, L. D., & Scarborough, D. L. (1989). Language-specific lexical access of homographs by bilinguals. *Journal of Experimental Psychology: Learning, Memory, and Cognition*, 15, 305-315.

Goodman, K. S. (1970). Reading: A psycholinguistic guessing game. In H. Singer & R. B. Ruddell (Eds.). *Theoretical models and processes of reading*. Newark, DE: International Reading Association.

Goswami, U. & Bryant, P. (1990). *Phonological skills and learning to read*. Sussex: Erlbaum.

Grainger, J. & Beauvillain, C. (1987). Language blocking and lexical access in bilinguals. *Quarterly Journal of Experimental Psychology*, 39A, 295-319.

Hague, S. & Olejnik, S. (1989). *Text structure: Does awareness transfer from first language to second language?* Paper presented at the meeting of the American Educational Research Association, San Francisco, CA.

Henderson, L. & Chard, J. (1980). The readers' implicit knowledge of orthographic structure. In U. Frith (Ed.). *Cognitive processes in spelling.* (pp. 85-116). New York: Academic Press.

Hornberger, N. H. (1990). Continua of biliteracy. *Review of Educational Research*, 59, 271-296.

Horowitz, R. & Samuels, S. J. (Eds.) (1987). *Comprehending oral and written language.* New York: Academic Press.

Ianco-Worrall, A. (1972). Bilingualism and cognitive development. *Child Development*, 43, 1390-1400.

James, C. T. (1975). The role of semantic information on lexical decisions. *Journal of Experimental Psychology: Human Perception and Performance*, 1, 130-136.

James, M. O. (1987). ESL reading pedagogy: Implications of schema-theoretical research. In J. Devine, P. L. Carrell & D. E. Eskey (Eds.). *Research in reading in English as a second language.* (pp. 175-188). Washington, DC: TESOL.

Jared, D., McRae, K., & Seidenberg, M. S. (1990). The basis of consistency effects in naming. *Journal of Memory and Language*, 29, 687-715.

Katz, L., & Feldman, L. B. (1983). Relation between pronunciation and recognition of printed words in deep and shallow orthographies. *Journal of Experimental Psychology: Learning, Memory, and Cognition*, 9, 157-166.

Kellerman, E. (1986). An eye for an eye: Crosslinguistic constraints on the development of the L2 lexicon. In E. Kellerman & M. Sharwood Smith (Eds.). *Crosslinguistic influences in second language acquisition*, (pp. 35-47). New York: Pergamon Press.

Kellerman, E. & Sharwood Smith, M. (Eds.) (1986). *Crosslinguistic influences in second language acquisition.* New York: Pergamon Press.

Kilborn, K., & Ito, T. (1989). Sentence processing strategies in adult bilinguals. In B. MacWhinney & E. Bates (Eds.). *The crosslinguistic study of sentence processing.* (pp. 257-291). Cambridge, UK: Cambridge University Press.

Kirsner, K., Smith, M., Lockhart, R., King, M., & Jain, M. (1984). The bilingual lexicon: Language-specific units in an integrated network. *Journal of Verbal Learning and Verbal Behavior*, 23, 519-539.

Lado, R. (1957). *Linguistics across cultures*. Ann Arbor: University of Michigan Press.

MacWhinney, B. & Bates, E. (Eds.) (1989). *The crosslinguistic study of sentence processing*. Cambridge: Cambridge University Press.

Madrid, D. L., & Garcia, E. E. (1985). The effect of language transfer on bilingual proficiency. In E. E. Garcia & R. V. Padilla (Eds.). *Advances in bilingual education research*. (pp. 27-52). Tucson, AZ: The University of Arizona Press.

Mason, J. & Allen, J. (1986). A review of emergent literacy with implications for research and practice in reading. In E. Rothkopf (Ed.). *Review of Research in Education*. (pp. 205-238). Washington, DC: American Educational Research Association.

McCusker, L. X., Hillinger, M. L., & Bias, R. G. (1981). Phonological recoding and reading. *Psychological Bulletin*, 89, 217-245.

McKay, S. L., & Wong, S. C. (Eds.). (1988). *Language diversity: Problem or resource*. New York: Newbury House.

McLaughlin, B. (1984). *Second-language acquisition in childhood: Volume 2*. School-age children. Hillsdale, NJ: Erlbaum.

Nagy, W. E., García, G. E., Durgunoğlu, A. Y. & Hancin, B. J. (1991). *Spanish-English bilingual children's use and recognition of cognates in English reading*. Paper presented at the meeting of the American Educational Research Association, Chicago, IL.

Nas, G. (1983). Visual word recognition in bilinguals: Evidence for a cooperation between visual and sound-based codes during access to a common lexical store. *Journal of Verbal Learning and Verbal Behavior*, 22, 526-534.

Odlin, T. (1989). *Language transfer*. Cambridge: Cambridge University Press.

Potter, M. C., So, K-F, Von Eckardt, B., & Feldman, L. B. (1984). Lexical and conceptual representation in beginning and proficient bilinguals. *Journal of Verbal Learning and Verbal Behavior*, 23, 23-38.

Rayner, K. & Pollatsek, A. (1989). *The psychology of reading*. Englewood Cliffs, NJ: Prentice-Hall.

Ringbom, H. (1987). *The role of the first language in foreign language learning.* Philadelphia: Multilingual Matters.

Robinett, B. W., & Schacter, J. (Eds.). (1983). *Second language learning.* Ann Arbor: The University of Michigan Press.

Saville-Troike, M. (1984). What really matters in second-language learning for academic achievement? *TESOL Quarterly,* 18, 199-219.

Scarborough, D., Gerard, L., & Cortese, C. (1984). Independence of lexical access in bilingual word recognition. *Journal of Verbal Learning and Verbal Behavior,* 23, 84-99.

Seidenberg, M. S. (1985). The time course of information activation and utilization in visual word recognition. In D. Besner, T. G. Waller, & G. E. MacKinnon (Eds.). *Reading research: Advances in theory and practice.* Vol. 5 (pp. 199-252). New York: Academic Press.

Seidenberg, M. S. (1989). Visual word recognition and naming: A computational model and its implications. In W. D. Marslen-Wilson (Ed.). *Lexical representation and process.* (pp. 25-74). Cambridge, MA: MIT Press.

Seidenberg, M. S. (1990). Lexical access: Another theoretical soupstone? In D.A. Balota, G. B. Flores d'Arcais & K. Rayner (Eds.). *Comprehension processes in reading.* (pp. 33-72). Hillsdale, NJ: Erlbaum.

Seidenberg, M. & McClelland, J. L. (1989). A distributed developmental model of visual word recognition and naming. *Psychological Review,* 96, 523-568.

Sharwood Smith, M. & Kellerman, E. (1986). Crosslinguistic influence in second language acquisition: An introduction. In E. Kellerman & M. Sharwood Smith (Eds.). *Crosslinguistic influence in second language acquisition.* (pp. 1-9). New York: Pergamon Press.

Slobin, D. I. & Bever, T. G. (1982). Children use canonical sentence schemas: A cross-linguistic study of word order and inflections. *Cognition,* 12, 229-265.

Stanovich, K. E. (1980). Toward an interactive-compensatory model of individual differences in the development of reading fluency. *Reading Research Quarterly,* 16, 32-71.

Stanovich, K. E. (1986). Matthew effects in reading: Some consequences of individual differences in the acquisition of literacy. *Reading Research Quarterly,* 21, 360-407.

Steffensen, M. S. (1987).The effect of context and culture on children's L2 reading: A review. In J. Devine, P. L. Carrell & D. E. Eskey (Eds.). *Research in reading in English as a second language.* (pp. 41-54). Washington, DC: TESOL.

Steffensen, M. S., & Joag-dev, C. (1984). Cultural knowledge and reading. In J. C. Alderson & A. H. Urquhart (Eds.). *Reading in a foreign language.* (pp. 48-61). London: Longman.

Steffensen, M. S., Joag-dev, C. & Anderson, R. C. (1979). A cross-cultural perspective on reading comprehension. *Reading Research Quarterly,* 15, 10-29.

Tunmer, W., & Nesdale, A. (1985). Phonemic segmentation skill and beginning reading. *Journal of Educational Psychology,* 77, 417-427.

Tyler, A. & Nagy, W. (1989). The acquisition of English derivational morphology. *Journal of Memory and Language,* 28, 649-667.

Wagner, R. K. & Torgesen, J. K. (1987). The nature of phonological processing and its causal role in the acquisition of reading skills: A meta-analysis. *Merrill-Palmer Quarterly,* 34, 261-279.

Weber, R. (1991). Linguistic diversity and reading in American society. In R. Barr, M. Kamil, P. Mosenthal & P. D. Pearson (Eds.). *The Handbook of reading research: Volume II.* (pp. 97-119). New York: Longman.

White, L. (1989). The adjacency condition on case assignment: Do L2 learners observe the Subset principle? In S. M. Gass & J. Schacter (Eds.). *Linguistic perspectives on second language acquisition.* (pp. 134-158). Cambridge, UK: Cambridge University Press.

Yaden, D. B. (1986). Reading research in metalinguistic awareness: A classification of findings according to focus and methodology. In D. B. Yaden & S. Templeton (Eds.). *Metalinguistic awareness and beginning literacy,* (pp. 41-62). Portsmouth, NH: Heinemann.

Yopp, H. (1988). The validity and reliability of phonemic awareness tests. *Reading Research Quarterly,* 23, 159-177.

Cognitive Processing in Bilinguals – R.J. Harris (Editor)
413

Auditory and Visual Speech Perception in Alphabetic and Non-alphabetic Chinese-Dutch Bilinguals

Beatrice de Gelder and Jean Vroomen
Tilburg University

Abstract

Chinese subjects were compared with Dutch controls on a speech-categorisation task in which they had to identify either auditory, visual, or audio-visual speech stimuli. Chinese subjects behave differently from native Dutch speakers on the categorisation of the auditory stimuli from a /ba-da/ continuum. Moreover, they were worse in lipreading /ba/ or /da/. When the Chinese subjects were divided into two subgroups as a function of whether they did master the alphabetic writing system, the results suggest a clear influence of alphabetic skills on speech sound categorisation.

Introduction

Learning to understand and speak a second language involves getting acquainted with a so far unfamiliar phonological system. That the mismatch between familiar and new phonological system can be a major obstacle is evident in one's intuitive and introspective evidence. Very little is known about how the phonology of a second language is acquired and the way native and second language sound systems interact. The categorical perception paradigm offers a tool for investigating an area in which linguistic experience might have effects.

Since its discovery in the late sixties (Liberman, Cooper, Shankweiler, and Studdert-Kennedy, 1967), the phenomenon of categorical perception offers an important source of evidence for arguing that speech is special. Categorical perception phenomena have been observed both with newborn infants and with adults (see Kuhl, 1990 for an overview). Yet, the basis of this well replicated phenomenon remains unclear and the inferences that can be drawn from the phenomenon to the representations and processes underlying speech perception remain hazardous.

The empirical reasons for this theoretical uncertainty are fairly straightforward. Very little is presently known about the influence of linguistic experience on speech processing. One crucial aspect of linguistic experience concerns phonological development itself. Very little is known about the development of the infants's categorisation ability over time. Data that would allow theories to build a bridge between the infant and the adult data are still lacking.

The infants' growing experience with language might affect its early categorisation ability. Clearly, the interpretation of the infants' categorical perception data needs to be put in the context of the development of the lexicon. The occurrence of developmental disorders offers a window into phonological development. Young retarded readers show a less steep categorical perception function than chronological and reading age controls (de Gelder & Vroomen, 1988; Werker & Tees, 1987). The poorer performance of this group is not due to poor alphabetic skills but suggests a phonological coding deficit manifesting itself on the occasion of reading acquisition. Nevertheless, experience with written language might be another source of phonological development and variability in categorisation performance.

The matter of the ontogenesis of phonological processing gets more complicated when we look also at visual speech categorisation. Kuhl and Meltzoff (1982) have shown that infants detect the equivalence between spoken and seen phonemes and have a preference for stimuli showing a cross-modal match. Yet, studies by Massaro, Thompson, Barron, and Laren (1986) show that there is a development in the ability to perceive visual speech. This increasing importance of visual speech over time is surprising given data which suggest that the auditory and the visual speech modality extract information from a common, abstract code (e.g., Massaro, 1987).

A second crucial aspect of linguistic experience concerns cross-linguistic influences. Within the categorical perception paradigm, cross-linguistic studies are a valuable source of information on the units of speech processing. At present, very few cross-linguistic studies of categorical perception are available. Here also, only the two extremes of the developmental continuum are represented. Young infants are sensitive to phonetic contrasts not active in their native language (Best et al., 1988; Werker & Tees, 1984), but have lost this ability by the end of the first year. From the available evidence it appears that experience with native language has an influence on phonetic boundaries (for a review, see Repp, 1984). For example, evidence for a cross-language difference between English and Japanese speakers was found for discrimination along the /r/-/l/ contrast (Miyawaki et al., 1975). Japanese subjects show no categorical perception of a contrast without phonemic value in their language. This leads one to ask whether acquiring a second language would modify this situation, or also, whether for the contrast that are active in the native language one would obtain comparable categorisation data across native speakers of two different languages.

It is not clear whether these data suggest a loss of the discrimination ability or a reorganisation within the phonological system in such a way that non-native language distinctions are no longer easily accessed. Werker & Tees (1984) have investigated this question. Their findings suggest that when given enough practice and adapting the testing procedures adult listeners can regain their ability to distinguish non-native contrasts and return to a phonetic or even an auditory mode of responding as opposed to a phonemic one. Such data would favour the reorganisation view.

The present study adds new data to the cross-linguistic aspect of categorical perception. Indirectly it also throws light on the issue of development. Our aim was to find out (1) whether Chinese bilinguals speaking Chinese having acquired Dutch at adult age would differ from native Dutch speakers in auditory categorisation, visual identification of lipread speech, and the visual influence on auditory categorisation, and (2) whether acquaintance with an alphabetic script would make any difference above and beyond the differences observed between bi-lingual Chinese and native Dutch speakers.

There are major differences between the sound systems of Dutch and Chinese. Spoken Chinese (Cantonese, Mandarin) is a syllabic language consisting of combinations of consonants, diphthongs, consonantic vowels and consonants. Yet, there is a major degree of overlap between the Chinese and the Dutch sound systems. For example, the syllables /ba/ and /da/ figure prominently in Dutch as well as in Chinese. Against that background there is no reason to expect major differences in auditory categorisation.

Visual speech identification performance offers a complementary source of information on speech sound categorisation as vision and audition represent two autonomous but very closely linked input modalities for speech. Adults with normal hearing combine the auditory and visual speech information in normal circumstances as well as under impoverished conditions (e.g., Massaro, 1987). Individual differences in lipreading ability have been noted but should not been taken as an indication that lipreading skill is under the control of such general factors as intelligence or verbal ability (Jeffers & Barley, 1971). No comparative data are available on visual speech identification as a function of the specific phonology of the native language. A final aspect of bimodal input situations concerns the influence of the input of one modality on the processing of the information in the other modality. Available studies predict that the visual influence will be a function of the subjects' lipreading skills. In populations where there is a suggestion of a deficit in phonological processing we have observed reduced influence of the visual input on the auditory processing (de Gelder & Vroomen, 1988; 1990; 1991). Thus there is no reason to expect reduced visual influence purely as a consequence of non-native language experience.

However, a critical aspect of the present study concerns the possible influence of the scripts the subject masters on his performance in the categorical perception task. Of the few available studies engaging in cross-linguistic comparison none has paid attention to the differences in orthographies between the languages and the possible influence of these differences. In contrast with Chinese, Dutch has an alphabetic and surface orthography. It is well known that alphabetic reading skills go hand in hand with phonemic awareness skills. Non-alphabetic readers cannot perform phonemic segmentation tasks (Read, Yun-Fei, Hong-Yin, & Bao-Qing, 1986) while their Chinese bi-scriptal counterparts manage well (de Gelder, Vroomen, & Bertelson, 1990). Of course, performance on meta-phonological tasks as examined in the above studies is a different matter than speech categorisation. The present study makes a beginning with the study if this complex issue. On this occasion we wanted to check whether differences in orthographic skills between the two groups of native Chinese speakers might be a source of variability in the categorisation task. If so, bi-scriptal Chinese subjects would differ from monoscriptal ones on the auditory categorisation and on the visual identification task. The differences would be less though than the one observed between monoscriptal Chinese and Dutch speakers.

Method

Subjects

Two groups of subjects were tested, a group of 18 Chinese subjects and a group of 17 Dutch controls. The Chinese subjects (14 female and 4 male) came from Mainland China and a few had spend some years in Hong Kong. Most of them worked in Chinese restaurants. The mean age of the Chinese subject was 30;9 year (range from 16;0 to 53;0 year). They had spend about 5;6 year in the Netherlands. The control group consisted of 9 male and 8 female native speakers of Dutch (mean age = 33;6 year). None of the subjects reported any hearing or seeing deficit.

Stimuli

Subjects were presented a colour videotape prepared by Massaro (see Massaro & Cohen, 1983, Experiment 2) showing a speaker seated in front of a wood panel. The speaker's head filled about two thirds of the screen. The tape was made by copying the original video tape and replacing the natural sound track with synthetic speech. A nine-step /ba/ to /da/ auditory continuum was used. It was created as follows. Tokens of the speaker's /ba/s and /da/s were analyzed using linear prediction to derive a set of parameters for driving a software-formant serial-resonator speech synthesizer (Klatt, 1980). By altering the parametric information regarding the first 80 msec of the syllable, a set of nine 400-msec syllables covering the range of /ba/ to /da/ was created. During the first 80 msec, Formant 1 (F1) went from 250 Hz to 700 Hz following a negatively accelerated path. The F2 followed a negatively accelerated path to 1199 Hz from one of nine values equally spaced between 1000 and 2000 Hz from most /ba/-like to most /da/-like, respectively. The F3 followed a linear transition to 2729 Hz from one of nine values equally spaced between 2200 and 3200 Hz. All other stimulus characteristics were identical for the nine auditory syllables.

Procedure

Nine levels along the auditory /ba/ to /da/ continuum were factorially combined with two possible visual articulations, /ba/ or /da/. These 18 trials represent the bimodal condition. There was also an auditory-alone and a visual-alone condition. In the auditory-alone condition, one of the nine auditory stimuli was presented, but the speaker did not move his mouth. In the visual-alone condition, the speaker articulated either /ba/ or /da/, but no auditory speech was presented. In this case, the subject had to rely entirely on lip-reading. In every block of 54 trials, there were 18 bimodal conditions, 18 auditory-alone conditions, and 18 visual-alone conditions. The experiment consisted of 5-1/2 blocks of trials preceded by 10 practice trials for a total of 307 trials. There was a 5-min break after 160 trials. Subjects were tested individually in a quiet room. They viewed a 63 cm television monitor which presented both the auditory and the visual dimensions of the speech stimuli. Subject sat about 2 meter from the monitor. The audio was set at a comfortable listening level. Subjects were told of the three different kind of trials: The bimodal trials, the auditory-alone trials, and the visual-alone trials. They were instructed to report orally whether the speaker said /ba/ or /da/. The experimenter sat next to the subject and noted the responses and determined whether the subject was watching the screen at the time of the speech presentation. If this criterion was not met, the trial was disregarded.

Results

The results show that Chinese subjects are less categorical in their labelling of the /ba-da/ continuum and that they are worse in lipreading than the controls. The effect of the visual information on the bimodal labelling was not significantly different between the two groups.

We first consider the robustness of auditory categories. Figure 1 displays the proportion of /da/ responses as a function of the nine levels of the auditory continuum and the three levels of the visual variable, a /ba/, none, or a /da/ articulation, separately for the two groups. An analysis of variance (ANOVA) was performed on the proportion of /da/ responses with group as between subjects variable and the auditory and visual factors as within subjects variables. As expected, the average proportion of /da/ responses increased as the auditory stimulus moved from the /ba/ to the /da/ end of the continuum [$F(8,264) = 271.0$, $p < .001$]. There was also a large effect of the visual variable [$F(2,66) = 135.3$, $p < .001$]. The average proportion of /da/ responses increased from .290 for the /ba/ visual stimulus, .529 for the neutral stimulus, to .772 for the /da/ visual stimulus. The interaction of the auditory and the visual variable was significant [$F(16,528) = 15.3$, $p < .001$], because the effect of the visual variable is larger at the ambiguous levels of the auditory continuum. These findings are in agreement with earlier studies (cf. Massaro, et al.,1986; Massaro, 1987).

The only effect in which the group variable was significant was a second order interaction among the group, auditory, and visual factors [$F(16,528) = 2.37$, $p < .002$]. In order to explore this, a separate ANOVA with group as between subjects factor was performed on the proportion of /da/ responses in the neutral visual articulation condition. These data are replotted in figure 2. There was a main effect of the auditory variable [$F(8,264 = 356.8$, $p < .001$], and a significant interaction between the groups and the auditory variable [$F(8,264) = 6.32$, $p < .001$]. Inspection of figure 2 suggests that the Chinese subjects were less categorical in the identification of the stimuli. That is, the labelling function for the Chinese subjects is less steep than that of the control group.

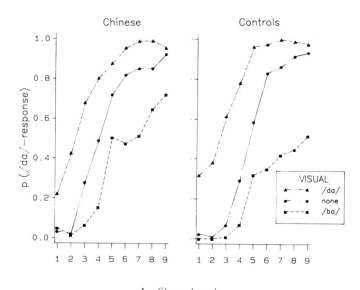

Figure 1. Proportion of /da/-responses as a function of the auditory and visual levels for the Chinese subjects and controls.

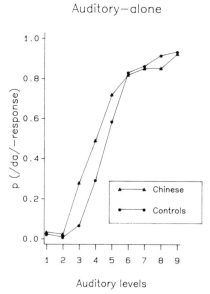

Figure 2. Proportion of /da/-responses as a function of the auditory levels for the Chinese subjects and for the controls.

To analyze this, the individual proportions of /da/ responses were submitted to a logit transformation from which the values of the phoneme boundaries and the slopes are obtained (Finney, 1964). These are determined by regressively computing the cumulative normal distribution which is closest, by a maximum likelihood criterion, to the data. The mean of the resulting distribution is the interpolated 50% crossover point (phoneme boundary) and the slope is a measure of the degree of the sharpness with which phoneme categories are distinguished from one another. In a two-tailed *t-test*, there was a marginally significant difference in the place of the phoneme boundary [$t(33) = 2.03$, $p = .06$]. The mean boundaries were located at 4.34 and 4.93 stimulus units for the Chinese and the controls, respectively. The slopes of the labelling functions were significantly different [$t(33) = 2.46$, $p < .02$]. The mean slope (in degrees) was 40.8 for the Chinese subjects and 49.9 for the controls. Thus, Chinese subjects were less categorical in the identification of the /ba-da/ continuum.

We now turn to the results on visual speech identification. In the visual-only condition, the proportion of correct responses was determined. The Chinese subjects were worse in lip-reading than the controls [$t(33) = 2.93$, $p < .01$]. The average percentage of correct responses was 80.3 for the Chinese and 93.7 for the controls.

In order to measure the contribution of the visual source to the bimodal speech events, the individual percentage of /da/ responses given a visual /ba/ was subtracted from the percentage of /da/ responses given a visual /da/. The mean contribution of the visual source was 41.6 for the Chinese group and 54.0 for the controls. This difference fell short of significance [$t(33) = 1.68$, $p = .10$].

A correlation between subjects' proportion correct in the visual-only condition and the steepness of the labelling function in the audio-visual condition with a neutral articulation was computed. The correlation between these variables was significant for the combined results, $r = .521$, $p < .001$. For the two groups separately, the correlation was positive but fell short of significance in the control group (Chinese, $r = .519$, $p < .02$; control group, $r = .255$, $p = .16$). In general, the results show a positive relationship between the ability to lipread and the degree of categorical speech perception.

As already argued, we wanted to know whether alphabetic reading skill has an influence on speech categorisation. For that reason, the Chinese group was divided into two sub-groups: one group consisted of non-alphabetic Chinese subjects who could not read an alphabetic script (Dutch or any other alphabetic script), but who were fluent readers of the Chinese logographic script; the other group of Chinese subjects could read logographic Chinese as well as the Dutch alphabetic script (See Table 1 for details of the subjects). The group was split on the basis of an alphabetic reading test which required reading aloud 20 mono and bisyllabic pseudo words. Pseudo words were created by changing one letter from real words. Subjects who could not read more than 50 percent correct were assigned to the non-alphabetic group; subjects who read more were assigned to the alphabetic group. The mean percentage correct was 13.6 for the non-alphabetic group and 82.0 for the alphabetic group. Subjects were also given a reading test in which they had to read 20 Dutch mono- and bisyllabic high frequency words. The mean percentage correct on this reading test was for the non-alphabetic group 49.3 percent and for the alphabetic group 96.5 percent. In a logographic reading test subjects had to read 20 logographs of nouns. Both Chinese groups performed errorless on this task. The non-alphabetic group consisted of 1 male and 7 female with a mean age of 29;10 year. They had been living for about 2;6 year in the Netherlands. The alphabetic Chinese group consisted of 3 male and 7 female subjects (mean age = 31;6). These subjects had been to Dutch reading classes and had acquired a basic alphabetic reading skill. To assess the reading level of the control group, these subjects were given a standardized speed reading test (Brus & Voeten, 1973). On average they read 100.1 real words in 1 minute and were all within normal range.

Table 1

Details of the Chinese Sub-Groups

Group	N	Age	Real	Reading % correct Pseudo	Logographic
Non-alphabetic	8	29;10	49.3	13.6	100
Alphabetic	10	31;6	96.5	82.0	100

In the following analyses, we compared the three groups (non-alphabetic Chinese, alphabetic Chinese, and controls) on their labelling of the stimuli. Figure 3 displays the proportion of /da/ responses separately for the three groups. Note that the control group is the same as in the previous analyses. An ANOVA was performed on the proportion of /da/ responses with group as between subjects variable and the auditory and visual factors as within subjects variables. As in the previous analyses, the auditory [$F(8,256) = 246.4$, $p < .001$] and visual [$F(2,64) = 109.7$, $p < .001$] stimulus effects were significant, as was the interaction between these two variables [$F(16,512) = 13.0$, $p < .001$]. There was also a significant second order interaction of the group by auditory by visual factor [$F(32,512) = 1.71$, $p < .01$].

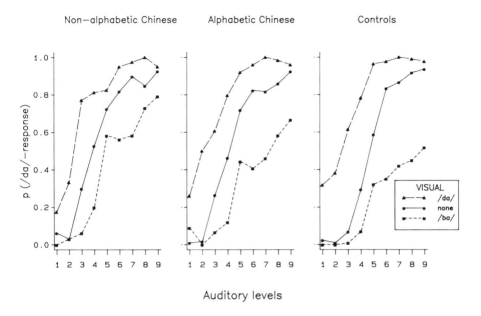

Figure 3. Proportion of /da/-responses as a function of the auditory and visual levels for the non-alphabetic Chinese, alphabetic Chinese, and controls.

A separate ANOVA with group as between subjects variable was performed on the proportion of /da/ responses in the neutral visual articulation condition. These data are presented in figure 4. There was a main effect of the auditory variable [F(8,256) = 305.1, p < .001], and a significant interaction between the groups and the auditory variable [F(16,256) = 3.27, p < .001]. Submitting the data to a logit transformation revealed that there were no significant differences in the place of the phoneme boundary [F(2,32) = 2.05, p = .14]. The mean boundaries were at 4.27, 4.40, and 4.93 stimulus units for the non-alphabetic Chinese, alphabetic Chinese and the controls, respectively. The slopes of the labelling functions were different [F(2,32) = 3.83, p < .05]. The mean slopes (in degrees) were 37.3, 43.6 and 49.9 for the non-alphabetic Chinese, alphabetic Chinese, and controls, respectively. *Post hoc* analyses (Fisher's LSD) showed that the non-alphabetic Chinese were less categorical in their labelling than the controls (α = .05), but they did not differ from the alphabetic Chinese. Alphabetic Chinese did not differ significantly from the controls.

The difference in steepness of categorization is not depending on the length of the stay in Holland as is shown by the absence of significant correlation between the steepness parameter and the length of stay (for both groups r = 0.13).

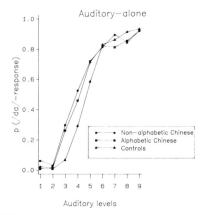

Figure 4. Proportion of /da/-responses as a function of the auditory levels for the non-alphabetic Chinese, alphabetic Chinese, and controls.

There was also a significant difference in lipreading performance between the three groups [F(2,32) = 10.9, p < .001]. The average percentage of correct responses was 70.0 for non-alphabetic Chinese, 88.5 for alphabetic Chinese, and 93.7 for the controls. *Post hoc* analyses showed that non-alphabetic Chinese performed worse than alphabetic Chinese and the controls (Fisher's LSD, α = .01).

The mean contribution of the visual source in the bimodal conditions was 36.0 for the non-alphabetic group, 46.1 for the alphabetic Chinese, and 54.0 for the controls. This difference felt short of significance [F(2,32) = 1.88, p = .16]. Table 2 summarizes the results.

Table 2

Performance on the Speech Identification Test for the Three Groups

Group	Steepness auditory categorization	Lipreading % correct	Visual dominance
Non-alphabetic Chinese	37.3	70.0	36.0
Alphabetic Chinese	43.6	88.5	46.1
Controls	49.9	93.7	54.0

Discussion

The present study suggests that experience with native language leaves its mark on the way speakers make speech sound categorisations, irrespective of whether speech sounds are presented auditorially, visually, or bimodally. Speakers learning a second language in adulthood remain different from the native speakers of that language. At the same time, the data suggest a second kind of effect of experience with language, this time occurring on the occasion of learning to read the alphabetic script of the non-native language. This second experience appears to narrow the gap between native and non-native speakers, creating an intermediate category between the two other groups. If so, the possibility that orthographic skills exercise an influence on speech categorisation must be taken seriously.

The most surprising fact suggested by these data is that the phoneme boundary is less marked for Chinese subjects than it is for the native Dutch speakers. What aspects of linguistic experience might explain this fact? How might linguistic experience affect speech sound perception and what factors might drive it? A central factor so far appears to be the role of a non-native contrast in the speaker's native language. A recent proposal by Best, McRoberts, and Sithole (1988) distinguishes four alternatives: (a) the two stimuli are assimilated to a single category; (b) the two stimuli are assimilated to opposing native language categories; (c) one stimulus is privileged because taken as representing a better example of the category; (d) neither member is assimilated to a native category. Unlike in the study by Miyawaki et al. (1975) the present study did not present the subjects with a stimuli without phonemic value in their native language. The syllables /ba/ vs. /da/ are as common in Chinese as they are in Dutch. Moreover, the subjects were all familiar with spoken Dutch.

Is the categorical perceptual difference observed here suggestive of a difference in phonemic vs. phonetic or acoustic discrimination difference between the groups? It is clear that the audiovisual presentation of the stimuli strongly induces a speech mode of listening even in the auditory-only condition where the speakers' face was not moving. But more convincingly, the fact that categorisation differences between the three groups show up in the auditory as well as in the visual presentation modality strongly suggests that cognitive-linguistic and not peripheral differences exist between the groups.

Two other aspects of the data are straightforward. Steepness of auditory categorisation is a good predictor of success on the lipreading task, at least in neurologically unimpaired subjects. The data from visual speech identification offer new support for that view. The results on auditory speech categorisation do not lead us to expect a very high performance on the visual discrimination task in the two groups of Chinese subjects. Likewise, the results on the influence of visual information on auditory categorisation are predicted by earlier studies. Werker (1991) mentions the finding of a similar cross-linguistic difference in audio-visual speech perception and an effect of the visual information that is different as a function of the native language of the subjects (French vs. English). The representation activated as a consequence of a mismatch between the auditory and the visual input, the so called McGurk illusion (McGurk & MacDonald, 1976) is thus different for English and for French speakers watching the same stimuli.

Finally, we turn to the influence from experience with written language, e.g. learning to read Dutch. It is clear from the present data that the categorisation performance of bi-scriptal Chinese speakers differs from that of the mono-scriptal Chinese. Yet, at present there is little known about whether reading skill or orthography influences speech perception. But there is reason to believe that cross-modal influences between spoken language representation and written language representation do occur. In contrast, what is well documented is that alphabetic scripts promote phonemic awareness (see Bertelson & de Gelder, 1990 for an overview). The syllabic phonology of Chinese does not encourage an explicit segmental representation of speech. Whether we are dealing with an effect of having acquired basic reading skill or with an effect of the teaching methods is not clear. In the domain of metaphonological skills the same question crops up and is currently still debated in research on reading acquisition with young children (Bertelson & de Gelder, 1990). It is likely that in the course of reading instruction a good deal of attention has been devoted to building up awareness of internal sounds structures. Although the speech categorisation task is not a metaphonological awareness task, subjects may have profited from their recently acquired skills at segmental analysis and they may have become able to focus attention in a more structured way on phonemic differences.

Acknowledgement Note

This work was partially supported by the Tilburg VF research program. We are indebted to D. Massaro for use of the test materials and to E. Vianen and M. van Zon for assistance with testing the subjects. We are grateful to O. Tzeng for comments on the manuscript.

References

Bertelson, P., & de Gelder, B. (1990). The emergence of phonological awareness. In I. Mattingly and M. Studdert-Kennedy (Eds.), *The motor theory of speech perception.* (Pp. 393-412). Hillsdale, NJ: Lawrence Erlbaum Associates.

Best, C. T., McRoberts, G. W., & Sithole, N. N. (1988). The phonological basis of perceptual loss of nonnative contrasts: Maintenance and discrimination among Zulu Clicks by English-speaking adults and infants. *Journal of Experimental Psychology: Human Perception and Performance,* 14, 245-260.

Brus, B. T., & Voeten, M. J. M. (1973). *Een minuut test. Vorm A en B.* Nijmegen: Berkhout.

de Gelder, B., & Vroomen, J. (1988, August). *Bimodal speech perception in young dyslexics.* Paper presented at the 6th Australian Language and Speech Conference. Sydney.

de Gelder, B., & Vroomen, J. (1990, July). *Poor readers are poor lipreaders.* Paper presented at the Applied Psychology Conference, Kyoto.

de Gelder, B., & Vroomen, J. (1991). Phonological deficits beneath the surface of reading-acquisition problems. *Psychological Research,* 53, 88-97.

de Gelder, B., Vroomen, J., & Bertelson, P. (1990, January). *Segmental abilities in bi-scriptal Chinese.* Paper presented at the Experimental Psychology Society, London.

Finney, D. J. (1964). *Probit analysis.* Cambridge: Cambridge University Press.

Jeffers, J., & Barley, M. (1971). *Speechreading.* Springfield, IL: Thomas.

Klatt, D. H. (1980). Software for a cascade/parallel formant synthesizer. *Journal of the Acoustical Society of America,* 67, 905-917.

Kuhl, P. (1990). On babies, birds, modules, and mechanisms: A comparative approach to the acquisition of vocal communication. In R. J. Dooling and S. H. Hulse (Eds.), *The comparative psychology of audition* (Pp. 379-419). Hillsdale, NJ: Lawrence Erlbaum Associates.

Kuhl, P., & Meltzoff, A. N. (1982). The bimodal perception of speech in infancy. *Science,* 218, 1138-1141.

Liberman, A. M., Cooper, F. S., Shankweiler, D. P., & Studdert-Kennedy, M. (1967). Perception of the speech code. *Psychological Review,* 74, 431-461.

Massaro, D. W. (1987). *Speech perception by ear and eye: A paradigm for psychological inquiry.* Hillsdale, NJ: Lawrence Erlbaum Associates.

Massaro, D. W., & Cohen, M. M. (1983). Evaluation and integration of visual and auditory information in speech perception. *Journal of Experimental Psychology: Human Perception and Performance,* 9, 753-771.

Massaro, D. W., Thompson, L. A., Barron, B., & Laren, E. (1986). Developmental changes in visual and auditory contributions to speech perception. *Journal of Experimental Child Psychology,* 41, 93-113.

McGurk, H., & MacDonald, J. (1976). Hearing lips and seeing voices. *Nature,* 264, 746-748.

Miyawaki, K., Strange, W., Verbrugge, R., Liberman, A. M., Jenkins, J. J., & Fujimura, O. (1975). An effect of linguistic experience: The discrimination of /r/ and /l/ by native speakers of Japanese and English. *Perception and Psychophysics*, 17, 9-16.

Read, C., Yun-Fei, Z., Hong-Yin, N., & Bao-Qing, D. (1986). The ability to manipulate speech sounds depends on knowing alphabetic writing. *Cognition*, 24, 31-44.

Repp, B. H. (1984). Categorical perception: Issues, methods and findings. In N. J. Lass (Ed.), *Speech and language: Advances in basic research and practice. (Vol. 10)*, (Pp. 310-330). New York: Academic Press.

Werker, J. F. (1991). Ontogeny of speech perception. In I. G. Mattingly and M. Studdert-Kennedy (Eds.), *Modularity and the motor theory of speech perception.* (Pp. 91-110). Hillsdale, NJ: Lawrence Erlbaum Associates.

Werker, J. F. & Tees, R. C. (1984). Cross-language speech perception: Evidence for perceptual reorganisation during the first year of life. *Infant Behavior and Development*, 7, 49-63.

Werker, J. F. & Tees, R. C. (1987). Speech perception in severely disabled and average reading disabled children. *Canadian Journal of Psychology*, 41, 48-61.

Cognitive Processing in Bilinguals – R.J. Harris (Editor)
© *1992 Elsevier Science Publishers B.V. All rights reserved.*
427

A Study of Interlingual and Intralingual Stroop Effect in Three Different Scripts:
Logograph, Syllabary, and Alphabet

Wei Ling Lee
Tan Tock Seng Hospital, Singapore

Ghim Choo Wee
Ministry of Education, Singapore

Ovid J. L. Tzeng and Daisy L. Hung
University of California, Riverside
and
The Salk Institute for Biological Studies, San Diego

Abstract

One hundred and sixty-seven Chinese, 24 Malay and 24 Indian children of
Singapore, bilingual in both English and their mother tongues (Chinese,
Malay, and Tamil, respectively) were tested with the Stroop color-naming
tasks in both languages under intralingual and interlingual conditions. The
interference effect was found for each and every language, with respect to
both intra- and inter-language conditions. The Chinese words were not found
to cause more interference than the English words, and the reduction in
interference in the switch language situation was the same for all three
bilingual groups. These results contradict the predictions made by the
orthography-specific hypothesis in which logographic script is expected to
induce greater intralanguage interference than the sound-based scripts
(syllabary and alphabet) and the reduction of interference from intra- to
interlanguage condition is expected to increase as the difference between two
orthographic structures increases. A further analysis suggests that the speed
of decoding color words and the speed of generating color names may
combine to determine the magnitude of the Stroop effect. Under such a
conceptualization, it is meaningless to assign any important role to the
orthographic factor in the interpretation of the bilingual Stroop effect. In fact,
the Stroop effect itself, regardless of the context of bilingualism, is better
handled by an activation-suppression model of selective attention which
accounts for all data observed in the present study as well as those observed
in the previous literature.

The many different writing systems in use today can be divided into two broad
categories. The first category are those in which each symbol represents a single
morpheme, and the written symbol is mapped directly onto meaning. Examples
include Chinese Hanji and Japanese Kanji which are essentially the same as the
Chinese Hanji with certain changes in meaning due to historical as well as
socio-cultural reasons. In the second category, each symbol represents a speech sound,

and the relation of sign to meaning is mediated through the phonological system of the spoken language. Writing systems in this category can be further subdivided into alphabetic scripts such as English and Malay in which each written symbol represents a phoneme; and syllabic scripts such as Tamil and Japanese Kana, where each written symbol represents a syllable.

A theoretical question of practical importance is whether reading different types of scripts requires different information processing strategies. A positive answer would have important implications for how reading should be taught in different countries using different writing systems. Indeed, there is some experimental and clinical evidence supporting this theoretical position. Only a few examples will be cited here. It has long been noted that in processing linguistic materials, the mode of presentation has a differential effect on memory in the two different scripts. For English readers, the auditory presentation (listening) produces better recall performance than visual presentation (reading); however, the opposite is true for the Chinese readers (Tzeng & Wang, 1983; Hue, Fang, & Hsu, in press). Such an orthographic-specific effect has also been confirmed by results from neuro-psychological observations. For example, Sasanuma (1974) reported that the ability to read Kanji (logographic) or Kana (syllabic) script could be selectively impaired in adult Japanese patients who become aphasic, depending on the exact site of the lesion. Similarly, Hasuike, Tzeng, and Hung (1986) surveyed more than 20 studies employing visual half-field presentation technique to examine the pattern of cerebral asymmetry and a right visual field (left-hemisphere) advantage for the recognition of phonetically based symbols such as English words or Japanese Kana scripts, and a left visual field advantage for the recognition of single Chinese characters. Even though these data lead to a general consensus among researchers in that processing of logographic characters may be less subjected to the influence of phonological information in the language, implications from these visual hemi-field experiments are much in dispute, mainly due to the many problematic aspects of their procedures (Sergent & Hellige, 1986).

Another approach to investigating the different information processing strategies used in reading different scripts is to use the Stroop interference paradigm (Stroop, 1935). The interference in the Stroop color-word test is the greater time required to name a series of color patches when the patches are themselves incongruent color names (e.g., GREEN written in red ink) than when the patches are simple meaningless colored patches. Biederman and Tsao (1979) found a greater interference effect for Chinese subjects in a Chinese-version Stroop color-naming task than for American subjects in an English version. They attributed this difference to the possibility that there may be fundamental differences in the perceptual demands of reading Chinese and English. Since the perception of color and the direct accessing of meaning from a pattern's configuration are presumed to be right hemisphere functions, they suggested that during the Stroop test these two functions might be competing for the same perceptual capacity of the right hemisphere. This competition could have been avoided in the English Stroop test because reading English and naming colors are executed by different hemispheric mechanisms.

Biederman and Tsao's finding and their account for the data are interesting and immediately provoked a series of studies from all over the world to further examine effect of orthographic variations on reading (Hung & Tzeng, 1981; Tzeng & Hung, 1988). Critics (e.g., Smith & Kirsner, 1982) pointed to the fact that two totally different subject populations were tested in Biederman and Tsao's study and the thus, the results could easily be accounted for by the subject, rather than orthographic, factor. In an attempt to circumvent the problem of subject variations, investigators then focused on the Japanese writing system in which the same readers could be tested under two different scripts, namely, Kanji logographs and Kana symbols. Data from several studies upheld the orthographic- specific hypothesis (Hatta, 1981; Hatta, Katoh, & Aitani, 1982; Fang, Tzeng, & Alva, 1981) with the results that for the same Japanese reader a Kanji- Stroop test produced more interference than a Kana-Stroop test.

The Japanese evidence is far from conclusive, however. A major problem lies in the fact that in everyday ordinary reading materials, the color names are always written in Kanji logographs and thus, when readers were facing both Kanji and Kana color terms, their naming for the former is more representative of natural reading while their naming for the latter is contrived to meet the experimental demands. That is, with the Japanese subjects in a Stroop experiment under two scripts, the subject variable and the spoken language efficiency may be equated, but the orthographic variable is certainly a confound which is difficult to overcome.

The methodological problem can be reasonably resolved in Singapore in which school children are brought up to be bilinguals as well as literate in bi-scripts. Since they are competent in two languages, their reading of either script written in its natural style should give an excellent opportunity to examine the orthographic-specific hypothesis with regard to the Stroop effect. In addition, Singapore has several unique bilingual populations in which various bi-scriptal combinations are present. For example, the Chinese-English bilingual children are learning both logographic and alphabetic scripts; the Malay-English bilinguals are learning two types of alphabetic scripts; and the Indian-English bilinguals are learning both syllabic and alphabetic scripts. Examinations of the Stroop interference effect across these different bilingual groups with respect to the distinctive orthographic properties would give a wide range of possibilities for theoretical considerations.

If Biederman and Tsao's orthographic-specific hypothesis is true, then one would expect that in a subject who is bilingual in both Chinese and English, the interference when naming Chinese color-words in Chinese would be more than when naming English color-words in English. On the other hand, in a subject bilingual in English and Malay, we would not expect much difference in the interference when naming the Malay color-word in Malay compared to naming English color-words in English. This is because Malay and English both use alphabetic scripts. In fact, modern Malay script utilizes the same alphabet as English, and each alphabet represent the same or very similar phonemes in Malay as they do in English. The two writing systems differ in that the grapheme-phoneme conversion rules are very regular in Malay, whilst there are frequent exceptions in English. The expected findings in a subject bilingual in Tamil and English would be similar to that of the Malay-English bilingual. This is because Tamil is a syllabic script which has very regular grapheme-syllable conversion rules. Though the syllables are made up of one or more letters, each syllable has a distinct configuration different from its constituent letters. Indian children learning to read are taught how to read the syllables and combine the syllables to form words. Only later, do they learn the individual letter which make up the syllables.

Another point of interest when studying the Stroop interference paradigm in bilinguals is the reduction of the interference in the interlingual situation compared to the intralingual situation. It is well known the when bilinguals are asked to name the color of a color-word in a different language than that in which the word is written, the interference is less than if the task is to name it the color of a color-word written in the same language. It has been postulated that the greater the difference between the orthographic structure of the two languages, the greater the reduction in interference in the switch language situation (Fang, et al., 1981). This reduction was postulated to reflect the difference in the demand on the same central processor due to orthographic similarity. It was thought that because the greater the orthographic similarity between the two languages, the stronger will be the competition for the same information processing mechanisms and thus, the smaller will be the reduction of Stroop interference from the intra- to the interlingual condition.

The present study examined intralingual as well as interlingual Stroop color-word tests with Chinese, Malay and Indian children in Singapore who were bilingual in English and their mother tongue. With such a wide range of orthographic variations, we hoped to replicate Biederman and Tsao's finding that Chinese color-words caused more interference than English words. In addition, we also hypothesized that reading a logographic script involved a different information processing mechanism than sound-based alphabetic script such as Tamil syllabary and English alphabet. Hence, the reduction in interference in the interlingual Stroop situation was expected to be greatest for the Chinese-English situation, less for the Tamil-English, and much less for Malay-English situations.

Method

Subjects

Two hundred and fifteen third-grade children were randomly selected from two schools, 167 were Chinese, 24 were Malay and 24 were Indians. The age range was 9.0 to 11.0 years with a mean age of 9.5 years. The children had all been studying English as the first written language and written forms of their mother tongue as a second written language in school for at least 3 years. The mother tongue was Mandarin, Malay and Tamil for the Chinese, Malay and Indian children, respectively. At home, most children spoke their mother tongue, whereas at school, English was the medium of instruction and the first language. From the speed of color naming in English and their mother tongue, the children of all three races could be considered to be equally fluent in both languages. In this paper, the written form of the mother tongue will be abbreviated as L2, the official title of the subject matter used in the schools.

Materials

Nine types of stimulus boards were prepared:

1. Colored XXX (control board).
2. Black English color words.
3. Black Chinese color words.
4. Black Malay color words.
5. Black Tamil color words.
6. Color-word board in English.
7. Color-word board in Chinese.
8. Color-word board in Malay.
9. Color-word board in Tamil.

The control board had 5 columns (22.5 cm each) by 10 rows (18 cm each) of colored XXX. The XXX were written in red, green or blue and measured 0.8 cm tall by 2.0 cm wide. The three colors occurred randomly except that no color occurred twice in succession. The second, third, fourth and fifth boards were constructed with five columns of 10 words each. The words were names of colors (red, green and blue) written in black. The color names occurred randomly except that no word occurred twice in succession. The English, Malay and Tamil words measured 1.7 - 2.5 cm wide and 0.8 cm tall. The Chinese characters measured 1.5 x 1.5 cm each. The color name in the 4 different languages were as follows:

1. English: red, green, blue.
2. Chinese: hong, ching, lan.
3. Malay: maira, hijau, biru.
4. Tamil: sivapu, pachai, nilum.

Procedure

The children were tested individually. Each child was given 8 tasks which were divided into two 4-task blocks. The first block included:

1. Color naming of colored XXX in English.
2. Color naming of colored XXX in L2.
3. Reading color names written in black English words.
4. Reading color names written in black words in L2.

The above 4 tasks were always administered before the subsequent block of 4 tasks. This is to ensure that the children were able to read all the words, and were able to distinguish the various colors. The order in which the above four tasks were administered was randomized. The following 4 tasks were then administered in the second block.

1. Color naming of English color-words in English.
2. Color naming of L2 color-words in L2.
3. Color naming of English color-words in L2.
4. Color naming of L2 color-words in English.

The sequence in which the latter 4 tasks were administered was also randomized. Before the experiment started, the child sat at a table while the stimulus boards were placed face down on the table. The experimenter explained the task and procedure to the child. The child was asked to perform each task as quickly and as accurately as possible and to correct mistakes where possible. The child was asked not to point to the items. In the tasks involving color-words, it was specially emphasized not to read the words but to name their colors instead. Each time a stimulus board was to be displayed, the child was informed of the type of task to be performed. The stimulus board was turned face down as soon as the task was completed. Time to complete the task for the entire board (50 stimulus items) was recorded to the nearest 0.1 sec with a stopwatch.

Results and Discussion

Measures

Eight measures were derived from the time taken to complete each of the eight tasks. A list of these measures and a summary of results from these measures across the three ethnic groups is presented in Table 1.

Table 1

Mean Color Naming Times (in Sec) for the Eight Different Conditions for the Three Bilingual Groups

Condition	Chinese-English	Malay-English	Tamil-English
A: name 50 colored XXX in English	51.4	56.2	51.4
B: name 50 colored XXX in L2	50.0	53.9	63.0
C: read 50 black English color names	36.5	32.5	32.9
D: read 50 black L2 color names	38.8	34.7	42.1
E: name the ink color of 50 English color-words in English	88.3	96.6	92.4
F: name the ink color 50 L2 color-words in L2	84.0	95.5	96.3
G: name the ink color of 50 English color-words in L2	77.2	87.1	83.5
H: name the ink color of 50 L2 color-words in English	71.6	82.5	74.4

In addition, from the above measures difference scores were computed to indicate the amount of interference in various intra- and inter-language conditions with appropriate control measures.

A-B: difference in time to name 50 colored XXX in English compared to L2. (A-B).
C-D: difference in time to read 50 English words compared to 50 L2 words. (C-D).
STR/E: interference of English color-words on color naming in English.(E-A).
STR/L2: interference of L2 color-words on color naming in L2. (F-B).
INTER/E: difference in magnitude of interference when color-words and
    response were both in English compared to the situation where stimuli
    were color-words in L2 but response was in English. (E-A-H+B).

A summary of these derived measures for the three ethnic groups is presented in Table 2. The analysis of the results for each ethnic group will be presented separately, followed by comparisons among various language groups.

Table 2

Paired T-Tests Comparing the Difference in Time Taken to Read Color Names or to Name Colors for Each Child

CHINESE: N=167

Variable	Mean (sec)	Std Error	t	Prob>
A-B	1.43	0.907	1.574	0.1175
C-D	-2.32	0.596	-3.896	0.0001
STR/E	36.95	1.365	27.059	0.0001
STR/L2	33.98	1.306	26.024	0.0001
STR/E/L2	2.96	1.411	2.100	0.0372
INTER/E	-16.74	1.108	-15.102	0.0001

MALAY: N=24

Variable	Mean	Std Error	t	Prob>
A-B	2.33	2.307	1.012	0.3223
C-D	-2.20	1.223	-1.802	0.0847
STR/L2	40.30	3.434	11.736	0.0001
STR/E/L2	41.63	2.817	14.778	0.0001
INTER/E	-1.33	3.985	-0.334	0.7425

TAMIL: N=24

Variable	Mean	Std Error	t	Prob>
A-B	-11.53	2.654	-4.345	0.0002
C-D	-9.18	1.215	-7.557	0.0001
STR/E	40.95	3.076	13.313	0.0001
STR/L2	33.48	3.971	8.432	0.0001
STR/E/L2	7.467	4.316	1.730	0.0970
INTER/E	-18.004	2.778	-6.480	0.0001

Chinese Children

An inspection of the times in Table 1 shows that there is no difference in the speed of color naming in English compared to Chinese, indicating that the Chinese children were equally competent in naming the colors of both languages. A statistical analysis with a paired-t test on the difference scores (A-B) supports this conclusion. If anything, there was a slight but significant difference in speed of reading the Chinese words compared to English words (C-D), even though English was taught as the first written language in Singapore. Importantly, a significant interference effect was observed for both intralingual Stroop conditions. However, the interference was greater when the stimulus and response language were both in English (STR/E) than in Chinese (STR/L2). This result is in sharp contrast to those obtained by Biederman and Tsao (1979) in which Chinese subjects were compared with English-speaking subjects and greater interference was observed for the former group. The discrepancy has a serious implication for our conceptualization of the relationship between writing systems and learning to read. We will discuss these issues in depth after examining the Stroop effects in other bilingual groups. The result also confirmed the expectation that there would be a significant reduction in interference in the interlingual situation (INTER/E). Again, we will reserve our analysis for the magnitude of reduction until we have a chance to have a look at results of other groups. Suffice it to say that all the significant effects are supported by statistical analysis, as shown in Table 2.

Malay Children

The Malay children did not show a significant difference in the speed of color naming in English compared to Malay (A-B). Though they were slightly slower in reading Malay words compared to English (C-D), this did not reach statistical significance. This difference was not unexpected as the Malay words were each 2 syllables long compared to 1 syllable in the case of the English words. As expected, there was a significant interference in the intralingual situation (STR/E and STR/L2) which was significantly reduced in the interlingual situation (INTER/E). However, there was no significant difference in the magnitude of the intralingual interference in English and Malay. That is, the magnitude of interference caused by Malay color-words on response in Malay was the same as with English color-words on response in English. Statistical analyses and their respective results are presented in Table 2.

Indian Children

The findings in the Indian children were very similar to that in the Malay children except that the Indian children took longer to name colors and to read words in Tamil compared to English. Again, this is not unexpected as the Tamil words had 2 to 3 syllables per word compared to one syllable in the case of the English words. Subjects showed significant intralingual Stroop interference effects for both English and Tamil, with the latter producing significantly greater interference than the former. However, since both scripts are presumably sound-based, such a difference is certainly unexpected based upon previous orthographic-specificity account. There is also a significant reduction of interference from intra- to inter-lingual conditions. These results and their statistical tests are presented in Table 2.

Cross-Script Comparisons of Intra- and Inter-lingual Stroop Effects

From the above results and their statistical analyses, it is clear that in each ethnic group of the three different bilingual settings (Chinese-English bilinguals, Malay-English bilinguals, and Tamil-English bilinguals), the Stroop color interference effect was convincingly demonstrated for each of the two written languages as well as for the inter-language color naming tasks. The question of import is whether the magnitude of the interference differs systematically from one type of script to the other. Many researchers (Biederman & Tsao, 1979; Hatta, 1981) have given an positive answer. However, methodological deficiencies as pointed out above have considerably weakened their theoretical stipulations. Thus, it is important to reexamine the scriptal effect with more or less balanced bilingual readers in our Singapore populations.

It should be noted that the three bilingual groups showed equivalent amounts of interference in the English Stroop task (37, 40, and 41 sec for Chinese-English, Malay-English, and Tamil-English bilingual groups, respectively), indicating that all three groups of children are subjected to a similar degree of color naming interference in English, a common language shared by all of them. Now let us use the English language as a reference point and compare the magnitude of the Stroop interference of the L2 across the three ethnic groups.

Table 2 shows that the intralanguage Stroop interference indeed varies across languages, with significantly greater interference in the alphabetic Malay language (41.63 sec) than in the logographic Chinese and syllabic Tamil languages (33.98 sec and 33.48, respectively), $F(2, 212) = 9.76$, p<.01. Since these three groups of bilingual subjects showed an equivalent amount of interference in the English Stroop task, the difference cannot be attributed to the subject factor. However, the observed differences cannot be accounted for by above-mentioned orthographic hypothesis either. Ironically, the pattern of the differences is just the opposite to what has been predicted from an orthographic hypothesis. Hence, we have the first sign of failure by the orthographic hypothesis to account for the intralanguage Stroop data of the three bilingual groups.

There is another aspect of the orthographic hypothesis which makes a specific prediction about the interlanguage Stroop interference effects. Past studies have consistently shown that for bilinguals an interlanguage Stroop task produces significant less interference than an intralanguage Stroop task. Fang, et al. (1981) made an extensive review of the literature of bilingual Stroop experiments and noted that the magnitude of reduction of interference from intra- to inter-language task seemed to increase as the similarity of the orthographic structures of the two competing languages increased. They postulated that similar orthographies would compete for the same processing mechanism and thus switching from one to the other would not make much difference in terms of processing demand; consequently, little reduction of interference would be expected from intra- to inter-language Stroop task.

Viewing from such an orthographic-specific processing perspective, we should expect to find the greatest reduction of interference from the intra- to inter-language Stroop task in the Chinese-English (logographic vs. alphabetic) case, and the least reduction in the Malay-English (both alphabetic) case. Unfortunately, data obtained in the present study are far from supportive of the orthographic hypothesis. Let us look at the entries of INTER/E for all three languages at Table 2, which depict differences in magnitude of interference when color-words and response are both in English, compared to the situation where stimuli are written in L2 (one of the three languages) but response is in English. From top to bottom, the amounts of time reduced for Chinese-English, Malay-English, and Tamil-English are 16.74 sec, 14.03 sec, and 18.00 sec, respectively, $F(2, 212) < 1$. Therefore, results from the present three groups of bilingual readers with various combinations of scripts showed that no systematic relationship was found between the magnitude of the Stroop effect and the nature of the script.

These null findings essentially undermine the two most important predictions of the orthographic hypothesis with respect to both the intra- and inter- language Stroop interference effects. We have to conclude that the orthographic factor <u>by itself</u> has nothing to do with the degree of the Stroop interference. This conclusion immediately raises two questions: Why was there the excitement for the orthography-specific hypothesis in the early years of this research? And, given our conclusion of the irrelevance of the orthographic factor, how can we account for the previous data which seem to support such a hypothesis?

The answer to the first question seems to be an easy one in retrospect. When group differences are obtained, there is a tendency to account for them in terms of the most salient differences between the groups, which in this case is the linguistic descriptions of the different types of written scripts. Methodologically speaking, nothing is wrong with this as long as the theorist stipulates his/her propositional account within the same level of description, i.e., without attempting to stipulate underlying **psychological** or **neurological** mechanisms in order to account for the differences. Unfortunately, in recent years, we have seen many model builders incorrectly assume that a linguistic description must have an implied knowledge of language structure, which then provides an independent rationale for the proposed specialized mechanism (or neurolinguistic pathway) in order to access the knowledge. For instance, the first orthography-specific account for the cross-language Stroop effect assumed that the reading of logographic script (Chinese) and the processing of color information may compete for the same "perceptual capacities" in the right hemisphere (Biederman & Tsao, 1979, p. 130). As cogently pointed out by Paradis, Hagiwara, and Hildebrandt (1985), "This claim is somewhat surprising in view of the fact that both kanji naming and color naming are generally impaired subsequent to **left** hemisphere lesion." (p. 55). The mistake was made because many theorists were ready to believe that the alphabetic and logograghic script ought to be processed differently even if there had never been data to disprove the null hypotheses.

The second question is more difficult to answer, but it actually is a more pertinent theoretical question to raise against the interpretation of the cross-language Stroop interference effect. Since the seminal work of Preston and Lambert (1969), the consistent results from the bilingual Stroop test is that both the intralingual condition and the interlingual condition takes more time to name than a control condition of naming solid color patches. Since the bilingual subjects were not able to inhibit the processing of the irrelevant color word in the other language, the result of a consistent interlingual interference by itself argues strongly against the suggestion of a bilingual switch mechanism. This inability to "switch off" the irrelevant other language provides the rationale for the competition hypothesis, which in turn provides a sensible account for the finding that the interlingual conditions induces much less interference than the intralingual account. In addition, it stimulates the idea that the amount of reduction in the Stroop interference from the intralingual to interlingual conditions may be a function of the similarity between the orthographic structures of the two languages. Comparing their own data for Chinese-English and Japanese-English bilinguals, and also data from other bilingual studies in the literature, Fang, et al., (1981) were able to show the magnitude of reduction in interference between intralanguage and interlanguage conditions is greatest between Chinese and English and least between French and English, with other languages ranked in between. On the surface, these data and other similar findings seem to give a strong support for the orthography-specific view of the Stroop interference effect.

However, these results were not always reproducible (see Hildebrandt, 1981; Smith & Kirsner, 1982; Obler & Albert, 1978), but the negative findings, for whatever reasons, tended to be ignored. Procedural differences may account for some of the discrepancies. But a particularly serious problem of comparison across these different studies is the lack of control for bilingualism: Not all of the studies used fluent bilinguals! Different degrees of bilingualism affect decoding times as well as response generation times and such massive confounding makes the results from intralingual and interlingual Stroop tasks very difficult, if not impossible, to interpret. The seemingly clear relation between the orthographic factor and the magnitude of Stroop interference could easily be a reflection of different degrees of bilingualism.

Due to the Government's emphatic demand on bilingual education, Singapore's children, regardless of their ethnic origin, are required to learn English as well as their respective native languages. This unique bilingual setting makes it possible to have three different bilingual groups comparable in terms of language competence. Consequently, results from the present study with bilingual children in Singapore provide a much better test of the validity of the orthography-specific hypothesis. With respect to the issue of bilingualism, all three groups of bilingual children have English as their first formal written language at school and they all have to learn to read their own native language as a second written language. Based upon their more or less equal response times in naming color words in black ink or color patches in English, all three bilingual groups should be considered equivalent in terms of their English proficiency. This equivalence is corroborated by the fact that in the English Stroop task, all three bilingual subjects shows equal amounts of intralanguage Stroop interference. Since Chinese is the native language for the Chinese-English bilingual children, Malay is the native language for the Malay-English bilinguals, and Tamil is the native language for the Indian-English bilinguals, there is no reason to suspect the equivalence in their native language proficiency in these three different bilingual groups. Again, this conclusion is corroborated by the non-significant differences in naming color words and color patches in their respective native languages.

The experimental manipulations are by no means non-sensitive in the present study. Both intra- and interlingual Stroop tasks resulted in highly significant interference for each and every language condition. But the most important fact is that there was no systematic relationship between the orthographic factor and the magnitude of the Stroop interference. In fact, the data here and those in the past literature seem to be better accounted for by one of the current theories of selective attention (Neill, 1977; Tipper & Driver, 1988; Tzeng & Hung, in press). Under the conceptualization of the activation-suppression model, attention "refers to selection from available, competing environmental and internal stimuli, of specific information for conscious processing." (Posner & Rafal, 1987, p. 138). Objects are in general processed in a parallel fashion and equivalent information is available for both relevant and irrelevant objects. Selection involves, at least in part, the selective inhibition of the ignored objects. If selective inhibition occurs after initial activation, changes in its magnitude would be expected on occasions where irrelevant memory structures have not yet undergone inhibition. Indeed, when Neill and Westberry (1987, Experiment 1), in a modified Stroop-like experiment which specifically looked at the development of inhibition as a function of speed in extracting information from the relevant and irrelevant dimensions, manipulated speed- accuracy trade-off by instructional emphasis on either accuracy or speed, changes in the magnitude of inhibitions were observed. In other words, a delay in processing the relevant dimension would allow time for greater interference from the irrelevant dimension to develop. This observation in the selective attentional studies has a direct implication for the interpretation of the bilingual Stroop effect. That is, for a bilingual subject, the degree of bilingualism matters a great deal because the time required for decoding the printed word in one language and the time required to generate an articulatory code for the ink color in another language combine to determine the magnitude of interlanguage Stroop interference.

Such an explanation also gives an excellent account for the Japanese data in which logographic Kanji induces much greater Stroop interference than the syllabic Kana script. This is because most studies comparing reading of Kanji and Kana have also shown that color names written in Kana were read faster than when they were written in Kanji (Feldman & Turvey 1980), in spite of the fact that in daily life, the color names are usually written in Kanji script. That is, speed differences in decoding words printed in different scripts play a determining role in the magnitude of the Stroop effect. The **orthography-specific** Stroop interference effect observed in the past literature is no more than the manifestation of such a difference in decoding speed due to phonological factors. In other words, the orthographic factor is relevant because it happens to relate to the phonological factor indirectly.

Acknowledgement Note

The research reported here was supported in part by a research grant from the National Science Council of Singapore to Wei Ling Lee, and in part by a grant from CCK Cultural Foundation to Daisy Hung and in part by a research grant from the National Science Council of the Republic of China (NSC 80-0301-H194-05) to Ovid Tzeng. We are grateful for the full support from the Singapore Primary School District. Many teachers helped in the various phases of the study; to them, we express our sincere appreciation.

References

Biederman, I., & Tsao. Y.C. (1979). On processing Chinese ideographs and English words: Some implications from Stroop-test results. *Cognitive Psychology*, 11, 125-132.

Fang, S. P., Tzeng, O. J. L., & Alva, E. (1981). Intra- versus inter-language Stroop interference effect in bilingual subjects. *Memory & Cognition*, 9, 609-617.

Feldman, L. B., & Turvey, M. T. (1980). Words written in Kana are named faster than the same words written in Kanji. *Language and Speech*, 23, 141-147.

Hasuike, R., Tzeng, O. J. L., & Hung, D. L. (1986). Script effects and cerebral lateralization. In J. Vaid (Ed.), *Language processing in bilinguals: Psycholinguistic and neuropsychological perspectives*. NJ: Lawrence Erlbaum, pp. 275-288.

Hatta, T. (1981). Differential processing of kanji and kana stimuli in Japanese people: Some implications from Stroop-test results. *Neuropsychologia*, 19, 87-93.

Hatta, T., Katoh, H., & Aitani, N. (1982). Does single kanji process dominantly in the right hemisphere? Some implications from Stroop-test results. *International Journal of Neuroscience*, 18, 67-72.

Hildebrandt, N. (1981). The Stroop effect with Japanese-English bilinguals. (Kinjo University Annuals), English Department, No. 22.

Hue, C. W., Fang, D., & Hsu, K. Y. (in press). Immediate serial recall of Chinese characters: A study of input modality effect. *Acta Psychologica*.

Hung, D. L., & Tzeng, O. J. L. (1981). Orthographic variations and visual information processing. *Psychological Bulletin*, 90, 377-414.

Neill, W. T. (1977). Inhibitory and facilitatory processes in selective attention. *Journal of Experimental Psychology: Human Perception and Performance, 3*, 444-450.

Neill, W. T., & Westberry, R. L. (1987). Selective attention and the suppression of cognitive noise. *Journal of Experimental Psychology: Learning, Memory and Cognition, 13*, 327-334.

Obler, L. K., & Albert, M. L. (1978). A monitor system for bilingual language processing. In M. Paradis (Ed.), *Aspects of bilingualism.* Columbia, South Carolina: Hornbeam Press, pp. 156-164.

Paradis, M., Hagiwara, H., & Hildebrandt, N. (1985). *Neurolinguistic aspects of the Japanese writing system.* New York: Academic Press.

Posner, M. I., & Rafal, D. (1987). Cognitive theories of attention and rehabilitation of attentional deficits. In M. J. Meier, A. L. Benton, A. L. Diller, & C. Livingston (Eds.), *Neuropsychological rehabilitation.* New York: Guilford Press.

Preston, M. S., & Lambert, W. E. (1969). Interlingual interference in a bilingual version of the Stroop color-word task. *Journal of Verbal Learning and Verbal Behavior, 8*, 295-301.

Sasanuma, S. (1974). Impairment of written language in Japanese aphasics: Kana vs Kanji processing. *Journal of Chinese Linguistics, 2*, 141-57.

Sergent, J., & Hellige, J. (1986). Role of input factors in visual-field asymmetries. *Brain and Cognition, 5*, 174-199.

Smith, M. C., & Kirsner, K. (1982). Language and orthography as irrelevant features in color-word and picture-word Stroop interference. *Quarterly Journal of Experimental Psychology, 34A*, 153-170.

Stroop, J. R. (1935). Studies of interference in serial verbal reaction. *Journal of Experimental Psychology, 18*, 643-662.

Tipper, S. P., & Driver, J. (1988). Negative priming between pictures and words in a selective attention task: Evidence for semantic processing of ignored stimuli. *Memory and Cognition, 16*, 64-70.

Tzeng, O. J. L., & Hung, D. L. (1988). Cerebral organization: Clues from scriptal effects on lateralization. In I-M. Liu, H-C. Chen, & M. J. Chen (Eds.), *Cognitive aspects of the Chinese language, Vol. I.* Hong Kong: Asian Research Service, pp. 119-139.

Tzeng, O. J. L., & Hung, D. L. (in press). Location-specific inhibition in visual selective attention. *Psychological Science*.

Tzeng, O. J. L., & Wang, W. S-Y. (1983). The first two R's. *American Scientist*, <u>71</u>, 238-243.

Cognitive Processing in Bilinguals – R.J. Harris (Editor)
443

Code-switching and Language Dominance

Abdelâli Bentahila and Eirlys E. Davies
Sidi Mohamed Ben Abdellah University

Abstract

Whereas recent research on code-switching has focussed largely on the search for syntactic constraints, this paper argues that more attention should be paid to the influence of social and psychological variables on switching patterns. A comparison of the discourse of two types of Moroccan bilingual reveals striking differences in the types of switch used. An attempt is made to relate the patterns favoured by each group to aspects of their language background, in particular to the contrast between balanced bilinguals and those dominant in one language.

The phenomenon of code-switching (which we may define informally here as the use by a bilingual of more than one language within a single utterance or exchange, as opposed to the choice of different languages in different contexts) has attracted a great deal of attention in the past twenty years, and there is now a considerable body of literature reporting on switching in a wide variety of communities, involving many different pairs of languages. The issue that has received most attention is the search for structural constraints which can account for the ways in which the two languages can be combined. There have been a number of proposals for possibly universal syntactic constraints on code-switching; those which have been most discussed are probably the Equivalence Constraint and Free Morpheme Constraint, as formulated by Poplack (1980), and the Government Constraint proposed by Di Sciullo, Muysken and Singh (1986). However, each of these has met with considerable criticism, and with reports by other researchers of bilingual communities where it does not appear to be valid. For instance, counter-examples to the Equivalence Constraint are reported in language pairs such as Adanme-English (Nartey, 1982), Arabic-French (Bentahila & Davies, 1983), French/English-Bantu languages (Kamwangamalu, 1984), Hebrew-Spanish (Berk-Seligson, 1986) and Swahili-English (Scotton, 1988), while violations of the Free Morpheme Constraint are recorded for Navajo-English (Canfield, 1980), Adanme-English (Nartey, 1982), Yoruba-English (Goke-Pariola, 1983), Arabic-French (Bentahila & Davies, 1983), Dutch-Turkish (Boeschoten & Verhoeven, 1987), German-English (Clyne, 1987), Swahili-English (Scotton, 1988) and Maori-English (Eliasson, 1989), and exceptions to the Government Constraint are found in pairs such as Arabic-French (Bentahila & Davies, 1983), German-English (Clyne, 1987) and Dutch-Arabic (Nortier, 1989). Poplack and her associates have defended the Equivalence and Free Morpheme Constraints by arguing that certain purported counter-examples should not be regarded as switches at all, but are instances of some other phenomenon; thus Sankoff, Poplack and Vanniarajan (1986) draw a distinction between switching and nonce-borrowing, and Nait M'Barek and Sankoff (1988) argue for a distinction between both of these and a third pattern they label constituent insertion.

There is no space here for an evaluation of the various positions in this debate, but we feel it safe to say that, whether or not these further distinctions prove to be justified on independent grounds, it must be acknowledged that the patterns found in many communities' mixed language utterances are not well captured by any of these constraints. The reason why the search for universal constraints has not been more successful, we suspect, is that it has tended to focus almost exclusively on the syntactic dimension of code-switching, treating switching patterns as purely structural phenomena rather than setting them within a social and psychological context. This tendency to attribute all features of code-switched discourse to the influence of syntactic principles seems reminiscent of the Generative Semantics movement of the late sixties and early seventies, which began from the assumption that all aspects of the meaning of a string must be derivable from its underlying structure. With the development of pragmatics, this approach has of course long been forsaken by theoretical linguists, and in our opinion exclusively syntactic treatments of code-switching must go the same way. In their place should come accounts which, while recognizing that syntactic principles do have a part to play in determining which types of switch are likely to occur, treat them as only one among a number of variables which might influence this issue. In particular, we feel that more attention should be paid to potentially influential aspects of the users of code-switching, which might include their degree of proficiency in each of the languages, the extent to which and domains in which they use each language, their attitudes towards their languages and towards mixing them, and the functions each language tends to fulfill in their everyday life and discourse. Most of the studies oriented towards the search for syntactic constraints have paid little attention to such variables, but have focussed on the similarities which can be found between switching patterns in very different communities using different language pairs. To see the effect of specific variables, however, it is desirable to compare relatively similar groups, using the same language pair, and contrasting only with regard to features such as those just listed. One attempt at such a comparison is reported here.

The concept of language dominance
    We should like to look in particular at one aspect of the bilingual's make-up, for which we shall use the cover term language dominance, although we recognize that this label may be found vague or even misleading. There are in fact several criteria which could be invoked to justify describing a bilingual individual as dominant in one language rather than the other. One could characterize as dominant the language a bilingual is not proficient in, or that which he uses most, or one could take a temporal view and use the term to identify the language which the bilingual acquired first, in infancy, in contrast to one learnt later in life. We shall not discuss the potential interactions between these three criteria here, since the group we shall describe as dominant conforms to the prototype case where all three criteria are satisfied. It is important to note, however, that we are treating dominance only as a property of the individual speaker. We are not concerned here with its application at the social level, to describe the language which is most used or most prestigious in a particular community, or with its application at the level of discourse, to describe the language which predominates in a particular conversation, exchange, or utterance.

Our term dominant language should therefore be clearly distinguished from the label matrix language which is used by Myers-Scotton in her recently developed theory, the Matrix Language Frame Model of code-switching, which postulates that in any discourse involving code-switching it is possible to distinguish between what she calls a matrix language and an embedded language. Some of Myers-Scotton's earlier remarks about the definition of a matrix language make it sound similar to what we have called a dominant language; notably we may cite her remarks that "the ML is generally the language in which speakers have the higher proficiency" (1990, p. 66), and, later on the same page, that it is "generally the more dominant language in the community in terms of the number of domains in which it is the more unmarked choice" and also "the language more unmarked for the specific type of interaction in which the CS [code-switching] utterances occur". However, further still down the page and in a later paper, Myers-Scotton (1991) makes it clear that the crucial criterion for determining the matrix language is discourse-based. She proposes that the Matrix language is the language of more morphemes in an interaction involving code-switching, and notes that it may even change within the course of a single conversation. In contrast, of course, what we have called a bilingual's dominant language will not vary even though some of his own interactions may involve a much heavier use of the other, non-dominant language. Accordingly, then, although there are clearly interesting links between Myers-Scotton's concept and what we are called language dominance, we feel that these are too complex to be explored here.

The earlier literature on code-switching does, however, contain a few claims which seem to relate to our notion of language dominance. For instance, in an analysis of the speech of a Danish-English bilingual child, Petersen (1988) postulates a constraint to the effect that, in word-internal code-switching, grammatical morphemes of the dominant language may co-occur with lexical morphemes of either language, whereas grammatical morphemes of the non-dominant language may co-occur only with lexical morphemes of the same language. Others have attempted to compare bilingual groups differing with regard to dominance. For instance, Pfaff (1990), in a study of Turkish-German bilingual children, reports differences between the Turkish-dominant and the German-dominant children with regard to the types of switch favoured. Finally, contrasts have been reported between bilinguals who are clearly dominant (in the sense of more proficient) in one of their languages and balanced bilinguals, who are equally fluent in both. Poplack (1980), in a study of Puerto Ricans, found that those who claimed to be less proficient in English tended to switch to English for fillers, tags, or idiomatic expressions, while those fluent in both Spanish and English switched more between sentences and between constituents of a sentence, which she considers to be the type of switch requiring greatest proficiency in the two languages. Nortier (1989) likewise found that among Dutch-Arabic bilinguals more intrasentential switches were used by fairly balanced bilinguals than by those clearly dominant in either Dutch or Arabic. On the other hand, Berk-Seligson (1986) found no significant differences between balanced and dominant Hebrew-Spanish bilinguals with regard to the types of switch they favoured.

Method

Subjects

The study reported here is concerned with the links between language dominance and the code-switching patterns of Moroccan bilinguals. It therefore sets out to compare two groups of Moroccans who can be considered to belong to the same bilingual community, having Moroccan Arabic as their first acquired and home language and French as a second language learned through the medium of formal education. Members of the first group, whom we shall refer to as the older generation, were born between 1939 and 1951, while those of the second, younger group were all born in the late sixties and early seventies. Both groups could be considered to be relatively highly educated; the younger bilinguals were all either in the last years of secondary education or pursuing a university education when they were recorded, while the older informants were all receiving or had received some kind of higher education, and included teachers, engineers and medical personnel.

Despite these basic similarities, the age difference between the two groups has made them slightly different types of bilinguals. The older group received their early education either when Morocco was still a French protectorate or in the decade following independence, which means that they acquired literacy in French and Arabic simultaneously, used French extensively as a medium of instruction for other subjects, and pursued their higher education through the medium of French alone. These people have a very high degree of proficiency in French, and could plausibly be described as balanced bilinguals, able to communicate with perfect ease in either language. The younger group, however, were educated at a time when the post-independence policy of Arabisation was already well under way; they began learning French at a later age than the older group, and used Arabic as the medium of instruction for all subjects except scientific ones and French itself. Accordingly, although they can express themselves adequately in French, both in speech and writing, they do not possess the fluency of the older bilinguals, and have far less experience of using French than these. According to all three of the criteria mentioned earlier, then, the members of this group can be described as Arabic-dominant bilinguals.

Procedure

The study involves the comparison of two sets of tape recordings. The first consists of approximately six hours of informal conversation between friends and acquaintances belonging to the older generation, and the second of approximately two and half hours of recording of similar conversation involving only members of the younger group.

Results and Discussion

An initial comparison can be made by examining the frequency of particular categories of switch in each data set, as shown in Tables 1 and 2.

Table 1

Tokens of Switch Types in Two Generations' Discourse

Switch Type	No. of Occurrences	
	Older Generation	Younger Generation
1) For whole clause	193	44
2) For whole NP	125	394
3) For whole PP	9	5
4) For adverb/AdvP	108	56
5) For filler/tag/parenthetical	55	27
6) Within NP: - between Det and Det	30	93
- between Det and N	14	8
- between N and Adj	46	25
- between N and possessive pronoun	17	21
7) For conjunction alone (between two clauses both in the other language)	25	2
8) For preposition alone (preceded and followed by items in the other language)	34	3
9) For pronoun alone	28	2
10) Within verb (between bound and root morphemes)	17	73
11) Other	56	35
TOTALS	757	788

Table 2

Switch Types in Order of Frequency

Older Generation

Switch Type	No. of Occurrences	%
1) For whole clause	193	25.5%
2) For whole NP	125	16.5%
3) For adverb/AdvP	108	14.2%
4) For filler/tag/parenthetical	55	7.2%
5) Between N and Adj	46	6.1%
6) For preposition alone	34	4.5%
7) Between Det and Det	30	3.9%
8) For pronoun alone	28	3.7%
9) For conjunction alone	25	3.3%
10) Within verb (word-internal)	17	2.2%
11) Between N and possessive pronoun	17	2.2%
12) Between Det and N	14	1.8%
13) For whole PP	9	1.2%

Younger Generation

Switch Type	No. of Occurrences	%
1) For whole NP	394	50.0%
2) Between Det and Det	93	11.8%
3) Within verb (word-internal)	73	9.3%
4) For adverb/AdvP	56	7.1%
5) For whole clause	44	5.6%
6) For filler/tag/parenthetical	27	3.4%
7) Between N and Adj	25	3.1%
8) Between N and possessive pronoun	21	2.7%
9) Between Det and N	8	1.0%
10) For whole PP	5	0.6%
11) For preposition alone	3	0.4%
12) For conjunction alone	2	0.2%
13) For pronoun alone	2	0.2%

This quantitative analysis reveals some quite clear contrasts between the two groups with regard to the frequency with which they use certain types of switches. In the first place, we may note that switching between whole clauses (either independent sentences or those conjoined by either co-ordination or subordination) is the most common pattern used by the older generation, whereas it constitutes less than 6% of the younger generation's switches. The latter group instead shows a very strong preference for switches for a whole noun phrase, which constitute a remarkable 50% of their total number of switches. This contrast does not corroborate Poplack's observation, noted above, that greater use of intrasentential switches is associated with balanced rather than dominant bilinguals. Another notable difference concerns the use of switching within a single word, a strategy which appears to violate Poplack's Free Morpheme Constraint. Rare in the speech of the older group, this proves to be the third most common pattern used by the younger group. Finally, some other types of switch which have been considered strange or impossible are found quite extensively in the discourse of the older group but are almost nonexistent in that of the younger generation; these are the switches for isolated grammatical items such as prepositions, conjunctions or pronouns, which would appear to be proscribed by Joshi's (1985) Closed Class Item Constraint, but which together make up more than 11% of the older group's switches.

We should like to suggest that these contrasts can all be related to the major difference between these otherwise very similar groups, namely the fact that the older speakers are balanced bilinguals whereas the younger ones are definitely dominant in Arabic. To show this, it is necessary to consider how the switches are exploited within stretches of discourse, rather than merely categorizing and listing them. The following extracts from the recordings may be considered representative of the types of pattern that recur.

Sample 1 (Older generation)

"waħed nuba kunt ana w thami. On s'est arreté juste au feu rouge, on parlait. kunna bYina nmfiw l marrakef ma nmfiw l marrakef w kunt qri;t. Il m'a vu enseigner w dakfi, w ʒa:ji:n lhena, on habitait ici waqef, il faut voir, ħda le dix-septième étage f dak le feu rouge faf zawlu ʒʒerda lwstanija Σad sawbulha lgas et j'étais devant, il y avait une centaine de voitures derrière moi w ana waqef. J'attends le feu rouge pour changer. waħed ssaΣa comme ça je démarre, je démarre jaΣni w kant dak la semaine djal tajzawlu les permis. Je démarre hakda w nna:s kulhum waqfi:n muraj."

"Once there were Thami and I. We stopped just at the traffic lights, we were talking. We were wondering whether to go to Marrakesh or not to go to Marrakesh, and I had been teaching. He had seen me teaching and so on, and we were coming here, we lived here. I was waiting, you should have seen, near the seventeen storey building at that-the traffic light where they have taken away the garden in the middle and have just done the concrete, and I was in the front, there were about a hundred cars behind me and I was waiting. I was waiting for the red light to change. At a certain moment, like that, I drove off, I drove off, I mean, and it was that-the week where they take away the driving licences. I drove off like that and all the people were waiting behind me."

Sample 2 (Older generation)

"walakin ça dépend de quel degré de connaissance djal la personne, li?anna à un moment donné, lorsque, par exemple, moi je veux apprendre l'anglais, pas pour apprendre la culture w la civilisation anglaise, c'est pour pouvoir m'en servir soit pour faire en marche un appareil wlla apprendre certains techniques, c'est tout. D'ailleurs, même le francais, je n'ai pas besoin d'apprendre la civilisation française. Ca me sert seulement pour étudier, c'est tout."

"but that depends on the degree of knowledge of the person, because at a given moment, when, for instance, I want to learn English, [it is] not in order to learn about English culture and civilisation, it's to be able to use it either to use a machine or to learn certain techniques, that's all. Besides, even French, I don't need to learn about French civilisation. I use it only to study, that's all."

Sample 3 (Younger generation)

"tajʒiw tajdiru dak la régulation djal les naissances, bhal daba tajbYiw jħaddu nsel. tajħesbu bħal daba tajʒiw tajdiru dak l calcul f le cycle, bhal ʃi mra tatħsib wla ʃi haʒa, tajdrubu lhasab l spermatozoide tajƩi:ʃ talt ijem, w l'ovule tajderbu lhaseb tatƩi:ʃ jumajen, w l'ovulation tatkun rbaƩṭaʃ ljum après les règles, quatorze jours après les règles tatkun l'ovulation. donc baʃ tajderbu lħasab tatƩi;ʃ dak sspermatozoide kebl talt ijem, w talt ijem min bƩd ?idan sttijem. mumkin Ʃawd dak la réproduction chez des spermaphytes, Ʃand dak les végétaux w zaƩma Ʃla ?asas zaƩma lmuhim f had la réproduction, liʒanna les hormones huma zaƩma ħaʒa lmuhima f l'hypophyse. L'hypophyse c'est une glande, une glande sexuelle. hija lli tatsecréterna les hormones lli tajagiw matalan Ʃla les testicules."

"They come and do that-the limitation of the births, for example they want to limit births, they count for example they come and do that calculation within the cycle, for example a woman counts or something, they do the calculation that a sperm lives three days, and the egg they do the calculation that it lives two days, and the ovulation takes place fourteen days after menstruation, fourteen days after menstruation there is the ovulation. So in order to do the calculation, that sperm lives three days before, and three days afterwards, thus six days. It's possible also that- the reproduction in the spermaphytes, in those-the plants, and that is on the basis of that is, the important thing in this-the reproduction, because the hormones they are, that is, the important thing in the hypophysis. The hypophysis is a gland, a sexual gland, it's that which secretes [Arabic inflections] for us the hormones which act [Arabic inflections] for instance on the testicles."

Sample 4 (Younger generation)

A: w <u>la structure fonctionnaire</u> hija djal Taylor. bħal daba Yir waħed kajaΣţi bezzaf djal <u>les ordres</u> l <u>les ouvriers.</u> w kajemkin l <u>les travailleurs</u> <u>jexecutiw</u> dak <u>les ordres</u>, walajini b ħurija djalhum, fehmti? <u>L'autorité</u> kataΣţi ħaq l <u>le chef</u> baƒ <u>jcommander</u>, w baƒ dik ţţalabat djalu zaΣma lxrin <u>jexecutiw</u> <u>leurs ordres.</u>   had <u>l'autorité institutionelle</u> katΣţi had <u>le droit</u>hada, fehmti?

B: zaΣma waxxa huma kaj<u>executiw</u> dak <u>l'ordre</u>, Yir <u>par volonté.</u>

A: ijjah, Yir <u>par liberté.</u>

A: And <u>the bureaucratic structure</u> is that of Taylor. For example only one person gives a lot of <u>the orders</u> to <u>the workers.</u> And it is possible for <u>the workers</u> to <u>execute</u> [Arabic inflections] those-<u>the orders</u>, but with their own freedom, do you understand?   <u>The authority</u> gives the right to <u>the chief</u> to <u>command</u>   [Arabic inflections], and for his demands, that is, the others to <u>execute</u> [Arabic inflections] <u>their orders.</u>   This-<u>the institutional authority</u> gives this <u>the right</u> this one, do you understand?

B: That is, although they <u>execute</u> [Arabic inflections] that-<u>the order</u>, [it is] only <u>by their own will.</u>

A: Yes, only <u>by freedom.</u>

The tendency for the older group to use frequent switches between one clause and the next is clearly seen in Sample 1, where there is an almost regular alternation between a statement in one language and one in the other. Rather than being mainly French or mainly Arabic, the discourse involves an almost equal use of each language, and each plays an essential role in the unfolding of the story that is being told, since some important details are provided in one language and some in the other. This pattern is very frequent in the recordings of the older group, and would seem to reflect quite well the position of these balanced bilinguals, who are equally at home in both languages for such information discussion. However, it is scarce in the speech of the younger group, who, not being as fluent or at ease in French as the older generation, rarely use French as the vehicle for complete speech acts.

Instead, as a scrutiny of samples 3 and 4 will reveal, this younger group uses extensive switching back and forth for smaller constituents within clauses, following certain very recurrent strategies. In particular, they very regularly switch from Arabic to French for a noun accompanied by its article and sometimes by other modifiers, a pattern which is also used by the older generation, but to a much lesser extent. These French strings may constitute complete NPs in themselves, or they may form part of a larger NP in which the switch occurs between an Arabic determiner and a French one (the second most frequent category of switch for the younger group). An example of this second type is, in the first line of sample 3, *dak la régulation*; in the translations such examples have been given word-for-word representations, as in *that-the limitation.* The fact that this pattern does not conform to the Equivalence Constraint has led Nait M'Barek and Sankoff (1988) to exclude such examples from the class of code-switches, instead coining the term constituent insertion to describe them; but whatever name they are given, the fact that they are so excessively exploited by this younger generation requires an explanation.

Samples 3 and 4 also offer several illustrations of the other slightly controversial strategy favoured by the younger but not the older group - that of switching within a single word, between root and bound morphemes. All the 73 instances of this pattern in the younger group's discourse consist of switching between a French verb stem and various Arabic grammatical morphemes which are attached to it and which signal tense and aspect, together with the person, number and gender of its subject and/or object. Two such examples are found in the last sentence of sample 3: *tatsecretena* is composed of the French verb *secreter* preceded by the morphemes (ta) (durative aspect marker) and (t) (third person feminine subject marker) and followed by (na) (first person plural object marker), while in the same line, the stem of the French verb *agir* is accompanied by Arabic (ta) (durative) (j) (third person masculine subject marker) and (w) (plural subject marker). The frequency of these examples is, as we have already noted, all the more remarkable because they constitute potential counter-examples to the Free Morpheme Constraint; those who wish to maintain this constraint may relabel such examples as nonce-borrowings, but again the label chosen does not affect the point we are making here, which is that our two generations sharply contrast in the extent to which they use them.

We would like to suggest that the much greater frequency of both these patterns within the younger generation's discourse can be traced to a single overall strategy, which is exemplified in longer stretches of discourse like those in samples 3 and 4. The constant switching back and forth between Arabic and French in these samples is far from random, but conforms to a general tendency; French is extensively used for vocabulary items such as verbs, adverbs and especially nouns, whereas Arabic is resorted to for the grammatical elements such as conjunctions, prepositions, demonstratives, pronouns, as well as for fillers and commonplace everyday vocabulary. It will be noted that both the samples given involve discussion of relatively technical matters; sample 3 is taken from a discussion by students of the content of a biology lesson, while in sample 4 the speakers are discussing material from a secretarial studies course. In fact, this pattern seems to be adopted especially when members of the younger generation need to talk, in an informal setting, about specialized subjects which they have studied through the medium of French. The tendency to resort to French for lexical items is thus related to the greater availability of the French terms for people who are used to dealing with such topics, in a formal educational context, exclusively through the medium of French. One might then ask why, if they are experienced in discussing these topics in French, they do not simply adopt this language for the duration of such topics of discussion, instead of using this technique of constant switching back and forth. Here again we can invoke the notion of language dominance. While these younger Moroccans can express themselves in French if need be, French remains for them very much a secondary language, associated with specific domains, notably the context of formal education. For them, the normal medium for informal discussion such as the kind of chat between friends recorded in our data is undoubtedly Arabic rather than French; this is attested by the many quite long stretches of conversation entirely in Arabic which are found in the discourse of the younger group but not that of the older generation. In fact, then, the style found in extracts like 3 and 4 can be considered to result from the conflicting needs of these Arabic-dominant bilinguals; they clearly need to resort to French for the lexis required for such technical topics, yet French alone would seem an unnatural and over-formal choice for this kind of in-group chat. The solution, as samples 3 and 4 show, is a type of discourse which, though it draws heavily on French vocabulary, nevertheless can be considered to be basically Arabic, since it is this language which contributes the grammatical elements forming the framework within which the French elements are set.

The two particular switching patterns which characterize this style can both be considered instances of this general strategy for resolving such conflicts. The occurrence of French verb stems combined with Arabic inflections need not be regarded as some kind of aberration with requires an exceptional treatment, but can instead be seen as a natural outcome of this technique of combining French vocabulary with Arabic grammatical items. The use of French nouns within Arabic contexts seems equally clearly motivated, though the fact that these nouns are so frequently accompanied by French determiners rather than Arabic ones might initially seem rather puzzling. However, we have argued elsewhere (Bentahila & Davies, 1991) that this tendency may be related to the way Moroccans originally learn French, in a formal school context which requires conscious learning and memorization of rules and vocabulary. In such a context, French nouns tend to be memorized along with the appropriate article, since this serves to indicate the gender of the noun which would otherwise have to be memorized separately. Accordingly, noun and article tend to be stored as a closely linked sequence, which makes it perhaps less than surprising than when Moroccans call up a French noun for use in code-switching discourse, they tend to use the appropriate article too.

In fact, then, when the peculiarities of the younger generation's switching patterns are seen in the context of these bilinguals' particular background and communicative needs, they appear neither arbitrary nor surprising. Their tendency to use French lexis set within a clearly Arabic background structure can be understood once we recognize their special characteristics; these are bilinguals who have a strong preference for Arabic, their dominant language, yet who cannot do without French as a source of vocabulary when dealing with technical subject matter. On the other hand, the fact that the style illustrated in samples 3 and 4 is not characteristic of the speech of the older generation also seems readily explainable. Since they are quite at ease in sustaining informal conversation that is dominated by French, the older group is unlikely to experience the kind of conflict we have outlined above, and therefore will not need to resort to the complex code-switching patterns exemplified in samples 3 and 4. Instead, if they find themselves discussing a topic where the relevant vocabulary is more available to them in French, the most natural solution for them will be to opt for French grammatical elements as well. The result will be discourse where French clearly predominates, with only rare and relatively brief excursions into Arabic.

Sample 2 provides an illustration of this type of discourse, which is very common in the speech of the older group but practically nonexistent in our recordings of the younger bilinguals.

The few switches we do find here involve the use of an isolated Arabic grammatical element within an otherwise uninterrupted stream of French. In sample 2, for instance, there are repeated switches to Arabic for conjunctions (<u>walakin</u> (but), <u>li?anna</u> (because) <u>w</u> (and) and <u>wlla</u> (or)), as well as one switch for the preposition <u>djal</u> (of). Like the two switch patterns most characteristic of the younger group, these switches may attract attention because they do not conform to one of the postulated syntactic constraints, this time the constraint proposed by Joshi (1985) mentioned earlier. However, once again our interest here is not in validating constraints but in finding reasons for the patterns which do occur. The frequent exploitation of this type of switch by our balanced older bilinguals can hardly be traced to an inability to use the corresponding French grammatical items, or even to the fact that the Arabic items have greater availability for them; these speakers are perfectly capable of speaking pure French, including appropriate French conjunctions, prepositions, and other grammatical elements, whenever they wish to. The last proviso seems important, however, for again context seems to play its part in influencing the choices made. Although many of the older speakers recorded regularly hold conversations exclusively in French, notably in work contexts or in the presence of non-Arabic speakers, their discourse in the informal conversations between intimates which we recorded, even where strongly dominated by French, tends to feature regular brief switches of the type seen in sample 2. These switches seem to serve as markers of a certain informality, in the sense that they prevent the impression of carefulness which the exclusive use of French might present. More than this, they can be seen as in-group markers, symbolizing the Moroccan identity of these people. It is perhaps precisely because their own French is so fluent and native-like that these bilinguals have developed the habit of incorporating into their speech a minimal amount of Arabic, just sufficient to mark them as clearly Moroccans. The Arabic items occurring in discourse like sample 2 make almost no contribution to the message that is being conveyed, and so they do not disrupt the flow of information conveyed in French - a non-Arabic-speaking French speaker would have no difficulty in following the conversation perfectly - but they do appear to have a significant symbolic value.

Indeed, we might again invoke the notion of dominance here, though only with respect to the third of the criteria we noted as contributing to the definition of this concept. For although these older bilinguals may be balanced in the sense that they possess similarly high proficiency in both languages, and use them both regularly in everyday contexts, there still remains a difference between the two for them; Arabic is the language they acquired in infancy, in the home setting, whereas French was introduced to them only later, in an educational setting. In this respect, Arabic may be considered to possess a certain primacy over French, and its use for the occasional very basic function word such as a preposition or conjunction, even in discourse which is clearly essentially French, could be considered to reflect this difference of status. We do not find the converse pattern, where discourse in Arabic is interspersed with

French grammatical items here and there; on the contrary, where Arabic functions as the basic vehicle for an exchange, the switches to French tend to be for lexical items such as nouns, verbs and adverbs, as is the case in samples 3 and 4.

Finally, we may note that the almost complete absence of these types of switch form the discourse of the younger group is quite simply due to the fact that they never produce the kind of almost exclusively French discourse in which such switches fulfil their symbolic function. Their use of French in our recordings never goes beyond the extent illustrated in samples 3 and 4, where, as we have seen, it is not simply isolated grammatical items which are in Arabic, but the vast majority of all function words. Nevertheless, one may draw some sort of parallel between the strategies of the two groups, in that both the older group's tendency to resort to Arabic for function words even when speaking mainly French, and the younger group's tendency to rely on Arabic grammatical structures in conjunction with French lexis, could be seen as testifying to the essential primacy of Arabic as the first language of both groups.

To conclude, we may recall that the quantitative analysis presented in Tables 1 and 2 was sufficient to reveal striking differences between our two groups, the balanced and the Arabic-dominant bilinguals, with regard to the syntactic categories of switch they use most. However, we have tried to show that, in order to gain some understanding of the relationship between language dominance and the preference for certain types of switch, it is necessary to look beyond mere figures and examine the functioning of the various types of switch within the discourse of the two groups. Thus we saw that the preference for switching between clauses among the members of the older generation reflected their tendency to assign the two languages similar discourse functions and communicative loads, whereas the relative rarity of such switches in the younger group's speech corresponded to the quite different status of French here, where instead of serving as a medium for complete statements it tends to function merely as a source of vocabulary in discourse which is still essentially Arabic in structure. The same contrast between the two groups is reflected in the fact that the younger group does not exploit the heavily French-dominated style, characterized by occasional symbolic switches to Arabic for function rather than content items, which is also favoured by the older generation.

We can see, then, that language dominance does appear to have an influence on patterns of code-switching, but that the relationship between the two is not a matter of simple one-to-one correspondences, as has perhaps been implied by some of the previous general statements on this issue, such as the claim that balanced bilinguals use the supposedly more difficult intrasentential switches more than dominant bilinguals (a claim which, incidentally, is not borne out by our data). Rather, we would suggest, language dominance is one factor among others which is likely to influence a bilingual's language choice and communicative strategies, and these in turn may lead him to favor particular switch patterns which fulfil his specific discourse needs. In accounting for the highly distinctive patterns which characterize the discourse of our two groups of speakers, we have made reference to specific features of these bilinguals' language background. In other communities or subgroups, different combinations of features may lead to the adoption of other switching strategies. The quite striking contrasts in code-switching patterns which seem to have resulted from the relatively small differences between our two groups can, we hope, serve as an illustration of how important it is to explore these interactions between background features, communicative functions and structural configurations. Instead of assuming that the absence of a particular type of switch from one or many communities' repertoires must be accounted for in terms of a syntactic constraint proscribing it, and then having to make further ad hoc provisions when another group is found to use this switch type after all, we should at least consider the possibility that its distribution may be traceable to features of bilinguals' background and communicative needs. As we have seen, members of one group may simply have little or no need to use a particular type of switch, while for another group it may constitute a convenient and therefore regularly exploited means of expression. We accordingly end with a plea that, as a counterbalance to the tendency to search for purely syntactic constraints on code-switching, more attention be paid to the other factors which may turn out to have a part to play in explaining this complex and diverse phenomenon.

Author Notes

While the recordings of the older generation were made by one of the authors, those of the younger generation include recordings made by our students Abdelkader Oujdi and Khammar Nami, and we are grateful to them for access to these recordings. The representation of Moroccan Arabic used here is a form of phonemic transcription based mainly on International Phonetic Alphabet conventions, but with some modifications: /ʕ/ represents a voiced pharyngeal fricative, /ʔ/ a glottal stop, and /ʃ/ a voiceless palato-alveolar fricative, while the vowel symbol /e/ has been used to symbolize the central vowel schwa. The translations of the sample extracts are in places word-for-word formulations involving non-English structures, where these have been considered necessary to show the syntactic patterning of the switches, but elsewhere a more idiomatic translation has been preferred.

Any inquiries or correspondence should be addressed to the authors at the following address: 133 Mimosas, Avenue Moulay Kamel, Fes, Morocco.

References

Bentahila, A. & Davies, E. E. (1983). The syntax of Arabic-French code-switching, *Lingua*, 59, 301-330.

Bentahila, A. & Davies, E. E. (1991). *Constraints on code-switching: A look beyond grammar*. Paper presented at the European Science Foundation Symposiumo Code-Switching, Barcelona, Spain.

Berk-Seligson, S. (1986). Linguistic constraints on intrasentential code-switching: A study of Spanish-Hebrew bilingualism. *Language in Society*, 15, 313-348.

Boeschoten, H. & Verhoeven, L. Th. (1987). Language-mixing in children's speech: Dutch language use in Turkish discourse. *Language Learning*, 37, 191-215.

Canfield, K. (1980). A note on Navajo-English code-mixing. *Anthropological Linguistics*, 22, 218-220.

Clyne, M. (1987). Constraints on code-switching: How universal are they? *Linguistics*, 25, 739-764.

Di Sciullo, A. -M., Muysken, P. & Singh, R. (1986). Government and code-mixing. *Journal of Linguistics*, 22, 1-24.

Eliasson, S. (1989). English-Maori language contact: Code-switching and the free-morpheme constraint. *Reports from Uppsala University Department of Linguistics*, 18, 1-28.

Goke-Pariola, A. (1983). Code-mixing among Yoruba-English bilinguals. *Anthropological Linguistics*, 25, 39-46.

Joshi, A. (1985). Processing of sentences with intrasentential code-switching. In D. Dowty, L. Karttunen & A. Zwicky (Eds.), *Natural language parsing: Psychological, computational and theoretical perspectives*. Cambridge, England: Cambridge University Press.

Kamwangamalu, N. M. (1984). Some morphosyntactic aspects of French-Bantu code-mixing: Evidence for universal constraints. *Papers from the Twentieth Regional Meeting of the Chicago Linguistic Society*, 157-170.

Myers-Scotton, C. (1990). Intersections between social motivations and structural processing in code-switching. *Papers for the Workshop on Constraints, Conditions and Models*. Strasbourg: European Science Foundation Network on Code-Switching and Language Contact.

Myers-Scotton, C. (1991). *Whither code-switching? Prospects for cross-field collaboration: Production-based models of code-switching*. Paper presented at the European Science Foundation Symposium on Code-Switching, Barcelona, Spain.

Nait M'Barek, M. & Sankoff, D. (1988). Le discours mixte arabe-français: Emprunts ou alternances de langues? *Canadian Journal of Linguistics*, 33, 143-154.

Nartey, J. N. A. (1982). Code-switching, interference or faddism? Language use among educated Ghanaians. *Anthropological Linguistics*, 24, 183-192.

Nortier, J. (1989). *Dutch and Moroccan Arabic in contact: Code-switching among Moroccans in the Netherlands*. Doctoral thesis, University of Amsterdam.

Petersen, J. (1988). Word-internal code-switching constraints in a bilingual child's grammar. *Linguistics*, 26, 479-493.

Pfaff, C. (1990). Mixing and linguistic convergence in migrant speech communities: Linguistic constraints, social conditions and models of acquisition. *Papers for the Workshop on Constraints, Conditions and Models*. Strasbourg: European Science Foundation Network on Code-Switching and Language Contact.

Poplack, S. (1980). Sometimes I'll start a sentence in Spanish y termino en español: Toward a typology of code-switching. *Linguistics*, 18, 581-618.

Sankoff, D., Poplack, S., & Vanniarajan, S. (1986). The case of the nonce loan in Tamil. *University of Montreal Technical Report No. 1348*.

Scotton, C. M. (1988). Code-switching and types of multilingual communities. In P. Lowenberg (Ed.), *Language spread and language policy: Issues, implications and case studies*. Georgetown University Round Table on Language and Linguistics. Washington, D. C.: Georgetown University Press.

Cognitive Processing in Bilinguals – R.J. Harris (Editor)

Cultural Influences of a Reading Text on the Concept Formation
of Second-language Learners of Two Nigerian Ethnic Groups

M. J. Lasisi and A. S. Onyehalu
Obafemi Awolowo University

Abstract

The vital importance of ecocultural factors in cognitive behaviour has been stressed by researchers in psychology and related fields. In the present study, the influence of the cultural identity of two Nigerian ethnic groups on their comprehension of a literary prose passage was examined. Subjects consisted of 93 Ibo-English bilingual undergraduate students and 95 Yoruba-English bilingual undergraduate students, all majoring in Education. Findings, in large part, confirmed significant effects of cultural beliefs and identity in the analysis and appreciation of the textual material by subjects.

Introduction

The second-language reader's conceptualization of the author's aim in a literary work is dependent on the type of background experience brought to the reading situation that will, in turn, endow the text with personal meaning in terms of how the reader responds to the text, the effect the text has on that reader, and how the personal meaning affects the reader's interpretation (Bettelheim & Zelan, 1982). These are characteristics that are brought forward from early reading experience and that remain valid in adulthood as the reader continues to search for meaning in the text. It is further postulated that meaning is derived from the text in accordance with, first, the conscious and unconscious preoccupations of the reader and, second, whether or not the material addresses these preoccupations.

Accordingly, a literary text, by the very nature of this genre, subtly and precisely draws on a system of meaning to form its literal and implied messages that are accepted or rejected by the reader. Thus, reader reactions are stimulated on more than one level of the reader's consciousness. Consequently, the reader responds to both types of messages with conscious and unconscious reactions. The result is that the meaning intended by the author and the meaning derived by the reader may be similar, but not identical. This is due to the influence of the personal concerns of the reader and the way these influences affect the conceptualizations of the text.

Although this may be true in general, the theory may need modification when investigating bilingual learners. Perhaps the second-language reader's tendency to accept or reject the text is activated by concepts embedded in culture rather than intrinsically caused by psychoanalytic thought processes. In other words, from within the unconscious, the reader responds to culture first and other preoccupations second. If the second-language reader's personal concerns in terms of culture are directly related to the text, he or she thus becomes emotionally involved in what is being read. The extent to which the reader's personal reactions may distort the basic intention of the text may depend on how well the readers can control their cultural emotions, so to speak, and their ability to use abstract reasoning to visualize what is not in their culture.

In this light, previous research has shown that prior knowledge greatly enhances reading comprehension when scores for culture-based and non-culture-based material are compared (Reynolds, Taylor, Steffensen, Shirey & Anderson, 1982,; Langer, 1984; Steffensen, Joag-Dev & Anderson, 1979). Research has also been carried out at the secondary school level, comparing the two ethnic groups used in this study (Ibos and Yorubas) in relation to basic recognition and comprehension of primarily concrete objects that were outside the culture (Lasisi & Falodun, 1988).

However, the present study attempts to go deeper by comparing concept formation of the two Nigerian groups in relation to the notions of physical strength, individuality, human productiveness, and the effect of magical powers when these ideas are presented in an indigenous culture-based literary work. Although the two groups are within the same larger Nigerian culture, they form two distinct social sub-groups characterized by variant attitudes towards common traits (Adediran, 1980; Ademola, 1971; Akinjogbin, 1980).

On the one hand, the Ibos appear to place value on displays of physical strength as evidenced by wrestling matches and the conferring of warrior titles. Emanating from the prestige given to muscular prowess is the esteem given to the individual's ability to defend the community. In addition, this group views as productive, primarily those activities that benefit the larger community in a material way. It is interesting to note the popular belief that due to the Ibo man's near consuming respect for physical strength, the belief by this group in magical powers is minimal. Without doubt, Ibo culture has its share of witches and wizards who threaten havoc. Nevertheless, Ibo witches and wizards are believed to warn the offender before acting. Thus, even in witchcraft, the Ibo relies on the power of self first rather than on herbal weapons or the supernatural (Opeola, 1986, 1988).

On the other hand, the Yoruba group does not consider physical size or combat ability as deciding factors in overcoming an opponent. On the contrary, the Yoruba stresses the importance of cunning and wit as measures to defeat an enemy. Using the information gathered from this psychological assessment of the opponent, a decision is made whether to apply "juju" (magic) to winning the situation. Generally, no attempt is made to discuss the situation with the enemy. Rather, the assumption is that the enemy willfully carried out the offence in question. Moreover, before one could commit such an act, the offender is believed to have acquired a personal brand of supernatural power that was used to cause the initial offence. The tendency of this group, it is believed, is to act in secret, before the enemy can find a more effective means of retaliation. By the same token, the traditional belief is that Yoruba witches are unforgiving. As such, they give no warning before attacking their victims (Opeola,1986).

Lastly, music and dance are vital to the lives of this group since these art forms embody the totality of Yoruba culture. Unlike the Ibos who primarily view dance and music as unproductive activities, the Yorubas meticulously fit song and dance steps to form a complex presentation of various aspects of the culture. Thus, song and dance reinforce the Yoruba's sense of tradition. As a result of these differences, the essential question the present study addresses is this: how does culture affect the higher order concepts the young adult Nigerian readers form as they interact with a text that is written in the context of another social group?

Previous work done by Lasisi and Falodun (1988), though at a more literal level of comprehension, provides insight into answering this question. Their study, which compared Ibos and Yorubas, revealed evidence that the influence of background knowledge has an overriding effect on the reading comprehension of the Nigerian reader. Both groups were exposed to the sequencing of text material whose context differed culturally but whose content storywise was similar. Though the two culturally distinct passages were written primarily in English, several words were kept in the first language of each group.

The sequencing of presentation of the two texts was varied to find if the culture-based passage presented first as against the non-culture-based presented second, influenced the comprehension of culturally adverse material. Sequencing had an effect for both groups primarily where the test questions were culture-based as against non-culture-based or where, in a single instance, comparison was made between two sets of culture-based questions. At no time did a set of non-culture-based scores show superiority over culture-related material.

Further investigation (Lasisi, Falodun & Onyehalu, 1988) studied the effect of cultural medium of presentation, language, and sequence of cultural/foreign and first language/second-language presentation on the reading comprehension of bilingual Yoruba subjects. Previous studies concerning schema theory were upheld in that scores for culturally related second-language text were superior to scores for foreign based passages also written in English. Results were similar when scores for foreign based second-language passages translated to the mother-tongue were compared with scores for culture-based first language passages.

Thus, it appears that sequencing of text and presentation of translated foreign based text material to the first language play second fiddle to the influence of culture. As Lipson (1982, 1983) illustrates, much of the information in a non-culture-based passage will be rejected because it is considered culturally adverse by the reader. This act is thought by the researcher to be founded in a failure to resolve cultural conflicts between prior knowledge and new information.

The attempt by the Nigerian reader to resolve this conflict may be dependent on whether or not the reader has both the cultural and linguistic background appropriate for the text (Onochie, 1987). Onochie (1986) observed the responses of Ibo subjects for a cloze procedure test on culture-based sentences (Ibo) and non-culture-based sentences (Hausa). The sentences were given in the context of both cultures. Without the aid of clues, the subjects were asked to supply the missing words. Results indicated that the answers were always in harmony with the cultural context of the sentences. As in other studies cited here that involve Ibo and Yoruba subjects, culture and background experience seem to be powerful factors in second-language learning.

However, there are times, such as those of examination conditions for an acclaimed non-culture-based literary work, when readers are not free to reject a text because it is not in harmony with their schemas. In such instances, the individual is expected to read extensively by focusing on the author's ideas rather than relating them effectively to oneself (Block, 1986). Therefore, the foundation question of the present research returns. How does the reader approximate the concepts intended by a text that is embedded in an unfamiliar social context? Finally, how will these approximations of concept differ from those of subjects for whom the text is culturally relevant?

Method

Subjects

The study made use of two categories of randomly selected subjects from two distinct ethnic groups in Nigeria. One group was the Ibo-English bilinguals (23 males and 70 females). The second group was the Yoruba-English bilinguals (45 females and 51 males). The subjects were third and fourth year university students majoring in Education. Average age range was 15 to 25 years. The Ibo speaking subjects attended Anambra State University of Technology, Enugu in Eastern Nigeria while the Yoruba speakers attended Ogun State University, Ago-Iwoye near Ijebu-Ode in Western Nigeria.

Instrument and Procedure

Subjects were given a two-part questionnaire and a comprehension passage taken from Chinua Achebe's (1958) acclaimed novel, *Things Fall Apart*. Part one of the questionnaire, which contained five questions, was administered prior to the subjects being exposed to the text. Part two was comprised of six comprehension questions.

Chapter one of the Achebe novel was used as the reading passage because of its cultural significance. Since Achebe is a novelist born into the Ibo ethnic group, his writing has a conspicuously Ibo cultural background.

Part one of the questionnaire elicited the views of the subjects on strategic cultural issues which featured prominently in the novel, e.g. concept of physical strength, value of music, and belief about witchcraft. Issues raised in the second part bore a parallel relationship to those in the first part. Essentially, they sought to determine the extent respondents brought to bear their original cultural values, experiences, and background to their appreciation and comprehension of the passage. The assumption, as stated earlier, was that the Ibo subjects on whose culture the story is based, would comprehend more precisely the ideas put across by the author. In other words, the Ibos would be in a better stead than their Yoruba counterparts to use their practical experience to support their comprehension of the passage. Thus, a difference was expected between the means of the groups that would imply the influence of culture on comprehension of concepts.

Bio-data of the subjects in terms of sex and age group was sought in the second part of the questionnaire. The validity of the instrument was ascertained on the opinion of lecturers in the area of Literature in English in this university. The greater bulk of the analysis was based on frequencies which showed the number of subjects who responded to each item and in a particular manner. Items were rated on a continuum that ranged from reliance on concrete physical reality on the one end to reliance on emotional-psychological feelings on the other end. Some responses were stated as percentages.

Results

In the first part of the questionnaire, questions were asked of the Ibo and Yoruba bilinguals on cultural issues of a general nature that in addition, related to the contents of a passage taken from Achebe's novel. Alternative responses were provided for each item so that vital clues concerning outstanding differences and similarities of cultural background values and practices were provided. Highlights are as follows:

Their concepts of "a man of strength" differ significantly. The Ibo subjects emphasised concrete physical strength and physical cleverness while the Yorubas emphasised psychological and emotional qualities of the mind (chi-square = 12.01, df = 3; p<.05). On whether physical strength should be considered important, 89 out of 91 respondents (97.80%) among the Ibos answered in the affirmative while 77 out of 95 Yorubas (81.05%) responded in the affirmative. The difference is statistically significant (chi-square = 113.16, df = 1; p<.05).

When asked to rate "intelligence," "cunning," and "juju" (magic) as effective strategies for problem-solving, no significant difference was found in the choices of both groups with respect to "intelligence". However, significant differences in favour of the Yorubas existed in their ratings of cunning, and magic as shown in Table 1.

Table 1

Group preferences for effective means of solving serious problems

(a) Intelligence

Ranking

	1st	2nd	3rd	Total
Ibo	72	4	8	84
Yoruba	66	9	18	93
	138	13	26	n = 177

Not significant

(b) Cunning

Ranking

	1st	2nd	3rd	Total
Ibo	6	70	8	84
Yoruba	10	61	23	94
	16	131	31	n = 178

Chi-square = 8.34, df = 2; p<.05.

(c) Juju (Magic)

Ranking

	1st	2nd	3rd	Total
Ibo	7	9	69	85
Yoruba	18	23	52	93
	25	32	121	n = 178

Chi-square = 13.02, df = 2; p<.05

The above results, especially in the area of cunning and magic, are in line with known differences in the cultural beliefs of the Ibo and Yoruba ethnic groups. The Yoruba are more inclined to believe in metaphysical forces and wit as effective means of solving problems than the Ibos, who have a greater tendency to rely on their physical strength and concrete reality.

The last of the pretest questions related to notions about witchcraft in terms of whether it is perceived as a reality or mere artifact. The responses are instructive. Among the Ibos, 47 out of 93 (50.53%) responded in the affirmative while 46 out of 93 (49.46%) responded negatively. On the other hand, 82 out of 95 Yorubas (86.31%) believed in witchcraft while only 13 out 95 (13.68%) rejected the idea, and the difference in the Ibo and Yoruba responses is quite statistically significant (Chi-square = 27.93; df = 1; p<.05).

Posttest

Subjects were later exposed to the Achebe passage and six comprehension questions. While the Ibo and Yoruba cultural practices are not entirely divorced from one another, the passage is more strongly rooted in Ibo tradition than that of the Yoruba. Thus, the aim of the researchers was to determine the extent of the influence of culture on the various concepts found in the text. This aim has its basis in schema theory. The theory maintains that the greater the congruence between new information and past experience the better the text is comprehended.

The comprehension questions measured the reactions of the subjects to five major issues. The first was whether the subjects considered victory in a wrestling match, as described extensively in the passage, to be a prestigious achievement. Their responses on a 5-point Likert scale showed a significant difference in favour of the Ibo subjects. The Ibos felt more strongly that it was a prestigious feat than the Yorubas (Chi-square = 36.82; df = 4; p<.05). The result appears in Table 2.

Table 2

Assessment of wrestling as a prestigious achievement in the story (frequencies)

Options[1]	A	B	C	D	E	Total
Ibo Group	66	26	0	0	1	73
Yoruba Group	27	52	5	5	4	93
	93	78	5	5	5	166

(Chi-square = 36.82; df = 4; p<.05)

[1]A - E represent the continuum from strongly agree to strongly disagree.

Equally of interest are the reasons adduced by subjects for their choices. Subjected to chi-square analysis, the reasons manifested a significant difference. The Ibo subjects regarded wrestling as tied to respect and honour, as a unique achievement, as having great cultural value, and as a manifestation of physical fitness and health. This was not so of the Yoruba group where 28.35% of the respondents considered it as valueless. Table 3 shows the response.

Table 3

Rationale for choices in Table 2 (frequencies)

Options[1]	A	B	C	D	E	F	G	Total
Ibo Group	36	8	1	19	4	2	0	70
Yoruba Group	33	4	2	4	2	3	19	67
	69	12	3	23	6	5	19	137

(Chi-square = 31.39; df = 6; $p<.05$)

[1]A = respect, honour, admiration   E = physical fitness and health
B = initiates fear   F = it is an admirable art form
C = highlights uniqueness   G = has no worth
D = culture says it is prestigious

The second question asked whether Okonkwo, the great wrestler, could be regarded as a man of prestige. Ibo subjects agreed more significantly with this proposal than their Yoruba counterparts (chi-square = 10.37; df = 4; $p<.05$) as shown in Table 4.

Table 4

Agreement with presentation of Okonkwo as prestigious (frequencies)

Options[1]	A	B	C	D	E	Total
Ibo Group	55	34	1	1	1	92
Yoruba Group	32	50	1	3	2	88
	87	84	2	4	3	180

(chi-square = 10.37, df = 4; $p<.05$)

[1]A - E represent the continuum from strongly agree to strongly disagree.

The third question sought subjects' assessment of Okonkwo, the hero of the story as (a) physically handsome, and (b) figuratively handsome. Concerning physical handsomeness the two groups differed significantly while no significant difference was observed in their ratings of Okonkwo as figuratively handsome (See Tables 5a and b).

Table 5a: Is Okonkwo physically handsome? (frequencies)

Options	Yes	No	Total
Ibo	53	39	92
Yoruba	29	64	93
	82	103	185

(chi-square = 13.08; df = 1; p<.05)

Table 5b: Is Okonkwo figuratively handsome? (frequencies)

Options	Yes	No	Total
Ibo	59	32	91
Yoruba	53	37	90
	122	69	181

(Not significant)

The fourth question sought respondents' views as to whether Unoka, the father of Okonkwo, is a responsible person or not. Only 3 out of 93 Ibos (3.22%) responded in the affirmative. The bulk of subjects on either side perceived Unoka as irresponsible. There was no significant difference in the views of the two groups on this matter.

The reasons for the verdict concerning the character of Unoka differed significantly between the Ibo and Yoruba ethnic groups (chi-square = 21.04; df = 7; p<.05). Fifty-four out of 89 Ibos (60.67%) chastised Unoka for lack of hardwork, being a man of easy virtue, being a debtor and for having taken no traditional title, as against 28 out of all Yorubas (30.76%) who held the same views. More Yorubas than Ibos, however, showed sympathy for Unoka for his being a generous public entertainer and in fact, for being law-abiding in spite of his poverty.

The final question based on the text required the subjects to estimate what Unoka's indulgence in playing the flute indicated about his character. The views of the two groups of subjects differed significantly (chi-square = 36.71; df = 6; p<.05). Ibo responses reproved Unoka for being a mere clown, dreading manly activities, not being serious about life, and being too jolly and easy-going. While some Yoruba subjects shared some of the same views, a sizable proportion of them respected Unoka for contributing meaningfully to social life through his music and for consistently expressing his musical talent.

Discussion

The major hypothesis of this study is that bilingual readers tend to bring to a comprehension passage vital elements from their cultural background that invariably shapes the notions and conclusions they derive from the text. It is, therefore, postulated that even when Ibo and Yoruba subjects are exposed to the same reading passage, they are likely to emerge with slightly different impressions coloured by their different cultural identities and beliefs.

Previous studies based on schema theory support the proposition that comprehension is not a mere matter of applying linguistics (Anderson, Reynolds, Shallert, & Goetz, 1977; Lasisi & Onyehalu, 1986). Bartlett (1932) has unequivocally stressed the importance of the reader's background knowledge on the comprehension of text materials. It has been equally argued that a text is never fully explicit, and this therefore necessitates a high level of application of previous knowledge in rationalizing the text. This position becomes even more real when the second and subsequent language learners are considered.

In the present research, Ibo and Yoruba subjects were demonstrated to process relatively different cultural identities. Analysis of scores for an unambiguous literary passage (Achebe) indicated that the two groups emerged with slightly different impressions and attitudes about the passage even when the subjects for study were carefully matched by levels of education and major fields of study. Thus, when questioned concerning the status of wrestling as a prestigious feat, the Ibos coming from a more aggressive and assertive ethnic group readily supported the idea. Also, the reasons for the answers were indicative of the cultural background of the subjects. These values were not as strongly held in the Yoruba group. Consistent with the above situation is the response of the subjects concerning the reputation of Okonkwo as a man of prestige. More Ibos than Yorubas based the character's prestige on physical prowess.

Again, consistent with the foregoing argument and based on the different cultures of the subjects, when asked to rate Okonkwo, the hero of the Achebe story, as physically handsome or not, a higher ratio of the Ibo than Yoruba subjects agreed that Okonkwo was really a handsome lad. They seem to be actually responding to the demands of their respective cultures. It is, however, important to note that when asked whether Okonkwo was figuratively handsome, there was a "catching up" by the

Yoruba subjects as there was no longer any significant difference in their choices. This obviously seems to give credit to Yoruba readers for being able to decenter themselves from their dominant culture in order to actually perceive Okonkwo as presented by the story-teller.

The last portions of the results of this study centered on the portrayal of Unoka, the father of Okonkwo, as dedicating his entire life to producing music and entertainment with his flute while paying no attention to the other necessities of life. In judging Unoka's level of responsibility, the majority of Ibo subjects wrote him off as a lazy, unachieving man while only a minority of the Yoruba subjects felt that way. In Ibo culture, while it is usual to entertain the audience with music and dancing on certain occasions, the Ibos have less respect for entertainers who devote their life to drumming and dancing. This resentment among the Yorubas is much less acute because of the cultural link between Yoruba tradition and the dance and music art forms. The significance of Unoka's predilection for his flute was seen by the Ibos as dreading manly activities, playing the clown, and/or not being serious enough with life. In their culture, patronage of professional musicians during social functions is less frequent than in Yoruba culture. Yoruba subjects were clearly more tolerant in assessing Unoka. They acknowledged his entertainment function as an essential service and seem to recognise his right to freely express his musical talent.

In the final analysis, it has to be restated that cognition does not take place in isolation. Several researchers within the cognitive developmental model (Ehindero, 1982, 1984; Hamlyn, 1971; Onyehalu, 1983, 1985; Piaget, 1950; Piaget & Inhelder, 1969), individually and in concert, have attested to the inevitable impact of a multitude of factors--social influences, cultural influences, motivational factors, the role of emotion, experience and so on--which become relevant in the attainment of concepts and the evolution of logical behaviour. The domain of reading comprehension is no exception to the rule. Readers invariably bring previously conceived notions of reality into their interpretation and analysis of literary work. They examine new information in the light of what they already know and systematically try to reconcile them if cognitive conflict is to be avoided.

Again, the scenario can be likened to the figure-ground postulation in the psychology of perception. This postulation implies that the viewer perceives an object for what it is only when the object is seen vis-à-vis its background, and both the object and the background help to mutually give precise meaning to each other. The bilingual subjects in the current study attempted to understand and interpret the prose passage in the light of their indigenous cultures. Hence, the responses and reactions to the same text material by subjects of comparable academic exposure have been largely different but defensible. As a matter of fact, bilinguals should be conceptualised as belonging to two worlds and living a dual existence. There is the world of their indigenous culture and first language. There is also the world created by the second language and its separate culture. The bilingual struggles to adapt to both.

References

Adediran, A. (1980). Yoruba ethnic groups or a Yoruba ethnic group? Department of History, University of Ife Seminar Papers 1979-80, 5, 48-64.

Ademola, I. (1971). The Eastern Yoruba country before Oduduwa. Department of History, University of Ife Seminar Papers 1970-71, 1, 34-73.

Akinjogbin, I. A. (1980). The concept of origin in Yoruba history: the Ife example. Department of History, University of Ife Seminar Papers 1979-80, 5, 65-80.

Anderson, R. C., Reynolds, R. E., Schallert, D. L., & Goetz, E. T. (1977). Frameworks for comprehending discourse. *Educational Research Journal*, 14, 367-381.

Bartlett, F. C. (1932). *Remembering*. Cambridge: Harvard University Press.

Bettelheim, B. & Zelan, K. (1982). *On learning to read: the child's fascination with meaning*. New York: Knopf.

Block, E. (1986). The comprehension strategies of second language readers. *TESOL Quarterly*, 20, 463-494.

Ehindero, O. J. (1982). A developmental analysis of certain Piagetian concepts among some Nigerian children. *Journal of Research in Science Teaching*, 19, 45-52.

Ehindero, O. J. (1984). The effects of ecocultural factors in operational thought among some Nigerian adolescents. *Journal of Research in Science Teaching*, 19, 451-457.

Hamlyn, D. W. (1971). Epistemology and conceptual development. In T. Mischel (Ed.) *Cognitive development and epistemology*. New York: Academic Press.

Langer, J. A. (1984). Examining background knowledge and text comprehension. *Reading Research Quarterly*, 19, 468-481.

Lasisi, M. J., & Falodun, S. (1988). The effect of within-culture differences on the reading comprehension of form I pupils in Nigerian secondary schools. *Ife Studies in English Language*, 2, 29-37.

Lasisi, M. J. & Onyehalu, A. S. (1986). Multiple exposure to cultural and foreign prose as a factor in comprehension performance of bilingual learners. *Reading Improvement*, 23, 201-211.

Lasisi, M. J., Falodun, S., & Onyehalu, A. S. (1988). The comprehension of first and second language prose. *Journal of Research in Reading*, 11, 26-35.

Lipson, M. Y. (1982). Learning new information from text: the role of prior knowledge and reading ability. *Journal of Reading Behavior,* 14, 243-261.

Lipson, M. Y. (1983). The influence of religious affiliation on children's memory for text information. *Reading Research Quarterly,* 18, 448-457.

Onochie, E. O. (1986). Readability measures in a second language: A comparative study of the Fry formula and the cloze procedure. Unpublished doctoral dissertation, University of Ibadan, Nigeria.

Onochie, E. O. (1987). Schema theory of reading: implication for primary reading instruction in a second language situation. *Proceedings of the Second Biennial Conference of the Reading Association of Nigeria,* 4, 129-140.

Onyehalu, A. S. (1983). Feedback and performance of Piagetian conservation tasks in a developing country. *American Journal of Psychology,* 96, 65-73.

Onyehalu, A. S. (1985). A test of Piaget's horizontal decalage in Nigeria. *Perceptual and Motor Skills,* 61, 355-361.

Opeola, S. M. (1986, September). Use of spiritual and herbal weapons in Yoruba warfare. Paper presented at the conference on the Centenary of the 1886 Kiriji/Ekitiparapo Peace Treaty, Obafemi Awolowo University, Ile-Ife, Nigeria.

Opeola, S. M. (1988). Yoruba traditional methods of contraception. Paper presented at the meeting of Nigeria 04, Family Planning Service Project: Fifth Year Workshop Activities of the Department of Obstetrics and Gynaecology, Obafemi Awolowo University, Nigeria.

Piaget, J. (1950). *The psychology of intelligence.* London: Routledge and Kegan Paul.

Piaget, J. & Inhelder, B. (1969). *The psychology of the child.* London: Routledge and Kegan Paul.

Reynolds, R. E., Taylor, M. A. Steffensen, M. S., Shirey, L. L., & Anderson, R. C. (1982). Cultural schemata and reading comprehension. *Reading Research Quarterly,* 3, 353-366.

Steffensen, M. S., Joag-Dev., C., & Anderson, R. C. (1979). A cross-cultural perspective on reading comprehension. *Reading Research Quarterly,* 15, 10-29.

Part VI:

METALINGUISTIC SKILLS IN BILINGUALS

Cognitive Processing in Bilinguals – R.J. Harris (Editor)
© 1992 Elsevier Science Publishers B.V. All rights reserved.

Language Awareness and Language Separation in the Young Bilingual Child

Lenore N. Arnberg
Stockholm University

Peter W. Arnberg
Swedish Road and Traffic Research Institute

Abstract

One of the main research questions raised in connection with early bilingual language acquisition has concerned the child's differentiation of the two languages. Earlier research investigating this issue has suggested two hypotheses concerning language differentiation; i.e., that the child separates the languages from the beginning or that the separation process is a gradual one. Despite a number of studies in the area, it has not yet been possible to resolve this issue, and support for both positions has been found. The present study takes a different approach in investigating language separation, suggesting that two types of learning processes may be involved. Using Vygotsky's (1978) framework, one involves elementary and the other involves higher mental functioning. The purpose of the study was to investigate the role of higher mental functioning in the child's ability to separate the two languages. Eighteen bilingual children ranging in age from 1;8 to 4;0 participated in the study. The findings showed preliminary support for the role of bilingual awareness in language separation in that children who showed an awareness of the two languages in a specially designed bilingual awareness task showed significantly less mixing than those who did not show this awareness.

One of the main research questions asked in connection with early bilingual language acquisition has concerned the child's differentiation of the two languages. This issue is important in light of the suggestion that the bilingual child must learn to sort out the two lexical and syntactic systems before any real progress can be made in acquiring either code (Vihman & McLaughlin, 1982). Earlier studies have supported two opposing viewpoints concerning the differentiation process, namely, that the child is able to differentiate the languages from the beginning or that the differentiation process is a gradual one (see Arnberg & Arnberg, 1985, for a review of the literature). Although quantitatively speaking, more studies have supported the latter position, several recent studies have questioned the "gradual differentiation hypothesis" (see, e.g., de Houwer, 1987; Meisel, 1989), and Genesee (1989) concluded that "the case for undifferentiated language development in bilingual children is far from established." As was the case with earlier authors (see, e.g., Lindholm & Padilla, 1977, 1978; Padilla & Liebman, 1975), these authors do not see the occurrence of language mixing, i.e., the "indiscriminate combinations of elements from each language (Redlinger & Park, 1980, p. 337)," as offering counter-evidence for the "initial differentiation" hypothesis. However, whereas mixing was earlier explained by factors such as a lack of a lexical entry in one of the languages, momentarily forgetting one of the words, or a greater saliency of one of the words, current explanations of mixing have involved different factors.

For example, De Houwer (1987) and Meisel (1989), who discuss differentiation mainly at the morphosyntactic level, attribute mixing at the lexical level to a failure in pragmatic or sociolinguistic competence. In connection with this, De Houwer suggests the following:

> Even if most of the bilingual child's early two- and three-word utterances contain lexical items from both languages and even if the child produces these "mixed utterances" in a variety of sociolinguistic situations, there is little reason to speak of a "hybrid system" or "one medium of communication." Clearly, the child draws on all her vocabulary knowledge, and does not address one person entirely in one language. In other words, the child has yet to acquire a particular type of sociolinguistic knowledge (p. 105).

A similar explanation is offered by Meisel (1989).

> The child may well use two different grammatical systems, as evidenced by distinct word order patterns, etc., and he may still choose the "wrong" language occasionally. Which language is the "right" or "wrong" one is usually determined by the same sociolinguistic factors as in code-switching, e.g., interlocutor, topic, etc. In other words, there is a deficiency in the PRAGMATIC COMPETENCE. Even though the two grammatical systems have been internalized, the child might still violate the rules which govern switching, e.g., in the case of the children discussed here, speaking German to the French-speaking mother (p. 21).

Meisel (1989) subsequently suggests that different terms be used to distinguish the two phenomena, i.e, "mixing" to refer to the above failure in the pragmatic competence and "fusion" to refer to the inability to separate the two grammatical systems. Thus, he summarizes the findings from his study as indicating that:

> Bilinguals are capable of differentiating grammatical systems; fusion is not necessarily a characteristic of bilingual language development, but mixing may occur until codeswitching is firmly established as a strategy of bilingual pragmatic competence (p. 21).

Meisel (1989) seems to be suggesting that there is a dissociation between language differentiation at the lexical and syntactic levels, a viewpoint also advocated by Klausen and Plunkett (1987). Although the present study does not investigate mixing at the syntactic level, the idea that language mixing at different linguistic levels should have different causes is questioned. The present paper, instead, presents a new approach in explaining language mixing, the implication being that this will apply to all linguistic levels.

Observations of Bilingual Children Acquiring
Two Languages from an Early Age

It is easy to recognize at least one reason for the disagreement among researchers with regard to the differentiation process in bilingual children when one examines the research literature; namely, there appears to be support for both positions! The following observations appear frequently in studies of young bilingual children:

1. Many children appear to mix the languages extensively initially, i.e., when speaking one of the languages, 30 – 40% of the child's utterances may contain words or phrases from the other language. Recently, however, many of the earlier studies reporting this finding have been criticized for their failure to control for mixing in the input which the child has been exposed to, e.g., among parents. Nevertheless, this result has also been found in studies where the child was exposed to a strict separation of the languages in input (see Saunders, 1988; Schlyter, 1987).

2. Occasionally, children are reported in the literature who appear to mix the languages minimally or not at all. These children have nearly always been raised according to a one person: one language strategy (see, e.g., Bergman, 1976).

3. Even among children who mix the languages, large portions of their utterances are in fact in the correct language. This occurs even during conditions where input in the two languages highly favors one language or the other. This seems to indicate that, even at an early age, the child adjusts his/her use of the two languages on some level at least some of the time, depending on factors such as the interlocutor, situation, subject being spoken about, etc. (see, e.g., L. Arnberg, 1981, 1987).

4. Somewhere between the ages of two and four, most studies have shown a major change in the nature of the child's mixing pattern, mixing at this time decreasing to approximately 1–2% of the child's utterances. Furthermore, when mixed utterances do appear, these frequently resemble adult-like utterances in which both languages are used. For example, there is a decrease in mixing at the phrasal level and an increase in the insertion of single lexical items, these frequently consisting of nouns for which adequate translation equivalents do not exist. In other words, the child's mixed utterances more and more resemble code-switching, i.e., they demonstrate an ability to SELECT the language according to the interlocutor, situational context, etc. (see, e.g., Redlinger & Park, 1980; Vihman, 1982).

The above results may initially seem difficult to synthesize. We would like to suggest that one way of handling these conflicting findings is to propose that there may be two types of learning processes involved in language separation; using Vygotsky's (1978) framework, one involves elementary and the other involves higher mental functions. A brief description of these learning processes and their application to language separation in the bilingual child is presented below.

Elementary Mental Functions

With regard to the first process, a very young child, or even an unborn child, might, in a primitive way, gradually begin to separate the two languages exposed to. This process appears to be similar to that proposed by Kesner (1980) for animal learning, involving five salient attributes characterizing mnemonic information. These consist of: 1) a spatial attribute; 2) a temporal attribute; 3) an affect attribute; 4) a sensory-perceptual attribute; and 5) a response attribute. Considering the first two attributes, a spatial attribute within this framework would involve the coding and storage of specific stimuli representing places. Applying this to a bilingual context, if English is spoken in the home and Swedish outside the home, the child will tend to connect the languages with these contexts. The "time" attribute in a bilingual context might, e.g., lead to English words and phrases being stored together when they co-occur within the same time span.

Other researchers have also brought up the parallel between elementary mental functions and animal learning. For example, Cole (1985) suggests that the distinction between elementary and higher mental functions has arisen in psychology in response to the need for distinguishing psychological phenomena found in both humans and animals from those found only in humans. Similarly, Vygotsky (1978) suggests a parallel between higher animals' problem-solving ability and elementary mental functions.

Some examples from our research with Swedish-English speaking children in Sweden, as well as from the literature, may serve to illustrate language separation behavior occurring at this level. For example, during this stage, an English-Swedish speaking child was observed to have switched to English at his day nursery whenever the English-speaking mother's car came into view. In another case, a bilingual child was observed to have switched to Swedish during the English-speaking recording session when hearing the Swedish ice cream truck pass by. A third example can be seen in the tendency for young bilingual children to associate their languages with different rooms in their bilingual day nursery (Nauclér, 1984).

Higher Mental Functions

The second type of learning process involves that which Vygotsky (1978) has referred to as higher mental functioning. In order to understand the difference between this type of mental functioning and that described earlier, it is useful to recognize several characteristics attributed by Vygotsky to higher mental functions. These include: 1) the shift of control from the environment to the individual, i.e., the emergence of voluntary regulation; 2) the emergence of conscious realization of mental processes; and 3) the use of signs to mediate higher mental functions. Elementary mental functions are thus characterized by the absence of these attributes.

With regard to the first characteristic, Vygotsky (1978, p. 39) suggests that "the central characteristic of elementary functions is that they are totally and directly determined by stimulation from the environment. For higher mental functions, the central feature is self-generated stimulation, that is, the creation and use of artificial stimuli which become the immediate causes of behavior." With regard to the emergence of conscious realization of mental processes, the second attribute, Vygotsky refers to an intellectualization and mastery of higher psychological functions. Finally, with regard to the third attribute, Vygotsky refers to the existence of psychological tools or signs, the most important of these being language, which can be used to control one's own and others' behavior.

Thus, when applying these phenomena to the bilingual child, when higher mental functions are involved in language separation behavior, the child no longer simply "reacts" to stimulation from the environment, but instead directs his/her attention in some way to the dual language presentation, is able to reflect upon the two languages used and to eventually talk about this, and can exercise control in the use of the languages. The following examples may serve to illustrate language separation occurring at this level:

In the first example, the child shows evidence of the realization that a referent can have two labels. Although the child may have used the two translation equivalents spontaneously in speech to each parent at an earlier stage, he/she is now able to comment on this.

(Mother and child, age 2;3, are playing with a farmyard and animals, and the mother asks the child to name one of the animals.)

Mother	Child
What's this here?	
	En ko (A cow)
A cow?	
	Ja (Yes)
T'isn't a cow	
	Ja
It's a h...	
	Horse
It's a horse, yes	
	(pause and then with great excitement) Mamma, den kan kalla häst (Mommy, it can call horse)
Yes, yes. You can call it a... Pappa calls it a "häst," doesn't he?	

The child at this stage also shows the ability to immediately correct itself if the wrong language is used by mistake, to state specifically when it does not know a word in one of the languages, rather than merely inserting a word from the other language as occurs at an earlier stage (see Imedadze, 1960), and the ability to translate.

In the next example, the child seems to recognize not only that words can refer to the extralinguistic context, but that there are also interconnections between the words themselves, these occurring in each language. This would appear to be an example of the formation of genuine concepts in which, according to Vygotsky (1934, p. 196), there is "simultaneously a relationship to an object and a relationship to another concept, that is, the initial elements of a system of concepts."

(The child, age 2;3, and the mother are playing with a play grocery store, discussing the various items for sale)

Mother   Child

That's milk
                          Milk (with great excitement)
                          Cow! Cow!
Cow, yes. Oh wow! (obviously
pleased)

In the final example, the child, although at a somewhat older age, shows the ability to verbalize an understanding of the bilingual situation:

(The conversation takes place between the experimenter and a girl, age 5;0.)

E: How do you know when to speak English and when to speak Swedish?
C: YOU speak English. My daddy speaks Swedish and he also speaks a little English.
E: Do you ever speak English at your day nursery?
C: No.
E: Why not?
C: Cause that my Swedish talk. Then I speak Swedish. Then the others wouldn't know and the babies there wouldn't know, so I will have to speak Swedish there.
E: When you go to America, do you ever speak Swedish there?
C: Yes to mormor (grandma) cause she's gonna come to us some day. When she says "yes" and then it's "ja" in Swedish.

Conclusions

In summary, what has been suggested is that there may be two different types of learning processes involved in language separation in the bilingual child; using Vygotsky's (1978) terminology, one involving elementary and the other involving higher mental functioning. This framework may be useful in explaining the above mentioned conflicting observations with regard to language development in bilingual children:

1. <u>Some individual children may not mix the languages at all:</u> One explanation for this may be that such children, with whom the parents have been highly consistent in using a one person: one language strategy and for whom the languages have been balanced, separate the languages because they strictly associate each language with a specific person, i.e., they are using elementary mental functioning. It is highly important here to consider the research design of the study. Frequently data are reported for child–parent interactions alone and there is no way of knowing if similar language separation behavior would have occurred had the child interacted with other speakers of each language.

2. <u>Why for the majority of children, language mixing does occur:</u> For most children at least, it is suggested that a learning process involving higher mental functioning will be a more efficient strategy in learning to separate the languages than one involving elementary mental functions. Most children may thus mix the languages because they are not yet aware of the bilingual presentation in the environment, in other words, they do not use higher mental functioning in separating the languages.

3. <u>Why children who mix do not do so all of the time:</u> the lack of mixing in some cases may be due to the fact that elementary mental functioning is also involved in language separation.

4. <u>Why most children stop mixing the languages by approximately age four:</u> At this time nearly all children are able to use higher mental functioning in language separation. This does not mean, however, that elementary functions completely cease to operate at this level (see P. Arnberg, 1972, for a discussion of parallel processing as presented in the theories of Kendler & Kendler, 1962, 1970, and Neisser, 1967).

The Transition from Elementary to Higher Mental Functions

As was Vygotsky's general strategy in studying child development, an important task is to explain how mental functions first appearing in an elementary form are transformed into a higher form.

In her review of six current theories of developmental psychology, Miller (1989) concludes that, as no one theory satisfactorily explains development, it is critical that researchers draw on the content, methods and theoretical concepts of different theories. Following this line of reasoning, in suggesting several hypotheses for how the child moves from elementary to higher mental functioning in the language separation process, we would like to draw on three theories in developmental psychology. These are Piaget's cognitive-stage theory, Gibson's perceptual-development theory, and Vygotsky's theory concerning the relation between language and thought.

Piaget's Cognitive-stage Theory

Piaget's theory describes changes in how children acquire knowledge about the world, first through the development of sensorimotor schemes based on physical actions which become increasingly intentionalized and coordinated. The child then acquires symbolic ability and gradually, from semilogical reasoning, reaches the stage of concrete operations, followed by the stage of formal operations. Thought progressively becomes increasingly organized, one stage building upon the next. In explaining how development occurs, Piaget places great importance on the notion of adaptation, involving the complementary processes of assimilation and accommodation, which occur as the organism constantly strives toward a state of equilibrium.

For the purposes of this paper, one of the most criticized aspects of Piaget's theory concerns his claim that cognitive development proceeds through a series of stages. In summarizing Piaget's notion of stages, it is suggested that these are "structured wholes that emerge from and transform a previous stage, follow an invariant and universal sequence and proceed from an unstable period of transition into a final stable period" (Miller, 1989, p. 41). The universal aspect of the stages should be recognized, this being an inevitable outcome, given the nature of the human organism (its physical structures and cognitive functions) and of the environment (Miller, 1989, p. 76).

Piaget's cognitive-stage theory can be applied in several different ways in addressing questions concerning language awareness and language mixing/separation in bilingual children. For example, Van Kleeck (1982), in considering the development of metalinguistic awareness in general (in relation to which the case of awareness of two languages in the bilingual child can be said to be an example), suggests that there are cognitive correlates of metalinguistic skills. She predicts (and cites evidence to support her claims) that the types of metalinguistic skills appearing in the preoperational stage (age 2 to 7) will be qualitatively different from those appearing in the stage of concrete operations (age 7 to 11). This is due to the child's ability to decenter during the latter stage, i.e., to attend to more than one aspect of a situation simultaneously and to consider relationships between these aspects. Thus, a child in the stage of concrete operations can, during a metalinguistic task, shift his/her thinking between form and content, a task which the preoperational child finds difficult. Although focusing on monolingual children, the idea presented here is, thus, that the child will not be able to perform certain metalinguistic tasks until a certain cognitive stage is reached. (Although of course many neo-Piagetian theorists are highly critical of the notion of stages, the idea of stages in the more classical Piagetian sense will be retained here.)

A second suggestion in the literature which would fit into a stage approach, although in terms of linguistic rather than cognitive stages, is that the child separates the languages when a certain syntactic level has been reached (Schlyter, 1987). The children in the study reported had all learned to separate their languages by the end of stage III (see Crystal, Fletcher & Garman, 1976), at which time morphology, language-specific word order and other grammatical devices have appeared. Schlyter (1987) thus concluded that "it is reasonable that when the child develops language-specific grammatical patterns, he/she should be able to separate the languages lexically, i.e., not mix them" (p. 46). Although not explained in this way, it would seem reasonable to interpret this suggestion in terms of the notions of assimilation and accommodation. The child would thus assimilate information about the two languages (thus producing mixed utterances at times) until a stage is reached at which language-specific grammatical patterns appear. At this time, the child is forced into a state of disequilibrium, at which time he/she must accommodate his/her present structures to meet the demands of reality, this hypothetically leading to language separation, with a concomitant awareness of the two languages. Awareness thus results from disequilibrium, i.e., when automatic regulations used in performing certain intentional acts are no longer sufficient in reaching a goal (Piaget, 1974). According to this hypothesis, a specific linguistic stage should always result in the child's separating the languages.

In summary, this theory predicts a similar development for all children. The child learns to separate the languages when it has reached a certain stage of development, this being expressed either in terms of cognitive or linguistic structures. The theory leaves the separation process more or less up to the child and does not highlight the need of any specific training or intervention from adults.

Gibson's Theory of Perceptual Development

Although Piaget's theory has had an enormous influence in the field of developmental psychology, as mentioned earlier, there has been much criticism of his notion of stages (see Miller, 1989). It is thus useful to examine other theoretical approaches, one of these being Gibson's (1969) theory of perceptual development.

One of Gibson's (1969) major claims is that the world is structured and that the child gradually becomes more and more aware of this structure. In other words, children learn by becoming increasingly aware of the information which is already present in stimulation. Unlike Piaget who believes that the child "constructs" his knowledge through the formation of schemes based on physical actions upon the world, Gibson suggests that stimulation is a rich source of information, the child's task being to learn to extract more and more information from stimulation.

There are many levels of information in stimulation. At first the child discriminates objects by means of one or more distinct features. At higher levels the child can attend not only to features but to patterns and relationships between them as well as doing this in an efficient and optimal way. An example taken from adult perceptual learning may serve to illustrate this process. For example, when listening to an orchestral work for the first time, one's perception is rather undifferentiated. Only after several exposures to the music is the listener able to pick out the various themes, to differentiate the various instruments, etc. Thus, although the same information has always been present in stimulation, one must learn to perceive it. This example highlights another issue, namely, that Gibson (1969) does not believe that the perceptual learning process is essentially different between children and adults. When presented with a new situation, adults must also learn to perceive. Likewise, in a familiar situation, such as locating a favorite box of cookies on the kitchen shelf, the child may also be highly efficient in perception. (Nevertheless, adults can probably pick up needed information more economically than children as they have a better understanding of the task).

For Gibson, then, perceptual development is nearly synonymous with attentional development. The child learns to ignore nonessential stimulation which makes the learning and thinking process economical. This of course makes it possible to understand complex structures when the familiarity process has sorted out irrelevant information. This process occurs as a result of the child's experience in the world, including feedback from his/her own actions and instruction from adults. An important point which Gibson also makes with regard to experience concerns task specificity, i.e., the fact that there are goals and needs specific to each situation. Perception is thus always motivated by goals important to the individual.

Thus, rather than a stage at which the child, in general, becomes aware and conscious (Vygotsky) or can use certain mental operations (Piaget), the child from a very early age is able to discriminate features in the world. An important aspect of Gibson's (1969) theory is thus that it attributes a potential for awareness to the child from the start, the child being different from an adult mainly due to its lack of knowledge of the world's structures as well as of methods for perceiving these. This naturally places learning in a new light, as we no longer need to wait for the child to reach a certain stage before teaching something. (It is of course important to consider the child's prior knowledge in a specific learning area, however.) The authors thus feel that an adjustment to the child's developmental level and interests is of major concern; nevertheless, in some specific learning areas, it may be possible to teach the child without an overemphasis on these factors.

In applying this line of thinking to the bilingual child, one can hypothesize that the child's experience in a given situation (in this case in connection with using the two languages) will play a major role in determining when language separation will occur. For example, if the child is placed in critical situations in which he/she is forced to discriminate between the languages due to, e.g., having failed to communicate as a result of using the "wrong" language with a monolingual speaker, it is likely that language awareness will occur, regardless of the child's cognitive or linguistic stage.

There is some support for this idea from the literature. For example, Levelt, Sinclair and Jarvella (1978, pp. 8-9) consider the role of "moments of failure" to be important in increasing awareness:

> A major cause for linguistic awareness could be failure in communication, that is, in speaking or understanding. Repairs made while speaking, or the registering of WHAT? while listening, may occur when automatic processing fails to yield the result being sought: a speech error is corrected or there is an attempt to remedy a lapse in understanding. Conscious intervention is then required and the language user is – momentarily at least – in some fashion aware of the linguistic entity that caused the problem.

The role of attentional factors is also supported in a study by Robinson and Robinson (1981). This study focused on the importance of the explicitness of adults' discussion of communication failures in enhancing the development of the child's understanding of the reason for these failures. The results showed that children who showed an appreciation of message inadequacy had mothers who had signalled explicit rather than nonexplicit non- understanding on occasions when communication failures had occurred.

In conclusion, from this theory we can predict that there will be differences among children concerning when they learn to separate the languages deriving from the varying experiences which different bilingual children are likely to have in connection with using their two languages. More specifically, it is predicted that those experiences which draw the child's attention to the dual language presentation in an explicit way are likely to have a positive influence on the child's ability to separate the languages.

Vygotsky's Theory Concerning the Relation Between Language and Thought

Vygotsky's theory (see Wertsch, 1985) is an important complement to the two earlier presented theories, as it differs from them in several important respects. For example, the theory deals specifically with the role of language in development which neither of the other theories do. Vygotsky's theory also allows for more specific predictions concerning the role which social factors, especially adults, play in the developmental process.

The theory is a stage theory, although the stages would appear to be less fixed than is the case with Piaget. For example, Vygotsky views development not as a steady stream of quantitative increments but in terms of fundamental qualitative transformations or "revolutions" associated with changes in psychological tools (Wertsch, 1985). The tendency to view development in terms of stages can also be seen in the distinction made between two lines of development, the natural line and the social or cultural line. The natural line is associated with elementary mental functions and the social line with higher mental functions. It is also suggested that the natural line ceases to play an active role in ontogenetic change after an early period and that the social line then predominates.

Vygotsky's theory focuses nearly only on the social line, and he particularly con-centrates on changes in the way that language mediates higher mental functions. An important issue focused on concerns two properties of human language, i.e., its potential to be used in abstract, decontextualized reflection and its potential to be rooted in contextualization. These two tendencies are referred to respectively as the "symbolic" and the "indicative" functions of language. Although both of these aspects of language are involved in higher mental functioning, the symbolic, decontextualized use of language is seen as the most advanced form of higher mental functioning and an emphasis is thus placed on tracing its development. One of the ways in which this development is accounted for is by investigating how concepts or word meanings develop from "unorganized heaps" to genuine or scientific concepts, the latter involving the symbolic, decontextualized use of language.

Vygotsky (see Wertsch, 1985) thus views the development of genuine or scientific concepts as of the utmost importance in the evolution of higher mental processes. He attributes this development mainly to learning in formal school settings due to the tendency in such settings for language to be used to talk ABOUT language (that is, on decontextualized, metalinguistic reflection) as opposed to talking about nonlinguistic reality. The importance which he places on scientific concepts can be seen in the following citation:

> Scientific concepts (as opposed to everyday concepts), with their unique relationship to objects, with their mediation through other concepts, with their internal hierarchical system of interrelationships among themselves are the area in which the conscious realization of concepts, that is, their generalization and mastery, emerges first and foremost. Once the new structure of generalization emerges in one sphere of thought, it is transferred, as any structure is, as a well-known principle of activity, without any training to any other area of thought and concepts. Thus, conscious realization enters through the gates of scientific concepts. (Vygotsky, 1934, p. 193-194, in Wertsch, 1985.)

The main implication of Vygotsky's theory for language awareness in the bilingual child would appear to be in terms of the potential which the bilingual child has to come into contact with language used in a symbolic, decontextualized way from an early age. Although this use of language is mainly attributed to formal, educational settings, one could hypothesize that a bilingual situation enhances the potential for language to be used to talk ABOUT language. Naturally, however, the extent to which this occurs is likely to vary among individual families.

In relation to more specific claims concerning the bilingual child, one can thus hypothesize, as was the case with Gibson's theory, that there will be individual differences among children concerning when they learn to separate the languages. Unlike Gibson, however, rather than being the result of experiences which draw the child's attention to various aspects of the bilingual situation, this is more likely to be due to the child's metalinguistic experiences in the home, i.e., the way in which parents talk about the two languages. For example, parents may talk about the languages in a contextualized or decontextualized way. For example, they may use strategies such as "mommy says X; daddy says Y" or "at home you say X and at preschool you say Y" which could be considered more "contextualized" than, e.g., "in English it's called X and in Swedish it's called Y." In connection with decontextualization, some parents might also talk about languages in general, that words in different languages may mean the same thing, etc. (Of course many parents probably begin with a more contextualized strategy, gradually moving to a more decontextualized one.)

A major difference from Gibson's theory, however, is that for Vygotsky, the child's bilingual awareness can be expected to have much greater generalization to other areas, extending beyond the specific task at hand to other areas of thought and concepts.

Conclusions

The above discussion concerning how the bilingual child learns to separate the two languages has not focused on all of the ways in which the three theories discussed differ regarding the predictions they may make concerning the separation process. Also, the focus on these particular three theories does not mean that there are not other factors which are also important in explaining language separation. For example, imitation and observational learning (see Bandura, 1977) would also seem to be involved in this process.

These three theories, however, seem to focus on a central issue in the language separation process, namely, whether separation occurs at a specific stage in the child's development or whether it is more likely the result of the child's particular experiences in connection with the use of the two languages, these being more directly linguistic as well as non-linguistic in nature.

Purpose of the Present Study

The purpose of the present study was to further investigate the concept of awareness in relation to the bilingual child's ability to separate his/her two languages. The idea of awareness is not an entirely new one (see, e.g., Arnberg & Arnberg, 1985; Ferguson, 1980; McLaughlin, 1984; Saunders, 1988; Vihman & McLaughlin, 1982). In connection with this, Klausen and Plunkett (1987, p. 3) have also suggested the need for some internal reorganizational process if the child is to differentiate the two linguistic systems. Nevertheless, there has remained a need to more fully investigate the concept as well as to systematically relate it to language mixing/language separation.

In connection with this, the following two research questions have been addressed:

1. Are children who are aware of the bilingual presentation able to separate the languages to a greater extent than those who are not?

2. Does the development of awareness follow a similar pattern for all children, i.e., occurring at a specific linguistic or cognitive point in the child's development, or does it vary individually depending on the child's experiences in using the languages?

Method

Subjects

The data reported here have been collected in connection with two studies: 1) a cross-sectional study of 18 English-Swedish speaking children between the ages of 1;8 to 4;0; and 2) a longitudinal study of 3 English-Swedish speaking and 1 Russian-Swedish speaking child between the ages of 1;7 to 2;3 at the onset of the study. The present paper concentrates mainly on the data from the cross-sectional study. (The data from the longitudinal study will be published in a separate paper.)

With regard to the cross-sectional data, all of the children were of middle class background, residing in a large urban area in Sweden. The only requirement for the study was that they be as balanced as possible in their use of the two languages. Eight of the children attended an English-speaking day nursery, five attended a Swedish-speaking day nursery and five children were cared for in the home. Ten girls and 8 boys were represented in the sample.

Experimenters

The experimenters consisted of a native English-speaking adult, a native Swedish-speaking adult, and a native Russian-speaking adult. Although all the adults had some knowledge of the second language, due to the difficulty of finding monolinguals in Sweden, they exclusively used the designated language in the presence of the child. All adults were unfamiliar to the child at the onset of the study but visited the child at least once prior to the recording session in order to become acquainted with the child. The parents were close by but not present during the recording sessions; thus, the data represent child–adult interaction in a situation in which the adult was not the child's caregiver.

Stimulus Materials

The stimulus materials consisted of toys which were brought to the child's home/preschool and which were the same for all of the children. These consisted of, e.g., a farmyard and animals, a dollhouse, a play kitchen and a play grocery store.

Bilingual Awareness Measures

With regard to the awareness measures, an important point made by McLaughlin (1984), frequently overlooked, is the following:

> "The argument that the bilingual child separates the languages when he or she is aware that there are two systems in the environment is circular unless some criterion is provided for assessing what is meant by this awareness – other than that the child separates the languages" (p. 192).

This point is extremely important in light of the fact that many studies of bilingual children have involved children interacting with their (bilingual) parents and where there is no way of determining from the child's utterances alone whether the mixing of the lexical items is due to the child's lack of awareness of the bilingual presentation or is instead a reflection of the child's sensitivity to the fact that he/she is interacting with a bilingual speaker.

A suggestion in the literature was used as the basis for the operational definition of awareness used in the present study, namely, that the child can be said to be aware when it ceases to adopt words from one language to the other, but instead asks for the corresponding word when it is unknown in one of the languages (Imedadze, 1960). This observation was supported in prestudies where we found that in a word test, younger children frequently substituted the word from the other language when an item was not known in one of the languages, while older children nearly always stated in some way when they did not know a word (see Arnberg & Arnberg, 1985).

The method developed thus consisted of a simple picture-naming task in which the child was asked to label the pictures in each language on separate occasions. The responses were classified in the following categories: 1) correct language responses; 2) incorrect language responses; and 3) responses consisting of a designation in some way that the word was not known (e.g., "I don't know," silence, etc.). A lack of awareness was felt to be associated with a large percentage of "wrong language responses" for items not known, while awareness was felt to be associated with a large percentage of "I don't know" type responses for items not known. We were naturally most interested in the child's responses when a word was known in one language but not the other. The percentage of responses in each category was based on the total items answered in each language version of the test.

In addition, parents and experimenters were asked to rate each child on a 9-grade "awareness" scale where "1" indicated "no awareness of the bilingual presentation" and "9" indicated "full awareness of the bilingual presentation." Parents were also asked to explain, with the help of concrete examples, why they had rated the child as they had.

Language Development Measures

A one-half-hour speech sample was collected from each child in each of the languages during natural play situations involving the child and the experimenter. The speech samples were audio-taped and transcribed immediately following the sessions.

Each speech sample was analyzed for the following:
    MLU in words
    Percentage of mixed utterances
    Other observations of the child's language behavior demonstrating
        an awareness/nonawareness of the bilingual presentation

In addition, the English samples were analyzed using the developmental model *Language Assessment, Remediation and Screening Procedure* (LARSP) (see Crystal, Fletcher & Garman, 1976). This model was chosen due to its comprehensiveness (see Klee & Fitzgerald, 1985).

Parental Interviews

The mothers of all the children were interviewed, and in cases where the mother was not the English-speaking parent, the English-speaking fathers were interviewed as well. The parents were asked to provide general background information concerning the family as well as information about the child's bilingual upbringing and development.

Procedure

All subjects were tested in one language on one day and in the second language approximately one week later. Half were initially tested in English and half in Swedish. All were tested in their homes except for the subjects attending the English-speaking day nursery who were tested at their day nursery. All data collection took place in a quiet room.

The subjects were first allowed time to become accustomed to the experimenter. This was followed by the picture-naming test (requiring approximately fifteen minutes) and the speech sample collection (thirty minutes).

Results

Language Awareness and Language Separation

The results from the picture-naming task showed that one group of children gave a high percentage of "wrong language" responses for items not known and a low percentage of responses designating in some way that they did not know the word (e.g., "I don't know). These children were classified as "unaware." A second group of children showed the opposite trend, i.e., giving a high percentage of responses designating that they did not know the word and a low percentage of "wrong language" responses. This group was classified as "aware." Although there were a few exceptions, in general there was high agreement between the parent/experimenter judgements and the results from the picturenaming task.

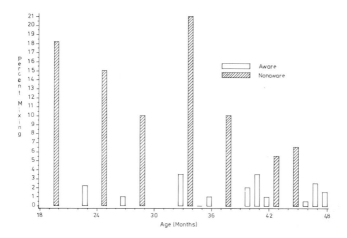

Figure 1. The Percentage of Mixing (Both Languages Combined) in Aware and Nonaware Children of Different Ages (N = 18). The Results Show a Higher Percentage of Mixing in the Nonaware Group.

The mean score for language mixing in the "aware" group was 1.7%, and the mean score for language mixing in the "nonaware" group was 12.3% (see Figure 1). The analysis of variance indicated a main effect of awareness ($\underline{F}(1,16) = 34.81$, $\underline{p} <$ .0001). No effects for age were found.

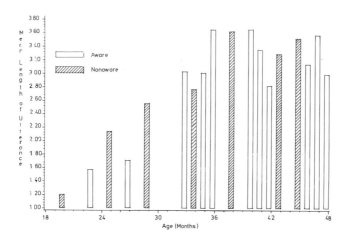

Figure 2. Mean Length of Utterance in Words (English) Presented for Aware and Nonaware Children of Different Ages (N = 18). As Can Be Seen, the Two Groups Do Not Differ With Regard to MLU.

If awareness is not connected with age, a second question concerns whether or not there are any other differences between the aware and the nonaware children. For example, is it the case that the aware children were more advanced in their linguistic development than the unaware children?

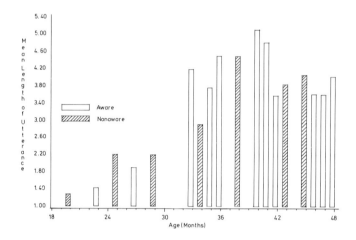

Figure 3. Mean Length of Utterance in Words (Swedish) Presented for Aware and Nonaware Children of Different Ages (N = 18). As Can Be Seen, the Two Groups Do Not Differ with Regard to MLU.

The results from Figures 2 and 3 do not show a significant difference between the aware and the nonaware children in their language development as measured by Mean Length of Utterance (in words) in either language. Because MLU is a very rough measure of language development, however, the aware and the nonaware children were also compared in terms of the results from the analysis of the English transcripts using *the Language Assessment, Remediation and Screening Procedure* (LARSP) (see Crystal, Fletcher & Garman, 1976). A single score for each child was calculated in the following way. Considering clause-level structures only, the percentage of clause-level structures at each stage level (from Stage II to VIII) was calculated and this was multiplied by the number for each stage, these scores then being summed together.

Example of derivation of single LARSP score:

Stage II	Stage III	Stage IV
30%	60%	10%
60	180	40

Total score = 280

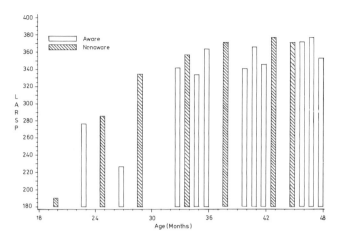

Figure 4. LARSP Profile Scores (In English) Presented for Aware and Nonaware Children of Different Ages (N = 18). As Can Be Seen, the Two Groups Do Not Differ with Regard to the Scores.

The results (see Figure 4) were similar to those concerning the MLU scores in that there was not a significant difference between the aware and the unaware children with regard to the scores based on this model.

Individual Differences in the Development of Awareness

The above results with regard to the children's MLU and LARSP scores do not support the role of either age or linguistic level alone in determining when awareness develops. Although we of course do not know the exact onset of awareness in the aware children, if linguistic level alone were the determining factor, it should not be the case that nonaware children show a more advanced linguistic development than the aware children do. Yet, this is precisely what we find for some of the children. If linguistic level or age is not the determining factor, which factors do contribute to the child's becoming aware and subsequently ceasing to mix the language? In order to investigate this issue, the results from the parental interviews were examined.

In the earlier background to this paper, two groups of factors were discussed which were felt to facilitate the development of awareness: 1) those factors serving to increase the child's attention to various aspects of the bilingual situation; and 2) those factors related to the ways in which parents focused on the bilingual situation in a metalinguistic sense.

The presence of a number of factors in the first category was found to have varied among the different children in the study. For example, several of the parents described their children's having experienced a "linguistic shock" at an early age, resulting from the child's (unsuccessful) attempts to communicate with monolingual grandparents in the minority language country (see Arnberg & Arnberg, 1985). According to the parents, these events had had a dramatic effect in decreasing language mixing. Attention to aspects of the bilingual situation is also felt to be enhanced through the exposure to the two languages in a wide variety of situations. Clearly, the children had had varying experiences in this regard as was evidenced by reports concerning visits to the minority language country, contact with other native speakers, attendance at a bilingual nursery school, and exposure to the minority language in the mass media for the different children. Finally, even the strategy in the home for raising the child bilingually may increase the child's attention to the dual language presentation. Strategies in which the languages are connected with a specific person or location are felt to be more helpful in this regard than those where, e.g., parents use the two languages interchangeably.

Children were also found to vary in the extent to which their parents focused on the bilingual situation in a metalinguistic sense. For example, some parents reported that they frequently used strategies such as "mommy says X, daddy says Y," eventually replacing this with "in English it's called X, in Swedish it's called Y," while other parents reported that they never spoke about the languages in this way. Some parents reported that they always repeated the word in the correct language when the child mixed the languages, while others reported that they never did this. It is felt that this strategy may enhance the child's realization that a referent can have two labels. Some parents had also begun literacy training; for example, in one family, signs with the words for the object in each language, printed in large letters, had been fastened to common objects in the home. Finally, parents varied in the extent to which they talked about the minority language when it appeared on television and in other mass media forms and when preparing the child for a trip to the minority language country.

Can Awareness be Trained?

In connection with the above variation in the backgrounds of the children concerning the presence of factors facilitating the development of awareness, we became interested in whether or not children can be "trained" to become aware. In order to investigate this issue, two of the four parents in the longitudinal study were randomly selected, to whom instructions would be given concerning "awareness training," the other two children serving as "controls." One of the "experimental" children, N, however, was found to have already been aware at the onset of the study. In this case the mother, a linguist, had naturally on her own provided the child with the type of input found to be favorable in enhancing awareness.

The second child, I, was 1;7 during the initial visit and mixing the languages at 28% (both languages combined). Shortly thereafter the "awareness concept" was explained to the mother and ways were explained to her concerning how she might help in developing bilingual awareness in the child. By the end of a four month period, the child showed bilingual awareness on the word test and according to parental/experimenter judgements. Mixing of the languages (both languages combined) had also decreased dramatically from 28% at age 1;7 to 2% at age 1;11 (see Figure 5). In contrast, the two "control children" did not show evidence of an increase in awareness on either of the measures. Their mixing rates at the conclusion of the period studied were approximately 9%. (Their ages at this time were 2;2 and 2;6).

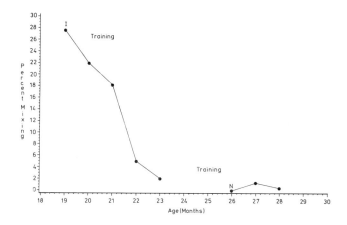

Figure 5. Effects of Training on Language Separation in Two Children (Both Languages Combined). The Results for I Show Progressively Less Mixing During a Four Month Period as a Result of Training. For N, Training Was Carried Out by the Mother Prior to the Onset of the Study.

Discussion

Elementary and Higher Mental Processes

The results give support to the earlier suggestion concerning two different processes that are involved in language separation. The concept of "awareness" has here been used to exemplify the higher mental processing, and the child's ability to state specifically when it does not know a word rather than automatically giving the word in the other language in a test situation has been used here to operationalize the concept. The results from parental interviews and from parental and experimenter judgements have also supported the picture of a change in understanding or a becoming aware of the dual language presentation. This change seems also to stimulate an extensive decrease in mixing. This has been strongly supported by the results from the longitudinal study, and the group differences between the "aware" and the "unaware" children in the cross-sectional study indirectly gave support in the same direction. Thus, the earlier question concerning whether children who are aware of the bilingual presentation are able to separate the languages to a greater extent than those who are not can be answered in the affirmative.

How Does the Child Become Aware?

Both the results from the longitudinal study and the interview results from the crosssectional study suggest that, as Vygotsky claims, parents and others interacting with the child have an important influence in developing awareness. Further support for this is offered by the fact that considerable age differences were found concerning when the child becomes aware. Nor was any strong relationship found between linguistic level and awareness, which would have supported the suggestion that a certain linguistic level leads automatically to awareness. Nevertheless, it is possible that linguistic level may be a factor when the differences between the languages involved are more distinct than was the case in the present study.

The results are also in line with Gibson's theory of perceptual development, suggesting that when the child can become aware of specific aspects of reality, e.g., the recognition that there are two languages in the environment, may be rather independent of the child's general developmental level. The results are thus positive in the sense that they give good hope to parents and preschool teachers that the bilingual child's awareness of the two languages can in fact be influenced at an early age. Thus, in response to the earlier hypothesis concerning whether the development of awareness follows a similar pattern in all children or whether it is subject to individual differences depending on the child's experiences in connection with the use of the two languages, the latter alternative seems to be supported by the present findings.

The Positive Effects of Awareness

It would seem obvious that a better understanding of reality will have a positive influence on learning. Several examples of how this may apply to the bilingual child are given below.

The main implication of this paper has been that an early awareness can be expected to assist the bilingual child in organizing the two languages and in eliminating a possible confusion between them, as evidenced by mixing. On a more psychological note, awareness may also be important in establishing positive attitudes toward bilingualism. If the child is frequently teased or ridiculed by other children when using words from the wrong language, he/she may choose to reject one of the languages. Finally, with regard to the child's cognitive development, within a Vygotskian perspective at least, an early awareness should generalize to other areas of concept learning and thinking.

Further Research

In a world in which bilingual individuals are becoming more and more necessary, not to mention the enormous individual benefits of bilingualism, it is perhaps time to develop methods for utilizing the tremendous potential for bilingualism represented during the preschool years. This paper has been an attempt to translate theoretical considerations into concepts which can be used by those coming into contact with such children, e.g, parents and preschool teachers. The concept of making the child aware or recognizing that there are two languages in the environment seems to be an easy one for parents to understand, and it may also be a strong tool in helping the child to learn the two languages. The task before us is considerable, however, including further establishing the importance of awareness, studying its effects, and developing methods in which awareness can be trained in the home and preschool settings.

To be able to answer some of the above questions, it is essential that longitudinal studies be carried out involving children who have undergone some type of "awareness training" and control group children. Such studies should optimally include languages which grammatically differ to a greater extent than is the case with English and Swedish, in order to, e.g., investigate the possible effects of awareness on separation at the morphosyntactic level. (An important theoretical question which needs to be empirically investigated, of course, is whether or not awareness is in fact necessary for separation at this level.) In a longitudinal study in which the factor of awareness is experimentally controlled, it will also be possible to study the effects of an early awareness on the child's long-term development in each of the languages. This issue is nearly impossible to study unless there is random assignment of matched children to experimental and control groups due to the fact that in correlational studies, those parents who naturally enhance their children's awareness of the dual language presentation at an early age are also likely to be those who provide other types of input which are favorable for language development in general.

References

Arnberg, L. (1981). Early childhood bilingualism in the mixed-lingual family (Doctoral dissertation, Linkoping University). *University Microfilms International, 82-70,003.*

Arnberg, L. (1987). *Raising children bilingually: The pre-school years.* Clevedon: Multilingual Matters Ltd.

Arnberg, L. & Arnberg, P. (1985). The relation between code differentiation and language mixing in bilingual three- to four-year-old children. *The Bilingual Review,* 12, 20-32.

Arnberg, P. (1972). *Haptic studies of attention processes during solving, overlearning, extinction, and superstition in concept learning.* Summary. (Doctoral dissertation, University of Stockholm).

Bandura, A. (1977). *Social learning theory.* Englewood Cliffs, NJ: Prentice-Hall.

Bergman, C.R. (1976). Interference vs independent development in infant bilingualism. In G. D. Keller, R. V. Teschner, & S. Viera (Eds.), *Bilingualism in the bicentennial and beyond.* New York: Bilingual Press.

Cole, M. (1985). The zone of proximal development: Where culture and cognition create each other. In V. Wertsch (Ed.), *Culture, communication and cognition: Vygotskian perspectives.* New York: Cambridge University Press.

Crystal, D., Fletcher, P., & Garman, M. (1976). *The grammatical analysis of language disability: A procedure for assessment and remediation.* New York: Elsevier.

De Houwer, A. (1987). *Two at a time: An exploration of how children acquire two languages from birth.* Doctoral Dissertation, Free University of Brussels.

Ferguson, C. A. (1980). *"Auf Deutsch, duck": Language separation in young bilinguals.* Manuscript.

Genesee, F. (1989). Early bilingual development: One language or two? *Journal of Child Language, 16,* 161-179.

Gibson, E. (1969). *Principles of perceptual learning and development.* New York: Appleton-Century-Crofts.

Imedadze, N. U. K. (1960). Pssckhologicheskoy, prirode rannego dvuyazychiya. *Voprosy Psikkologii, 6,* 60-69.

Kendler, H. H., & Kendler, T. S. (1962). Vertical and horizontal processes in problem-solving. *Psychological Review, 69,* 1-16.

Kendler, H. H., & Kendler, T. S. (1970). Developmental processes in discrimination learning. *Human Development, 13,* 65-89.

Kesner, R. P. (1980). An attribute analysis of memory: The role of the hippocampus. *Physiological Psychology, 8,* 189-197.

Klausen, T., & Plunkett, K. (1987). *The development of Danish-English bilingualism.* Paper presented at the Second International Congress of Applied Psycholinguistics, July 27-31, 1987, Kassel, West Germany.

Klee, T., & Fitzgerald, M. D. (1985). The relation between grammatical development and mean length of utterance in morphemes. *Journal of Child Language, 12,* 251-268.

Levelt, W. J. M., Sinclair, A. & Jarvella, R. J. (1978). Causes and functions of linguistic awareness in language acquisition: Some introductory remarks. In A . Sinclair, R. J. Jarvella, & W. J. Levelt (Eds.), *The child's conception of language*. Berlin: Springer.

Lindholm, K. J., & Padilla, A. M. (1977). Language mixing in bilingual children. *Journal of Child Language*, 5, 327-335.

Lindholm, K. J., & Padilla, A. M. (1978). Child bilingualism: Report on language mixing, switching, and translations. *Linguistics*, 211, 23-44.

McLaughlin, B. (1984). *Second-language acquisition in childhood: Volume 1. Preschool children*. Hillsdale, NJ: Lawrence Erlbaum Associates.

Meisel, J. M. (1989). Early differentiation of languages in bilingual children. In K. Hyltenstam & L. Obler (Eds.), *Bilingualism across the lifespan: Aspects of acquisition, maturity and loss*. Cambridge: Cambridge University Press.

Miller. P. H. (1989). *Theories of developmental psychology* (2nd ed.). New York: W.H. Freeman and Company.

Nauclér, K. (1984). *Språkväxling i en tvåspråkig förskolegrupp*. University of Gothenburg, SPRINS-report No.26.

Neisser, U. (1967). *Cognitive psychology*. New York: Appleton-Century-Crofts.

Padilla, A. M., & Liebman, E. (1975). Language acquisition in the bilingual child. *Bilingual Review*, 2, 34-55.

Piaget, J. (1974). *La prise de conscience*. Paris: Presses Universitaires de France.

Redlinger, W. E. & Park, T-Z. (1980). Language mixing in young bilinguals. *Journal of Child Language*, 7, 337-352.

Robinson, E. J., & Robinson, W. P. (1981). Ways of reacting to communication failure in relation to the development of the child's understanding about verbal communication. *European Journal of Social Psychology*, 11, 189-208.

Saunders, G. (1988). *Bilingual children: From birth to teens*. Clevedon: Multilingual Matters Ltd.

Schlyter, S. (1987). Language mixing and linguistic level in three bilingual children. *Scandinavian Working Papers on Bilingualism*, 7, 29-48.

Van Kleeck, A. (1982). The emergence of linguistic awareness: A cognitive framework. *Merrill-Palmer Quarterly*, 28(2), 237-265.

Vihman, M. M. (1982). The acquisition of morphology by a bilingual child: A whole-word approach. *Applied Psycholinguistics*, 3, 141-160.

Vihman, M. M., & McLaughlin, B. (1982). Bilingualism and second language acquisition in preschool children. In E. J. Brainard & M. Pressley (Eds.), *Verbal processes in children. Progress in cognitive development research.* New York: Springer-Verlag.

Vygotsky, L. S. (1934). *Thinking and speech: Psychological investigations.* Moscow and Leningrad: Gosudarstvennoe Sotsial'no-Ekonomicheskoe Izdatel'stvo.

Vygotsky, L.S. (1978). *Mind in society: The development of higher psychological processes.* Cambridge, Mass.: Harvard University Press.

Wertsch, V. (1985). *Vygotsky and the social formation of mind.* Cambridge, Mass.: Harvard University Press.

Cognitive Processing in Bilinguals – R.J. Harris (Editor)
© *1992 Elsevier Science Publishers B.V. All rights reserved.*

Selective Attention in Cognitive Processing: The Bilingual Edge

Ellen Bialystok
York University

Selective attention is identified as a unique cognitive process in which bilingual children demonstrate consistent advantages over monolingual children. The construct is explained in general terms and then operationalized within a specific framework for metalinguistic skills. Research comparing bilingual and monolingual children solving tasks in which bilingual children excel in problems requiring high levels of selective attention is reported. The analysis is applied to other cognitive domains to explore the extent to which the selective attention advantage for bilingual children extends beyond language competence.

Ever since the results of early research reporting severe cognitive disadvantages for bilingual children were vitiated by methodological arguments (reviewed in Hakuta, 1986), researchers have been struggling to determine what the proper interaction between a child's cognition and a child's bilingualism might be. Numerous studies have explored this issue, and in many cases comparisons between bilingual and properly-selected monolingual control groups have yielded evidence of advantages for the bilingual group. Hamers and Blanc (1989) compiled a list of these studies and report that bilingual advantages have been observed for the following cognitive functions: reconstruction of a perceptual situation, verbal and nonverbal intelligence, verbal originality, verbal divergence, semantic relations, Piagetian concept formation, divergent thinking, nonverbal perceptual tasks, verbal transformation and symbol substitution, and a variety of metalinguistic tasks. At first glance, the list appears to be a heterogeneous collection of disparate findings. Hamers and Blanc, however, argue that the list is consistent and points to a unified achievement that links the variety of tasks and outcomes. Specifically, they claim that the "cognitive advantages...seem to be mainly at the level of a higher creativity and reorganization of information" (1989, p.50). What is the nature of this "creativity" and "reorganization" that distinguishes bilingual children from their peers? How can these descriptions be operationalized in terms of cognitive processing? And why should bilingual children enjoy an advantage in these areas? These are the questions to be addressed in this chapter.

The approach I will take is to examine the achievements of bilingual children by considering the problems in which they excel as being those that are dependent upon high levels of selective attention. The argument is that bilingual children develop more advanced levels of control over selective attention than monolingual children do. This advantage is traced to the enriched opportunity for learning language and learning about language that is available to children who are learning to attend to two linguistic systems.

Definitions of Attention

Selective attention is a specialized function of the larger construct of attention, but the general concept of attention itself is greatly in need of explanation. Phenomenally, we can distinguish between performances in which we "pay attention" and those we can perform with apparently little concern for the underlying operations. But this criterion may be misleading. As Jackendoff (1987) points out, there is an important distinction to be made between *attention,* which is a cognitive process, and *consciousness,* which is our awareness of some process. The expedient of examining our awareness of a particular cognitive process probably tells us little or nothing about the way in which attention has been allocated during that process. For this reason, introspective procedures are incapable of yielding informative descriptions of attentional processes.

We must begin, therefore, by finding a way of defining and measuring attention that makes the construct appropriate for research and theory building. The research strategy will ultimately be to compare the attentional demands of different kinds of problems in order to isolate those problems for which the demands on selective attention are consistently high. The hypothesis is that these problems will be solved better by bilingual children.

One means of explicating a vague or difficult concept is to itemise the components that it entails. Enns (1990) has effectively applied this procedure to attention and as a result has both increased the explicitness and operationalization of the definition. Such concretization is an essential prerequisite to carrying out research. In Enns' scheme, the highest level construct that characterizes attention is called *selectivity.* This selectivity is a restriction in the domain to which attention can be applied. Such restriction is both an acknowledgment of and a means of dealing with the space-time limitations of the sensory systems and the finite capacity of brain processes.

Selectivity, in Enns' (1990) hierarchy, is reflected in four component features of attention: integration, filtering, search, and priming. Integration is the attention needed to compare two entities to make such decisions as similarity judgments. Selectivity is needed to allocate attention to the attributes needed to make these judgments. Filtering is the attention needed to suppress processing of irrelevant information. Enns argues that children's poor performance in filtering is attributable to their inefficient selectivity processes. They are unable to determine what is irrelevant and so should not be attended to. Search is the use of attention to locate a target entity. Again, selectivity is necessary to guide the search, particularly when the cues for the search are symbolic rather than concrete. Priming refers to the effect of repeated stimuli on attention so that children become better at solving problems than they would if new strategies were needed each time. Selectivity appears to have its most important role here in breaking the set in order to produce the flexible responses required by different situations. Selectivity, then, is the central aspect of attention that motivates the components of the system.

On this analysis, attention stands at the centre of cognitive functioning and selectivity, or selective attention, is the preeminent variety. But what is the relation between the development of attention and the development of cognition and how might this relation change for bilingual children? If attention is indeed a central mechanism of cognitive performance, and selectivity is the highest form of attention, then a link between bilingualism and the development of selective attention is critical in understanding the intellectual performance of bilingual children.

The development of attentional abilities, in particular those related to selectivity, may be a central aspect of what is entailed by intellectual development. In an interesting interpretation of Piaget's theory of development, Gold (1987) identifies three themes that permeate Piaget's work. The first is reversibility and refers to the ability to compensate for changes in the environment in order to preserve stasis. The second is the child's gradual escape from domination by perceptual features, what he calls 'perceptual seduction'. These two themes are both rooted in mechanisms responsible for attention and will be discussed below. The third, the profundity of cognitive developmental change, is essentially a recognition that the changes described by developmental theory are not superficial modifications of performance but rather reflections of radical alterations in the cognitive system. This is not so much an implication of Piaget's view as a restatement of it. It is certainly a necessary implication of a structuralist theory.

Let us then examine the first two themes that Gold identifies. My claim is that both these themes are reflections of a common developing ability for selective attention. Consider first reversibility. Reversible thought is the ability to compensate for operations or events that destroy the equilibrium of a system. The conservation problems are classic examples of such problems in which an operation must be performed or imagined that would restore a display to its original perceptual state. In reversible thought, the child recognizes that properties such as quantity remain stable across certain perceptual transformations and that the original stasis could be restored by a compensating operation. If balls in a line are stretched out, the line can be restored by pushing them back together; if water in a beaker changes the proportion of the vessel it fills in a new container, it can be returned to the original beaker. In general, reversible thought is the ability to correct for changes in equilibrium brought about by externally-imposed change.

Reversibility can be achieved by either compensation (needed for the conservation tasks) or by inversion (needed for the class inclusion task). In the case of compensation, the child needs to understand that what is lacking in one dimension is compensated by another, so that the two together form an equilibrium. In the case of inversion, the child needs to see the objects as both the whole set and the component subsets at the same time. The main cognitive requirement of reversible thought, then, is the ability to consider two competing aspects of a problem at the same time - two dimensions that give information, two operations that have different effects, or two analyses of a group that combine or partition the whole. Children below about 6 years of age fail the various conservation tasks because they are unable to attend to these two relevant dimensions or operations. As Gold (1987, p.10) describes it: "the child who fails a conservation task does so because he focuses too much on one of the changes which occur, at the expense of the other, complementary change. The older and conserving child, by contrast...attends to exactly the correct extent to each of the changes which occur". Similarly, children fail the class inclusion tasks because they fail to consider an item as both an individual object and a member of a larger class of objects. The ability to attend to two competing pieces of information requires control of attention. In particular, it requires selective attention in the sense described by Enns.

The second theme, perceptual seduction, is the child's increasing ability to resist the natural pull towards perceptually salient features and include a greater variety of information for consideration and for perceptual processing. This freedom from perceptual seduction is stated more directly in terms of the attentional demands: "In order to find these cues she has to withdraw attention from those perceptual features which attract it spontaneously; she has to *direct* her attention actively, rather than simply have it directed for her" (Gold, 1987, p.28, italics original). This notion of becoming free from slavishness to perceptual dominance and being able to control the focus of attention is considered by Gold not only to be a critical achievement in its own right, but also to be the basis for reversible thought. Hence the two themes converge on the need to control the focus of attention so that relevant, and not simply dominant, information is included in problem-solving.

The movement from perceptual seduction into perceptual autonomy (my term), therefore, is a crucial aspect of intellectual development. If bilingualism influences the development of this selectivity of attention, then one would expect bilingualism to have profound implications for children's cognitive development. Let us, then, examine the evidence that suggests that bilingual children develop selective attention more rapidly or more easily than monolingual children.

Control of Attentional Processing

One of the important developments of children's language proficiency in the early school years is their increasing skill at what has been called by a number of researchers "metalinguistic abilities". Although the precise definition and list of accomplishments that entail metalinguistic abilities differ across different research programmes, the concept of the child's increasing skill at being able to consider language as a logical system, or a formal problem space, as opposed to a means for communication that has in itself no inherent interest, is constant across usages. Children, that is, become able to think about language in addition to being able to think through language. These metalinguistic abilities have been implicated in children's ability to learn literacy skills and in their progress with aspects of cognitive development.

My research in children's metalinguistic abilities has taken the approach that these abilities can be explained by recourse to two underlying cognitive processes called *analysis of representational structures* and *control of attentional processing* (see Bialystok in press, for description). Analysis of representational structures refers to the child's ability to create mental representations of linguistic information at increasingly detailed levels of structure. Knowledge that had been implicit can be redescribed so that it is represented in an explicit structure that allows access to the detail and components of that knowledge (cf. Karmiloff-Smith, 1986). Although implicit representations of language are adequate for conversational uses of language, more explicit representations become necessary for literate uses.

Control of attentional processing refers to the child's ability to direct attention to specific aspects of either a stimulus field or a mental representation as problems are solved in real time. The need for control is most apparent when a problem contains conflict or ambiguity. In these cases, two or more mental representations may be constructed, each of which bears some relation to the problem. The correct solution, however, requires attending to only one of these possible representations. Attending to the competing representation may either simply slow down the process of solving the problem or sometimes mislead the child to the incorrect solution.

Most problem situations present some degree of ambiguity. Even the simple act of carrying on a conversation provides the speaker with at least two alternative signals to which attention can be paid: the use and structure of the formal symbol system and the set of meanings that symbol system has been invoked to represent. These alternatives are scarcely noticed in conversational uses of language since the meaning is so clearly the relevant level of representation for language comprehension and production. Other uses of language, however, and in particular metalinguistic ones, demand different degrees of attention to these two aspects.

Metalinguistic (and other linguistic) problems require different levels of involvement of each of these two processes of analysis and control. Hence, different metalinguistic problems are not necessarily equivalent but can be described in comparable terms by virtue of their cognitive demands on these two processes. The framework, therefore, provides a means for determining the processing demands of specific tasks. Analyzing the demands of different tasks produces a classification in which tasks with similar demands can be identified. A detailed description of these relative placements of metalinguistic tasks and the empirical evidence that supports those positions is provided elsewhere (Bialystok, in press). The primary developmental claim of this framework is that each of these two cognitive processes develops in response to different experiences. The argument is that literacy is important in advancing the child's level of analysis of linguistic representations and that bilingualism confers an advantage on children in their development of control of attentional processing.

Metalinguistic problems that require the highest levels of control of processing are those in which the solution depends on paying attention to some aspect of the language input that is not salient, not usual, or not expected. To count the number of words in a sentence, for example, the child must overcome the natural strategy of paying attention to meaning in order to pay attention to the word boundaries (e.g., Fox and Routh, 1975). Another example is the symbol substitution problem developed by Ben-Zeev (1977) in which children are required to substitute arbitrary words into sentences (e.g., "They are good children") creating nonsense (e.g., "Spaghetti are good children"). The natural tendency to attend to meaning prevents young children from solving this problem. The sun-moon problem developed by Piaget (1929) is a further example of this type of problem. Children must decide what the sun and moon would be called if they switched names and which one would be up in the sky at night (the sun would). The trick is to dissociate the word from its usual meaning; that is, children must not pay attention to what they know these words usually mean. These problems are all difficult because their solution demands unusual attentional strategies that must be executed in the context of compelling alternatives. Ignoring meanings is an extremely difficult problem. Stroop (1935) demonstrated long ago that if you show subjects printed cards with names of colours written in different colours of ink and ask them only to say what the colour of the ink is, the colour word itself provides hopeless interference when the two do not match.

These metalinguistic problems that place high demands on control of processing are the tasks in which bilingual children demonstrate a significant advantage over monolingual children. One task that we have developed illustrates this point most clearly. Grammaticality judgment tasks have been used frequently to assess children's growing ability to make metalinguistic decisions (de Villiers & de Villiers, 1972; Gleitman & Gleitman, 1979; Hakes, 1980). In the standard version, children are presented with sentences and asked to comment on their grammatical acceptability. This problem addresses knowledge of language structure; they must recognize a sentence as deviating from a standard pattern. In some versions, they must further make appropriate corrections to the sentence in order to repair it. The items that are especially difficult are those which contain a grammatical error, because children must not only detect this error but also override a prevailing response bias to accept sentences and reject these as incorrect. For this reason, the standard version of the grammaticality judgment problem is a metalinguistic test of analysis of representational structure.

The demands change, however, when the problem is slightly modified. If the sentence is grammatically correct but contains a semantic error, such as "Apples grow on noses", the child must ignore the silly meaning and realize that the grammatical pattern is acceptable. The problem in this case is not to detect syntactic deviation but to resist rejecting a sentence that is semantically anomalous. Children must *avoid* attending to meaning. Sentence meaning, as I have pointed out above, is very alluring (c.f. Stroop test). Although these sentences make minimal demands on the child's level of analysis of representational structures, they make high demands on the child's control of processing. Even with a response bias towards accepting sentences, children overwhelmingly claim that these sentences are unacceptable and reject them. Nonetheless, bilingual children have repeatedly been shown to solve these high control judgments more successfully than comparable monolingual children (e.g. Bialystok, 1986, 1988).

In sum, studies in which metalinguistic tasks have been classified for their demands on either analysis of representational structures or control of processing have shown that bilingual children consistently solve the high control problems better than monolingual children of the same age. Metalinguistic problems in which analysis of representational structures is the primary component responsible for the solution show no advantage for bilingual children.

Applying this analysis to other research produces the same distribution. A number of studies comparing the performance of bilingual and monolingual children on a battery of metalinguistic tasks have demonstrated bilingual advantages only for those tasks that, according to the present analysis, demand high levels of control of processing (Edwards & Christophersen, 1988; Galambos & Goldin-Meadow, 1990; Smith & Tager-Flusberg, 1982). The effect has also been demonstrated with adults. In a large-scale study of the cognitive and metalinguistic abilities of adult Liberian males as a function of the experiences of literacy and schooling, Scribner and Cole (1981) found a complex pattern of results in which individual groups who have had particular experiences showed specialized advantages in some tasks in their large test battery. Among the patterns, the bilingual subjects performed better than monolingual subjects on metalinguistic and cognitive tests that involved, according to the present analysis, high levels of control of processing.

Cognition and Control

The general result from the metalinguistic studies is that bilingual children have a specific advantage in processing linguistic information in problems that place a high burden on control of attentional processing. Bilingual children, that is, are better able to intentionally control the focus of their attention on linguistic input than are monolingual children. They are less distracted by salient features of the input, such as meaning, and can more easily isolate specific aspects of the input, such as form, to arrive at various kinds of metalinguistic judgments. To what extent does this advantage translate into a general cognitive benefit?

One problem that appears to engage a similar process of controlling attention is the Embedded Figures Task that was originally developed as a measure of the cognitive style construct field-dependence-independence (Witkin, Dyk, Faterson, Goodenough, & Karp, 1962). Field-independent processing is characterized by the ability to break down a perceptual field into its components and to attend to individual parts of the whole; field-independent processing is a more holistic style in which the perceiver processes the larger patterns but does not pay attention to the detailed structure of the whole. In the Embedded Figures Test, a simple shape is concealed inside a complex pattern and the subject must find the outline of that simple shape (Witkin, Oltman, Raskin, & Karp, 1971). Subjects who can solve these problems are considered to be field independent.

In addition to measuring a stylistic variable among subjects, the Embedded Figures Test also captures a component of spatial ability. In a review of the literature, Messick (1976) reports that across a large number of studies, consistent positive relations were found between scores on the Embedded Figures Test and such spatial ability tests as Spatial Relations, Morrisby Shapes, Form Board, Card Rotations, Paper Folding, 3-D Cube Rotations, and others. Hence, any relation between performance on the Embedded Figures Task and metalinguistic tests based on control of processing would constitute evidence for some transfer effects of selective attention across domains. On the surface, these tasks have little in common: Embedded Figures is spatial and metalinguistic tasks are linguistic; Embedded Figures is written and metalinguistic tasks are oral; Embedded Figures is group administered and metalinguistic tasks are individual. Only their common need to deliberately focus attentional resources appears to unite them.

Evidence from a number of studies has demonstrated the common basis of children's performance on measures of field-dependence-independence and control of processing on cognitive tasks. Huteau and Rajchenback, cited in Kogan (1983, p.687), report that field-dependence-independence differentiated performance only for those Piagetian tasks that required overcoming an embedded figurative context. Hence, it was related to volume conservation but not to permutations in 14-year-olds, and to liquid conservation but not to seriation in 7-year-olds. The two conservation problems require children to overcome distracting perceptual cues in order to focus on the logic of the operation (cf. Gold, 1987).   Liben (1978) showed a correlation between field-dependence-independence and performance on the water level task developed by Piaget and Inhelder (1956). High school students were asked to draw a line indicating the water line in a half-filled bottle that has been tilted between 0^0 and 90^0. The problem is to focus only on the environmental horizontal and not make the line parallel to the bottom of the bottle. The correlation remained high even when spatial ability (measured by the Guildford-Zimmerman Test of Spatial Orientation) was held constant. Pascual-Leone (1989) similarly reports strong correlations between these tasks. These results provide evidence for a common cognitive process between the Embedded Figures Task and various cognitive tasks that involve selective attention.

A more recent demonstration of this relation in my own laboratory has shown a relation between children's performance on the Embedded Figures Task and metalinguistic tests of control using regression analyses. Children's performance on metalinguistic tests of control significantly predicted their performance on the Embedded Figures Task, even after age, verbal ability, and spatial ability had been accounted for. The children's performance on metalinguistic tests of analysis of representational structures had no relation to their performance on the Embedded Figures Task. The conclusion was that the Embedded Figures Task depended on the same type of control of processing for its solution as did the metalinguistic tasks.

If this is the case, then bilingual children who have already demonstrated superiority in metalinguistic tasks measuring control of processing should also reveal an advantage over monolingual children in solving the Embedded Figures Task. Bilingual children, that is, should be more field independent than monolingual children. A strong significant relation of this type has been found in a longitudinal study of young bilingual children (Maggie Bruck, 1991, personal communication).

Although many studies have explored the relation between field independence and the ability to acquire a second language, the results of these studies have often produced ambiguous and contradictory results (e.g., Alptekin & Atakan, 1990; Genesec & Hamayan, 1980; Hansen & Stansfield, 1981; Naiman, Frohlich, Stern, & Todesco,

1978; Tucker, Hamayan & Genesee, 1976). The vagaries of these results challenge the interpretation that field independence *per se* has any direct influence on second language acquisition. An examination of the measures of second language proficiency, however, shows some systematicity between the measure used and the emergence of a relation with field independence. The single most enduring effect between these constructs is when second language ability is measured by a cloze test. The cloze test requires subjects to alternately focus on the forms and meanings of a passage broken up by deletions and therefore poses the greatest challenge to control of processing. Again, a generalized effect between a second language skill and a dramatically different cognitive measure, in this case, field independence, is carried through a common reliance on control of attentional processing.

If bilingual children enjoy a processing advantage for problems which require high levels of selective attention, how broadly can this advantage be detected? The superior performance of bilingual children on metalinguistic tests is the most conservative demonstration of the theoretical claim that the source of the advantage is in the general process of selective attention. All the constructs and measures remain within the domain of language. The relation between bilingualism and field independence through selective attention is a more ambitious claim. In this case the domains are starkly different from each other. Here the relations are much more limited, but probably more compelling where they exist because of the vast differences between the domains. A third case is intermediary to these two. Children's acquisition of numeracy and cardinality, or the understanding of the way in which numbers refer to quantities, shares certain similarities with children's acquisition of language but remains, nonetheless, a distinct system. Like language, children's acquisition of concepts of number goes through stages in which they are progressively able to solve more difficult problems. Also like language, the various problems they solve along the way vary in their demands for analysis of representational structures and control of attentional processing. Do bilingual children demonstrate an advantage over monolingual children in solving problems with number that require high levels of control of processing?

Ongoing research in our laboratory has begun to address this question. We are developing tasks that are analogous to the metalinguistic tasks used in our research by creating problems that vary in their demands for analyzed representations of knowledge and control of attentional processing. One of these problems is a task that ostensibly examines children's understanding of the concept that numbers stand for quantities, but the task is presented in a perceptually-distracting context. Children are shown towers made out of either lego blocks or duplo blocks. Lego and duplo are identical except that the duplo blocks are eight times the volume - they are twice as wide, twice as long, and twice as thick. Hence, a tower built out of duplo would need twice as many lego blocks to reach the same height. Children are told that the towers are apartment buildings, and that one family lives in each block. Sometimes the blocks are big and sometimes small, but they always have just one family in them. Two apartment towers are shown to the child and the child is asked to judge which tower can hold more families. They understand that the solution depends on the relative number of blocks and not the relative height of the two towers. The critical case is one in which a lego and duplo tower are presented for comparison and the lego tower contains more blocks even though the duplo tower is taller. Children must focus only on the number of blocks and choose the lego tower. This problem is difficult because it requires high levels of control of processing. In a study of monolingual and bilingual children between 3 and 5 years of age, bilingual children performed consistently better than monolingual children on this problem.

These studies together point to a consistent advantage that bilingual children enjoy over monolingual children in one aspect of cognitive processing. How can this interpretation apply to the list of tasks cited by Hamers and Blanc (1989) at the beginning of this chapter that have shown advantages for bilingual subjects? Their list was diverse and included both verbal and nonverbal problems. The argument I have presented in this chapter is that the tasks and instruments that have been used to assess these skills share a common basis in a cognitive requirement for high levels of selective attention. What Hamers and Blanc refer to as "higher creativity and reorganization of information" is the manifestation of greater control over selective attention. Reconstruction of a perceptual situation can occur only when attention is disengaged from the salient locus of attention. Verbal tests of originality and divergence similarly require the perception of novel associations, that is, attention to nonsalient relations. This need for selective attention is characteristic of the problems in which bilingual advantages have been found. This common basis is also the essential development that characterizes movement into Piagetian operational thought, according to the interpretation by Gold (1987). In his view, the critical theme is the child's increasing ability to escape from perceptual seduction. This requires selective attention. Hence, on those Piagetian tasks in which overcoming perceptual cues is most relevant to the solution, bilingual children should demonstrate an advantage over monolingual peers.

Why do bilingual children develop advanced levels of selective attention? Several features of their early experience with two languages may lead them to develop more sensitive means for controlling attention to linguistic input. They are used to hearing things referred to in two different ways, and this can alert them earlier to the arbitrariness of referential forms. They are used to attending to the language that is being spoken as well as the meanings, and this can help them attend to forms and to distinguish between relevant and irrelevant linguistic variation. They may need to address different people in different languages, and this can enhance their flexible access to a variety of forms that have the same meaning. They frequently need to learn different conventions for marking such social relations as politeness, and this can signal to them that there is a pragmatic dimension to word meanings as well as a semantic one. Although bilingual children are not gaining privileged knowledge through this experience, they are learning about the structure and function of language earlier than their monolingual peers. The cognitive processes they have deployed in this learning appear to be general, and there is evidence that the selective attention of bilingual children is enhanced across all domains. If selective attention is as important to intellectual development as Piaget appeared to imply, then this bilingual edge is a considerable advantage.

References

Alptekin, C., & Atakan, S. (1990). Field dependence-independence and hemisphericity as variables in L2 achievement. *Second Language Research, 6,* 135-149.

Ben-Zeev, S. (1977). The influence of bilingualism on cognitive strategy and cognitive development. *Child Development, 48,* 1009-1018.

Bialystok, E. (1986). Factors in the growth of linguistic awareness. *Child Development, 57,* 498-510.

Bialystok, E. (1988). Levels of bilingualism and levels of linguistic awareness. *Developmental Psychology, 24,* 560-567.

Bialystok, E. (in press). Metalinguistic awareness: The development of children's representations of language. In C. Pratt and A. F. Garton (Eds.), *The development and use of representation in children.* London: Wiley.

De Villiers, P. A., & de Villiers, J. G. (1972). Early judgements of semantic acceptability by children. *Journal of Psycholinguistic Research, 1,* 290-310.

Edwards, D. & Christophersen, H. (1988). Bilingualism, literacy and meta-linguistic awareness in preschool children. *British Journal of Developmental Psychology, 6,* 235-244.

Enns, J.T. (1990). Relations between components of visual attention. In J.T. Enns (Ed), *The development of attention: Research and theory.* Amsterdam: Elsevier Science Publishers.

Fox, B., & Routh, D.K. (1975). Analyzing spoken language into words, syllables and phonemes: A developmental study. *Journal of Psycholinguistic Research, 4,* 331-342.

Galambos, S. J., & Goldin-Meadow, S. (1990). The effects of learning two languages on levels of metalinguistic awareness. *Cognition, 34,* 1-56.

Genesee, F., & Hamayan, E. (1980). Individual differences in second language learning. *Applied Psycholinguistics, 1,* 95-110.

Gleitman, L. R., & Gleitman, H. (1979). Language use and language judgment. In C.F. Fillmore, D. Kempler, & W. S.-Y. Wang (Eds.), *Individual differences in language ability and language behavior.* New York: Academic Press.

Gold, R. (1987). *The description of cognitive development.* Oxford: Clarendon Press.

Hakes, D. (1980). *The development of metalinguistic abilities in children.* New York: Springer-Verlag.

Hakuta, K. (1986). *Mirror of language.* New York: Basic Books.

Hamers, J.F., & Blanc, M.H. (1989). *Bilinguality and bilingualism.* Cambridge: Cambridge University Press.

Hansen, J., & Stansfield, C. (1981). The relationship of field dependent-independent cognitive styles to foreign language achievement. *Language Learning, 31,* 49-367.

Jackendoff, R. (1987). *Consciousness and the computational mind.* New York: Academic Press.

Karmiloff-Smith, A. (1986). From metaprocess to conscious access: Evidence from children's metalinguistic and repair data. *Cognition, 28,* 95-147.

Kogan, N. (1983). Stylistic variation in childhood and adolescence. In J. H. Flavell & E. M. Markman (Eds.), *Handbook of child psychology: Vol. III: Cognitive development.* New York: Wiley.

Liben, L. S. (1978). Performance on Piagetian spatial tasks as a function of sex, field dependence, and training. *Merrill-Palmer Quarterly, 24,* 97-110.

Messick, S. (1976). Personality consistencies in cognition and creativity. In S. Messick and Associates (Eds.), *Individuality in learning* (pp. 4-22). San Francisco: Jossey-Bass.

Naiman, N., Frohlich, M., Stern, H., & Todesco, A. (1978). *The good language learner.* Toronto: Ontario Institute for Studies in Education.

Pascual-Leone, J. (1989). An organismic process model of Witkin's field-dependence-independence. In T. Globerson & T. Zelniker (Eds.), *Cognitive style and cognitive development.* Norwood, NJ: Ablex.

Piaget, J. (1929). *The child's conception of the world.* London: Routledge & Kegan Paul.

Piaget, J., & Inhelder, B. (1956). *The child's conception of space.* London: Routledge & Kegan Paul.

Scribner, S., & Cole, M. (1981). *The psychology of literacy.* Cambridge, MA: Harvard University Press.

Smith, C. L., & Tager-Flusberg, H. (1982). Metalinguistic awareness and language development. *Journal of Experimental Child Psychology, 34,* 449-468.

Stroop, J.R. (1935). Studies of interference in serial verbal reactions. *Journal of Experimental Psychology, 18,* 643-662.

Tucker, G. R., Hamayan, E., & Genesee, F. (1976). Affective, cognitive, and social factors in second language acquisition. *Canadian Modern Language Review, 23,* 214-226.

Witkin, H. A., Dyk, R. B., Faterson, H. F., Goodenough, D. R., & Karp, S. A. (1962). *Psychological differentiation.* New York: Wiley.

Witkin, H. A., Oltman, P. K., Raskin, E., & Karp, S. A. (1971). *A manual for the children's embedded figures test.* Palo Alto, Calif.: Consulting Psychologists Press.

Cognitive Processing in Bilinguals – R.J. Harris (Editor)
© *1992 Elsevier Science Publishers B.V. All rights reserved.*

Translation Ability: A Natural Bilingual and Metalinguistic Skill

Marguerite E. Malakoff
Yale University

Abstract

The study of translation ability provides an avenue to understanding the cognitive-linguistic experience that is particular to bilingual children. Translation is a bilingual skill; it has also been called a metalinguistic skill *par excellance*. There has been little research on translation ability in bilingual children, despite calls for such research based on anecdotal and indirect evidence. This chapter reports the findings from a series of studies that have shown that grade school students are competent translators who are not easily misled by deliberate translation pitfalls, and who show no evidence of linguistic confusion when translating.

Background Issues

The bilingual child has long been an object of curiosity and observation. For close to a century, scholars and educators have studied the effects of bilingualism on cognitive and linguistic abilities. The question has generally focused on two issues: 1) how a child with more than one language mentally organizes (or fails to organize) language; and 2) the effects of speaking two languages on cognitive and linguistic development. These questions grew out of a *monolingual norm assumption*: the belief that monolingualism is the cognitive-linguistic norm and that the child's cognitive system is fragile and designed to cope with only one language (Malakoff, 1988).

As a result of this view, most studies on bilingualism have focused on comparing bilinguals to monolinguals, and most measures used have been derived from and for a monolingual sample. Bilingual performance is measured against monolingual performance, and bilinguals are "handicapped" or "cognitively enhanced" according to how they measure up to their monolingual counterparts. Such designs assume that the cognitive-linguistic experience of the two populations is comparable. However, as Grosjean (1985 and the present volume) has noted, the bilingual is not "the sum of two complete or incomplete monolinguals"; rather, the bilingual has a "unique and specific linguistic configuration." (1985 p. 467). Doyle, Champagne, and Segalowitz (1978) for example, in a study comparing preschool monolingual and bilingual children, found that, although the monolingual children had a larger vocabulary in the dominant language, the *verbal fluency* of the bilingual children was superior to that of the monolinguals. While there is much to be learned from comparing monolingual and bilingual development, the cognitive-linguistic development of bilingual children requires study in its own right.

Bilinguals differ from monolinguals in a very major way: the bilingual child experiences the world through two languages--two languages used in *alternation*. That is, for the bilingual, linguistic experience is spread over two languages: experience is encoded in *either* of two languages and can be expressed in *both* languages, and the information representation can be *transferred* between the two languages. Perhaps the most explicit process through which this transfer occurs is translation. Swain, Dumas, and Naiman (1974) suggested many years ago that translation provides a viable tool for research on cognitive linguistic development in bilingual children; nonetheless, translation has until recently received little attention within developmental psychology.

In this chapter, the term *translation* is used to refer to all modes of reformulating a message from one language (the Source Language) into a message in another language (the Target Language). That is, the term *translation* is used regardless of whether the Source or Target Language message is oral or written; for example, oral to written and written to oral would both be considered translation. This is different than the case in the literature on professional translation, which makes the distinction between translation and interpretation, where translation refers to the written modality and interpretation to the oral modality.

The term bilingualism also requires a working definition. *Bilingualism* has become a social term to cover populations with different proficiencies and linguistic backgrounds, from monolinguals beginning a second language to persons fluent in two languages. In this chapter, *bilingual* is used to mean a person who is able "to produce a complete meaningful utterance" in two languages (Haugen, 1956: 6). Bilingualism does not imply equal mastery of two languages, but rather the ability to use two languages; hence it is best described in terms of degree of bilingual fluency (DeAvila & Duncan, 1980).

Of particular interest to researchers has been the effect of bilingualism on cognitive development. Many early researchers concluded that bilingualism had a negative impact on development (e.g., Anastasi & Cordova, 1953; Saer, 1924; F. Smith, 1923; M. Smith, 1939). Bilingualism was thought to cause children to become mentally confused--at best, to be a mental burden for developing children. However, as early as 1928, there already existed a debate over the validity of these negative conclusions, and the counterargument had been presented that bilingualism, in fact, develops intellectual abilities through the comparison and differentiation of two language systems (Braunhausen, 1928). More recent research does not support the view that simply speaking two languages taxes either the cognitive or the linguistic system. (For reviews, see Hakuta, 1986; McLaughlin, 1984; Romaine, 1989). On the contrary, there is evidence suggesting that bilingualism has a positive effect on cognitive development when both languages are supported emotionally and academically by the community and the society at large, that is, when both languages are positively viewed and valued by the community.

Bilingualism and Natural Translation

Gerver, in a discussion of the psycholinguistic properties of translation, wryly noted that he could "not start with the admission that the reviewer was almost defeated by the vast literature on the topic." (Gerver, 1976: 165). The situation has changed little: if the empirical literature on adult translation is still scarce, that on children is barren. Most references to and evidence of child translation in the literature is indirect: from anecdotes within case studies of bilingual language acquisition (Clyne, 1987; Leopold, 1939-1949; Levy, 1985; Ronjat, 1913. See also Romaine, 1989, for a review), or from empirical studies where translation was observed or used as a research tool, but was not studied (see Harley, 1986; Paivio, Clark, & Lambert, 1979; Swain, 1972; Swain, Naiman, & Dumas, 1974). The more recent *science of translation* literature discusses the linguistic nature of translation (see Nida, 1976; Seleskovitch, 1976; Wilss, 1982); however, there exists little *empirical* discussion of translation from a linguistic, psycholinguistic, or sociolinguistic perspective, much less from a developmental perspective.

Linguistic diversity and bilingualism is the norm for most societies, and bilingual children are present in almost every country in the world. For most bilingual children, translation is a part of their everyday activity--a part of their bilingual life, and an aspect of their linguistic ability and bilingualism about which developmental psychologists and psycholinguists know very little. Until recently, bilingualism has been viewed with a wary eye--especially when children are from a minority language community and families of lower socio-economic status. The greater issue has been on keeping the two languages separate and reaching proficiency in the majority language, rather than the study of bilingual development. Thus there has been a lack of interest in child translation on the part of psychologists and second language researchers. In sum, translation has generally not been considered to be within the reach of the average bilingual child.

In addition, and regardless of whether the focus is on minority language students or middle class children, the emphasis in both education and in research has been on the *process* of second-language acquisition. Also, translation, an educational method in second-language instruction since Roman times, fell out of fashion in the post-war era. The combined discrediting of translation in education and the focus on second-language acquisition have also contributed to the lack of interest in translation as a bilingual skill.

Translation is typically viewed as a valuable skill available only to linguistically sophisticated bilinguals with professional training. It is not a skill that is considered to be within the cognitive and linguistic repertoire of just any bilingual child. Harris and Sherwood (1978), however, argue that all bilingual children can translate from an early age. In support of this argument, they cite the prevalence of spontaneous translation in preschool children; the small exposure to a new language that older children need before starting to translate; and the lack of correlation, in children, between the ability to translate and instruction in translation. Shannon (1987) has documented children interpreting for adults in medical, legal, and administrative situations. Other recent studies with a variety of bilingual populations have also shown that bilingual children who have no special training can translate material that is within their level of comprehension (Hakuta & Malakoff, 1987; Hakuta et al., 1988; Harris, 1980).

Brian Harris adopted the term *natural translation* to refer to translation by naive child translators--bilingual children without any special training in translation (see Harris, 1977; 1980; Harris & Sherwood, 1978). He contrasts this type of translation with that done by highly trained and experienced professional translators. The term "natural" refers to the *cognitive skills* involved, not to the translation situation, per se. That is, natural translation is done by the child who has received no formal training in translation and is relying on a set of natural linguistic and cognitive skills. Natural translation is concomitant to bilingualism--just as the ability to communicate is naturally inherent in the ability to speak a language. It is not a learned skill, such as learning a foreign language in an educational setting, but rather, it is a skill that develops from a natural and existing base, in the same way that a mother-tongue language abilities develop.

Translation then is a bilingual activity: it is a linguistic activity to which all bilinguals have access by the very fact that they are bilingual. However, bilingualism in itself does not make a person a good translator; that is, bilingual proficiency[1] is not synonymous with translation ability (see Carroll, 1978; Nida, 1976). Translation ability may be thought of as the product of an interplay between bilingual proficiency and metalinguistic skills. For a given metalinguistic level, there can be a range of bilingual proficiencies, and for a given bilingual repertoire, there can be a range in metalinguistic awareness.

Bilingualism and Metalinguistic Awareness

Metalinguistic awareness is one of the cognitive abilities in which bilingual children seem to be superior. Metalinguistic awareness is the ability to think flexibly and abstractly about language; it refers to an awareness of the formal linguistic features of language and the ability to reflect thereupon. Metalinguistic awareness allows the individual to step back from the comprehension or production of an utterance in order to consider the *linguistic form* and *structure* underlying the meaning of the utterance. Thus a metalinguistic task is one which requires the individual to think about the *linguistic nature* of the message: to attend to and reflect on the structural features of language. To be metalinguistically aware, then, is to know how to approach and solve certain types of problems which themselves demand certain cognitive and linguistic skills. Metalinguistic tasks include detection of ambiguity (Galambos & Goldin-Meadow, 1990), and segmenting sentences or words into their constituents (Bowey & Patel, 1988). These language problems all require both an awareness of language as a system and the ability to access and manipulate knowledge about that system. Metalinguistic awareness, however, does not refer to a knowledge of the linguistic terms, per se. That is, a child may be able to perform well on the metalinguistic task of phonemic segmentation or detection of ambiguity without knowing what the terms *phoneme* or *ambiguity* mean.

A variety of evidence suggests that bilingualism enhances children's awareness of the languages they are learning to speak. Vygotsky (1962) claimed that bilingualism permits children to view their language as a system among others, and thereby enhances their linguistic awareness. Studies of middle class child bilinguals have generally shown that bilingualism enhances metalinguistic development. Preschool bilinguals are aware of the arbitrary relationship of names and objects at a younger age than monolingual children (Ben-Zeev, 1977; Ianco-Worall, 1972). Case studies of bilingual acquisition report expressions of metalinguistic awareness before the age of three (Clyne, 1987; Leopold, 1949). Research has also found an enhancing effect of early bilingualism among school-age children (Balkan, 1970; Ben-Zeev, 1988; Bialystok, 1988; Cummins, 1978, Galambos & Hakuta, 1988), although these studies were based primarily on middle class population. However, recent research has also found a similar cognitive advantage of bilingualism among minority language students who are still in the process of learning a second language (Galambos & Hakuta, 1988; Hakuta & Diaz, 1984).

Translation as a Bilingual Ability

Preliminary Studies

Our investigation of translation ability began with a set of preliminary studies conducted in the New Haven public schools (Hakuta & Malakoff, 1987; Hakuta et al., 1988; Malakoff & Hakuta, 1991). The first study examined the properties of translation among "expert" child translators--children who had some experience translating, most frequently for their families. The goal of this study was to investigate the psycholinguistic properties of translation among a select group of "experts." The second study explored the distribution of translation ability among a less select group of bilingual fourth graders.

For the first study (Hakuta & Malakoff, 1987), 16 Spanish-English bilinguals (8 boys, 8 girls) were recruited through a local advocacy agency that offered after-school and summer educational programs. The students had just completed either the fourth or fifth grade; the mean age was 10.7, with a range from 9 to 12 years. All were fluent bilinguals and had experience translating. The students completed a battery of translation tasks in which they were to translate words, sentences and stories from English to Spanish and Spanish to English. In all cases, the source language message was presented via a computer screen and the student's responses were given orally. Ability to translate was assessed by measuring the time it took to produce the translation and by analyzing the types of errors made. In addition, we asked the students to produce a story translation in written form. Finally, students completed measures of language proficiency in both English and Spanish and tasks designed to measure linguistic and cognitive abilities.

The results showed that, although the translation tasks included ample opportunity for grammatical errors, students were very good translators. The translation tasks were constructed to include "pitfalls" designed to elicit intrusion errors, that is, where vocabulary or grammatical structures from the source language intrude into the target language. An example is (from Hakuta, 1990):

> Source sentence: *La luna blanca brilla en la noche.*
> Translation: The moon white shines in the night.

Such errors, however, were very infrequent: students were not being "taken in" by the translation pitfalls. The low frequency of intrusion errors also shows that students have little difficulty maintaining a separation between their two languages. This finding supports the argument by sociolinguists that code-switching is a deliberate linguistic activity and is not a reflection of linguistic confusion (e.g., Zentenella, 1981). Our expert translators maintained linguistic separation when the task demanded it, and they could code-switch when the social situation warranted the use of both languages, such as when they were with other bilinguals.

A second finding was that translation speed on the word translation tasks was better predicted by proficiency in the target language of the translation than by proficiency in the source language. That is, when translating from English into Spanish, translation speed is better predicted by Spanish proficiency than by English proficiency. Another measure, in addition to language proficiency, also showed a strong relationship with translation ability. In this task, students were asked to identify whether words appearing on a computer screen were Spanish or English (the tasks included only words which could not be identified based on superficial cues, such as accent marks). This measure of linguistic flexibility was a stronger predictor of translation speed than was language proficiency. We believe this second measure to reflect a form of metalinguistic awareness.

The second study was designed to investigate the distribution of translation ability in a less selected group of bilingual students. The sixteen subjects in the first study had been selected based on their status as "expert" translators; they were thus not a random sample of bilingual students. The students in the second study were 52 fourth and fifth grade Spanish-English students currently in the bilingual program. The only constraint on their participation was that they be able to complete the written story translation task in both directions, as judged by their teacher. These students were given only the story translation task which could be easily adapted to a group administered written test.

The results from this second study indicated that translation is a skill that is widely distributed among bilingual children. Overall, overlooking spelling errors, the fourth and fifth grade students produced excellent translations. The error analyses show a good consistency in error patterns between the two groups of students, suggesting that the more selected "expert" translators did not reflect unusual translation ability. The low rate of intrusion errors for both samples is evidence of the separation of languages in terms of their structure.

A Study of Translation Ability in Fifth Through Seventh Grade Students

The preliminary studies exposed psycholinguistic properties of translation within a selected group of bilingual students and the distribution of written translation ability only within a random sample of bilingual students. While the second study established that translation ability is a widely distributed skill among bilingual students, it did not examine the effects of language proficiency, bilingual fluency, modality of task or age on translation performance.

Method

To further investigate some of the questions raised by these preliminary studies as well as to further examine the distribution of translation ability among bilingual students, a study was conducted with 92 French-English bilingual students attending an international school in Geneva, Switzerland. *Fluent and Non-fluent bilinguals* from the fifth through seventh grades were included in the study. All students were attending an English language program (in a school with both English and French primary language programs) and receiving French language arts instruction. *Non-Fluent* bilinguals were advanced second-language learners of French who were fluent in English; *Fluent bilinguals* were students who spoke both French and English fluently.

Four similar translation tasks were developed, crossing direction of translation (into French or English) with modality of task (oral or written). Each task consisted of 20 sentences, each of which contained specific translation "pitfalls." These pitfalls were specifically designed to elicit *source language errors*, that is, errors that reflect interference of the structure or phrasing of the source language sentence. Each task sentence contained similar difficulties across languages; that is, any given sentence had the same type of difficulty across tasks and languages. Two translation versions were developed within each language; students received different versions for the oral and the written tasks. The correspondence of version and modality was balanced within grade and level.

Within each translation task, each sentence was scored for the *Global Quality* of the translation, the mean rate of *Source Language Errors*, and accuracy of the Target Language *Meaning*. A measure of the accuracy of meaning was included to assess whether students were providing semantically accurate translations. One indication of how well students understand the purpose of a translation task is how well they communicate the original meaning in the Target Language, regardless of the grammatical correctness of the target language sentence or even the specific choice of words. That is, the Target Language sentence (or translation) can have errors and still communicate the intention of the original source language message.

A *Global Score* was given for the overall quality of the target language sentence, including, but not exclusive, to the pitfall phrase. This score reflected whether the sentence was correct, contained minor errors, was incomprehensible or wrong, or was incomplete. The accuracy of *Meaning* was scored in a similar manner as the Global Score, but only grammatical errors that modified the meaning of the translation or made it incomprehensible were taken into account. That is, if a sentence contained grammatical errors that did not interfere with the meaning, its meaning would be considered to be correct. In addition, a *Meaning Score* was given only if the sentence was at least partially completed.

Source Language Errors (SLE) are errors in the target language sentence (that is, the translation) that can be attributed to the influence or interference of the source language sentence structure or lexicon. Examples are word inversions, inappropriate use of "of the" for possession, false cognates, and literal translations of expressions. To ensure comparability across translation versions, source language errors were only recorded if they occurred within a pitfall phrase. Any SLE outside of the pitfall phrase were included only in the Global Quality and/or Meaning score.

Language proficiency was also assessed in both English and French. The measures were designed to assess fluency *within* each language relative to other students. An open-ended Cloze test was used to assess language proficiency. Each cloze test was developed from a passage in a popular children's book in its respective language.

Results and Discussion

The results from this study are consistent with the claim that translation skill is a widely distributed ability among bilingual children. Overall, the students had little difficulty either understanding the demands of or completing the translation tasks. Collapsed across all students and items, the students completed close to 99 percent of the task items when the translation was oral. On these tasks, students did receive minimal experimenter prompting, such as "give it a try" or "Just do your best." However, even on the written translation tasks, where students received no experimenter encouragement, students completed over 95 percent of the items.

The findings also show that students are not easily misled by translation pitfalls designed specifically to elicit linguistic confusion at potential points of structural or lexical conflict between the two languages. Overall, students translated over 90 percent of the items with only minor errors: over 50 percent were completed without any error and students avoided translation pitfalls on close to 70 percent of the items. Non-fluent bilinguals avoided the pitfalls on over 65 percent of the items while Fluent bilinguals avoided the pitfalls on 72 percent. The percentage of "wrong" translations rarely exceeded five percent for any grade or fluency level. Reinforcing these results is the comparison of the meaning of the translation with the original source sentence. Collapsed across all tasks, the translations matched the original source language meaning for over 76 percent of the task items.

As is the case with many other cognitive-linguistic abilities, translation ability showed grade-related improvements, regardless of task or degree of fluency. Modality of the translation task, on the other hand, had little effect on translation performance. Students showed a similar rate of Source language errors whether the task was oral or written. However, Non-fluent students were more likely to leave items incomplete when the task was written than when it was oral.

Translation ability does not require a high degree of fluency in both Source and Target Languages. Although the degree of fluency certainly influences performance on the translation tasks, Non-fluent students were nonetheless good translators who were able to complete over 40 percent of the items without being misled by the translation pitfalls. When the target language was the non-instructional and weaker language, Non-fluent students translated close to half the items without error; when the target language was the instructional language, they completed over 60 percent of the items without error.

As would be expected, Fluency had a greater impact on translation performance when the target language of the translation was not the primary language of instruction. That is, students were able to translate more easily *from* a weaker language than *into* a weaker language. This is consistent with the literature on language acquisition and second language learning that draws the distinction between competence in comprehension and that in production.

The findings supported the earlier findings that proficiency in the target language of the translation is a better predictor of translation performance than proficiency in the source language. This interaction between language proficiency and direction of translation was reflected in both the Global quality of the translation and the rate of source language errors. However, these findings must be somewhat qualified if language proficiency in the two languages is very unbalanced, as was the case among the Non-fluent bilinguals. In this case, fluency in the weaker was a predictor of translation performance when it was the source language, although to a lesser degree than when it was target language.

The Importance of the Type of Pitfall: A Pilot Study

One question raised by the studies so far discussed is the importance of the type of translation pitfall or point of linguistic conflict. To begin to examine the question, we conducted a small pilot study among bilingual French-English third through seventh graders attending an international school in New York City. Of particular interest was whether there was a difference if the point of potential confusion was structural--such as word order, the construction of possessives or negation--or if the point of potential confusion was lexical--such as idioms, expressions, or false cognates. The translation tasks were thus constructed with two types of translation pitfalls: *structure-based and lexical-based.* Structure-based refers to the situation where the grammatical structure from the source language intrudes into the target language sentence. For example:

> Source language: J'ai une grande maison <u>bleue</u>.
> Literal translation: I have a big house <u>blue</u>.

Lexical-based errors, on the other hand, occur when a source language lexical item or expression is inserted into the target language. The translation may be anomalous while being grammatically correct. For example:

Source language: C'est une amie très <u>sympathique</u> (She's a very
                              <u>nice</u> friend).
Literal translation: She's a very sympathetic friend.

Source language: Il fait un froid de canard. (It is extremely cold).
Literal translation: It is cold like ducks.

French-English bilingual students were identified by their French language arts
teachers based on their high level of fluency in both French and English. Five to seven
students were identified at each grade. Most students spoke French with at least one
parent and all were receiving academic support in French for five hours per week.
The students were asked to orally translate a short pen-pal letter and a series of
isolated sentences. Both tasks contained pitfall phrases that were based either on
difference between the two languages that were structural, false cognates, or
expressions. Students translated in both directions. They were also permitted to ask
questions or comment as they translated.

Overall, the students were good translators and had little difficulty conveying
accurately the meaning of the original message across languages. The students made
few source language errors, regardless of grade level or target language. Nor did they
use false cognates or make lexical intrusion errors. (Unlike a false cognate, a lexical
intrusion item does not exist in the target language). As would be expected, the third
grade students had the greatest difficulty translating. They also showed the highest
incidence of translation errors and were more likely to leave sentences incomplete.
By the sixth and seventh grades, however, the translation was generally as fluent and
almost as rapid as if the student were reading the letter aloud in the target language.

The results of the error analysis, however, suggested that the type of pitfall
might be important. Errors involving idioms and expressions were more common than
structure-related errors at all grade levels and for both target languages. While the
error rate in the two oldest grades was lower than in the two youngest grades for
structure-based errors, there was no grade-related difference on items involving idioms
and expressions. That is, although the older students made virtually no structure-
related errors, they were as likely to make lexical-based errors as the younger students.
However, older students reacted differently to these errors than did the younger
students. Most sixth and seventh graders who made errors on the idioms and
expressions showed and frequently expressed dissatisfaction with their translation and
great frustration with their inability to produce a more acceptable translation. Third
and fourth graders on the other hand, appeared to be less aware of their mistakes.
This suggests that while older students were unable to provide correct translations, they
were nonetheless aware of the conflict between the two languages and the insufficiency
of their translation. Such awareness appeared to be less common among the younger
students. This awareness is believed to reflect greater levels of metalinguistic
awareness.

Implications for Further Research

The studies summarized in this chapter support the claim that bilingual students are good translators as early as the third or fourth grade--all the studies reflected a high quality of translation and a low incidence of intrusion errors. Even the youngest students showed little evidence of linguistic confusion; although the translations were not perfect, there was little evidence of word-for-word translations, errors of false cognates, or lexical intrusions. The last study discussed, however, suggests that while students are not misled by differences in linguistic structure, they have greater difficulty with idiomatic expressions. Avoiding errors when translating idioms and expressions requires an understanding of the connotative differences between two languages, in addition to being aware of the structural differences. That is, the translator must be aware that a given combination of words, although grammatically correct, does not carry the same meaning in two languages.

This awareness and the ability to produce good translations are, we believe, related to a variety of metalinguistic skills. This relationship and the delineation of the relevant skills requires further research. Bilingual development is thought to enhance metalinguistic awareness through the increased experience with the separation of form (words) and meaning and the contrasting of different linguistic structures. Translation, and children's views of translation, offer a tool to gain additional insight into the relationship between metalinguistic awareness and bilingualism. For example, in the last study described, students were asked to judge and explain the adequacy of certain translations. Bilingual students as young as the third grade demonstrated a sophisticated understanding of how language works. Here are some examples:

> *You can't say it in English. I don't know why you can say it in French. I always wondered why jus d'orange--juice of orange--about two years ago I just stopped a moment before I was going to get the juice and then--jus--jus d'orange--juice of--Oh--now it makes sense. So you see, sometimes it can make sense in English and sometimes it can't. But it's just the way you say it.* David, age 9; grade 3.

> *It doesn't sound right in English. Well, maybe if every time--if--let's say it was fish blue--we say it all our lives--it would sound correct. That's just the way people say it.* Caterina, age 11; grade 5.

> *What a winter we had. It was--j'essaie de penser à un proverbe en anglais--(*I'm trying to think of a proverb in English)--*It was a chilling winter.* Pierre, age 13; grade 7; translating the French idiom: un froid de canard (literally: a cold of the ducks).

Translation ability needs to be examined at younger ages. To understand the nature of translation ability and its potential as a tool for research and education, it must be studied in much younger children and particularly pre-literate children. It is clear that by the fourth and fifth grades, bilingual students are already good translators. There is also evidence that

third graders have little difficulty translating both letters and isolated sentences given
without context. However, this evidence also suggested that younger students may not
approach the task in the same way as older bilinguals. Third graders appear to
translate more spontaneously, whereas the older students appear to regard translation
as a language-based task and to be more aware of explicit governing rules. This
question, however, remains a matter for further research.

Footnote

[1]The term *bilingual proficiency* is used to underline the "unique and specific linguistic
configuration" (Grosjean, 1985: 467) inherent in bilingualism, and avoid the implication
that the language proficiency of the bilingual is the sum of two monolingual
proficiencies.

References

Anastasi, A. & Cordova, F. (1953). Some effects of bilingualism upon the intelligence
test performance of Puerto Rican children in New York City. *Journal of
Educational Psychology*, 44, 1-19.

Balkan, L. (1970). Les effets du bilingüisme français-anglais sur les aptitudes
intellectuelles. [The effects of French-English bilingualism on intellectual
aptitude.] Bruxelles: Almev.

Ben-Zeev, S. (1977). The influence of bilingualism on cognitive strategy and cognitive
development. *Child Development*, 48, 1009-1018.

Bialystok, E. (1988). Levels of bilingualism and levels of linguistic awareness.
Developmental Psychology, 24, 560-567.

Bowey, J. A. & Patel, R. K. (1988). Metalinguistic ability and early reading
achievement. *Applied Psycholinguistics*, 9, 367-384.

Braunhausen, N. (1928). Le bilinguisme et la famille. In BIE (Bureau International
de l'Education) International Conference on Bilingualism, April 2-5, 1928,
Luxembourg. Geneva, Switzerland: BIE.

Carroll, J. B. (1978). Linguistic abilities in translators and interpreters. In D. Gerver
& H. W. Sinaiko (Eds.) *Language interpretation and communication*. New York:
Plenum Press.

Clyne, M. (1987). Don't you get bored speaking only English? Expressions of
metalinguistic awareness in a bilingual child. In R. Steele and T. Treadgold (Eds.)
Essays in honour of Michael Halliday. Philadelphia: John Benjamins Publishing
Co.

Cummins, J. (1978). Educational implications of mother-tongue maintenance in minority language groups. *Canadian Modern Language Review*, 34, 855-883.

De Avila, E. A. & Duncan, S. E. (1980). Definition and measurement of bilingual students. In *Bilingual program, policy, and assessment issues*. Sacramento, CA.: California State Department of Education, 1980.

Doyle, A., Champagne, M., & Segalowitz, N. (1978). Some issues on the assessment of linguistic consequences of early bilingualism. In M. Paradis (Ed.) *Aspects of bilingualism* (pp. 13-20). Columbia, SC: Hornbeam Press.

Galambos, S. & Hakuta, K. (1988). Subject-specific and task-specific characteristics of metalinguistic awareness in bilingual children. *Applied Psycholinguistics*, 9, 141-162.

Galambos, S., & Goldin-Meadow, S. (1990). The effects of learning two languages on levels of metalinguistic awareness. *Cognition*, 34, 1-56.

Gerver, D. (1976). In D. Gerver & H. W. Sinaiko (Eds.) *Language interpretation and communication*. New York: Plenum Press.

Grosjean, F. (1985). The bilingual as a competent but specific speaker-hearer. *Journal of Multilingual and Multicultural Development*, 6, 467-477.

Hakuta, K. (1986). *The mirror of language*. New York: Basic Books.

Hakuta, K. (1990). Language and cognition in bilingual children. In A. M. Padilla, H. H. Fairchild, & C. M. Valadez (Eds.) *Bilingual Education: Issues and Strategies* (pp. 47-59). Newbury Park: Sage.

Hakuta, K., & Diaz, R. M. (1984). The relationship between bilingualism and cognitive ability: A critical discussion and some longitudinal data. In K. E. Nelson (Ed.) *Children's language*, Vol. 5. Hillsdale, NJ: Lawrence Erlbaum Associates.

Hakuta, K., & Malakoff, M. (1987). Translation skills in bilingual children. Paper presented at SRCD, April 25, Baltimore, MD.

Hakuta, K., Gould, L., Malakoff, M., Rivera, M., & Rodriguez-Landsberg, M. (1988). Translation and interpretation in bilingual Puerto-Rican students. Paper presented at AERA, New Orleans, April, 1988.

Harley, B. (1986). *Age in second language acquisition*. Avon, England: Multilingual Matters, No. 22.

Harris, B. (1977). The importance of natural translation. *Working Papers in Bilingualism* (OISE, Toronto), 12, 96-114.

Harris, B. (1980). How a three-year old translates. In *Patterns of Bilingualism*. RELC Anthology Series 8. Singapore: National University of Singapore Press.

Harris, B., & Sherwood, B. (1978). Translating as an innate skill. In D. Gerver & H. W. Sinaiko (Eds.) *Language interpretation and communication*. New York: Plenum Press.

Haugen, E. (1956). *Bilingualism in America*. University of Alabama: University of Alabama Press.

Ianco-Worall, A. (1972). Bilingualism and cognitive development. *Child Development*, 43, 1390-1400.

Leopold, W. F. (1939-1949). *Speech development of a bilingual child: A linguist's record (4 volumes)*. Evanston, Ill: Northwestern University Press.

Levy, Y. (1985). Theoretical gains from the study of bilingualism: a case report. *Language Learning*, 35, 541-554.

Malakoff, M. E. (1988). The effect of language of instruction on reasoning in bilingual children. *Applied Psycholinguistics*, 9, 17-38.

Malakoff, M. E., & Hakuta, K. (1991). Translation skill and metalinguistic awareness in bilinguals. In E. Bialystok (Ed.) *Language processing and language awareness in bilingual children*. NY: Oxford University Press.

McLaughlin, B. (1984). *Second-language acquisition in childhood: Vol. 1*. Hillsdale: Lawrence Erlbaum Associates.

Nida, E. A. (1976). A framework for the analysis and evaluation of theories of translation. In R. W. Brislin (Ed.) *Translation: Applications and Research*. New York: Gardner Press, Inc.

Paivio, A., Clark, N. & Lambert, W. E. (1979). Bilingual coding theory and semantic repetition effects on recall. Unpublished manuscript. University of Western Ontario.

Romaine, S. (1989). *Bilingualism*. New York: Basil Blackwell.

Ronjat, J. (1913). *Le developpement du langage observé chez un enfant bilingue*. Paris: Champion.

Saer, D. (1924). The effect of bilingualism on intelligence. *British Journal of Psychology*, 14, 25-38.

Seleskovitch, D. (1976). Interpretation, a psychological approach to translation. In R. W. Brislin (Ed.) *Translation: Applications and Research*, New York: Gardner Press.

Shannon, S. (1987). *English in the Barrio: A sociolinguistic study of second language contact.* Unpublished doctoral dissertation, Stanford University, Stanford.

Smith, F. (1923). Bilingualism and mental development. *British Journal of Psychology*, 13, 19-25.

Smith, M. E. (1939). Some light on the problem of bilingualism as found from a study of the progress in mastery of English among pre-school children of non-American ancestry in Hawaii. *Genetic Psychology Monographs*, 21, 119-284.

Swain, M. (1972). Bilingualism as a first language. Unpublished doctoral dissertation. University of California, Irvine.

Swain, M., Dumas, G., & Naiman, N. (1974). Alternatives to spontaneous speech: Elicited translation and imitation as indicators of second language competence. *Working Papers on Bilingualism*, 3, 63-79.

Vygotsky, L. S. (1962). *Thought and language.* Cambridge, Mass: M.I.T. Press.

Wilss, W. (1982). *The science of translation.* Tübingen: Gunter Narr Verlag.

Zentenella, A. (1981). Language variety among Puerto Ricans. In C. A. Ferguson & S. B. Heath (Eds.) *Language in the USA* (pp. 218-238). Cambridge: Cambridge University Press.

Cognitive Processing in Bilinguals - R.J. Harris (Editor)
© *1992 Elsevier Science Publishers B.V. All rights reserved.*

Metalinguistic Awareness
in Second- and Third-language Learning

Jacqueline Thomas
Texas A&I University

Abstract

After providing a brief introduction to the concept of metalinguistic awareness, this chapter reviews research which has investigated the role of metalinguistic awareness in second language learning. Included is a theoretical discussion of the nature of linguistic knowledge and of the advantages bilinguals are thought to possess in terms of metalinguistic awareness. The chapter concludes with a look at research into language learning strategies. The author proposes that looking at differences between monolingual and bilingual students in language learning strategies and beliefs about the process of language learning promises to be a fruitful area of research.

Interest in the concept of metalinguistic awareness has been growing recently in the fields of psychology and language education, with particular focus on reading. The relationship between metalinguistic awareness and language learning promises to be a fruitful area of research for those interested in multilingualism. At the same time, there is increasing interest in language learning strategies, variables affecting a student's choice of such strategies, and strategy training. The purpose of this chapter is to present an overview of recent research dealing with aspects of metalinguistic awareness and to posit a link betweeen metalinguistic awareness and a student's choice of language learning strategies.

Metalinguistic awareness may be defined as an individual's ability to focus attention on language as an object in and of itself, to reflect upon language, and to evaluate it. Most young children treat language as transparent, to use Cazden's (1975) image. They look through language to meaning rather than at language unless "something interferes with the normally smooth process" of communication and language "becomes for some moments opaque" (Cazden, 1975, p.28). Much research has been conducted into children's metalinguistic development (e.g., Hakes, 1980; Tunmer et al., 1984) and it is commonly assumed that it is a special kind of language performance, that it is cognitively demanding, and that it is related to literacy (e.g. Vygotsky, 1962). Yopp (1988) reports four general types of metalinguistic ability: phonological awareness, word awareness, syntactic awareness, and pragmatic awareness. A growing body of evidence indicates that metalinguistic awareness plays a significant role in reading achievement, according to Yopp. However, discussion of the relationship between metalinguistic awareness and reading instruction falls outside the scope of this paper.

Metalinguistic Awareness, Second Language Learning, and Bilingualism

The distinction made by Bialystok (1978) between explicit and implicit knowledge has been very helpful in furthering the understanding of metalinguistic awareness in second language learning research.   In her seminal article describing a theoretical model of second language learning, Bialystok proposed that information about a language may be represented in the learner's mind as explicit linguistic knowledge, implicit linguistic knowledge, or other knowledge.   Initially Bialystok suggested that facts stored as explicit linguistic knowledge could be articulated in contrast to automatic information that is used spontaneously and is represented in implicit linguistic knowledge.   The distinction between the two knowledge sources is defined in terms of function: explicit knowledge "acts as a buffer for new information about the language" (Bialystok, 1978, p. 72); stores information which is represented explicitly; and articulates information that is represented in implicit knowledge.   Implicit linguistic knowledge contains "all the information about the target language necessary for most spontaneous comprehension and production tasks" (p.73).   Thus it is implicit knowledge in Bialystok's model that functions communicatively.

Interestingly, knowledge about other languages is assigned to other knowledge in Bialystok's tentative model, along with information about the target culture and knowledge of the world.   There is a strong argument for including knowledge about other languages within explicit or implicit knowledge (depending how aware the learner is of the language as a system), since it is potentially a resource for the language learner to aid in the formation of hypotheses about the target language.   Gass (1983) includes knowledge of other languages in her discussion of avoidance and transfer as they relate to metalingusitc awareness and second language intuitions.

In her model Bialystok makes a further distinction between formal and functional practicing as language learning strategies: formal practicing focuses on the language code and may increase the learner's explicit knowledge of the code (for example by studying a grammar book outside class) or automatise explicit knowledge so that it is transferred to implicit knowledge (for example by using language drills and exercises). Functional practising involves sampling authentic language input (via movies, talks with native speakers, and reading in the target language) with a communicative purpose. Another strategy in this model is monitoring: information from explicit linguistic knowledge is brought to the language task to improve the response that is generated by implicit knowledge (compare Krashen, 1977).

Subsequently Bialystok (1981) adopted the terms analyzed and nonanalyzed knowledge for explicit and implicit knowledge to avoid the tendency to associate explicit with conscious knowledge of language rules.   She no longer assumes that the ability to articulate conscious facts is a criterion for researchers to determine what explicit knowledge is (Bialystok, 1981 quoted by Odlin, 1986).   As Sharwood Smith (1981) points out, only some learners are able to talk about what they have become aware of.   In addition Sharwood Smith notes that, because learners are unable to articulate rules or facts about language does not mean that they are not aware, either dimly or clearly, of the structure of the language they are learning. Even though he associates the ability to analyse language in a conscious manner with a separate skill fostered in formal classroom teaching, Sorace (1985) found in her study that students develop the ability to make rules explicit relatively late, even when they have studied the target language in a formal environment. In fact she found that her students assimilated and reproduced a particular grammar rule in different ways and suggests that "what learners use are in fact their own reformulations of rules, which are different from the pedagogical rules that they are taught in the classroom" (p. 250). Odlin (1986) terms these idyosyncratic reformulations "caricatures."

In contrast to Bialystok's emphasis on the non-communicative functions of explicit or analyzed knowledge, Odlin (1986) presents evidence to suggest that metalinguistic knowledge often has communicative functions. Indeed Odlin is reluctant to dichotomize awareness of forms and awareness of functions and proposes that researchers think in terms of accessibility: formal linguistic knowledge is less accessible than functional metalinguistic awareness, although he admits that forms and functions can be intertwined in metalinguistic awareness. He cites research by Huerta (1978) suggesting that bilinguals who code-switch are often aware of their lexical choices. In other words they use formal linguistic knowledge with a communicative purpose. Similarly Sorace found it difficult to explain why the subjects in her study showed a growing interaction between their metalinguistic knowledge and their productive use of the target language if the function of formal knowledge is limited to monitoring. She argues, like Odlin, for a productive function for metalinguistic awareness, which would account for hesitations, self-corrections, and restatement of utterances. Odlin has suggested that there is evidence that "the most successful individuals are able to detect errors that especially interfere with discourse comprehension" (p. 138). Gass (1983) has similarly noted the facilitative role played by metalinguistic abilities in both learning to communicate and actually communicating: conscious repairs can keep the conversation from failing altogether when break-downs in communication have taken place.

In her later work Bialystok (1986) defines metalinguistic ability as an emerging ability that reflects gradual progess with underlying cognitive skills which she refers to as the analysis of knowledge and the control of cognitive operations. As language development takes place so the child structures and organizes an implicit body of language and gradually moves toward "representations of knowledge that include explicit features for the structure of that knowledge" (p.15). This is what Bialystok means by analysis of language. Control of cognitive operations refers to the degree of intentionality of cognitive processing involved in solving specific problems. In relation to control in language Bialystok argues that as children develop they are freed from focusing on the meaning of language to treat language as a system.

In her recent book on communication strategies Bialystok (1990) has developed the concept of analysis of linguistic knowledge and control of linguistic processing as components of language processing. According to Bialystok, these two components develop in approximate synchrony, unless special circumstances occur to affect the mastery of one of them, e.g., schooling and bilingualism. In the second case bilingual children advance in their control of processing because they are able to recognize the arbitrary nature of the form-meaning relation in language. Three studies conducted in the 70s (Ben-Zeev, 1977; Feldman & Shen, 1971; and Ianco-Worrall, 1972) found that bilingual children performed significantly better than monolingual children on tasks involving the switching of names of objects in a sentence. These studies replicate early work by Piaget (1929). Based on the results of these and other such studies (e.g., Cummins, 1978; Slobin, 1978; and Van Kleeck, 1982), it is hypothesized that bilingual children have an advantage over monolingual children "in the acceleration of the control function involved in the solution to linguistic and metalinguistic problems (Bialystok, 1986, p. 17). Bialystok quotes a study by Vihman and McLaughlin (1982) in which a 2-year-old bilingual could differentiate between languages, what objects would be called in each language, and who could be expected to understand the different labels. As Bialystok points out, such control problems would be very difficult for most children who do not normally attend to the language itself at this early age, but rather to the meaning of language. Similarly Odlin quotes studies by Heeschen (1978) and by Galambos and Goldin-Meadow (1983) which also indicate that being bilingual promotes metalinguistic awareness. Heeschen "suggests that there may be increased linguistic reflectiveness in multilingual situations regardless of whether or not the society is literate" (Gass, 1983, p.277).

In a study by Thomas (1988) English-Spanish bilinguals were found to have advantages over monolingual English students when learning French in a formal classroom environment. The college students with prior knowledge of Spanish performed significantly better than the monolingual students on tests of vocabulary (recognition of cognates) and grammar (selecting a grammatically appropriate closure for a sentence stem) where there was time for them to exploit their explicit or analyzed linguistic knowledge. Thomas suggests that students used their metalinguistic awareness to facilitate their performance on the tasks focused on language forms. In addition, the bilingual students learning French as a third language produced compositions that were ranked as more comprehensible to native speakers of French than did their monolingual counterparts. Thomas concludes that the bilingual subjects' metalinguistic awareness also functioned to monitor linguistic output on a communicative task where their attention was focused on the message.

Further analyses revealed that those students who had studied Spanish formally for at least two years had additional advantages over the bilingual students who had acquired Spanish informally at home: they performed significantly better on the grammar test but not on the vocabulary test, regardless of whether they used Spanish actively or passively at home. It is hypothesized that their experience in a formal language learning environment had more impact on grammatical sensitivity than on the recognition of cognates. In this case schooling seems to have increased their awareness of language as an object in and of itself.

An error analysis (Thomas, 1985) conducted on the subjects' compositions investigated differences between the errors of monolingual students, bilingual students who had acquired Spanish informally at home and bilingual students who had studied Spanish formally. The analysis revealed that the bilingual students who had developed at least minimal literacy skills in Spanish produced the lowest percentage of errors in all the structures analyzed and they also attempted more structures than either of the other groups. Thomas suggests that this group of students was able to avoid interference, exploit positive transfer and develop more effective strategies for producing acceptable written commmunication due to their awareness of Spanish as a system.

Mägiste (1984; 1986) has also argued for the advantages bilinguals have when learning a third language. She makes a distinction between subjects who use their home languages actively or passively rather than whether their linguistic knowledge is explicit and analyzed or implicit and unanalyzed. In her study measuring response time on different verbal tasks Mägiste (1986) found that at a very elementary level of third language learning prior languages that are known only passively do not cause as much interference as languages that are practiced more actively at home. She interprets the results of her study in terms of strategy and hypothesizes that "By mainly concentrating on one language and knowing the other latently, a student chooses a strategy that maximizes positive transfer effects" (p. 117). This suggests that subjects are making a conscious choice but since Mägiste does not report whether her German-Swedish bilinguals had received schooling in their third language, it is difficult to know at what level of awareness these students were functioning.

The Relationship between Metalinguistic Awareness, Beliefs about Language Learning, and Choice of Language Learning Strategies

According to Oxford et al., (1990), while all language learners use strategies, the more effective students use them "more consciously, more purposefully, more appropriately, and more frequently" (p. 199) than less effective students. The results of studies investigating the role of metalinguistic awareness in the success of second and third language learning have led this researcher to hypothesize that students' prior linguistic experience affects the strategies they subsequently adopt, their level of consciousness about which strategies are effective, and their ultimate success in the foreign language learning classroom.

The implications of research into language learning strategies are important for teachers and teacher training (Oxford, 1990; Oxford & Crookall, 1989). Training in language-learning strategies is possible but can be "adversely affected by learners' dysfunctional attitudes and beliefs" (Oxford et al., 1990, p. 200). Therefore, the contribution of learners' beliefs to their language learning strategies cannot be underestimated. Since learners' beliefs and attitudes depend upon their background, research into the relationship between choice of language learning strategies and the kind of prior linguistic experiences which affect that choice is important.

Horwitz (1985; 1988), Wenden (1987), and Elbaum (1989) have investigated students' beliefs about language learning. The results of Horwitz's study underline the importance of providing students with the underlying rationale for classroom practices to minimize the possible clash between students' expectations based on their beliefs about what the language learning process involves and specific language learning activities. Students' beliefs, according to Horwitz, could limit their potential success at language learning. Studies reported to date indicate that beliefs may be influenced by current instructional practices (e.g., Horwitz, 1988) or by previous informal contact with the target language (e.g., Elbaum, 1989). However, little research has been conducted into the relationship between students' prior linguistic experiences in general and their beliefs about the language learning process. When bilinguals learn a third language semantically related to one of the languages they know, do they form different beliefs and develop different strategies from monolingual students learning the same target language? Do those bilinguals assumed to have explicit/analyzed linguistic knowledge differ in their beliefs and strategies from those who have implicit/nonanalyzed knowledge?

Thomas (1990) conducted a small-scale study to investigate monolingual and bilingual students' beliefs about language learning and the relationship between students' beliefs and their previous language instruction and/or informal contact with another language at home. The study was designed to discover if learners of French as a second language would assign more or less importance to grammar in their definition of what it means to be able to communicate in another language, compared to English-Spanish bilinguals learning French as a third language. Given the opportunity to design the "perfect" language learning curriculum, would learners of French as a second language assign more or fewer hours to "explicit" or formal classroom activities such as "doing exercises in a foreign language textbook" and "studying a reference book in English that explains the grammatical structure of the language" (see Appendix for complete list of activities) than their colleagues learning French as a third language?

It was hypothesized that bilingual students who had grown up hearing Spanish used as a form of communication would be aware that languages can be learned without formally studying the grammar of the language and through less explicit or functional activities such as "having conversations in the language with people who encourage you to try and do not correct your errors," or "reading foreign language newspapers, magazines, or books for enjoyment." It was further hypothesized that students who had developed some awareness of Spanish as language in and of itself through formal study would assign more importance to the role of grammar in their beliefs about the nature of communicative competence than bilinguals who had only been exposed to Spanish informally. It was hypothesized that they might also choose more explicit activities in designing the optimal language learning environment.

Method

Subjects

Approximately half the students learning French at Texas A&I University in South Texas, USA come from bilingual communities where Spanish is spoken in the home and in informal social situations. However, Spanish does not enjoy equal status with English in the community and no content courses are offered in Spanish at the university. Some of the English-Spanish bilingual students have formally studied Spanish, while others have only informal knowledge of the language. In this study it was assumed that those students who had received formal training in Spanish had greater access to explicit linguistic knowledge which they could use to make comparisons with for the purpose of developing language learning strategies. The other half of the students are monolingual English speakers who have little or no prior foreign language learning experience.

Data were collected from 32 students who were registered for beginning and intermediate French classes in the spring of 1990. Of the total sample 19 students were monolingual English speakers with no formal exposure to another language. They were all learners of French as a second language. The remaining 13 students comprised those students who had grown up in a bilingual home, six of whom had studied Spanish formally for at least two years.

Materials

At the end of the semester the 12 beginning students and the 20 intermediate students in the sample were asked to complete a very slightly modified version of the experimental tasks of Elbaum's (1989) Implicit Theories Assessment (ITA). This instrument deals with students' beliefs about the nature of communicative competence and the amount of time that should ideally be assigned to communicative and metalingustic language learning activities in the "perfect" foreign language learning classroom. In the first task subjects are asked to read non-technical definitions of the four components of communicative competence based on the theoretical models of Canale (1983) and Canale and Swain (1987). The subjects weight each component based on their perception of its contribution to a student's ability to communicate in another language.

In the second task subjects design their "ideal" foreign language learning program. Presented with 10 activities which are either explicit or metalinguistic on the one hand or implicit and communicative on the other, the subjects must indicate how many hours per week they believe should be devoted to the various activities in order to develop communicative competence. The subjects in this study were told to fill 10 hours per week with the activities because this figure corresponds to the three hours of class time and seven hours of out-of-class time that students are expected to spend on studying a foreign language each week.

In addition to completing the two assessment tasks of the ITA, subjects in the present study were asked to complete a language background questionnaire. Students reported their knowledge of Spanish (they self-rated their ability to read, write, understand, and speak the language) and the nature of Spanish usage in their homes. Based on their responses to this questionnaire students were assigned to one of three groups for purposes of comparison: those with no knowledge of another language, those from a bilingual home with formal knowledge of Spanish, and those from a bilingual home with informal knowledge of Spanish. Two sets of scores are discussed for monolingual and bilingual subjects: the mean weight accorded to grammar and the three other components in students' definitions of communicative competence (expressed as percentages) and the rankings of activities according to the number of hours assigned by students in designing the optimal language learning program.

Results and Discussion

The means scores of beginning students' beliefs about communicative competence are shown in Table 1.

Table 1

Mean Scores of Beginning Students' Beliefs about Communicative Competence

	Grammar	Vocabulary	Social Use	Strategies
Monolinguals N=7	30	31.4	18.6	20
Bilinguals N=3*	26.7	25	15	33.3

*Two beginning students failed to complete this task.

After one semester of instruction in French the beginning bilingual students learning French as a third language assigned a little less importance to the contributions of grammar (3.3% less), vocabulary (6.4% less), and knowledge of how to use language correctly in social situations (3.6% less) than did the monolingual students. In fact the monolingual students believed that over 60% of one's ability to communicate could be attributed to knowledge of grammar and vocabulary combined. The bilingual students assigned more importance to knowledge of strategies to get around their limitations (13.3% more) than did their monolingual counterparts. The prior experience of Spanish-speaking students seems to have made a difference in what they think it means to be able to communicate in a foreign language. Bilingual students in South Texas are used to applying such strategies as code-switching in order to get around their limitations (for example not finding the Spanish word for a certain cultural concept). It is hypothesized that they have developed an awareness that knowledge of such strategies is a component of communicative competence.

The mean scores of intermediate students' beliefs about communicative competence are shown in Table 2.

Table 2

Mean Scores of Intermediate Students' Beliefs about Communicative Competence

	Grammar	Vocabulary	Social Use	Strategies
Monolinguals N=10	22	29.5	16.8	31.7
Bilinguals N=10	31.2	34.2	15.9	18.7

After two or more semesters of instruction in French the bilingual students in this sample assigned less importance to strategies (13% less) than did the monolingual English-speaking students and more importance to grammar and vocabulary (9.2% and 4.7% more respectively). The French program at Texas A&I University provides students with few opportunities in beginning classes to develop strategies to overcome linguistic limitations like the ones bilingual students are used to using in Spanish outside of class. These intermediate students appear to reflect the pattern of instruction which emphasizes knowledge of grammar and vocabulary in their beliefs about what contributes to a person's ability to communicate in another language, as Horwitz (1988) has suggested. Interestingly, monolingual students in the intermediate stages of study are more aware of the role played by knowledge of strategies than bilingual students at the same stage of study. The monolinguals' exposure to formal instruction in a foreign language appears to have taught them that knowing French grammar and vocabulary just is not enough to facilitate communication.

Regarding students' beliefs about the best possible combination of activities needed to develop communicative competence, opinions seem to vary according to students' linguistic background. The rankings that the monolingual and bilingual subjects (beginning and intermediate students combined) gave to the ten language learning activities are given in descending order in Table 3. (See Thomas, 1990 for a further break-down of the data.)

Table 3

Students' Rankings of Explicit and Implicit Language Learning Activities
(Beginning and Intermediate Students Combined)

Monolinguals N=19	Bilinguals N=13
1. Error correction	1. Conversations
2. Talks	2. Error correction
3. Exercises	3. Memorization
4. Read to learn	4. Exercises
5. Memorization	5. Reference grammar
6. Tapes	6. Diary
7. Diary	Talks
8. Read for fun	8. Tapes
Conversations	Read to learn
10. Reference Grammar	10. Read for fun

While error correction is ranked first or second by both monolingual and bilingual subjects, conversations is ranked first by bilinguals but eighth by monolinguals. Students from a monolingual home making their first contact with another language have had no experience of conversations with people who might encourage them to try to communicate without correcting their errors. Their attempts to communicate in the target language have been almost exclusively with the teacher whose role is clearly to correct their utterances either directly or indirectly through modeling. Students from a bilingual home, on the other hand, have probably had experiences with their grandparents or other relatives and family friends where the focus of attention was on the message rather than on the language itself. The bilingual subjects appear to have been able to conceptualize conversations with people who do not correct their errors and believe that this would be helpful in developing communicative skills in French.

Monolingual students ranked talks second, while bilinguals ranked the same activity equal eighth. In this case the bilinguals appear to be more realistic, perhaps realizing from their own experience that language learning must be interactive for it to be effective. They may have attended talks in Spanish where they experienced difficulty in understanding. Monolinguals experiencing foreign language instruction for the first time, on the other hand, often naively believe that they can learn through osmosis. Their belief that going to talks by people who speak the language would be particularly effective might reflect this naiveté.

The rankings that the bilinguals with formal training in Spanish and those without (beginning and intermediate combined) gave to the ten language learning activities are given in descending order in Table 4.

Table 4

Bilingual Students' Rankings of Language Learning Activities

Bilinguals with formal training N=6	Bilinguals without formal training N=7
1. Conversations	1. Conversations
2. Error correction	2. Reference grammar
3. Exercises	3. Error correction
4. Memorization	Memorization
5. Talks	5. Exercises
6. Tapes	6. Read to learn
Diary	Diary
8. Read to learn	8. Tapes
9. Reference grammar	9. Talks
10. Read for fun	10. Read for fun

Both bilinguals with formal training in Spanish and those without allocated more hours to conversations than any other activity. Both groups of students were aware that communicating with someone who encourages the learner to try without correcting their errors could be an effective activity if it were included in the foreign language learning classroom. These same students are aware, however, that getting someone who is proficient in the language to correct errors can complement natural conversations with a focus on meaning. This latter activity was either ranked second or equal third by the two groups of bilingual subjects. Contrary to expectations, the bilingual students with access to formal knowledge of Spanish did not allocate more hours to explicit classroom activities than those with only informal exposure to Spanish. Their bilingual experience seems to have led them to realize the potential advantage of having conversations focused on meaning regardless of whether they had studied Spanish formally or not. Perhaps, as Odlin has suggested, in their minds they combined awareness of forms with awareness of functions.

Much more research needs to be done. Understanding the nature of the relationship between metalinguistic awareness, second language learning and bilingualism will provide insights into cognitive processing in bilinguals. The advantages bilinguals have over monolinguals will have to be further explored, especially in the area of language learning strategies.

References

Ben-Zeev, S. (1977). Mechanisms by which childhood bilingualism affects understanding of language and cognitive structures. In P. A. Hornby (Ed.), *Bilingualism: Psychological, social, and educational implications*. New York: Academic Press.

Bialystok, E. (1978). A theoretical model of second language learning. *Language Learning*, 28, 69-83.

Bialystok, E. (1981). The role of linguistic knowledge in second language use. *Studies in Second Language Acquisition*, 4, 31-35.

Bialystok, E. (1986). Children's concept of word. *Journal of Psycholinguistic Research*, 15, 13-32.

Bialystok, E. (1990). *Communication strategies: A Psychological analysis of second-language use*. Oxford: Basil Blackwell.

Canale, M. (1983). From communicative competence to communicative language pedagogy. In J. Richards & R. Schmidt (Eds.), *Language and Communication*. London: Longman.

Canale, M. & Swain, M. (1987). Some theories of communicative competence. In W. Rutherford & M. Sharwood Smith (Eds.), *Grammar and Second Language Teaching*. New York: Newbury House.

Cazden, C. (1975). Play and metalinguistic awareness. *Urban Review*, 7, 28-39.

Cummins, J. (1978). Bilingualism and the development of metalinguistic awareness. *Journal of Cross-Cultural Psychology*, 9, 131-149.

Elbaum, B. (1989). An analytic research design for the study of learners' beliefs about language learning. Paper presented at the second annual "Research Perspectives in Adult Language Learning and Acquisition" conference, Columbus, Ohio.

Feldman, C. & Shen, M. (1971). Some language-related cognitive advantages of bilingual five-year-olds. *The Journal of Genetic Psychology*, 118, 235-244.

Galambos, S., & Goldin-Meadow, S. (1983). Learning a second language and metalinguistic awareness. In A. Chukerman, M. Marks, & J. Richardson (Eds.), *Papers from the Nineteenth Regional Meeting*. Chicago: Chicago Linguistic Society.

Gass, S. (1983). The development of L2 intuitions. *TESOL*, 17, 273-291.

Hakes, D. T. (Ed.) (1980). *The development of metalinguistic abilities in children*. New York: Springer Verlag.

Heeschen, V. (1978). The metalinguistic vocabulary of a speech community in the highlands of Irian Jaya. In A. Sinclair, R. J. Jarvella, & W. J. M. Levelt (Eds.), *The child's conception of language* (pp. 155-187). New York: Springer-Verlag.

Horwitz, E. (1985). Using student beliefs about language learning and teaching in the foreign language methods course. *Foreign Language Annals*, 18, 333-340.

Horwitz, E. (1988). The beliefs about language learning of beginning university foreign language students. *Modern Language Journal*, 72, 283-294.

Huerta, A. (1978). Code-switching among Spanish-English bilinguals: A sociolinguistic perspective. Unpublished dissertation, University of Texas.

Ianco-Worrall, A. (1972). Bilingualism and cognitive development. *Child Development*, 43, 1390-1400.

Krashen, S. D. (1977). The Monitor Model for adult second language performance. In M. Burt & M. Finocchiaro (Eds.), *English as a second language*. New York: Regents.

Mägiste, E. (1984). Learning a third language. *Journal of Multilingual and Multicultural Development*, 5, 415-421.

Mägiste, E. (1986). Selected issues in second and third language learning. In J. Vaid (Ed.), *Language processing in bilinguals: Psycholinguistic and neuropsychological perspectives* (pp. 97-122). Hillsdale, New Jersey: Lawrence Erlbaum.

Odlin, T. (1986). On the nature and use of explicit knowledge. *International Review of Applied Linguistics in Language Teaching*, 24, 123-144.

Oxford, R. (1990). *Language learning strategies: What every teacher should know.* New York: Newbury House/Harper & Row.

Oxford, R. & Crookall, D. (1989). Language learning strategies: Methods, findings and instructional implications. *Modern Language Journal*, 73, 404-419.

Oxford, R., Crookall, D., Cohen, A., Lavine, R., Nyikos, M., & Sutter, W. (1990). Strategy training for language learners: Six situational case studies and a training model. *Foreign Language Annals*, 22, 197-216.

Piaget, J. (1929). *The child's conception of the world.* London: Routledge & Kegan Paul.

Sharwood Smith, M. A. (1981). Consciousness-raising and the second language learner. *Applied Linguistics*, 2, 159-168.

Slobin, D. (1978). A case study of early language awareness. In A. Sinclair, R. J. Jarvella, & W. J. M. Levelt (Eds.), *The child's conception of language*. New York: Springer-Verlag.

Sorace, A. (1985). Metalinguistic knowledge and language use in acquisition-poor environments. *Applied Linguistics*, 3, 239-254.

Thomas, J. (1985). The role played by prior linguistic experience   in second and third language learning. In R. Hall, Jr. (Ed.). *The Eleventh Linguistic Association of Canada and United States Forum 1984*. Columbia, South Carolina: Hornbeam Press.

Thomas, J. (1988). The role played by metalinguistic awareness in second and third language learning. *Journal of Multilingual and Multicultural Development*, 9, 235-246.

Thomas, J. (1990). A study of the relationsihp between learners' beliefs about language learning, effective language learning strategies, previous language instruction and contact with another language in the home. Paper presented at the third annual "Research Perspectives in Adult Language Learning and Acquisition" conference, Columbus, Ohio.

Tunmer, W. E., Pratt, C. & Herriman, M. L. (Eds.). (1984). *Metalinguistic awareness in children*. New York: Springer-Verlag.

Van Kleeck, A. (1982). The emergence of linguistic awareness: A cognitive framework. *Merrill-Palmer Quarterly*, 28, 237-265.

Vihman, M. M. & McLaughlin, B. (1982). Bilingualism and second language acquisition in preschool children. In C. J. Brainerd & M. Pressley (Eds.), *Verbal processes in children*. New York: Springer-Verlag.

Vygotsky, L.S. (1962). *Thought and language*. Cambridge, MA: M.I.T. Press.

Wenden, A. (1987). How to be a successful language learner: Insights and prescriptions from L2 learners. In A. Wenden & J. Rubin (Eds.). *Learner strategies in language learning*. Englewood Cliffs, NJ: Prentice Hall International.

Yopp, H. K. (1988). Metalinguistic awareness and bilingualism. *Journal of Educational Issues of Language Minority Students*, 3, 49-56.

Appendix

Explicit activities

1. Doing the exercises in a foreign language textbook.

2. Listening to tape-recorded sentences and repeating them.

3. Memorizing words and expressions used in the language.

4. Studying a reference book in English that explains the grammatical structures of the language.

5. Getting someone who is proficient in the language to correct your errors.

Implicit activities

1. Having conversations in the language with people who encourage you to try and do not correct your errors.

2. Using foreign language books and newspapers to learn more about a subject that interests you.

3. Going to talks by people who speak the language.

4. Reading foreign language newspapers, magazines, or books for enjoyment.

5. Keeping a personal diary that you write in the language.

Part VII:

CEREBRAL LATERALIZATION IN BILINGUALS

Cognitive Processing in Bilinguals – R.J. Harris (Editor)
1992 Elsevier Science Publishers B.V.

Leaning to the Right: Hemispheric Involvement in Bilinguals

Edith Mägiste

Uppsala University

Abstract

A dichotic listening task of stepwise addition was given to 40 right-handed German-Swedish bilingual students. In the visual modality, the frequency and direction of conjugate lateral eye movements to verbal, spatial and emotional tasks was investigated in 36 students. The results provided evidence that the two techniques are sensitive indicators of different degrees of bilingualism as well as sensitive measures of hemispheric asymmetry. More left hemisphere involvement was observed in students with a clearly dominant language, whereas balanced bilinguals showed more bilateral involvement. No evidence was found for the age or stage hypothesis.

There is evidence from studies using EEG, visual half-field and dichotic listening techniques that bilinguals seem to be less lateralized to the left hemisphere than monolingual subjects. When solving verbal tasks, relatively more bilateral involvement was found for L1 (Gordon, 1980), L2 (Sussman, Franklin & Simon, 1982) or both languages (Genesee, Hamers, Lambert, Mononen, Seitz & Starck, 1978); however, no laterality differences based on bilingualism were obtained by Galloway and Sarcella (1982) or Piazza and Zatorre (1981). Obviously, there is still much inconsistency presumably due to several factors, such as proficiency level and familiarity with the task, gender, age, and context of acquisition of L2. These factors seem to interact in one way or another (Vaid, 1983).

To control for some of these variables, a developmental study was performed with German-Swedish bilingual students. With increasing bilingualism a gradual shift to the right hemisphere was observed in both early and late bilinguals to the same extent and in L1 and L2 for similar languages (Mägiste, 1987). Measures in the two languages were taken on the word level for tachistoscopic tests and on both word and sentence level for dichotic listening. However, the right-ear advantage (REA) for verbal material which generally is experienced in right-handed monolingual subjects varied considerably in strength depending on the task. Immediate recall of two longer sentences from one ear, when competitive stimulation was given to the other ear, did not in most cases lead to a REA, probably due to the memory load of the task. A more sensitive measure of lateralization was the repetition of two-word pairs, where the demands on concentration and motivation are more limited compared to sentences. The most marked REA in this study was obtained when subjects were asked which word in a pair they recognized best.

Stepwise addition should be a task which can be expected to elicit a clear REA, indicating predominantly left-hemisphere (LH) processing. The task contains both linguistic elements and requires a sequential analytic approach, the characteristic mode of the LH. In the visual modality, recent research has shown that conjugate lateral eye movements under certain laboratory conditions are indicators of hemispheric activation. Generally, the results suggest predominantly left-eye movements indicating right-hemisphere involvement when subjects reflect upon spatial tasks. On tasks demanding analysis of verbal features, mainly looking to the right indicates LH dominance (Kinsbourne, 1974; Krikorian & Rafales, 1982; Walker, Wade & Waldman, 1982). These findings are in line with neuroanatomical and behavioral evidence indicating that the right hemisphere subserves visuo-spatial functions, whereas the left hemisphere is dominant for verbal and language functions. So far lateral eye movements as a method have not been used in bilingual subjects to find out whether or not they differ from monolinguals in processing strategies.

Thus, one purpose of the present study was to determine whether subjects varying in degree of bilingualism would show laterality differences in processing simple arithmetical operations and other verbal, spatial and emotional information. Another purpose was to evaluate the sensitivity of two more uncommon techniques for measuring laterality in the visual and auditory modality.

An excellent opportunity to measure certain parameters of bilingualism is provided by the German School in Stockholm which offers German-Swedish bilingual schooling. What makes this school especially interesting is that each grade includes students with a wide range of residence times in Sweden, so that all degrees of bilingual proficiency can be found. Generally, students from this school show a native proficiency in the German and Swedish languages after 4-6 years of residence in Sweden (Mägiste, 1979; 1980; 1984; 1986).

In the first study, a German-dominant group was compared to a German-Swedish balanced group. Such a design permits further testing of the stage hypothesis which would predict more bilateral involvement in Swedish for the German dominant group who is at the beginning of L2 acquisition (Silverberg, Bentin, Gaziel, Obler & Albert, 1979). It is also possible to test the age hypothesis, according to which a language acquired after puberty will be less late-realized due to a greater functional independence between L1 and L2 when L2 is acquired later in Life (Gordon, 1980). Since all subjects in the balanced group had learned L2 clearly before puberty, no differential lateralization effect between the two languages should be expected in this group from the age hypothesis.

Experiment 1: Stepwise addition

Method

Subjects

Forty German-Swedish bilingual students (20 boys, 20 girls) in the age range 14-

16 years participated for payment. All were normal hearing, right-handed students from the German School in Stockholm, where instruction is in German and Swedish at both elementary and high-school levels with German as the dominant classroom language. The students are taught Swedish history, political science and Swedish language in Swedish by Swedish teachers, while all other topics are taught by German teachers.

For all subjects, German was the first language and the language of the home, at least during the initial years of residence in Sweden. Swedish was acquired outside the home in a natural milieu. Thus, both languages were learned in informal environments as well as in formal teaching situations in school. Generally, after some years of bilingual training the students handled each language with the competence of a native speaker.

The students were divided into two language groups according to residence time in Sweden and 5-point rating scales: a German dominant group consisted of 20 students who had resided between three months and four years in Sweden with a mean of two years; a German-Swedish balanced group of 20 students with a residence time between five and 16 years in Sweden with a mean of 12 years. They rated their language skills as about equally good in German and Swedish in terms of reading, writing, understanding and speaking. All subjects in the balanced group had learned both languages before puberty and had a native competence in them. In the German-dominant group, German was handled with the competence of a native speaker, while Swedish, the weaker language, was not.

Material. A dichotic listening task of 80 simple arithmetical items was used in both German and Swedish. In each language, 40 operations were constructed requiring stepwise addition. The base number was always a two-digit number and the three addends were 1 as the minimum and 5 as the maximum. For example: $58 + 2 + 4 + 5 = ?$ The operations were presented binaurally across two channels and heard through a stereo headset at 85 dB with a noise ratio of 60 dB.

Procedure. Subjects were tested individually. Each subject started the session by filling in the questionnaire about handedness (Oldfield, 1971) and language background. The dichotic listening task was presented on two tapes, one for each language. Subjects were told in advance to focus their attention on items arriving at a specific ear. For half of the tasks which were presented in competition, subjects were instructed to solve the operations they head in the right ear, for the other half subjects concentrated on the left ear to solve the tasks. Conditions and languages were counterbalanced across subjects. At the beginning of a new condition subjects were given some practice trials.

Results

Figure 1 shows the mean percentages of correctly solved arithmetical operations in German and Swedish languages for the two groups varying in degree of bilingualism.

As regards LH-performance, the subjects were instructed to attend to the right ear, in
RH-performance the subjects attended to the left ear.

For each language a 2 X 2 analysis of variance was carried out on the data
presented in Figure 1 with language group (dominant German versus German-Swedish
balanced) as a between-groups factor and condition (forced-left and forced-right) as
a within-subjects factor.

When German was the language of response, the main effect of language group
was significant, $F(1,38) = 6.52$, $p<.05$, as well as the main effect of condition, $F(1,38)$
$= 42.05$, $p<.001$. As indicated by the left panel of Figure 1, the German-dominant
group shows clearly marked differences in performance between the two hemispheres
in favor of the left hemisphere (LH), whereas the German-Swedish balanced group
(right panel) is more balanced in skills; there is only a slight, nonsignificant tendency
for better performance in the left hemisphere, which practically means that subjects
in this group performed about equally well regardless of which ear they attended to.
This differential performance of the two groups also becomes evident in the highly
significant group X task interaction, $F(1,38) = 16.62$, $p<.0001$.

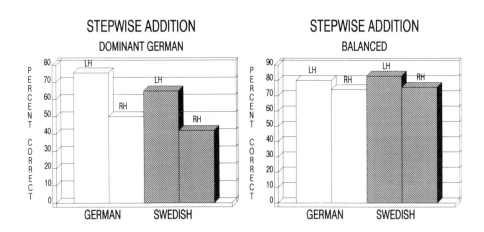

Figure 1. Percent correctly solved operations in German-Swedish bilinguals: A clear
lateralization effect to the LH in the German dominant group, more bilateral
involvement in the balanced group.

A corresponding result was obtained when Swedish was the language of response. The man effects of group, F(1.38) = 17.18, p<.001, and condition, F(1,38) = 15.59, p<.001, reached significance, as well as the group X task interaction, F(1,38) = 4.1, p<.05. The balanced group solved about the same number of arithmetic problems in Swedish as in German with only slightly better performance when attention was directed to the right ear. The German dominant group, on the other hand, solved clearly fewer problems in their weaker language and their performance differed considerably depending on which ear they attended to. In this group a well pronounced REA was observed.

Discussion

The results provide evidence for more LH-involvement in German and Swedish for the German-dominant group and about equal LH- and RH-involvement for both languages in the balanced group. Thus, a pronounced REA was found in the German-dominant group. In both languages, the percentages of correctly solved arithmetic tasks was 22-26% higher when the right ear was stimulated, indicating LH-involvement. This result gives no support for the stage hypothesis according to which the performance in Swedish, L2, should be less lateralized than in L1. Actually, the lateralization pattern is about the same for the weaker and the better language. There is just a higher error rate in the weaker language which affects LH- and RH-performance to the same extent. The result is in line with findings obtained by Mägiste (1987), Sanchez, Manga, Babecki and de Tembleque (1988), and Vaid and Genesee (1980).

As proficiency in L2 increases and approaches native-like competence as is the case in the German-Swedish balanced group, LH-performance is only slightly better than RH-performance, indicating nearly perfect bilateral involvement. Since all subjects in this balanced group had acquired the second language before puberty, there is no evidence for the age hypothesis either, which would predict a bilateral effect only if L2 is acquired after puberty.

The number of correctly solved problems when attention was focused on the right ear was about the same for the balanced group when compared to the performance in German for the German-dominant group. The main difference between the two groups is the greater RH-involvement in the balanced group which results in a very clear reduction of the REA. As is also evident from the significant interaction effects between the groups, the balanced subjects perceived more from the left ear, perhaps due to a better ability to screen out irrelevant information from the right ear. As a result, the subjects in this group solved in either language more arithmetic operations than the German-dominant group in their better language. This is an interesting finding, if it is a valid one. It would indicate more brain activity in bilinguals who are about equally adept at two languages. These students are dealing actively daily with two languages. In addition, they learn two or three other languages as foreign languages. This means a constant confrontation with different language and norm systems. Since the brain is comparable to a muscle that works better with more training, these young bilingual people utilize the capacity of the brain to a greater extent than people who are mainly concentrating on one language. Therefore, it is perhaps not surprising that bilingualism might be one factor that increases the general arousal level in the brain.

Experiment 2: Conjugate lateral eye movements

The purpose of this study was to find out if a comparable lateralization pattern could be obtained in bilinguals by using conjugate lateral eye movements. With this technique it is important to avoid confrontations with the experimenter. In a face-to-face situation, subjects usually break eye contact with the questioner when reflecting upon the task and move eyes in only one direction irrespective of the type of question asked. For this reason, the questions in the present study were prerecorded on a tape-recorder and during the experiment subject and experimenter were in separate rooms.

There were four types of questions following the taxonomy of Schwartz, Davidson and Maer (1975): verbal, spatial, verbal-emotional, and spatial-emotional. On the basis of previous results with monolingual subjects, verbal questions yielded predominantly rightward movements, whereas spatial questions results in more leftward movements. Emotional questions elicited mostly leftward movements, especially spatial-emotional questions. If lateral eye movements are a sensitive measure of differential hemispheric functioning in monolingual and bilingual subjects, the general expectations should be more leftward movements on all tasks in bilinguals when compared to monolinguals. Since subjects were from the German School in Stockholm with the same language background and curriculum as the subjects in Experiment 1, the eye movements for questions in L1 (German) and L2 (Swedish) should be about equivalent. The most pronounced differences between monolingual and bilingual performance were expected in answers to verbal questions, as this condition contains much abstract information and thus measures language most purely. The spatial and emotional elements in the other conditions might override parameters of language and bilingualism as indicated by Tucker, Roth, Arneson, and Buckingham (1977), who reported predominantly left eye movements to emotionally disturbing tasks.

Method

Subjects. Thirty-six right-handed subjects (18 males, 18 females) participated for payment. Half of them were Swedish monolingual students of psychology in the age range 19-39 years. In a strict sense this group was not monolingual, since the subjects knew at least one more foreign language. However, their knowledge was far from the language proficiency of the bilingual group who handled their languages with the competence of a native speaker. The bilingual group were students from the German School in Stockholm. Their age range was 17-20 years. All bilingual subjects had acquired the two languages in a bilingual environment before 12 years of age.

Questions. Subjects were exposed to 40 questions in Swedish read in successive order from a tape-recorder. There were 10 questions of each category of the same kind used by Schwartz et al. (1975). For example: a verbal non-emotional question was "What is the main difference between work and play?"; a verbal emotional question "Say a sentence where the words razor and artery are included"; a spatial question "Visualize a Swedish crown put in your hands with the face of the king up. In what direction is he looking?"; a spatial emotional question "Visualize and report your immediate reactions when you enter an unfamiliar hotel room, just closing the door and reaching for the light when an arm suddenly is twisted around your neck". Forty equivalent sentences were constructed in German. Order of presentation of conditions and languages (in case of bilingual subjects) were counterbalanced across subjects.

Apparatus and procedure. The direction of eye movements was studied using a Sony video camera hidden behind a white screen which was 4 m in front of the subject. The subject was seated in an arm-chair and instructed to gaze at the center of the screen where the telescopic lens was hidden, marked through a small hole. To avoid unwanted head movements and looking around, the laboratory environment was completely neutral and painted white. The 40 questions were heard from a recorder placed behind the screen. After each question there was a short rest intended for the subject's answer. The pause varied with the type of the question. There responses were picked up by a closed videosystem and transferred to a Finlux Monitor (28 inches) in the next room where the experimenter counted the eye movements. The subject was left alone during the entire session which took 30 minutes for the monolingual and 60 minutes for the bilingual subjects.

Scoring of eye movements. All eye movements were scored from the video tape that followed the cessation of the question and continued as long as the subject formulated the answer. Movements within the clock positions 1 and 5 were considered left movements, and the movements with the 7 to 11 were considered right movements. If the eyes were not visible or went up and down, the trial was discarded. The videotapes were scored twice.

Results

The results were analyzed by a 2 X 2 X 4 factorial ANOVA with two language groups (mono-, bilinguals), two sexes, and four conditions (verbal, spatial, verbal-emotional, spatial-emotional). Two separate analyses were carried out, one for each language.

Table 1 shows the mean percentages of eye movements to the left and to the right when Swedish was the language of response. In line with the expectations, the direction of eye movements varied according to the condition as indicated by a significant main effect $F(3,96) = 8.73$, $p < .01$. Generally, more right movements were registered to verbal and spatial than to emotional questions. This was most pronounced in the verbal condition for monolingual boys who showed 50.2% more eye movements to the right, indicating a clear lateralization to the left hemisphere. This LH-preference for verbal tasks was much less marked in both monolingual and bilingual girls who directed only a few more eye movements to the right leading to a difference around 10% in favor of the left hemisphere.

Table 1.   Mean Percent Eye Movements to the Left and to the Right and Mean Differences as a Function of Group and Condition. A Negative Sign Indicates Predominantly Right Hemisphere Activity, a Positive Difference Indicates Mainly Left Hemisphere Involvement.

Language and condition	% eye movements			% eye movements		
Swedish	Monolingual boys			Monolingual girls		
	left	right	diff	left	right	diff
verbal	24.9	75.1	50.2	43.2	56.9	13.7
spatial	31.7	68.4	36.7	56.3	43.7	-12.6
verbal emot	36.1	63.9	27.8	55.2	44.8	-10.4
spatial emot	54.0	46.0	-8.0	58.1	42.0	-16.1
Swedish	Bilingual boys			Bilingual girls		
	left	right	diff	left	right	diff
verbal	45.1	54.9	9.8	45.1	54.9	9.8
spatial	45.9	54.1	8.2	60.6	39.4	-21.2
verbal emot	57.9	42.1	-15.8	54.4	45.6	- 8.8
spatial emot	53.6	46.4	- 7.2	55.1	44.9	-10.2
German	left	right	diff	left	right	diff
verbal	53.7	46.3	- 7.4	48.0	52.0	4.0
spatial	61.1	38.9	-22.2	61.9	38.1	-23.8
verbal emot	56.0	44.1	-11.9	54.0	46.0	- 8.0
spatial emot	58.7	41.3	-17.4	53.5	46.5	- 7.0

Relatively more bilateral involvement for girls was also observed on the spatial and emotional tasks and confirmed by the significant main effect of gender $F(1,32) = 4.74$, $p < .05$. The main effect of group, however, did not reach significance in Swedish, $F(1,32) = 2.62$, $p > .05$, mainly due to the results for girls. As can be seen in Table 1, bilingual boys were clearly less lateralized than monolingual boys, since the amount of differences between left and right movements generally is much smaller. Bilingual girls, on the other hand, do not differ as much from monolingual girls, so that the results for bilingual boys and girls taken together only show tendencies in the expected direction of more bilateral involvement in bilinguals.

When German was the response language, the ANOVA revealed a significant main effect of group $F(1,32) = 5.38$, $p < .05$, indicating that bilingualism affected the direction of eye movements. As can be seen in the lower part of Table 1, bilinguals showed clearly more left movements on most tasks than monolinguals. This becomes evident by the numerous negative differences for bilingual subjects, indicating predominantly right-hemisphere involvement.

In line with the results on the Swedish tasks, the main effect of conditions was significant in German, too, $F(3,96) = 7.34$, $p < .01$. Generally, most right movements were observed on the verbal task and most left movements on the spatial emotional task, indicating processing differences in hemispheric activity.

There were two significant interaction effects, group X gender, $F(1,32) = 4.64$, $p < .05$, and group X condition, $F(3,96) = 3.6$, $p < .05$. Monolingual boys responded clearly more often with right eye movements to all questions, with the exception of spatial emotional questions. Bilingual boys, in contrast, responded to all questions with mainly leftward movements, indicating right-hemisphere dominance which was least pronounced in response to verbal questions. Girls, on the other hand, responded with slightly more right movements only to verbal questions, which was somewhat more pronounced in monolingual than in bilingual subjects. On all other tasks, left movements dominated to a varying degree indicating more right hemisphere involvement in girls.

Discussion

The present results provide evidence that conjugate lateral eye movements can be rather sensitive indicators of hemispheric functioning. Significantly more rightward eye movements were found in response to verbal questions, compared to the three other types of questions. Conversely, a greater number of left movements was generally found to spatial and emotional than to verbal questions. In monolingual boys, however, rightward movements dominated also on the spatial and verbal-emotional tasks, but were less pronounced when compared to the verbal questions. Thus, the results for girls in the present study were more consistent with the data reported by Schwartz et al. (1975) than were those for boys.

The main predictions for bilingual subjects were confirmed to a great extent. Generally, bilinguals were less lateralized to the left hemisphere than monolinguals. This effect of relatively more bilateral involvement was evident in both L1 (German) and L2 (Swedish), but reached significance only in L1. The verbal condition differentiated best between the two language groups as indicated by monolinguals' predominantly more rightward movements, which decreased about 40% or even turned into leftward movements. These processing differences for verbal tasks were most pronounced for boys. Girls seemed to process verbal information by using bilateral strategies to a greater extent, and bilingualism does not change this pattern dramatically.

It is quite obvious that the emotional component overrides the verbal component on the emotional questions, as indicated by predominantly more left eye movements. As a measure of differential lateralization between mono- and bilingual subjects, emotional questions seem less sensitive than purely verbal features. It may very well be the case that the individual differences in perceived emotionality are far greater than those experienced on verbal tasks.

One main problem with the present method is finding an adequate level of difficulty that fits most subjects. As pointed out by Ehrlichman and Weinberger (1978), some questions are more likely to elicit eye movements than others. Questions that call for highly overlearned, immediately available, and syntactically simple responses do not tend to elicit eye movements, whereas questions that require more complex cognitive operations for retrieval or formulation of the answer do tend to elicit eye movements. In future research, careful work should be done to find appropriate questions, preferably too difficult rather than too easy. In this perspective, the use of conjugate lateral eye movements in studies of differential hemispheric asymmetry seems to be a reliable and easy technique, not requiring advanced equipment for its application.

Concluding Remarks

According to the present findings, bilinguals seem to be less lateralized to the left hemisphere in both languages when compared to monolinguals. This result somewhat reduces the controversy in connection with the lateralization of similar languages. There appears to be no evidence for the stage hypothesis, which suggests that right-hemisphere involvement is more likely in the beginning than in the advanced stages of language acquisition. On the basis of the present studies, right-hemisphere involvement was a long-lasting effect observed in highly proficient bilinguals with equivalent performance in their two languages and who had acquired the languages early in life. Neither was there much evidence for the age hypothesis, according to which a language acquired after puberty will be less lateralized owing to a greater functional independence between L1 and L2 when L2 is acquired later in life. Since all subjects clearly learned Swedish before puberty, the age hypothesis should not predict any differences at all between the two language groups in the present studies.

In conclusion, the expectations from the age and stage hypotheses were not confirmed. However, the dichotic listening task of stepwise addition and conjugate lateral eye movements are seemingly sensitive indicators of different degrees of bilingualism as well as sensitive tools for measuring differences in the lateralization pattern of the brain. It would be interesting if similar studies on other groups of bilinguals could be done to test for the validity of the present findings.

References

Ehrlichman, H. & Weinberger, A. (1978). Lateral eye movements and hemispheric asymmetry: A critical review. *Psychological Bulletin, 85*, 1080-1101.

Galloway, L. & Scarcella, R. (1982). Cerebral organization in adult second language acquisition: Is the right hemisphere more involved? *Brain and Language*, 16, 56-60.

Genesee, F., Hamers, J., Lambert, W. E., Mononen, L., Seitz, M., & Starck, R. (1978). Language processing in bilinguals. *Brain and Language*, 5, 1-12.

Gordon, H. W. (1980). Cerebral organization in bilinguals: Vol. I. Lateralization. *Brain and Language*, 9, 255-268.

Kinsbourne, M. (1974). Direction of gaze and distribution of cerebral thought processes. *Neuropsychologia*, 12, 279-281.

Krikorian, R. & Rafales, L. (1982). Emotional stimulation, defensive orientation and hemispheric activation. *Brain & Cognition*, 1, 371-380.

Mägiste, E. (1979). The competing language systems of the multilingual: A developmental study of decoding and encoding processes. *Journal of Verbal Learning and Verbal Behavior*, 18, 79-89.

Mägiste, E. (1980). Memory for numbers in monolinguals and bilinguals. *Acta Psychologica*, 46, 63-68.

Mägiste, E. (1984). Stroop tasks and dichotic translation: The development of interference patterns in bilinguals. *Journal of Experimental Psychology: Learning, Memory, and Cognition*, 10, 304-315.

Mägiste, E. (1986). Selected issues in second and third language learning. In J. Vaid (Ed.), *Language processing in bilinguals: Psycholinguistic and neuropsychological perspectives*. Hillsdale, New Jersey: Erlbaum, pp. 97-122.

Mägiste, E. (1987). Changes in the lateralization pattern of two immigrant groups in Sweden, *International and Intercultural Communication Annual, Volume 11: Cross cultural adaptation: Current theory and research*. Beverly Hills: Sage, pp. 233-251.

Oldfield, R. C. (1971). The assessment and analysis of handedness: The Edinburgh Inventory. *Neuropsychologia*, 9, 97-113.

Piazza, D. & Zatorre, R. (1981). Right ear advantage for dichotic listening in bilingual children. *Brain and Language*, 13, 389-396.

Sanchez, P., Manga, D., Babecki, P., & de Tembleque, R. R. (1988). Language lateralization in bilingual speakers. Paper presented at the *"Primeras Jornadas de Estudios Canadienses en España"*. Madrid, Spain.

Schwartz, G. E., Davidson, R. J., & Maer, F. (1975). Right hemisphere lateralization for emotion in the human brain: Interaction with cognition. *Science*, 190, 286-288.

Silverberg, R., Bentin, S., Gaziel, T., Obler, L., & Albert, M. (1979). Shift of visual field preference for English words in native Hebrew speakers. *Brain and Language*, 8, 184-190.

Sussman, H., Franklin, P., & Simon, T. (1982). Bilingual speech: bilingual control? *Brain and Language*, 15, 125-142.

Tucker, D. M., Roth, R. S., Arneson, B. A., & Buckingham, V. (1977). Right hemisphere activation during stress. *Neuropsychologia*, 15, 691-700.

Vaid, J. (1983). Bilingualism and brain lateralization. In S. Segalowitz (Ed.,), *Language functions and brain organization*. New York: Academic Press, pp. 315-339.

Vaid, J. & Genesee, F. (1980). Neuropsychological approaches to bilingualism: A critical review. *Canadian Journal of Psychology*, 34, 417-445.

Walker, E., Wade, S., & Waldman, I. (1982). The effect of lateral visual fixation on response latency to verbal and spatial questions. *Brain & Cognition*, 1, 399-404.

Cognitive Processing in Bilinguals – *R.J. Harris (Editor)*

Differential Cerebral Lateralization of Chinese-English
Bilingual Functions?

Rumjahn Hoosain
University of Hong Kong

Abstract

Chinese-English bilinguals in Hong Kong provide a good test of
the hypothesis of greater right hemisphere involvement in
bilingual language functioning, particularly from the point of
view of the nature of languages involved. However, studies
using hemifield and bilateral visual presentation, monaural
presentation, dichotic listening, as well as time-sharing tasks
provided little support for the hypothesis. A review of the
Chinese-English aphasia literature was similarly non-supportive.
Some experimental findings of greater ambilaterality for second
language functions might only reflect task difficulty.

While it is generally accepted that the left cerebral hemisphere is dominant for
language functions, the possibility that bilinguals have a lateralization pattern different
from monolinguals has received a lot of attention since the work of Albert and Obler
(1978). That bilingual functions are less left lateralized, and more specifically that
second language functions involve the right hemisphere more, have been suggested
(Albert & Obler, 1978; Vaid, 1983). More recently, it is felt that such views are not
justified by evidence in the literature and there is the suggestion that we should "move
on to more productive research" (Paradis, 1990, p. 576). In this paper I review
experimental and clinical data on Chinese-English bilinguals. If bilingual lateralization
patterns are different the chances of obtaining such evidence should be good with
these subjects.

Discussions of bilingual lateralization often recognize a number of variables that
are taken to be conducive to differential lateralization. These include language specific
factors, involving ways in which languages of the bilingual differ from each other, and
language acquisitional factors, involving the manner of second language acquisition as
well as the age and stage of second language acquisition. It has been suggested that
the greater the first and second languages are different,and the more the contexts of
acquisition of the two languages are different, the more likely it is that lateralization
of the second language will differ from the left dominance pattern for the native
language (Vaid, 1983).

Chinese-English Bilinguals

One major difference between Chinese and English is in terms of the relation
between script, sound, and meaning in the written language (see Hoosain, 1991a). This

is usually indicated by labelling the two languages as ideographic and alphabetic respectively. The script-sound relations in Chinese is on a one- to-one basis, with no grapheme-to-phoneme conversion rules (with pronunciations "spelt-out" in the latter case). As a result of differences between Chinese and English orthographies, the manner of information processing can differ. For example, eye-movement patterns in adult Chinese readers and the nature of reading problems in Chinese children are quite different from those of English speakers (Stern, 1978; Woo & Hoosain, 1984). Chinese is a tonal language. Nine tones are used in the Cantonese dialect spoken by the bilingual Hong Kong subjects referred to later. This use of tonal variation to indicate meaning results in the sing-song appearance of Chinese speech to non-speakers. In language structure, Chinese grammar is said to be "meagre" (Kalgren, 1949). Chinese grammar as such is not taught in schools, for example, in Hong Kong. In contrast, English grammar is given a lot of formal treatment in these schools. Thus, the manner of learning and processing Chinese compared with English can involve diverse processes.

The course of bilingual acquisition follows a typical pattern for the vast majority of the University of Hong Kong undergraduates used in studies by the author, reported later (they all participated as subjects in the experiments in connection with taking an Introduction to Psychology course). They are all native Chinese (Cantonese) speakers, and Cantonese is spoken at home as well as amongst peers. English is learned at school, in a formal manner. It is taught as a school subject in grade school through high school and is officially the medium of instruction in high school for most of the subjects, although a variable amount of Chinese or mixed speech could be actually used in the classroom. English is the medium of instruction at the university. But it is safe to say that most subjects seldom have any extended conversation in English, lasting longer than a couple of sentences. They would read their daily Chinese newspapers but would only occasionally read English newspapers. Thus, the bilingual language acquisition conditions for Chinese and English are very dissimilar, and, according to some views, could be expected to show a less comparable pattern of hemispheric involvement for the two languages (Vaid, 1983).

In terms of the stage hypothesis (Galloway & Krashen, 1980), there should be greater left hemisphere involvement in second language processing in the final stages of second language acquisition. However, there is some sense in which the Hong Kong Chinese-English bilinguals should not be considered as reaching the final stages of bilingualism. It is true that these undergraduates have reached some kind of plateau of accomplishment in their second language acquisition, somewhat comparable to that of many beginning foreign students found in American universities.

There has been concern that a lot of findings in the bilingual lateralization literature are either nonsignificant or contradicting each other (Paradis, 1990). To a large extent, methodological problems (e.g., Fennell, Bowers, & Satz, 1977; Sussman, 1989) and the lack of comparability between studies have led to a feeling of absence of progress. Different studies can employ diverse types of bilingual subjects, acquiring their languages under different circumstances and in different manners, and the languages involved could be different. One alternative would be for different procedures to be used by the same investigators on the same type of subjects, to provide some in-depth picture of the situation. This article reviews a number of studies carried out by the author on Chinese-English bilinguals in Hong Kong, using bilateral and hemifield presentation, monaural and dichotic listening, as well as time-sharing tasks to look at various aspects of bilingual functioning and the possibility of a different lateralization pattern for the two languages involved. Other experimental studies as well as aphasia studies are also reviewed.

Visual Studies

Three separate studies have been conducted comparing the lateralization of Chinese and English functions in visual tasks (Hoosain, 1986, in press; Hoosain & Shiu, 1989), all using Chinese-English bilinguals at the University of Hong Kong described above. In the first study (Hoosain, 1986), high frequency two-character Chinese words and three-lettered English words were presented in a visual hemifield procedure, with items shown in the right or left visual field so that the sensory information is initially conveyed to the contralateral hemisphere. The two Chinese characters in each item, as well as the three English letters were aligned vertically. Each item was shown for 150 ms, and subjects were asked to produce the translation equivalent of each presented item (in Chinese or in English) in the other language as soon as possible. Response times for each translation and error rate were obtained.

It took the subjects about a second to translate the high frequency words in the experiment. Response times were faster for items shown in the right visual field, for both Chinese and English words, although the differences did not quite reach statistical significance. However, error rates for translating both Chinese and English words were significantly smaller when the items were shown in the right visual field. It would seem that lateralization patterns for the translation tasks in the two languages are similar, both favoring visual information initially conveyed to the left hemisphere.

Hoosain and Shiu (1989) conducted a more purely visual study. Pairs of items were presented on the two sides of the fixation point simultaneously for 120 ms. Each item could be a high frequency two-character Chinese word, a high frequency four- letter and two-syllable English word, or a four-digit random number. The pair of items could be Chinese-Chinese, Chinese- English, or Chinese-number in these bilateral presentations. Error rates showed that, whether paired with another Chinese word, an English word, or a number, Chinese words were seen significantly better when shown in the right visual field. Similarly, English words (which were always paired with Chinese words) were seen significantly better when they appeared in the right visual field rather than the left. Thus, both languages indicated a left hemisphere superiority in visual processing.

Hoosain (in press) tested right-handed and left-handed subjects, as well as handedness-switched subjects who were born left-handed but forced to switch their preferred hand to the right during childhood. They were shown common two-character

Chinese words and three-letter English words, with constituent characters or letters aligned vertically. Exposure time was adjusted for each individual subject. For right-handed subjects, there was a significantly greater number who identified more of the words shown in the right visual field than those shown in the left visual field, similarly so for Chinese and English words. Although both left-handed subjects and handedness switched subjects identified more Chinese and English words presented in the right visual field compared with the left, the numbers were not significant. Thus, there was no cerebral lateralization difference between identifying Chinese and English words. Both kinds of items showed a left hemisphere advantage, although it was significant only for the right-handed subjects. Left-handers are known to show a weaker left lateralization and it appears that handedness switched subjects function similarly to ordinary left handers.

To summarise, in various experimental tasks involving visual perception of Chinese and English words, the Hong Kong Chinese- English bilingual undergraduates did not display any differential lateralization for Chinese compared to English. Incidentally, while there have been periodic reports that visual perception of Chinese words is more right lateralized than that of English, due to its ideographic characteristic, it is now quite clear that this is not a valid factor and universal perceptual factors such as exposure time and the quality of the sensory signal are responsible for such findings (Hasuike, Tzeng, & Hung, 1986; Ho & Hoosain, 1989; Hoosain, 1991a).

There are a few other studies reported in the literature involving Chinese-English bilinguals in perception of Chinese and English words. Kershner and Jeng (1972) tested right-handed Taiwanese Chinese graduate students in the U.S. They were shown Chinese and English words as well as geometric forms in hemifield or bilateral presentation. In the case of both Chinese and English words, subjects were able to write down what they had seen better when the items were shown in the right visual field. This pattern was obtained for the hemifield as well as the bilateral presentation procedures. For the geometric forms, performance was better when items were presented in the left visual field using the hemifield presentation procedure, although no significant difference was found with the bilateral presentation procedure.

Hardyck, Tzeng, and Wang (1977) tested bilinguals who were fluent in reading Chinese and English. Single-character words and their English translation equivalents were used. No signifcant response time and accuracy results were found with these subjects when pairs of Chinese-Chinese, Chinese-English, or English-English items were presented either in the same hemifield or bilaterally, and subjects had to indicate whether items had the same physical shape or not, or whether they had the same meaning or not. Hardyck, Tzeng, and Wang (1978) used similar materials, but about 5 minutes after the tachistoscopic presentation subjects were asked to recall the items presented. There was a significant difference in recall performance in favor of Chinese words shown in the right visual field compared to the left, and there was a similar but nonsignificant difference for English. This was the first experimental study that provided indication of differential lateralization -- a weaker left lateralization for English.

But this finding of Hardyck et al. should be evaluated in connection with their report that response times in the initial tachistoscopic presentation were faster for first language compared with second language words. Most of the bilingual subjects had Chinese as their first language, although a few had English as first language. Thus, the majority of the subjects actually spent more time with the English words than with Chinese words during initial presentation. The longer dwell times for English items also meant that there was a greater opportunity for interhemisphere commmunication in processing English items.

To conclude, experimental visual studies of Chinese and English with bilingual subjects do not point to differential lateralization for the two languages. The only exception (Hardyck et al., 1978), showing weaker lateralization for English, involves longer processing times. This issue will be discussed later.

Auditory Studies

Reports on auditory studies of Chinese-English bilinguals are rare in the literature. Hoosain (1984) performed a digit span test on Chinese-English bilingual undergraduates. The standard procedure for such tests was used, except that each set of random numbers, starting with a short sequence and ending with a sequence too long for the subject, was presented only to the right or left ear over a set of earphones. Also, both forward digit span and backward digit span were determined, for Chinese and for English. The digit spans obtained by this monaural procedure showed a significant right ear (left hemisphere) superiority for forward digit span in Chinese. No other condition showed any significant laterality difference, although there was still a nonsignificant right ear superiority for forward digit span in English.

On the face of it, this would be a second indication (apart from that of Hardyck et al., 1978) of weaker lateralization of English functions in Chinese-English bilinguals. The weaker lateralization for the backward digit condition (for both Chinese and English) can be considered in terms of the view that operations to produce backward digt sequences involve the right hemisphere more (Rudel & Denckla, 1974). But the weaker lateralization for the forward digit span in English is reminiscent of the finding of Hardyck et al., only now in the auditory mode rather than the visual. The actual forward digit span for English was smaller than for Chinese, that is, subjects found memorizing English numbers more difficult. In the case of tachistoscopic presentation in the Hardyck et al. study, response times were longer for second language items (which was English for most of the subjects). Again, this means that weaker lateralization was found with the more difficult language.

In a dichotic listening study (Hoosain, 1991b), Chinese- English bilingual undergraduates at the University of Hong Kong heard two groups of four common two-character Chinese words (or four common two-syllable English words), each group through one ear, using a set of earphones. The percentages of correct recall of Chinese items were 62.4% for those presented to the right ear and 43.3% for the left ear. Thus, there was a right ear or left hemisphere superiority effect. For English, the corresponding results were 49.0% and 34.3% respectively. Although the English performance was not as good as that for Chinese, there was a similar right ear, left hemisphere superiority effect.

The two auditory studies provide mixed results for the differential lateralization hypothesis. The monaural study showed some indication of weaker lateralization for English, but then subjects found the English digit span test more difficult than Chinese. The dichotic listening study showed similar left lateralization for both Chinese and English, even though English words were more difficult to recall.

Time-sharing Studies

There are only a couple of studies using the time-sharing paradigm (Hoosain, 1990; Hoosain & Shiu, 1989). In both studies, undergraduates at the University of Hong Kong were asked to count backwards by 3's (e.g., to say "97, 94, 91, etc." when given "97") in either Chinese or English. They were also asked to perform a standard finger tapping test, with the right or left index finger. After baseline measures for these tasks were obtained, subjects were asked to simultaneously engage in finger tapping with the right or left hand and backward counting in Chinese or English. Finger tapping is controlled by the contralateral hemisphere. When compared with baseline tapping or counting scores, changes in the respective performances during the time-sharing trials would indicate the extent to which the right or left hemisphere is engaged in the backward counting task in either language.

In the time-sharing trials, there was an increase in backward counts performed but a decrease in the number of taps made, when compared with the respective baseline measures. The possibility that one of the concurrent tasks could be carried out better than baseline performance has been acknowledged (Kinsbourne & Cook, 1971), although there could also be some practice effect. In these two experiments, it appeared that subjects attended to the counting tasks more than to tapping during the time-sharing trials. This pattern was found in both studies. Hoosain and Shiu (1989) found that concurrent counting affected right-hand tapping (controlled by the left hemisphere) more than left-hand tapping, and similarly so for both languages. This indicated that both Chinese and English backward counting was lateralized in the left hemisphere. The effect of concurrent counting on tapping performance did not show any significant lateralization pattern.

On the other hand, Hoosain (1990) found some indication of right hemisphere involvement in second language functioning. This time, the effect of concurrent counting on tapping performance did not show any significant lateralization pattern. But when subjects were counting in Chinese, improvement in counting was greater during tapping with the left hand rather than the right. When counting in English, improvement was greater during tapping with the right hand. This would suggest that the left hemisphere is more concerned with counting in Chinese and the right hemisphere more concerned with counting in English. This particular finding provided perhaps the strongest single indication of right hemisphere involvement in English functioning.

Thus, the two time-sharing studies produced contradictory findings. In a review of the time-sharing paradigm, Sussman (1989) warned that concurrent tapping disruption rates can be affected by discrepant baseline tapping speed of the dominant and nondominant hands. But in the case of Hoosain (1990) we had a significant interaction effect of language and hand used on the enhancement of backward counting. In any case, the contradictory results from the above two studies, one showing left lateralization for both languages and one showing left hemisphere lateralization for Chinese but right lateralization for English, reminds us of the contradictory picture for bilingual laterality pointed out by Paradis (1990).

There is also a question of the reliability of the time- sharing procedure. We had enhanced tapping in one study and enhanced counting in another, although identical procedures were used on similar subjects. Enhanced performance during time-sharing, particular involving the hand contralateral to the language hemisphere, is seldom found (Kinsbourne & Cook, 1971). It might be noted that the Hong Kong subjects tend to have very high baseline scores in the first place, averaging over 110 taps with the right hand and 14 backward counts, in 20 seconds. The subjects in Hoosain (1990) had even better baseline Chinese backward counting, averaging 16.0 counts.

Aphasia Studies

There are about a dozen individually reported cases of aphasia in Chinese-English bilinguals in the literature. Although there are indications of intrahemisphere differences in locations for Chinese and English processes, there is no overall picture of differential lateralization for the two languages. The earliest reported case was that of Lyman, Kwan, and Chao (1938). A patient from Shanghai who was fluent in both Chinese and English had a large left occipito-parietal fibroblastoma. His Chinese as well as English speech and oral comprehension were good. He had some difficulties with reading English, but his reading of Chinese was very much worse. His written English was also better than Chinese. For a few decades, this study had a prominent position in the literature on Chinese aphasia and provided support for the idea of differential lateralization of the two languages of the bilingual. It is also consistent with greater ambilaterality for the second language of the bilingual.

April and his colleagues (April & Tse, 1977; April & Han, 1980) reported on two cases of crossed aphasia in Chinese-English bilinguals living in New York. The two right-handed Chinese males had right hemisphere lesions resulting in aphasia. The first patient had his Chinese functions affected more than English, and it was suggested that the right hemisphere might be more involved with using an ideographic language. However, the second patient did not show any significant difference between Chinese and English performance. April and Han (1980) also reported that a review of unspecified numbers of Chinese patients in New York and in Taiwan did not indicate an incidence of crossed aphasia above the 4% from the European literature. While many of the Taiwan patients may not be Chinese-English bilinguals, the New York patients should most likely be bilingual. The actual number of cases that were examined was not reported by April and Han, but it was apparently enough to convince the authors to give up the idea of differential lateralization amongst the Chinese (although the authors focused on altered lateralization due to use of the nonalphabetic Chinese language rather than bilingual differential lateralization as such).

T'sou (1978) reported on a female Chinese-English bilingual in Hong Kong with a left posterior temporo-parietal hemorrhage resulting in conduction aphasia. Both Chinese and English were affected, although there were some variations due to language characteristics. Thus, she had problems particularly with the low falling tone in Cantonese, and mirror image reversal in English (saying <u>dog</u> instead of <u>god</u>).

In the above four cases, the patients were all Chinese dominant, although that of Lyman et al. was fluent in English. Rapport, Tan, and Whitaker (1983) studied a total of seven right- handed polyglots in Malaysia. All were fluent in English and at least one Chinese dialect, and in some cases English was the dominant language. Some also spoke Malay. Different combinations of the Wada test (with one or the other cerebral hemisphere being temporarily incapacitated), cortical stimulation (while subjects were engaged in object naming or silent reading), and clinical tests were carried out on the patients. Five of the seven patients had left and two had right hemisphere lesions.

Rapport et al. found no pattern of greater right hemisphere involvement in language functions, either for Chinese or for the other languages. There were two cases of weaker lateralization, with indication of right hemisphere involvement. But, in one case, the patient was a young female with a laterality quotient of +75. In the other case, the patient could have mixed cerebral dominance as a result of congenital vascular anomaly in the left hemisphere. All the patients were left hemisphere dominant for the languages or dialects tested. Cortical stimulation did provide evidence that different languages or dialects could occupy different loci within the same left hemisphere.

The Chinese-English aphasia literature does not generally support a conclusion of greater right hemisphere involvement for the second language, or indeed greater right hemisphere involvement for either language. The two cases of crossed aphasia reported by April and his colleagues could well fall within the category of reports that are selective in favor of the unusual, and they were more than counterbalanced by the absence of a higher incidence of crossed-aphasia amongst Chinese patients reviewed in New York and in Taiwan. Unfortunately, the actual number of cases considered by April and Han (1980) is not known, although in the New York sample, it was from two hospitals over two years in the city, and one of the hospitals treats a large Chinese population. This would apparently amount to an unselected group study (Solin, 1989).

Conclusion

The available experimental and aphasia studies, on the whole, do not present a picture of any pattern of differential lateralization of Chinese-English bilingual functions. Even so, there are a small number of reports going against the trend that need to be considered. There are two experimental studies showing a weaker lateralization for English (Hardyck et al., 1978, Experiment 2; Hoosain, 1984). In both cases, performance for English items was poorer, with subjects requiring more response time and recalling fewer items respectively. There is indication that tasks based on visual information taking more than one second to complete tend not to obtain significant lateralization effects (Hoosain, 1991a). In these cases, interhemisphere communication probably plays a greater role and the quest for lateralization effect is doomed. A similar situation could be found where a more difficult task requires greater effort. Given that second language functioning tends to be poorer (slower, with smaller short-term memory capacity, etc.) for most bilinguals, there is a built-in bias for findings what could be taken as weaker lateralization of second language functions. These findings do not necessarily mean that the locus of processing has moved away from the left hemisphere, or that right-hemisphere based processes or strategies are dominantly being used for the second language.

In the case of the time-sharing studies showing contradictory results (Hoosain, 1990; Hoosain & Shiu, 1989) further work needs to be done to clarify the reliability of the of the procedure, particularly in view of questions concerning the paradigm (Sussman, 1989). Out of the eleven cases of aphasia reported, only three were consistent with the hypothesis of differential lateralization as a result of Chinese-English bilingual experience. The two cases of crossed aphasia reported by April and his colleagues are offset by their own reference to larger samples of left lateralization for language. The case of Lyman et al. (1938) would have to remain in its place in the classical literature, without us knowing whether it was selected because of its unusual features (we do not even know the handedness of the patient).

References

Albert, M. L., & Obler, L. K. (1978). *The bilingual brain: Neuropsychological and neurolinguistic aspects of bilingualism*. New York: Academic Press.

April, R. S., & Han, M. (1980). Crossed aphasia in a right-handed bilingual Chinese man: A second case. *Archives of Neurology, 37*, 342-346.

April, R. S., & Tse, P. C. (1977). Crossed aphasia in a Chinese bilingual dextral. *Archives of Neurology, 34*, 766-770.

Fennell, E. B., Bowers, D., & Satz, P. (1977). Within-modal and cross-modal reliabilities of two laterality tests. *Brain and Language, 4*, 63-69.

Galloway, L., & Krashen, S. D. (1980). Cerebral organization inbilingualism and second language. In R. C. Scarcella & S. D. Krashen (Eds.), *Research in second language acquisition* (pp. 74-80). Rowley, MA: Newbury House.

Hardyck, C., Tzeng, O. J. L., & Wang, W. S.-Y. (1977). Cerebral lateralization effects in visual half-field experiments. *Nature, 269*, 705-707.

Hardyck, C., Tzeng, O. J. L., & Wang, W. S.-Y. (1978). Cerebral lateralization of function and bilingual decision processes: Is thinking lateralized? *Brain and Language, 5*, 56-71.

Hasuike, R., Tzeng, O. J. L., & Hung, D. L. (1986). Script effects and cerebral lateralization: The case of Chinese characters. In J. Vaid (Ed.), *Language processing in bilinguals: Psycholinguistic and neuropsychological perspectives* (pp. 275-288). Hillsdale, NJ: Erlbaum.

Ho, S. K., & Hoosain, R. (1989). Right hemisphere advantage in lexical decision with two-character Chinese words. *Brain and Language, 37*, 606-615.

Hoosain, R. (1984). Lateralization of bilingual digit span functions. *Perceptual and Motor Skills, 58*, 21-22.

Hoosain, R. (1986). Psychological and orthographic variables for translation asymmetry. In H. S. R. Kao & R. Hoosain (Eds.), *Linguistics, psychology, and the Chinese language* (pp.203-216). Hong Kong: University of Hong Kong Centre of Asian Studies.

Hoosain, R. (1990, August). Cerebral lateralization of bilingual vocal-auditory functioning. Paper presented at the meeting of the American Psychological Association, Boston.

Hoosain, R. (1991a). *Psycholinguistic implications for linguistic relativity: A case study of Chinese*. Hillsdale, NJ: Erlbaum.

Hoosain, R. (1991b). Dichotic listening of Chinese and English words by bilinguals. Unpublished manuscript, University of Hong Kong, Hong Kong.

Hoosain, R. (in press). Cerebral lateralization of bilingual unctions after handedness switch in childhood. *Journal of Genetic Psychology*.

Hoosain, R., & Shiu, L. P. (1989). Cerebral lateralization of Chinese-English bilingual functions. *Neuropsychologia, 27*, 705-712.

Kalgren, B. (1949). *The Chinese language*. New York: Ronald.

Kershner, J. R., & Jeng, G. R. (1972). Dual functional hemispheric asymmetry in visual perception: Effects of ocular dominance and post-exposure processes. *Neuropsychologia*, 10, 437-445.

Kinsbourne, M., & Cook, J. (1971). Generalized and lateralized effect of concurrent verbalization on a unimanual skill. *Quarterly Journal of Experimental Psychology*, 23, 341-343.

Lyman, R. S., Kwan, S. T., & Chao, W. H. (1938). Left occipital-parietal brain tumour with observations on alexia and agraphia in Chinese and English. *The Chinese Medical Journal*, 54, 491-515.

Paradis, M. (1990). Language lateralization in bilinguals: Enough already! *Brain and Language*, 39, 576-586.

Rapport, R. L., Tan, C. T., & Whitaker, H. A. (1983). Language function and dysfunction among Chinese- and English-speaking polyglots: Cortical stimulation, Wada testing, and clinical studies. *Brain and Language*, 18, 342-366.

Rudel, R. G., & Denckla, M. B. (1974). Relation of forward and backward digit repetition to neurological impairment in children with learning disabilities. *Neuropsychologia*, 12, 109-118.

Solin, D. (1989). The systematic misrepresentation of bilingual-crossed aphasia data and its consequences. *Brain and Language*, 36, 92-116.

Stern, J. A. (1978). Eye movements, reading, and cognition. In J.W. Senders, D. F. Fisher, & R. A. Monty (Eds.), *Eye movements and the higher psychological functions* (pp. 145-155). Hillsdale, NJ: Erlbaum.

Sussman, H. M. (1989). A reassessment of the time-sharing paradigm with ANCOVA. *Brain and Language*, 37, 514-520.

T'sou, B. K. (1978). Some preliminary observations on aphasia in a Chinese bilingual. *Acta Psychologica Taiwanica*, 20, 57-64.

Vaid, J. (1983). Bilingualism and brain lateralization. In S. J. Segalowitz (Ed.), *Language functions and brain organization* (pp. 315-339). New York: Academic Press.

Woo, E. Y. C., & Hoosain, R. (1984). Visual and auditory functions of Chinese dyslexics. *Psychologia*, 27, 164-170.

Authors

Doris Aaronson is Professor of Psychology, New York University, 6 Washington Place, 8th floor, New York NY 10003 USA

Jeanette Altarriba is Postdoctoral Research Associate, Department of Psychology, University of Massachusetts, Tobin Hall, Amherst MA 01003 USA

Lenore Negrin Arnberg is Associate Professor at the Centre for Research on Bilingualism, Stockholm University, S-106 91, Stockholm, Sweden

Peter Wilhelm Arnberg is Research Director at the National Swedish Road and Traffic Research Institute, S-581 01, Linköping, Sweden

Cecile Beauvillain is Research Scientist with CNRS at the Laboratoire de Psychologie Expérimentale, Université René Descartes, 28 Rue Serpente, 75006 Paris, France

Abdelâli Bentahila is Professor on Faculty of Arts at Sidi Mohamed Ben Abdullah University, Villa 133 Mimosas, Ave. Moulay Kamel, Fes, Morocco

Ellen Bialystok is Professor of Psychology, 4700 Keele St., York University, North York ON M3J 1P3, Canada

Gordon D. A. Brown is Senior Lecturer in the Department of Psychology, University of Wales, Bangor, Gwynedd, Wales LL57 2DG, United Kingdom

Hsuan-Chih Chen is Senior Lecturer in Psychology, Department of Psychology, The Chinese University of Hong Kong, Shatin N.T., Hong Kong

Helena-Fivi Chitiri is a recent doctoral graduate from the Ontario Institute for Studies in Education, University of Toronto, 252 Bloor St. W., Toronto ON M5S 1V6 Canada

Eirlys E. Davies is Professor on Faculty of Arts at Sidi Mohamed Ben Abdullah University, Villa 133 Mimosas, Ave. Moulay Kamel, Fes, Morocco

Ton Dijkstra is Lecturer in Psychology at the University of Nijmegen, St. Annastraat, Nijmegen, The Netherlands

Estelle A. Doctor is Associate Professor at the Department of Psychology, University of the Witwatersrand, P.O. Wits, 2050 Johannesburg, South Africa

Aydin Y. Durgunoglu is Senior Scientist and Visiting Assistant Professor at the Center for the Study of Reading, University of Illinois, 51 Gerty Drive, Champaign IL 61820 USA

Nick C. Ellis is Senior Lecturer in Psychology at the University College of North Wales, Bangor, Gwynedd, Wales LL57 2DG United Kingdom

Cheryl Frenck-Mestre is Research Scientist with CNRS at Centre de Recherche en Psychologie Cognitive, Université de Provence, 29 Ave. Robert Schuman, 13621 Aix-en-Provence, France

Beatrice de Gelder is Professor of Psychology, Tilburg University, P.O. Box 90153, Tilburg 5000 LE, The Netherlands

Jonathan Grainger is Research Scientist with CNRS at the Laboratoire de Psychologie Expérimentale, Université René Descartes, 28 Rue Serpente, 75006 Paris, France

François Grosjean is Professor of Linguistics and Director of the Speech and Language Processing Laboratory, University of Neuchâtel, Ave. du 1er mars 26, CH-2000 Neuchâtel, Switzerland

Barbara J. Hancin is a Doctoral Candidate, Department of Linguistics, University of Illinois, 707 S. Mathews Ave., Urbana IL 61801 USA

Michael Harrington is a Doctoral Candidate in the Program in Experimental Psychology at the University of California, Santa Cruz, Psychology Board, Kerr Hall, Santa Cruz CA 95064 USA

Richard Jackson Harris is Professor of Psychology at Kansas State University, Bluemont Hall, Manhattan KS 66506-5302 USA

L. Kathy Heilenman is Associate Professor of French at the University of Iowa, Department of French and Italian, Iowa City IA 52242 USA

Roberto Heredia is a Doctoral Candidate in Experimental Psychology, Clark Kerr Hall, University of California Santa Cruz, Santa Cruz CA 95064 USA

Rumjahn Hoosain is Senior Lecturer, Department of Psychology, University of Hong Kong, Pokfulam Road, Hong Kong

Charles Hulme is Reader in Psychology, Department of Psychology, University of York, York Y01 5DD United Kingdom

Daisy L. Hung is at Department of Psychology, University of California-Riverside, Riverside CA 92521 and The Salk Institute for Biological Studies

Kenneth Hyltenstam is Acting Professor of Bilingualism at Centre for Research on Bilingualism, Stockholm University, S-106 91 Stockholm, Sweden

Catharine W. Keatley is a Research Associate in Psychology at Tilburg University, P.O. Box 90153, Tilburg 5000 LE, The Netherlands

Kerry Kilborn is now Lecturer at the Department of Psychology, 56 Hillhead St., University of Glasgow, Glasgow, Scotland G12 9YR United Kingdom

Denise Klein is Postgraduate Researcher at the Department of Psychology, University of the Witwatersrand, P.O. Wits, 2050 Johannesburg, South Africa

Judith F. Kroll is Professor of Psychology, Department of Psychology and Education, Mount Holyoke College, South Hadley MA 01075 USA

Monica J. Lasisi is Lecturer in the Institute of Education, Faculty of Education, Obafemi Awolowo University, Ile-Ife, Nigeria

Wei Ling Lee is at Tan Tock Seng Hospital, Singapore

Edith Mägiste is Docent (Associate Professor), Department of Psychology, Uppsala University, Box 1854, S-751 48, Uppsala, Sweden

Brian MacWhinney is Professor of Psychology, Carnegie Mellon University, Pittsburgh PA 15213 USA

Marguerite E. Malakoff is Postdoctoral Researcher at the Yale Child Study Center, Department of Psychology, P.O. Box 11A, Yale Station, Yale University, New Haven CT 06520-7447 USA

Janet L. McDonald is Assistant Professor of Psychology at Louisiana State University, Baton Rouge LA 70803 USA

Barry McLaughlin is Professor of Psychology, Clark Kerr Hall, University of California Santa Cruz, Santa Cruz CA 95064 USA

Elizabeth Marie McGhee Nelson is a Doctoral Candidate in Psychology at Kansas State University, Bluemont Hall, Manhattan KS 66506-5302 USA

Anthony S. Onyehalu is Senior Lecturer in Educational Foundations and Counselling in the Faculty of Education, Obafemi Awolowo University, Ile-Ife, Nigeria

J. Y. Opoku is Senior Lecturer and Head of Department of Psychology at University of Ghana, P.O. Box 84, Legon, Ghana

Michael Palij is Research Associate in Department of Psychology, New York University, 6 Washington Place, 8th floor, New York NY 10003 USA

Alexandra Sholl is Graduate Student in Cognitive Psychology, Tobin Hall, University of Massachusetts at Amherst, Amherst MA 01003 USA

Yilin Sun is a Doctoral Candidate at The Ontario Institute for Studies in Education, University of Toronto, 252 Bloor St., W., Toronto ON M5S 1V6 Canada

Insup Taylor is Professor at The McLuhan Program in Culture and Technology, University of Toronto, 39A Queen's Park Crescent E., Toronto ON M5S 1A1 Canada

Jacqueline Thomas is Associate Professor of French at Texas A & I University, Department of Language and Literature, Campus Box 162, Kingsville TX 78364 USA

Ovid J. L. Tzeng is Professor of Psychology, University of California-Riverside, Riverside CA 92521 USA and at the Salk Institute for Biological Studies

Jyotsna Vaid is Associate Professor of Psychology, Texas A & M University, College Station TX 77843 USA

Marianne C. Votaw is a Doctoral Candidate in Psychology at the University of Virginia, Gilmer Hall, Charlottesville VA 22903 USA

Jean Vroomen is Research Associate in Psychology at Tilburg University, P.O. Box 90153, Tilburg 5000 LE, The Netherlands

Ghim Choo Wee is with the Ministry of Education, Singapore

Dale M. Willows is Associate Professor of Curriculum and Special Education at the Ontario Institute for Studies in Education, University of Toronto, 252 Bloor St. W., Toronto ON M5S 1V6 Canada

Subject Index

A

Acquisition, age of 68-71
Activation of meaning 400-401
Aphasia 567-568
Articulatory suppression 116-117, 140-141
Assimilation, linguistic 3
Associations, cross-language 17-18
Attention, selective 501-510
Automatization 377-378
Awareness, language 475-497
Awareness, metalinguistic 475-546, 518-519, 531-541

B

Bilingual (wholistic) view of bilingualism 54-56
Bilingual interactive activation model 210-211

C

Calculation, mental 143-149
Child, bilingual 57-58, 351-367, 475-497, 501-510, 515-526
Chinese-English bilinguals 76-84, 289-293, 561-562
Chinese alphabetic vs. non-alphabetic bilinguals 413-424
Code-switching 443-456
Cognates, priming effects with 38-40
Cohort model 338-339, 344
Comparison hypothesis 76
Competence, communicative 536-541
Competition model 325, 344, 345, 371-386
Completeness 352
Context effect on word recognition 213
Control
- of attentional process 507-510
- failure of 353
Counting 149-150
Critical period 383-384
Cue validity 373-374
Cultural influences on comprehension 459-469

D

Definition of bilingualism 5, 16-17, 51-84, 299-300, 515-516
Dichotic listening task 550-554, 565
Digit span task 115-117
Diglossia 4-5
Dominance, language 443-456

E

Eye movements, conjugate lateral 554-558

F

Family trees of languages 12-14
Forgetting, language 56-57
Form-function mappings 372
Fossilization 353, 383-384
Functional restructuring 382-383

G

Generational differences in code-switching 446-456
Gibson's theory of perceptual development 483-485
Greek orthography recognition 287-289

H

History of bilingualism research 15-49

I

Ibos 459-569
Inactive language, influence of 32-33
Independence model 91-100
Instruction in L2 and Competition Model 384-385
Intelligence
- and bilingualism 7
- testing 141-142
Interdependence model 91-100
Interference effects 223-225
Interference on Stroop task 30-32, 258-261, 427-440

K

K.T. (case study) 245-248
Knowledge, background 402, 459-469

L

Language background 63-84
Language learning, beliefs about 535-536
Language switch 18-20
Language, memory for 23-24
Lateralization, cerebral 549-569
Lexical acquisition 377
see also Word Recognition

Lexical decision task 33-40, 212-213,
221-233, 268-274
Lexicosemantic networks 299-316

M

Masking, visual 160-161
Measurement of bilingualism 5-6, 74
Memory
- implicit-explicit 92-100
- episodic 158-160
- conceptual vs. lexical 191-204
- bilingual 91-204
- span in L2 109-118
Mental functions, elementary vs. higher 478-480
Mentalinguistic abilities 402-404, 475-545
Mixed speech, processing of 60-61
Mixing, language 477
Modularity 347
Monolingual (fractional) view of
bilingualism 52-54
Morphological processing 399-400
Multilingualism vs. bilingualism 10

N

Native speakers, who and what? 64-68
Neighborhood effects 215-217
Noun animacy cues 329-334
Number words 265-278
Numbers, digit naming 139, 143

O

On-line integration 337-349
Organization in recall 22-23
Orthographic depth hypothesis 284-286
Orthographic processing in reading 394-399
Orthographic constraints in word
recognition 221-233
Orthographies, comparison of 396-397, 427-440
Overview of book 7-9

P

Personality and bilingualism 6
Phonological processing
- in word recognition 237-249
- in reading 394-396
- transfer of 375-377
Piaget's theory of cognitive development
481-483
Pitfalls in translation 523-526

Priming 35-40, 161-170, 199-200, 214, 268-274
Proactive interference, release from 21-22

R

Reaction time measures 27-40
Reading
- and short-term memory 106-107, 125-132
- word recognition in 283-297
- cross-language transfer 391-404
Regionalism and language 4
Repetition
- effect on recall 24-27
- cross-language 34-35

S

Scripts, writing see Orthographies
Semilingualism 58
Separation, language 475-497
Short-term memory 105-155
Speech perception 413-424
Stepwise addition task 550-554
Stroop color-word task 30-32, 258-261, 427-440
Subject pools, psychology 66-68, 72-75
Syntax
- through translation 378-379
- role in L2 processing 323-367, 401-402

T

Third-language learning 536-541
Time-sharing task 566-567
Trace model 348
Transfer
- semantic 175-188
- L1-L2 transfer in reading 391-404
- of learning 20-21, 371-411
Translation
- equivalents 157-170, 175-189
- latencies 197-198
- and syntactic learning 378-379
- ability 515-526

U

Ultimate attainment in L2 351-367

V

Verb agreement cues 329-334
Vygotsky's theory of language and
thought 485-487

Author Index
(boldface = complete reference)